A GUIDE TO THE EQUITY

A GUIDE TO THE

Equity
Markets
of Hong Kong

PAUL B. McGUINNESS

OXFORD
UNIVERSITY PRESS

OXFORD
UNIVERSITY PRESS

Oxford University Press is a department of the University of Oxford.
It furthers the University's objective of excellence in research, scholarship,
and education by publishing worldwide in

Oxford New York

Athens Auckland Bangkok Bogotá Buenos Aires Calcutta
Cape Town Chennai Dar es Salaam Delhi Florence Hong Kong Istanbul
Karachi Kuala Lumpur Madrid Melbourne Mexico City Mumbai
Nairobi Paris São Paulo Singapore Taipei Tokyo Toronto Warsaw

with associated companies in Berlin Ibadan

Oxford is a registered trade mark of Oxford University Press

Published in the United States
by Oxford University Press Inc., New York

© Oxford University Press 1999

First published 1999
This impression (lowest digit)
1 3 5 7 9 10 8 6 4 2

British Library Cataloguing in Publication Data
available

Library of Congress Cataloguing-in-Publication Data

McGuinness, Paul, 1963 —
A guide to the equity markets of Hong Kong / Paul McGuinness.
p. cm.
Includes bibliographical references.
ISBN 0-19-592076-7
1. Stock exchanges—China—Hong Kong. I. Title
HG5802.M384 1999
332.64′25125—dc21
99-33006
CIP

Printed in Hong Kong
Published by Oxford University Press (China) Ltd
18th Floor, Warwick House East, Taikoo Place, 979 King's Road, Quarry Bay
Hong Kong

Acknowledgements

It has been my privilege to live and work in Hong Kong since the late summer of 1989. Apart from the obvious cultural and culinary benefits offered by this cosmopolitan gem, I have also been fortunate to share in one of the world's greatest 'experiments' in free-market or 'laissez-faire' economics. For any academic professing some level of scholarship in the field, Hong Kong offers a rich vein of potential research materials and topics. Hopefully, some of this will infuse the pages of this text.

As with all endeavours in the literary field, the support of several people has been crucial. A special debt is owed to those that gave generously of their time by patiently reading several of my chapters. Apart from the comments received by anonymous reviewers—selected by OUP—special thanks are due to a number of personal friends. Hopefully, seeing their names in print will encourage them to add this text to their existing collection of readings. Levity aside, a personal debt of gratitude is owed to Benjamin C. Ostrov, Stephen Keef, David Sharam and Kevin Keasey for offering useful criticisms and pointers. I would also like to thank Ling Fung and Hudson Yau for providing assistance in the collection of data materials, necessary in the construction of several figures in the text. The assistance of numerous people in the financial services industry is also acknowledged at various points in the book. Special thanks are due to W.L. Ying, Elton Cheng, Kevin Cheng and Peter So for graciously dealing with various enquiries. It would also be remiss of me not to mention the knowledge and experience gained from years of interaction with the business community and our own student body. All of this has undoubtedly sharpened my awareness of the market and the players that operate in it. This does not mean to say that insights into the accumulation of mammon have been generated at the same time. Even if they had, reasons of self-interest might lead me to hold back a little. Writers of finance texts habitually trot-out the same warning: this book is not a 'get-rich-quick' guide. What the text might do, though, is offer a guide for those interested in the operation and structure of particular aspects of the markets. Insights into the more mundane as well as the more exotic—like the equity derivative—feature widely, all of which is explained in the preface. Apart from helping those confronted by university examinations, the text probably has something of value for a wider audience; even for those who toil daily at the market's coal-face. Leaving aside all of this, any shortcomings in meeting the objectives of this text lay squarely at my door.

A final vote of thanks is also due to my family. Nothing could have been achieved without their support. In this, I have been truly blessed. Accordingly, I dedicate this book to my nearest and dearest, Polly, Claire and Charlotte, and to the memory and sacrifices borne by my parents, Patrick Joseph and Patricia Mary.

Contents

Abbreviations and Acronyms

ADR	American Depositary Receipt
ADS	American Depositary Share
CAPM	Capital Asset Pricing Model
CCASS	Central Clearing and Settlement System
CI	Certificate of Indebtedness
DEM	Deutsche Mark
EFIL	Exchange Fund Investment Ltd.
EMP	Efficient Markets Paradigm
GB	Pounds Sterling
HIBOR	Hong Kong Inter-Bank Offer Rate
HKD	Hong Kong Dollar
HKFE	Hong Kong Futures Exchange Ltd.
HKMA	Hong Kong Monetary Authority
HKMC	Hong Kong Mortgage Corporation Ltd.
HKSAR	Hong Kong Special Administrative Region of the People's Republic of China (see SAR)
HKSCC	Hong Kong Securities Clearing Company Ltd.
HKT	Hong Kong Time
Hong Kong Codes	Hong Kong Codes on Takeovers and Mergers and Share Repurchases
HSI	Hang Seng Index
IPO	Initial Public Offering
JPY	Japanese Yen
Listing rules	The Rules Governing the Listing of Securities on the Stock Exchange of Hong Kong Ltd.
LIBOR	London Inter-Bank Offer Rate
LSE	London Stock Exchange
M&As	Mergers and Acquisitions
MPF	Mandatory Provident Fund (Scheme)
NASDAQ	National Association of Securities Dealers Automated Quotation (market/system)
NAV	Net Asset Value
NIB	Note-issuing Bank
NPV	Net Present Value
NYSE	New York Stock Exchange
OTC market	Over-the-Counter market
PRC	People's Republic of China
RTGS	Real Time Gross Settlement (system)
SAR	Special Administrative Region (see HKSAR)
SEAQ	(London) Stock Exchange Automated Quotation (system)
SEHK	(The) Stock Exchange of Hong Kong Ltd.
SEOCH	Stock Exchange Options Clearing House

SFC	Securities and Futures Commission
USD	United States Dollar
VAR	Value-at-Risk

1 billion = 1,000,000,000

$ sign, unless accompanied by the prefix HK, refers to United States Dollars

Tables and Figures

Tables

Appendices

Figures

Preface

Background

Equity markets 'house' equity securities. Equity securities, in turn, represent paper claims, or ownership entitlements, to corporate income streams. The owners of these pieces of paper also receive voting rights. It is this feature which makes the equity security rather different to debt-based paper claims: ownership of the securities conveys ownership rights in the underlying issuing company. Leaving aside this rather crude definition, the remit of this text is to explore these securities, and the markets where they trade, in one of the world's premier financial centres.

Is this, then, a text about the Stock Exchange of Hong Kong (SEHK) and the principal product it trades, the ordinary share? Not quite. The Exchange and the securities it 'houses' are clearly central to the deliberations in this text, but so are a whole range of derivative products written on equity securities, many of which trade on the Hong Kong Futures Exchange (HKFE). A number of overseas markets also trade Hong Kong stocks in a variety of forms. In other words, Hong Kong equity markets are considered in a rather broad sense. A variety of regulatory structures, clearing bodies, and governmental agencies also fall under the spotlight. This text, then, is not a descriptive account of one particular marketplace or body.

The institutions, markets, and regulators that lubricate the movement of capital are one thing. But how do the various market players and issuers benefit from such securities? What do we mean by speculation, hedging, arbitrage, shorting the index, buying a put, and so forth? These are all key questions, but they need to be answered in a particular market context. Hong Kong is unique. Its economy and markets are infused with facets of Western capitalism and Chinese business practice. 'So is Singapore', I hear you say. But is Singapore really the natural home to Mainland Chinese investment? The 'H' share, the 'red-chip', and the 'violet' stock all give Hong Kong a distinctive hue.

Motivations

Teachers of finance in Hong Kong habitually complain about the absence of reference materials on all manner of local market issues. Convincing local students that the appropriate reference text for a course in finance— and financial markets in particular—should be American-based requires some imagination. Audiences around the world might also question the marginal contribution of a new text on US financial markets, given the huge number of books already in circulation. The same cannot be said about a similar text focusing on Hong Kong or the Mainland. The potential audience is also a compelling factor, with the Special Administrative Region's (SAR's) financial institutions and markets at the very epicentre of China's financial system.

The timing of this book might also raise a few eyebrows, coming into print just after the Asian currency crisis of 1997/8; however, these events have not, in my opinion, diminished its value. In some respects, the opposite is true. Despite some erosion in market values, Hong Kong has fared better than most of its neighbours. Why? The trite response is to cite Hong Kong's fundamental strength, transparent legal and regulatory structures, and its unfettered investment and trade environment. Recent events have reinforced these points more than ever. The lessons learned from the Asian currency crisis also help to sharpen the focus of certain key areas. The interplay between Hong Kong's Currency Board system and the pricing of local securities being one.

Even with the 1997–8 nadir in Asian markets, Hong Kong's equity markets still boast a position in the upper echelon of world markets,[1] as well as an enviable level of market development and sophistication. In some ways, this reflects changes instituted after the last major market fall-out, in October 1987. This event paved the way for new financial regulations, trading systems, and risk-management policies—providing the impetus for the stellar returns of the following decade. Between June 1995 and June 1997 alone, market capitalization levels on stocks traded on the SEHK almost doubled.[2] In this light, the 1997–8 malaise represents a retreat from recent gains. It has not, as some commentators have argued, put Asia back a decade or more. As with the 1987 correction, the malady may well yield longer-term benefits.

Key Equity Market Developments

The commitment of the People's Republic of China (PRC) to the SAR, as established prior to the 30 June 1997 change of sovereignty and enshrined in the Basic Law, will also be critical to Hong Kong's resurgence. This commitment has been evident for some time. The slew of PRC-incorporated, state enterprise listings (known as 'H' shares), between 1993 and 1998, underline this fact. This commitment has also been manifest in other obvious ways: through new investments, stock acquisitions, and rising trading turnovers locally. The gelling of old and new, or of a proven and stable regulatory framework with a flood of new Mainland investment, has been a feature of the markets for some time.

Investment and political change are but part of the new landscape. Developments in trading technology and new products have also added a certain sophistication and lustre to the markets. The establishment of the Automated Matching System (AMS) for the execution of SEHK trades, the move to scripless electronic settlement and clearing, and the rash of new equity-based derivatives were notable highlights, which will be dealt with extensively in this text.

Structure of the Text

The text is written with an applied approach in mind. Accordingly, greater emphasis is placed on the structure of local equity markets and products, and their specific uses, than on descriptive content or theory. This objective is amplified by the use of case studies, empirical analyses, and specific examples throughout. This approach lends itself to a wide audience of potential readers—encompassing students, academics, investors, and analysts—and allows the distinctive features and mechanisms in the market to be more easily appreciated.

Local issues of concern in the equity markets are also appraised from international and regional perspectives. Benchmark comparisons with major regional markets, such as Japan's, feature widely. Comparison with markets such as the United Kingdom, due to its historical influence, and the United States, by virtue of its arsenal of investment funds and significance in trading, also inevitably follow.

Fourteen chapters of analysis are set out, each forming part of an integrated overview of Hong Kong's equity markets. Chapter 1 sets the scene by comparing the local market to its regional and global competitors. The ascent of the SEHK—to become the Pacific-Basin's second largest equity market and one of the world's premier markets in terms of value and turnover—is appraised through both statistical and historical narratives. The characteristics of the local market are then assessed in Chapter 2 with particular attention given to listing characteristics of issuers on the local Exchange and the market's regulatory bodies. Trading mechanics and equity funds management then feature in Chapter 3. Developments in the local funds industry are explored, given the rapid growth in this sector and the effect of managed funds on underlying equity values. The increasing involvement of overseas institutions and offshore-registered funds in the trading of local equities is part-and-parcel of the internationalization of the local market. The influx of red-chip and 'H' share listings on the SEHK, and the migration of some stock trading in Hong Kong market constituents to London and New York, are also explored in Chapter 1 and, at greater length, in Chapters 4 and 7.

Pricing issues—or more precisely, the risk–reward trade-off—for various classes of listed stock are addressed in Chapter 4. Conceptual issues relating to risk and return are first set out and appraised within the context of the efficient markets paradigm (EMP). While viewed by some practitioners as the product of fanciful thinking or 'ivory tower' leanings, the concept of market efficiency is at the core of all pricing relationships. In a 'nutshell', absolute market efficiency tells us that prices respond fully and quickly to new information. Obvious trading rules, allowing one to consistently outperform some risk-adjusted benchmark, should not, therefore, be readily apparent. Most studies of the EMP directly test this proposition.

The pertinent question is: how well does the EMP hold up in the local markets? Local market studies suggest a number of inefficiencies or anomalous pricing patterns. While modest departures from efficiency inevitably plague all markets, the question is always one of degree. Are Hong Kong's markets less efficient than other markets of similar size? Based upon regional comparisons—as we will see in Chapter 4—they are not. The ease of entry and exit into the local market, where dealings are devoid of local capital gains and income taxes, exchange-controls, and stock ownership restrictions, is one reason for this. Another is the transparency of the market, engendered by clearly defined regulatory codes and practices, which enhance trading interest and liquidity. The increased competition resulting from such transparency is also likely to limit the scope for price-manipulation. In many other smaller markets, a lack of transparency serves as an impediment to both price-discovery and market growth.

Chapters 5, 6, and 7 explore the actual listing process and the principal role of the equity market as a vehicle for corporate fund-raising. This primary market role is first assessed—in Chapter 5—for initial public offerings (IPOs) of stock, which rose sharply in number during the 1990s, and then, in Chapter 6, for seasoned stocks. The latter concerns new issues of stock by companies with an established listing on the market. In a typical year, funding raised through seasoned issues easily exceeds that from its unseasoned counterpart, the IPO. It is partly because of this that many firms seek listing in the first place. The option to 'tap' the market for funds—once listed—is clearly an attractive one. This material is extended in Chapter 7 by considering the recent trend towards dual-listing and/or dual-trading. Dual-trading, without formal listing of the stock on an overseas exchange, is increasingly popular. London's Stock Exchange Automated Quotation system (SEAQ) for trading makes this possible in its international sector—known as the SEAQ International market—for a wide range of locally-listed stocks. In the absence of listing, however, London plays a subordinate role to the SEHK since all fund-raising activities necessarily occur in each stock's home setting, where formal listed status has been established. The upward spiral in SEHK trading turnover during the 1990s also confirms the SEHK's undisputed role as the principal market for the trading of Hong Kong and mainland PRC stocks.

A small number of locally-listed stocks have also sought additional listings—and, by definition, access to alternative primary market outlets—in recent years. Markets in London, Singapore, Australia, and Japan have figured in this trend. The creation of American Depositary Receipt (ADR) programmes in both Hong Kong and Mainland PRC stocks are also notable. Driven largely by the needs of United States institutions, facing restrictions on the purchase of foreign stocks, the ADR offers a route for such investors to gain exposure to non-US stocks. The complexities of the ADR are spelt out in Chapter 7. In brief, they arise where the underlying scrip (share certificates) are retained by a custodian in the issuing company's home market. The receipts, backed by the scrip, are then issued directly in the United States through a depositary institution. For investors, all of the benefits associated with the underlying stock pass without prejudice to the receipt holder. For those reluctant to venture outside their own familiar

market surroundings, depositary receipts are a convenient substitute for
direct stock ownership. They also allow for dividend returns in US dollars.
ADR programmes therefore feature as a serious alternative to direct stock
listings.

Chapter 8 provides coverage of the antithetic of the new stock issue—
the share repurchase. This involves a corporation buying back its own
stock and, locally, results in the immediate cancellation of the scrip. While
new issues increase the number of shares in issue and siphon funds from
the market, repurchases do the reverse: reducing the number of shares in
circulation and injecting funds into the market. New issues are almost
always pitched during bull markets whereas buy-backs typically appear
in bear markets. The massive increase in local buy-back activity in the last
quarter of 1997 in Hong Kong is indicative of this. These conditions also
saw a number of new issues postponed or shelved. What should be
emphasised though is the scale of repurchase activity. A recent commentary
in *Forbes* magazine highlights that, for 1996 and the early part of 1997, the
number of shares repurchased in the United States was only slightly below
the number issued.[3] As in the US market, share repurchases in Hong
Kong are far from trivial and, as such, warrant detailed attention. For the
purposes of this text, this is undertaken by considering repurchase activity
in tandem with two related areas: director share dealings and corporate
dividend policy. As share repurchases reduce the number of shares in
circulation and inject funds into the market for a stock, a repurchase
typically has a positive effect on the underlying share value, inducing
capital gains for those retaining shares. In this sense, the share repurchase
is like a dividend. Likewise, the share repurchase has some similarities
with director purchases of stocks. While both act to support underlying
stock prices by injecting funds into the market for the stock, a notable
difference also exists. Share repurchases—unlike director purchases—are
conducted in the name of the underlying corporation and, as such, lead
to a cancellation in the shares acquired. Director dealings in contrast have
no effect on the number of shares in issue.

An array of corporate restructuring activities, relating to acquisitions,
privatizations, corporate spin-offs, demergers, and buy-outs, are then
investigated in Chapter 9. All of these activities are central to an
understanding of the dynamism and life of listed stocks. The recent debt
crisis spawned by the Asian currency crisis reminds us that de-listings of
stocks—many of which are a direct consequence of corporate liquidation—
are as natural to a market as its primary function. Similar sentiments also
apply to other major corporate events such as acquisitions, divestments,
and spin-offs. Evaluation of all of these activities naturally follows on
from the material in Chapters 5 to 8.

Developments in equity derivatives are sketched out in the final section
of this text. Options, warrants, convertibles, and swaps are discussed in
Chapters 10 and 11, and futures in Chapter 12. These markets have grown
from virtually nothing in the last ten years or so to a stage where many
are now major bases for derivative trading in Asia. The SEHK's warrant

market, which essentially lists instruments on underlying equity stocks or equity baskets, is viewed as one of the largest and most active in the world. Similar comments can be made about Hang Seng Index futures contracts traded on the Hong Kong Futures Exchange (HKFE), which attract considerable volumes. More recent developments in stock futures and stock options complement the impressive array of exchange-traded equity derivatives now available.

As well as an understanding of the essential features and functions of the products making up Hong Kong's equity derivatives market, the impact of the products on underlying cash positions and markets is also explored. In this vein, issues of risk management—including the rise to prominence of the value-at-risk (VAR) model—are examined. This material forms the content of the penultimate chapter—Chapter 13. In Chapter 14, an overview of market trends and likely future developments in Hong Kong's financial markets is ventured. Developments in equities and equity derivatives are stressed as well as a series of initiatives to jump-start debt markets. In the former area, particular attention is given to the emergence of Internet trading and the development of new ownership structures for exchange-trading bodies. The SAR government's intervention of August 1998 in Hong Kong's equity and futures markets is also assessed.

Overview

While the issues covered make some inroads into an understanding of the structure and functions of Hong Kong's equity markets, one should always be aware of, firstly, the relative importance of these markets, both regionally and globally; and secondly, the huge potential for further capital appreciation and primary market activity as corporate China seeks funding for a slew of capital infrastructure projects, as it emerges from developing country status to one as a fully-fledged global market player. Hong Kong will serve as a central pillar in this process with its equity markets fulfilling a much needed funding role.

The resilience of local corporations in particular, and the SAR economy in general, during the recent economic downturn also bodes well. Various commentators are learning to distinguish between those parts of Asia that have weathered the storm of falling currencies—which include mainland China, the SAR, Singapore, and Taiwan—and those countries that bore the brunt of the crisis—Thailand, Malaysia, Indonesia, South Korea, and, to a lesser extent, Japan. The experiences of 1997–8 suggest that Hong Kong is reasonably robust and that its authorities are able to defend the economy when called upon; as with the defence of the Hong Kong dollar (HKD) link to the US dollar (USD). The economy has, however, been blighted by a small number of high-profile liquidations—Peregrine, CA Pacific, and Forluxe Securities, to name but three. Currency exposure, in one way or another, has been the driving force behind many of the corporate bankruptcies in Asia. Corporations with USD-denominated loans made to parties unable to meet their obligations, due to devaluations in the debtor-corporation's own currency, provide one obvious instance. The demise of Peregrine can be explained along such lines. The erosion of capital bases, in Thailand, Indonesia, and Malaysia, in particular, have also been critical. This has had a truly debilitating effect on corporations in these countries, preventing them from exploiting the one real benefit of a devaluation: favourable export conditions. To add to their woes, rising import costs have inflicted a crippling blow to those with capital but reliance on foreign inputs.

In Hong Kong, currency values have been stable, thanks to the operation of the Currency Board and the economy's fundamental strength. The falling currencies elsewhere, as any casual observer will appreciate, have had pronounced effects in other areas: asset price deflation being the most obvious, with falls in property and securities values providing the most visible evidence of this. Not surprisingly, this has triggered increases in unemployment and falls in GDP growth. Problems on the Mainland, such as the GITIC bankruptcy, have also undermined confidence. Creditor concerns, triggered by the demise of this ITIC (International Trust & Investment Company), have certainly added to the risk premium in the markets. Once this recedes, as Mainland debt restructuring programmes take effect, and the economies of Asia rebuild their capital bases, Hong Kong's markets will undoubtedly spring back to life. Hong Kong's fundamentals are compelling enough reason for this assessment.

At the time of going to press, plans to consolidate the SEHK, HKFE, and the three associated clearing bodies into one listed unit were aired. While Chapters 2 and 14 paint the broad picture, one can only speculate, at this juncture, on the manner and effects of these changes. Similar sentiments also apply to the government's interest in upgrading the SAR's 'financial architecture' and its much-touted 'hi-tech' drive. Nothing stands still, especially in Hong Kong. Excuses aside, much of the text, especially in relation to broad principles and functions, has a certain 'durability' which should help insulate it from the ravages of time.

Paul B. McGuinness
The Chinese University of Hong Kong
September 1999

1.   Monthly Statistics for June 1997 and December 1998, provided by Federation Internationale des Bourses de Valuers (FIBV), reveal that the SEHK, based upon the 'market value of shares of domestic listed companies', fell from sixth to eleventh place in the global rankings.
2.   The 'market value of shares of domestic listed companies' on the SEHK was US$551.1 billion, as of June 1997, compared with US$277.2 billion two years earlier (FIBV Monthly Statistics, June 1995 and June 1997).
3.   See Hulbert (1997).

1. Introduction to Hong Kong's Equity Markets and Their Place in the Global Pecking Order

As a starting point, the essential differences between three broad groups of security type—money, capital, and derivative market instruments—are drawn.[1] As subsets of equity securities feature in only the last two categories, money markets and their instruments, though highly significant in their own right, fall outside this text's remit. Nonetheless, differentiating the money market instrument from its capital and derivative market counterpart serves a useful function.

Money market securities are debt-based and include, amongst other things, the local counterpart of the (US- or UK-based) Treasury bill—the Exchange Fund bill—certificates of deposit, repurchase agreements, and commercial paper. These are all short-term in nature, having a maturity, from their original date of issue, of 12 months or less. In contrast, capital market instruments have a maturity, from their original date of issue, of more than one year. These include securities such as government and corporate bonds, convertible debt, common (ordinary) stock, and preferred stock. In recent years, a third broad category of security type—the derivative—has emerged, with the majority written on underlying capital market securities. Derivatives, while much maligned by those with only a cursory knowledge of finance, can be defined as instruments whose values reflect—or are related to—some other underlying security. They are also characterized by leverage (gearing) which allows the investor to obtain exposure to contract values well in excess of the deposit placed (known as the margin) to open up the position. By magnifying percentage returns, this property strikes fear into the hearts of those less acquainted with the real purpose of derivatives: to hedge risk. When used to hedge, the instruments, instead of magnifying volatility, reduce it. In short, they help to 'lock in' overall returns—after netting out one's exposure in the underlying cash position and the hedge instrument itself—to a narrow range of possible values. This function is key to all derivatives, which include futures, forward contracts, options, warrants, convertibles, and swaps. Details of all of these follow in Chapters 10 to 13.

All equity-based securities in Hong Kong are related in one way or another to either ordinary stock or preferred stock. The former is by far the most important and, for the SEHK, accounts for the lion's share of market value and turnover.[2] The essential differences between the two are examined in Section 1.1. The distinctions between corporate equity—encompassing both ordinary and preferred share capital—and corporate debt are then drawn in Section 1.2. This distinction not only helps to explain how debt and equity function within the corporate setting but reveals how debtholders and shareholders interact.

The characteristics of local stock-issuing companies and their shareholding structures feature in Section 1.3. Two main issues emerge: the predominance of foreign-incorporated companies and the concentration of stockholdings, with a clear controlling share interest evident in most listed companies. The existence of separate categories of stock, such as the China-incorporated 'H' share, and a glut of 'red-chips' add a further dimension to the market. All in all, the intermingling of old and new, or the fusion of long-standing blue-chip companies with new China-play stocks, gives the local market a very distinctive hue. As pointed out in the preface, shades of blue, red, and purple capture the new configuration of colours.

Market structures for equity trading are then addressed in Section 1.4 where a key demarcation is drawn between exchange-traded and over-the-counter (OTC) markets. The question of where stocks trade, in view of the 'internationalization' of stock trading, is also entertained. London trading of Hong Kong stocks, and its impact upon the local market, is central to this discussion. All in all, a rather sanguine tale emerges with feedback trading between London and Hong Kong boosting volumes in both markets. Dramatic increases in turnover during the early to mid-1990s, when dual-trading of Hong Kong counters increased significantly, bears testimony to this. The huge volume gains on the SEHK also point to its hegemony in the trading of local and Mainland stocks.

Material on the relative importance of Hong Kong's equity market is then offered in Section 1.5. As most market-watchers are aware, the SEHK—at least, in terms of value—is second only to Japan in Asia. Hong Kong's engine of growth has been the property sector. With a bias towards property-related investment, particularly in the larger 'blue-chips', equity and property markets have inevitably moved in synch. The influence of real estate is clearly critical to an understanding of local equity markets and is taken up in Section 1.6.

Structural and regulatory reform have also been key in fashioning the market's ascent. Much of this reform has been born out of adversity. The October 1987 crash, which spawned the *Report of the Securities Review Committee* (1988), is a good example of this. The changes triggered by this report—including the establishment of an independent regulatory body, the Securities and Futures Commission (SFC)—were key in raising market transparency and order to new levels. A maelstrom of other changes, principally in the area of trading, settlement, and clearing, also followed on the heels of the report. It is this proactive response to instability and crisis that marks out Hong Kong as a real financial 'tiger'. This theme is reflected in Section 1.7.

1.1   A Taxonomy of Equity Share Classifications

The Distinctions between Ordinary (Common) Stock and Preferred Stock

Despite their differences, both ordinary and preference shares offer income payments to their shareholders in the form of dividends. Unlike interest payments on debt, which are treated as an expense item, these dividends represent an appropriation from a corporation's after-tax profits and, as such, offer no offset against taxable income.

The priority of dividend payment, and its actual level, best characterize the difference between ordinary and preferred share capital. In the former, dividends are best described as discretionary payments determined, in the first instance, by the underlying company's directors. Once ratified by the shareholders at a company's Annual General Meeting, the dividends take on declared status.[3] If, in any year, earnings after interest and tax (EAIT)—also known as earnings attributable to stockholders—are small or negative, dividends may not be paid. In contrast, the preference share provides investors with a 'fixed' dividend which ranks ahead of ordinary share dividend. This dividend is fixed in the sense that if sufficient EAIT exists to pay the preference dividend, it will be paid. A shortfall of EAIT below the promised preference dividend may mean either partial payment or non-payment. This situation can be remedied if the preferred stock is cumulative, as any shortfall can be added on to future years' dividend payments. Participating preference shares add a further wrinkle as, in good years, a supplementary dividend payment may be granted to holders of preference share. In theory, preference shares could have both cumulative and participatory features, although the former is far more likely than the latter.

In sum, preference shares rank ahead of ordinary shares in the queue for dividends and, logically, offer much greater certainty with respect to income returns. As always, a trade-off exists: preference shareholders (excepting the participating share) forfeit the possibility of enhanced dividend; whilst ordinary shareholders embrace greater uncertainty in exchange for it.

Preferred shareholders also have a claim on corporate assets—in the event of liquidation—which ranks ahead of ordinary shareholders, but behind that of the company's creditors. Ordinary shareholders have one clear advantage over preferred shareholders, though: voting rights. Many preferred shares confer absolutely no voting rights and therefore give preference shareholders little opportunity to voice their opinions. In contrast, ordinary shareholders exercise control by, amongst other things, nominating and voting for a company's board of directors.

Ordinary shares and some types of preferred shares can also be distinguished in terms of their life expectancy. Some types of preference stock, such as redeemable preferred shares, have a finite life. In most cases, these are structured with a definite redemption date and a given set of redemption terms which allow the issuer to purchase the securities from the investor at a predetermined price. In other cases, the stock may be 'callable' over some defined time interval, again on predetermined terms. Some preferred shares are also convertible, allowing the investor to convert the stock into the underlying ordinary shares of the issuer. It must be stressed that this is an option exercisable by the investor only and, if unexercised, leaves the preferred shares intact. Where conversion is chosen, the investor surrenders the preferred shares in exchange for a predetermined number of new shares in the issuing company. Locally, Tem Fat Hing Fung (Holdings) Ltd's Exchange-listed preferred stock is a good example of such a security. It is also redeemable and cumulative and, accordingly, attracts the convoluted label of a convertible, cumulative, redeemable preference stock.[4]

In some jurisdictions, ordinary and preferred stocks are joined by a third category of stock: the deferred stock. These are almost an anachronism with only one such stock listing—the Peninsular & Oriental Steam Navigation Co's deferred stock—evident on the SEHK. In general, the deferred stockholder is at the back of the queue when it comes to dividends—with preference and ordinary shareholders having prior claims—but receives enhanced voting rights as compensation.

Classes of Ordinary Stock and their Relationship to Par Values and the Place of Incorporation of the Stock-Issuing Company

Distinctions can also be made between various classes of ordinary share: the 'A', 'B', and 'H' share distinctions being readily apparent locally. The 'H' share, which will be examined in greater detail in Section 1.3, is a Mainland-incorporated enterprise listed on the SEHK. 'A' and 'B' shares are ordinary shares issued by a given company that carry the same voting rights but carry differential par values. To understand the 'A'/'B' share distinction, some appreciation of the difference between par and market values is required.

Par Values vs. Market Values

A stock's par value should not be confused with its market value. At one level, a share may have a par value even if, due to the stock being unlisted, a market valuation is not available. At another, the par value of a listed stock should remain constant despite variations in a stock's market value. The only exception to this rule, is where a stock split or stock consolidation (i.e., reverse split) is mandated, in which case a proportional change in par value occurs. This complication is considered in Section 6.1.

What, then, is the point of a par value? At the most obvious level, it plays a role in determining dividends on preference shares. A 7.5% preference stock, for instance, promises a dividend per share of $0.075 per annum if the share's par value is $1. But as some preferred stocks around the globe promise dividends in dollar terms—without reference to the par—even this role for the par is somewhat secondary. Its principal role lies, in fact, within the accounting sphere. Together with the issued share capital (ISC) account of a company, the par tells the reader the precise number of shares in issue of a certain type. An ISC balance of $100 million, for shares of par of $2.00, suggests 50 million shares in issue, for example. If these 50 million shares had been issued in one batch at a market price of $3.00 some time earlier, funding of $150 million would have been raised. As the ISC account only reflects part of this amount—the product of par and number of shares issued—the difference must be captured somewhere else within the book-keeping system. This difference, equal to selling price less par, all multiplied by the number of issued shares, shows up as a credit of $50 million in the issuer's share premium account. The $150 million debit entry, corresponding to the $100 million ISC and $50 million share premium credit entries, finds its way to current assets. Beyond this accounting meaning, the par offers little value. Indeed, some countries, such as Australia and New Zealand, have taken steps to remove it entirely: the upshot being a consolidation of ISC and share premium accounts.

The 'A' and 'B' Share Distinction
Par values are still very much in use locally. As argued earlier, certain corporations also have ordinary stock in issue with differential pars. The 'A' and 'B' ordinary share distinction—as in Swire Pacific 'A' and 'B' stock, where par values of $0.60 and $0.12 prevail—is indicative of this.[5] While both types of share carry the same voting rights, dividends are paid in proportion to the par. Accordingly, one Swire Pacific 'A' stock attracts a dividend five times that of its 'B' cousin.[6] The 'A'/'B' share distinction now carries more novelty value than anything else, given restrictions on listed companies issuing separate tranches of such shares.[7]

As a final point in this area, the 'A' and 'B' share distinction used for stock listings in the Mainland markets of Shanghai and Shenzhen is quite different. Shares categorized as such are segmented with 'A' shares only available to Mainland investors and 'B' shares, denominated in USD and HKD, restricted to non-mainland residents. A similar local/foreign or 'A'/'B' share dichotomy is also apparent in Thailand. Greater detail on this issue, in relation to Shanghai and Shenzhen listed stocks, follows in Section 7.2.

1.2 The Distinction between Corporate Debt and Corporate Equity

Debt securities, whether of a short-term or long-term nature, enjoy income claims on a company's assets ahead of preference and ordinary shareholders. The reasoning is simple: debt interest is an expense for the debtor company while shareholder income (i.e., dividends) is an appropriation from earnings after interest and taxes. With a given interest rate on debt, debtholders (creditors) clearly enjoy a fixed claim on the income stream of the debtor firm and the ordinary shareholders a residual claim. Preference shareholders, as we saw earlier, have an intermediate claim with their fixed dividend ranking ahead of ordinary shareholders but behind creditors. The same comments also essentially sum up the capital claims enjoyed by the three parties, although the precise conditions for repayment may vary from one jurisdiction to another. These conditions are largely governed by a company's articles (and place) of incorporation. For Hong Kong-incorporated companies, the provisions of Sections 163–165 of the *Companies Ordinance* apply. These relate to the 'Proof and Ranking of Claims' in both forced and voluntary liquidations; the former occurring where creditors pursue court sanction and the latter where debtors freely embark upon winding-up procedures.

In most jurisdictions, capital repayments will likely accrue to short-term creditors, long-term creditors, preference shareholders, and ordinary shareholders in that order of priority. Issues of debt seniority may also surface for debts of a particular term, with more established debts ranking ahead of newer ones. Debts with specific security—where the debtor pledges collateral (involving either personal or corporate assets)—are also likely to rank ahead of all unsecured claims. To illustrate the effects of corporate liquidation on the claimants, consider the balance sheet for a fictitious entity ABC Ltd shown in Exhibit 1.1. For simplicity, assume that all debts are unsecured.

Exhibit 1.1

BALANCE SHEET OF ABC LTD.

	$million		$million
Assets 11,200	Owner's Equity:		
	Issued Share Capital, Ordinary Shares	3,000	
	Preference Shares	1,500	
			4,500
	Share Premium, Ordinary Shares	500	
	Preference Shares	—	
			500
	Accumulated Profits (Ordinary Shares)	2,200	
			2,200
	Debt: Long-Term Liabilities	3,800	
	Short-Term Liabilities	200	
			4,000
11,200			11,200

The first thing to note is that accounting conventions require that assets be recorded at historic cost.[8] As such, the market (or disposable) value of the firm's assets is likely to stray from balance sheet values. While the fixed capital claim of the debtholders—equal to the face or principal amount of their debt—can be read from the balance sheet, the same is not true for the equityholders. A second thing to note is that accumulated profits—sums remaining after dividends that are ploughed back into owners' equity—are assumed to accrue solely to ordinary shareholders.[9]

To illustrate the liquidation process, suppose ABC's assets are disposed of for $7 billion. Ignoring liquidation expenses (which would, in all likelihood, be paid first), the following sequence of payments would likely result: $200 million to short-term creditors; $3.8 billion to long-term creditors; $1.5 billion to preference shareholders; and, whatever remains, $1.5 billion in this case, to ordinary shareholders. As the ordinary shareholders only receive a fraction of their book claim (= $5.7 billion), they clearly face most of the risk. As argued, they receive compensation for this risk given their voting rights.

Had the disposable value of the assets in ABC been $20 billion, the picture would have been rather different: creditors and preferred stockholders would have received their fixed claim return of $4 billion and $1.5 billion, respectively, leaving the rest—$14.5 billion—for the ordinary stockholders. Ordinary stockholders would have come out well ahead, garnering nearly three times their book claim of $5.7 billion.

The Inherent Conflict between Debt and Equityholders

As far as creditors are concerned, their position is secure as long as asset valuations in ABC remain at or above $4 billion. Valuations below this would lead them to forfeit some of their claim. Equityholders would not be liable for this shortfall, though, given their limited liability status. In effect, the residual claim for the ordinary shareholders has a lower bound of zero. The upshot for creditors (debtholders) is obvious: when the equityholders' residual claim approaches zero, the riskiness of the debtholders' position increases markedly. The risk attitudes of the equityholders are also likely to change in the process. Knowing that their limited liability status protects them against creditor losses, ordinary shareholders may wish to endorse more speculative investment projects. If returns from these projects are poor, firm value is likely to slip further with the creditors suffering the downside. On the other hand, if the projects generate strong returns, firm value is likely to increase with the equityholders enjoying all the upside gain in value by virtue of their residual claim. It is precisely because of this that creditors write restrictive (protective) covenants with equityholders whenever debt financing is arranged. These contracts typically require equityholders to maintain working capital levels—defined loosely as current assets less current liabilities—at prescribed levels and to limit dividend payments. Some agreements may also give creditors a voice—and, in some cases, a veto—

over any subsequent borrowing and investment decisions made by the debtor company. In such a contractual arrangement, the creditor is the principal and the equityholder the agent.[10]

The Corporate Balance Sheet as a 'Snap-Shot' of Investment vs. Financing Sources

In a general sense, the assets shown on a balance sheet capture the corporation's investments. The requisite financing—liabilities and owners' equity—appear on the opposite side of the sheet. The investment process can be viewed in action by considering the effect on the balance sheet of asset expansion. Referring to the position in Exhibit 1.1, suppose company ABC wishes to expand its fixed asset base by $1 billion. Suppose this investment—perhaps reflecting the purchase of land, plant, and machinery, or buildings—is financed by a new issue of stock. Given a par for the ordinary stock in ABC of $10 (which, given an ISC balance of $3 billion, suggests 300 million shares already in issue) and a selling price of $20 per share, the company would need to sell an additional 50 million shares to raise the target amount. In accounting terms, debits to assets of $1 billion and credits of $500 million to the ISC account for ordinary stock (= 50 million shares at $10 per share) and the ordinary share premium account (= 50 million shares at $20–$10) would do the trick. It is this kind of financing operation that underpins the role of equity markets. The same might also be said of the debt markets, had corporate bond financing been used, or of the banking system, had an approach to the banks been made.

1.3   Characteristic Features of Local Stock-Issuing Companies and their Shareholders

Corporate Domicile/Incorporation and the Emergence of 'China-Play' Stocks

The par value of a company's stock, as described in Section 1.1, and a host of other details pertinent to a company's legal structure, reflect that company's articles of association. These articles, in turn, depend upon the jurisdiction chosen. Rather confusingly, a company can set up its own legal constitution—and thus domicile—in a very different location to the majority of its business interests and fixed assets. This is particularly true of SEHK listed companies with a majority now incorporated outside the SAR: the preferred locales being Bermuda, the Cayman Islands, and the Cook Islands. The effect of this migration—a trend which has been noticeable since Jardine Matheson's decision in 1984 to change its incorporation from Hong Kong to Bermuda—caused some alarm initially. But as more and more companies followed suit, it became clear that, in most cases, such moves were having little or no effect upon the physical location of assets and business interests. Far from causing waves, then, the trend, which took hold in the late 1980s and early 1990s, had only a ripple effect on the markets. The jurisdictions chosen had something to do with this. All, due to their British dependent territory status and/or Commonwealth ties, dovetailed very closely with corporate regulations in the Crown Colony (and those of its heir and successor, the SAR).

In a relocation of domicile, a new holding company is set up in a foreign locale. This involves the new holding company issuing shares to replace those of the previously constituted holding company.[11] Why have so many locally-listed companies pursued such a course of action? Most accounts reflect two themes: firstly the tax savings flowing from such relocations; and secondly the elimination of uncertainty relating to possible tax changes, and other corporate-based regulations, in the light of Hong Kong's change of sovereignty. The second issue may be seen as a logical response to uncertainty, and is consistent with the timing of most of the relocations which occurred between the mid-1980s and early 1990s. The tax savings argument is less obvious. Any corporate income earned on Hong Kong-based assets invites local corporate tax consequences, no matter where the underlying company is domiciled. The tax issue relates, instead, to savings in real estate and capital duties. Given the active new issues market in Hong Kong, relocation may result in substantial capital duty savings.[12]

The Influx of Mainland Incorporated 'H' Shares

The trend to offshore incorporation has also occurred alongside a rash of listings of mainland China-incorporated companies. These state-owned Enterprises (SOEs), which trade on the SEHK under the guise of the 'H' share, form the constituents of the *Hang Seng China Enterprises Index*. As of the 1998 year-end, they numbered 42.[13] In relation to Chapter 19A of the *Rules Governing The Listing of Securities on The Stock Exchange of Hong Kong Ltd* (hereafter *Listing Rules*), which sets out listing requirements for 'Issuers Incorporated in the People's Republic of China', 'H' shares are 'overseas listed foreign shares which are listed on the Exchange and subscribed for and traded in Hong Kong dollars'. Foreign shares are in turn 'issued by a PRC issuer under PRC law, the par value of which is denominated in renminbi, and which are subscribed for in a currency other than renminbi.'[14]

As with the first issue by Tsingtao Breweries in September 1993, and all successive 'H' share listings, listing requires the assent of both the SEHK and the PRC state authorities. Once authorized for listing, the 'H' share usually comes to market through an initial public offering (IPO) where new and/or existing shares are offered to local and international investors.[15] This route to listing, which is examined in Chapter 5, allows some diversification in the ownership base of the new entrant. Nonetheless, it still leaves the existing owner—the PRC state and any other connected parties—holding the lion's share of the outstanding stock. Counterparts to the 'H' share, like the 'N', 'S', 'L', and 'T' share are also readily apparent and refer to Chinese SOE listings in New York, Singapore, London, and Tokyo, respectively.

The Red-Chip Stock

Unlike the 'H' share, the red-chip stock is issued by a company with incorporated status outside the Mainland. These stocks are currently tracked by the *Hang Seng China-Affiliated Corporations Index*. At the 1998 year-end there were 46. As with the 'H' share, the red-chip is characterized by Mainland majority control. This may stem directly from the PRC state, provincial or municipal parties or indeed any companies controlled by such concerns.[16] For Hong Kong listed stocks, control refers to an ownership interest of 35% or more of the outstanding stock controlled by an individual entity or collection of entities which, in the parlance of the local takeover code, are deemed to 'act in concert'.

Notable differences in the business activities of underlying 'H' share and red-chip companies are evident. Most of the former have specific business interests which lie, in the main, in areas of heavy engineering, transportation, and power production.[17] In contrast, red-chip companies span a wider number of industries and are considerably more diversified in their asset-base. They also have more assets in non-Mainland jurisdictions. This is especially true of red chips that were engineered via 'backdoor' listing, a topic that is taken up in Chapter 9. In brief, this involved the acquisition of listed companies and the subsequent injection of the acquirer's assets into the listed 'shell'. This gave rise, especially during the early 1990s, when such activity was particularly marked, to companies with varying configurations of Mainland and local assets. Over time—as more and more Mainland assets have been ploughed into these entities—some of the red chips have begun to mirror another type of stock: the 'China-concept' entity. Companies issuing such shares have a predilection towards Mainland investment but, unlike their red-chip and 'H' share counterparts, have little or no Mainland ownership. Companies such as Cheung Kong Infrastructure and New World Infrastructure best represent this kind of stock.

The Distribution of Shareholdings: the 25% 'Public' Interest Requirement and the 35% Control Threshold

The issue of shareholder control serves as a cornerstone of the SFC's *Hong Kong Codes on Takeovers and Mergers and Share Repurchases* (hereafter, the *Hong Kong Codes*). It therefore carries great significance for all stocks listed on the market. Control exists when a party, or group of parties acting in concert, controls 35% or more of a listed company's stock.[18] Similar principles relating to majority control are also recognized in jurisdictions like the United Kingdom, Singapore, and Malaysia, with specified trigger points in these jurisdictions varying between 25% and 33%.[19] While the *Hong Kong Codes* is not a part of statute, it carries considerable force by virtue of the fact that '. . . The Rules Governing the Listing of Securities on The Stock Exchange of Hong Kong Limited expressly require compliance with the Codes.' (*Hong Kong Codes*, 1.4, p. 1.2, April 1996).

The significance of the 35% control level is that it acts as a potential trigger for corporate acquisition. If a party, or group of parties deemed to be acting in concert, raise their ownership interest in an entity from a level below 35% to a level above this threshold, Rule 26.1 of the *Hong Kong Codes* comes into force. This stipulates that—in the absence of an SFC granted waiver—a general offer must be made to all other parties holding shares. So, if a party Q has 33 million shares in a company C, constituting a 33% shareholding, and increases its holdings by a further 3 million shares to a 36% interest, Q breaches the trigger. In the absence of a waiver, Q would then be compelled to make an offer to buy the 64 million shares held by other investors.

For reasons of brevity, the offer price set and the conditions for success for a general offering are not discussed here. Details of both are carefully set out in Chapter 9. The issue here is why does a holding of 35% or more—and not a holding of 50% or more—constitute control? Part of the answer lies, perhaps, with the fact that listed companies must 'normally' be able to demonstrate a public interest holding in their stocks of at least 25% (where the market capitalization of their stock is not in excess of HK$4 billion). This is reflected, amongst other things, in Rule 8.08 of the *Listing Rules*.[20] This public interest essentially comprises holdings by parties who are judged not to be 'connected persons of the issuer'.[21] What constitutes a connected person? According to the *Listing Rules*, 'in relation to a company other than a PRC issuer, and other than any subsidiaries of a PRC issuer, means a director, chief executive, or substantial shareholder of such company or any of its subsidiaries or an associate of any of them . . . .'[22] A substantial shareholder is, in turn, a party able to control at least 10% of a company's voting stock.[23]

Shares constituting the public interest of a company's stock may be widely dispersed. As such, there is a high probability that a large proportion of them will not be mobilized in corporate decision-making. As such, a shareholding of less than 50% should defeat most challenges. If we go to an extreme and assume that none of the shares held by the public are mobilized, someone able to mobilize 37.5% or more of a company's oustanding shares would achieve de facto control. The possibility of being able to wield control with a slightly lower percentage may be one of the reasons behind the 35% threshold adopted in Hong Kong. With a 35% stockholding, one can realistically gamble on wresting corporate control. A certain amount of apathy amongst the other 40% of investors, constituting the non-public interest, or their inability to achieve consensus, would lend support to this.

A substantial number of SEHK listed stocks—including all 'H' share companies—have clear controlling interests (as defined by the interpretation given to control in the *Hong Kong Codes*)[24]. Most listed

Asian companies are subject to a clearly defined controlling influence. The story in the West is rather different, where more diffuse shareholding structures exist. The Asian model has its admirers, though, especially those that seek a clear channel of communication between principal owners and managers. On the downside, minority stockholders provide a much weaker check or balance against the policies of major stockholders in a typical Asian corporation. In this setting, issues of corporate governance are of even greater import. The irony is that many Asian countries lag well behind in these stakes.

There is also evidence that certain groups of investors control a disproportionate number of locally-based stocks through cross-holdings and/or interlocking directorships. Mok et al. (1992) provide compelling evidence for this in terms of the dominance of family groupings. Although their analysis is now a little dated—given their use of data for December 1989—the general thrust of their arguments may still hold. Employing a criterion of 'family control',[25] they examined Hong Kong's 77 largest corporations, which accounted for 75% of the market's value at the time. They discovered that nine families were able to wield control over stocks making up around 50% of the market's value.[26] Results of this kind suggest that the actions of major players—whether unintentionally motivated or not—are likely to have a pronounced effect on market prices. The role of these players and other major investors, such as overseas institutions, are key to any understanding of liquidity and price behaviour. Not surprisingly, many local commentators refer to these major players as de facto market-makers. While actual market-making violates the provisions of the Securities Ordinance, being tantamount to market manipulation, the term de facto market-maker does not necessarily carry a pejorative meaning. It refers only to the disproportionate influence such investors' trades have on the overall market.

1.4   Issues of Where and How Stocks Trade: Over-the-Counter (OTC) vs. Exchange-Traded Markets and the Internationalization of Stock Trading

While most attention will focus on exchange-traded products within this text, other types of market structure—such as the over-the-counter (OTC) market—cannot simply be relegated to a footnote. In the derivatives area alone, OTC market transactions are huge, as we will see in Chapters 10 to 13. Certain derivatives such as swaps and forward contracts are exclusive to such markets. Foreign exchange and debt markets, like the Euro-bond market, also function as OTC markets. In some quarters, equity trades also operate OTC. What then is an OTC market and how does it differ from an organized exchange?

Primary and Secondary Market Functions in Relation to the Two Types of Market

The principal difference is that OTC markets are not centred on, nor confined to, a particular trading location or exchange. Quite often, these products are customized and arranged privately with, in many cases, little scope for subsequent trading of the securities. Any party buying the security directly from the issuer is therefore assumed to have an intention to hold the security until its defined settlement or maturity date. In contrast, exchange-traded products, notably derivatives and corporate bonds, have standardized terms and typically attract trading interest once in issue.

A market that offers liquidity after the initial sale of the securities is commonly described as a secondary market. As the securities are already in issue, trades in such a secondary market represent wealth transfers between buyers and sellers which completely bypass the original issuer of the securities. In contrast, securities are first issued in a primary market where governments, in the case of debt issues, and corporations, in the case of equity and debt issues, raise funds directly from the market.

The success of any market depends critically upon the interaction of both the primary and secondary market functions. Subscription to IPOs and other primary market offers is unlikely to occur, for instance, unless a secondary market is available for unwinding such positions. As is the case with OTC products, however, secondary markets may not necessarily materialize. Even for some exchange-traded products—for example the majority of the SEHK's listed debt—little or no secondary market trading may be evident. The potential buyer should, of course, be compensated for this illiquidity through the addition of a liquidity premium to the asset's return. If a corporate bond—which represents a stream of fixed future cash-flow payments from the bond issuer to the buyer—is expected to be illiquid once in issue, the issuer will need to mark down the price to achieve a sale. For the given stream of cash-flow returns, the buyer therefore receives an increased yield on the investment to compensate for the security's perceived illiquidity.

To appreciate the above, note that the yield—or, more precisely, yield to maturity or redemption yield—of a bond equates to a common discount rate. This rate sets the present value of a bond's future cash flow equal to its invoice price. A bond with market price of $928.61 (per $1,000 of face, par, or principal value) with exactly two years to maturity and a coupon rate of 3% per annum payable in two equal—and equally spaced—instalments per year, would command a yield y (= 0.07 or 7%) given by,

$$\$928.61 \quad = \quad \frac{15}{(1+y)^{1/2}} \quad + \quad \frac{15}{(1+y)^{1}} \quad + \quad \frac{15}{(1+y)^{3/2}} \quad + \quad \frac{1015}{(1+y)^{2}}$$

As the market price of the bond depends, amongst other things, on liquidity, a deterioration in its marketability would result in a lower price and enhanced yield. The inflation in yield would duly compensate for the perceived illiquidity. Similar arguments should also apply to any other illiquid security. As one might expect, such arguments are typically of greater import for products traded OTC.

The Issue of Credit or Counterparty Risk

As we shall also learn in later chapters, positions opened on an exchange afford much greater protection against counterparty default. For derivatives, in particular, the counterparties to an exchange-trade receive the protection of the exchange's clearing house which guarantees the profits and losses on all positions. This guarantee—which, for reasons of credibility, must be backed by a sufficiently large fund—means that the clearing house operates as a de facto counterparty to every open position. This function, which is crucial to the success of exchange-traded derivatives, is known as novation. The protection afforded by this also makes it easier to generate secondary market interest in such markets.

OTC Trading in Stocks

OTC markets can also be found in the direct trading of stocks. These, as with OTC derivative trades, can take the form of private arrangements between particular buyers and sellers where, typically, little prospect for subsequent secondary market trading exists. Dealings in some American Depositary Receipts (ADRs), which feature in Section 7.4, are like this. Due to regulations imposed by the US authorities, such instruments proxy directly for the underlying share and convey all benefits of the underlying share to the holder. They are not derivatives as such, as the ADR has a defined relationship with the share and is directly convertible into a given number of such shares. In this sense, processes of arbitrage should ensure that the ADR's value is approximately equal to the value of the underlying stock backing the ADR.

Some active secondary markets have some features in common with OTC markets. The National Association of Securities Dealers Automated Quotation (NASDAQ) market in the US, where trading is conducted through a telecommunications system with screen-based bid and offer prices generated by dealers in numerous locations, could be described as such. As it has no specific trading location, it resembles an OTC market. If, however, we assume that a trading system with a clear ownership or membership structure is not an OTC market, NASDAQ falls outside the OTC definition.

London Trading in Hong Kong Stocks

In a sense, London trading of Hong Kong stocks in SEAQ International resembles NASDAQ given, at least until recently, its total reliance upon a competitive dealer-based system similar to NASDAQ's. As most Hong Kong stocks trading on SEAQ International are not listed in London, the forum provides—as with OTC markets in general—a secondary market only. Despite this limitation, the market has made considerable inroads into the trading of Hong Kong stocks. So much so, that a separate index for the London trading of Hong Kong stocks, the Hang Seng London Reference Index, was established in December 1994. The growing influence of London largely reflects a time-zone advantage, which allows effective 'back-to-back' trading in many of Hong Kong's largest stocks. The internationalization of stock trading is a key feature of the Hong Kong equities field and highlights the increasing visibility of local stocks.

1.5   International Comparisons of Exchange-Traded Equity Markets

To provide some indication of the growing importance of Hong Kong stock trading, global comparisons of equity market values are helpful. Market value is typically captured by the market capitalization of listed equities in the various exchanges. For an individual stock, this is equal to the number of shares listed in that stock multiplied by the prevailing price. For the market as a whole, market capitalization is derived by summing the market capitalization values for all constituent stocks.

Table 1.1 provides some indication of the relative importance of major markets where the value of domestic stock listings in the principal exchange of various countries are compared. One drawback is that certain markets, like the US NASDAQ market and Japan's Osaka market—which are sizeable in their own right—are necessarily excluded because of this approach. While overshadowed by the size of the New York Stock Exchange, NASDAQ is the world's second largest stock exchange in terms of value. Osaka, in turn, is larger than Germany's Deutsche Borse.[27] There may also be some confusion over the precise meaning of a domestic stock listing. It is taken here to reflect the categorization given to it by the actual exchanges in question.

Asia-Pacific markets are well represented with four of the top 20 markets hailing from the region. This representation would have been even greater had June 1997, rather than December 1998, figures been relied upon. The Asian currency crisis—despite the retention of the HKD/USD linked rate locally—resulted in Hong Kong falling from sixth in the rankings to eleventh, all within the space of eighteen months.

In spite of the havoc wreaked by the Asian currency crisis, the data reported in Table 1.2 indicate that Hong Kong's market grew in value by a staggering 4,596% (i.e., 47 times) between 1976 and 1998. As with some other markets on the Pacific-Rim, a considerable portion of this growth is due to new listings of stock, principally IPOs. Again, much of this has occurred in recent years. During the 1990s alone, the number of listed companies rose by over 120%. A similar story of burgeoning growth is indicated when analysing the daily dollar value of trading volumes of the market in the 1970s and 1980s, which pales when compared with recent levels. The record daily SEHK turnover of around HK$79 billion, which

Table 1.1   Global Comparisons of the Market Capitalization of Domestic Listed Companies and Trading Turnover in Major Stock Markets

Country	Representative Bourse	June 94 M.Cap. Rank	June 95 M.Cap. Rank	June 96 M.Cap. Rank	June 97 M.Cap. Rank	Dec. 97 M.Cap. Rank	Dec. 98 M.Cap. Rank	Market Capitalization as of Dec. 98 (US$billions)	Turnover for 1997 (US$billions)#
USA	New York	1	1	1	1	1	1	10,271.9	5,777.6
Japan	Tokyo	2	2	2	2	2	2	2,439.5	896.1
UK	London	3	3	3	3	3	3	2,297.7	1,989.5(*)
Germany	Deutsche B./F'ft	4	4	4	4	4	4	1,094.3	1,067.7(*)
France	Paris	5	5	5	5	5	5	985.2	1,414.1(*)
Switzerland	Zurich	8	6	7	8	6	6	689.2	568.9(*)
Netherlands	Amsterdam	11	9	9	9	8	7	603.2	280.9(*)
Italy	Milan	13	15	13	12	10	8	569.7	203.3
Canada	Toronto	6	7	6	7	7	9	543.4	305.2
Spain	Madrid	17	16	15	13	12	10	402.2	424.3(*)
Hong Kong	Hong Kong	7	8	8	6	9	11	343.6	453.7
Australia	Sydney	10	12	10	11	11	12	328.9	171.0
Sweden	Stockholm	21	17	16	16	14	13	278.7	175.8(*)
Taiwan	Taipei	12	13	14	10	13	14	260.0	1,308.6
Belgium	Brussels	22	20	22	19	18	15	247.6	33.9
S.Africa	Johannesburg	9	10	12	15	16	16	168.5*	44.7
Brazil	Rio De Janeiro	–	–	–	–	–	17	162.0	26.7
	Sao Paulo	20	–	17	–	15	–	–	190.7
Finland	Helsinki	29	25	27	25	22	18	154.8	36.3
S. Korea	Seoul	16	14	18	17	29	19	114.6	170.8
Denmark	Copenhagen	24	23	25	20	20	20	98.9	46.7(*)

Source: Data for market capitalization levels extracted from *Federation Internationale des Bourses de Valeurs (FIBV) Monthly statistics* for various issues (July 1995; July 1997; and January 1998). Data for turnover extracted from FIBV Annual statistics (see http://www.fibv.com).

Notes:
a   Only the largest exchange, in terms of share capitalization, is shown for each country.
b   Turnover figures include trades in investment funds.
*   Capitalization figures in FIBV for Johannesburg are based upon domestic and foreign shares and investment funds.
#   Turnover figures reported by FIBV are typically reported as 'Trading System View' figures or as 'Regulated Environment View' figures. Where the latter are used the (*) label is applied to the figures.

Table 1.2   Historical Guide to the Growth of Hong Kong's Equity
Market

Year	No. of Listed Securities**	No. of Listed Companies	Market Capitalisation*** (HK$millions) of Listed Stocks	Average Daily Stock Trading Turnover (HK$millions)
1976	319	295	56,675	53.2
1977	315	284	51,278	24.9
1978	298	265	65,939	112.5
1979	298	262	112,809	104.2
1980	309	262	209,752	388.9
1981	335	269	232,331	434.3
1982	342	273	131,640	187.1
1983	351	277	142,093	150.5
1984	348	278	184,642	196.8
1985	340	279	269,511	307.0
1986	335	253	419,281	498.5
1987	412	276	419,612	1,509.8
1988	479	304	580,378	804.4
1989	479	298	605,010	1,216.0
1990	520	299	650,410	1,164.2
1991	597	357	949,172	1,347.2
1992	749	413	1,332,184	2,802.3
1993	891	477	2,975,379	4,910.3
1994	1006	529	2,085,182	4,586.4
1995	1033	542	2,348,310	3,347.4
1996	1272	583	3,475,965	5,671.7
1997	1533	658	3,202,093	15,465.1
1998	1246	680	2,661,712	6,887.1
1999#	1166	688	3,590,380	6,339.4

Source: For the years 1976–1996, SEHK *Fact Book 1996* p. 94 and p. 97; for 1997, SEHK *Monthly Bulletin* (January 1998, p. 8–9); for 1998 (December), SEHK *Monthly Bulletin* (January 1999, p. 8–9); and for 1999#, SEHK *Monthly Bulletin* (July 1999, p. 8–9).
Notes: ** Includes ordinary and preference shares, warrants, debt, and unit trust securities and rights listings.
*** Figures reported show the market value of ordinary stock listings only (securities listed as preference shares, warrants, debt and unit trusts are excluded). The addition of figures for preference shares and warrants would have raised market capitalization levels to HK$3,219 billion as of December 1997 and HK$2,676 billion as of December 1998 (see SEHK *Monthly Bulletin*, January 1998, p. 9 & January 1999, p. 9).
# Reflects average daily value turnover for 1999 up to the end of June.

occurred during August of 1998, also demonstrates the strength of the Exchange's trading system: the Automated Matching System (AMS).

In the global scheme of things, the SEHK ranks eighth in terms of turnover (see Table 1.1). Hong Kong's standing is even more impressive if one considers turnover per dollar of market value. From 20 or more markets covered in Table 1.1, only five—Germany, France, Hong Kong, Taiwan, and Spain—were able to generate annual turnover in excess of their closing market capitalization levels for the 1997 year-end. Taiwan's ratio is particularly impressive.

The exclusion of foreign stock listings from the data in Table 1.1 may have some impact upon international comparisons of both market value and turnover. Certain markets, like the London Stock Exchange (LSE), benefit considerably from foreign stock trades and listings. As of the 1997 year-end, for example, the LSE reported 526 of its 2,991 listings as being international companies. More importantly, these listings accounted for a greater proportion of the market's value than domestic listings (see also Table 1.3 for an overview of the importance of foreign/international companies in various exchanges).[28]

Table 1.3   Global Comparison of (Domestic and Foreign) Company Quotations in Major Markets: Numbers of Companies Listed and Turnover Value

Market/ Exchanges	No. of Companies Listed		No. of Foreign Listings as a % of Domestic Listings* ((2) ÷ (1) × 100)	Ratio of Turnover Values in Foreign to Domestic Companies Multiplied by 100 **
	Domestic* (1)	Foreign* (2)		
1. NASDAQ	4,627	441	9.53	4.57
2. New York	2,722	392	14.40	13.02
3. London	2,399	522	21.76	137.75
4. Tokyo	1,838	52	2.83	0.16
5. Toronto	1,384	49	3.54	0.18
6. Australian	1,162	60	5.16	0.73
7. Paris	784	178	22.70	2.55
8. Korea	748	–	–	–
9. Germany	741	–	–	4.71
10. American	708	62	8.76	na

Rankings made in terms of the number of domestic listings.
Foreign is taken to be synonymous with 'international'.
*   Figures obtained from London Stock Exchange's *Fact File* (1999, p. 39), which provides details of 28 markets. Columns (1) and (2) reflect positions as of 31 December, 1998.
**   Figures determined from domestic and 'international' values disclosed in London Stock Exchange's *Fact File* (1998, p. 41), which relates to turnover value for 1997.

The incorporation of foreign stocks into the market capitalization figures for the various markets would show that, as before, the top three jurisdictions are easily distinguishable from the rest. However, the magnitude of capitalization differences would likely be squeezed. Such comparisons suggest, therefore, that the size of the London equity market is severely underestimated when only domestic stock listings are taken into account. For Hong Kong, relatively few of its listed stocks are recognized as being foreign, which means that analysing domestic—as opposed to 'domestic plus foreign'—stock listings makes little difference, as is probably the case with most other markets.

In some jurisdictions, a stock might be viewed as foreign if its domicile or place of incorporation lies outside the country where it is listed. If this criterion were rigidly followed, more than half of the listed stocks on the SEHK would be viewed as foreign. In fact, all Hong Kong listed companies that have domiciled overseas have done so in Common Law jurisdictions. As a result, the legal framework governing such companies dovetails with that for SAR incorporated companies, and will continue to do so by virtue of provisions in the Basic Law which uphold the use of Common Law post-handover.[29]

As only a small number of non-Hong Kong domiciled companies are regarded as foreign listed companies by the Exchange, overseas domicile is not the defining characteristic of a foreign stock listing on the SEHK. If the majority of the assets in a company are located in the SAR or Mainland, the SEHK views a listing in this company as a domestic one, regardless of its place of domicile. As of the close of 1996, the *Fact Book 1966*, pp. 101–106 revealed that 382 of the 583 companies listed on the Exchange were incorporated outside Hong Kong. Of these, 22 were China-incorporated 'H' shares. As with the lion's share of the remainder of companies with foreign incorporation (338 in total), these were deemed local stocks. By definition, companies recognized as foreign had, in addition to overseas incorporation, assets that were broadly based outside Hong Kong and the Mainland. Guidelines adopted by other exchanges, in defining domestic stock listings, implicit in the information in Table 1.1, may vary, however.

Cross-Holdings and the Inflation of Market Capitalization Figures

One issue that may drive market capitalization levels are cross-holdings. Japan in particular, through cross-holding structures like the *keiretsu*, arguably experiences some inflation in its capitalization numbers. Cross-holding structures are cartel-like arrangements in which each of the constituent members tacitly agree to buy the others' new shares. The underlying mechanism is spelled out in Ferguson and Hitzig's (1993) excellent account. In brief, if one takes a club of ten companies and each issues new shares, the shares will be divided among nine parties on each occasion. Taken to an extreme, all of the funds raised from a company's new issue will be returned to the buying companies when they, in turn, make new shares. If this happens, market capitalization levels can rise without any corresponding increase in any of the companies' real assets. This is a startling insight. Though exaggerated in its proportions here, it has led some to question the actual (or cross-holding adjusted) value of certain markets. Various estimates for Japan, where this kind of cross-holding arrangement is most prolific, suggest that anything between 24% and 49% of the market's value should be shaved from published figures.[30] In short, cross-holdings represent a form of 'double-counting'. If these mutual holdings are spread across enough players they easily slip between the cracks when consolidating accounts.[31] There is some consolation for Japan, though. If Osaka's capitalization figures were added on to Tokyo's, a good deal of the suggested adjustment for cross-holding effects would be offset.[32]

The *keiretsu*, or the interlinking of Japanese companies in particular business sectors, is taken up further in Section 9.1. As it ties up the ownership structure of companies within such groups, takeovers are virtually eliminated.

Listed Securities Other than Equity Stocks

The international comparisons drawn thus far, in keeping with market-based comparisons elsewhere, are exclusively based on stock listings. This reflects a widely held view that the majority of value, in most exchanges, stems from such securities. This is certainly the case if one studies the detailed figures for the SEHK. While figures are not easily attainable on the value of the debt market and the various unit trusts listed, their contribution to total market value is probably negligible. The much larger warrant market—with 271 listings as of November 1998—accounted for less than 1% of the value of all stock listings.[33] The exclusion of warrants, debt securities and unit trusts from the earlier data does not, therefore, pose a serious problem when evaluating the absolute value of the Exchange's listed securities.

Some other exchanges—like Luxembourg and Vienna—trade very little equity but play a significant role in the trading of debt securities. If one adds the value of listed debt to that of listed equity, a rather different picture emerges to the one presented in Tables 1.1–1.3. This picture is reflected in Appendix 1.1. While, once again, the top tier—New York, Tokyo, and London—stand out from the crowd, second-tier rankings change considerably. Comparison with earlier tables is complicated by the inclusion of more than one exchange per country—as with Tokyo and Osaka for Japan and the NYSE and NASDAQ for the United States. Nonetheless, their inclusion suggests that Japan and the United States have a distinct edge over their rivals in the trading of listed equity and debt. Having said that, the Euro-bond market—which operates largely through London—is not factored into the figures given its operation as a 'floating' dealer-based market outside the confines of any organized exchange. Similarly, the figures in Appendix 1.1, largely ignore the value of OTC positions in both long-term debt and equity.

A Brief Overview of Hong Kong's Debt Markets

All in all, activity in Hong Kong's debt markets pales when compared with the local equity market. Liquidity in Exchange-listed debt securities, for example, appears weak, despite over 250 listings.[34] The securities also make minimal contribution to the Exchange's overall value, as mentioned. As is true in most jurisdictions, secondary market activity—especially for corporate debt securities—occurs mainly in the more opaque OTC arena.

The Hong Kong Monetary Authority (HKMA) also provides a debt market through its issue of Exchange Fund bills and notes. These really provide a means for mopping up excess liquidity in the inter-bank market rather than a source of explicit financing for the SAR government. A history of budget surpluses—excepting the more recent deficit for 1998—allied to a mountain of reserves mean that government operations require little or no public borrowing. At the end of the 1997 reporting year, the HKMA's audited accounts showed an accumulated surplus of over HK$385 billion (nearly US$50 billion) on the government reserves it is charged to manage. This reflected surpluses in two distinct funds: HK$190 billion in the Exchange Fund and HK$195 billion in the Land Fund.[35] The sheer size of these figures mean that the Hong Kong SAR government holds a veritable treasure chest of reserves.

Exchange Fund bills and notes clearly figure as liabilities in the accounts of the Exchange Fund. The bills, which are akin to US or UK Treasury bills in structure, are sold as zero-coupon securities by the Fund at a deep discount to their principal (face) value and are issued with four maturities: approximating to one, three, six, and 12 months from their date of issue. Exhibit 1.2 provides an example of such a zero-coupon, deep-discount bill.

Exhibit 1.2   The Calculation of Yield for a Treasury Bill Security

Consider a Treasury Bill in country X with the following terms: maturity, from date of issue, three months; principal $1,000; and redemption price $1,000. If the Bill were issued for $982, this amount would go to the Treasury's coffers. The Treasury would, in turn, be obliged to repurchase the Bill for $1,000 three months later. The yield (on a compound annualised basis) at the time of issue is, $\{[1 + (18/982)]^{365/90} - 1\} \times 100 = 7.64\%$.

Exchange Fund notes, in contrast, have a maturity greater than one year—reaching a maximum of 10 years—and are sold with a fixed coupon. Trades in the bills and notes are organized by the HKMA through a group of earmarked 'market-makers' (dealers) with subsequent settlement and clearing handled through the HKMA's in-house Central Moneymarkets Unit (CMU). Debt issues by the Hong Kong Airport Authority, Mass Transit Railway Corporation (MTRC), and the recently formed Hong Kong Mortgage Corporation (HKMC)—which is 100% owned by the Exchange Fund—also complement this market.

The HKMC which has been charged with creating a secondary mortgage market in Hong Kong is seen as a key vehicle in developing Hong Kong's debt markets. With a brief, amongst other things, to buy outstanding bank mortgages and use them as backing (collateral) for issues of fixed-interest debt securities, it is hoped that the HKMC can significantly deepen debt markets in the SAR. Demand for these securities is likely to come largely from investors in the Mandatory Provident Fund (MPF) Scheme. Both the MPF, and the role of the HKMC, are taken up in much greater detail in Section 14.1. Suffice to say, the authorities in Hong Kong's fledgling debt markets, like their counterparts in many other markets in Asia, are ready to do battle to create more vibrant debt markets. While partly designed to broaden investor choice and lower funding costs for issuers, more active debt markets, as argued later in Chapter 14, will likely spur equity market development as well.

The Wider Spectrum of Financial Markets

Markets for commodities, foreign exchange, derivatives, and short-term debt instruments (i.e., money market securities and other debts of maturity one year or less) are also excluded from Tables 1.1 to 1.3. Even if products such as listed derivatives were factored into the picture, the exclusion of OTC positions—which in the derivatives field account for about 50% of all positions[36]—would render comparisons somewhat artificial. Because of this, and the fact that markets for a number of other security types are not explicitly considered, only a partial insight into the relative importance of various countries' financial markets is offered. In terms of the equities picture, however, Hong Kong is, by any recognized measure, an eminent player.

1.6   The Dependency of Equity and Property Markets

The ascent of Hong Kong's equity markets owes much to the ebullience of real estate markets. The coupling of both real estate and equity markets reflects the dominance of real estate assets in the balance sheets of most Hong Kong listed companies. Property stocks also account for nearly 20% of the SEHK's market capitalization and about 25% of its turnover.[37] Given that listed companies in all sectors are heavily laden with property assets and investments, the influence of real estate is all-pervasive. Comparison of the performance of the Hang Seng Index (HSI) with property-based capital value indices easily bears this out (see Figure 1.1).[38] The association between residential property prices and the HSI is particularly striking.

By virtue of the huge demand for mortgage borrowings, necessary in financing property acquisitions, Hong Kong's equity market is also one of the most interest rate-sensitive. The finance sector, where most of this lending arises, accounts, like the property sector itself, for a disproportionately large slice of the SEHK's overall value, about 29% at the end of 1998.[39]

Figure 1.1 Comparison of the Performance of the HSI and Property
Market Sectors in Hong Kong: January 1984 – January 1999

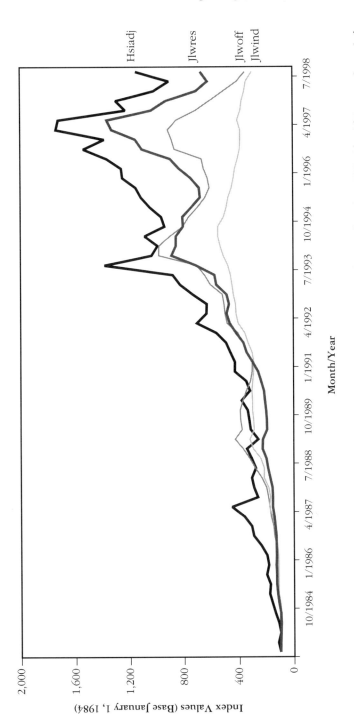

HSI ADJ = Hang Seng Index; Office = JLW Office Sector Index; Industrial = JLW Industrial Sector Index; Residential = JLW Residential Property Sector Index. HSI Values were the closing values obtaining on the first day of the relevant month. The base for the HSI of 100 corresponded to 874.94 points. All JLW Capital Indices were set at a base of 100 as of January 1984.

Sources: Datastream for HSI and Jones Lang Wootton for all property indices (defined as Jones Lang Wootton Capital Value Indices).

Over the years, demand for borrowing has been particularly pronounced in office and residential sectors. Demand for industrial spacing, though strong, has fallen some way behind. 'De-industrialization', or the relocation of textile and manufacturing businesses to the Mainland, and the establishment of a service-based economy in the last 20 years or so, largely explain this. Nonetheless, the interest rate conditions of the past and the perennial problem of insufficient land—exacerbated by population growth, unfavourable topography, and limited land supply—caused an escalation of prices in the 1980s and 1990s in all sectors. Based upon the cumulative returns in the capital value indices shown in Figure 1.1, the residential sector has easily outperformed all other sectors, growing in value by over 900% between the 1983 and 1997 year-ends.[40] Those who failed to enter this market clearly have good reason to rue their misfortune.

There is some consolation for those that opted for equities instead given an even greater cumulative percentage return on the HSI over the same period. This, however, provides consolation rather than compensation. Given the leverage (borrowing) offered on property deals, the typical speculator would have generated profits well in excess of the percentage returns on the underlying capital values. A large residential property purchased at the 1983 year-end for HK$1 million, for example, would have risen, by the 1997 year-end, to approximately HK$10.3 million in value, using the *Jones Lang Wootton Capital Value Index* for residential properties. Had this purchase been financed by a down-payment of HK$300,000, and borrowings of HK$700,000, the return on the down-payment would have been well over 3,300%, before interest charges. Of course, interest and the actual repayment of the loan would have eaten in to some of this gain. Even so, this still would have left the investor with a huge percentage return on the initial investment. Unless an investor had had access to a margin facility with a broker, equity returns would have lagged some way behind. Undoubtedly, this lesson in the use of margin is the story behind many of the 'rags-to-riches' stories of the 1980s and 1990s. Sadly, it also explains some of the losses suffered during 1997/8 where retreats in property values, for some parties, probably exceeded down-payments. In sum, leverage and margin trading are not for the faint-hearted. The greater the leverage gained, the greater the volatility of one's percentage returns. This is a theme that recurs time and time again. A host of derivative products, including warrants featured in Chapter 11.3 reflect such leverage. While the speculative play of choice for many retail investors, huge losses, particularly during the final quarter of 1997 (see Section 11.3), will not have endeared the typical investor to derivatives.

The Interest Rate Story

Low interest rates were behind the explosion in property and equity market values in the 1980s and 1990s. These rates were essentially inherited from the US as Hong Kong took its lead from the United States Federal Reserve, by virtue of the Hong Kong dollar's exchange rate 'peg' to the US dollar. As bank deposits and other fixed-interest bearing securities offered little appeal, given their negative real returns for most of the period, capital sought out the potentially higher returns in real estate and equity markets. More importantly, real borrowing costs were negative for much of the period. This is reflected in Figure 1.2, where one-month HIBOR ('Hong Kong Inter-Bank Offer Rate'), prime and inflation rates, for month-end data between December 1985 and May 1999, are compared. For much of this period, the prime rate—the rate at which local banks lend to their best credit-rated customers—was substantially below the inflation rate, the latter being measured by the Hong Kong government's Consumer Price Index (CPI) 'A'. This gap was most pronounced between 1989 and early 1995 and, not surprisingly, led to cheap money washing into the property and equity sectors. Even for retail investors, facing borrowing rates of prime plus 100 or 200 basis points, funding costs would have been negative for much of the period. The precise method for calculating real interest rates is set out in Exhibit 1.3.

Exhibit 1.3   The Computation of Real Interest Rates

Real interest rates are inferred by taking the difference between nominal (money) rates and expected inflation rates. This stems from Fisher's (1930) seminal writings on interest rates. In precise terms, Fisher's insights are typically captured through the following identity:

$$1 + r_m \equiv (1 + r_r) \times (1 + r_i^e)$$
$$r_m = r_r + r_i^e + (r_r \times r_i^e) \approx r_r + r_{ie}$$
$$\Rightarrow r_r \approx r_m - r_{ie}$$

r_m is the money rate of interest; r_r the real rate of interest; and r_{ie} the expected inflation rate.

The HIBOR, as shown in Figure 1.2, captures a bank's cost of funding. When a bank requires additional or emergency funds, it will typically borrow from other banks at HIBOR. As most banks try to lend to prime or near-prime quality customers, one would expect the prime-HIBOR differential to be strongly positive. This was the case for virtually the whole period covered in Figure 1.2.

The fourth quarter of 1997 saw a reversal in this relation, however. When concerns surrounding the Thai, Indonesian, and Malaysian currencies surfaced, the fear of a domino effect across Asia prompted an outflow of HKD deposits from the banking system, forcing banks to seek additional liquidity in the inter-bank market. Not surprisingly, inter-bank rates rose sharply. This, in turn, precipitated increases in the prime rate of 150 basis points between October 1997 and January 1998. Despite these increases, local banks faced an unpalatable funding situation: the immediate costs of funding (HIBOR) were still higher than lending returns (prime). Further

Figure 1.2 Comparison of HIBOR, Prime and Inflation Rates in Hong Kong: December 1985 – May 1999

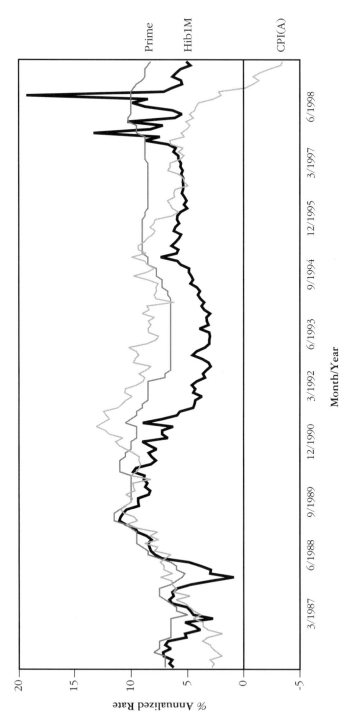

Series 1 - HIBOR (1-month)$; Series 2 = Prime Rate$; Series 3 = CPI(A) Inflation Rate*
All rates used were month-end Values. $ Middle rates (mid-point of bid less ask rates) were used for HIBOR and Prime.
* Inflation rates were calculated on a year-on-year basis; CPI(A) observation used in 1998 and 1999 were mid-month values.

Source of data: Datastream.

adjustments to the prime could have been made. The potentially devastating effects of such moves, on equity and property values, and, by connection, bank loans (assets), probably weighed against such a decision. In any event, the pressure on HIBOR soon abated. The normal positive prime–HIBOR relation was, in fact, a feature of most of 1998. Some short-lived perturbations in HIBOR were striking, particularly during the latter part of August 1998, when hedge funds were allegedly borrowing (and selling) large sums of Hong Kong dollars. This issue is taken up in Section 12.8. More on the relationship between banking, interest rates, and equity values follows in Section 2.2.

1.7   Equity Market Performance and Structural Change

Major structural developments in the markets have also had a strong influence on overall equity market performance. Adversity has driven much of this. The events of October 1987 are a case in point. The restructuring of trading, settlement, clearing, and risk-management systems in the aftermath of this crisis ushered in a new era of stability and ebullience in the markets.

Preliminary insights into the general association between structural change and market performance can be gleaned by plotting the performance of the Hang Seng Index (HSI) against indices for the world's top three equity markets (see Figure 1.3). In both absolute and relative terms, the Hong Kong market has been a star performer. Between June 1970 and June 1997, the HSI grew by over 8,200% (or a factor of 83.79 times). This translates to a compound annual growth rate of 17.82%.[41] Compared to the best of the three major markets—the United Kingdom, which increased in value by over 1,600% between 1970 and 1997—the result is impressive. Detailed figures for returns in each of the years underpinning these comparisons are shown in Table 1.4. It should be borne in mind that none of the indices used are adjusted for dividends. Returns indicated in Figure 1.3 and Table 1.4 do not, therefore, reflect the markets' overall performance. Factoring in such dividends might well change the rankings. It would certainly alter the magnitude of return differences.

Aside from the October 1987 crash, the unification of stock exchange trading in April 1986 was, perhaps, the key market event of the 1980s. The steep upturn in equity values in the post-1986 period—even with the inclusion of the October 1987 'blip' in prices—is readily apparent in Figures 1.1 and 1.3. Unification, by consolidating liquidity and price-discovery, undoubtedly spurred the markets. The volume benefits of unification are clearly evident in Table 1.2.

The new unified exchange—The Stock Exchange of Hong Kong Ltd— superseded four separate exchanges: the Far East Stock Exchange (FESE), the Kowloon Stock Exchange (KSE), the Kam Ngan Stock Exchange (KNSE), and the Hong Kong Stock Exchange (HKSE). The earlier splintering of

Figure 1.3 Cumulative Return Comparisons (Mid 1970, Base = 100) for
the Period 30 June 1970 to 30 June 1988: HK, USA, Japan
and UK

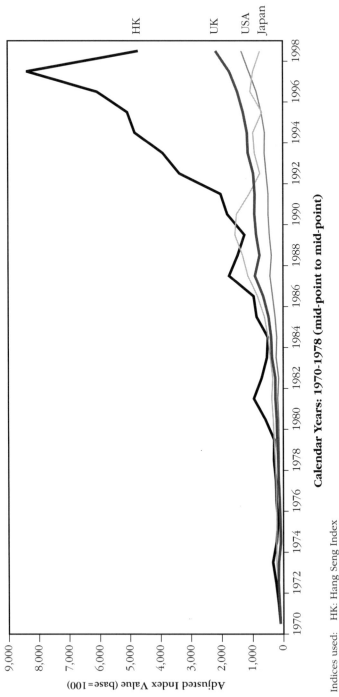

Indices used: HK: Hang Seng Index
                US: Dow-Jones Composite 65 Stock Average
                Japan: Nikkei 225 Stock Average
                UK: FTSE All Share

Returns calculated on a mid-year to mid-point basis (not adjusted for dividends).
Source of data: Datastream.

Table 1.4   Comparative Summary of Annual Returns in HK, the USA,
Japan, and the UK: Mid 1970 – Mid 1998

ANNUAL (%) RETURNS MEASURED ON A JUNE TO JUNE BASIS[2]

Year[1]	HK[3]	USA[4]	Japan[5]	UK[6]
1970–71	61.26	40.49	23.17	33.66
1971–72	49.35	3.09	43.29	22.91
1972–73	42.67	-12.12	25.31	-7.01
1973–74	-35.92[7]	-11.07	-1.30	-45.12
1974–75	-19.57[7]	10.84	-2.24	21.70
1975–76	28.52	16.34	5.34	21.22
1976–77	6.49	0.38	5.04	22.70
1977–78	26.68	-9.44	10.78	10.48
1978–79	-3.15	4.35	13.46	17.66
1979–80	97.81	6.52	9.53	8.74
1980–81	62.57	20.40	14.51	18.93
1981–82	-26.28	-16.30	-8.31	0.69
1982–83	-24.58	54.46	22.97	42.17
1983–84	-6.56	-10.18	16.99	6.28
1984–85	74.30	25.52	24.13	22.10
1985–86	10.73	31.85	37.05	36.97
1986–87	82.75	24.86	36.94	41.36
1987–88	-15.94	-11.69	14.86	-16.49
1988–89	-14.88	17.75	18.65	14.40
1989–90	44.17	9.24	-3.06	6.32
1990–91	11.91	-0.06	-27.08	-0.86
1991–92	66.38	13.10	-31.51	4.77
1992–93	16.31	10.92	22.81	17.73
1993–94	23.37	-1.80	5.38	2.17
1994–95	5.12	18.66	-29.68	10.94
1995–96	19.71	22.40	55.20	14.34
1996–97	37.89	28.03	-8.55	17.68
1997–98	-43.78	21.93	-23.17	25.59
Mean (%)	20.62	11.02	9.66	13.29
St. Dev. (%)	37.62	17.25	21.68	17.88
Min (%)	-43.78	-16.30	-31.51	-45.12
Max (%)	97.81	54.46	55.20	42.17
N	28	28	28	28

Notes:
[1] All returns are calculated on a mid-year to mid-year basis (1970–71 return is between 30 June 1970 and 30 June 1971.
[2] None of the returns are adjusted for dividends. Percentage returns are based upon the following price indices:
[3] Hang Seng Index;
[4] Dow-Jones Composite 65 Stock Average;
[5] Nikkei 225 Stock Average; and
[6] FTSE All Share.
[7] The 1973–5 malaise in Hong Kong's market is slightly obscured by taking mid-year to mid-year returns. Over six monthly cycles starting from 30 June 1973 and ending in 30 June 1975, HSI values in chronological order were 623.19, 433.68, 399.66, 171.11, and 321.20 points. Returns over the four six-month periods were -30.41%, -7.84%, -57.19% and 87.72%.
Source of index data: Datastream.

trades probably meant that no one market achieved desirable levels of liquidity, though it is generally conceded that the Far East Stock Exchange captured the lion's share of pre-unification turnover.[42] Pricing differentials for individual stocks quoted on two or more of the pre-unification markets were also commonly reported, although processes of abitrage should have reined in any substantial price discrepancies.

Of the pre-unification exchanges, the Hong Kong Stock Exchange had the longest history. Its roots were firmly established in the British colonial community in 1914, although stock trading had been set up by its antecedent—a local association of stockbrokers—in 1891.[43] The first major boom in local stock trading coincided with the emergence of the three other pre-unification exchanges in the 1969–72 period. The FESE was the first of these to open in December 1969, followed by the KNSE in March 1971, and the KSE in January 1972.[44] This period of change was marked by a flood of new stock listings. This onslaught of activity, mirroring investors' growing appetite for stock trading, owed much to the lax listing requirements on each of the four exchanges. In hindsight, it is perhaps not that surprising that market values crumbled in 1973. The onset of the oil crisis, in the second-half of 1973, compounded the weak sentiment of the time, and led to a precipitous fall in the market. The Index, in fact, shed approximately 90% of its value between March 1973 and January 1975.[45] The crashes of October 1987, and the financial crisis of 1997–8, appear as mere ripples compared with the tidal wave of 1973–5.

While the devastation of the 1973–5 market shake-out spelled doom and gloom for legions of local investors and brokerage firms, a number of positive elements emerged. One was a call for more rigorous listing requirements in each of the exchanges. This, in addition to the rupturing of market confidence, sounded the death-knell for the local IPO market and saw listings slow to a trickle in the subsequent 1975–9 period (see Chapter 5, Table 5.1).

Despite sluggish world growth in the mid to late 1970s—reflected by the poor performance of the US and Japanese equity markets as shown in Figure 1.3—Hong Kong's equity market fared better than most. As Hong Kong's market had been beaten into the ground between 1973 and 1975, some recovery from the bargain-basement price levels of early 1975 was, perhaps, inevitable. This tells only part of the story, though. The upturn also owed something to a series of government-led initiatives which helped lower the risk-premium on local stocks. Amongst other measures, the authorities sought to assuage investors' fears through the promulgation of The Protection of Investors Ordinance and investor compensation schemes, in 1974.[46] Consultative discussions on a unified stock trading system were also initiated in the late 1970s, leading to the enactment of the Stock Exchanges Unification Ordinance and the incorporation of the unified body in 1980.[47]

Other developments, such as the Hong Kong government's public-housing scheme initiated in the early 1970s were also significant. Under the wings of a new, progressive governor, Sir Murray MacLehose, an ambitious plan was hatched to provide large sections of the community with housing stock at subsidised rentals. As reported in Wong (1976), MacLehose's plan marked a sea-change from previous governmental initiatives in the area of resettlement.[48] By releasing pressure on the incomes of countless households, significant sums of money would have been freed-up in the intervening years. Some of this would have found its way into the markets. The positive effects on consumer spending and, therefore, corporate earnings, would also have buoyed market sentiment.[49]

A strategic shift away from manufacturing into services would also have contributed to the market's ascent. The PRC's 'open-door' policy of the late 1970s being crucial to this. This gave scores of local entrepreneurs, wishing to exploit an abundant supply of cheap labour, the opportunity to relocate only a few miles away from Hong Kong. In short, the opening-up of China revitalized local industry. Services—essentially, the marketing and shipment of goods through Hong Kong—were also spurred to new heights. This growth helped fill the employment gap left by the transfer of Hong Kong's manufacturing base.

While the mid- to late 1970s were characterized by some degree of market ebullience, the years immediately following were marred by political disputes between the then sovereign power—the United Kingdom—and the PRC over the status of the 99-year land lease on the New Territories. This lease was set to expire on 30 June 1997. The issue visibly surfaced in 1981 when local property developers sought assurances from the then Hong Kong government as to the lease's continuation. These were deemed to be critical to mooted property developments at the time.[50] These approaches set in motion negotiations between the lessor—a party that vehemently opposed the legitimacy of the lease—and the lessee, the UK government. The tortuous and protracted nature of these negotiations triggered a confidence crisis, throwing property and the local currency into free fall. As shown in Table 1.4, the onset of these negotiations pushed local stocks into a three-year bear market. The HKD also came under severe pressure. Following a 'run' on local bank deposits, which came to a head in September 1983, the government decided to abandon the floating exchange-rate system in favour of a Currency Board system (as described in Section 2.2). This came into effect in October 1983 and saw the Hong Kong dollar 'pegged' to the US dollar at the rate of HK$7.8:US$1. Accounts at the time, suggest that this measure, more than any other, built confidence in the run-up to 1997.

The impasse surrounding Hong Kong's post-1997 status was essentially resolved by a Joint Declaration in late 1984 between the then sovereign and the PRC government. Realizing that proposals for a continuation of its lease on the New Territories were unacceptable to the lessor, the British government somewhat reluctantly negotiated a new administrative structure for Hong Kong. The Joint Declaration, and the subsequent promulgation of the Basic Law in 1991, signalled Hong Kong's transition from a British dependent territory to a PRC Special Administrative Region (effective from 1 July 1997). The Joint Declaration, while far from being universally welcomed, at least helped to calm the business community by laying out a framework of change. This framework included a promise that the new SAR would enjoy 'a high degree of autonomy' post-handover.[51] This, in turn, would be achieved under a much lauded 'one country, two systems' principle.

Ironically, while China's paramount leader Deng Xiaoping took much of the credit for the principle, it aptly described Britain's own approach to its governing of the United Kingdom and several of its British Isles' dependencies (officially lying outside the UK). These included the Isle of Man and Channel Islands, which were subject to the UK's own foreign policy directives but enjoyed substantial freedoms with regard to their own political constitutions, law-making powers, and tax-setting privileges. The novelty of the 'one country, two systems' principle was not one of concept, therefore, but one of implementation. Never had such a principle been proposed for two systems that *prima facie* seemed so ideologically incompatible.

The breakthrough in negotiations injected new life into a hitherto lacklustre market that saw HSI values rise four-fold between July 1984 and the summer of 1987. This remarkable bull market also ushered in unified stock trading and the creation of the HKFE's highly successful HSI futures contract (in 1986). The latter became the *pièce de résistance* of the HKFE. Its successful launch saw the product amass huge volumes. Within its first year, it became the most actively traded stock index futures contract outside the United States.[52] Accounts of this period, including Robert Fell's excellent narrative in 'Crisis and Change', suggest a time of unbridled optimism in the markets. This was to be short-lived, however, given the reverberations of the global equity markets disaster of October 1987. This, as mentioned earlier, exposed serious flaws in the markets' trading and regulatory structures. In the words of Robert Fell, 'The events of October 1987 would show that success could be a cruel mistress.'

Accounts of the 1987 crash—including the collapse of the HKFE's guarantee fund and the temporary closure of the markets—have now entered into local folklore. Due to the highly leveraged nature of futures, the market fall triggered huge losses for investors with net long positions in HSI futures. In many cases, investors were unable to cover their losses (if positions were offset) or were unable to meet margin calls (where positions remained open). While much of this is recounted in detail in Section 12.8, the bare bones of the episode centred on the HKFE's responsibility to guarantee profits on its constituent members' (registered brokerage firms) positions. Unfortunately, the guarantee fund underpinning this commitment proved to be ludicrously inadequate, forcing the Hong Kong government to prop up the market with an injection of about HK$2 billion.[53]

A complete and thorough review of the overall organization of securities trading followed in the shape of the *Report of the Securities Review Committee*, chaired by Ian Hay-Davison. Various reforms were duly implemented. In addition to laying the groundwork for a complete overhaul of the HKFE's risk-management systems, a number of other major developments unfurled, the establishment of the Securities and Futures Commission being one of the first, pushing the Officer of the Commissioner of Securities into obsolescence. Enjoying much greater independence than its forebear, and a host of new regulatory powers, the SFC quickly went to work. The promulgation of the Hong Kong Codes on Takeovers and Mergers in 1992 (which was subsequently integrated with the SFC's 1991 Hong Kong Codes on Share Repurchases) was significant in its early years of operation. Statutory changes also followed. The enactment of the Disclosure of Interests Ordinance (1991) was significant in this regard.

Regulatory changes were only part of the package of renewal. New directions in the process of settlement and clearing were also instigated, leading to the implementation of the Central Clearing and Settlement System (CCASS) in 1992. This system, described in Section 3.3, saw a move away from physical stock (scrip) transfers to a scripless, electronic clearing and settlement system.

Despite some order being introduced by the positive and swift reactions of the Hong Kong government and its two exchanges, new challenges soon unfolded. The events at Tiananmen Square on 4 June 1989, which saw the deployment of the PRC state's apparatus in quelling student unrest in Beijing just eight years prior to Hong Kong's reversion to the Mainland, seriously undermined confidence. Markets responded swiftly, falling approximately 22% in value on news of the crackdown.[54] Property values followed suit. Hong Kong was again confronted by crisis. Initiatives following Tiananmen, like the UK/HK Nationality package and the funding of major infrastructural projects in Hong Kong—the Chek Lap Kok Airport Development being the most obvious one—served to rekindle confidence. Assurances from the ruling sovereign and its designated successor, on various matters pertaining to the transition, were also key in calming markets and assuaging the concerns of many in the business community. For one reason or another the feared capital flight was stemmed.

The arrival of a new governor, Chris Patten, with an agenda of electoral reform, in 1992 led to a deterioration in relations between the incumbent and prospective sovereign powers. With the mooted changes, and Beijing's fiery response to them, equity values entered a period of extreme volatility with the HSI seemingly moving in sync with the fortunes of Patten's package of reforms. Despite this, the HSI, along with the real estate sector, forged strongly upward during the five-year term of Hong Kong's last governor (see Figure 1.1). The resolution of several issues of uncertainty, despite an impasse between Beijing and London on several issues, such as the funding of the new airport, were particularly significant in the run-up to the handover. The stellar returns of the 1995 to 1997 period, as noted in the preface, captured the markets' response. The Asian financial crisis of 1997/8 clearly tempered this. Nonetheless, the SAR's remarkable resilience reflects its inherent economic strength. Hong Kong is also accustomed to adversity, as the foregoing testifies. If earlier crises are anything to go by, the recent lessons learned will set a new agenda for Hong Kong's markets, as discussed in Chapter 14.

1.8 Concluding Remarks

Hong Kong and its equity markets have experienced enormous changes that, from the vantage point of the late 1960s or early 1970s, would have seemed highly implausible. By all recognized criteria, local markets have obtained a legitimacy and cachet well beyond expectations. Active primary and liquid secondary markets have also powered growth in the overall economy.

Major challenges still exist, though such as the control of real estate prices. The events of 1997 and 1998 may have taken some 'heat' out of this market, but capital costs and office rents still appear unreasonably high. The SAR government will, therefore, need to be vigilant in checking further hikes in values. The fact that nearly 85% of the SAR's GDP is derived from services—which depend critically upon the affordability of rents for their viability—is reason enough for this assessment.[55] Long-term restraint of prices is therefore essential, and is likely to come in the form of supply-side adjustments.[56] With the currency devaluations of 1997 and 1998, business costs in much of Asia have been pared to the bone. In the absence of a similar currency devaluation in Hong Kong, which no responsible business leader welcomes, the message is clear: costs must fall and productivity rise. Signs of this are already emerging.

A substantial portion of the SAR's income derives from financial services. The markets, and all the ancillary services relating to them, are fundamental to Hong Kong's longer-term prosperity. Free and unfettered capital flows are the key. Low taxes, the rule of law, and the PRC's commitment to the present economic system augur well on this front. Calls for further trading concessions, such as the deregulation of brokerage commissions and the elimination of stamp duty on securities transactions, may grow louder in the years ahead. Moves to restructure the ownership and running of exchange bodies—as in Australia, Sweden, and the Netherlands (see Sections 2.1 and 14.3)—are also in the pipeline. In short, financial competition is intensifying and radical solutions to secure and capture market share require some thought.

For some, the territory's well-earned reputation as an unfettered port of call for securities trading was blighted by the SAR government's August 1998 intervention in its own stock and futures markets. For others, the intervention 'rescued' Hong Kong and its markets from parasitic attacks by speculators. The various arguments pertaining to both schools of thought are assessed at length throughout this text (particularly in Section 12.8 and Section 14.2) Whatever one's view, the intervention by virtue of its scale and intensity was simply unparalleled. Financial historians will, no doubt, see the event as a milestone—and some, perhaps, as a millstone—for Hong Kong's government.

Appendix 1.1   Global Comparison of the Market Value of Total Listed
Equity and Debt in Major Markets

		Total Equity & Debt Value (US$ million)
1.	New York	6,984,531
2.	Tokyo	5,503,957*
3.	London	5,341,886
4.	Osaka	4,851,335
5.	German	2,419,485*
6.	Luxembourg	1,824,361
7.	Chicago	1,230,211* #
8.	Paris	1,167,223* #
9.	NASDAQ	803,170#
10.	Vienna	651,776

Source: Figures computed from available information in the LSE's *Quality of Markets Review*, Spring Edition 1995, p.86 (£1.00 is assumed to be equal to US$1.60).

Figures for fixed interest bearing securities (i.e., debt, consist of securities in the corporate and public sectors as well as foreign debt); * Indicates that data relating to the value of foreign equity is not available in the source; and # indicates that some or all of data on the value of fixed interest bearing listed securities is not available in the source.

Notes

1.   The author would like to acknowledge the comments of an anonymous reviewer for earlier comments on this chapter.
2.   As of November 1998, 683 ordinary and five preference shares were listed on the Exchange. Warrants, debt securities and unit trusts, totalling 271, 258, and 27, respectively, were also listed (see *SEHK Monthly Bulletin* (Dec. 1998, p. 9)). Equity options, which trade separately on the Exchange, can also be added to these listings.
3.   As we shall see in Section 8.3, Hong Kong companies pay dividends twice yearly. Only the 'final' dividend for the reporting year—which is typically much larger than the 'interim' payment—is subject to such AGM approval.
4.   See Wardley Cards for Tem Fat Hing Fung (Holdings) Ltd, (prep: 30-3-98, Card 03) for description of its share capital.
5.   See *SEHK Monthly Bulletin* (Dec. 1999, p. 84).
6.   Interestingly, the ratio of market prices in the 'A' and 'B' shares for this stock typically exceeds the ratio of dividend payments (per share). Liquidity factors may account for this. With typically greater volume in 'A' shares, some discount on the 'B' may be required to compensate for their relative illiquidity. Studies in the US, such as Lease, McConnell and Mikkelson's (1983), are interesting because they compare different classes of stock with the same dividend streams but differential voting rights: the opposite of the above. They find that in companies where such classes exist (but without preference shares) the shares with greater voting power trade at a noticeable premium (see p. 469).
7.   Restrictions on companies issuing 'B' shares were announced in April 1987 (see *Fact Book 1996*, p. 90). Rule 8.11, 8-4, 10/95, *Rules Governing the Listing of Securities on The Stock Exchange of Hong Kong Ltd* should be referred to for precise details.

8. The guideline 'lower of cost or market value' is also often heard and reflects the general principle of prudence which underpins historic-cost accounting conventions.

9. Where participating preference shares are in issue, the picture would be different, as these qualify for capital and dividends in excess of their 'fixed' claims.

10. The two parties to this arrangement are part of an agency relationship. Many other applications exist in economics and finance. Jensen and Meckling (1976, pp. 308–10) provide a particularly good overview of the essential characteristics of such agency contracts.

11. Cheung and Lui (1992, p. 380) point to two trading effects: price risk, occasioned by trading suspensions during the actual period of restructuring, and the spur to trading volumes around the immediate announcement of a relocation.

12. This point is made very clearly in Anonymous (May 1993b): 'Duty payable on an increase in authorized or issued capital can be mitigated with the transfer of corporate domicile from Hong Kong. Capital duties are significantly less in many foreign jurisdictions. For example, there is no capital duty payable in Bermuda except an annual share registration fee . . .' (p. 27).

13. Among the various selection criteria for entry into this index is the following condition, which reflects the condition of PRC state 'majority control': '1. The company should have at least 35% shareholding directly held by either: a. China entities which are deemed to include state-owned organizations, provincial or municipal authorities in China, or b. Listed or privately owned Hong Kong companies (Hong Kong or overseas incorporated) which are controlled by 1a. above. . . .' (*Hang Seng China Enterprises Index* brochure, HSI Services Ltd).

14. Rule 19A.04, 19A-5, 11/94, Listing Rules.

15. Although the more recent issue of Huaneng Power International Inc in January of 1998 indicates that listing can be achieved through other routes, for example the introduction, which is discussed in some detail in Chapter 7.

16. See *Hang Seng China-Affiliated Corporations Index* brochure, HSI Services Ltd for specific details.

17. CATIC Shenzhen Holdings Ltd's 'H' share listing in September 1997 is one exception given its role as a holding company for a broad range of business operations (see Reuters (September 1997)).

18. See Hong Kong Codes (see pp. 2.1–2.3, March 1992) for precise definitions.

19. See Chandrasegar and Baratham (1993, p. 7) for comparison of control levels in Hong Kong, Singapore, and Malaysia.

20. Rule 8.08, 8-02/8-03 of the *Listing Rules* also provides for the possibility of a lower public interest for stocks with a capitalization exceeding HK$4 billion.

21. Readers are advised to refer to the precise definition of public interest spelled out in Rule 8.24, 8-7, 10/95, ibid. In verbatim: 'The Exchange will not regard any connected person of the issuer as a member of "the public" or shares held by a connected person as being "in public hands". In addition the Exchange will not recognize as a member of "the public": (1) any person whose acquisition of securities has been financed directly or indirectly by a connected person; (2) any person who is accustomed to take instructions from a connected person in relation to the acquisition, disposal, voting or other disposition of securities of the issuer registered in his name or otherwise held by him.' (Rule 8.24, quotation marks used as shown).

22. See ibid., Chapter 1, 'General Interpretation', 1-3, 12/94. The definition for a PRC issuer and accompanying notes in the description of a 'connected person' are not reported here. The meaning of 'connected person' can be extended when, among other things, certain issues in Chapter 14 (*ibid.*) come into play (see 'General Interpretation', 1–3, 12/94 and Chapter 14).

23. For a precise definition, see ibid., 1-8, 12/94.

24. See Note 18 earlier.

25. They note that: 'a "family-controlled company" is defined as one in which 10% or more of its shares are held either by an identified family with family member(s) holding seat(s) on the board of directors of the company, or by a holding company that satisfies the same criterion.' (Mok et al. (1992, p. 282) quotation marks shown as used).

    Mok et al. note that the Jardine group does not satisfy the above but treat it as an exceptional case, and note that: 'the group is considered family controlled because the Keswick family is largest shareholder, and because the intricate network of stockholdings and directorships has ensured the family's effective control over the group.' (p. 282).

26. See Table 2 in Mok et al. (1992, p.282).

27. For precise figures, see http://www.fibv.com/.

28. 'International companies' accounted for about 66% of the LSE's overall equity market value of around GBP4,231 billion as of the 1998 year-end (see *Fact File*, 1999, p. 39 & 49).

29. Specifically, see Article 8.

30. McDonald (1989) deduces a 24% adjustment based upon his analysis of 75 industrial firms in Japan in 1987. A number of years later, Goldman Sachs came up with an adjusted index for Japan by netting out cross-holding effects. They indicated an even larger discount: shaving the overall market's value by approximately 49% (see Anonymous, October 1996b).

31. Ferguson and Hitzig (1993) note that this could be achieved in the US. In other words, consolidation of accounts can completely miss the mutual ownership arrangement. With felicity they note, 'GAAP has gaps'. GAAP refers to Generally Accepted Accounting Principles.

32. There is also some evidence that cross-holding structures making up the *keiretsu* are slowly being unwound (see Levinson (1992), for instance).

33. See SEHK *Monthly Bulletin* (Dec. 1998, p. 9).

34. Figures for August 1998, for instance, reveal that turnover in these securities accounted for less than 0.01% of ordinary stock turnover (*SEHK Monthly Bulletin*, 1998, September p. 9).

35. See HKMA *Annual Report* (1997, pp. 77 & 93). Total assets in the two funds, at the 31 December year-end, summed to approximately HK$832 billion.

36. Estimates in *The Economist*, for the 1994 year-end (see Anonymous, March 1995, p. 22), show that outstanding exchange-traded derivatives and OTC positions summed to approximately US$11 trillion and US$12 trillion, respectively.

37. See the SEHK *Monthly Bulletin* (Feb. 1998, p. 9) for precise figures.

38. Thanks are expressed to Jones Lang Wootton for the provision of this data. The HSI in the comparison in Figure 1 is adjusted to reflect a base of 100 as of the 1983 year-end.

39. See SEHK *Monthly Bulletin* (Dec. 1998, p. 9).

40. Thanks are due to Jones Lang Wootton for providing the data for these comparisons, and to Mark Clavey, in particular, for answering enquiries about this data. Increases reflect 'Large and Luxury' residential values.

41. The HSI as of 30 June 1970 stood at 181.37 points and rose to 15,196.79 points as of 30 June 1997. In other words, an 8,278.89% gain. The annual compound rate is r, such that $(1 + r)^{27} = (1 + 82.7889)$.

42. Empirical studies such as Larson and Morse's (1987) bear this out.

43. See *Fact Book 1986*, p. 88 for a description of the early origins of stock trading.

44. See *Fact Book* (various issues) for the precise opening dates.

45. Wong's (1991) detailed account of this tumultuous period is highly recommended.

46. See *Fact Book 1996*, p. 88 for details of various market-related changes initiated in 1974.

47. Ibid. (p. 89) for details of the train of initiatives leading up to these events.

48. In relation to Sir Murray MacLehose's radical plan, Wong (1976) reports: 'at the opening session of the Legislative Council in October 1972, he announced his plans of providing public housing to practically everyone in Hong Kong—a ten-year target of 1.8 million. . . . he gave the first green signal for public housing for the urban population to expand into the suburban and rural new territories.' (p. 291).

49. Particular thanks are due to Ben Ostrov for sharing his thoughts on the public housing developments of the 1970s.

50. See Goodstadt (1981) for more detailed discussion of the positions of local banks and property developers with regard to the airing of the lease issue in 1981.

51. See Joint Declaration, S. 3(2). A commitment that the PRC's policies, as laid out in S. 3, would 'remain unchanged for 50 years.', was also set out (see S. 3 (12)).

52. See Pierog et al. (1987) for comparisons of futures exchanges at this time and affirmation of the HSI futures global ranking.

53. This was a loan package, referred to as the 'lifeboat' (see Schoenfeld (1987) for details).

54. As reflected by changes in the HSI Services Ltd's HSI barometer.

55. According to Hong Kong Trade Development Council figures, the proportion of 1996 GDP was 84.4% (see http://www.tdc.org.hk/).

56. In the immediate aftermath of the handover, the Chief Executive, Tung Cheehwa, announced a series of long-term initiatives aimed at limiting further increases in property prices. These initiations revolve around an ambitious plan to increase the supply of building land and housing in Hong Kong over a five-year term.

2. The Structure and Characteristics of Hong Kong's Equity Markets

Hong Kong's securities market machinery essentially comprises two exchange forums, the SEHK and HKFE, and three associated clearing houses, the Hong Kong Securities Clearing Co Ltd (HKSCC), the Stock Exchange Options Clearing House (SEOCH), and the HKFE Clearing Corporation Ltd. The functions of the clearing houses are addressed later in this text. All three are essentially linked to the constituent exchanges. Not surprisingly, the SEOCH and HKFE Clearing Corporation are simply extensions of the SEHK and HKFE (as discussed in Sections 10.6 and 12.8). The HKSCC is slightly different, as it is limited by guarantee, with the Exchange shouldering 50% of this responsibility. The remainder of the guarantee is underwritten by five banks. The HKSCC essentially deals with clearing and settlement issues in all securities traded on the Exchange, other than traded equity options. The nature of clearing and settlement, and the precise functions of the HKSCC, are addressed in detail in Section 3.3.

Proposals to merge the two exchanges and the associated clearing bodies, in March 1999,[1] reflect deep-seated concerns that the existing structures are, to some degree, unwieldy and inefficient. Why are there three clearing and settlement bodies, when one generic body could do much the same job for the constituent products? The same line of reasoning can also be applied to trading and regulation. Are two separate exchanges with separate self-regulatory features really necessary?

Authorities all over the world are embracing reform. This essentially translates into the consolidation and harmonization of existing structures and regulatory platforms. Imminent moves are expected in both of these areas in light of the recent proposals in Hong Kong (see Note 1). If approved by members of the SEHK and HKFE, a three-tiered plan will unfold,[2] leading to the de-mutualization of both exchanges, their consolidation into one new unified body, and the subsequent listing of this unified entity on its own market. The Hong Kong authorities are not the first to hatch such a plan. The Australian Stock Exchange (ASX) has already listed on its own exchange and the Singaporean authorities hatched plans similar to Hong Kong's five months earlier.[3] Nonetheless, Hong Kong's mooted reforms represent a bold and radical initiative. Before any serious examination of such moves can be made, some background on the structure of the markets and the regulatory regime currently in place is required. Detailed consideration of the proposed reforms is provided later in Section 14.4.

The structure of the SEHK and HKFE is first explored in Section 2.1. Both forums, through ruling bodies, supervise their member brokers and the various companies and issuers on the markets. These ascribed self-regulatory features dovetail with and support the regulatory work of the markets' designated regulator, the Securities and Futures Commission (SFC). This body was set up under statute in 1989 as an independent entity. It is, by definition, central to all surveillance and enforcement procedures in the securities arena.

Banking and currency sector regulation are then assessed in Section 2.2. Far from being tangential to the securities markets, banking and exchange-rate management are critical in shaping the performance and stability of the debt, equity, and property markets. The activities of the Hong Kong Monetary Authority (HKMA) are pivotal in this. Its prescribed management of the Exchange Fund and local Currency Board system give it a key role in. influencing interest rates and, by connection, the smooth flow of capital in and out of the securities markets. The HKMA's intervention in the local stock and futures markets in August 1998 also provides evidence of its direct involvement in the markets. In short, the HKMA, and the Exchange Fund and Currency Board under its remit, are central to an evaluation of local securities markets.

As the Currency Board has been a permanent feature of Hong Kong's economy since 1983, it is accorded special attention in Section 2.3. The general role of interest rates, in shaping equity and debt security values, is also addressed in this section. An overview of the regulatory structure of the markets then follows in Section 2.4.

2.1 Market Regulation and the Role of the Self-Regulatory Exchanges

As argued at the outset, consolidation is the mood of the day in the securities markets. Regulatory powers are not immune to this, and must also move with the times. Initiatives such as rationalizing financial services regulations, as seen in the United Kingdom, look more and more prescient by the day. Under the auspices of a newly formed regulatory body, the Financial Services Authority (FSA), regulatory functions from a range of diverse financial services areas, spanning insurance, banking, and securities trading, are scheduled to pass into the charge of the new unit. With the Bank of England's acquiescence, certain regulatory functions in the banking domain have already been transferred to the new body.

What is the essential motivation behind the rationalization of regulatory control? The short answer is that regulatory powers are often segmented whereas the financial services industry is increasingly unified. As more and more financial institutions take on multifaceted roles, a single issue of concern can arouse the attention of any number of regulators from supposedly distinct fields. This cannot be efficient. Traditional regulatory regimes resemble some MBA programmes; the underlying ethos is that business can be subdivided into finance, accounting, marketing, and management. If only life were so simple. Regulators, like MBA schools, have to adapt to the new business environment where, increasingly, the financial conglomerate dominates. This is partly due to the global boom in mergers and acquisitions, it is also a reflection of increased global competition where effective performance dictates certain economies of scale. Attempts within particular organizations to weld certain aspects of commercial and investment banking, insurance, and securities activities are a reaction to this. Glass-Steagall apart, which limits the integration of some of these services in the United States,[4] a number of countries have recognized the incompatibility of traditional systems in overseeing the new consolidated enterprise. Instead of telling Japan to reform, a number of Western countries should take heed of their own message. What was successful yesterday may not be so tomorrow.

Is a super regulator likely on the local scene? Recent press reports suggest it might be, although one should be sceptical of such accounts. Without wanting to denigrate the press, the need for consolidation in the SAR seems less pressing than might be the case elsewhere. Regulatory control in the financial services arena is far from fragmented. Three bodies—the SFC, the HKMA and the Office of the Commissioner of Insurance—are charged with supervision of the bulk of local financial service activities.[5] The proposed merger of the exchanges (see Note 1) may affect this situation. Considerable regulatory change, with possibilities of consolidation in certain areas, will be required to ensure that the new unified body performs as it is intended to. More on this issue follows in Section 14.4.

The local authorities have been making their own contribution towards rationalization in other ways. The release of the Composite Securities and Futures Bill,[6] which aims to consolidate eleven Government Ordinances that bear upon securities market trading, is a good example of this. While not directly related to regulation, the consolidation of securities laws will add clarity and precision to the enforcement and regulation of the markets.

The Principal Regulatory Bodies

The principal regulator in the securities field is the SFC. The exchange bodies, the SEHK and HKFE, bolster this role by embracing a self-regulatory approach to their own markets. This approach relates to the governance of members, issuers, and dealers (where appropriate). The HKMA, given its role in the enforcement of exchange-rate stability, also plays a part, albeit an indirect one, in the maintenance of orderly markets. The activities and responsibilities of this body are therefore assessed alongside those of the SFC, SEHK, and HKFE. Issues of insurance and, therefore, the role of the Office of the Commissioner of Insurance, though extremely important, lie outside this text's remit and are left to others to deliberate.

Before turning to the SFC and HKMA, the structure, governance, and self-regulatory roles of the two exchanges are first assessed. The proposed merger of the two bodies, as outlined in Note 1, is also briefly assessed. Extensive discussion on this issue is provided in Section 14.4.

The Stock Exchange of Hong Kong (SEHK) Ltd.
The *Stock Exchange Unification Ordinance* of 1980[7] (Part III, Issue 14, p. 10) set the stage for the creation of the SEHK, which commenced trading in 1986. As noted in Section 1.7, the SEHK was created from the unification of four separate exchanges.

The precise organizational role of the SEHK and its status are succinctly summarized in its Annual Report. For reasons of clarity, this is quoted verbatim here:

> The Stock Exchange of Hong Kong Limited (the Exchange) is a company incorporated under the Companies Ordinance with limited liability, and is recognised by the Securities and Futures Commission under the Stock Exchanges Unification Ordinance as the sole exchange with the exclusive right to establish, operate and maintain a stock market in Hong Kong. Under Section 27A of the Stock Exchange Unification Ordinance, the Exchange has the duty to ensure an orderly and fair market in securities traded through its facilities. In performing this duty, the Exchange is required to act in the interests of the public, having particular regard to the interests of the investing public, and ensure that where these interests conflict with any other interests that the Exchange is required to serve under any other law, the former shall prevail. (*SEHK Annual Report*, 1998, p. 60, parentheses used as shown).

Two essential issues emerge from the SEHK's organizational description: its exclusive licence to operate a securities exchange and its prescribed role in ensuring a fair market in securities trading. While its exchange licence is firmly enshrined in statute, its duties and responsibilities may change from time to time. The recent decision by the Exchange's Ruling Council to adopt the status of a public body, in relation to the Prevention of Bribery Ordinance,[8] is an example of this. Proposals to merge the Exchange with the HKFE will, if approved, trigger far more wide-ranging consequences. Although some things will remain much as they are at present, the recent policy paper on the issue indicates that the new merged body will enjoy monopoly status.[9] This means, amongst other things, that the exchanges, and their associated clearing bodies, will continue to perform public duties.[10] The paper also makes it clear that the SFC will retain its supervisory role of the markets. Nonetheless, changes to the regulatory role of the SEHK are expected.[11]

The Existing Membership Structure of the Exchange
Ownership of the Exchange is currently vested in the hands of its constituent members. The existing members' role, apart from one of ownership, is to provide the brokerage (agency) function for investors to enable them to buy and sell in the market. As of December 1998, there were 562 members in total. Of these, 492 were classified as trading members and 70 non-trading members. The breakdown of the individual and corporate membership within each of these categories, as well as the number of shares held by each, is reported in Exhibit 2.1. While the precise conditions

for corporate and individual membership differ, a new applicant under either category must be 'registered under the Securities Ordinance as a dealer'.[12,13]

Exhibit 2.1   Breakdown of Membership of the SEHK

	Trading Members		Non-Trading Members		Total
	Individual	Corporate	Individual	Corporate	
No. of Members*	103	389	53	17	562
Shares	112	738	53	26	929

Source: http://www.sehk.com (10 December 1998)
Note: * Fact Book 1997, p. 112 indicates that as of the 1997 year-end, the number of overseas members totalled 105 (from 555 members in total).

The Exchange also boasts a strong contingent of foreign brokers. In 1997, the Exchange reported that 18% of its members were classified as corporate overseas members.[14] Not all markets in Asia are receptive to such membership groupings. Taiwan's exchange (the TSE) excludes such parties, for instance.[15]

The differential between the number of SEHK members and membership shares is explained by some parties, principally corporate members, holding multiple shares. The shares themselves are transferable between outgoing members and new applicants (which include existing members seeking additional share interest).

From the Exchange's shareholdings, a Ruling Council of 31 representatives is selected. The chairman and chief executive of the Exchange serve at the pinnacle of this Council. The self-regulatory remit of this body, which reflects the broader duties of the Exchange itself, broadly relate to two sets of constituents: Exchange members and the companies supplying the listed securities. As mentioned earlier, the Exchange's self-regulatory role must also be compatible with, and geared to, the general regulatory requirements enforced by the SFC.

Revenue Sources of the Exchange
The single most important source of Exchange revenue derives from a transaction levy. This is charged on both the buy and sell side of all trades recorded on the Exchange. As shown in Exhibit 2.2, revenues derived from this source have accounted for a third or more of Exchange revenues in recent years (33.28% in 1995/6; 43.72% in 1996/7; and 38.8% in 1997/8). As shown in Section 3.1, this item represents a fraction of an investor's overall transaction costs, accounting for only 0.011% of the value of an executed order. It is easily overshadowed by brokerage commission (of at least 0.25% of stock value; Chapter 3, note 8).

Exhibit 2.2   Breakdown of Turnover (Revenues) from the SEHK's
Operations

	1998 HK$'000	1997 HK$'000	1996 HK$'000
Transaction levy: the Exchange's entitlement*	447,832	345,326	149,739
Listing Fees	215,902	181,910	138,772
Stock information income	227,387	112,485	71,080
Income from members:			
• monthly subscription and others	106,340	72,645	45,489
• options trading related activities	12,378	10,063	9,199
• unclaimed brokerage	20,634	21,052	4,634
Interest income**	99,036	29,088	14,968
Rental	2,184	2,424	2,400
Recovery of Brokers' Fidelity Insurance	7,903	8,826	9,385
Others	13,937	6,014	4,221
	1,153,533	789,833	449,887

1996 and 1997 Figures extracted (with the exception of footnote **, footnote * shown below) from the SEHK's *Annual Report 1997*, p. 57 (Note 3)

1997 and 1998 Figures extracted (with the exception of the footnote **, footnote * shown below) from the SEHK's *Annual Report 1998*, p. 64 (Note 3)

Footnote * from the SEHK's *Annual Report 1997*, p. 57 reads as, 'The Exchange was entitled to 54% (1996: 54%) of the transaction levy collected with the remaining 46% (1996: 46%) being paid to the SFC.' (Note 3, brackets as shown).

Footnote * from the SEHK's *Annual Report 1998*, p. 64 (Note 3) reads as: 'For the period from 1 July 1997 to 31 March 1998, the Exchange was entitled to 54% (1996/97:54%) of the transaction levy received, while the remaining 46% (1996/97:46%) was paid to the SFC. From 1 April 1998 onwards, the Exchange was entitled to 54.55% of the transaction levy received, while the SFC was entitled to 36.36%, and the remaining 9.09% was credited directly to the Development Reserve.' (Note 3, brackets as shown).

Accounting year: July 01 – June 30.

Despite the fact that the Exchange receives only part of the transaction levy (around 54%, see the notes to Exhibit 2.2), its contribution to revenues is substantial, as the above testifies. This is especially so when volumes soar, as they did in the third quarter (July to September) of 1997.[16] Average daily turnover during this period was HK$23.858 billion. To appreciate the spike in volumes during these three months, comparison with average daily turnover levels for 1997 and 1996 of HK$9.405 billion and HK$4.180 billion, is helpful.[17] The increased revenues to the Exchange in 1997/8 were driven largely by the surge in volumes between July and September 1997.[18]

To really appreciate the importance of the transaction levy, the combined contribution of ongoing listing fees and initial listing fees[19] for new entrants to the market, and stock information income—the second and third major contributors to revenues in 1997/8—fell slightly short of the levy's contribution (38.4%, as compared to 38.8%). The Exchange also generated a significant amount of income from Member subscriptions and other payments.

The 1995-97 Success Story
Exchange turnover for the 1997/8 financial year, of more than HK$1,153 million, represented a sharp increase of 46% over the corresponding level for 1996/7. More strikingly, turnover had grown by 156% relative to the 1995/6 position, which was an impressive result over a mere two-year period. Surplus figures yield a similar story, rising from levels of HK$20.4 million in 1995/6 to HK$388.9 million in 1997/8.[20] These profit increases are of little direct benefit to members though as dividends, under the existing regime, cannot be paid out to the Exchange's shareholders (members).[21, 22] The proposed reform of the Exchange and the HKFE (see Note 1) will radically alter this picture, however. Amongst other things, the proposal will make shareholders, in the new consolidated exchange, eligible for dividend payments. They will also be able to trade their ownership rights freely once the shares in the new entity are listed.[23] Currently, the surplus is subject to certain guidelines laid down by the Financial Secretary.[24]

Stamp duty is also set against SEHK trades and collected by the Exchange on behalf of the Hong Kong government. In 1998, an amount slightly in excess of HK$9.03 billion was added to the government's coffers through such means.[25] Two specific taxes make up overall stamp duty revenues on stock trading: *ad valorem* and transfer deed stamp duty. Discussions over the years suggest, particularly in the case of the *ad valorem* component, that it is somewhat unpopular with investors—as perhaps all taxes are. Calls for its reduction, or removal, as a way of instilling greater competitiveness in the local markets, are routinely heard.[26]

The Hong Kong Futures Exchange (HKFE)
Like the SEHK, the local futures exchange also has a membership structure. Many of these membership firms, either through subsidiaries or related entities, have a presence in both markets.

The origins of the HKFE can be traced back to the creation of the Hong Kong Commodities Exchange (HKCE) in 1976.[27] Up until the establishment in 1984 of the HKFE, which superseded the HKCE, futures contracts had revolved around commodities like cotton, sugar, soybeans and gold.[28] The de-listing of cotton, sugar, and soybean contracts, in October 1981, August 1992, and February 1992, respectively,[29] and the subsequent development of financial futures, under the auspices of the newly named HKFE, completely revolutionized futures trading in Hong Kong.[30] The most momentous of these changes was the introduction of Hang Seng

Index (HSI) futures in May of 1986. This contract, since its very inception, has accounted for the lion's share of the HKFE's turnover. Almost from the day of its launch, aggregate volumes in existing soybean, sugar, and gold contracts were relegated to rather marginal status by the fledgling product.[31]

As HSI futures volumes have also driven commission revenues, it is true to say that the profitability of the HKFE has been interwoven with the fortunes of this product. The story of this product, therefore, yields key insights into the rise, fall, and re-emergence of the Futures Exchange. Comparison of figures for the operating surplus of the Exchange with volume levels in its premier product testify to this (see Table 2.1 and Figure 2.1).

Table 2.1 The Operating Surplus (Post-Tax) of the HKFE: 1987–1998

Year	Operating Surplus* (HK$ millions)[1,2]	Annual Volumes in HSI Futures** (No. of Contracts)
1987	15.9	3,611,329
1988	(11.4)	140,155
1989	(8.6)	235,976
1990	(3.5)	236,002
1991	(1.0)	499,262
1992	6.6	1,089,027
1993	45.8	2,415,739
1994	154.3	4,192,571
1995	105.0	4,546,613
1996	120.6	4,656,084
1997	284.9	6,446,696
1998	307.2	6,969,708

* Compiled from various HKFE *Annual Reports*
** Compiled from volumes, courtesy of the HKFE

Notes:
[1] Accounting year-end is 31 December. Figures for 1997 therefore reflect results for the financial year 1 January, 1997 to 31 December, 1997 inclusive.
[2] Results shown are those reflecting consolidated operations (i.e., those of the HKFE and of its clearing units).

The fall in this story, as illustrated in Section 1.7, corresponds to the October 1987 crash and its aftermath. The crash shook the very foundations of local futures trading by exposing gaping holes in guarantee and risk-management systems. Volumes in HSI futures bore the brunt, shrinking to a tiny fraction of pre-crash levels. While the resulting confidence crisis was prolonged, the inevitable restructuring of risk-management systems ushered in a new, stronger platform for futures trading. Much of the detail surrounding this process of rejuvenation is set out in Section 12.8.

Figure 2.1 HSI Futures Volume (Number of Contracts): May 1986 – May
1999

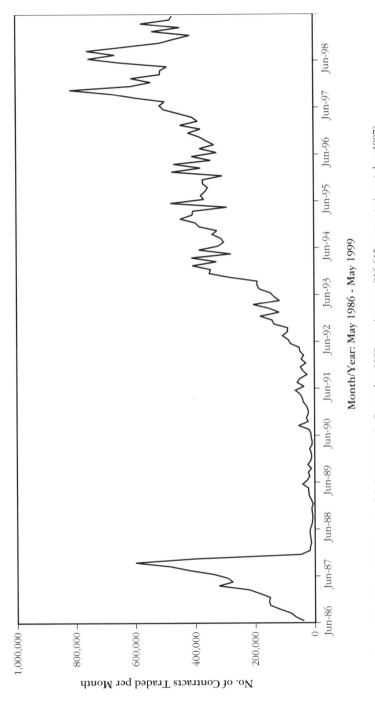

Month/Year: May 1986 - May 1999

Range of monthly volumes (minimum = 5,919 contracts in December 1988; maximum = 816,615 contracts in october 1997).

Source: Volume data was provided by the Hong Kong Futures Exchange

By 1992 the HKFE's restructuring programme was bearing fruit, with substantial improvements in HSI futures volumes being the visible evidence of this. These volumes mushroomed over the following five years, climbing to unprecedented heights by the final quarter of 1997.

Income Sources of the Exchange

As we shall learn in Chapter 12, futures trading is conducted on a margin basis with deposits, representing a fraction of the contract value, placed by clients with their members. Member firms are, in turn, required to place the net margin of their clients, relating to the aggregate number of 'live' positions opened through the member, on deposit with the HKFE Clearing Corporation Ltd (hereafter the 'Clearing Corp'). Interest payable on these deposits is the most obvious cost for the Clearing Corp and the HKFE in the maintenance of these arrangements. However, by paying a lower interest rate on these deposits than its investment rate, the Exchange, as is true of essentially all futures exchanges, is able to generate an interest differential on margin funds held by the Clearing Corp.[32] The interest generated from such margin balances constitutes the major source of income for most futures exchanges. The HKFE is no exception, with this component accounting for about two-thirds of its total revenue in 1997. The other sources of revenue, apart from sundry income, reflected transaction and clearing fees and membership fees, which accounted for approximately 20% and 0.5%, respectively, of total revenues.[33]

Comparison of the Hong Kong SAR's two Exchanges: the HKFE and SEHK

The SEHK essentially provides the cash markets and the HKFE the derivatives market, although in the last ten years or so derivatives have also emerged on the SEHK. Its assemblage of traded equity options and warrants gives it some standing in the trading of equity derivatives. The HKFE by its very nature is a market for financial futures and options, notwithstanding its listing of gold futures.[34] Despite their obvious product differences, the two exchanges are very similar in some other important respects. They both share a membership structure and perform self-regulatory roles in relation to their constituent members and the suppliers of the securities on the markets. The precise roles of the HKFE are set out in the Commodities Trading Ordinance and in its own 'Rules', written in two volumes for the HKFE itself and its wholly-owned subsidiary, the HKFE Clearing Corporation Ltd.

The HKFE's Membership Structure

At the close of the 1997 financial year, the HKFE had 135 members, each holding at least one share in the Exchange. The obligations and duties of the constituent members are not easily summarized, however, given four particular categories of membership. Most members (131) fall into the category of futures commission merchants (CMs) which allows them to trade in three ways: on client account, on principal account, and as a floor agent for other members. The remaining registered members were classified as either Brokers (3) or merchant traders (1). The former is much like a CM, apart from the fact that the first of the three trading roles of the CM—trading on client account—falls outside its remit. Merchant traders are rather different and, as well as engaging in principal trading, are able to act as 'a merchant in a deliverable commodity traded on the Exchange'. The final type of member—the trader—is only permitted to trade on principal account.

Separate membership of the HKFE's wholly-owned clearing company, the HKFE Clearing Corporation Ltd., leads to further membership categories. Of the 135 HKFE Members detailed above, 114 were members of the Clearing Corp and were registered as either general clearing members or individual clearing members.[35] Specific details on the roles of each, and of the general duties and requirements of HKFE members, are again, for pedagogical reasons, examined in Chapter 12 of this text.

The Effects of the Proposed Merger of the SEHK and HKFE on its Existing Members

With increased global competition, a number of exchanges have chosen to convert, either partially or fully, to a corporate structure. This allows original membership stakes to be converted into publicly traded shares. This not only makes existing member shares more tradeable, it also opens up exchanges to ownership configurations that, hitherto, were unheard of. The Australian Stock Exchange (ASX) is, perhaps, the best example of this new breed of exchange. Shares in ASX are also quoted on the exchange it organizes.[36] Hong Kong's three-tiered plan (see note 1)—to 'de-mutualize' the SEHK and HKFE, merge them, and list the new unified body— represents the latest move in this game. This comes on the heels of Singapore's recent announcement to do the same.

The mood for change is largely driven by certain perceived weaknesses in membership structures. Many see the traditional model as a medium for ensuring that members' interests rank ahead of market users'.[37] Resistance to change may also be a problem, with some members banding together to ward off moves that might threaten their interests. This reaction is one that is often ascribed to small brokers in such structures. Failures in various markets to institute changes in areas such as broker commission rates—a subject taken up in Section 3.1—is one manifestation of such resistance. Many see competition in this area as essential in attracting foreign institutional investment. In essence, what may be good for individual members, namely the preservation of the status quo, may militate against the interest of the overall market. Not surprisingly, then, membership structures are under review in a number of markets. More diversified ownership structures, where trading members and users gain representation, would arguably promote the kind of commercial orientation many exchanges now seek. In most of the models offered for de-mutualization, members are able to relinquish ownership rights (i.e., to sell tradeable shares in a listed exchange company, representing their old member stakes) without affecting their trading rights as 'trading members'. This allows ownership and trading rights to be separated and is at the very core of the SEHK/HKFE reform proposals.[38]

The Market's Independent Regulator: The Securities and Futures Commission (SFC)

As we saw in Section 1.7 the SFC largely grew out of the recommendations of the *Report of the Securities Review Committee*, which were released in the aftermath of the October 1987 crash. This paved the way for the enactment of the Securities and Futures Commission Ordinance, and the SFC's creation in 1989.

As regulatory control of securities and their markets had been spread across a number of governmental bodies prior to the creation of the SFC, the existing structures appeared unwieldy and ill-coordinated. They also lacked independence. The creation of a new independent body and the elimination of the erstwhile regulatory Commissions, and by connection the Office of the Commissioner for Securities and Commodities Trading, marked a sea-change in regulatory reform.

At the time of the crash, two bodies, the Securities Commission and the Commodities Trading Commission, were given primacy in securities market regulation and surveillance. As explained in the *Report of the Securities Review Committee* (1988, p. 224), the two bodies were entrusted with two principal duties: the enforcement of the major ordinances of the day, the Securities Ordinance and Commodities Trading Ordinance, and of the supervision of a range of activities on the SEHK and HKFE. Without going into specific details of the roles of each, and of the government-appointed Commissioner, it became apparent that the two Commissions had been marginalized in a number of substantive ways. Robert Fell, who arrived at the Exchange as its Chief Executive in November 1987, sums this up in his narrative of the decision to close the Exchange in the midst of the crash (for four days between Tuesday, 20 October and Friday, 23 October 1987).

> No one seems to have bothered about the position of the Securities Commission whose remit included the duty of closing the exchange for up to five days because of 'financial crisis, whether in Hong Kong or elsewhere, or other circumstances, which is likely to prevent orderly trading'. No one seems to have questioned the legality of the proposal; more important, no one seems to have wondered about the implications for the financial markets generally.' (Fell (1992, p. 195), quotation marks shown as used).[39]

Unlike its forebears, then, the SFC was born out of statute and set up as a separate unit standing outside the confines of the Hong Kong government's Civil Service. Notwithstanding this, the government performs a number of key roles in supervising the SFC's regulatory mandate. These, as enunciated in an SFC statement relating to its 'Accountability', require that:

The SFC is responsible to the government for the discharge of its responsibilities, and reports to the Financial Secretary. It is obliged to consult the Financial Secretary prior to exercising certain of its powers and when making certain rules. The Chairman and Executive Directors of the SFC are appointed by the Chief Executive of the HKSAR and its annual budget must be approved by the Chief Executive and tabled before the provisional legislative council of the HKSAR.' (Securities & Futures Commission (information handbook), p.2 ('Accountability'); the term 'provisional' in the last line refers to the status of the HKSAR's legislative body prior to the first elections in the newly formed SAR).

The potential funding role provided by the Hong Kong government is just that, given the body's exclusive reliance upon other sources of revenue in recent years.[40] These income sources have principally been derived from two sources: levies (reflecting defined shares of the transaction levies collected by the SEHK and HKFE), and a range of fees and charges. Recent figures show that the former, for both the 1996/7 and 1997/8 financial years, accounted for well over half of the organization's income. Lastly, as the organization has a non-profit-making orientation, any surplus of income over expenditures is free of tax.[41]

The Regulatory Scope of the SFC
The SFC, as shown in Figure 2.2, is structured with regulatory powers to oversee the activities of the SEHK and the HKFE and their associated clearing houses/companies. As the diagram shows, and as stated earlier, each of the bodies also accepts a self-regulatory role. In the case of the two exchanges, this relates to members and issuers. For the three clearing houses, governance duties extend to clearing members/participants.

The SFC is also vested with powers in four other broad areas of activity, pertaining to the regulation of 'financial intermediaries other than Exchange Members', mergers and acquisitions, the offering of investment products, and to areas of activity that fall within the general province of market malpractice.

Its central regulatory role is set to stay and may actually grow in significance, when the proposed merger of the SEHK and HKFE, and the new entity's subsequent listing, come into effect.[42] The consolidation and reforms to this regulatory framework will naturally unfold as the mooted reforms near.

2.2 The Interrelationship of Banking, Monetary and Equity Markets

The Role of the Hong Kong Monetary Authority (HKMA)

As noted earlier, the SFC is not the only regulator in the financial services arena. The Hong Kong Monetary Authority (HKMA) and the Office of the Commissioner of Insurance are also notable players, though for the purpose of this text, the former is considerably more important than the latter.

Figure 2.2 Regulatory Purview of the SFC

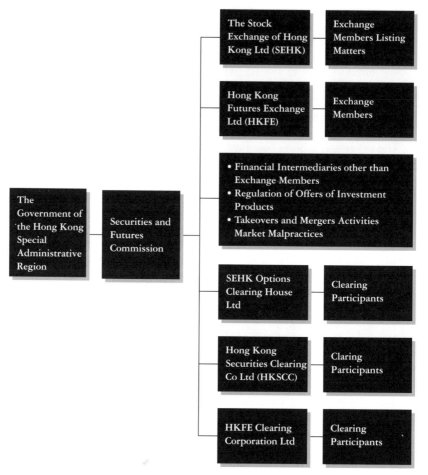

Diagram adapted from the Securities and Futures Commission Annual Report 1998–99: Making the Markets Work Better, p. 1.

The HKMA was born out of marriage between two government bodies—the Office of the Exchange Fund and the Office of the Commissioner of Banking—in 1993. As we discussed in Chapter 1, the HKMA plays a pivotal role in the SAR's financial system through its role in banking supervision and the management of the government's Exchange and Land Funds. By virtue of its jurisdiction over the Exchange Fund , it also plays a key role in maintaining the Currency Board system.[43] This is part and parcel of its task of ensuring exchange-rate stability. It is, perhaps, this last role that gives the HKMA such a significant presence in the overall financial system. As the linchpin to general interest rate behaviour and, by connection, asset price behaviour, the Currency Board system is critical to our appreciation of property, and debt and equity markets. It would certainly be a huge oversight to exclude the workings of this system from a text of this sort.

The Currency Board System

The Background to the 'Peg'

The current linked exchange-rate system between the Hong Kong dollar and US dollar was set up in October 1983. Prior to this a floating exchange-rate system had been in operation. This system came under heavy fire during the late summer of 1983 as Sino-British relations deteriorated. The political impasse between the then sovereign and the territory's sovereign-designate triggered massive selling of HKD bank deposits. Perhaps the best account of the time is offered by Lui.[44] He reports that the local currency fell from a value for the 1982 year-end of HK$6.515 against the greenback to an all-time nadir, in September 1983, of HK$9.60. Most of this decline was in fact concentrated in one month, September 1983. Amongst other things, this triggered a severe bout of asset inflation as consumers stockpiled retail and consumer goods in anticipation of further declines in currency values. Decisive action came in the form of a new 'linked exchange-rate system', implemented in October of the same year. This change proved to be an immensely stable arrangement. The resilience of this new system largely reflects the commitment afforded to it by successive administrations. In many ways, its political underpinnings are as important as its economic ones.

The linked exchange-rate system (Currency Board) may have been boldly implemented, but it was far from original. As argued in Jao's (1998, pp. 219–21) excellent narrative, the 1983 measure represented a return to a situation that had characterized the Hong Kong of old: the Sterling Exchange Standard. Apart from the 1941–5 interlude, marking the Japanese occupation, this currency regime had stood firm between 1935 and 1972.[45] The mechanism suggested in 1983 therefore marked a new beginning to the Currency Board, albeit with a new 'sovereign' currency as backing.[46]

Is the 'Peg' Really a Peg?

The quotation marks give the answer away. It is not. Not that many people appreciate this, as anyone reading the financial pages would know. Genuine pegged exchange-rate systems involve a central bank anchoring a currency's value to a given exchange-rate level (or range of values), with a particular foreign currency serving as the designated anchor.[47] As explained in Section 14.4, a number of Asian countries saw fit to follow such a policy in the 1990s, 'shadowing' the US dollar within specified limits. This policy proved to be a little misguided given the strong appreciation of the US dollar between 1995 and 1997 (see Figure 14.1). Hong Kong, of course, also suffered in much the same way given its direct link with the US dollar.

The pegging or targeting of a currency is achieved through direct intervention in the markets. When a currency, subject to such an arrangement, depreciates below a target level, the central bank buys from the local float. When the opposite occurs it sells from its existing holdings into the float. As the HKMA is not strictly a central bank, one might argue that this is the reason why the pegged exchange-rate system does not operate locally. This may be so, but misses the essential truth of the Currency Board system: it works without the need for direct market intervention.

Key Features of the Currency Board: NIBs and CIs
Hong Kong's Currency Board system rests on a commitment by its designated note-issuing banks (NIBs), HSBC, the Standard Chartered Bank and the Bank of China, to buy and sell Hong Kong dollars at the prescribed linked rate of HK$7.8:US$1. It is this commitment, and not direct intervention by the HKMA, that characterizes a Currency Board system. One can also be sure that the monetary base under such a system is also backed by the requisite amount of foreign currency to allow complete conversion of all the local currency in circulation into the reference currency of choice. This captures the essence of a Currency Board. This backing comes about through the use of Certificates of Indebtedness (CIs) which are issued by the Exchange Fund whenever a NIB releases HKD banknotes into circulation. Each CI must be backed with USD assets (at the linked rate) placed by the NIBs with the Exchange Fund. In this way, the CIs become liabilities of the Exchange Fund and assets of the NIBs. Similarly, when the NIBs buy Hong Kong dollars from the HKMA they redeem the requisite number of CIs from the Exchange Fund, and receive US dollars at the prescribed linked rate. The upshot is that the CI base and, therefore, the US dollar asset base of the Exchange Fund, is always sufficient to allow complete conversion of HKD banknotes at the linked rate.

As the NIBs also commit to buy and sell banknotes with all licensed banks at the linked rate, transactions in banknotes are inevitably consummated at the linked rate. It would be futile, for instance, for any bank to try to sell banknotes at a higher rate, simply because a buying counterparty could never be found (given the option for that counterparty to buy from the NIBs at the more advantageous linked rate). In this sense, then, only bank deposits can trade at a premium or a discount to the linked rate. It is the market for these bank deposits that essentially determines the market rate for HKD foreign exchange. The markets for banknotes and deposits are not entirely separate, however, which suggests potential for arbitrage. Arbitrage, in a pure sense, represents a riskless profit opportunity. This is achieved by taking opposite positions in the same underlying asset in two different markets. To illustrate, suppose a higher rate of exchange is available on HKD deposits in the foreign exchange market. An arbitrageur could then buy Hong Kong dollars at the linked rate from one of the NIBs and, after converting the amount to bank deposit form, could sell the deposit for profit in the foreign exchange market. Due to transaction costs and other limitations, it is generally recognized that such arbitrage has limited scope.[48] As illustrated later in this section, interest rate adjustments are far more important in aligning the market and linked rates.

The 'Monetary Base of the Currency Board: Bank Notes and the Clearing Balance

The essential monetary base for the Currency Board system reflects the value of local banknotes in issue. This is captured by the Exchange Fund's CI liabilities and, as of the 1997 year-end, totalled just over HK$87 billion.[49] This is not the definitive measure of the monetary base, however. The clearing balance held by the HKMA, for immediate settlement and clearing of banknote transactions, must also be added to this figure.[50, 51] This clearing balance at the 1997 year-end, as indicated in the HKMA's annual report, was HK$296 million (p. 77). The overall figure for the monetary base should not be confused with official money supply figures.[52]

The clearing balance reflects a requirement for all licensed banks in the SAR to hold a clearing account with the HKMA, which is used for clearing and settling all inter-bank transactions as well as direct sales and purchases of currency with the Exchange Fund (see notes 50 and 51). This coincided in December 1996 with the introduction of a state-of-the-art settlement system for inter-bank transactions: the Real Time Gross Settlement System (RTGS).[53] As previously discussed, the clearing balance, across all banks, gives us a measure of inter-bank liquidity. The use of RTGS essentially imposes the full rigour of the linked exchange-rate system on all inter-bank transactions in a timely and secure fashion.

The net balance on banks' clearing accounts increase when a net sale of US dollars is made to the Exchange Fund. This invites the currency board operation into full play with the HKMA buying the net amount and crediting a corresponding amount of Hong Kong dollars to the aggregate clearing balance, in accordance with the link. In the local parlance of the HKMA, this is a currency inflow. More accurately, those banks with sales of US dollars receive credits to their clearing balances whilst those with purchases incur debits.

As the net clearing balance represents the effective level of inter-bank liquidity, its precise balance will be closely related to the rate at which banks lend/borrow with one another: the Hong Kong Inter-bank Offer Rate (HIBOR). This issue, which is central to the workings of the Currency Board, is taken up in the following.

The Role of Interest Rates

When market rates deviate from the linked rate, interest rate adjustments, through the market-determined HIBOR, come into play. The events of October 1997, when huge selling of Hong Kong dollars occurred, best illustrate this. For a variety of reasons, cash calls from speculators and investors led to a flow of US dollars from the banking system, with a surfeit of Hong Kong dollars flowing in. A minority of banks may also have been shorting the currency. That is, borrowing Hong Kong dollars and selling them to the HKMA at the linked rate. The purchase of US dollars from the HKMA, for whatever reason, precipitated a capital outflow or shrinkage in the banks' net clearing balance. An escalation of inter-bank rates (HIBOR) naturally followed. A number of banks, seeking to stave-off a 'negative' balance on their clearing accounts, added to this pressure by chasing Hong Kong dollars in the inter-bank market. This is where the self-balancing mechanism comes in. Increased inter-bank rates choke off the desire of speculators to short the currency (i.e., to borrow it, and sell it). They also encourage banks to buy Hong Kong dollars from the HKMA (at the linked rate) and lend the amounts to other banks, that need Hong Kong dollars, at attractive rates. This self-correcting buying pressure increases banks' net clearing balance and eases interest rate pressure. This is the manner in which interest rates and the clearing balances held by the HKMA are inextricably linked. Quite simply, a Currency Board system operates through interest rate adjustments. As long as selling pressure of the Hong Kong dollar persists, interest rates will do their job and hover above their normal range.

When banks are heavy net buyers of Hong Kong dollars from the HKMA (i.e, a currency inflow occurs) the mechanism works in reverse. In such circumstances, the monetary base will increase and banks will have excess HKD liquidity. The surfeit of funds available in the inter-bank market causes interest rates on the Hong Kong dollar to fall relative to the US dollar. This increases the incentive to buy US dollars. This inevitably leads to a subsequent fall in the banks' clearing balances as they approach the Exchange Fund for US dollars, at the linked rate. The capital outflow reduces the availability of the local currency in the inter-bank market, thus raising interest rates. Again, interest rates and the net clearing balance move in a counter-fashion.

What is the normal range for HIBOR? As we saw in Section 1.6, the prime rate, at least over extended periods, should exceed HIBOR. If it does not, banks essentially lose money. This is because the returns on their largest loans, often made at prime to their best credit-rated customers, are often financed by inter-bank loans. During late 1997, the extent of Hong Kong dollar selling was such that a negative differential between prime and HIBOR occurred on a number of occasions. The incentive for Hong Kong banks to adjust prime rates above HIBOR may not be an option either. Raising prime rates during a market when interest rates are rising and property and equity markets are falling may be disastrous for the economy. It would also be counter-productive for the banks, as it would undermine the quality of their loan assets.

Liquidity Adjustments Achieved Through Exchange Fund Bills and Notes and the Discount Window
The foregoing, while capturing the essence of the negative interest rate/clearing-balance relation, is a little over-simplified. Mechanisms exist, for instance, for the HKMA to influence liquidity. One of course, is through

the issue of Exchange Fund bills and notes, described in Section 1.5. It is possible for the HKMA to draw down excess liquidity in the banking sector by selling bills or notes to the banks. This would have the effect of supporting HIBOR and easing any 'capital inflow' problem. One of the reasons why such bills and notes are desirable, apart from the yield they offer, is that they count as eligible securities for banks wishing to obtain additional liquidity through the HKMA's *discount window*. This window recently supplanted the Liquidity Adjustment Facility (LAF), which had been in place since 1992.

The old LAF system operated with two rates—an offer and a bid. It gave banks the opportunity to borrow (at the offer rate) from the HKMA during specified periods after the closure of the daily inter-bank market.[54] In other words, had banks not shored up a short-fall in HKD liquidity by the end of inter-bank trading hours, they could do so through the LAF. The offer rate was reflected in overnight repurchase agreements with eligible securities sold at a discount to an agreed repurchase price. Liquidity could also be transferred to the HKMA through the LAF bid rate. Changes to these arrangements, in September 1998, saw the elimination of the bid rate and the replacement of the LAF offer rate by a base rate (in relation to the new discount window)[55].

Prior to these changes, the LAF had played a critical role in adjusting liquidity. In brief, LAF offer and bid rates were determined by the HKMA as a collar within which overnight HIBOR rates could vary.[56] As we saw in October 1997, when excessive speculation against the Hong Kong dollar was apparent, the HKMA threatened to charge rates well above quoted offer rates to penalize parties deemed to be repeat borrowers. This threat was probably useful in two respects. Firstly, it penalized banks looking to open up short positions by borrowing Hong Kong dollar funds from the HKMA. Secondly, and perhaps more importantly, it imposed significant costs on those with existing short positions in the Hong Kong dollar. The effect of the measure, where funds were already tight, was to add pressure to already spiralling interest rates, so much so that, on 23 October 1997, overnight HIBOR rates hit levels of about 300%.[57] Pressure on rates soon abated, however, as banks switched from selling Hong Kong dollars to selling US dollars (to other banks and the speculators themselves) with the HKMA, as required under the Currency Board, facilitating the currency 'inflow'.

Manipulative Plays against the Currency Board
A currency board stabilizes the exchange rate at the cost of increased interest rate volatility. Speculators wishing to short the Hong Kong dollar also appreciate this and can bargain, if their speculative plays drain inter-bank liquidity sufficiently, on a precipitous fall in stock and bond values. This may well have been behind some of the speculative attacks of 1997 and 1998. The August 1998 assault on the currency allegedly involved a 'double-play' where speculators sold Hong Kong dollars short while holding short stock positions (i.e., positions where an investor has borrowed and

sold an asset with a future commitment to repurchase) or short HSI futures positions (i.e., selling futures). The currency attacks, especially with the HKD/USD link seemingly impregnable, led to sharp increases in interest rates. Huge gains were amassed on outstanding futures positions, which more than offset any currency losses. The attacks against the currency were allegedly designed to exploit the predictable interest rate effects. With concomitant falls in the HSI equally predictable, huge gains on HSI futures would have been possible. The leverage on such contracts would account for this.

Prominent local academic Chen Nai-Fu articulated the view that speculators were likely to sell currency forward rather than spot.[58] We know from Chapter 1 that forward contracts entail the parties to such agreements promising to buy (or sell) some underlying asset at a future delivery date at a price determined in the forward contract. Selling Hong Kong dollars forward simply entails agreeing to sell the currency in exchange for another at some future date. One advantage to a forward contract is the convenience it offers. Payment does not have to be made until the future delivery date. In the meantime, any HKD funds assigned to the future delivery payment can be parked in the HIBOR market for handsome interest returns.[59] This works on the premise that such forward selling triggers movements in HIBOR.

The speculator, with a commitment to sell Hong Kong dollars forward, gains if subsequent selling in the spot market drives up local interest rates. In the words of Professor Chen, 'A common strategy of currency speculators is that they will sell a large amount of currency in the forward market, perhaps with a knock at the spot market to start the panic.'[60] In one sense, the gain arises because speculators are able to offset their forward position for profit by buying the currency forward (for the same delivery date) at a lower price.

The theorem of Interest Rate Parity (IRP) underpins the above. This tells us that the ratio of forward to spot rates, between currencies X and Y, equates to the ratio of one plus their interest rates. Formally,

$$F_{X/Y}/S_{X/Y} \; = \; S_{Y/X}/F_{Y/X} \; = \; (1 + r_X)/(1 + r_Y)$$

Exhibit 2.3 highlights the principle. IRP tells us that when a currency X (relative to Y) is weaker forward than spot, its interest rate should be higher (than Y's). This theorem has been known for many years and dates back to Keynes' writings on the subject.[61] In relation to the foregoing, IRP suggests that if a 'panic' in a currency can be engineered, interest rates will rise as the currency's forward discount rises. In some countries, such a 'panic' might simply drive spot and forward rates down without appreciably changing the spot–forward differential. In places like Hong Kong, where a currency board operates, the HKD spot rate would likely be less affected than the forward rate. The experience of late 1997 and early 1998 provides telling evidence of this. Speculators, as noted, probably

Exhibit 2.3   The Workings of Interest Rate Parity (IRP)

The principle of IRP, or covered interest rate arbitrage, can be illustrated by considering two actively traded currencies. The Swiss Franc (X) and the US dollar (Y) are used for this purpose. Given spot and (six-month) forward rates, as shown below, and respective six-month London Inter-Bank Offer Rates (LIBOR) of 5.07781% and 1.4625%, IRP tells us that,

$$\frac{1.3757 \text{ SFR/USD}}{1.4004 \text{ SFR/USD}} = \frac{0.7141 \text{ USD/SFR}}{0.7269 \text{ USD/SFR}} = \frac{1 + 0.007286}{1 + 0.025075} = 0.982/3$$

As all reported interest rates are annualized, the appropriate interest rate for an investment for six months, in the above, is equal to $[(1 + 0.014625)^{0.5} - 1]$ for the Swiss franc and $[(1 + 0.0507781)^{0.5} - 1]$ for the US dollar.[62] The data indicates that the theorem holds, albeit with some very slight rounding error.

In essence, IRP tells us that a currency with a lower interest rate trades at a forward premium. The reason for this is provided in Figure 2.3 where two investment strategies are considered: one where US dollars are invested at USD LIBOR for six months and the other where US dollars are converted to Swiss francs at spot and invested at SFR LIBOR. The second strategy also requires that Swiss francs be sold forward against the US dollar at the outset to allow US dollar proceeds to be generated at the investment's conclusion. Both strategies yield almost an identical payoff. The difference of US$29.25 would, in any event, be easily eliminated by transaction costs.

IRP derives from arbitrage. Any significant discrepancy between the two strategies described in Figure 2.3 invites opportunities for riskless profit. To illustrate, suppose Scenario 1 offers significantly higher US dollar proceeds than Scenario 2. In other words, US dollar interest rates are higher than IRP would suggest. Arbitrageurs should simultaneously borrow SFR 140,040, convert the amount to US$100,000 spot and invest the sum at USD LIBOR for six months, and sell the proceeds forward for Swiss Francs. An excess of Swiss Francs, after settling the loan and interest, will then be guaranteed In six months' time.[63] Some spread will be evident though and, along with other transaction costs, means arbitrage opportunities will only occur when departures from IRP are sufficient to cover these costs.. This surplus is an arbitrage (riskless) profit.[64]

Is IRP Valid in practice? A slew of studies (see Marston (1976), Cosandier and Lang (1981), and Thornton (1989) for good examples) suggest it is. Accounts like Marston's, and Cosandier and Lang's indicate that IRP holds strongly in the Euro-currency market, where large bank transactions dominate.[65]

gained by being able to buy back the same forward contract at a cheaper price.

In theory, then—and maybe in practice—currency speculators can profit on both sides of the 'double-play'. Deliberate manipulation of securities prices, through such manoeuvres, would surely also suggest market

Figure 2.3   An Illustration of the Principle of Interest Rate Parity

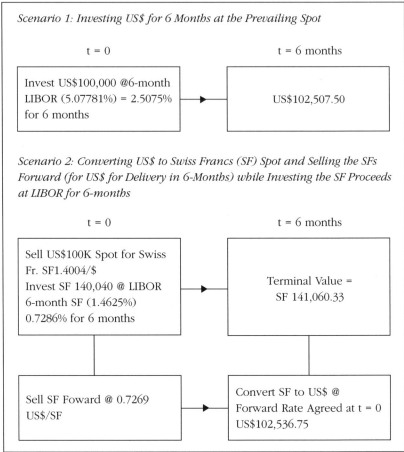

Scenario 1: Investing US$ for 6 Months at the Prevailing Spot

t = 0   t = 6 months

Invest US$100,000 @6-month
LIBOR (5.07781%) = 2.5075%   US$102,507.50
for 6 months

Scenario 2: Converting US$ to Swiss Francs (SF) Spot and Selling the SFs Forward (for US$ for Delivery in 6-Months) while Investing the SF Proceeds at LIBOR for 6-months

t = 0   t = 6 months

Sell US$100K Spot for Swiss
Fr. SF1.4004/$
Invest SF 140,040 @ LIBOR   Terminal Value =
6-month SF (1.4625%)   SF 141,060.33
0.7286% for 6 months

Sell SF Foward @ 0.7269   Convert SF to US$ @
US$/SF   Forward Rate Agreed at t = 0
                                        US$102,536.75

Data Sources:
- Spot and Forward Exchange Rates were taken from the Asian Wall Street Journal (12 January 1999, p. 24) and referred to rates in NY as of 11 January 1999.
- Interest Rates used were LIBOR raes reported in the Markets Post of the South China Morning Post (12 January 1999, p. 11).

Notes: US$ LIBOR interest for six-months, $(1 + 0.0507781)^{0.05} - 1 = 0.025075$
SF LIBOR interest for six-months, $(1 + 0.014625)^{0.5} - 1 = 0.007286$

manipulation. If proven, this charge would likely incriminate the offender under the terms of the Securities Ordinance.

The HKMA is all too familiar with the manipulative 'double-play' strategy described, given the events of August 1998. Certain unnamed hedge funds were deemed to be selling substantial numbers of HSI futures contracts whilst simultaneously selling the local currency (in both the spot and forward markets). This practice caused the HKMA to take unprecedented action by intervening in the equity and futures markets to counter such strategies. To really appreciate how it worked, deeper understanding of futures and futures trading strategies is required. This issue is revisited in Section 12.8.

At this stage, it is worth considering the ways in which the HKMA has modified the Currency Board system in the wake of the August 1998 hedge-fund ploy. The intention behind these measures was to weaken the speculator's hand. The changes instituted, numbering seven in total, provided, amongst other things, for increased liquidity in the inter-bank market.[66] Estimates at the time suggested that the measures had raised this from around HK$1.8 billion to HK$30 billion.[67] The newly created discount window, as described earlier, formed a key part of this, allowing investors to tap the increased funding by placing collateral, largely Exchange Fund bill and note paper, with the HKMA on a repurchase ('repo') basis. The various changes, by enhancing inter-bank liquidity, have generally had a calming effect on the markets. The sharp reduction in HIBOR volatility in the weeks following the September 1998 initiative (see Figure 1.2) duly reflect this result.

2.3   The Connection between the Currency Board and Equity and Debt Security Values

The General Impact on Stock Values

The hikes in HIBOR, resulting from the intense selling of the Hong Kong dollar at various points during 1997 and 1998, provide ample evidence of the negative relation between interest rates (in general) and stock values. At one level this negative relation reflects the cost of funding stock purchases, either through borrowing arrangements, directly with the banks or via margin accounts (to be discussed in Section 3.1). Whenever such costs rise, buying demand clearly wanes. On another level, increased interest rates impose additional costs on retail investors; increased mortgage repayment charges being one. As cash flow constraints tighten, the incentive to realize any stockholdings clearly increases. This is one of the reasons why fixed-interest rate mortgage schemes hold such appeal for the Hong Kong SAR government. Being able to lock in interest rate costs not only provides greater certainty and budgetary control for retail investors but also helps insulate the equity market from undue swings in interest rates. This issue is taken up further in Section 14.1, where debt-market developments in the SAR are analysed.

Periods of rising interest rates also make bank deposits and other less risky investment vehicles more attractive. With deposit rates rising during the latter part of 1997 and early part of 1998, many saw an opportunity to redirect their investments from stocks to deposits. For banks as well, lending at HIBOR held greater appeal than an investment in the local equity market. While currency risk was partly behind the inflation in nominal returns on local bank deposits, with many seeing this as compensation for the risk of the 'peg' breaking, currency risk remained a concern whether investing in local stocks or HKD currency deposits. The asset deflation caused by rising interest rates also meant that the real returns on the deposits were at least equal to nominal returns. A very different situation to the one prevailing in the late 1980s and early 1990s when real rates of borrowing were either negative or close to zero (see Figure 1.).

The Currency Risk Premium
By late 1998, the pressure on the local currency had abated somewhat with interest rates, both HIBOR and prime, falling to normal levels. This change, in turn, contributed to a revival in local stock values, partly due to the elimination, or diminution, of the currency 'risk premium'. This can be understood in terms of the present value model which tells us that a stock's price equates to the present value of all expected income receipts (dividends) from holding it. In sum:

$$P_{0J} = \frac{E(D_{1J})}{1 + K_{eJ}} + \frac{E(D_{2J})}{(1 + K_{eJ})^2} + \dots + \frac{E(D_{nJ})}{(1 + K_{eJ})^n}$$

Where P_{0J} is the current ex-dividend price of stock J; $E(D_{tJ})$ is the expected dividend at time. t for stock J; and K_{eJ} represents equityholders' required rate of return (cost of capital) for J.

Within this model, risk relates to the perceived level of variance around expected dividend payments. Where this variance is deemed to be large, investors will discount the expected dividend stream at a much higher rate. This rate of discount, described as the *cost of equity capital* for the stock, represents some aggregate of investors' required rates of return. Greater risk, manifest in a higher cost of equity capital, results in some discount on the stock price. This duly raises the stock's expected return. With currency risk, essentially the risk that the linked rate will be broken, investors were forced to give serious thought to the expected US dollar value of the dividend payments. Even if the link were perceived to be in no imminent danger, the fear that it would eventually break, leading to lower equivalent USD dividends, was sufficient to drive many investors for cover. With the reduction in HIBOR volatility following the HKMA's September 1998 drive to widen the pool of bank liquidity, fears on this front seemed to recede and stock prices rallied. The risk premium had seemingly been cut: the amount being the difference between the cost of equity capital (K_{eJ}) for a representative stock J before and after the 1998 initiative.

The General Impact of Interest Rates on Bond Values

The general impact of interest rate movements on bond prices can be gleaned by considered a bond pricing example.[68] Suppose we have a bond with exactly three years to maturity paying a coupon of 7%. The bond's asking price is $105.68 (per $100 of principal) and, as is customary, pays coupons in two equally spaced instalments per year. This suggests six future payments to the bondholder (creditor), the first of $3.50 in six months' time and the last of $103.50 (principal plus final coupon instalment) in 36 months'. Essentially, the yield (y) on the bond is inferred by setting its purchase price (asking price) equal to the present value of the cashflow returns as shown in Exhibit 2.4, Panel A.

Exhibit 2.4   Case Illustration of a 7% Three Year Bond
(Face Value = $100)

Panel A

$$105.68 = \frac{3.5}{(1+y)^{1/2}} + \frac{3.5}{(1+y)^1} + \frac{3.5}{(1+y)^{3/2}} + \frac{3.5}{(1+y)^2} + \frac{3.5}{(1+y)^{5/2}} + \frac{103.5}{(1+y)^3}$$

y = 0.05.
y is the bond's yield to maturity (or redemption yield).

Panel B

$$105.68 = \frac{3.5}{(1+r_{0,1})^{1/2}} + \frac{3.5}{(1+r_{0,1})^1} + \frac{3.5}{(1+r_{0,2})^{3/2}} + \frac{3.5}{(1+r_{0,2})^2} + \frac{3.5}{(1+r_{0,3})^{5/2}} + \frac{103.5}{(1+r_{0,3})^3}$$

$r_{0,1}$, $r_{0,2}$ and $r_{0,3}$ are one-, two-, and three-year spot rates.
$r_{0,1}$ = 2.4% (= 0.024); $r_{0,2}$ = 3.75%; and $r_{0,3}$ = 5.10% provides one solution to the above. These rates reflect positive term structure.

A yield of 5% (0.05) obtains (by solving y). In practice, it is not the yield, or a set of constant intertemporal discount rates, that determines a bond's value. The individual discount rates do this. These are normally referred to as spot rates and are used by investors to discount each constituent future cash-flow return back to a present value. To highlight this process, the pricing equation in Panel A of Exhibit 2.4 is re-expressed, using the spot rates, in Panel B.

Each period spot (discount) rate could be different. The following sequence of spot rates would solve the equation in Panel B: $r_{0,1}$ = 2.4% (= 0.024); $r_{0,2}$ = 3.75%; and $r_{0,3}$ = 5.10%. These rates represent the market's perception of the required rates of return on each of the cash-flow returns in the bond. Once the price of the bond is determined from these discount rates, a yield (y = 0.05 in this case) is inferred. It is wise to remember that spot rates determine bond prices. Yields are subsequently inferred from this price. In turn, the yield only equates to the spot rates when constant (or flat) term structure obtains. Most of the time, we see positive term structure, characterized by rising discount rates as shown in Exhibit 2.4, Panel B. The yield, though, provides a useful measure as it tells us the annualized compound rate of return on the bond if we acquire it (at the price on which the yield is based) and hold it all the way through to maturity.

We can also see that the spot rate used for discounting the final, and largest, cash-flow payment from the bond ($r_{0,3}$) has a much greater bearing on the bond's total valuation than any other spot rate. Not surprisingly, then, the yield rate tends to gravitate towards this final-year spot rate.

The Role of Inflation

Inflationary expectations are always critical to asset valuations. We can illustrate this for the bond in Exhibit 2.4. Suppose investors anticipate inflation to be around 3% per annum during the next two years. Reference to the well-known Fisher identity, introduced in Chapter 1, Exhibit 1.3, tells us that a yield (nominal rate of return) of 5% provides for a real rate of approximately 2% under such circumstances. Many have interpreted Fisher's (1930) account of interest rates to mean that nominal rates simply adjust to reflect increased rates of *expected* inflation. In this way, real rates would be forever constant. This is not quite true, though, as Fisher himself declares. He notes that nominal rates may not adjust fully to changes in anticipated inflation.[69] Nonetheless, a lot of effort has been directed to test the proposition of a constant real rate of return on various asset classes. Clearly different types of assets will offer different real rates. The question is are real rates for a particular class of asset approximately constant? Studies like Crowder and Hoffman's (1996), for US Treasury bills between 1952 and 1991, are generally supportive of this contention.[70]

Assuming investors insist on a constant real rate, an increase in inflationary expectations suggests a compensating increase of the same in a bond's yield. This is achieved by an appropriate correction to the bond's price. The story might go like this: if bank deposit rates increase in an economy by 25 basis points in response to an increase in expected inflation rates of 25 basis points, some investors might shift from government bonds to bank deposits. If the two types of security are viewed as being of a similar credit-rating they would, to all intents and purposes, be close substitutes. A shift to the higher yielding asset would then precipitate a fall in the government bond's price. In theory, this should continue until the yield on the bond is again competitive with that on the deposit.

In short, assets of a particular risk-class and maturity should offer similar nominal rates of return (and, therefore, similar real rates). While not testing this thesis, Ibbotson and Sinquefield (1979), again for the United States, give some idea of the average nominal and real rates of return on particular assets. They consider annualized returns over the period 1925 to 1978 and note that the arithmetic mean returns for common stocks, long-term corporate bonds, long-term government bonds and Treasury bills in the United States were 11.2%, 4.1%, 3.4%, and 2.5%, respectively.[71] In other words, in a typical year, common stocks generated returns 870 basis points higher than United States Treasury bills. This is taken in Ibbotson and Sinquefield as the risk premium for common stock (i.e., the compensation in return for the increased risk of investing in common stocks). The topic of risk and return features more prominently in Sections 4. 1 and 4.2.

In relation to real returns, Ibbotson and Sinquefeld note that the mean differential between the arithmetic returns on Treasury bills and the rate of inflation is approximately zero.[72] In other words, Treasury bills generate real returns of zero on average, while common stocks generate levels equivalent to their risk premium, on average.

Inflation, Interest Rates and the Currency Board

How does this all fit in with the Currency Board? Essentially, such a board prevents the textbook version of the Fisher equation—that is the preservation of real rates of return of a given asset class—from working. We know this already from discussions in Section 1.6. As interest rates in Hong Kong broadly follow those in the United States, because of the exchange-rate link, interest rate movements in Hong Kong are driven by inflationary expectations in the United States. Local inflationary expectations have comparatively little effect. This means that fixed-interest bearing securities, like bank deposits, sometimes offer negative real rates of return; which was, in fact, the case for much of the late 1980s and early 1990s (see Figure 1.2). This result pushed investment away from fixed-interest bearing securities in to the equity and property market sectors. Negative borrowing costs (in real terms) were largely responsible for the ensuing 'bubble' in these markets. Under a floating exchange-rate regime, interest rates have a much better chance of adjusting to preserve positive real rates.

Returning to our earlier comments surrounding the Currency Board's associated 'risk premium', certain implications hold for fixed-interest bearing securities like bonds. A fear, real or imagined, that the Hong Kong dollar might depreciate in the short- to medium-term would force yields for medium-term bonds to mushroom (with prices doing the opposite). This is one of the reasons why the yield curve on short- to medium-term Exchange Fund notes had such a strong positive gradient for much of late 1997 and early 1998.[73] Its return to a mildly positive shape in late 1998 was comforting because it was symptomatic of a decline in the currency's 'risk premium'.

Issues of Credit Risk

Predicting general interest rate movements may be the key to anticipating market movements—so long as the predictions are more timely than everyone else's. These hunches still only form part of the equation, however, especially when bond investments are considered. Deteriorating credit-ratings for the bond issuer can easily offset any gains emanating from interest rate cuts. Investors shorting Asian corporate bonds (i.e., borrowing them from other investors and selling them in anticipation of lower prices) prior to credit rating down grades would have had much to celebrate in late 1997 and early 1998. Actual downgrades, coupled with rising interest (spot or discount) rates, contributed to sharp price declines on a range of Asian bonds.

Erroneous judgements relating to changes in interest rate expectations and credit-ratings clearly come at a fairly hefty price. So do those pertaining to yield spreads, if the recent troubles of Long-Term Capital Management (LTCM) are anything to go by. Reports at the time suggested that LTCM was, amongst other things, betting on a narrowing yield spread between a selection of risky corporate bonds and US Treasury bonds.[74] Given the negative relation between bond prices and yields, a narrowing of the yields would have resulted in profits when long in corporate bonds and short in Treasuries. As the very opposite, a widening of the spread, occurred, the strategy resulted in large losses. This débâcle is revisited in Section 3.5 where hedge funds fall under the spotlight.

Rejoinders about currency risk also apply. Devaluations of other currencies, as we saw with the Russian rouble in 1998, can spark unexpected movements across bond markets. This devaluation triggered what some described as a 'flight to quality', where holdings shifted from shares and riskier corporate bonds into more secure sovereign bond and bank deposit havens. For any corporation with loans, or export exposure, to a country with a weakening currency, the risk of losses inevitably figures in credit-rating agencies' assessments of that corporation. Even with bonds denominated in US dollars (or Hong Kong dollars), the fall-out can be severe. In short, interest rate expectations, credit-rating changes, and currency risks are all interwoven and particular views relating to each should be well established before taking a short or long punt in bonds.

2.4 Concluding Remarks

The essential structures governing the workings of the local equity and debt markets have been set out in the foregoing. This entailed comment on the institutional arrangements, with particular reference to the regulatory powers vested in bodies like the SFC and HKMA, as well as on the essential role of the Currency Board in shaping the key variable to all security values: interest rates. With this background, attention now turns to the actual structure of equity investment, which can involve direct stock investment or indirect access to underlying stock through either fund or derivative investments. Investments through the first two of these routes are considered in Chapter 3.

Notes

1.   See *A Policy Paper on Securities and Futures Market Reform*, 1999.
2.   In the light of such approval, the requisite legislation for the establishment of the new entity would follow (see Ibid., pp. 31–2 for the proposed 'Timeframe for Reform'). By the same token, the Policy Paper makes it clear that, even without members' approval, steps will be taken to implement the essence of the reforms (Ibid., para 10.2, pp. 32–3).
3.   See speech, Deputy Prime Minister of Singapore, Lee Hsien Loong (1998).
4.   This Act came into force in 1933 in the US. It is examined briefly in Chapter 9 (Note 12).

5.   The Financial Services Bureau, an organ of the HKSAR government, recognizes the three bodies as the 'principal' regulators in the local financial services industry (see FSB homepage at http:/www.info.gov.hk/fsb).

6.   See *A Draft for a Composite Securities and Futures Bill* (1996). See Low (1998) for useful overview of the principal ordinances.

7.   Rule 27(1) grants the body, '. . . the exclusive right to establish, operate and maintain a stock market in Hong Kong.'

8.   See SEHK News Release (1998).

9.   See *A Policy Paper on Securities and Futures Market Reform*, 1999 (Para. 15, Executive Summary, and 8.14 in particular).

10.   Ibid. (Para. 8.14).

11.   For one, the paper, under the heading, 'listing of the NewCo' (a reference to the proposed merged entity), states that, 'It would be inappropriate for the SEHK to supervise its own holding company.' (Ibid., Para. 8.14(d)).

12.   See *Fact Book 1997*, p. 111 for a summary of this dealership requirement, and a range of others, for individual and corporate membership on the Exchange. The dealership requirement is extended for corporate members to read 'registered under Securities Ordinance as dealer and have at least one director registered as dealer' (*Fact Book 1997*, p. 111).

13.   The SFC, through its licensing division, is responsible for granting dealership status.

14.   See *Fact Book 1997*, p. 112 for detailed figures.

15.   See Harrison (1997, p. 49) for an excellent summary of 'Restrictions on Foreign Participation' in 10 Pacific-Rim markets.

16.   In other words, the first quarter of the 1997/8 financial year.

17.   All figures were determined from SEHK *Annual Report*, 1998 ('Average Daily Turnover' table, p. 23).

18.   The stellar performance of the Exchange between 1995–6 and 1997–8 should also be emphasized. This period saw a notable spike in volumes, up to the end of 1997 (see Table 1.2). Primary markets moved in tow with the number of new security listings climbing from 20 in 1995, to 49 in 1996, to 82 in 1997 (See *Fact Book 1997*, p. 4).

19.   These likely reflect annual or other fees, charged to all companies holding listed securities.

20.   See SEHK *Annual Reports* (1997, p. 58; 1998, p. 51).

21.   The SEHK's *Annual Report*, 1998 makes this clear. It states, 'Under the Memorandum and Articles of Association of the Exchange, the Exchange shall not pay dividends to its Members. The assets of the Exchange will only be available for distribution among its Members upon winding up of the Exchange' (p. 68, Note 9).

22.   Reforms in 1991 curtailed the possibility of dividend payment to SEHK Members. This, and other changes, were effected by the SFC following the Members' rejection of a motion to convert the SEHK into a non-profit making entity (see Paisley (1991) for a detailed account of these reforms).

23.   See *A Policy Paper on Securities and Futures Market Reform*, 1999 (Para. 8.8).

24.   One requirement is that the SEHK ensures it, '. . . has appropriated the excess of transaction levy income over one-third of its budgeted recurrent expenses to the Development Reserve in accordance with the budget guidelines approved by the Financial Secretary in May 1996.' (SEHK *Annual Report*, 1998, p. 77). For the period 1 July 1997 to 30 June 1998, this met with a transfer of over HK$234.7 million to the Development Reserve (ibid.).

25.   Ibid. (p. 1).

26.   A recent cut in this duty should help placate those with such concerns. Its level was trimmed by one-sixth from HK$1.50 (to HK$1.25) per HK$1,000 of order value (see *Fact Book 1997*, p. 10 for details).

27. For details of the events leading up to the creation of the HKCE, see Report of the Securities Review Committee (1988, pp. 399–400).

28. For reasons of brevity, the historical developments leading up to the establishment of the HKFE are not entertained here. For an excellent narrative of the events surrounding this change, see Freris (1991, pp. 142–3).

29. The initial listing dates in cotton, sugar, soybeans and gold were May 1977, November 1977, November 1979, and August 1980, respectively. Thanks are due to the HKFE for the provision of both the initial listing and de-listing dates in these commodity futures contracts.

30. Trading in physical gold on The Chinese Gold & Silver Exchange Society has, of course, been evident in Hong Kong since the turn of the twentieth century.

31. According to the Report of the Securities Review Committee (p. 404), dollar volumes in HSI futures contributed to 81.6% of total HKFE dollar turnover during 1986. This is all the more remarkable given that HSI futures were only available for the last eight months of the year.

32. For the 1997 year-end, HKFE's interest income amounted to around HK$473 million as compared with interest expenses of approximately HK$207 million (HKFE *Annual Report* (1997, p. 36)).

33. All figures and percentages are drawn from the HKFE's *Annual Report* 1997.

34. Notwithstanding this, provision is made, via a HKFE connection with the New York Mercantile Exchange (NYMEX), for Member firms (and their investors) to trade in a range of commodity and energy futures on NYMEX.

35. The precise numbers of HKFE and Clearing Corp members were obtained from the HKFE's *Annual Report* (1997).

36. See Anonymous (October 1998b) for an account of ASX's listing and the pricing of its stock.

37. More extreme views see membership structures as being akin to an 'old boys' club'. A recent high profile editorial (see *Review* Editorial (1998)) makes this very point in relation to the 'typical Asian stock exchange'.

38. See *A Policy Paper on Securities and Futures Market Reform*, 1999.

39. The *Report of the Securities Review Committee* also expressed opinions on such lines, noting in its published findings in May 1988 that, '. . . the Commissions seem to have become advisory committees, except that when the October crisis came, they were not even asked for their advice . . .' (p. 227).

40. The SFC Annual Report (1998, p. 72, Note 2), for the year ending 31 March 1998, reports that such appropriations have not occurred since the period ending 31 March 1994.

41. See the Securities and Futures Commission Ordinance, Part II, S. 3(3).

42. See *A Policy Paper on Securities and Futures Market Reform*, 1999 (Para. 8.17).

43. This is reflected in the Exchange Fund Ordinance (Cap. 66) which, amongst other things, places the Fund under the Financial Secretary's charge (S.3). The Ordinance, in turn, vests the Financial Secretary with powers to appoint a 'monetary authority' (S.5A) and delegate the various powers and duties, wrested under the Ordinance, to this 'person' (S.5B).

44. See Lui (1991, p. 188), in particular, for an excellent historical summary of local exchange-rate systems.

45. See Jao (1998, p. 221) for precise details.

46. Jao also provides a useful documentary of the Currency Board's British antecedents, with reference to its use in British colonies in the late nineteenth and early twentieth centuries (see ibid.).

47. This point was elegantly made in a recent speech by the Chief Executive of the HKMA, Joseph Yam (see Yam (1998)).

48. The *Report on Financial Market Review* (1998, pp. 21–2) makes this very point, with bank note handling charges cited as a principal cost in such arbitrage.

Lui (1991, p. 205) also makes it very clear that such arbitrage is limited by, amongst other things, licensed banks being the only parties capable of operating at the linked rate.

49. See HKMA *Annual Report* (1997, p. 21 & 77).

50. A precise definition for the monetary base is, '. . . the sum of banknotes issued and the balance of the banking system (the reserve balance or clearing balance) held with the currency board for the purpose of effecting the clearing and settlement of transactions between the banks themselves and between the currency board and banks.' (*Report of Financial Market Review*, 1998, p. 20).

51. The HKMA announced, in early 1999, new 'backing arrangements for coins in circulation' whereby coins will be issued and redeemed at the linked rate. The changes were penned for 1 April 1999 (HKMA Press Release, 1999). In the following, clearing balance refers to the clearing account balance plus securities eligible for repo. See Yaum (1998b) for discussion of how Exchange Fund paper can also function as part of the monetary base.

52. The widely used HKD M3 money supply figure was reported to be around HK$1,641 billion at the 1997 year-end (see HKMA (1998, p. 17)). This captures the HKD value of transaction balances, as well as an array of bank deposit and negotiable certificate of deposit balances, held locally. For detailed discussion of this and other widely used money supply measures, see Beecham's (1996, pp. 15–20) excellent summary.

53. Between 1988 and the commencement of RTGS, a clearing role had been established via the now defunct Clearing House of the Hong Kong Association of Banks. This gave rise to the so-called accounting arrangements in the clearance of balances with the Exchange Fund (see Monetary Management Department, HKMA (1997a, pp. 22–4) for useful background on this).

54. Specific details are ignored here for reasons of brevity. For a detailed account of the LAF and its history, see HKMA (1997a, pp. 24–5).

55. See HKMA press release (September 1998).

56. Although movements outside of this range were possible (see HKMA (1997b, pp. 35) for diagrammatic representation of this using actual data). Since its introduction, LAF rates had been fixed, with an official bid-offer spread of 300 basis points set in October 1997 superseding the previous 200 point arrangement.

57. See Chan and Ku (1997) for an account of the penal rate threat, through the LAF, during this period. Thanks are due to Hugh Thomas for helpful comments on the Currency Board in the foregoing.

58. See Chen (1997).

59. Ibid.

60. Ibid.

61. See Keynes (1929, pp. 137–9 in particular). He spells out the IRP argument as follows, 'If money becomes dearer in London, the discount of forward *dollars* diminishes or gives way to a premium.' (p. 137, emphasis added). 'Dearer' money in this context refers to an increase in interest rates on sterling (relative to the dollar). In keeping with this quotation, this triggers a shrinking forward premium (or widening discount) on sterling. Keynes ascribes the whole adjustment process to arbitrage (p. 138).

62. The *Asian Wall Street Journal* (12 January, 1999, p. 24) was used to determine spot and forward exchange rate (for NY transactions as at 11 Jan, 1999) with LIBOR interest rates gleaned from the Markets Post of the *South China Morning Post* (12 January, 1999, p. 11).

63. LIBOR lending and borrowing rates, for a currency, are assumed to be approximately equal.

64. Leaving aside any pressure on rates, the arbitrage process would likely increase the forward premium on the Swiss franc, through spot buying and forward selling pressures. Any residual profit opportunities would be lapped up by others. Arbitrage, as we will see time and time again in this text, is key to ensuring competitive pricing.

65. As mentioned in Section 1.5, the Euro-currency markets are dealer-based with most bargains struck in London or Luxembourg. Interest rates in these deals, as reflected in the example in Exhibit 2.4, utilize market-determined LIBOR rates.

66. See HKMA press release (September 1998).

67. See Yiu (1998) for discussion of the basis for this estimate.

68. See Section 1.4 for an earlier comparable example.

69. In particular, Fisher (1930) opines that, '. . . when prices are rising, the rate of interest tends to be high but not as high as it should be to compensate for the rise; and when prices are falling, the rate of interest tends to be low, but not as low as it should be to compensate for the fall', (p. 43, an accompanying note is not shown).

70. They report, '. . . considerable support for a traditional "tax-adjusted" Fisher equation. . . . a 1% increase in inflation yields a 1.34% increase in the nominal interest rate. After adjusting for tax effects, this "Fisher effect" is insignificantly different from unity.' (p. 115, quotation marks used as shown).

71. See Ibbotson and Sinquefield (1979, Table III, p. 43).

72. Ibid.

73. A yield curve is constructed using fixed-interest-bearing government securities of a particular country. It represents a plot of the time to maturity of that security against its yield. Normally, bonds and notes of similar coupon rates are chosen for this purpose.

74. See Zuckerman (1998) for an excellent account.

3. Mechanisms for Stock and Equity Funds Investment and the Microstructure of Equity Markets

Issues relating to the actual mechanics of stock investment are discussed in the first section of this chapter with materials organized to cover essential terminology, the selection and operation of brokerage accounts, and trading costs. Issues of market microstructure then follow in Sections 3.2 and 3.3 where trade execution and post-trade arrangements—namely, clearing and settlement—are investigated.

Although the material in Sections 3.1 to 3.3 focuses entirely on trades in individual stocks, investments through managed fund portfolios, or collective investment schemes, as they are known locally, cannot be ignored. As more and more trading appears to be driven by institutions, and more and more retail investors appear open to the merits of fund management, markets in virtually all jurisdictions are increasingly fund- and institutionally-driven. Excepting investment trusts, where secondary-market trading occurs in the units or shares of the fund, the effects on the markets are indirect. Only the assets or securities making up the funds are actively traded. The fact that many of these securities are Hong Kong-based means that the market is often driven by the whims and judgements of the fund manager, especially when portfolios are re-balanced to change their exposure to the local market. It must be said, however, that institutions operating like fund managers—but with arsenals of funds representing proprietary assets—can do much the same thing. Whatever the precise form of this investment, it is clear that institutional players are more and more a part of Pacific-Rim markets, despite their retreat in late 1997 and 1998.

The creation of compulsory savings schemes are also significant in driving the demand for investment funds. As the Mandatory Provident Fund Scheme (MPF) now has legislative approval, we should see some activity on this front. The MPF, as a private-sector based retirement scheme, will require both employer and employee contributions. With much of this funding going into a variety of bond, money-market, and equity funds, managed funds will soon be of relevance to all. Accordingly, issues relating to funds management feature in Section 3.4. An analysis of the much-denigrated hedge fund naturally follows on from this in Section 3.5. Concluding remarks then follow in Section 3.6.

3.1 The Mechanics of Security Investment

As outlined in Section 2.1, secondary trading on a membership-based exchange requires that investors route orders through recognized members of that exchange. Similar comments apply when investing in derivatives listed on futures exchanges. Trades executed outside exchanges, on so-called over-the-counter markets, are rather different. Membership structures do not exist in such an environment. Nevertheless, most still trade through designated brokers.

Brokerage (Member) Trades: Principal and Agency Trades

Recognized brokerages (or exchange members) typically trade in two ways: as an agent for a client or as a principal. In the latter, the broker trades for the underlying brokerage firm. Agency trading arises where the broker acts as an agent for another principal, namely his/her client. Information on the precise nature of a broker's trade—whether it be an agency or principal trade—is likely to be conveyed to the relevant exchange authorities at, or shortly after, trade execution.

Surveys conducted by the SEHK indicate that most trades on the Exchange are agency based. According to the *Fact Book 1997*, in relation to the 'Members Transaction Survey 1997', only 5% of the dollar value of trading volume (i.e. turnover) arose through 'members' principal trading'.[1] The remainder of trading was split between 'individuals' and 'institutions' with the former responsible for 56% of overall turnover and the latter 39%. Most important of all, perhaps, is the fact that most of the turnover from individuals originated locally with 53% of overall turnover stemming from this source.[2] In short, the importance of retail investors cannot be understated. In some of the larger overseas markets, retail players only account for a few percentage points of turnover. Why is Hong Kong so different? In markets like the United States and United Kingdom, retail players typically seek out fund investment rather than direct stock investment. The reverse is essentially true in most of Asia. Discussions in Section 3.4 will shed some light on the reasons behind this.

Discretionary and Non-Discretionary Brokerage Accounts

The type of brokerage account chosen by an investor depends upon the requirements of the client. In a discretionary account, the client may rely on the research skills of the brokerage firm and allow the account representative to buy or sell according to the brokerage firm's judgement of market conditions and opportunities. Alternatively, the account may be non-discretionary, where specific instructions are required from the client before any position is taken or liquidated. A hybrid of discretionary and non-discretionary features is also possible where the account representative is given some latitude in buying and selling, subject to specific client instructions. One instruction that is commonly employed is the 'stop-loss' order. An instruction to 'cap' losses within 5% of investment cost would necessitate positions being closed-out whenever this limit is breached. Stop-loss orders are much more critical in futures trading given the margin (to be discussed) implicit in such contracts, which, like any form of gearing (leverage), magnifies percentage returns.

Even though a stop-loss order is specified, it may not work. When prices enter a downward spiral it may be virtually impossible to sell stock. The cataclysmic falls in Asian markets during several trading days in October 1997 remind us of this. Such precipitous falls in value occur precisely because buyer sentiment is poor. Buyers simply wait in the wings until prices move into a range compatible with their views. Without buy orders no one can sell. Sellers accordingly adjust their transaction prices to try to match those of the buyers. In a surging bull market, the opposite is true. During periods of market ebullience, buyers easily outnumber sellers. Sellers therefore call the tune and wait until the former offer prices consistent with their offer demands.

Some investors may also elect to have their brokerage accounts in nominee form[3] where trades register in the name of the brokerage. In such cases, all benefits from security holdings pass to the client via the brokerage firm. This form of account may be particularly useful when investors are required to settle transactions in different overseas markets. Extra assistance with settlement and other issues—such as dividend payments and corporate announcements—may be warranted in certain markets. Certain custodial services, which essentially safeguard security returns and ownership rights, may also be offered.

Transaction Costs

Bid-Asking Spreads

The first significant cost item to recover in a stock trade is the bid-asking spread. As investors have to buy at the prevailing ask price and sell at the bid, the higher asking price means an immediate loss on the capital value of any purchase. This spread in Hong Kong is probably around 0.5% of the value of stock, on average.[4] Stock purchased for $101.00 (the asking price) will therefore have a re-sale value immediately afterwards of $100.50 (bid). As the minimum spread or 'tick' size is governed by the rules of the exchange where the order is placed, spread sizes are usually fairly stable. In the foregoing, a one-spread increase—or an 'up-tick' movement—would cover the initial bid-asking differential.[5] This would lead to new bid and asking prices of $101.00 and $101.50.

Bid-asking spreads are evident in all markets and trading systems. However, the spread carries different meaning depending upon whether the market is dealer-based or not. 'Quote-driven' markets are examples of the former where registered dealers, trading on their own account, provide quotes for brokers to buy and sell securities. In this setting, the broker acts on behalf of a client while a dealer, registered by an exchange or trading system, buys and sells securities on his/her own account and, in so doing, creates a market for such securities.

Markets like NASDAQ and the London Stock Exchange's SEAQ system,[6] operate through market-makers. Normally, the quotes provided are firm for the time they appear on a screen but are subject to continual adjustment by dealers. In this kind of quote-driven system, dealers charge a bid-asking spread to cover transaction costs as well as the risk of adverse selection.[7] In addition, the spread may move in response to a deficit or surplus in their holdings of the stock.

In order-driven systems—such as the SEHK's system for stock trading—buy and sell orders are matched automatically. This system, which is explored in greater detail in Section 3.2 allows buy and sell orders to be matched at a single price. This is where quantity and price limit orders overlap (e.g., S wishes to sell 1,000 shares of stock X for at least $0.90 while B wishes to buy the same number of X shares for a price no higher than $0.90). Within such a system, the bid-asking spread reflects a perceived difference for being able to buy and sell a security with immediate effect. As dealers are not usually present in such a trading system, brokers simply submit orders at particular prices into the order-matching system. The bulk of the transaction costs of trading are not therefore reflected in the spread.

'Out-of-Pocket' Expenses
Transaction costs for SEHK stock trades are evaluated in McGuinness (1997a). Using figures reported by Research & Planning at the SEHK, total buying or selling costs for 'blue-chip' counters during 1995 were noted to be approximately 0.41% of stock value (see Table 3.1). As a result, the round-trip costs, arrived at by buying *and* selling the same stock, sum to about 1.30% of stock value (= 2@0.41% plus the spread of 0.50%). Other than the spread, the transaction costs reflect three major items: brokerage commission, an Exchange/SFC transaction levy, and stamp duty.[8] The brokerage commission, applies to parties on both sides of the transaction, and typically constitutes the largest portion of these costs. A minimum value of 0.25% of stock value is stipulated.[9] Experience suggests that retail investors can be charged commission rates well in excess of this, however, with levels of 0.5% not that uncommon.

Transaction costs may also be higher where stocks are traded in odd-lot form (i.e., as fractions of board lots). In general terms, there is little liquidity in such trading and additional charges are likely when conducting such business.

Fixed Versus Negotiable Brokerage Commissions
The deregulation of brokerage commissions in the last twenty years or so means that negotiable commission rates are now commonplace in virtually all European and North American markets (as highlighted in Table 3.2). The so-called 'big-bangs' that ushered in the era of variable commissions began in the United States in 1975 and in Europe in 1986 (through the United Kingdom's Financial Services Act of 1986). Apart from notable exceptions like Australia, which deregulated its commission rates as long ago as 1984, most Asian markets still cling to a regime of fixed rates.[10] Japan proposes to breakaway from this club by the close of 1999, a move which may ring in similar changes in the rest of Asia, if international investors see some competitive advantage in this.

Table 3.1   Transaction Costs for HSI Constituent Stocks: Summary Evidence

TRANSACTION COST FOR 1995 FOR 33 HSI CONSTITUENT STOCKS

Turnover (HK$)	Transaction Costs (HK$)	Average Daily Transaction Cost (HK$)
528,204,197,957	2,181,483,338	8,831,916

Source: Research & Planning Department of the Stock Exchange of Hong Kong Ltd for all HSI constituent stocks (as defined at 02/96, for all trading days in 1995).

Notes: Transaction costs in the *Research & Planning Department*'s calculations are based on: Brokerage = 0.25%; Transaction Levy = 0.013%; and Stamp Duty = HK$1.50 per HK$1,000 of stock. Average transaction costs per side, for HSI constituent stocks, are, HK$(2,181,483, 338/528,204,197,957) × 100 = 0.413% of stock value (per side).

Extracted from McGuinness (1997a, p. 464).

Table 3.2   Historical Guide to the Deregulation of Brokerage Commissions

Market	Change from Fixed to Negotiable Brokerage Commission Rates
USA	1975[1]
Canada	1983[2]
Australia	1984[3]
UK	1986
France	1989[4]
Switzerland	1991[5]
Japan	1999 (proposed)[6]

Notes: For excellent reviews of the changes, see:
[1]   Anonymous (1975)
[2]   El-Baroudi (1992)
[3]   Smiles (1984)
[4]   Humphreys (1990)
[5]   Anonymous (May 1993a)
[6]   Koseki (1997)

Despite the use of fixed brokerage commissions, most would admit that trading costs in Hong Kong are reasonably competitive. This is especially so when comparison is made with other markets in the region. Drawing such comparisons is far from easy. Differences in tax regimes provides an obvious complication. Thankfully, Harrison's (1997) assiduous work renders such a research enterprise unnecessary. He provides an excellent summary of 'Transaction costs and taxes for foreign institutional investors' in ten Asian markets, including Hong Kong. The figures unearthed suggest that Hong Kong has a clear competitive advantage over a number of markets in Asia. This holds in relation to direct transaction costs, and especially so, when dividend withholding and capital gains taxes are factored into the picture.[11] Hong Kong is the only market among those scrutinized (except China) that offers full exemptions in both areas.[12]

Trading Costs in Local Stocks in Hong Kong and London

Hong Kong also appears to be competitive with London in relation to the trades of given sets of stocks in the two jurisdictions. In a recent SFC-commissioned study of overseas trading in Hong Kong stocks, Chang et al. (SFC, 1997) report an average bid-asking spread, for eighteen Hong Kong stocks traded in London, of 1.71%. They also note that this served as a good indicator of total round-trip costs, given that, 'there is no explicit commission other than bid-ask spread for institutional trades' (p. 14).

At face value, London costs would appear substantially higher. This may be misleading, however, as some investors, through a process of negotiation with dealers, may be able to extract prices within displayed quotes. Naik, Neuberger, and Viswanathan (1994) note that negotiations on SEAQ, and quote-driven markets in general, are typically welcomed by dealers insofar as they help dealers to become informed. The favourable prices offered can therefore be seen as a reward for such information.[13] In this light, it is difficult to gauge the actual costs associated with London trading of Hong Kong stocks. Given the fact that the London market is overwhelmingly institutionally-driven, one would expect such negotiations to be commonplace.[14]

Cash and Margin Accounts for Stock Investment

Most retail investors probably prefer to pay the full cost of stock purchase at the time of the trade (or at least within the required settlement period). The more adventurous might, in contrast, seek leverage by opening a margin account. Instead of paying for stock outright, the broker commits to pay a part of the stock's acquisition value. Essentially, the client borrows from the broker. The residual, which is the fraction of the purchase price paid by the client, is called the margin.

Despite the fact that they often entail significant running costs, margin accounts are offered by a number of local brokerage houses. These costs are passed on to the margin investor principally through interest charged on the loan balance. Enquiries with a number of local brokerage houses suggest that this might be as much as prime+300 basis points. Other transaction costs involved in buying and selling shares seem to be comparable with those for cash-only accounts. Margin facilities are not always offered by brokerage firms. Even for firms that engage in such activities, only the best credit-rated clients are likely to enjoy such a service.

The key attraction of margin is that it raises the absolute percentage rate of return on an investor's initial outlay. The extent of this depends, of course, upon the level of margin offered. Most margin accounts require more margin (i.e., a higher percentage of the purchase value of the stock to be paid) in higher-risk and/or less liquid stocks. Enquiries with local brokerage firms suggest that initial margins of 50% are available for 'blue-chip' investments but rise to 70–80% when so-called second or third-line stocks are considered. Margins will also be typically maintained at this level. This means that if a stock is purchased for a market price of $50 using a 60% margin facility, $20 is borrowed by the investor at the time of purchase. As the margin percentage has to be maintained, a fall in the stock's value to $40.00 results in a fall in the investor's margin interest to 50% (= ($40-loan)/$40.00). This would trigger a margin call of $4.00 to maintain the margin level at 60%. In the process, the payment would reduce the investor's loan balance to $16.00 (= 40%) and increases his/her margin balance to $24.00. As such calls must normally be settled within the day, funds must always be on standby. Failure to meet a call would likely result in a client's position being liquidated and interest charged on the arrears.

The margin conditions also mean that if stock prices rise, investors are able to withdraw excess funds from their accounts. If interest is not paid on such excess margin balances, withdrawals are very likely. Illustration of the operation of a margin account, and the various margin calls and withdrawals evident in such an account, feature in Exhibit 3.1. An investor with a 50% initial (and maintenance) margin facility is considered. If 1,000 shares of stock X are purchased at date t=0 for $2 per share and the share price closes on subsequent days (t=1, t=2 and t=3) at $2.10, $2.00 and $1.70, respectively, margin adjustments would occur as shown.

Exhibit 3.1   Illustration of the Operation of a Margin Account

Date	Closing Stock Price	Investment Value		Actual Margin	Loan	Margin (%)
t = 1	$2.10	$2,100	Bal.	$1,100	$1,000	52.38%
⇒ (Margin Wdl $50.00)			Adj. Bal.	$1,050	$1,050	50.00%
t = 2	$2.00	$2,000	Bal.	$950	$1,050	47.50%
⇒ (Margin call $50.00)			Adj. Bal.	$1,000	$1,000	50.00%
t = 3	$1.70	$1,700	Bal.	$700	$1,000	41.18%
⇒ (Margin call $150.00)			Adj. Bal.	$850	$850	50.00%

The effect upon rates of return should also be readily apparent. Between t = 0 and t = 1, for example, the percentage return on the cash purchase of stock X would have been 5% (= ($100/$2,000) × 100). For the margin investor, the return would have been twice this figure (= ($100/$1,000) × 100). Had the share price at t = 1, fallen to $1.90 instead, the returns would again have differed by a factor of two. This time, however, the percentage returns would have read -5% for the cash account investor and -10% for the margin investor.

This insight into leverage gives some idea of the increased volatility facing the margin investor. Such facilities are clearly not for the faint-hearted. Brokerage firms are only too aware of the risk of default on such positions. The demise of the CA Pacific Group in early 1998 is a stark reminder. In this case, CA Pacific Finance Ltd, a margin-trading arm of CA Pacific Securities Ltd, faced a massive default on one of its clients' margin accounts. These losses caused widespread concern as they occurred in the accounts of an unregulated finance company. Had the losses been racked up in CA Pacific's securities trading arm, CA Pacific Securities Ltd, the SFC would have been given some jurisdiction over the margin trading activities.

The demise of CA Pacific awakened market participants to a regulatory loophole: the practice of registered (regulated) brokerage firms operating margin trading services in unregulated finance companies. A recent press release on proposed changes to the regulation of share margin financing, which requires legislative approval for its passage, suggests the imminent plugging of this loophole.[15]

Long and Short Positions

When a security is purchased, the underlying investor is said to be in a long position. This also describes the position of an investor holding securities in his/her portfolio. A subsequent sale of such securities then represents a liquidation of this position. In formal terms, the investor would be closing-out his/her long position.

A minority of investors may also short stock from time to time. Such short-selling activities involve the sale of stock that is not currently owned by the investor.[16] In other words, the investor is said to be short or out of the stock and, to ensure that the stock is vested in the interests of the buyer, he/she must borrow it. So-called 'naked' short-selling, where an investor shorts stock without an underlying borrowing commitment at the point of sale, is illegal in Hong Kong and a number of other jurisdictions. Locally, the provisions of Section 80(1) of the Securities Ordinance are pertinent. As indicated in a recent SFC press release, 'Any Person who contravenes Section 80(1) shall be guilty of an offence and shall be liable on conviction to a fine of $10,000 and imprisonment for six months . . . .'[17]

Issues relating to the eligibility of securities for short-selling, stock-borrowing and lending agreements, and the conditions applying to members and their agents engaged in such activities, are set out in various provisions and schedules of the *Rules of the Exchange*.[18] In many markets, including Hong Kong, short-selling is also subject to a 'tick-rule'. A 'tick', as mentioned earlier, refers to a spread in a particular security. This rule normally means that a security can only be short-sold at the asking price (i.e., the prevailing bid plus one spread).[19]

The important question is why would an investor go short? The motivation for many may be a speculative one where the investor anticipates an imminent fall in the value of the underlying stock. If investors' beliefs are substantiated, they are then able to return the stock to the lender (by buying it back in the market) at a discount to the original sale price. Other motivations for short-selling, like hedging and arbitrage, are also important. These are explored further in chapters 10 to 12, in relation to derivatives.

Stock Borrowing Arrangements for Short Positions

In a number of jurisdictions, stock borrowing can be arranged within one's own brokerage firm. This occurs with little difficulty for accounts held in *nominee* form in certain markets, with the brokerage firm able to lend and borrow scrip between such accounts. In such cases, interest is not normally charged as the sale proceeds are held by the brokerage firm in the form of a *lien* (i.e., on behalf of the client until the stock borrowing is repaid). Returns on the proceeds thus accrue to the brokerage firm during the term of the short position. In certain jurisdictions, both stock borrowing and supporting security for the loan—collateral—may be required before a short-sale can be executed.[20] So, even if borrowing occurs internally, the collateral placed allows the sale proceeds to pass without delay to the seller.

Investors could also borrow stock from a third party. A number of custodian banks specifically provide services in this area. Where borrowing is arranged through such means, the sale proceeds accrue to the investor. The interest earned on such monies, during the term of the borrowing arrangement, then serves to defray interest charges on the loan. Issues of collateral still remain.

Risks Entailed When Short

Short positions come with some risk for both borrower and lender. For the borrower, the principal risk is that share prices rise rather than fall, imposing capital losses on the short-seller. For the lender, a rise in the underlying stock's price also poses a risk. If the share price increase is substantial, the borrower may not be able to finance the stock repurchase (and, therefore, pay back the lender). To guard against this eventuality, a prudent lender would always insist on some form of collateral. The regulations relating to this vary from jurisdiction to jurisdiction, but typically require collateral in excess of the sale proceeds.[21] A stock borrower required to place collateral of 110%, in accordance with the rules of a particular jurisdiction, would therefore be placing securities (or funds) equal to the value of a loan, plus margin equal to 10% of the loan.

In certain jurisdictions, where borrowing is carried out internally, through an investor's own broker, all proceeds from the short-sale might be retained by the broker. Separate margin payments would then have to be placed. Whether sale proceeds are retained or collateral is placed, the borrower's pledged funds (or securities) serve to protect the lender against possible default. This may not afford complete protection, however, for two reasons: (i) the value of the stock shorted may rise above the value of the collateral/funds placed; and (ii) collateral value, where securities are pledged, can fall. Both of these risks are usually handled by 'marking-to-market' the pledged collateral/funds. With a 110% requirement, this would necessitate the pledged asset value being maintained at 110% of the borrowed stock's value. Where a shortfall occurs, a margin call would be triggered. Failure to meet this would be tantamount to default. This, depending upon the precise terms of the arrangement, would allow the lender to terminate the stock loan. If the borrower fails to return the stock, the lender could, justifiably, realize the collateral/funds placed under his/her control.

To illustrate, suppose L lends stock X to borrower B, whereupon B sells X for $100. This necessitates collateral of $110 being placed with L (given a 110% requirement). As B loses (L gains) with subsequent price increases in X, an increase in the stock's value from $100 to $101 would necessitate additional margin from B of $1.10. In contrast, a decline in stock value would allow some drawing down of B's placed collateral/ liquid funds.

Dividends and Short Positions
If the underlying stock goes *ex-dividend* during the term of the stock borrowing arrangement, a further complication arises. As shown in Figure 3.1, an ex-dividend date typically follows a dividend announcement by four to five weeks, and precedes actual payment by two to three weeks. The precise timetable of events, as discussed in Section 8.3, is dependent upon the stock involved but, once the dividend is announced, the subsequent ex-dividend and payment dates become known to all. What, then, is the significance of the ex-dividend date? Investors purchasing stock prior to the ex-dividend date receive the dividend on the stock at t = 2 (in Figure 3.1). This is true even if they sell their share(s) shortly after the ex-date (between t = 1 and t = 2 in Figure 3.1). In contrast, anyone buying the share on the ex-date or thereafter does so without entitlement to the dividend payment at t = 2. To ensure a fair market, then, the price of the underlying stock should fall by the value of the dividend on the ex-date.

If just prior to the ex-date the stock was priced at $10, and a dividend per share of $0.30 was promised, the share price should fall to $9.70 at the open of the ex-date. This assumes the overall market is flat between the close of trade on the day prior to the ex-date and the subsequent open.[22] It also represents a fair and predictable adjustment. If the investor buys one share just prior to the ex-date, he pays $10 but receives dividend income of $0.30 a few weeks later. Buying on the ex-date means no dividend payment but a lower payment price of $9.70, as compensation. Tax effects, which are ignored in the above, might blur the adjustment a little. If stock investors typically pay a 20% (income) tax on dividends, their net distribution—assuming they bought the stock ahead of the ex-date—would be $0.24. This would suggest a drop-off in prices at the ex-dividend date of the stock of the same. As tax on financial income earned in Hong Kong typically carries no tax liability, a tax adjustment is not necessary. The ex-date drop of $0.30 as argued would seemingly still

Figure 3.1 The Ex-dividend Date and its Likely Impact upon Share Prices

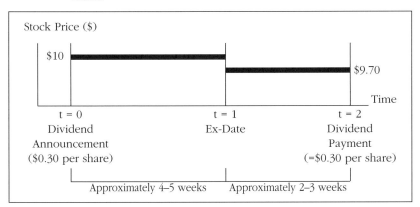

t = 0 – t = 1: Eligible period for purchasing stock with access to dividends at t = 2 (Cum-Dividend Period).
t = 1 – t = 2: Ex-dividend Period.

Notes: Cum-dividend period runs up to the close of trading on the business day immediately prior to the ex-dividend date; ex-dividend period runs from t = 1 onwards.

apply.[23] In the final analysis, however, it is an empirical question whether ex-dividend date stock price adjustments conform squarely with theory (or expectations).

What are the implications for the short-seller/stock borrower who sells stock prior to such an ex-date, but has a commitment to close out the position some time later? As the dividend payment bypasses the lender and goes to a third party (i.e., the party that originally acquired the stock from the short-seller or some other party if the stock was subject to further secondary market trading prior to the ex-date), the stock borrower will need to reimburse the lender for the dividend per share 'lost' on the stock. The short-seller/borrower should not be unduly troubled by this, however, as the ex-date decline in the underlying share's value should compensate him/her for this additional charge. It does, however, pose a further administrative issue for stock lender and borrower.

3.2 Trading Systems

Call and Continuous Markets

At the simplest level, securities trading can be organized through either call or continuous markets. The former is akin to an auction where all orders and associated prices are collected and collated. From these orders, market-clearing bid and asking prices are determined. Orders are then executed simultaneously at a given market-clearing price. The use of limit orders (i.e., a buyer will only transact if the asking price is at $x or below and a seller will only transact if the bid price is at $y or above) means that a set of prices can typically be found to satisfy most of the orders. A good example of a call market is the London gold market.[24] Many other markets—such as the New York Stock Exchange (NYSE)—operate a call mechanism at the market open. This often helps to clear orders that may have accumulated overnight. Other markets may operate a so-called pre-opening session, ostensibly for the same purpose. Thereafter, trades are likely to be executed in a continuous fashion as they arrive on the market. Many major exchanges, like the SEHK, are continuous at the open and thereafter.

Order- and Quote-Driven Markets

Markets can also be categorized in terms of the specific trading system used, as we saw earlier in this chapter. To recap, a theoretical dichotomy can be drawn between order-driven and quote-driven systems. In practical terms, some markets—like the SEHK's equity options market—operate through hybrid systems, where the properties of each kind of system have a specific function (see Section 10.6). A broad outline of the distinguishing features of 'order-' and quote driven markets are entertained herein.

In order-driven systems, buy and sell orders are submitted by brokers, on behalf of clients, into an order-matching system. As a result, the order flow dictates market-clearing prices. Most markets for stock trading in Asia, including the SEHK's, operate this kind of system. A quote-driven system, in contrast, relies upon dealers (or market-makers), recognized by the particular exchange where they trade, posting buy and sell quotes in securities. The dealers, who act as principals, are trading on proprietary account and form prices based upon their perception of the order-flow. So, instead of orders directly determining prices—as with order-driven systems—quoted prices reflect the perceived order-flow. In most quote-driven systems, the dealer provides firm prices which, for the time they appear on the trading-screen, represent a commitment by the dealer to either buy—in the case of the bid—or sell—in the case of the ask—at the displayed price. Of course, dealers are likely to adjust prices continually as new information and their perception of the order-flow changes.

Where a number of dealers are registered, a competitive market-making system emerges. This enables brokers to sift through screen-based quotes to select the most favourable bid or offer price. NASDAQ and the London Stock Exchange (LSE), as we saw earlier, are examples of this kind of competitive market-making system.[25] Interestingly, some markets, like the LSE, have started to move away from this kind of system. Since October 1997, some of the largest stocks on the LSE have traded through an order-driven matching system. The established quote-driven system centres on its Stock Exchange Automated Quotation (SEAQ) system which—as more and more stocks pass into the new order-matching system—will likely take on a secondary role. Over the longer term, the changes may sound the death-knell for certain market-makers. Despite the move to an order-driven system, however, some order-driven features have always been apparent on the LSE through its inter-dealer broker market. This allows dealers the opportunity to lay off excess inventory, and cover short positions, through a matching facility. As a market purely for dealers and, because of allowable delays in the communication of trades by dealers, it affords dealers an opportunity to unwind positions in a timely fashion.[26] The size of these trades is not to be underestimated. Reliable estimates suggest that they have accounted for around one-third of the LSE's total stock turnover.[27]

A range of other competitive dealer-based systems also exists in a variety of other securities and markets. The trading of Eurodollar bonds and foreign exchange being prime examples. Most of these markets operate as parallel markets—or floating markets—in products listed on major European exchanges. Further discussion of such securities follows in Section 11.6.

As an aside, Eurodollar securities which essentially involve the trading of securities in currencies foreign to the actual trading locale, should not be confused with Euro-denominated securities. Until recent times, it was customary to refer to Eurodollar securities as Euro-securities. The advent of the Euro currency has changed all that. Eurodollar securities need not, therefore, be denominated in the Euro; however, bonds issued in London in the Euro would technically be Euro-securities under the old definition.

Local examples of quote-driven trading systems can also be found. The trading of HKMA Exchange Fund bill and notes, as we saw in Section 1.5, are good examples. The foreign counterpart to the Exchange Fund bill—the ubiquitous Treasury bill—also typically trades through such dealer-based systems. The same can be said of an array of corporate bond securities around the globe which, like Eurobonds and other Euro-securities, trade on systems parallel to recognized exchanges. The perennial problem, though, is one of finding market-makers prepared to commit to provide firm prices and, therefore, liquidity in classes of security that are naturally illiquid. Even where market-makers provide firm prices, the spreads posted may leave a bitter taste for those with a pressing need to trade. But as market-makers need to be compensated for the risk of being unable to unwind excess inventory holdings or short positions, this is the inevitable price of doing business. Most studies of bid–ask spreads—which deal, almost exclusively, with quote-driven systems—consistently point to liquidity as the overriding factor in the determination of spread levels.[28]

The Effects of Liquidity on Spread Size

At a fairly simple level, the impact of liquidity on spread size can be appreciated by inspecting US Treasury notes and bonds. These are essentially US government securities, and enjoy the highest possible credit-rating. To all intents and purposes, US Treasury securities, as with the government debt securities of a number of other developed countries, have zero default risk. Aside from the maturity range of these instruments, where Treasury notes have a life of between two and 10 years, and Treasury bonds a life between 10 and 30 years (from their date of issue), a longer time remaining to maturity in both typically results in wider bid-asking spreads. What we infer from this is a decline in liquidity as the repayment date for the principal (face value) cash payment—which is by far the largest payment from debtor to creditor—stretches further and further into the future. Liquidity is likely to be considerably greater in a bond with only a few months remaining to maturity than one with 29 years, for instance. Anecdotally, spreads in the latter may exceed those in the former by a factor of five or six times. We would also expect the liquidity issue to drive prices lower in bonds and notes with a longer time remaining to maturity. As we should appreciate from Sections 1.4 and 2.3 this translates— at least, on average—to higher yields on longer-dated securities.

One other interesting observation concerns the US Treasury security with the longest remaining time to maturity: the long bond. This typically attracts more trading interest than bonds of slightly shorter maturity. This can be seen by comparing the long bond (i.e., the bond with 30 years to maturity) to Treasuries with maturities between 25 and 30 years. Accordingly, this long or 'bell-wether' bond, as it is sometimes known, typically attracts slimmer spreads and higher yields than bonds of slightly shorter maturity. Why is the long bond so actively traded? One reason is that pension funds, with long-term investment plans for clients, seek out the long bond simply because it minimizes reinvestment requirements. Consider a pension fund with a glut of liabilities due for payout in 25 to 35 years' time. By choosing to invest funds allocated for debt securities in the long bond rather than a Treasury with only 25 years to maturity, the fund manager only has to worry about reinvesting debt for clients with an expected retirement date more than 30 years away. For anyone planning to retire in, say, 29 years' time, secondary market conditions in the debt security—which will have only one-year remaining to maturity at that time—should ensure a relatively straightforward sale. Again, liquidity is the issue, with bonds with a shorter remaining time to maturity being far more saleable.

International Comparisons of Stock Trading Systems

Returning to the issue of trading systems, which system is best? Most American commentators, given the preponderance of quote-driven markets in the United States, would probably suggest the dealer-based system due to the guaranteed liquidity it affords.[29] But this may come at a cost in the form of unduly large spreads in all but the most liquid of securities. It may also be difficult to attract dealers to make some markets. In Asia, the majority of exchanges eschew such an approach, preferring instead an order-routing mechanism for stock trades.[30]

While trading systems vary considerably, most of the major exchanges now offer automated screen-based trading systems. These operate for both order-driven and quote-driven markets. The SEHK's Automatic Order Matching and Execution System (AMS) for stock trading is a good example of an electronic, fully-automated order-driven system. This was introduced in 1993. Initially, only back-up terminals were placed in the trading offices of members with trading restricted to the SEHK's trading floor. The second phase of the AMS project, instituted in 1996, changed all that with the installation of trading terminals in members' offices, thus facilitating both trading on and off the Exchange floor. Arguments about the desirability of trading floors, given the technology for trading from outside exchange premises, abound. London, for one, abandoned floor trading as long ago as 1986. Others like Hong Kong and New York clearly see some advantage in the retention of the visibility and immediacy offered by floor activities. As lucidly argued by Lee (1996a), 'those against floor trading seem to think the world sees the floor of the Stock Exchange as the centre of gravity of Hong Kong. To them, it is a symbol of irreplaceable prestige and Hong Kong's image as a financial centre, comparable only to Wall Street and the Tokyo Exchange, where floor trading still has social and political value.' (pp. 18–19).

Ultimately, the preferences of the member firms of any exchange hold sway in any decision for or against the retention of trading floors. The New York Stock Exchange (NYSE) also retains its floor trading presence for structural reasons. While stock trading occurs via market-makers, known as specialists on the NYSE, commission brokers and floor brokers provide assistance by providing a conduit for orders to directly enter the market.[31] In this sense, the NYSE's trading mechanism features aspects of both quote- and order-driven systems.

3.3 Settlement and Clearing Systems

Most major exchanges now allow their trades to be settled electronically without the need for physical transfer of share certificates (scrip) between buyer and seller. The move to scripless trading has been particularly marked in Asia. Singapore, perhaps, led the pace following its transition to scripless trading in 1987. Hong Kong, while starting later—following the introduction of its CCASS clearing and settlement system in 1992 for SEHK trades—has made the move from 'trade-to-trade' (or physical stock transfer) to a fully-fledged scripless system in a much shorter time.

Settlement and Clearing in Hong Kong: CCASS and the Role of the HKSCC

As mentioned in Chapter 2, three clearing houses are present in the local securities and futures field. While the Hong Kong Securities Clearing Co Ltd (HKSCC) is the clearing company for transactions relating to stocks and a variety of other SEHK-traded securities, traded-options on the SEHK, and products traded on the local futures exchange, clear through their own respective facilities. The features of each are explored in Chapters 10 and 12, respectively. Suffice it to say that some tie-ups between the clearing house entities have been established. For one, the clearing house for the SEHK's traded options market is recognized as a clearing agency participant of the HKSCC. This, amongst other things, enables the exercise of traded-options to be settled through the HKSCC's CCASS facility.

On a more topical note, proposed changes, detailed in the Financial Secretary's March 1999 budget, point to the eventual unification of all three clearing facilities. This would be an inevitable by-product of the proposed merger between the HKFE and SEHK, detailed in Chapter 2. The implications of this merger and the nature of new clearing arrangements, assuming such moves are endorsed, are taken up in Chapter 14.

The HKSCC is in fact limited by a guarantee shared by five banks, each of which contribute 10% to the guarantee, and the SEHK, which provides the remainder. The broad thrust of the HKSCC's operational and legal status can be described as follows:

> The company was incorporated in Hong Kong under the Companies Ordinance on 5 May 1989 and is limited by guarantee to the extent of $50 million. The Company has since 28 May 1992 been declared by the Securities and Futures Commission (Commission) to be a recognized clearing house. The Securities and Futures (Clearing Houses) Ordinance (Ordinance), which governs the recognition of clearing houses, specifies that a recognized clearing house's rules and memorandum and articles of association and any changes thereto, unless otherwise exempted, have to be approved by the Commission. The Company shall also make or amend rules as may be requested by the Commission. Amendments to the Company's rules and constitution, where not exempted, are therefore subject to the approval of the Commission. In all other aspects, the Company conducts its business as a self-regulated organisation. (HKSCC Annual Report, 1997/98, p. 37, parentheses shown as used).

Where electronic settlement exists, underlying scrip will likely be held in a central depository. In theory, all the seller's broker is required to do is inform the settlement and clearing company of the change of scrip ownership. Under CCASS, this is handled by the Exchange itself which transmits the requisite information to the HKSCC at the end of each trading day. Position statements are then returned to the broker participants via designated CCASS terminals.[32] The stock purchase and sale details are handled through an 'electronic book-entry' system in CCASS, where debit and credit entries are posted to participant stock accounts. For any buyer, funds must be credited to the bank account of the seller within the specified settlement period.

Unlike a bank deposit*ary*, a deposit*ory* is a vehicle for storing items of value. In this context, the items are security certificates. By immobilizing the certificates, settlement and clearing functions are executed more expeditiously and with fewer attendant risks. Risks pertaining to certificate loss and payment default, given the removal of cheque-based payments by an electronic payment system, are appreciably reduced. Add the labour cost savings, and the benefits of a central depository system are, to say the least, compelling.[33]

As of the 1997/8 financial year-end, HKSCC held nearly 49% of shares earmarked as eligible securities in its depository.[34] A range of other SEHK securities are also eligible for this service. According to the HKSCC:

> All equity securities, including derivatives, to be listed on the Stock Exchange, must be eligible for admission into CCASS. At present, securities admitted for clearing and settlement in CCASS are ordinary shares, preference shares, registered warrants, provisional allotment letters relating to nil-paid rights and debt securities listed on the Stock Exchange' (see http://www.hkclearing.com.hk/p15/htm (Jan. 1999)).

To many, the timely record of payment and security ownership change captures the whole settlement and clearing process. Clearing and settlement processes can, however, be disentangled. Clearing captures the first part of the process which involves the identification of each transactors' post-trade obligations. Settlement follows with the requisite transfer of funds and the appropriate debit (for the selling broker) and credit (for the buying broker) entries to stock ledgers to mark the security ownership change.[35] In the HKSCC's case the entries and payments are handled through the accounts of recognized participants. As of the HKSCC's 1998 financial year-end, broker (502) and custodian (63) participants accounted for nearly half of the total number (1,149) of participants. The brokers are, amongst other things, recognized members of the Exchange, whilst the custodians, as commercial banks, provide securities services for their clients that ultimately lead to all clients' transaction orders being routed to the Exchange through a recognized broker member. Other classes of HKSCC participant include clearing agency (1), stock pledgees (8) and investor participants (575).[36] The SEHK Options Clearing House Ltd, as noted, falls into the first category. A brief account of stock pledgee and investor participants follows later.

The Management of Exchange and Non-Exchange Trades by HKSCC

Trades passing through CCASS can be classified under two categories: 'Exchange Trades' and 'Non-Exchange Trades'. The former typically pass through a Centralized Netting System (CNS), which provides a guarantee to the buyer and seller, with regard to a transaction's settlement.[37] According to the Exchange, in 1997 '99.94% of Exchange trades were settled in CCASS, with 98.46% being settled through CNS.'[38] CNS involves a process of novation, which entails the clearing body interposing itself between buyer and seller. If the buyer fails to pay, for instance, the seller is protected by the clearing house's commitment to the terms of settlement. This commitment is supported by, amongst other things, a guarantee fund.

The netting aspect of CNS derives from the fact that all participants, in a particular security, are evaluated on their net or aggregate settlement exposure. If a broker participant P buys 2,000 X shares for client A at $2,000 and sells 1,000 X shares for client B at $1,200, the broker's net exposure—with regard to settlement—is a long position of 1,000 X shares at $800. This allows P's counterparty under novation, the HKSCC, to debit P's stock account only once (rather than twice, for each trade). It also guarantees the necessary payment which, in the absence of default by P, should result in debit instructions being transmitted to P's bank account. In the absence of netting and the electronic book-entry system, the trades described would have entailed two physical stock transfers for P with two accompanying cash instructions to be settled. This underlines the cost-savings of a netting-based, scripless settlement approach. CNS not only makes settlement more efficient and less risky, but also cheaper than its unnetted, trade-to-trade forebear.

In sum, netting arrangements ensure that at the end of each trading day, every participant's settlement obligations for particular stocks are determined by a single number (pertaining to the number of lots for stock delivery or receipt as well as the net dollar payment or receipt amount). Exhibit 3.2 provides an illustration of a theoretical netting arrangement for three participants, P, Q, and R, for trades in a stock Y.

Exhibit 3.2   An Illustration of Netting for Settlement Purposes

Participants	P	Q	R	
Trade #1	L 2,000 (@$1.00)		S 2,000 (@$1.00)	
Trade #2	S 1,000 (@$1.20)	L 1,000 (@$1.20)		
Trade #3		L 5,000 (@$1.50)	S 5,000 (@$1.50)	
Stock Bal.	L 1,000	L 6,000	S 7,000	0
Payment Bal.	($800)	($8,700)	$9,500	$0

Three trades are reported. Trade #3, for instance, refers to the purchase of 5,000 shares in Y at $1.50 per share through participant Q (with the selling broker being R). The letter L denotes a long (purchase) position and S a sell position in the reported trades.

Non-Exchange trades, other than transactions involving the clearing agency participant (as discussed earlier), are referred to as Settlement Instructions (SIs). According to HKSCC, 'SIs facilitate broker–custodian transactions, stock borrowing and lending, stock pledging and portfolio movements,' (http://www.hkclearing.com.hk/p4/htm (Jan. 1999)).

Registration and Nominee Services Provided by HKSCC

In addition to its clearing, settlement, and depository services, HKSCC also provides nominee and registration services. These functions are carried out by its two wholly-owned subsidiaries: HKSCC Nominees Ltd and HKSCC Registrars Ltd. The nominee services relate, amongst other things, to the transmission of benefits and corporate information to the broker participants. The nominee also acts in relation to instructions conveyed by brokers participants. The linkage with the other services provided by HKSCC results from shares in its central depository being registered in the name of HKSCC Nominees. In short, 'shares held in the CCASS depository are registered in the name of HKSCC Nominees Limited, the common nominee. They are fungible, and not earmarked for a particular participant. This does not change the beneficial ownership of the shares.' (http://www.hkclearing.com.hk/p11/htm (January 1999)).

The property of fungibility, in the above, suggests that certificates of a particular stock serve as direct substitutes for other certificates in that same stock. Precise details on registration services—as provided through HKSCC Registrars Ltd.—are explored later in this text, in Section 7.4.

In sum, the HKSCC essentially draws income from the fees it charges for the various services under its remit. Other than investors operating under the newly formed investor participant category—to be discussed below—these charges pass directly to an investor's broker or custodian. As noted by the Exchange:

> There are no charges levied by Hong Kong Securities Clearing Company on investors as investors settle with brokers or custodians outside the clearing and settlement system (CCASS). However, brokers or custodians have to pay fees for use of the clearing, settlement, custody and nominee services offered by CCASS. The decision on whether to pass these fees on to investors is at the discretion of the brokers or custodians.' (*Fact Book 1997*, p. 10).

The Emergence of Investor Participants
Recent changes have allowed a new type of HKSCC participant to emerge: the investor participant. Holders of such accounts are able to place their shares in the central depository and utilize the electronic book-entry system, as with brokers and custodians, but are afforded an additional benefit: physical and legal control of their shares. Notwithstanding this, trading instructions for such participants still pass through brokers or custodians. The latter may then channel trades through an accompanying broker affiliate (participant).

The Relation between Settlement Practice and Day-of-the-Week Returns

It has also been suggested that settlement regimes have an effect upon day-of-the-week returns. Marked day-of-the-week patterns have been observed routinely it seems ever since Fama's (1965) observation that US stock returns yield higher variances on Mondays. Subsequent studies, like Cross's (1973) and French's (1980), on the US situation, also point to a deflated mean return for Mondays, as measured by comparing the previous Friday closing price with the Monday close. The linkage between these day-of-the-week return observations and settlement largely stems from Jaffe and Westerfield's (1985) seminal work on the issue.

To illustrate the posited relation between settlement and day-of-the-week returns, let us consider Hong Kong's T+2 regime. This was introduced in 1992 just ahead of the introduction of CNS settlement. Under this regime, investors purchasing stock have two business days to pay. Purchases on Thursdays and Fridays appear particularly desirable as payment does not have to be made until the following Monday, in the former, and until the following Tuesday, in the latter. In contrast to purchases on Mondays, Tuesdays, and Wednesdays, then, Thursday and Friday purchases allow for two extra days of credit under a T+2 system. Sellers of stock, in contrast, would prefer to execute transactions on days other than Thursdays and Fridays. This being the case, a T+2 regime suggests that selling pressure during the first three business days of the week is displaced by buying pressure on the last two days. All other things being equal, this would suggest a perturbation in prices on Thursdays.[39]

Another way of appreciating this situation, is to look at close-close returns. The Thursday return is realized by purchasing stock just prior to the Wednesday close and selling it just prior to Thursday's close. This entails an interval of three calendar days between payment and receipt of cash (i.e., payment is required by Friday with cash receipts likely by the following Monday). As all other day-of-the-week returns suffer only a one-day gap between payment and receipt, some compensation in return must be given to the Thursday trader. This differential between cash payment and cash receipt in realizing each of the day-of-the-week returns is illustrated in Exhibit 3.3. Further consideration is given to this issue in Section 4.4.

Exhibit 3.3 Day-of-the-Week Returns and the Cash Payment-Receipt Issue for T+2 Settlement Terms

	Return Form	Payment Day	Receipt Day	No. of Days between Payments and Receipts
Monday Ret:	$M_{P\,(t,\,close)} - F_{P\,(t-1,\,close)}$	$Tues_t$	Wed_t	1
Tuesday Ret:	$Tu_{P\,(t,\,close)} - M_{P\,(t,\,close)}$	Wed_t	$Thur_t$	1
Wednesday Ret:	$W_{P\,(t,\,close)} - Tu_{P\,(t,\,close)}$	$Thur_t$	Fri_t	1
Thursday Ret:	$Th_{P\,(t,\,close)} - W_{P\,(t,\,close)}$	Fri_t	Mon_{t+1}	3
Friday Ret:	$F_{P\,(t,\,close)} - Th_{P\,(t,\,close)}$	Mon_{t+1}	$Tues_{t+1}$	1

Notes: M_P, Tu_P, W_P, Th_P, and F_P refer to stock prices for Monday, Tuesday, Wednesday, Thursday, and Friday respectively. Subscripts t and close refer to week t and the closing price of a particular day in week t.

3.4 Fund Investments

The comments drawn thus far relate to the mechanics and costs associated with direct stock investment. Investments through funds, which offer indirect access to equity stocks as well as to other securities, are rather different in both structure and in relation to running costs.

Essentially, a fund provides a repository for savings from a broad group of investors. These funds are then placed at the disposal of a fund manager who, in turn, invests the monies. Depending upon the objectives of the fund, an array of securities and markets can be accessed. This pool of investments is then represented by a number of fund shares or units. For many markets in Asia, purchase of these units represents the preferred route for investment, especially where foreign retail investment participation is restricted (e.g., Indonesia, Thailand, South Korea, and Taiwan). Increasingly though, emerging market stocks are trading outside of their own borders, making it easier to access shares directly.

Fund managers would claim that despite markets becoming more open, funds still offer a number of tangible benefits. Claims of this sort might often relate to two issues: the expertise the fund manager brings to bear and the transaction cost savings that the manager is able to generate from the scale of funds under his/her control. Many of the transaction cost savings arguments can be framed in terms of diversification where subscriptions are allocated across a wide range of markets and securities at relatively low cost. This also yields some reduction in return volatilities. To some this is a welcome benefit, to others it comes with a 'sting in the tail': a reduction in expected returns. Diversification benefits can also be obtained from a 'fund of funds' operation where the manager invests in a selection of funds created by other managers. Due to the sums under the manager's control, certain cost savings may be achieved and/or certain fees negotiated away. Individual retail investors trying to mimic this 'fund of funds' operation would either find the strategy prohibitively expensive or find their access stymied by minimum initial investment requirements.

There may also be tax advantages gleaned from funds registered and incorporated in offshore jurisdictions. In other words, the individual stocks may be in corporations from various far-flung markets where retail investors suffer punitive tax treatment when buying the stocks directly within these markets. Fund managers may also claim that their funds offer investors access to funds denominated in an investor's currency of choice (i.e., British stock and bond funds denominated in US dollars). This benefit may be illusory, however, if the underlying securities making up the fund's assets are acquired in the foreign currency. Remember that the fund unit valuations are determined by translating the values of the underlying securities into the investor's preferred currency. In this case, the investor would be worse off. Exposure to the foreign currency would still be evident and the costs of currency translation would reduce the value of the units.

Fund Valuation and the Concept of Net Asset Value Per Unit

The concept of net asset value (NAV) per unit is central to all explanations of investment fund value. This captures the value of the fund's total assets less any liabilities, all divided by the number of units or shares in the fund. In most funds, the liabilities are likely to be capital gains tax provisions. The NAV is typically computed on a daily basis using close-of-trade valuations for the assets of the fund. As these are almost always exchange-traded products, this exercise is relatively straightforward.

'Open-Ended' Funds

Open-ended funds in Hong Kong come in two forms: unit trusts and mutual fund companies. Sale of both of these in Hong Kong requires authorization from the Securities and Futures Commission (SFC). This regulatory feature, and many others, are contained in the SFC's Code on Unit Trusts and Mutual Funds. This Code was enacted in 1991 and represents a unifying code for the erstwhile code for unit trusts and code for mutual fund companies. The distinction between the unit trust and mutual fund company is essentially a legal one. Formal definitions are outlined in the Securities Ordinance of Hong Kong, under the definition of securities.[40]

The Law of Trusts, in turn, provides the statutory framework for unit trusts. As with UK unit trusts, such arrangements require the underlying assets of the fund to be protected by a trustee. This trustee then acts in the interests of the investors. While being an open-ended fund, the unit trust is very far removed from the US unit trust which serves as a third major funds vehicle in the US market—in addition to the open-ended fund (the US mutual fund) and closed-end fund.[41]

Mutual fund corporations in Hong Kong are not subject to a trust arrangement. However, as required by the Hong Kong Code on Unit Trusts and Mutual Funds, a fund without a trustee must have an appointed custodian. According to the Code, this party has responsibilities that, especially in regard to asset security, mirror many of those of the trustee. Notwithstanding the legal differences between the two structures, the vehicles are strikingly similar due to their open-ended nature.

Open-ended funds, or mutual funds as they are known in the United States, allow the number of units outstanding to fluctuate according to market demand. Existing unit-holders wishing to sell holdings sell them directly to the fund manager, who is obliged to redeem them at the prevailing bid price (= NAV per unit). Such redemptions lead to a reduction in the number of units outstanding. Managers sell new units—thus increasing the number in issue—when they receive orders from buying brokers. This time, however, the units are sold at the asking price, which typically includes a front-end loading. This means that the asking price is set at a premium to the unit's NAV (bid price). The size of this premium, which can vary between 1% and 7% of the NAV per unit, is often a bone of contention between local fund managers and investors. The introduction of 'no-load' funds in a number of markets in recent years, however, means that some funds can be purchased at their bid value.

'Closed-End' Funds

The nature of the open-ended fund mechanism means that all activity in the fund takes place directly with the fund manager. Secondary market trading is therefore unnecessary. In contrast, closed-end funds, like the Hong Kong investment trust, have units that, once in issue, necessitate secondary market trading. As the closed-end fund manager is not under an obligation to redeem units, sale of units by existing holders must be achieved by finding a buying counterparty. In this environment, investors wishing to buy or sell existing units must do so at prevailing market prices.[42] Depending upon supply and demand conditions, market prices can deviate substantially from NAV levels. This is an issue revisited later in this section.

Unit Trusts, Mutual Fund Corporations and Investment Trusts in the SAR

According to SFC statistics, 1,356 unit trusts and mutual funds were authorized for sale in the territory as of 31 March 1997. Of these, 972 were classified as 'sub-funds', 271 as 'single funds', and the remaining 113 as 'umbrella funds'.[43] Enquiries with the SFC indicate that the last category of fund is simply a structure housing 'sub-funds' which share the same managers, advisers, and trustee/custodian. In this sense, the 'umbrella' is not available for direct investment, but instead allows for convenient and less costly switching between the constituent 'sub-funds'. The distinguishing feature of the 'single fund' is that it is not part of an 'umbrella' structure.

Most of the funds authorized by the SFC are incorporated or domiciled overseas. As of 31 March 1997, only 6% of the 1,356 SFC authorized funds were incorporated locally. The preferred home, by far, was Luxembourg with 41% of the authorized funds incorporated in the Duchy.[44] A small number of authorized open-end funds have also listed on the SEHK in recent years.[45] As expected, little or no secondary market exists in such units as holders redeem their units directly with the fund manager, at the prevailing NAV per share. Why do managers list open-ended products? Despite an obvious lack of secondary market activity in such funds, managers may see listing as a way of raising the profile and visibility of their funds.[46] In other, less developed markets, it may be a means of attracting foreign investors. Many US institutions, for instance, will only invest in products that have listed status. One reason is that investor protection is enhanced through listing. This argument is often used to explain the reason behind some open-ended fund listings in Hong Kong. When many of them listed 20 or more years ago, there was a stronger need to shelter under the regulatory strength of exchange structures. As the overall market has become more transparent, this need may have waned. At the same time, however, the emergence of the

Exchange as a major exchange entity means that the first reason given—visibility—still holds. Even without secondary market trading, the cachet and visibility offered by listing may help the manager boost unit sales.

Investment trusts typically have listed status. Like all closed-end funds, a secondary market must be established. As such, investment trusts are usually regulated by the exchange where they list. This is clearly the case in Hong Kong, where the Exchange makes provision for these products under the guise of 'investment vehicles' in *The Rules Governing the Listing of Securities*.[47] As such the processes for their regulation and authorization differ somewhat from those for the open-ended unit trust and mutual fund company. In this regard, the *Hong Kong Investment Fund Yearbook, 1997* reports that: 'Closed-end funds listed on the Stock Exchange do not require SFC authorization, but all prospectuses to be registered with the Registrar General must first be vetted either by the Stock Exchange (in the case of prospectuses for companies that are to be listed) or the SFC (in the case of funds which are not to be listed).' (p. 31).

As of early 1998, 18 investment companies were listed on the Exchange. Active trading volumes were apparent in most of these.[48]

The 'Closed-End' Discount Conundrum: The Search for Answers

In most countries where closed-end funds trade, we routinely see unit prices trading at a discount to the corresponding NAVs of the units. Perusal of the *Financial Times*, for British investment companies and investment trusts, as defined therein, and to any quality US financial newspaper, bears this out. Reasons for the persistence of such closed-end discounts are less than straightforward. Malkiel's (1977) treatment of the issue gives us some clues. As a pioneer in this area of research, he laid the groundwork for a flood of later work on the topic. Amongst other things, he hypothesizes that discounts on closed-end funds arise for tax reasons. He opines that 'a commonly accepted rationale for the existence of discounts on closed-end fund shares is that investors face a built-in capital gains tax liability when they buy into shares with substantial amounts of unrealized capital appreciation.' (pp. 847–8).

In short, the prices of the units (shares) reflect the present value of after-tax returns to the investor. The NAVs, in contrast, capture the current market value of the fund's constituent assets less *realized* tax liabilities. The tax effects on accumulated gains on the underlying assets, which have not yet been realized, are not factored into the NAV computations.

Malkiel also recognizes the importance of a closed-end fund manager's policy towards the 'realization and distribution of capital gains'. He notes a number of possible effects from such policies. One he cites, is that 'a policy of realizing and distributing capital gains will tend to lower unrealized appreciation and thus limit future tax liabilities' (p. 850). Other issues aside, larger distributions should lower discounts. To test this issue, and several others, Malkiel adopted a regression approach using data on 24 US closed-end funds between 1967 and 1974. He found discount levels to be positively related to the amount of unrealized appreciation[49] and support for his postulated distribution effect.[50]

Subsequent studies have tended to focus on the time-series properties of such discounts. Most of these accounts stress the relationship between investor sentiment and discount size.[51,52] Another interesting avenue of research concerns the incentive to transform closed-end funds into open-ended funds. Such conversions would clearly eliminate any discount as open-ended funds must, by definition, trade at their NAVs.

As noted in Barclay, Holderness, and Pontiff (1993), the incentive to convert depends upon the level of managerial holdings in closed-end funds. They argue that 'if managers own a little of the funds, they would not benefit appreciably from the elimination of the discount, but would probably lose their jobs if the funds were opened. Consequently, managers resist open-ending proposals and the discounts persist. Following this reasoning discounts should decline as managerial stock ownership increases,' (p. 264). Their own results defy the logic of the above. They actually find higher discounts on US closed-end funds where managers hold a larger proportion of the units.

The foregoing discussions only really scrape the surface as far the closed-end discount is concerned. What we do know is that it is pervasive. It is also the product of market sentiment. It is not just a US based phenomenon either, as the opening comments to this subsection indicate. Cheng, Copeland, and O'Hanlon (1994), for a sample of 63 investment trust companies (ITCs) in the United Kingdom, point to mean discounts of between 14% and 23% for the years 1984 to 1989.[53] More importantly, Cheng et al. suggest the possibility of some inefficiencies in this market. They find that 'very substantial returns would be available to a strategy of selling one's existing holdings of low discount ITCs and replacing it (sic) by high discount ITCs' (p. 829).

Fund Charges and Returns

As we saw earlier, unit trusts and mutual funds in Hong Kong typically sell with a front-end loading. This raises the entry cost to levels well in excess of the fund's NAV per unit. This loading is typically measured as follows:

front-end loading = ((asking value − bid value)/asking value) × 100.

These loadings appear to be negotiable for the most part, with institutions and high-net-worth retail investors likely to achieve the best terms due to the amount of potential business they offer. Increased competition in the funds industry, with more and more authorized funds becoming available, should also contribute to lower loadings. It has been possible to access North American style 'no-load' funds in the territory since 1994 when the Regent Pacific Group introduced this product to local investors.[54] Anecdotal evidence suggests, however, that such no-load funds are still something of a rarity in Hong Kong. In other markets, like the United States, some 45% of open-ended funds have zero front-end loads.[55] This does not necessarily mean that 'no-load' funds are the preferred or cheapest route to pooled investment. Front-end charges may be replaced by levies elsewhere in the fund's overall cost structure.

Switching charges may also apply, although for fund movements within the umbrella structure described earlier, such costs are likely to be small. Switching may, in fact, be achieved on a bid-to-bid basis within such structures. Exit costs or liquidation charges may also apply in some funds. Redemptions prior to a prescribed maturity date, in fixed-maturity funds, would trigger such charges. Obviously, for closed-end funds, such penalties are not relevant as an investor sells units through an organized secondary market.

In addition to possible front-end and exit loadings, all managers, in both open-ended and closed-end funds, will levy management and administration charges. Based upon anecdotal evidence, these range between 1% and 2% of a unit's NAV per year. Some funds may also add separate fees for the services provided by the custodian or trustee. Whether these fees are included in the general management fee or not, it is customary to deduct general running costs from the fund's net asset value. In this sense, investors' NAVs reflect the value of their units net of all costs. Liquidation charges, if appropriate, may be taken out separately.

Fund Performance

Fund returns should be compared to the risk inherent in the underlying investment. A number of studies suggest that after accounting for transaction costs and risk, the average fund manager is unable to beat the appropriate benchmark; however, funds with superior performance are more likely to be better bets than other funds (see Grinblatt and Titman (1992), Goettzmann and Ibbotson (1994), and Gruber (1996)). Consistent evidence of superior performance suggests that fund manager expertise exists in some quarters. The onus is on the investor to seek out such managers. In other words, research pays. Plumping for the average does not.

One of the most interesting studies on fund performance is Gruber's (1996). He, like some others, considers the mounting evidence in the United States that actively-managed funds, on average, underperform passively-managed index funds. Based upon a large sample of US mutual funds, he notes first that mutual funds under-perform, relative to his principal benchmark, by an average of 65 basis points per annum. Much of this underperformance is driven by costs which he reports to be 133 basis point per annum. In view of this, Gruber posits that 'active management adds value, but that mutual funds charge the investors more than the value added.' (p. 789).

In contrast, Gruber reports a much lower level of underperformance in index funds, relative to their benchmark. This is approximately equivalent to their per annum costs. This brings Gruber back to the central question in his paper: 'Why do individuals continue to buy actively managed funds when such funds have lower risk adjusted returns than index funds?' (p. 790). As a solution, Gruber suggests that managerial expertise—an issue in actively-managed funds but not in the passive variety—is not priced into mutual fund NAVs. This expertise, as an intangible, may mean that funds are underpriced at their NAVs. Gruber's results are consistent with this assertion. He finds evidence of both strong predictability in fund performance and of money flows into those funds exhibiting superior performance.[56] At the same time, for the weaker funds, Gruber notes that redemptions may be limited by investor sophistication and restrictions imposed by pension funds and taxes.

Overview of Fund Investments in Pacific-Rim Markets

Retail investors often baulk at what they see as the prohibitive cost of fund investment. Brokerage accounts are much cheaper to run, for example. Discretionary services for little extra charge can also be supplied by the broker, and the development of so-called 'bank-in-one' or 'supermarket' accounts which provide all the traditional banking services plus brokerage services probably make this easier. By the same token, such accounts can also open up opportunities to fund investments.

There may also be cultural reasons governing the choice of investment vehicle. Retail investors within Asia may feel more comfortable when they have direct control over their own investments.[57] Why do you need a fund manager when you can invest yourself? Fund managers would cite reasons of expertise—their's—and time, as the compelling arguments.

Another impediment to a fund sale seems to be a widely-held view that diversification is a negative factor. It reduces expected returns. That is true. But it also reduces return volatility, which is the whole purpose of it. In the final analysis, fund investments are generally regarded as long-term investments. The front-end charges alone would suggest that they should be held for some time. Unless one can switch between funds in an umbrella style arrangement, moving in and out of funds would prove to be very expensive.

Innovations in Fund Products: Derivative Funds and Guaranteed Profit Funds

For those with more speculative tastes, certain funds now offer exposure to highly leveraged products like warrants. These are a little different to hedge funds, as we shall see in Section 3.5. Amongst other things, derivative funds allow investors exposure to derivatives using relatively small amounts of capital. Hedge funds do not. They are tailored for high-net-worth investors. All the same, hedge funds, like the derivative funds featured here, exploit leverage.

Guaranteed profit funds represent a development at the other end of the spectrum, with the target group typically being the more risk-averse. These products, particularly ones written on stock indices, are increasingly common. One of the first products of this kind made available to local investors was the Citi-Gestion SNC Capital Guarantee Fund which was issued on two baskets of indices in late 1994: one for Asia Pacific stock indices and the other for Latin American indices. A money-back guarantee was offered on the proviso that the units were held for the full three-year life of the fund. Early redemption of units was met with a penalty against the net asset value of each unit.[58] This feature, combined with the product's exposure to the upside returns on the index baskets, made it similar to, but not the same as, the US market-index certificate of deposit (MICD). This instrument was first issued in the late 1980s and offered both capital guarantee and exposure to the upside returns of one US stock index.[59]

While the MICD is now well known in the US market, it is but one of a range of index funds on offer in this market. As most of these come without a guarantee and follow a single index, they attract investors that seek broad exposure to one particular market. As they are passively-managed, they are generally cheaper than actively managed funds where fund managers stand ready to re-balance portfolios as market conditions dictate. For Hong Kong, only a handful of passive funds are available.[60] Considerable scope for the development of this market sector clearly exists.

3.5   Global Developments in Fund Management: The Hedge Fund

No account of fund management would be complete without reference to the hedge fund. Seen by some as the proverbial 'fly in the ointment', and the originator of the Asian financial crisis of 1997/8, the hedge fund has aroused considerable debate. Despite this, most politicians would find it difficult to define such a fund. To be fair, though, the hedge fund defies precise description. Nonetheless, all such funds share some common characteristics. For one, the funds cater to high-net-worth investors. The imposition of minimum investment levels of, often, several hundreds of thousands of US dollars is an obvious reminder of this. They also offer the fund manager a large slice of the investor's return, on top of the typical management and running charges.

In the United States, many hedge funds fall outside the ambit of the SEC due to their limited partnership status. Elsewhere, regulatory scrutiny is minimized by registering the funds offshore. In general terms, the regulatory control of hedge funds lags some way behind that of conventional investment funds.

The activities of hedge funds also bear some similarities. Many appear to adopt concurrent long and short positions in various assets. The fact that these positions appear to act in an offsetting manner, to some degree, probably accounts for the origin of the hedge prefix. In this vein, *The Economist*, opines that:

initially it described collective investment vehicles, often organized as private partnerships, that specialized in combining two investment techniques, short sales (borrowing a security and selling it in the hope of being able to repurchase it more cheaply before repaying the lender) and leverage (buying securities with borrowed money) in a way that reduced risk. By shorting a basket of stocks to protect against a general drop in equity prices, and then borrowing money to buy particular shares they deemed as undervalued, these funds "hedged" their positions so as to prosper whichever way the market moved.' (Anonymous (1998, June, p. 76), author's punctuation.)

The hedge rubric, as the above quotation suggests, is something of a misnomer. Effective hedging policies—elaborated on in later discussions in Chapters 10–12—help to radically reduce market exposure. The activities described above are not quite of this ilk. They, instead, reflect risky arbitrage where fund managers sense a valuation error on the asset involved on either the short or longside of the investment ploy. Sometimes valuation errors can be spotted on both sides of the ploy. Risk arises because the fund manager may be wrong about the under- or over-valuation of an asset or assets. The financial troubles of Long-Term Capital Management (LTCM) in the United States underline this. As briefly mentioned in Section 2.3, LTCM had, amongst other things, positioned itself to exploit a narrowing yield spread between a selection of risky corporate bonds and US Treasury bonds. It did this by taking long positions in the corporate bonds and short positions in the Treasury bonds.[61] As the very opposite— a widening of the spread—occurred, the strategy backfired. The prices of Treasuries rose (yields fell) and corporate bond prices fell (yields rose).

Riskless arbitrage, or just plain arbitrage, is rather different. This usually reflects the mispricing of a single asset. An example might be a stock that is traded in two markets. Allowing for foreign currency adjustments, an arbitrageur would seize on a marked price differential in the asset by buying the asset in the cheaper market and selling it in the 'expensive' market. With large numbers of buy and sell orders, the arbitrageur would likely squeeze the price differential. This not only helps in correcting market distortions, but also yields gains to the arbitrageur for little or no risk. This is quite different to the kind of risky arbitrage that is often part and parcel of hedge fund plays.

A Taxonomy of Hedge Funds

The level of risk in concurrent short and long plays can differ dramatically from one hedge fund to another depending upon the assets involved and the degree of leverage (gearing) in the fund. According to a recent summary by Gerson and Lehrman (1998), three types of hedge fund can be distinguished along such lines. The least risky of these have low gearing rates, as measured by the ratio of a fund's liabilities to its capital, and typically chase stocks. Slightly riskier funds, according to Gerson and Lehrman, are the so-called hybrids which involve more leverage and resort to plays not just in equities but also in other areas such as foreign exchange.

The riskiest of all are the so-called quasi-banks which, according to Gerson and Lehrman, are entities like LTCM, which are often leveraged at levels well in excess of those of a bank. The snag is that while they look like banks, they also fall outside the regulatory purview of the banking authorities.[62] Not surprisingly, Gerson and Lehrman conclude that authorities deliberate regulatory control of the quasi-bank fund rather differently to the other, less-risky types of hedge fund.

Recent studies of the role of hedge funds (see Anonymous (June 1998) for a summary) suggest that some hedge funds actually contribute to market stability. Blanket condemnation of hedge funds, therefore, seems ill-judged, despite the continuing stream of exhortations from politicians and other regulators clamouring for exactly that.

To regulators in Asia, the virtues of certain hedge funds do little to soften their image. The effects of the most rapacious of the creed are all too obvious with authorities in Hong Kong and Malaysia, in particular, directly challenging the alleged manipulation of their markets by some of these funds. In Hong Kong, this involved the SAR government, through the Hong Kong Monetary Authority (HKMA), intervening in both stock and futures markets in August of 1998. This was designed to thwart certain alleged funds profiting from a manipulative play involving short positions in Hong Kong dollars and HSI futures (see Section 2.2). In Malaysia, the reaction has been far more extreme given the imposition of a 'pegged' exchange-rate of the ringgit to the US dollar and the use of exchange controls. The latter basically prevents the ringgit from trading outside Malaysia. Whatever the pros and cons of these actions, a growing tide of opinion is voicing its discontent against the hedge fund. US commentators, notably Alan Greenspan, chairman of the Federal Reserve, have taken a more cautious view. At least in relation to US-based hedge funds, there is a fear that further regulation might push funds offshore into even less-regulated terrain.[63] This regulatory issue and others is taken up in the concluding chapter to this text.

3.6 Concluding Remarks

In sum, Hong Kong easily stands out as one of the most efficient and sophisticated markets in the Pacific Rim. Its trade execution systems and post-trade arrangements offer investors timely and secure systems for portfolio reallocations. Trading costs, especially in relation to individual stock trades, also appear attractive. This is in spite of minimum brokerage commissions. In most of the major markets outside of Asia, fixed commissions have been abolished. It remains to be seen whether such a change will occur locally. If it does, it will certainly give impetus to Internet brokerage services, which seem to thrive in truly competitive brokerage environments (see Chapter 14). The rise of fund management, and the hedge fund in particular, were also identified as key market developments. Both are returned to in later chapters.

Notes

1.   This survey covered Trades for the 12 month period from October 1996 (*Fact Book 1997*, p. 114).

2.   Ibid.

3.   Referred to as street name accounts in the United States.

4.   Chang et al. (p. 14, in SFC (1997)) suggest this figure as an approximate guide. Anecdotal evidence also confirms this. Using *SEHK Daily Quotation* sheets for 30 June 1995, spreads, measured as the closing rate bid–ask difference divided by closing price, for all 33 HSI constituents had a range between 0.190% and 2. 688% and a mean of 0.526%.

5.   The Exchange reports the minimum size for spreads, in relation to the HKD value of a share, via its spread table (see *Rules of the Exchange* (Second Schedule, Part A)).

6.   Notwithstanding a move, in some of the LSE's more liquid stocks, to an order-driven format (see Minto (1997) for discussion of the new trading system).

7.   Bid–ask spreads of dealers widen as informational asymmetries increase (see Glosten and Milgrom (1985)).

8.   Other second-order costs include a trading tariff, A.V. stamp duty, transfer deed stamp duty, and a transfer fee for the issue of new certificates (see *Fact Book 1998*, p. 14 for specific details). Like the first two, commissions and transaction levies apply on both buy and sell sides. There is also a minimum charge for brokerage commission of HK$50 (ibid.).

9.   See *Rules of the Exchange*, 534.1 (p. 5/14).

10.   Some, like the Stock Exchange of Singapore (SES), provide a sliding scale of rates, where the precise commission rate is linked to a transaction's value. Subject to $ minimum levels, these rates, for SES trades in 'stock, ordinary shares and preference shares, rights to a new issue and convertibles' were revised to a sliding scale of 0.95% to 0.285% with effect from 8 January 1999 (see SES Press Release (1999)).

11.   See Harrison (1997, p. 51).

12.   Ibid. (p. 51).

13.   In particular, Naik, Neuberger, and Viswanathan (1994) note that 'dealers often receive information which goes beyond the size and direction of the trade itself. For example, they learn something about the identity of the trader, whether he has traded before, whether he intends to trade in the future and what the motivation behind the trade is' (p. 1).

14.   The foregoing comparison of London and Hong Kong trading costs represents a summary of an earlier review of this area (see McGuinness, 1999a). 15. See SFC Press Release (1999).

16.   For the SEHK, its Rules tell us that, '"short-selling" means the sale of a security which: (i) the seller does not own; or (ii) is consummated by the delivery of a security borrowed by or for the account of the seller.' (Rules of the Exchange, Eleventh Schedule, 1).

17.   See *SFC Press Release* (1998). The content of S. 80(1) is also spelled out in the release. In verbatim,'a person shall not sell securities at or through the Unified Exchange unless, at the time he sells them, (a) he has or, where he is selling as agent, his principal has; or (b) he reasonably and honestly believes that he has, or where he is selling as agent, that his principal has, a presently exercisable and unconditional right to vest the securities in the purchaser of them.' (as quoted in *SFC Press Release* (September 1998).

18.   For a succinct summary of the key areas in the Securities Ordinance and Rules of the Exchange that bear upon short-selling, see *Eye on Securities* (1996).

19.   This so-called 'tick-rule' was reintroduced by the Exchange in September 1998. In sum, 'The tick rule stipulates that short sales of designated securities be

made at prices not below the best current asking prices.' (News Release, September 1998).

20. The Sixth Schedule, (13)(d), of the *Rules of the Exchange* suggest this.

21. The *Rules of the Exchange*, Sixth Schedule, (9)(a) inform us, amongst other things, that, in respect of borrowing arrangements for short-selling, this level should be at least 105%.

22. The ex-adjustment should still be apparent after adjusting for any market movement. Suppose that just prior to the ex-date, the market price was $10, but overnight the market fell by 5%. Assuming that the stock in question behaves like the overall market, its price at the open of the ex-date should fall to $9.20 (i.e., a 5% fall to $9.50 overnight less the necessary ex-adjustment of $0.30).

23. Overseas investors may face taxes on local dividends, levied by their own tax authorities. Capital gains charges, which are not levied locally, would also add a further complication. As Hong Kong shares have a strong local following, the ex-date 'drop-off' would likely be close to the gross dividend per share. The effects of taxes on ex-dividend day adjustments are examined in Section 8.3.

24. Fabozzi et al. (1994) note that, 'the London gold bullion market, which is a call market, and records prices at the "morning fix" and the "afternoon fix". These fixes take place at two call auctions which are held daily.' (p. 310).

25. The *Guide to the International Equity Market* (August 1994), published by the London Stock Exchange, states that, 'Market-makers are obliged to display continuous two-way prices at which they are prepared to deal in the SEAQ International firm quote securities in which they are registered.' (p. 20).

26. The 'window' provided between transacting and disclosure of the trade has undergone some revision in recent years (see Minto (1997) for an excellent summary of the changes).

27. See Hansch, Naik, and Viswanathan (1995, p. 43–4).

28. Glosten and Milgrom's (1985) study is one of the most commonly cited.

29. Madhavan's (1992) modelling approach offers useful insights with regard to issues like pricing efficiency.

30. Harrison (1997, p. 52) indicates that nine of the ten countries surveyed in his text trade stocks through an 'automated order matching' approach.

31. For a more detailed account of the NYSE trading system, see Alexander et al. (1993, pp. 48–53).

32. For details, see Hong Kong Securities Clearing Co home page (http://www.hkclearing.com.hk/p4/htm (Jan. 1999).

33. Most Asian countries now adopt central depositories. Harrison's (1997, p. 52) summary indicates that nine of the ten Asian markets covered in his text were, at the time of his analysis, either holding or shifting securities, into such depository systems.

34. See Hong Kong Securities Clearing Co Ltd's Annual Report 1997/98, p. 8.

35. Precise definitions, in relation to HKSCC's clearing and settlement operation, gleaned from its website, suggest the following: 'CCASS clearing services determine the stock and money obligations of participants to a securities transaction to deliver or receive either cash or securities. CCASS provides settlement services under which securities are credited or debited to participants' CCASS stock accounts and funds are recorded in the participants' money ledgers on settlement day.' (See http://www.hkclearing.com.hk/p4/htm (Jan. 1999)).

36. Detailed figures were extracted from the Hong Kong Securities Clearing Co Ltd's Annual Report 1997/98, p. 2.

37. The remainder are categorized as isolated trades. According to HKSCC, 'Exchange trades are settled under CNS system on a netting basis, unless isolated for settlement under the isolated trades system by the broker participants at the time of the transaction or by Hongkong Clearing for risk management purposes.' (See http://www.hkclearing.com.hk/p4/htm (Jan. 1999)).

38. See *Fact Book 1997*, p. 12.

39. The attractiveness of the T+2 system is also obvious when compared to the more typical T+5 regime in some of the bigger markets, like the New York and London Exchanges. For recent discussions of settlement systems in various markets, see Anonymous (Jul. 1996).

40. See Chapter 333, Issue 7.

41. Fabozzi et al. (1994) describe a unit trust in the US as being, 'similar to a closed-end fund in that the number of unit certificates is fixed. Unit trusts typically invest in bonds, and they differ in several ways from both mutual funds and closed-end funds that specialise in investing in bonds. First, there is no active trading of the bonds in the portfolio of the unit trust. . . .Second, unit trusts have a fixed termination date. . . . Third, unlike the mutual fund and closed-end fund investor, the unit trust investor knows that the portfolio consists of a specific collection of bonds' (p. 144).

42. US evidence suggests that managers of some closed-end funds may issue new units if demand is particularly strong. These funds would be more accurately described as quasi 'closed-end' funds.

43. See Securities Futures Commission, Insert 4 (of 9): Authorised Mutual Funds and Unit Trusts, 31 March 1997.

44. Ibid.

45. See Chapter 20 of *The Rules Governing the Listing of Securities* for detailed listing provisions.

46. Thirty such funds were listed on the Exchange as of December 1998 (See *SEHK Monthly Bulletin*, December 1998, pp. 126-127).

47. See Chapter 21.

48. Thanks are due to the Research & Planning Department of the Exchange for details of these listings.

49. This held for years 1967–72 in his study. For 1973 and 1974 the association turned negative. As Malkiel points out, market conditions meant that unrealized depreciation had generally displaced appreciation during this time (p. 854).

50. 'High distributions are associated with less unrealized appreciation and lower discounts.' (ibid., p. 55).

51. Malkiel himself notes that 'fund discounts narrow when the market falls and increase when the market rises' (ibid., p. 855).

52. One of the best of these accounts is offered in De Long and Shleifer (1992) in their review of such discounts.

53. See Cheng et al. (1994, p. 817).

54. See Leger (1994) for details of this development.

55. See Filsner (1997) for discussion of reported US evidence.

56. This is such that Gruber concludes that 'investors who supplied new cash flow benefit from this, for the risk adjusted returns earned on new cashflows (both into and out of funds) over the ten years of this study are positive and above the return earned by both the average active and average passive fund.' (p. 807).

57. See French (1997b) for a recent discussion of this issue.

58. Bennett, Chen, and McGuinness (1996) show that these open-ended funds were issued at a premium to a replicating portfolio—consisting of a zero-coupon bond and an arithmetic- average price call option which mirrored the pay-offs from each of the indices. This premium was argued to be reasonable—and an expected feature of such products—due to: '(i) the transaction costs associated with the construction of the products; and (ii) the absence of complete markets in stock index options (or futures)' (p. 266). The second issue refers to the difficulty for the issuer in hedging the product.

59. See King and Remolona (1987) for an account of the MICD.

60. See French (1997a) for discussion of single-market index funds in Hong Kong.

61. See Zuckerman (1998) for an excellent account.

62. Specifically they note, with regard to the US market that, 'Commercial banks are usually leveraged in the vicinity of 20-to-1, meaning that their equity capital equals 5% of their total assets. In order to control the potential losses from such leverage, the US Federal Reserve stipulates minimum capital-to-asset ratios based on the riskiness of a bank's investments. LTCM was leveraged as much as 300-to-1, and is subject to no comparable regulations.' (Gerson and Lehrman (1998, p. 12)).

63. See Anonymous, Review & Outlook (1998) for discussion of this position.

4. Concepts of Risk and Return, Market Efficiency, and Anomalous Stock Pricing Behaviour

A basic tenet of finance is that securities should be priced to reflect the trade-off between their risk and expected return. Within this framework, investors seek compensation for perceived risk in terms of increased stock returns. This perception of risk must be quantified to give it any real operational meaning. From a philosophical stance, a demarcation between risk and uncertainty can be made, with uncertainty—which presupposes some knowledge of future states of the world without reference being made to the probability of their actual occurrence—being a qualitative description of the future. The quantitative–qualitative divide between risk and uncertainty is well known and stems from the original distinction drawn in Knight.[1]

The precise measurement of risk is addressed from both theoretical and applied perspectives in Sections 4.1 and 4.2. For the latter, data for a selection of prominent locally-listed stocks is examined and various dimensions of risk calculated. The positive relation between risk and return is largely explained within the efficient markets paradigm (EMP) featured in Section 4.3. Widespread evidence of certain anomalies, which belie the risk-expected return trade-off, as postulated through the EMP, raise doubts as to its validity. While these anomalous return patterns—which include a catalogue of calendar and company size effects—appear in numerous markets, an evaluation of their significance in the Asia-Pacific region is warranted. This is entertained in Section 4.4. An overview of the relation between risk and return forms then follows in Section 4.5.

4.1 Risk Measurement for Common Stock

Finance theorists typically evaluate the risk of an asset with regard to the future volatility of its returns, which can be understood in terms of the widely-cited present value model, introduced in Section 2.3. This model tells us that the price of a stock should equal the present value of its expected income receipts (dividends). As a reminder, this model is shown again in Exhibit 4.1.

At face value, the present value model might require an investor to hold stock indefinitely, so as to reap all the dividends. This is not the case. Sale of the stock can easily be handled within the framework of the model. To illustrate, suppose stock S were sold at its ex-dividend price in period 2. The proceeds collected would equate to the discounted value of all dividends foregone between period 3 and n (for stock S in Exhibit 4.1). From the vantage point of period 0, the investor would

Exhibit 4.1   The Present Value Model for Common (Ordinary) Stock

$$P_{0,S} = \frac{E(D_{1,S})}{1 + K_{e,S}} + \frac{E(D_{2,S})}{(1 + K_{e,S})^2} + \ldots + \frac{E(D_{n,S})}{(1 + K_{e,S})^n}$$

where $P_{0,S}$ is the current ex-dividend price of stock S; $E(D_{t,S})$ is the expected dividend at time period t for stock S; and $K_{e,S}$ represents equityholders' required rate of return (cost of capital) for S.

receive three future cash flows: one cash flow in one period's time $(D_{1,S})$ and two cash flows in two period's time $(D_{2,S}$ and $P_{2,,S})$. The value of these pay-offs, determined by discounting their expected levels back to present, at the required rate of return (cost of equity capital) for the stock $K_{e,S}$, would equate to the stock's present value or opening price $P_{0,S}$. This is shown below:

$$P_{0,S} = \frac{E(D_{1,S})}{(1 + K_{e,S})} + \frac{E(P_{2,,S}) + E(D_{2,S})}{(1 + K_{e,S})^2}$$

This equation is clearly equivalent to the original $P_{0,S}$ value shown in Exhibit 4.1.

Risk relates to the perceived level of variance around the expected dividend payments. Greater risk—resulting in a higher cost of equity capital, $K_{e,S}$—leads to some discount on the stock price which duly raises the expected return. To illustrate, suppose that, at the very simplest level, dividend payments for a stock J are expected to be constant at a rate of $2.00 per year. If the variance around these expected values is perceived to be minimal, investors might employ a relatively low cost of capital of, for example, 10%. This would suggest a stock value of $20.[2] In contrast, a stock L offering the same expected stream of dividends in perpetuity may be regarded as a riskier proposition if investors perceive some variance around these payments. If this variance is substantial, investors would require suitable compensation before purchasing stock L. This increased risk would be reflected through the investors' cost of equity for L. If this were 15%, a stock value of $13.33 would be suggested.[3] As both J and L offer the same expected stream of dollar dividends, J clearly generates a higher expected rate of return than L. Greater perceived risk therefore translates to increased expected return.

Greater volatility in dividend payments, around an expected level, should also translate to greater volatility in future stock prices. In this sense, we can focus on either the volatility of future stock prices or dividend payments in capturing risk. Whichever is chosen, it is clear that risk is defined in an *ex-ante* sense (i.e., in a forward looking sense). Historical notions of volatility are therefore irrelevant unless there is evidence that risk levels on stocks exhibit some stability through time.

The Competitive Pricing of Stocks and the Elimination of Stochastic Dominance

In a competitive or efficient market, investors compare stocks in terms of their risk and expected return. Much theory tells us that these levels should be such that no stock stochastically dominates any other. In other words, if stock A appears to be less risky, when compared with B (i.e. the volatility of its prospective returns is lower), it should not offer an expected return higher than B's. The reverse of this should also apply.

For any increase in risk, we expect some form of compensation in terms of an increase in the expected or required rate of return, as noted in the foregoing. In equilibrium, then, all stocks of a given risk level should offer the same prospective rate of return. To illustrate, suppose a stock C has an expected rate of return, $E(R_C)$, of 21% and a standard deviation, $\sigma(R_C)$, around this mean of 19%. Suppose C, as shown below, stochastically dominates a stock A: for the same expected return, C has lower risk than A.

	Stock A	Stock B	Stock C	Stock D
E(R)	21.0%	15.0%	21.0%	11.0%
σ(R)	24.5%	17.3%	19.0%	15.0%

Given this picture, investors would shift from holding A to C. The effect of this would be to raise C's price and lower A's, thus generating a reduction (increase) in the expected rate of return on C (A). Selling and buying pressures should continue until no stock stochastically dominates any other. In other words, all stocks of a given risk level should offer similar expected percentage returns. In addition, if the perceived level of risk for a stock increases, a swift and complete downward revision to its price should occur. This is the guiding principle underlying the efficient markets paradigm, deriving directly from competitive market conditions.

The paradigm also tells us that only normal profits should be attainable on average. This is equivalent to saying that the net present value of a stock should be zero as, on average, such investments simply earn their required rate of return. That is, the present value of all cash-flow returns should equate to the stock's market price. In this environment, abnormal profit opportunities only arise where stocks are mispriced in relation to their risk characteristics. This is an important lesson and, as most teachers of economics will vouch, is critical to an understanding of perfect competition. A common misperception is that a perfectly competitive market—like the market for dairy milk, where there are huge numbers of suppliers and buyers—generates zero profit for the supplier. This view is patently false. Why would any one run a dairy farm if this were so? As the foregoing implies, a competitive market is one where expected returns equate, at least on average, to required rates of return. For the dairy farmer this means that his/her work yields a zero net present value. Not a zero profit. If dairy farmers typically require a 10% rate of return to make their businesses viable, and the market is highly competitive, they should, on average, expect rates of return of 10%.

Risk Measurement in Practice

Convention requires that risk be measured by the variance of an asset's future rates of return (or the standard deviation of these rates of return). While use of either variance or standard deviation is recommended, there is no reason, in theory, why other measures like the inter-quartile range of future rates of return could not be used. However, some assumptions of normality, or near-normality, make the former desirable. In such a world, the standard deviation functions as one of two parameters—the other being the mean—that uniquely characterize the future distribution of stock returns. Empirical scrutiny of stock returns suggests that this assumption may be an over-simplification given the presence of 'fat-tails' in stock distributions (see Hendricks, 1996, p. 41, for a concise review of this finding). In simple terms, large market movements occur more frequently than a normal return distribution would suggest.[4] While some discrepancy between theory and empirical fact clearly exists, the assumption of normality remains by virtue of (i) the statistical niceties it imparts, and (ii) the fact that it still approximates to empirical realities in major markets.

Accepting the standard deviation (or variance) as the cornerstone of risk measurement also allows a rather neat dissection of risk to be made. Equity portfolios that contain a number of different stocks often exhibit lower total return variances than those on constituent stocks. This stems from diversification and the insight that the total risk of any stock (i.e., the variance of its rates of returns) is composed of two parts: systematic and non-systematic (diversifiable) risk. The latter can be reduced (diversified) by combining the stock with other stocks in a portfolio, a point that is enshrined in modern portfolio theory (see Markowitz (1952)). This builds upon a mean-variance approach and reflects what we learned earlier: investors, deemed to be risk-averse, require increased expected returns from their investments for any increase in risk.

The major model derived from this insight, the Capital Asset Pricing Model (CAPM), tells us, amongst other things, that investors only price the systematic risk component of a stock's total risk. As the diversifiable risk component for any asset can be eliminated through diversification, investors do not seek nor need compensation for this, in terms of increased expected return. Any increment in a stock's total risk which is driven solely by diversifiable or specific risk should not, therefore, impact upon that stock's price. This is the essence of the CAPM.

The Difference between Hedging and Diversification

As a point of qualification, diversification is quite different from hedging. The latter allows one, at least in theory, to eliminate all market exposure.

This requires choosing a (hedge) asset with returns that have a negative correlation with an underlying investment position. The motivation is not to diversify risk but to lockin an established rate of return on the underlying position. A perfect hedge would therefore reduce total volatility on future returns to zero, which entails finding a hedge instrument with returns perfectly negatively correlated with one's cash (stock) position. Derivatives offer the best hope of this outcome.

Finding a stock to act as a hedge instrument for another stock position is an arduous task, simply because most stock returns are positively correlated. This correlation is evident when markets rise appreciably. Virtually all stocks move in the same direction. Similar comments apply when markets slide significantly. In most cases, then, the issue is one of degree of co-movement rather than direction.

Some negative associations can, however, be found if we look carefully. The performance of certain stocks, like Cafe De Coral during 1998, demonstrates this. This stock belied the overall trend of the market during 1998 and would have had returns negatively correlated with most Hong Kong stocks during this period. Between the end of July 1997—approximately two weeks before the market peaked—and the end of November 1998, the stock appreciated by more than 17%. Over the same 16-month period, the HSI fell by over 36% (see Exhibit 4.2). Clear evidence, therefore, of a negative correlation between this stock and the overall market.[5] Why? As a proprietor of fast-food outlets, Cafe De Coral probably captured business from consumers 'down-sizing' on their dining habits. The contraction of incomes during late 1997 and early 1998 would have driven this substitution effect. Earnings figures reported, in the notes to Exhibit 4.2, are consistent with this, especially given the surge in interim figures between 1 April and 30 September 1998.

Are such negative correlations expected in bull market as well? Probably not. In more buoyant times, an income effect would likely lift earnings in most companies, even those offering a staple of cheap substitute 'goods'.

Pricing Models for Common Stock: The Capital Asset Pricing Model (CAPM)

The CAPM is so central to finance theory that it probably features, in some form or other, in every finance course. The model, which is used for the specific purpose of pricing common stocks, was developed during the early to mid-1960s. Its final form reflects a number of contributions, although the initial impetus for the model is argued to stem from a paper by Treynor in 1961.[6] Subsequent contributions were then made in papers by Sharpe (1964), Lintner (1965), and Mossin (1966)[7]. As the theoretical underpinnings of the CAPM are presented in a litany of texts, this issue is not reassessed here. Instead, two other themes are addressed: (i) the intuition underpinning the model; and (ii) its applicability to the local market.

Exhibit 4.2   A Star Performer During the 1997/8 Downturn: Cafe De Coral

| | Cafe De Coral Share Price (HKD) | | | Hang Seng Index (pts) |
	High	Low	Close	Closing level for Month
July 1997	2.275	1.980	2.125*	16,365.71
Nov 1998	2.750	2.350	2.500**	10,402.32
% Change	20.88	18.69	17.65	-36.44

Notes: * Based upon 521,054,033 shares in issue.
        ** Based upon 509,308,033 shares in issue.

Profit attributable to shareholders rose from HK$140.995 million as of the 31 March 1997 year-end to HK$142.529 million as of the 31 March 1998 year-end. Interim profits attributable to shareholders also rose: climbing to HK$78.851 million for the six months ended September 1998 from HK$65.674 million for the six months ended September 1997.

   Dividends are ignored for Cafe De Coral. Factoring them in would clearly enhance the stock's returns. The same could be said about the HSI, as this is not adjusted for dividends either.

Source: Share data for July 1997 extracted from *The Securities Journal* July 1997 Trading Record (p. 5 & 20-21); for November 1998 extracted from the *SEHK Monthly Bulletin*, December 1998 (p. 5 & 20-21). Earnings data extracted from Cafe De Coral *Wardley Cards* (05, Prep: 25-1-99; 012, Prep: 25-1-99).

The CAPM result for any stock i can be shown as follows:

$$E(R_i) = R_f + \beta_i.[E(R_m) - Rf]$$

where $E(R_j)$ is the expected rate of return on security (common stock) j; R_f is the riskless rate of interest; $E(R_m)$ is the expected rate of return on the market portfolio (M); and $\beta_j = \sigma(R_j, R_m) / \sigma^2(R_m)$.

In brief, the CAPM result is derived from M, a well-diversified and optimal portfolio of risky securities. The β is the key to the model and, when multiplied by the excess market return, captures a stock's risk premium. That is, the premium of a stock's expected return over the riskless rate. Essentially, the higher the β the greater the risk premium.

The CAPM when shown graphically is referred to as the Security Market Line (SML). Points plotting off this line capture points of disequilibria. Stocks with returns above the line, for example, are underpriced, given their β levels. This underpricing essentially forces the stock's expected return above that predicted by the CAPM. This can be understood by noting that the expected return for a stock j captures the expected capital gain and dividend over the future holding period, all expressed as a proportion of the opening price $(P_{0,j})$.

$$E(R_j) = [E(P_{1,j}) - P_{0,j} + E(D_{1,j})]/P_{0',j} = (E(P_{1,j})/P_{0,j}) - 1 + [E(D_j/P_{0,j})].$$

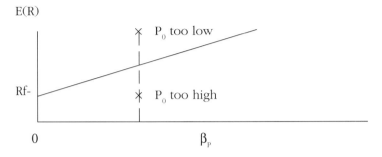

The converse, where stocks lie below the SML, indicates overpricing. In essence, points above the line represent positive NPV opportunities that should be gobbled up quickly. Points below the line also offer excess profits, but only for those willing to short the stocks. As a result, buying and selling pressures should ensure that stocks, at least on average, plot on the SML. In other words, stocks priced according to the CAPM offer zero NPV investments. As we argued earlier, this is the trademark of a perfectly competitive market, something exponents of the CAPM assume.

The assumption of perfect markets[8]—where markets are free of all frictions and transaction costs—also underpins the equilibrium outcome. Perfect competition necessarily follows from this. All that is required is that a large number of buyers and sellers inhabit the market. By implication this means all investors are price-takers. While perfect markets always imply perfect competition, the converse is not necessarily true. A perfect market, in addition to the assumptions required of perfect competition, also presupposes an absence of trading costs. In theory, perfect competition can accommodate such costs—a story standard texts always regale.

The Application of the CAPM: Theory & Practice

To illustrate the use of the CAPM, suppose the riskless rate of return, R_f, is 5%, the expected rate of return on the market index, $E(R_m)$, is 10% and the β for a stock K is 1.50. The CAPM would suggest that,

$$E(R_k) = 0.05 + (0.10 - 0.05) \times 1.50 = 0.125 \ (= 12.50\%).$$

Had the β on the stock been 1, instead, its expected return ($E(R_k)$) would have been equal to $E(R_M)$. This would hold whatever the market conditions. In essence, therefore, stocks with βs above 1 offer prospective returns higher than that for the market index. In general, for a stock i with $\beta_i > 1$, the following implications emerge:

If a bull market occurs, $E(R_i) > E(R_M)$; and
if a bear market occurs, $E(R_i) < E(R_M)$.

Based upon the above, it is desirable to buy high β stocks when anticipating an imminent bull market. Such stocks will rise, in percentage terms, more than other stocks. If, on the other hand, a bear market is anticipated, it makes sense to short high β stocks (and, perhaps, 'close' long positions). For a stock k with $\beta_k < 1$:

A bull market implies, $E(R_k) < E(R_M)$; and
a bear market implies the opposite.

More cautious investors, who are not sure which way the market is likely to move, may plump for low β stocks, however. These are clearly a safer bet if the market moves against the investor. Ordinarily, one thinks of utility stocks, like gas, electricity, and water companies, as being some of the least volatile in the market. One might find β's on such stocks between, perhaps, 0.5 and 0.8. β's in excess of 1, at least for Hong Kong listed companies, are likely to be found in the property sector. Many of the China-play stocks—'red-chips', 'H' shares, and China-concept stocks— are also likely to feature at the higher end of the spectrum.

β as an Indicator of Systematic Risk

As stressed earlier, the CAPM only prices systematic (non-diversifiable) risk. β essentially captures this systematic risk component. To help distinguish between the systematic and non-systematic components of risk for any stock, useful reference can be made to Sharpe's (1963) Market/ Diagonal model[9] which, as a forerunner to the CAPM, offers a simplified form of the relation between stock and market returns. Specifically, Sharpe's (1963) model, for a stock j, tells us that:

$$R_j = a_j + b_j.R_m + \varepsilon_j$$

where R_j is the rate of return on security j; R_m is the rate of return on a market index (m); a_j and b_j are constants; and $\varepsilon_j \sim N(0, \sigma_\varepsilon^2)$.

Comparison of Sharpe's model with the CAPM reveals that b_j, in the Market Model, is equivalent to β_j in the CAPM. Likewise, coefficient a_j corresponds to $R_f(1 - \beta_j)$. In this sense, a_j and b_j can be directly reconciled with the CAPM (moreover, if $\beta_j = 1$, $a_j = 0$).

Numerous texts also show that the total risk of a stock can be dichotomized by taking second moments around the mean of R_j in Sharpe's Market Model. In view of this, detailed elaboration of this result is not set out here. The final result, though, is shown below.

$$\sigma_j^2 = b_j^2. \sigma_m^2 + \sigma_\varepsilon^2$$
$$= \text{Systematic risk} + \text{Non-systematic risk}$$

The first component strips out that element of total risk that is systematically linked to the market's overall risk level—hence its description as systematic risk. This leaves the residual component which is specific or idiosyncratic to the individual security.

Due to its simplicity, the Market Model is often used in the estimation of stock β's. Section 4.2 provides an illustration of this for a selection of blue-chip and red-chip stocks listed on the SEHK.

4.2 Risk Measurement: A Hong Kong Case Study

As elsewhere, an *ex-post* approach to risk measurement is used. In view of the difficulties involved in formulating the *ex-ante* approach to risk measurement this is not too surprising. The view taken is that historical risk measures offer reasonable inferences into future levels. Empirical evidence generally bears this. Studies like Poterba and Summers' (1986) show that 'changes in current volatility have relatively small effects on volatility forecasts over even short horizons' (p. 1142). The upshot, therefore, is that forecasts of volatility, based upon historical measures, are probably quite stable and, to a large degree, unbiased.

The risk characteristics of ten stocks are examined in this section. These are outlined in Table 4.1 and include six constituents of the Hang Seng Index (HSI), namely HSBC Holdings, Swire Pacific 'A', The Hong Kong & China Gas Co, China Light & Power, Cheung Kong, and South China Morning Post Holdings (SCMP). These are essentially blue-chip stocks and, *prima facie*, should have βs considerably lower than typical China-play stocks. To capture the latter, two 'H' shares (Tsingtao Breweries and Maanshan Iron & Steel), and two red-chips (CNPC and China Everbright) are also featured in Table 4.1.

Like the blue-chip stocks, the China-plays chosen are high-profile stocks and, as such, command relatively high trading volumes. This means that the β estimates are likely to be more reliable. A great deal of evidence indicates that β estimates made for thinly-traded stocks are downwardly biased and, as such, require some adjustment. This adjustment exercise is far from straightforward, and is conveniently side-stepped here through careful stock selection.

Inspection of Table 4.1 reveals that the general risk characteristics of the stocks are as one might expect. In terms of total risk—captured by the variance surrounding the mean daily rate of return in the stocks—the blue-chips are significantly less risky than either the red-chips or 'H' shares featured. Total risk for the blue-chips varies between 2.38% and 6.65% over the October 1996–September 1997 sample period, with five of the six stocks recording levels below 4%. In contrast, all of the China-plays generate a variance in excess of 25%, although one can see that there is adequate compensation for this in terms of the larger mean daily returns. Had the analysis focused on the final quarter of 1997, instead, the results would have been less pleasing in respect of the China-play stocks. The extreme volatility and crumbling values of this period illustrate that, in *ex-post* terms, a negative relation between risk and return is a distinct possibility.

Table 4.1   The Sharpe (1963) Model Coefficients and Risk Characteristics for a Selection of Blue- and Red-Chip Hong Kong Stocks

	HSBC Holdings	Swire Pac. 'A'	HK & Ch. Gas Co.	Tsingtao Brew. 'H'	Maanshan I&S 'H'	CL&P	CNPC	Cheung Kong	China Everbright	SCMP
Market = HKSEAOI										
a	0.153	-0.146	0.060	-0.021	-0.048	0.006	0.657	0.046	0.805	0.173
	(2.235)*	(-1.693)	(0.740)	(-0.071)	(-0.187)	(0.070)	(1.920)	(0.539)	(2.264)*	(0.112)
b (= β)	0.876	1.027	0.752	1.807	2.404	0.903	2.350	1.132	2.449	0.658
	(15.899)*	(15.108)*	(11.727)*	(7.724)*	(11.966)*	(13.889)*	(8.720)*	(16.773)*	(8.737)*	(5.436)*
Market = HSI										
a	0.165	-0.123	0.090	0.073	0.062	0.030	0.766	0.067	0.931	0.028
	(2.761)*	(-1.474)	(1.106)	(0.235)	(0.219)	(0.355)	(2.128)*	(0.868)	(2.460)*	(0.183)
b (= β)	0.899	0.981	0.665	1.209	1.727	0.823	1.707	1.134	1.661	0.693
	(20.364)*	(16.036)*	(11.228)*	(5.313)*	(8.430)*	(13.554)*	(6.507)*	(20.320)*	(6.025)*	(6.293)*
Market = MSHKCI										
a	0.206	-0.094	0.111	0.116	0.116	0.050	0.824	0.098	0.986	0.050
	(2.836)*	(-1.173)	(1.352)	(0.371)	(0.410)	(0.598)	(2.275)*	(1.333)	(2.596)*	(0.328)
b (= β)	0.729	0.985	0.626	1.084	1.648	0.806	1.569	1.124	1.551	0.674
	(13.986)*	(17.345)*	(10.805)*	(4.892)*	(8.293)*	(13.905)*	(6.137)*	(21.809)*	(5.792)*	(6.358)*
Mean Ret. (%)	0.26	-0.02	0.17	0.19	0.24	0.10	0.94	0.17	1.10	0.10
Standard dev. σ_i (%)	1.54	1.88	1.58	5.28	5.10	1.74	6.23	1.99	6.49	2.58
N	256	256	254	260	258	252	260	256	260	254
Total Risk σ_i^2 (%)	2.38	3.55	2.51	27.86	26.01	3.04	38.86	3.96	42.06	6.65
Syst. Risk, $\beta_i^2 \times \sigma_m^2$ (%)	1.23	1.69	0.90	5.22	9.25	1.30	8.84	2.05	9.60	0.69
Spec. Risk, $\sigma_i^2 - \beta_i^2 \times \sigma_m^2$ (%)	1.15	1.86	1.61	22.64	16.76	1.74	30.02	1.91	32.46	5.96

	HKSEAOI	HSI	MSHKCI	
Mean (%)	0.12	0.10	0.07	⎞
St. Dev., σ (%)	1.27	1.37	1.42	⎟ Rounded to 2 d.p.
Var., σ^2 (%)	1.60	1.88	2.01	⎟
N	260	260	260	⎠

HKSEAOI = Hong Kong Stock Exchange All Ordinaries Index; HSI = Hang Seng Index; and MSHKCI = Morgan Stanley Capital Index (Hong Kong). Figures in parentheses are t statistics; * denotes significant t statistics (for two-tailed tests at the 5% level). The β used in the calculation of the systematic risk for each stock is that estimated from the market portfolio HKSEAOI (σ_m^2 = 1.60%).

All estimates are based upon daily stock returns using closing prices on stocks over the period 01-10-96 to 30-09-97, all of which were obtained from *Datastream International* in a form adjusted for all capital changes. Daily Returns using ex-dividend day prices were deleted from the analysis (i.e.,

The results in Table 4.1 also reveal the benefit of diversification with the total risk levels on the various indices—the Hong Kong Stock Exchange All Ordinaries Index (HKSEAOI), the HSI and the Morgan Stanley Hong Kong Capital Index (MSHKCI)—all noticeably lower than the levels for each of the ten stocks examined. The benefits of diversification are also demonstrated by considering portfolios within the ten stocks. As an example, an equally-weighted investment in Cheung Kong, Hong Kong & China Gas, Swire Pacific 'A' and SCMP was constructed. The net effect of this was a portfolio with a mean daily return equal to the average of means of the constituents and a risk value lower than all of the constituents (variance of daily returns = 2.10%; and n = 248 return observations). The resultant β on this portfolio—essentially an average of the individual constituent βs—is very close to 1 and the elimination of much of the diversifiable risk in the portfolio means that virtually all of the total risk is attributable to systematic risk.

The results in Table 4.1 are generally robust across the three indices used although the β estimates for the red-chip and 'H' shares differ somewhat in relation to the market benchmark. This underlines the point that β estimates are calculated relative to the chosen market index. By definition the chosen market index carries a β of 1. While the HSI and MSHKCI generate similar β estimates for the China-play stocks, notable differences emerge when the HKSEAOI is used as the market proxy. In contrast, all three indices produce generally consistent estimates for the blue-chips.

In essence, the returns on red-chip and 'H' shares would seem to correlate more closely with those on the HKSEAOI. Correlations of daily rates of return in the three major market indices with those for the established red-chip and 'H' share indices—the Hang Seng China-Affiliated Corporations Index (HSCAI) and the Hang Seng China Enterprises Index (HSCEI)—confirm this. These results are shown in Table 4.2 and, in a sense, explain why the Hang Seng Index Services Co Ltd was motivated to reconstitute the HSI in February of 1998 by replacing two constituents with China-related stocks. Certainly fears were expressed, especially prior to the market meltdown, in the fourth quarter of 1997, that the flagship index's link with the overall market was weakening due to a relative increase in volumes in red-chip and 'H' share counters. Notwithstanding this, the HSI carries a certain cachet with investors and is generally regarded as the market's barometer of confidence.

As the HKSEAOI, which is a value-weighted index of all stocks listed in Hong Kong, is much closer to the kind of index envisioned by the founding fathers of the asset-pricing models, all risk decompositions in Table 4.1 are made in relation to this index. With all red-chip and 'H' shares necessarily included in this index, correlations are as expected. Figures 4.1 and 4.2 highlight the movements in the daily and cumulative rates of return in the various indices.

Table 4.2   Correlations of Daily Rates of Return in Major Hong Kong
Market Indices: October 1996 – September 1997

	HKSEAOI	*HSI*	*MSHKCI*	*HSCAI*	*HSCEI*
HKSEAOI	1.0000	0.9453**	0.9290**	0.7511**	0.6712**
HSI	0.9453**	1.0000	0.9790**	0.5951**	0.5213**
MSHKCI	0.9290**	0.9790**	1.0000	0.5881**	0.5080**
HSCAI	0.7511**	0.5951**	0.5881**	1.0000	0.7461**
HSCEI	0.6712**	0.5213**	0.5080**	0.7461**	1.0000

n = 260.

* and ** indicate one-tailed significance at the 1% and 0.1% levels, respectively.
Notes: HKSEAOI = Hong Kong Stock Exchange All Ordinaries Index[@]
   HSI = Hang Seng Index[@]
   MSHKCI = Morgan Stanley Capital Index (Hong Kong)[@]
   HSCAI = Hang Seng China-Affiliated Corporations Index[#]
   HSCEI = Hang Seng China Enterprises Index[#]
Data sources: @ Data stream and # HSI Services Ltd

4.3 Market Efficiency

Earlier comments in this chapter prefaced the central role played by the efficient markets paradigm (EMP). Asset-pricing models, and established notions of risk and return, all derive directly from it.

In general terms, market efficiency implies that the prices of all traded assets reflect all available (relevant) information. This represents an absolute standard and, in practice, markets probably exhibit some degree of efficiency rather than complete efficiency. The arguments of Grossman and Stiglitz (1980), which provide a theoretical foundation for this insight, indicate that information gaps are always likely to remain in markets. They note that if prices perfectly reflect all relevant information (i.e., markets are efficient in a strict sense), no one has an incentive to carry out costly activities like securities analysis or information search. But if no one searches for information, markets cannot, by definition, impound all relevant information and, therefore, be efficient. Grossman and Stiglitz argue that in the presence of transaction costs, prices cannot fully reflect all relevant information. Consequently, investors who become informed receive some form of compensation for their efforts. In other words, investors will only incur costs in searching for information if prices do not fully reflect all information. Clearly, the return from this search activity must at least cover the transaction costs incurred.[10]

Despite the theoretical impossibility of absolute market efficiency, the general view, held until recently, was that markets were essentially efficient with only minor degrees of inefficiency being possible. This would seem to accommodate the Grossman and Stiglitz model and also the contention that market prices quickly adjust to new information.

Figure 4.1 Daily (%) Returns in Hong Kong Stocks using the Hong
Kong Stock Exchange All Ordinaries Index (HKSEAOI),
Hang Seng China Enterprises Index (HSCEI) and Hang Seng
China-Affiliated Corporations Index (HSCACI): October 1996
– 30 September 1997

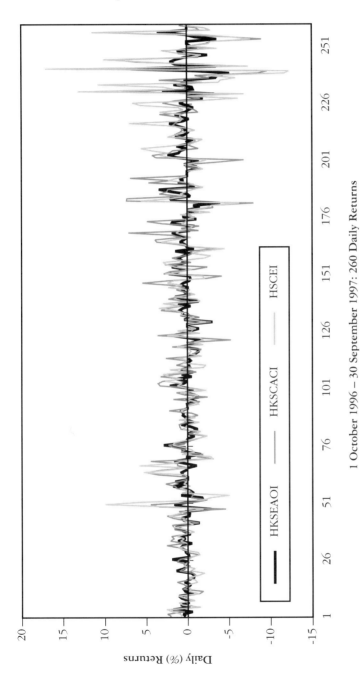

Figure 4.2 Cumulative Returns in Hong Kong Stocks; Comparison of the Hong Kong Stock Exchange All Ordinaries Index (HKSEAOI), Hang Seng China-Affiliated Corporations Index (HSCACI) and Hang Seng China Enterprises Index (HSCEI): 1 October 1996 – 30 September 1997

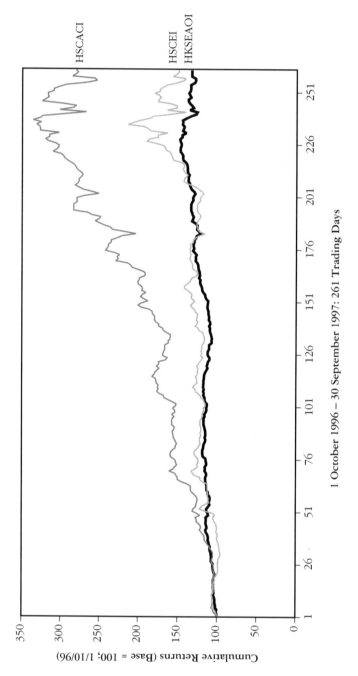

All three indices are unadjusted for dividends (cumulative returns therefore capture capital returns only). *Source of Data*: Closing daily values for the HKSEAOI were obtained from Datastream and closing values for the HSCACI and HSCEI were obtained from HSI Services Ltd.

Fama (1970) identifies three types of market efficiency: weak, semi-strong, and strong-form efficiency. Weak-form efficiency presupposes that asset prices reflect all relevant historical information. In other words, for an investor selecting stocks based upon historic price data, returns should not consistently outperform those on alternative assets of comparable risk. Likewise, an investor with a pool of well-diversified stocks should not be able to consistently 'beat the market' if weak-form efficiency holds. By implication, if such efficiency holds, all historic price analysis is futile.

Weak-Form Efficiency

A catalogue of recent studies suggest that even in the most developed and competitive of markets[11] some departures from weak-form efficiencies are evident. DeBondt and Thaler's (1985 and 1987) work, for instance, suggests that stock prices often overreact to new information and that predictable gains can be derived from the exploitation of this knowledge. The extent of such gains are, however, subject to considerable questioning (see Fama,1991, p. 1581-82, op. cit.). Furthermore, as Fama (1991) notes, tests of market efficiency are essentially a test of a 'joint hypothesis' where the financial researcher tests for market efficiency whilst assuming that the benchmark return model is correct. If the CAPM—which often serves as the return generating model—mis-specifies the risk–return relation, observed departures from it may be misleading. They may be driven, quite simply, by model error.

The existence of weak-form inefficiencies also helps to legitimize technical analysis which, despite being derided by proponents of the EMP, is widely practised. This practice relies upon the construction of statistical trend measures and charts from historic price series, all designed with the aim of deciphering future price movements. Until recently, most finance academics regarded technical analysis as an irrelevancy. Mounting evidence of weak-form inefficiencies has changed this perception somewhat. In this vein, recent studies, such as Brock, Lakonishok, and Le Baron's (1992), show that certain technical trading rules have predictive value. The profitability of these rules has also been assessed recently—in Bessembinder and Chan (1995) for six Asian markets, and in Hudson, Dempsey, and Keasey (1996) for the United Kingdom—after due account of transaction costs. In general terms, the studies confirm Brock et al.'s finding that the rules meet with some degree of predictive success; however, transaction costs are such that, in general terms, the rules are not profitable. Bessembinder and Chan (1995) note that relative to accepted round-trip trading costs, the rules they investigate would not have been profitable in Hong Kong, Japan, and Korea over the period 1975 to 1989. Although for the smaller markets in their study—Malaysia, Thailand, and Taiwan—they concede some potential for profit.

The technical trading rules identified in Brock et al. (1992) relate to buy and sell signals generated from assessments of (i) short- and long-term moving average series and (ii) movements in prices outside of defined trading ranges. A variant of (i)—where buy signals are triggered when a short-term moving average cuts a long term moving average, and sell signals triggered when the opposite occurs—is investigated in Wong's (1997) recent study of technical 'trend-chasers' in Hong Kong. By using various-moving average series, he notes: 'When market prices are higher than the moving average, it is a bullish signal and investors should hold long positions. For bearish signals (prices lower than the moving average), they should hold short positions or liquidate long positions' (p. 58, parentheses shown as used). Based upon this he simulates trading strategies in the HSI. Relative to this benchmark, he contends: 'some rule-based portfolios have a consistently and significantly superior market-timing ability regardless of investment horizon' (p. 62). While this study offers considerably more support for the role of the technical analyst than either Bessembinder and Chan's (1995) or Hudson et al.'s (1996), it still only offers a glimpse into the world of the technical analyst. First and foremost, do we really know how technical analysts behave? In reality, moving averages and other standard signal changes are but one part of an analyst's weaponry. Technical analysts may also buy and sell using rather subjective criteria. They are also unlikely to advertise trading rules that really work. All in all, existing tests of the art are a move in the right direction, but are still something of a shot in the dark.

To some, the widespread use of technical analysis suggests it must have merit. This is not necessarily so. If the various charts used serve as a marketing tool only and are targeted at the less-informed retail investor, they may yield income to the analyst but not the user. If indeed technical analysis is of direct value to the user, one needs to explain why the trading rules consistently outperform the market. At a cursory level, predictable price movements should eventually become obvious. Trading strategies would then emerge to exploit these underlying price patterns. This, in turn, would render them useless. This might mean that certain rules move in and out of vogue. Theory would also suggest competition between analysts, making it difficult for any one analyst to reap abnormal returns in a consistent fashion.

It is still too early to assess the real validity of technical analysis. For so long, researchers have viewed its proponents with derision and are only just waking up to the fact that their own description of reality is far from universally accepted. Critically, those working at the 'coal-face'—traders and others—probably place greater store by technical analysis than the EMP.

Semi-Strong-Form Efficiency

Assessments of technical analysis are also hampered by a problem endemic to all weak-form tests: the joint hypothesis issue (see Fama, 1991). Tests of semi-strong-form efficiency, where the null holds that all prices adjust swiftly and completely to publicly announced information, allow this issue to be sidestepped to some degree. The standard methodology used in such tests is the event study. Fama remarks, 'because they come closest to allowing a break between market efficiency and equilibrium pricing issues, event studies give the most direct evidence on efficiency. And the evidence is mostly supportive' (p. 1577).

Event studies focus on the timing and magnitude of market reactions to information disclosures. A gamut of disclosure types has been examined, relating to corporate earnings, dividends, capital changes, new issues, accounting policy changes, and many other corporate and macroeconomic-based events. Despite Fama's endorsement, these tests are not without problems. Often, the actual announcement date involves the release of residual information. Much of the information, relevant to any disclosure, may be pre-empted, or inferred, from earlier events. In addition, stock prices may react prior to a formal announcement due to information leakage by insiders. All that is required for semi-strong-form efficiency to hold, though, is that persistent abnormal return patterns are purged from post-announcement prices. A catalogue of evidence points to this being so.

The announcements of stock dividends and splits[12] are useful in illustrating event methodology. In both, new shares are issued free-of-charge to existing stockholders. However, some differences are evident between the distributions. These differences need to be briefly clarified before commenting on the announcement effects. To illustrate the difference, consider issues on 1-for-1 (one new share for every existing share held) terms in a representative stock RST with 50 million ($1.00 par) shares in issue. In both a 1-for-1 stock dividend and split, 50 million new shares would be given to existing shareholders, in proportion to their existing holdings. For the stock dividend, a capitalization of reserves would result. RST's issued share capital (ISC) would be credited with $50 million (50 million new shares @ $1.00 each) with its reserves debited with the same. A stock split, in contrast, would leave the ISC balance unchanged at $50 million due to a proportionate change in par. In the example, the 100 million shares outstanding after the split would command a new par of $0.50.

The burning question is: are stock dividends and splits of any benefit? The evidence seems to suggest yes.[13] To clarify, suppose that in our RST example, the 50 million shares in issue prior to either the 1-for-1 stock dividend or split, were priced at $10 per share. This suggests a market capitalization for RST of $500 million prior to either distribution. Theory would tell us that since no new funds are raised from the new shares in either distribution method, RST's market capitalization should remain at $500 million (i.e., 100 million shares at a new market price of $5 per share). No one should have gained or lost. If one had 1,000 shares worth $10 each prior to the distribution, one should have 2,000 afterwards, each worth $5. The evidence of Grinblatt et al. (1984), and others, points to a slight increase in the capitalization. Nonetheless, if this adjustment is swift and complete, so as to eliminate any subsequent systematic price movement, the market would still be efficient in a semi-strong sense. Unfortunately, Grinblatt et al. (1984) question even this.[14]

Like the post-announcement effect, the positive announcement effect is hard to fathom. As neither distribution method raises funds for the underlying firm, or effects changes to earnings or investment policies, the capitalization gains are a little puzzling. The increase may reflect a liquidity gain engendered by the reduction in board-lot cost.[15] Some retail investors faced with limited funds, and difficulties in trading odd-lots (fractions of lots), may have found the board lot-cost prohibitive before the distribution. After it, the cost may well be more acceptable, triggering an increase in demand from such investors.

Another favourite for event-study is the stock recommendation. If markets are truly efficient in a semi-strong-form, announcements of such information should offer market-watchers little benefit. Essentially, portfolios constructed using such 'tips' should generate risk-adjusted returns that are zero, on average, after transaction costs. A number of papers have dwelt on this issue. In general, results suggest only small degrees of inefficiency in major Western markets. Results for Asia are a little more mixed.

At one extreme, Dawson's (1982) study of the recommendations of one major Hong Kong securities firm suggests some inefficiencies. He examines 'tips' between August 1974 and October 1980. By taking the difference between the returns on a portfolio of stocks with 'buy' recommendations and the corresponding return on the HSI, for various periods following the recommendations, significant abnormal returns were evident. By subtracting market returns from the portfolio's returns, a β of 1 was assumed for his portfolio. This seemed reasonable given β estimates for the same period of around 0.96 (p. 20).[16] Little can be read in to the results, though, in view of the changes to the markets in the last 20 years or so. The increased depth and transparency of the local market would probably rule out such effects today. To know for sure, we would, of course, have to revisit the issue. Using a more recent period of data, Ariff, Goh, and Johnson (1990),[17] with reference to broker recommendations in Singapore between 1980 and 1985, find evidence of some abnormal returns from broker buy recommendations; however, these seem to be approximately offset by 'round-trip' transaction costs, more in keeping with the semi-strong efficient outcome.

Strong-Form Efficiency

The final form of market efficiency, as outlined in Fama (1970), is strong-form efficiency which requires that a market be efficient with respect to all available information (including private or insider information). In other words, insiders should not be able to earn excess returns from privileged information. Intense competition between insiders would explain this. Essentially, insiders would need to react more quickly than other parties privy to such private information. Studies like Seyhun's (1986) suggest that the first party to grasp the nettle wins. In other words, outsiders are unlikely to benefit even when an insider's trade is publicly announced. Of course, insiders may also have an incentive to disclose market-sensitive information to pre-empt other insiders from gaining.

Sanctions against insider trading may also limit the extent of strong-form efficiency, though. Insiders may be disinclined to profit from private information simply because of subsequent reprisals. Greater supervision of markets means, however, that private information is less likely to remain in the private domain. More efficiency, rather than less, inevitably follows under such circumstances.

Fund managers are often assumed to have more private information than other investors; however, examination of their performance is generally less than impressive. Several studies show that the average mutual fund generates returns, after transaction costs, that barely meet market or benchmark returns (see Fama (1991, pp. 1605–07) for a review of such studies). This means that any private information held by fund managers is either (i) quickly competed away, or (ii) that investors are as just as well-endowed with such information. It also raises questions as to the expertise of the typical fund manager. Nonetheless, managers with a proven track record of strong performance are more likely to repeat that kind of form than other managers, as indicated earlier (p. 97).

Some fund managers control huge sums. The decisions of some of these managers can, especially in smaller, less liquid markets, produce self-fulfilling returns. For markets to function efficiently, then, they must be sufficiently competitive on both the supply and demand sides.

4.4 Market Anomalies

Despite plenty of evidence supporting semi-strong efficiency, supporters of the EMP cannot rest easily on their convictions. The presence of numerous market anomalies is unsettling to say the least. The persistence of these anomalies suggest abnormal profit opportunities. If markets are truly efficient, investors should seize on such regularities. Their actions would alter prices and dim the prospect of gain for others pursuing similar trades. As a hypothetical example, suppose that whenever daffodils sprout, share prices rise. By observing weather conditions, the state of flora and history, investors could all make reasonable forecasts on the propitious date. The effect of this would be obvious: buying orders would hit the market just ahead of the key date. The sprouting of daffodils would then have little or no effect on the market. Similarly, if investors sense that a certain event will drive prices down they should short the market before it happens. Again, this will cancel out the effect. Competition, or efficiency, should ensure that if regularities recur (as all regularities do) the paper gains they promise are more than offset by the transaction costs necessary to remove them. This largely characterizes the day-of-the-week effect. Scholars have assessed virtually every nuance of this effect. They still find that transaction costs prevent profitable exploitation of the key regularity: a subdued Monday return. However, knowledge of the effect is still useful. If one plans to sell stock, it may be better to do so just before the Friday close than the following Monday open. Some of the other anomalies, like the turn-of-the-year effect, month-of-the year effect, and holiday effect, suggest profitable trading opportunities (after accounting for transaction costs). For illustrative purposes, a sample of these effects are evaluated within the context of Hong Kong's equity market.

Day-of-the-Week Patterns in Stock Returns

Day-of-the-week effects are apparent in many markets. The principal finding, when measuring returns on a close-close basis, is that Friday returns are typically higher than on other weekdays. Mondays—as mentioned—typically offer the lowest return of the week.[18] The shift from an inflated Friday return to a subdued Monday return is the characteristic of the weekend effect.

Table 4.3 summarizes day-of-the-week return patterns for Hong Kong. Without exception, the studies report subdued Monday returns and inflated Wednesday returns. While the latter has been widely reported in international surveys like Agrawal and Tandon's (1994)—where 13 of 19 countries exhibit this effect[19]—most discussion has focused on the 'weekend' effect. This has also been the case in Hong Kong despite the fact that none of the studies reviewed in Table 4.3 has been able to find a significant Monday effect.

Lee, Pettitt, and Swankoski's (1990) study allows us to extend local day-of-the-week findings to other Pacific-Rim markets. Their coverage of daily returns between 1980 and 1988 for Hong Kong, Japan, South Korea, Singapore, and Taiwan, shows that none of the markets exhibits a significant Monday return. However, four of the markets (Hong Kong, Japan, South Korea, and Singapore) have large positive Friday returns. This finding is also apparent in Table 4.3, for periods prior to 1990. Interestingly, Lee et al. also identify a significant negative Tuesday return for Japan, which confirms earlier evidence in Jaffe and Westerfield (1985). Due to global time-zone differences, Jaffe and Westerfield argue that Japan's Tuesday effect is a reaction to the Monday effect in the US.[20] Unlike most Asian markets, a strong negative Monday effect is apparent in many of the European and North American markets. Given the prominence of some of these markets, it is perhaps not too surprising that the effect spills over into Asia as a 'delayed Monday' (i.e., Asian Tuesday) effect.

Rogalski's (1984) explanation for the North American/European Monday effect is, perhaps, the most compelling. He notes that the majority of the 'weekend effect' is due to a non-trading effect between Friday close and Monday open. Rogalski (1984) also remarks that 'one possible explanation may be that, for whatever reason, information released on weekends is primarily negative' (Rogalski, 1984, p. 1614).[21] This being so, a rational investor might consider shorting stock just prior to the Friday close and

Table 4.3   Summary of Reported Day-of-the-Week Returns for the Hong Kong Market

MEAN % DAILY RATES OF RETURN ON THE HONG KONG MARKET

Study	Period	Mon	Tues	Wed	Tbu	Fri
Mok (1988, p. 96)	1/84– 9/87	0.1186	0.0491	0.2205*	0.2687*	0.1545
Ho (1990, p. 52)	1/75–11/87	-0.0299	0.0003	0.1590*	0.0999	0.2198*
Lee, Pettit & Swankoski (1990, p.270)	1/80–12/88	-0.073	0.007	0.234*	0.082	0.206*
Wong, Hui & Chan (1992, p. 51)	1/75– 5/88	-0.09	0.05	0.17*	0.06	0.51
Agrawal & Tandon (1994, P. 87)	2/73– 6/87	-0.088	-0.157*	0.173*	0.092	0.176*
Ho & Cheung (1994, p. 63)	1/75–12/89	-0.0546	0.0439	0.1683*	0.0828	0.2348*
McGuinness (1997a, p. 463)						
HK, Close-to-Close	12/94–3/96	-0.118	0.341*	0.163	0.159	-0.009
UK, Close-to-Close	12/94–3/96	-0.084	0.189	0.368*	0.041	-0.045
HK, Open-to-Open	12/94–3/96	-0.002	-0.092	0.145	0.295	-0.038

* Mean returns significantly different from zero, for t tests, at the 5% level (as indicated in the studies). Asterisks shown in Ho & Cheung (1994) and Wong et al (1992) indicate significant mean returns at the 1% level.

Notes:

(i) The Hong Kong market index is captured by the Hang Seng Index (HSI) in all the results reported above: See Mok (1987, p. 94); Ho (1990, p. 76); Lee et al (1990, p. 268), Wong et al (1992, p. 50), Agrawal & Tandon (1994, p.87). However, Mok (1990, p. 94 & 96) also reports returns using the Hong Kong Index and various sectoral indices of the market.

(ii) The mean daily rates of return reported are calculated on a close-close basis. In Mok (1988), Ho (1990), and Ho & Cheung (1994), returns are calculated in logarithmic form.

Table and Notes extracted from McGuinness (1997a, p. 464) with summary results from this study also incorporated for Hang Seng Index (HSI) returns measured on (i) a close-to-close basis and (ii) open-open basis for SEHK trading and for Hang Seng London Reference Index (HSLRI) returns measured for Hong Kong stocks trading in London's SEAQ International on a close-to-close basis.

closing-out the position at the following Monday open. Most accounts suggest that, after transaction costs, this would not be a worthwhile venture. If it were, one would be faced with the invidious task of explaining why such a profit opportunity is a systematic and recurring feature in markets. Any impediments against short-selling might offer one possibility but, in general terms, most day-of-the-week effects are more than offset by transaction costs. For Hong Kong, McGuinness's (1997a) study reveals that 'round-trip' transaction costs are sufficient to make all mean day-of-the-week returns negative. This holds even when excluding bid-asking spread costs, given 'round-trip' transaction costs of around 0.8% for blue-chip Hong Kong stock trades. In short, day-of-the-week return differences are an interesting and recurring feature in markets but their size does not, in general, suggest any violation of the EMP.[22]

A noteworthy change in the pattern of day-of-the-week returns in Hong Kong is the weakening of the Friday effect (see Table 4.3). The change in the magnitude of the Friday return is a likely reflection of changes to settlement.[23] Prior to June 1992, settlement was on a T+1 basis where stock payment had to be made within one business day of a transaction (with the scrip also registered in the buyer's name within this time). Under such a regime, Fridays were an opportune time to purchase stock given two extra calendar days of credit. For sellers, the opposite was true. The likely consequence of the buying and selling motivations under T+1 was increased selling pressure on Mondays through to Thursdays and increased buying pressure on Fridays. The result being an inflation in Friday returns. The shift to T+2 terms in 1992 signalled a clear change. Thursday returns are likely to be higher under such a regime. Table 4.3 reflects this result, given a strengthening of the Thursday return and weakening of the Friday return, for data post-1992 (see Section 3.3, p. 90 also).

As a final point, McGuinness's (1997a) study is the only one in Table 4.3 that incorporates data on day-of-the-week patterns for Hong Kong stocks traded in London. This does not reflect an oversight on the part of other researchers. The SEAQ International market for Hong Kong stock trading was at a formative stage until the early 1990s. Trading volumes have since risen dramatically .

To reiterate, whilst a range of day-of-the-week return patterns is evident in various markets, transaction costs would likely wipe out any gains when trading on the effects.

The Holiday Effect

The holiday effect, which results in large returns on days immediately preceding holidays, appears to be of greater significance. Ariel (1990) sums up the significance of this effect for the United States as follows: 'on average the pre-holiday return equals nine to fourteen times the return accruing on non-pre-holidays. Over one-third of the return accruing to the broad market over the 1963–82 period is attributable to eight trading days prior to holidays each year', (p. 1624).

Tests in Ariel also indicate that while the volatility of pre-holiday returns is slightly higher than on other trading days, the increase cannot explain the huge differential in mean returns between the day prior to a holiday and other days (given significant t and non-parametric test results for these differences). Ariel (1990, p. 1623) also reports that the pre-holiday effect is largely independent of day-of-the-week effects.

In Hong Kong and other Chinese societies, the Lunar New Year holiday carries particular significance and has been meted out for special attention. A number of commentators have pointed to a strong run-up in stock prices on the trading day immediately prior to this holiday. Mok (1990, p. 87), for data between 1975 and 1990, confirms this effect for Hong Kong and two other Asian markets with strong Chinese characteristics: Taiwan and Singapore. For the 16 years of his data, Mok notes that price increases occurred on the Lunar New Year's Eve for Hong Kong, Taiwan and Singapore on 16, 15, and 14 occasions respectively. This compares with 11 increases in London and only 5 in New York over the same period.

Various reasons for the Lunar New Year's effect have been offered. Deliberations on this issue, like Tsang's (1996), suggest two key factors: (i) the injection of new money into the market and property sectors as a result of bonus payments just prior to the new year; and (ii) the onset of the 'corporate reporting season'. With regard to the latter, Tsang remarks:

> Most blue-chip companies in Hong Kong make their annual results announcements between mid-February and mid-April. The steady growth trend in corporate earnings over the past ten years gives rise to a long-standing bullish expectation for future results. The closer the corporate reporting season, the greater the inclination for the markets to trade on current-year profits, resulting in lower price/earnings valuation. (p. 20).

Tsang also notes that strong post-holiday returns are greeted as an auspicious start to the new year. Investors might, therefore, be inclined to submit buy rather than sell orders on the opening day of trading, as a way of inviting a self-fulfilling prophecy. Mean returns in both Mok (1990) and Tsang (1996) suggests some merit to this, but the fact remains that the pre-holiday effect is far more pronounced than any post-holiday effect.[24]

Like the Lunar New Year, there is strong evidence of a pre-Western New Year effect. This also seems to spill over into Asian markets. Mok (1990) finds evidence of this effect for Hong Kong, Taiwan, and Singapore, characterized by an appreciable rise in share prices in the opening days of the Western new year. This is, essentially, the story behind the January effect.

The January or 'Turn-of-the Year' Effect

Like the holiday effect, the January effect does appear to be significant after adjustments for transaction costs. This return is typically measured by comparing price changes between the last trading days of December and January. Gultekin and Gultekin (1983),[25] in respect of an equally-weighted NYSE index, for the 1947–79 period, report a mean US January return of 4.50%. This compares with an average mean for all other months of 0.80%.[26] This is a startling difference. Even when comparing January's mean return with that for the second highest month, December, a differential of over 2.14 times is apparent.

To regard the January return as a 'month-of-the-year effect' may be something of a simplification, though. Keim (1983) notes that in the United States 'more than fifty per cent of the January premium is attributable to large abnormal returns during the first week of trading in the year, particularly on the first trading day' (p. 31). The effect is therefore inter-meshed, not surprisingly, with the 'the turn-of-the-year effect'.

The coincidence of fiscal and calendar years in the United States means that a 'tax-loss selling hypothesis' may underpin the January return. Dyl (1977), amongst others, notes that the capital gains tax code in the United States encourages investors, on the one hand, to realize losses prior to the tax year-end and, on the other, to defer gains. Higher year-end volumes in under-performing stocks, as noted in Dyl (1977), are consistent with this picture. In other countries, such as the United Kingdom, the 'tax-loss selling' effect may be even more pronounced due to the so-called 'bed-and-breakfasting' of securities, which entails investors selling loss-making stocks just prior to the year-end and buying them back almost immediately in the new tax year. This allows realized capital losses to act as a buffer against taxable capital gains. In the United States, such practices are heavily restricted. Operating under the guise of a 'wash sale', a period of at least 30 days must elapse between any sale and repurchase of a given stock straddling two tax years.[27]

If the 'tax-loss selling hypothesis' is relevant to the 'turn-of-the-year' effect, abnormally high April returns should also materialize in jurisdictions where an April-to-March tax year operates. The United Kingdom, like Hong Kong, falls into this category. Not surprisingly, stocks in the former experience a large inflation in returns during this month. Gultekin and Gultekin (1983, p. 475), using data for the 1959–79 period, report mean April returns of 3.129% in the United Kingdom, which easily exceed levels in all other months except January.[28]

The 'tax-loss selling' hypothesis also receives support in markets other than the United States and United Kingdom. Gultekin and Gultekin (1983, p. 479) report that for 13 of 17 countries, where monthly seasonal return patterns are evident, all but one, Australia, generate their highest mean monthly return at the beginning of a tax year.

The fact that a January effect is also apparent in countries that operate on a non-calendar tax year (such as the UK and Australia, in Gultekin and Gultekin's findings, and Hong Kong, as shown in Table 4.4) is also interesting. It suggests dependencies between markets. This may reflect the role of US investors in these markets, where gains realized fall under US tax codes. Tax treaties aside, this might lead to 'tax-loss selling' activities in respect of the US tax year-end, in these non-US markets. The absence

Table 4.4 Summary of Reported Month-of-the-Year Returns for the Hong Kong Market

Study	Sample Period	N		Jan	Feb	Mar	Apr	May	June	Jul	Aug	Sept	Oct	Nov	Dec
Chen (1989, p. 21)	Jan.65–Dec.76	33	(1)Mean(%)	7.44*	5.74	-2.53*	-1.78	2.78	0.77	1.71	-1.75	0.86	5.77	-4.10*	5.66
			(2)St.D.(%)	9.54	20.72	7.96	14.91	11.84	9.35	8.88	10.91	9.44	10.39	10.31	11.15
			CV (2/1)	1.28	3.61	-3.15	8.38	4.26	12.14	5.19	6.23	10.98	1.80	-2.51	1.97
Ho (1990, p. 62)	Jan.75–Nov.87	33	(1)Mean(%)	6.78^	1.77	-2.24	5.15^	1.13	2.56	2.01	0.87	-3.03	3.52	-0.02	4.85^
			(2)St.D.(%)	8.71	7.72	6.97	6.33	7.83	7.86	7.73	8.18	12.65	9.91	11.42	5.98
			CV (2/1)	1.28	4.36	-3.11	1.23	6.93	3.07	3.85	9.40	-4.17	2.82	-571.00	1.23
Pang (1988, p. 76) Jan.77–Dec.86															
Small Firm Ptf.		5	Mean(%)	4.44	-1.12	-1.54	3.16	0.76	-0.13	0.74	2.63	-1.02	1.43	-1.84	1.07
Large Firm Ptf.		5	Mean (%)	8.51@	-2.18	-0.58	5.65@	1.46	2.41	4.40@	1.04	-6.00@	7.21@	-1.70	3.71@
Cheung, Ho & Wong (1994, p. 228)	Jan.80–Dec.91	33	Mean Excess Return(%)	7.00^	2.48	-0.83	4.20^	0.71	1.83	3.39	-0.37	-1.85	1.18	0.49	4.66^

* Mean monthly returns significantly different from *overall mean monthly returns* at the 5% level (as reported in Chen, 1989).

^ Mean monthly returns significant from *zero* at the 5% level (as reported in Ho (1990)).

@ Mean monthly returns significant from *zero* at the 5% level (as reported in Pang, 1988).

Mean monthly excess returns significantly different from the *mean for other months* (as reported in Cheung et al. 1994).

N refers to the number of stocks in the portfolios/indices.

Notes:

(i) The Hong Kong market index is captured by the Hang Seng Index (HSI) in all the results reported, excepting Pang (1988): See Chen (1989, p.23); Ho (1990, p. 76); and Cheung, Ho and Wong (1994, p. 227). Pang utilizes data on 25 stocks and breaks them into portfolios. Only results for two of these portfolios are reported—the small and large firm portfolios—which contain five stocks each.

(ii) The mean rates of return reported in Pang (1988) and Ho (1990) are logarithmic and calculated on a close-close basis.

(iii) The mean rates of return reported in Cheung, Ho and Wong (1994) are expressed as excess market returns (=($ change in price of the index between month open and close plus the $ value of dividends received, all divided by the opening index) – risk free rate).

(iv) CV refers to the coefficient of variation and is reported as shown in Chen (1989) and estimated in Ho (1988) based upon the mean and standard deviation of the monthly returns reported. For Ho (1990), the CV figures reflect means and standard deviations rounded to 2 decimal places.

of capital gains taxes in Hong Kong suggests a greater role for the US tax-loss selling effect than in some other jurisdictions where part of the US capital gains liability may be paid, via tax treaty, in the locale where the gain occurs.[29] A more likely explanation for an almost ubiquitous January effect, is that buying and selling sentiment in New York simply spills over into overseas markets.

The studies outlined in Table 4.4 also report a marked April seasonal effect for Hong Kong. Again, this effect could be tax-induced; this time stemming from the activities of UK institutions in Hong Kong (see Pang, 1988, p. 81). As with the US institutions, British institutions have a sizeable presence in Hong Kong. As a means of defraying British capital gains taxes on overseas gains, many of them may well engage in tax-loss selling activities, in both Hong Kong and the United Kingdom, just prior to the fiscal year-end. This effect should still be significant but may have weakened during the 1990s, due to greater diversification in Hong Kong's investment base.[30]

Fund managers may also have a bearing on the 'turn-of-the-year' effect. As many managers are evaluated on a calendar year basis, portfolios may be rebalanced to contain proportionately more stocks at the beginning of the year. This flood of new money into the market may account at least partially for the January effect.

As noted throughout, the EMP tells us that investors should be able to identify regularities in returns and trade on them to their advantage. In so doing, anomalies like the January effect should be removed through offsetting price movements around the turn of the year. The persistence of such effects clearly raises serious doubts as to the efficiency of the markets. For Hong Kong, Chen's (1989) study is apposite. In relation to month-of-the-year effects, Chen demonstrates that trading rules devised from observed regularities would have yielded large excess returns over future holding periods. In other words, the effects conveyed considerable predictive power. Regularities gleaned between 1965 and 1976 were used to construct trading rules in Chen's study. These were then applied over a subsequent 1977 to 1986 test period. For one of these rules, designed to exploit the January effect, investors acquired stock at the December year-end and sold it at the following month-end. Funds realized were then put on deposit for the remaining eleven months of the year in anticipation of the next January effect. Chen shows that compared with the risk-adjusted benchmark, measured by weighting the annualized market returns and deposit-saving rates by 1/12 and 11/12, to reflect an investor's true exposure to the market from this strategy, a risk-adjusted excess return of 5.97% would have been earned (after transaction costs).

These results are also consistent with the risk-return ratios (CV) reported in Table 4.4 which show that, despite January mean returns being the highest of the year, the volatilities on these means are comparatively low (Chen, 1989; and Ho, 1990). Whether or not this attractive monthly return is still apparent is debatable.

The Firm Size Anomaly

There is also widespread evidence that risk-adjusted stock returns are inversely related to stock size. Risk-adjustments are typically obtained through the CAPM or some variant of it. In terms of the Sharpe Market Model, the risk-adjusted return for a stock j (RAR_j) can be expressed as follows:

$$RAR_j = R_j - \hat{R}_j = R_j - (\hat{a}_j + \hat{b}_j.R_m)$$

where $\hat{a}_j$ and $\hat{b}_j$ are estimates of the Market Model parameters for stock j; $\hat{R}_j$ is the predicted rate of return for stock j based upon these estimates; R_m the rate of return on the market portfolio; and R_j is j's actual return.

In most studies in this area, stock size is typically captured by a stock's market capitalization. For portfolios of 'low-cap' or small-firm stocks, average risk-adjusted returns ($R_{p,s} - \hat{R}_{p,s}$) typically exceed those on corresponding portfolios of large firms. Moreover, the effect tells us that small firm portfolios generate positive (abnormal) risk-adjusted returns on average. Banz's (1981) evidence, where risk-adjustments are expressed through the CAPM, is supportive of such an effect in the United States.[31]

Keim (1983) also reports that the firm size is closely related to the January effect in the United States. He notes that, 'the relation between abnormal returns and size is always negative and more pronounced in January than in any month. . . . Nearly fifty percent of the average magnitude of the size anomaly over the period 1963–79 is due to January abnormal returns,' (Keim, 1983, p. 31).

Roll (1983) contends that the positive association between the January and firm-size effects is due to investors selling proportionately more small-firm stock than large-firm stock at or near the fiscal year-end. As the typical small-firm exhibits greater risk than the typical large firm, it follows that small-firm stocks are more likely to feature as candidates for tax-loss selling. Roll also contends that, for reasons of liquidity and transaction costs, arbitrageurs may be unable to purge that part of the January effect relating to the small-firm effect. It goes without saying that the January effect still comes through strongly when only large firms are considered. Chen's (1989) evidence for Hong Kong testifies to this. The marked January effect he reports is based on returns on the HSI—a basket of the largest and most actively traded stocks in Hong Kong.

With regard to the firm-size effect, Pang's (1988) early study provides some limited evidence for its existence in Hong Kong (when examining risk-adjusted returns).[32] Cheung (1995), in a more recent analysis, also offers evidence in its favour for Hong Kong and several other Asia-Pacific markets. The perennial problem, especially in Asia, is the weak turnover in 'low-cap' stocks. This always makes β estimation something of a 'hit-or-miss' exercise. Even the adjustments to these estimates—the financial equivalent of reconstructing a building from its foundations—are open to question. Notwithstanding this point, the enterprise devoted to this issue is most impressive.[33] It is also an important area of endeavour, especially when researching some of the world's smaller markets where thin-trading is endemic.

β is not Everything

The foregoing material indicates that other variables like firm size should have a role to play in benchmark return models. Whilst not as elegant as the single-index asset-pricing models, multi-factor approaches, like Ross's (1976) Arbitrage Pricing Theory (APT) model and Sharpe's (1982) estimation approach, probably offer much greater explanatory power. Fama and French's (1992, pp. 427–9) empirical analysis gives greater resonance to such views. Fama and French argue that not only is β just a part of the story in explaining stock returns, but it is subordinate to other factors. In particular, they remark that 'unlike the simple relation between β and average return, the univariate relations between average return and size, leverage, earnings/price (E/P), and book-to-market equity are strong' (p. 428).

4.5   Concluding Remarks

Fama's rejoinder about the joint hypothesis always looms large when assessing market efficiency. Whenever departures from weak-form efficiency emerge, proponents of the EMP can always cast doubt on the results by claiming model error or some other methodological flaw. In short, there is no definitive equilibrium model. Even if a multi-factor approach is preferred, it is not obvious which factors should be included (nor their specific weightings). Nevertheless, single-index models offer an elegance and theoretical rigour that is hard to resist, which is probably why most academics cling to one form or another of the single-index model when evaluating stock returns.

To some extent, this issue can be avoided by testing efficiency in relation to Fama's semi-strong notion of efficiency, but a good number of these event-type tests still require a suitable benchmark model. How can we evaluate analysts' stock recommendations, for example, without assessing the risk of the underlying? Whilst there is much evidence around to support semi-strong efficiency, the existence of certain anomalies, like the month-of-the-year and holiday effect, are unsettling. In short, they contradict the EMP. Whilst only a few anomalies were considered here, it is apparent that some trading rules exist, even after taking account of transaction costs. This suggests some level of inefficiency, although in a number of cases critics would aver that the statistical evidence of inefficiency is a chimera or illusion. In other words, historical patterns do not necessarily convey predictive power, especially when this regularity is anticipated and provokes trading.

Whichever view holds sway, it is evident that the more developed and competitive a market is, the greater the degree of efficiency inherent in that market.

Notes

1.   For a recent discussion of this, founded on Knight's original distinction and later developments, see Machina and Rothschild (1990, p. 227–8).

2.   The present value of a perpetuity is simply the dollar payment in any period divided by the period discount rate.

3.   = $2/0.15.

4.   This point is readily accepted when applying the Value-At-Risk (VAR) concept to the risk-management of derivatives, a subject explored in Section 13.4. In this vein, Paul-Choudhury (1996) remarks that 'Outlying events (a technical euphemism for crashes) are more common in the real world than the normal distribution would suggest.' (p. 23, brackets appear as shown).

5.   The number of shares in issue between the two dates fell due to company-initiated buy-backs (see *Wardley Cards* for Cafe De Coral, 03, Prep: 25-1-99). These may have boosted sentiment in the stock slightly. Buy-backs were fairly common in a number of stocks during 1997/8. Companies often buy their stocks, for cancellation, precisely because they are 'good buys'.

6.   See Copeland and Weston (1983, p. 185 and p. 229) for reference to unpublished paper entitled 'Towards a Theory of the Market Value of Risky Assets' by Treynor, J., 1961.

7.   See Copeland and Weston (1983) for an overview of these historical developments.

8.   Many of the CAPM's assumptions stem from Markowitz's portfolio theory (see Copeland and Weston, p. 186 for further discussion of these assumptions).

9.   Though commonly labelled the Market Model, Sharpe (1963, p.281) refers to it as the Diagonal Model.

10. Grossman and Stiglitz (1980) also note that prices move closer to the absolute standard for market efficiency when information is more easily attained. However, as trading activity is a response to information asymmetries and/or differences in beliefs, trading volumes are likely to weaken as one moves closer to Grossman and Stiglitz's absolute standard.

11. See Fama's (1991, pp. 1577-1582) review of this evidence.

12. Stock dividends are also known as Bonus Issues or Capitalization issues.

13. Grinblatt et al. (1984) note, in their examination of both distribution methods, that 'on average, there is a significant increase in a firm's stock price at the announcement.' (p. 488).

14. They note, 'We have also documented post-announcement abnormal returns, particularly around the ex-dates of splits and stock dividends. The average magnitude of these ex-day returns exceeds that found previously for small stock dividends and is as large as the split or stock dividend announcement effect for some subsamples.' (Grinblatt et al. 1984, p. 488).

15. See Lakonishok and Lev (1987, p. 915-16) for a review of this argument.

16. Taking the difference between the return of a stock j and the market index M is equivalent to assuming j has β of 1. We can see this if we note that b_j in Sharpe's (1963) Market Model is equivalent to β_j. We also implicitly assume a_j is zero. Therefore, $R_j - (a_j + b_j.R_m)$ = risk adjusted return.

17. See Ariff and Johnson, *Securities Markets & Stock Pricing*, Ch. 15, 'An Analysis of Stockbrokers' Share Recommendations', pp. 153–65 (Ariff M., Goh, KKL and Johnson, LW).

18. See Cross (1973) and French (1980) for early studies for the US equity market and Jaffe and Westerfield (1985) for international comparisons.

19. See Agrawal and Tandon's (1994, p. 87) day-of-the-week return summary for time periods extending between 1971 and 1988. Other international surveys also report large mean returns for Wednesdays: Kim (1993, p. 60) notes that this day has the highest mean return of the week in the UK, Japan, and Canada; and Ho (1990, pp. 52–3), for seven of twelve countries, reports significant t statistics for this day's return.

20. In fact, for both Japan and Australia, Jaffe and Westerfield (1985) argue, 'Because of time zone differences, the pattern of daily returns in Australia and Japan could be identical to, but one day ahead of, the pattern in the U.S.' (p. 439).

21. Later studies by Smirlock and Starks (1986) and Harris (1986) also offer some support for the 'non-trading weekend' effect in the US.

22. Connolly's (1989) criticisms of day-of-the-week findings are also germane. He suggests that such effects are exaggerated. This is because standard F tests are biased against acceptance of the null, of insignificant differences in day-of-the-week returns, when using large samples.

23. See McGuinness (1997, p. 460) for detailed discussion of these changes.

24. Chan, Khanthavit, and Thomas (1996) identify holiday effects across four Asian markets: Malaysia, India, Singapore, and Thailand. They report, in addition to strong Lunar New Year effects in Singapore and Malaysia, evidence of religious and cultural holiday effects in one or more of the other markets.

25. For earlier evidence, see Rozeff and Kinney (1976).

26. See Gultekin and Gultekin (1983, p. 475) for detailed month-by-month means.

27. See Dyl (1977, p. 166) for further details of these restrictions and Gultekin and Gultekin (1983, p. 479) for a comparison of US 'wash sale' provisions with those in the UK.

28. Agrawal and Tandon (1994, p. 100) also confirm this for the UK for mean returns computed between 1971 and 1987. For 18 other countries analysed in this study, 13 also displayed a significant January return.

29. The growing influence of US institutions in Hong Kong suggests the argument is more valid now than it was in the 1970s or 80s. Pang (1988, p. 82) questions its validity for the 1977–86 period analysed in her study.

30. See Pang (1988) for earlier discussion of the role of overseas institutions in the 'tax-loss selling' hypothesis.

31. He reports that, 'On average, small NYSE firms have had significantly larger risk adjusted returns than large NYSE firms over a forty year period. . . .' (Banz (1981, p. 16)).

32. However, her results suggest a 'reverse firm size effect' when raw returns are examined which, almost paradoxically, given the higher risk-adjusted returns on small firms, suggests higher βs on larger firm stocks. Although, as she concedes, the β estimates for the small firms in her sample may well contain downward bias due to thin-trading.

33. See Ariff and Johnson (in *Securities Markets & Stock Pricing*, Ch. 8, pp. 79-84, 'The Effects of Thinness of Trading on Market Parameters') for an application of one of these approaches to thinly-traded stocks on the Singapore Stock Exchange (SES).

5. Primary Market Activities I: Initial Public Offerings (IPOs)

This chapter and the next focus on the capital raising functions of Hong Kong's equity markets.[1] As in other jurisdictions, a distinction can be drawn between unseasoned and seasoned stock issues. The first relates to the listing of companies that have not had their shares listed or 'seasoned' through market trading and is dealt with here. The second, which is the subject matter of Chapter 6, deals with new stock issues in companies with an established listed status. As many companies see an initial listing— obtained through an unseasoned offering—as a spingboard to a stream of future seasoned new issues, seasoned and unseasoned stock issues are inextricably linked.

In most markets, the unseasoned stock issue is achieved through an initial public offering (IPO). This stems from a requirement that listed companies be able to demonstrate a substantial holding of their shares in interests that are independent of the majority controlling shareholders, or parties thereto. This group of independent investors represents the public interest component of a listed company's stockholdings. For SEHK listings this normally amounts to at least 25% of the value of a company's listed shares. Although *The Rules Governing the Listing of Securities on The Stock Exchange of Hong Kong Ltd* (hereafter the *Listing Rules*) make provision for a lower public interest percentage where 'the expected market value of a new applicant at the time of listing' exceeds HK$4 billion.[2] In the case of PRC-incorporated issuers, Rule 8.08 is superseded by provisions set out in Rule 19A.14 of Chapter 19A of the *Listing Rules*.

Most private (unlisted) firms in Hong Kong are closely-held, typically with 100% of the stock owned by a group of family members or inter-connected partners. A public interest component in stockholdings is therefore rarely evident. Approval of a company's application for listing is inevitably contingent, therefore, on the establishment of a prescribed public interest level. As a result, a public offering of stock must occur before the company is admissible for stock listing. This then captures the real meaning of the term initial public offering: a public offering of stock pursuant to that stock's initial listing.

Until recently, virtually all IPOs in the territory were wholly organized and marketed in Hong Kong and as such were deserving of the label local IPO. The first 'H' share issue in 1993 changed all that by ushering in the global offering form. As we saw earlier, 'H' share issues relate to PRC-incorporated enterprises listing in Hong Kong. The global feature in such offerings arises from the fact that only a fraction of the shares is offered to the local market. These are normally made through a public offering with the rest placed overseas with an assortment of institutions. This describes what is now known as a combined offer. Initially, this was limited to 'H' share listings in Hong Kong; however, the offer method spread to non-'H' share companies in 1994 and 1995. Now it forms one of the standards for listing new stock on the Exchange, with major pronouncements on the subject dating back to 1994.[3]

As more and more offerings are of the combined form, the IPO of old, involving an exclusive offering of stock in Hong Kong, has been overshadowed to some degree. Nonetheless, clear understanding of it is necessary before moving on to consider the newer global form of offering. As such, the early material in this chapter deals exclusively with the more traditional IPO form. Before analysing the mechanisms, timetable, and costs involved in local IPOs, which figure in Section 5.3, the general pricing issues in IPOs (Section 5.1) and the underlying motivations of issuers are addressed (Section 5.2). Major developments in the Hong Kong IPO market are then considered (Section 5.4) followed by an examination of the more recent global/combined offering mechanism (Section 5.5). The IPO—both of the local and global form—is then examined from an investor's perspective (Section 5.6). This entails consideration of the application procedures and rationing schemes adopted in oversubscribed offerings. The penultimate section deals with the short- and long-term performance of IPO stocks (Section 5.7). Concluding remarks follow (Section 5.8).

5.1 The Pricing Issue in IPOs

Initial public offerings, whether of the local or global form, are notoriously difficult to price. The absence of prior market valuations in such stocks means that issuers, and their agents, have to give careful thought to a fair and realistic price for the stock. For companies already listed on the market—that is, seasoned companies—new stock issues are much easier to price. Existing stock values always provide a benchmark for evaluating the offer price for shares in such issues. In view of the difficulties involved in pricing IPOs, it is not surprising that most studies indicate considerably greater mispricing in IPOs than seasoned issues.

Listing, and the determination of a market price for the stock, occurs once all the shares on offer have been allocated to the public. These shares, and those retained by the founders/controlling parties, then stand ready for flotation on the market. Once dealing begins, the market's valuation for the stock quickly emerges. The extent of the mispricing can then be judged by taking the difference between the first listed (traded) price in the stock and the IPO offer price, all divided by offer price. The market, through its natural mechanism, determines a fair and competitive price for the stock as soon it is listed. A number of studies show that the mispricing in an IPO is largely determined within the first few minutes of listing.[4] This suggests a good deal of pricing efficiency.

Numerous studies tell us that IPO offer prices are typically set at a large discount to initial traded prices. The summary of initial returns to Asian

IPOs in Table 5.2 aptly demonstrates this. This data and the issues relating to it are taken up later. Nonetheless, the issue of underpricing (i.e., offer prices typically being set at a discount to initial traded prices) has perplexed many researchers given the fact that it seems to recur not just within the same market, but across markets. The issue is, perhaps, best dealt with by Rock (1986). He unravels the conundrum in terms of the rationing involved in allocating shares across applications. As IPOs typically involve a fixed number of shares on offer at a fixed offer price, rationing inevitably occurs whenever excess demand is evident. Much of this demand appears to be driven by the perceived underpricing of IPO stocks, which, as suggested in accounts like Rock's, is intimately related to the rationing mechanism itself. The intuition behind Rock's explanation of IPO underpricing, and others, is explored later.

5.2   The Motivations Underpinning IPOs

Social Prestige and the Promotion of the Company's Product and Business

What drives a company to transform itself from private to public status? At a very superficial level, one might feel that arguments of prestige or social cachet underpin entrepreneurs' decisions to float their companies on the market. The very process of the IPO means that the name of the company, its product and associated brand names come to the fore. This often begins well in advance of the listing date; however, the costs of arranging the IPO and new listing are far from cheap. It is not unusual for the direct costs of issue to consume 15% or more of the gross proceeds raised. The fact that entrepreneurs and their companies entertain such expensive ventures suggests something of value that, hopefully, transcends reasons of entrepreneurial hubris.

Risk Sharing and Capital Funding

The possibility of enticing new investment partners into the business's capital financing may be the draw card for the entrepreneur, allowing some risk-sharing or diversification of ownership, which may be a good thing when the entrepreneur feels that new blood may help steer the company forward into larger, more sophisticated markets. For most private companies going to market in Asia, though, one senses that this is not a major consideration. Capital expansion, which of course entails some diversification of ownership, is likely to be more important. Most IPOs, certainly in Hong Kong, involve offers of new shares rather than existing shares. As such, most of the funds raised accrue to the firms themselves and not to the original entrepreneurs. This would seem to bear out the capital expansion argument. Diversification of share ownership inevitably results, though, whichever route is taken. For many entrepreneurs this diversification issue is not an advantage, as such, but the cost of attracting much-needed funds.

The capital expansion motivation is easy to understand. Most small, private firms are heavily dependent upon the support of banks and other family members. This can only take a business so far. How many of the world's leading companies are private? Not many. The IPO then provides a platform for generating much needed funds. Platform is, perhaps, the right word as, once listed, the company can go back to the market for more and more funds. In other words, the financing benefits of a market listing are, at least in theory, ongoing. Many firms, once listed, tap the market year after year for new capital. Most of these seasoned issues are made through private placings in Hong Kong. These involve relatively small amounts of new stock placed with specific investors like investment banks and fund managers. For controlling shareholders wishing to raise large amount of capital, the rights offering is preferred. This is typically the largest of the seasoned issue methods and also avoids significant dilution in the controlling shareholder's stake because all the shares involved in the new issue are offered to existing stockholders in proportion to existing holdings. In sum, while seasoned issues via placings are cheaper than rights issues, both allow funding to be raised from fairly liquid pools of capital. This is not just an idle statement. The evidence points to much greater sums being raised, on most exchanges, from seasoned issues than unseasoned issues.

Enhancing or Establishing a Company's Credit Rating

Listed status can enhance a company's credit rating. In many cases, it allows a company to gain a credit rating for the first time. Once listed, a company attracts the gaze of analysts, researchers, and credit-rating agencies. The determination of its creditworthiness is critical if that company wants to issue marketable debt. Many credit-rating agencies are loath to step outside the listed-corporate arena. Even for a minority of private companies with a credit rating, listing provides some prospect for a credit upgrade. Why is this? In the eyes of the prime credit-rating agencies, a listed stock has access to a public market for funding that lies outside the realm of the typical private firm. This means that a company, once listed, need place less reliance on bank loans than hitherto. All other things being equal, this should enhance a potential creditor's confidence. Put another way, the same lender may be less enthusiastic about lending to a private company because of its seeming reliance upon bank financing, rather than the mix of debt and equity financing available to a publicly quoted body.

Improvements in credit ratings not only translate to easier access to debt financing, but also to cheaper funding. For debt issues this may mean a reduction in the discount offered on the debt and/or the provision of a lower coupon (interest) rate.

Founders/Controlling Shareholders Seeking to Liquidate Their Equity Stake

Issues of product promotion, capital expansion, and the preferential terms pertaining to new equity and debt financing are clearly the positive elements that most attach to the IPO. Care should be taken that these do not mask other self-serving motivations. It is quite possible that the founders/ controlling parties may see listing as an opportune way of selling-off equity on favourable terms. What this means is that IPOs are likely to be pitched during bull markets, possibly near their climax, and that a large proportion of the shares on offer, if not all, will be existing (rather than new) shares. Where all the shares on offer are new, the same suspicions are less likely to be aroused. In such circumstances, entrepreneurs commit to retain 100% of their previous holdings, although some dilution in their percentage interest inevitably follows from the new share issue, given the enlargement in the firm's equity base. Even this reassuring sight can be undermined if investors feel that entrepreneurs may start dumping their stock once the stock's secondary market has been established. Organized exchanges, being aware of such possibilities, try to assuage investors' fears by severely restricting such possibilities. For the SEHK, a moratorium on such sales is normally specified for the first six months of a stock's listing.[5]

This serves to lock in the share interest of the controllers for an appreciable period beyond the IPO,[6] essential in ensuring both a fair launch and a stable after-market price for the stock. Otherwise, it would be extremely difficult for entrepreneurs to sell IPO stock at anything other than basement prices. A legitimate fear of entrepreneurs driving stock prices downward in the initial listing period would drive all investors away from the IPO market.

5.3 The Characteristics of the Local IPO Form

The IPO Mechanism Deployed

Three particular forms of the local IPO mechanism are evident. These forms were apparent in virtually all IPOs in Hong Kong up until 1993. They still apply to a large number of IPOs coming to the market, but have been overshadowed to some extent by the arrival of the Global offering form. The general characteristic of the local IPO form is that all the shares on offer are offered locally. International book-building operations do not, therefore, characterize such offering forms. These features largely characterize the global offering described in Section 5.5.

Local IPOs generally occur through one of three routes:

(i)   an *offer for subscription* (or new issue of stock);
(ii) an *offer for sale* (offer of existing shares in issue); or
(iii) a combination of (i) and (ii).

The overriding feature in virtually all of these issue methods is the fixed supply of shares on offer and the fixed offer price. Although recent innovations in the global offering form mean that not all IPOs exhibit such features, adjustable offer prices are, in fact, common in the global offering due to the use of international book-building. Over-allotment options, granted by issuers to underwriters, where demand for offerings is likely to be strong, also feature widely in global IPOs.

The Offer for Sale

Of the three local IPO methods outlined, method (ii) is perhaps the simplest. This method involves pre-listing stockholders selling a proportion of their existing shares at a fixed price through the offering. As an example, suppose that company X has 100 million shares in issue, all privately owned by family F (the pre-listing stockholders). Suppose further that the company has obtained approval to list on a particular exchange through the sale of 25 million of its 100 million outstanding shares at $1 each. The funds raised from the offering will, after the necessary deduction of expenses, accrue to F. This will be guaranteed, even if the public fails to submit enough applications for the shares, given an underwriter's promise to buy any unallocated shares at the offer price. The same underwriting principle also applies to methods (i) and (iii).

The offer for sale is akin to a secondary market transaction. Funds are simply transferred from buyers (the public) to vendors (the pre-listing stockholders), without any funds passing to the underlying company. This would be described as a secondary offering by US practitioners. As the equity base of the company is not enlarged through such an offering, the number of outstanding shares listing on the market—100 million, in the case X—equals the number outstanding prior to the IPO. The only discernible change is that the pre-listing stockholders see their 100% interest whittled down to 75%, in the example considered.

The Offer for Public Subscription and Offer for Sale/Public Subscription Hybrid

In methods (i) and (iii), the offer for public subscription and the combination of offer for public subscription and offer for sale, the equity base of the issuing company is enlarged. This reflects the role of new shares which raise funds, after the deduction of expenses, for the issuing company. Accordingly, both an offer for subscription, and the new issue component of the combination method (iii), would be described as primary offerings by US commentators.

To illustrate, suppose that in an offer for subscription, a company Y, which has 150 million shares outstanding prior to issue, issues 50 million new shares at an offer price of $1. This leads to $50 million, less expenses, being credited to the working capital of the firm. Moreover, company Y enlarges its equity base to 200 million shares. All of the original 150 million shares owned by the pre-listing stockholders, and the 50 million new shares owned by the public, are listed. The pre-listing stockholders would therefore see a dilution in their interest from 100% to 75%, despite the retention of all pre-listing holdings.

For the third combination IPO method, dilution of pre-listing ownership arises from two sources: the enlargement of the company's equity base and the sale of existing pre-listing holdings. To illustrate, Exhibit 5.1 makes reference to Jackin International Holdings Ltd's 1996 combination offer for its listing on the SEHK.

Exhibit 5.1   Case Study of an IPO through an Offer for Subscription and an Offer for Sale

Jackin International Holdings Ltd's new listing on the SEHK in November 1996 was achieved through an IPO with the following terms: an offer of 74,250,000 new shares and an offer for sale of 16,500,000 'sale' shares to the public at HK$1.05 per share. 255,750,000 shares were in issue prior to the application for listing. The key features of the IPO are outlined below and are gleaned from the Jackin International Holdings Ltd's Prospectus (15 November, 1996).

1. Number of Shares Listed = no. of pre-listing shares + no. of new shares
   = 255.75 million + 74.25 million = 330 million shares

2. Gross Funds raised by Firm =
   HK$(74,250,000 × 1.05) = HK$77,962,500

3. Gross Funds raised by Vendors =
   HK$(16,500,000 × 1.05) = HK$17,325,000

4. Retention % = ((255.75 million − 16.5 million)/(255.75 million + 74.25 million)) × 100 = 72.5%. Percentage of equity retained by pre-listing shareholders

New listings can also be made by, amongst other things, placings and introductions, The introduction is considered later. The placing is also addressed later given its role in the global/combined offer form.[7]

The Significance of the Public Interest Component to Liquidity in Listed Stocks

In all the constructed examples, a retention percentage for pre-listing stockholders of 75% or lower is apparent. As the shares on offer are available to the public, this suggests a public interest component in the above of at least 25% of the (enlarged) equity base.[8]

The significance of the public interest component to majority control was spelled out in Section 1.3. As the public interest component typically represents a scattering of holdings, it was argued that a major shareholder could achieve effective control by holding 37.5% or less of a company's outstanding shares. This, of course, assumes that the stock held in the public interest is rarely mobilized against substantial shareholders. We can conjecture that the 35% ownership level, characterizing the threshold for 'control' in Hong Kong, provides some leeway for a higher public interest than 25%. It also provides for some apathy amongst the body of non-public interest shareholders.

The key question, perhaps, is why do so many exchanges around the world insist on a public interest component in listed stocks, and what is its real benefit? The answer really relates to liquidity. Shares held in public hands are, in fact, the most likely to turnover once a stock is listed. In contrast, pre-listing holdings are likely to be maintained for a significant period beyond the initial listing date for two reasons. Firstly, pre-listing stockholders may wish to keep their substantial interest intact. Secondly, as we have already seen, restrictions are generally imposed upon pre-listing stock holders which prevent them from liquidating the interest they retain.[9] This restriction is devised to safeguard the interests of all investors who purchase stock through the offer.

The IPO Timetable and Costs of Issue

Essential IPO issue details are disclosed in the prospectus document to an offering and are subject largely to provisions set out in Chapter 11A of the *Listing Rules*. Subscriptions for shares are then encouraged in the period between the prospectus becoming available and a deadline which is set just prior to the official listing date of the stocks.

When applying for shares in a Hong Kong IPO, applicants will be required to pay for the full cost of the shares under their application (i.e., the offer price multiplied by the number of shares applied for). Depending upon the level of subscriptions to the offering, applicants will then receive: (i) a full allotment under their application; (ii) a partial allotment of shares with the return of funds representing part of their rejected application; or (iii) a complete return of all application funds. The disclosure of allotment details, through the rationing scheme, is normally made a few days after the closing date for applications.

To illustrate the typical timetable of events in a Hong Kong IPO, useful reference can be made to the Jackin International Holdings Ltd IPO considered in Exhibit 5.1 earlier. Based upon the prospectus document for this issue (p. 5), the closing date for applications in this IPO was 20 November 1996. The rationing scheme was to be announced on or before 25 November 1996. Share certificates and/or cheque refunds were then scheduled to be posted on or before 26 November 1996 with listing of shares set for 28 November 1996. The eight-day period between the closing date in applications and the listing of shares is quite typical in Hong Kong IPOs.

For the issuing firm—or vendors, in the case of an offer for sale—the sale of all shares on offer is guaranteed by underwriting the offer. This entails, amongst other things, a commission cost of 2.5% of the gross proceeds from the offer. In return, the underwriters are obliged to buy up unallotted shares at the offer price.[10] Failure, in this context, means a subscription rate (SR) of less than 1 (i.e., less than 100%). A subscription rate of 0.80 (or 80%) would therefore see 20% of the shares on offer acquired by the underwriters, and their team of sub-underwriters, at the designated offer price.

The actual costs of an IPO are far from trivial. In the Jackin International Holdings Ltd case, featured in Exhibit 5.1, these amounted to about 18.89% of the total funds raised by the firm and vendors; however, as indicated in the prospectus document, the majority of the costs were covered by the issuing firm. As well as the 2.5% commission to underwriters, paid on all the offer shares, the prospectus reports that:

> Such commission, documentation fee and expenses, legal and other professional fees, and printing and other expenses relating to the initial public offering of the shares are estimated to amount in aggregate to approximately $18 million. The expenses in relation to the Offer will be payable by the Company and the Vendors in the proportion of approximately 82 per cent. and 18 per cent. respectively.' (*Jackin International Holdings Ltd Prospectus*, 15 November, 1996, p. 134–5).

In terms of gross funds raised, the foregoing suggests issue costs of approximately 18.9% for Jackin and 18.7% for the vendors.

While some costs are variable, such as the underwriter's commission, most costs are fixed. Large stock offerings should therefore be preferred as a means of spreading these costs. The value of the newly listed stock, with market capitalization of HK$346.5 million (based on the offer price), probably lies below the mean for other listings. As such, the percentage of funds absorbed in costs may be noticeably lower in larger offerings. Even allowing for some economies, IPO costs are far from trivial. This is a trademark of all IPO markets, though, and signals the importance attached to the event by issuing firms and pre-listing stockholders.

Key Information Disclosure Items

In addition to the standard accounting information and forecasts of future corporate earnings, reflected in a prospectus, investors would normally be looking for clues or 'signals' to help them fill in the complete picture. The percentage of equity retained in the firm by the pre-listing holders and the intended/disclosed uses for the funds raised would appear to be important in this regard.

The Retention (Percentage)

For simplicity, we will refer to the proportion of equity retained by pre-listing stockholders as the retention percentage. This is significant given evidence, in a number of studies and markets, of a strong positive relation between this percentage and the market value of newly listed stock. Most accounts defer to the Leland and Pyle (1977) signalling argument, in which pre-listing entrepreneurs bear a cost through such retentions by taking on a less diversified portfolio than would otherwise be required.[11] As with any signalling argument, such costs are only rationally incurred if future returns are expected to provide more than adequate compensation. Accordingly, pre-listing stockholders who retain a high proportion of their own stock signal positive expectations of future corporate earnings. Where such parties seek to reduce their ownership interest substantially below the normal 75% threshold, potential subscribers may well suspect the opposite. They would, quite rightly, view the issue with some suspicion. Pre-listing stockholders would then need to assuage the doubts of subscribers by rebutting the following: If the company is so good, why are you reducing your percentage stake substantially below the level required? This signalling issue would be further compounded if all shares on offer were existing shares.

Sometimes a large dilution in the pre-listing owners' stake may occur for good reason. Suppose an IPO is made to acquire a substantial amount of funds for a new investment project through a large new share issue. A substantial dilution effect may result even though lucrative returns from the project are likely. In this case it would be in the best interests of the issuing firm and its prospective shareholders if it undertook the project. How can the pre-listing stockholders lend an air of credibility to their plans, given the dilution effects resulting from the new issue? As existing shares are not being disposed of, their claims would at least have some credibility. To further buttress this credibility, they could provide specific details of the project at hand. This could be achieved by declaring such details through the prospectus as 'intended uses for funds raised'. While intended uses for funds raised are not the same as actual uses, investors are likely to scrutinize the information in this area carefully. The more vague the description of uses, the less convincing the plans.

Delineation of Intended uses for Funds Raised
In general terms, potential investors might be more inclined to pay a higher offer price for IPO stock where the balance of funds raised is directed to productive use. Statements specifically or indirectly suggesting the use of funds for debt repayment within the firm or simple additions to existing working levels might not be so warmly greeted. The latter might suggest, particularly to the more cautious investor, an absence of good investment projects. Issues of this kind are clearly important in explaining investors' demand for IPO shares and, ultimately, how the issuers fix the offer price. The number of disclosed uses for funds raised in an IPO may serve, for instance, as a proxy for the *ex-ante* uncertainty surrounding the after-market price in an IPO (see Beatty and Ritter, 1986). In other words, a more general or fragmented dissemination of funds creates a greater possible variance in the perceived levels of returns from the overall investment. This, in turn, translates to greater IPO underpricing, according to Beatty and Ritter (1986).

Obviously, funds raised from an offer for sale accrue solely to the vendors and have no impact whatsoever upon the firm's investment policy. To reiterate, this issue makes the offer for sale somewhat unattractive to the average investor. Very few IPOs, in fact, are constructed on this basis.[12] The negative signalling effect of a sell-off probably has more to do with this than anything else. Underwriters would likely recommend a lower offer price, relative to a comparable IPO involving a new issue, to overcome this problem.

5.4 Background and Developments in Hong Kong's IPO Market: An Historical Narrative

The growth of the Hong Kong market owes much to IPO activity. The inflation of the SEHK's market capitalization numbers stem from two sources: (i) the growth in seasoned stock values; and (ii) the additional value generated from unseasoned and seasoned issues of stock.

In many respects, (i) and (ii) are strongly linked as a bull market is often seen as a desirable market in which to pitch both IPOs and seasoned issues. From an issuer's viewpoint, a rising market provides an opportunity to generate a more favourable offering price at a reduced cost of equity capital.[13] Equally, investors seem to benefit from issues sold during bull market periods given evidence of increased initial returns from allocations of shares in such periods.[14] In this sense, market timing is critical to the success of an IPO. It is perhaps not too surprising, therefore, that the escalating returns of the 1990s have coincided with a flurry of IPO activity in Hong Kong. The scale of this upswing has been quite remarkable. As Table 5.1, shows activity rates in the 1990s dwarf rates in previous periods. The 363 issues made between 1991 and 1997, for instance, exceed all issues made between 1976 and 1990 by a factor of four. The upsurge in IPO activity in the 1990s was driven by two key factors: buoyant market conditions, and a surge in PRC-based investment due to the changing political and economic environment in Hong Kong.

Activity rates in the 1980s were also markedly higher than the decade before. In fact, for the 1975–9 period, only two IPOs were made in Hong Kong.[15] For the year preceding this, three new listings were made but only one of these, The Cross Harbour Tunnel Co. Ltd, was made through an IPO. In contrast, the 1969–73 period provided an extremely active IPO market. This period was one of discovery for share trading with three of Hong Kong's four pre-unification exchanges emerging at this time.[16] The lack of regulation in the markets at this time was undoubtedly a telling factor. The subsequent fall in stock values between 1973 and 1975, perhaps exacerbated by the proliferation of so many small, immature stocks on the markets, shattered confidence. In the process it erased much of investors' interest in IPOs. This lull in IPO activity continued for most of the 1974–9 period despite a sharp upturn in the economy towards the end of the 1970s.

The surge in IPO interest in recent years is manifest not only in terms of activity rates, but also in subscription levels. As an indication, six IPOs

Table 5.1 Overview of IPO Activity on the SEHK

Year	No. of IPOs	No. of Listed Companies	Market Capitalization (HK$millions)
1976	–	29	56,675
1977	1	284	51,278
1978	–	265	65,939
1979	1	262	112,809
1980	5	262	209,752
1981	12	269	232,331
1982	2	273	131,640
1983	4	277	142,093
1984	8	278	184,642
1985	4	279	269,511
1986	5	253	419,281
1987	15	276	419,612
1988	19	304	580,378
1989	5	298	605,010
1990	13	299	650,410
1991	48	357	949,172
1992	54	413	1,332,184
1993	62	477	2,975,379
1994	50	529	2,085,182
1995	25	542	2,348,310
1996	44	583	3,475,965
1997	79	658	3,202,630

Source: Data for the number of IPOs was determined from various SEHK *Fact Book 1986* to *Fact Book 1997.* The number of listed companies and the market capitalization of all listed securities was determined from the SEHK *Fact Book 1997*, p. 124.

Notes: The figures given do not take into account the listing of investment companies (i.e., investment trusts, unit trusts and mutual funds) or debt securities. Only ordinary stock listings made through an initial public offering (IPO) are recorded. New listings of stocks through alternative means, such as the introduction are excluded. Thirty-five of the 260 IPOs between 1993 and 1997 were global IPOs.

in 1997 alone attracted subscription rates of over 500 times the number of shares on offer, Beijing Enterprises Holdings being the most high profile, given a recorded subscription rate of 1,276 times.[17] In plain terms, given the requirement for full payment of shares at the time of application, the subscription level meant that a staggering 99.921% of aggregate funds received had to be returned to applicants.

The Denway Issue of 1993 and its Effects upon HIBOR

The frenzied level of investor interest in Hong Kong IPOs, signalled as early as 1993 when the Denway Investment issue broke all existing subscription records with a subscription rate of 658 times, alarmed many in the securities industry. With the full purchase price of the stock paid upfront in the applications, pressure on borrowing forced inter-bank rates (HIBOR) sharply upwards, necessitating an injection of HK$650 million into the inter-bank market by the HKMA.[18]

The Denway issue, in addition to several other highly subscribed offerings in 1993 and 1994, spawned renewed interest in alternative offering mechanisms. Amongst other things, it underpinned a 'Joint Policy Statement on Offering Mechanisms' by the SEHK/SFC in November 1994. This statement made reference to the use of alternative mechanisms such as the American style book-building approach in which 'roadshows' and other pre-IPO marketing methods could be used to determine a sustainable offer price. Despite changes to the offering mechanisms used in Hong Kong in recent years, subscription rates have exceeded 500 times in eight issues other than Denway: one further issue in 1993; two between 1994 and 1996; and five, as noted, in 1997.[19] In the majority of these in 1996 and 1997, though, the subscription rates relate to the much smaller public offer component of the combined (global) offer. The largest slice of shares, in such issues, were placed overseas via a book-building process.

The combined (global) IPO, which came to the fore in 1993, utilized a US-style book-building approach to allow underwriters greater insight into the potential demand for IPO shares. It represented a timely response to the undesirably high subscription rates experienced with one or two offerings in 1993 and 1994. The combined offer mechanism embodied a number of innovative features. At least the features appeared innovative in relation to the traditional local IPO that went before it. Over-allotment options, adjustable offer prices and 'claw-back' features were such mechanisms and were designed to stem much of the exuberant demand evident in IPO stocks in 1993 and 1994. These innovations are considered below.

5.5   The Emergence of the Global IPO

As noted in the foregoing, the global IPO reflects a combined offer form where a fraction of the shares on offer are offered in Hong Kong through a conventional public offering and the rest placed overseas via a book-building operation. The book-building aspect to the combined offering is, perhaps, its key distinguishing feature. This is a US-based practice, which involves some degree of pre-marketing of the stock. Detailed description of it is made in the recent SEHK/SFC Consultation Paper on Offering Mechanisms (1997, App. 4). Amongst other things, it allows the offer price to be fixed just ahead of formal trading. In other words, the book-building process of soliciting interest from investors via 'roadshows' and other means provides the necessary information about the viability of an offer price. Underwriters then gauge an offer price once the book has been built, so to speak. As noted in the SEHK/SFC Consultation Paper on Offering Mechanisms (1997, App. 4), in relation to book-building:

Underwriting does not occur until the final few hours of the book-building period just prior to the announcement of trading and immediately after the size and the issue price of the offer have been finalised. As the price is fixed on the basis of investor demand and as the duration between the time when the price is fixed and when trading is short, theoretically, the likelihood of the issue price being fixed at a great disparity to the actual trading price would be minimised—hence, better price discovery and price matches demand more accurately.' (App. 4, p. 1).

The consultation document indicates that the period of exposure facing underwriters in the conventional Hong Kong IPO approach is considerably longer. The price risks facing the underwriter therefore appear substantially greater under the more traditional approach (referred to as the local IPO here). What about the issuer? Benveniste and Busaba (1997), in their theoretical comparison of the book-building and fixed offer price approaches, shed some light on the issue. They note that 'book-building generates higher expected proceeds and exclusively provides an additional opportunity to sell additional shares at full value but, in the process, exposes the issuer to greater risk. In comparison, fixed price offerings priced at the cascade price guarantee the issuer certain proceeds' (p. 397). In short, then, the new approach should, at least in theory, reduce underpricing levels (at the cost of some increased uncertainty for the issuer).[20]

Types of Combined Offering Forms

The earliest combined offering forms in Hong Kong were evident in the 'H' share offerings made in 1993. These differed from earlier IPOs marketed in the territory in two important respects. For one, the offers were multi-jurisdictional with a public offer in Hong Kong and a slate of shares placed overseas. The second important innovation was that only the shares in the combined offer were eligible for listing.[21] The shares already in issue, typically being domestic shares, were only eligible for listing in the Mainland (or not for listing at all if they were classified as non-negotiable).

Without wishing to repeat the characteristic features of 'H' shares, outlined in Section 1.3, issued shares in PRC state enterprises are separated into domestic and foreign share categories. Domestic shares trading as 'A' shares in the Mainland cannot be traded outside the Mainland. Similarly, foreign shares, like 'H' shares in Hong Kong, cannot trade on the Mainland. This is an effective mechanism against takeover, since the number of domestic shares always exceeds the number of foreign shares.

A large number of global IPOs have also been used for stocks other than the 'H' share. In such cases all of the shares involved in the combined offer, the Hong Kong public offer and overseas placing, and all of the shares retained by the pre-listing stockholders, typically list locally.

Case Study of the Combined Offer Method

To illustrate the combined offer method, the 1996 combined offer of Kerry Properties Ltd is examined in Exhibit 5.2A. This case involved an offer for public subscription (of new shares) to local investors and a 'book-built' placing of shares to international institutional investors.

Exhibit 5.2A Case study of a global IPO involving international book-building

> Kerry Properties Ltd's new listing on the SEHK in August 1996 was achieved through an IPO with the following terms: an offer of 22.5 million new shares and a 'book-built' placing of 127.5 million shares at a 'maximum' offer price of HK$21.50.
>
> 850 million shares were in issue prior to the application for listing. Three relatively novel features were evident in this issue:
>
> (i) an *adjustable offer price* 'expected to be not less than $19.50 per share';
>
> (ii) an *over-allotment option* granted to the underwriter allowing the combined offer to be increased by as much as 15% (i.e, from 150 million shares to 172.5 million shares); and,
>
> (iii) a *'claw-back' option* allowing a certain number of shares to be transferred from the placing to the public offer depending upon the level of oversubscription.
>
> The key features above are gleaned from the *Kerry Properties Ltd Prospectus* (23 July 1996).

The Adjustable Offer Price, Over-Allotment Option and 'Claw-Back'
The adjustable offer price is the first interesting feature. This feature required subscribers to the public offering to lodge payments for shares at the maximum price, with the possibility of subsequent refunds if the final offer price was determined below this level. This final offer price essentially reflected the book-building operation involved in marketing shares to 'professional and institutional investors in Hong Kong, the United States, Europe and elsewhere under the placing.' (Kerry Properties Ltd prospectus, p. 23). In the Kerry Properties Ltd IPO, the prospectus revealed that 'The Price Determination Date is expected to be on or around 26 July 1996.' (p. 24). The key date specified being the closing date for applications in the public offer. In fact, the subscription rate for the public offering, of just over 100%, and the information gleaned from the book-building exercise saw a final offer price of HK$17.50.[22] This led to refunds of HK$4 per share to parties allotted shares in the public offer.

A further interesting feature, common in most of the combined offer mechanisms, is the 'claw-back' facility. In Kerry Properties Ltd's IPO, provisions were made (see prospectus, p. 24) for 15 million shares to be transferred from the placing to the public offering if the subscription rate (SR) to the public offering was greater than or equal to eight times. A transfer of only 7.5 million shares was provided for if the SR was such that $3 \leq SR < 8$. As it turned out, the 'claw-back' was not used.[23]

The 'claw-back' is seen as a way of ensuring a sufficiently large allocation of shares to local investors, especially where local demand is particularly strong. Despite this, it is readily apparent that the public interest component, when measured in terms of the proportion of listed shares allocated to non-pre-listing interests, is often noticeably lower in global IPOs than local IPOs. Of course, the combined offering mechanisms implicit in the global IPO form means that a large amount of new (or existing stock) can be widely spread across international institutions. The issues are also generally much larger than the local IPO so that the public interest component of 25% does not necessarily apply.[24] In other words, the stock allocated in the combined offer, as a proportion of the number of shares listed, may well be less than 25% (see Exhibit 5.2B in relation to the retention (%) figures in the Kerry Properties issue).

While the 'claw-back' facility was not used in Kerry Properties Ltd's offering, an over-allotment option was. As specified in the prospectus, this option was available to the underwriters for a period of '25 days from the Price Determination Date' (p. 23). In the event, 9.6765 million additional shares were issued, at the final offer price of HK$17.50, through the option.[25] The exercise of such over-allotment options—as reflected in a number of SEHK/SFC announcements/guidelines, culminating in the *Consultation Paper on Offering Mechanisms* (June 1997)—is viewed as a legitimate form of price stabilization.

Exhibit 5.2B   The Key Issue Statistics for the Kerry Properties Ltd IPO

1. Number of shares listed   = 850 million + 150 million + 9.6765 million
                               = 1009.6765 million shares.

2. Gross funds raised by firm = HK$ (159.6765 million × 17.50)
                               = HK$ 2,794.33875 million

3. Market capitalization (offer price*) = HK$ (1009.6765 × 17.50)
                                        = HK$ 17,669.339 million

4. Retention % = (850 m./1009.6765 million)) × 100 = 84.19%.

The key features above are gleaned from data disclosed in the Kerry Properties Ltd Prospectus (23 July 1996); Wardley Cards, Wardley Data Services Ltd (Kerry Properties Ltd, 02, prep: June 8 1996); and SEHK/SFC Consultation Paper on Offering Mechanisms (June 1997, Appendix 2, p. 2 for subscription and final offer price details). * Finalized price. 1–4 exclude 12 million shares issued shortly after listing (see Prospectus, p. 27, for proposal).

Consultations in 1997 and 1998 led the Exchange and the SFC to issue a joint policy statement in 1998, which stresses a minimum proportion of shares that should be offered to the public in Hong Kong, in relation to the overall number available for subscription. It also provides a precise formula for the amount and operation of the 'claw-back'.[26]

The Alternative Route to a New Listing: the Introduction

Thus far, only new listings through the IPO method have been considered. This is not the only route to a new listing, though, given the possibility of an introduction, which involves listing a company's issued shares on the market without a corresponding offer of shares. The forces of supply and demand then dictate the market price for the stock. Issues of initial pricing and fund-raising are therefore avoided when listing through this method.

While the introduction is simple and cheap, compared with the conventional IPO route for listing stock, very few non-listed companies are eligible for listing through this method. Given that many exchanges normally require that all listed stocks have a defined public interest component to their listed equity, only firms that can demonstrate a broad and diversified shareholder base are likely to qualify for listing through this method. As most private firms in Hong Kong, seeking listed status, are closely-held, often with one family or a few partners holding all of the stock, the chances of listing through an introduction are virtually nil.

In practice, the introduction method is rarely used. It may feature, though, where a company previously listed on an exchange has been de-listed for a short time, probably for reorganizational reasons, or where a company is spun-off from another listed company.

Demergers can also be introduced to the market in a similar manner. In such circumstances, the spun-off and de-merged companies essentially inherit the same ownership structure as the listed parent and, accordingly, qualify as stocks with an established public interest. This is not withstanding the fact that eligibility for listing hinges on a variety of other issues including a stock's expected market capitalization.

The introduction can also potentially be used for stocks with an existing listing overseas. The standard of investor protection on the overseas exchange, as well as the size of free-float in the stock's existing listing, would need to meet the standards set by the exchange where listing is sought. There are only a few examples of this kind of introduction locally; CM Telecom International Ltd's introduction in October 1997 is one such case. This stock was listed on the Singapore Stock Exchange (SES) prior to its introduction to the SEHK.

5.6 Application and Rationing Procedures in IPOs

Investors applying for shares, either through a local IPO or through the public offer component of a global IPO, will receive all the shares they apply for if the offering is undersubscribed. However, provisions are sometimes made in the global IPO for some or all of the public offer shares to be transferred to the placing component.[27] In any event, the lack of demand in such cases suggests an unfavourable offering price and the likelihood that the first listed price in the stock will be at a discount to the offer price (unless it is subject to adjustment). In general terms, a strong positive correlation between the subscription rate (SR) to an offering and its initial return is likely.[28] This means that investors have much to gain from an accurate assessment of the likely demand for an offering. Equally, they have much to lose if lodging an application for a poorly received offering. In some respects, clues can be gleaned from the media and from general hearsay in the run-up to the closing date in applications. Whatever the general feedback, investors would be advised to delay their final subscription decision to a time approaching the deadline date.

Timing issues are also pertinent to the issuer and the underwriter as, at least until recently, both were obliged to fix the offer price some days in advance of the agreed listing date. Pitching an IPO ahead of a bear market would raise considerable subscription risk and loss for the underwriter, even with a contingency discount built into the offer price. The prolonged bear market in 1994 in Hong Kong, and elsewhere, highlighted this. Five of the 50 IPOs launched in that year achieved subscription rates (SRs) lower than 1. The SRs were generally much lower in 1994 than the years before or after. In contrast, the bullish market of 1993 gave witness to much higher SR levels with all 62 offerings oversubscribed.

In cases where subscription rates exceed 1, shares must be rationed across applications. The precise form of the rationing scheme largely depends upon the SR in the offering[29]. The approaches adopted for rationing in Hong Kong appear to be quite similar to those adopted in markets like Singapore and the UK.[30]

In general, specific rationing terms are applied to particular application order sizes. Order sizes, in turn, reflect discrete numbers of lots where one lot is typically equivalent to 1,000 shares. In IPOs with relatively low SRs, a scaling approach seems to be favoured where all investors, applying for a given number of shares, receive a given proportion of the shares under their application. In a straightforward scaling approach, the proportion of shares received will generally decline as the size of the application increases. Whatever the terms of the scaling scheme, all applicants face a probability of one of receiving an allotment of shares.

For offerings with relatively high SRs, a combination of the scaling and balloting approach is typically employed. In this approach, balloting of applications is used to ration shares across the smallest application orders with scaling used for the larger applications. The rationing scheme in Wing Lee Holdings' (WLH) recent IPO demonstrates the general features of this kind of rationing scheme. This information reveals that the terms of ballots, used for the smallest application orders, improve with order size.[31] Nonetheless, for all order sizes subject to a ballot, the investor knows that the probability of receiving an allotment is less than one. For the larger orders, subjected to scaling, once again, the terms are such that the proportion of shares allocated declines with increasing application order size.

The expected number of shares received from an application divided by the number of shares applied for will also decrease with application lot size. On the surface, then, this suggests a bias in favour of the small investor. The reality is rather different, however. Comparison of an applicant for two lots in WLH with one for 5,000 shares reveals this. The former faced a probability of 14/2,926 (=0.0048) of receiving an allocation. For the successful 14 applicants, in this case, all received 2,000 shares. The remaining 2,912 investors received nothing. Whilst the 'approximate percentage of shares allocated to the total number of shares applied for' of 0.48% was higher than for any other application category, applicants applying for a large number of shares, like the 90 applicants for 5,000 lots, received, with probability one, 16,000 shares.

The fact that the probability of an applicant receiving an allocation of shares, as well as the actual number allocated, increases with order size means that large investors can act strategically to take up most of the fixed supply of shares on offer (see McGuinness (1993b)). To illustrate, consider the 79 applicants with orders for 70,000 lots in the Wing Lee Holdings IPO (see note 31). All of these applicants were allocated 216,000 shares each giving them, in total, 24.4% of all of the shares on offer in the IPO.[32] If considering all applicants with order sizes of 50,000 lots or more, the percentage rises to 40.2%. If considering all applicants with order sizes of 10,000 lots or more, a staggering 71.3% of the supply of shares is allocated. This means that investors prepared to front-up at least HK$10 million acquired nearly three-quarters of the issue. In all likelihood, most of the shares on offer would have been taken up by large institutions and corporate investors. The advantages of existing pools of liquidity, as well as reduced borrowing costs, clearly favour the large investor.

The nature of the rationing schemes in Hong Kong, and the gains from strategically placing large orders, have meant that small investors have effectively been 'squeezed out' of a number of the most lucrative offerings. Accordingly, the SFC and the SEHK, in a joint announcement dated 22 May 1997, instituted new rationing guidelines to ensure that small investors acquire a reasonable proportion of the shares on offer in all IPOs. In particular, they require that:

> The total number of securities available for public subscription (taking account of any claw-back feature in the case of issues which involve both placement and public subscription) are to be divided equally into two pools: pool A and pool B. The securities in pool A should be allocated on an equitable basis to applicants who have applied for securities in the value of HK$5 million or less. The securities in pool B should be allocated on an equitable basis to applicants who have applied for securities in the value of more than HK$5 million and up to the total value of pool B.' (*South China Morning Post*, Business Post, p. 2, 23 May, 1997, emphasis added).

The small investor, within the context of the above, is deemed to be a party with investment, at the application stage, of HK$5 million or less. Recent research on allocative mechanisms also suggests that approaches favouring smaller investors may also lead to higher offering prices for issuers and, hence, greater amounts of capital (see Chowdhry and Sherman, 1996).[33]

The market authorities also noted, in the same announcement, that existing rationing schemes, by encouraging investors to apply for large numbers of shares, may have a deleterious impact on short-term interest rates.[34] This was certainly the case in the Denway IPO[35] of 1993, mentioned earlier, and the more recent *Beijing Enterprises* issue (see Wong and Chan, 1997). The pooling of share applications, as described in the SFC/SEHK's joint announcement, has probably helped alleviate the pressure on interest rates to some degree by weakening the incentive of the bigger players to apply for inordinate numbers of shares.

5.7   The Underpricing and After-market Performance of IPOs

The sheer verve and excitement generated by Hong Kong IPOs in recent years would suggest that the IPOs in question are substantially underpriced at their initial offering price. This is reflected by the empirical evidence, when comparing initial market prices with offer prices. This underpricing phenomenon is common to virtually all markets.

Underpricing is typically determined with reference to the initial return an investor receives, given a full allocation of shares. This return is measured by assuming investors sell their allocation on the first date of listing. The convention in most studies is to compare the closing price of the stock on its first day of listing with the offer price. In initial return form, this gives rise to the IR measure below:

$$IR = ((P_M - P_O)/P_O) \times 100$$

where: P_M = First closing traded (market) price in the IPO shares, and
P_O = Offer price in the IPO shares.[36]

Measuring the initial return IR with respect to the opening traded price on the first date of listing, instead of the closing price, would probably make little difference to the overall magnitude of initial returns. This suggests an efficient pricing process for the listed stock with actual demand for the stock quickly impounded into the first available clearing price.

Details of the initial returns (underpricing levels) reported in various IPO studies in Pacific-Rim markets are shown in Table 5.2. The levels recorded in these markets are, in the main, higher than those typically reported in markets like the United States and the United Kingdom. Studies in these more established markets are numerous, and a detailed account

Table 5.2 Summary Review of the Levels of Underpricing Reported across Markets and Time Periods: Evidence for the Pacific Basin

	No. of Issues	Study Period	%	Return
Australia				
Finn and Higham (1988)	93	1966–78	29.2	M[1]
How and Low (1993)	523	1979–89	16.1	M[L,1]
Hong Kong				
Dawson and Hiraki (1985)	31	1979–84	10.9	U[1]
Dawson (1987)	21	1978–83	13.8	M[1]
McGuinness (1993)	92	1980–90	16.6	M[1]
Japan				
Dawson and Hiraki (1985)	114	1979–84	51.9	U[1]
Singapore				
Dawson (1984)	29	1979–83	37.5	U[1]
Wong and Chiang (1986)	48	1975–84	56.0	M[1]
Dawson (1987)	39	1978–83	38.4	M[1]
Koh and Walter (1989)	70	1973–87	27.0	r[1]
Saunders and Lim (1990)	17	1987–88	45.4	M[1]
Koh, Lim and Chin (1992)	53	1975–87	37.6	M[1]
Malaysia				
Dawson (1987)	21	1978–83	166.6	M[1]

*   Indicates the number of portfolios/groups of stocks analysed.
**   Indicates ordinary and preference shares included in study samples.
M[1]   Initial excess market returns between the first closing traded price in the new issue and the offering price.
M[L,1] Initial excess market returns between the first closing traded price in the new issue and the offering price measured in natural logarithmic form.
M[m]   Initial excess market return between the traded price one month after issue and the opening offer price.
U[1]   Initial return between the first closing traded price and the opening offer price unadjusted for changes in the market index.
r   Initial unadjusted returns less the continuously compounded risk-free return over the initial return holding period.

Extract: Keasey and McGuinness (1995, pp. 42–3, Table 1).

of these lie outside the scope of this book. Nonetheless, returns reported in two recent studies, by Aggarwal and Rivoli (1990) for the United States and Levis (1993) for the United Kingdom, are worth citing. Aggarwal and Rivoli (1990), for 1598 offerings between 1977 and 1987, and Levis (1993), for 123 offerings between 1985 and 1988, report initial IPO returns of 10. 7% and 8.6% respectively.[37] These are considerably lower than returns reported in Table 5.1 for Singapore, Japan, Australia, and Malaysia. Hong Kong can take some comfort from its initial return levels which lie closer to those in the larger, more developed markets. Data for recent findings in China offer less comforting reading, however. Mok and Hui (1998) point to underpricing in 'A' share IPOs in Shanghai of around 289% on average. This represents the mean market-adjusted return for issues made between 1990 and 1993. This result and the nature of China's 'A' share market feature in greater detail in Section 7.2. In brief, IPO underpricing probably provides a good measure of market maturity. As Shanghai develops, bearing in mind that it has only been in operation since late 1990, initial IPO returns are likely to moderate substantially.

Rock's (1986) Model of Underpricing

Given that the majority of IPOs appear underpriced at their initial offering price, investors might consider applying across all issues for a large numbers of shares. Based upon the comments made earlier, large application orders may be necessary in order to ensure a sufficiently large allocation of shares; however, this kind of strategy is a very risky one. The allocation practice in Hong Kong, and in many other countries including the United Kingdom, the United States, Australia, and Singapore, are such that a 'winner's curse', to use an expression brought into favour by Rock (1986), is evident in the allocation process.

This 'winner's curse' arises because investors are more likely to receive a large allocation of shares in offerings that are less attractively priced. This reflects the low subscription rates (SRs) that poorly priced offerings command. In cases of significant overpricing, the SRs may well be less than one so that all applicants receive a full allocation. In contrast, investors have a much lower chance of receiving shares in the more lucrative offerings which are likely to be substantially oversubscribed. In equilibrium, the 'winner's curse', for investors applying randomly for IPO shares, should result in investors receiving an overall rate of return just sufficient to cover their transaction costs. This point is argued in Rock's (1986) model of IPO underpricing.

Rock's (1986) model distinguishes between two types of IPO investor: the informed and uninformed investor. The former incurs search costs to decipher the true value of IPO stock and, accordingly, restrict their applications to underpriced issues. In contrast, uninformed investors, without any prior information, apply for all issues. With informed investors on the sidelines, they are overrepresented in overpriced issues. In underpriced issues, oversubscription occurs as both groups submit applications. This means that uninformed investors are likely to receive most of their application order in the overpriced issues but be squeezed out of the lucrative offerings. This is the 'winner's curse'. In view of this, Rock concludes that the majority of IPOs must be underpriced to compensate uninformed investors for the allocational bias they face. In essence, uninformed investors would only consider entering the IPO market, according to Rock, if their expected return, from an allocation of IPO shares, is greater than zero.

The Rock model has been lauded as the most convincing explanation for underpricing. This explanation can be tested where rationing schemes are disclosed. Initial investor returns from IPOs can be weighted by the probability of receiving an allocation of shares, determined from rationing schemes, and by taking into account the transaction costs associated with applications. McGuinness (1993b) shows that for Hong Kong offerings between 1980 and 1990, Rock's explanation has some empirical value. Specifically, McGuinness (1993b) notes that 'after adjustments for the winner's curse and the Hong Kong settlement mechanism, significant returns from random share applications are only attainable for relatively large applications. These significant returns range from 2.85% to 8.22%', (page 386).

Other attempts to test the Rock (1986) model, like Levis's (1990) analysis for UK IPOs, also indicate some evidence of excess returns from large, indiscriminantly placed applications. However, due to transaction costs, the returns diminish beyond a certain level. In contrast, Koh and Walter (1987) observe that initial returns in the Singaporean IPO market closely fit those predicted by the Rock model.

In addition to the Rock explanation, accounts of IPO underpricing are often framed using one of three other arguments:

(i)   *ex-ante* uncertainty arguments (see Beatty and Ritter,1986);
(ii)   insurance against litigation arguments (see Ibbotson,1975 and Tinic, 1988); and
(iii) signalling arguments (see Welch,1989).

Ex-ante uncertainty arguments have already been noted with regard to underpricing in relation to the prescribed uses for funds raised in an IPO. In a formal sense, Beatty and Ritter (1986) explore the concept of *ex-ante* uncertainty within the terms of Rock's (1986) underpricing model, so that explanations of underpricing are seen as being consistent with, if not complementary to, Rock's model.[38] *Ex-ante* uncertainty is defined in relation to the uncertainty surrounding the post-issue value of IPO stock. Suggested proxy measures include, amongst others, the standard deviation of post-listed returns (see, for example, Ritter,1984) as well as the number of different uses for funds raised disclosed in IPO prospectuses (see Beatty and Ritter,1986).[39]

A further proposition linked to the *ex-ante* uncertainty issue, which is developed and empirically confirmed in Beatty and Ritter (1986), is that underwriters who fail to enforce the relation between initial return levels and *ex-ante* uncertainty levels, subsequently lose IPO underwriting business. Connected with this, many studies also provide evidence of a negative association between investment banker quality and underpricing levels.[40] Johnson and Miller (1988) note further that the negative association reflects the fact that less prestigious banks underwrite and manage issues with relatively higher levels of *ex-ante* uncertainty. Confirmation of the negative relation between banker quality levels and *ex-ante* uncertainty levels is also noted in Carter and Manaster (1990)[41] for US IPOs.

Insurance against litigation arguments also feature widely as a possible explanation for IPO underpricing. Tinic (1988), for instance, argues that issuers and investment banks to IPOs may be compelled to underprice IPOs so as to avoid damages from potential litigants. He notes that if the initial performance of an IPO is unfavourable, investors may be more inclined to seek some form of redress by arguing that the issuing parties failed to demonstrate 'due-diligence' in relation to the 1933 SEC Act in the United States. This could relate to meaningful omissions of information or inaccurate disclosures. The potential risk of either, whether intentional or not, is substantial given the amount of information that has to be disclosed in the run-up to an IPO. In view of the risks of litigation, Tinic (1988) argues that issuing parties may wish to err on the side of caution by offering subscribers a higher initial return than might otherwise be the case. In lowering the offering price in this way, the issuing firm, or vendors, clearly consent to a reduced capital inflow. Consequently, some trade-off between the level of funds raised and the expected costs of litigation is suggested.[42]

More recently, Allen and Faulhaber (1989), Grinblatt and Hwang (1989), and Welch (1989) have devised models that suggest that underpricing may serve to reveal the post-issue (intrinsic) value of the issuing firm. In other words, underpricing acts as a signal of firm quality with the most valuable firms being able to recoup the capital lost from underpricing. For this to be true, the post-issue value of IPO firms' equity should be positively correlated with the level of initial returns in the offerings. McGuinness (1993c) confirms this for a sample of Hong Kong offerings and, simultaneously, notes that all the major implications of the Grinblatt and Hwang (1989) signalling model apply.

IPO underpricing, as noted in Welch (1989), may also be motivated by the possibility of achieving higher offer prices in subsequent seasoned issues. This argument is strengthened by evidence indicating the likelihood of new stock issues in the first few years of listing for a corporation.[43] The material presented in Chapter 6 also highlights the importance of this argument in Hong Kong, given considerably greater amounts of funding raised through seasoned equity issues than unseasoned issues.[44]

Longer-Term Performance of IPO stocks

Whatever the explanation for the actual magnitude of IPO underpricing, prices should adjust swiftly and fully in the initial listing period to reflect the intrinsic value of the stock. This is at least the position that exponents of the efficient markets hypothesis (EMH) would hold. Furthermore, given the risk of the stock, abnormal returns, across newly listed stocks, should not be apparent in the general post-listing period. The evidence indicates rather the opposite. Findings in numerous markets point to generally poor longer-term performance in IPOs (see Uhlir (1989; for West German IPOs), Ritter (1991; for US IPOs), McGuinness (1993a; for Hong Kong IPOs), Levis (1993; for UK IPOs), and Aggarwal et al. (1993; for Latin American IPOs)). This does not necessarily mean that post-listing prices fall below prices in the initial listing period. Instead it tells us that cumulative returns, measured from prices in the initial listing period, fail to keep up with an equivalent benchmark (market) return. The consistency of these post-listing IPO return results, raises questions about the validity of the EMH to the pricing of newly listed stocks. With such behaviour seemingly predictable, there may be scope for earning excess market returns by shorting IPO stock in the formative months of listing. If this were to occur, prices would adjust abruptly rather than trending downward (albeit in market-adjusted form). However, a number of markets restrict such activities on newly listed stock and this may explain why the trends persist.

What about corporate earnings performance? Does the earnings performance of a newly listed firm match its relative underperformance in the stock market? Evidence in studies like Jain and Kini's (1994), for the United States, broadly suggests yes. A subsequent study by Teoh, Welch, and Wong (1998), again for the US, point to some management of earnings at the time of IPO. They note in their conclusions: 'discretionary current accruals—which are under the control of management and proxy for earnings management—are high around the IPO relative to those of non-issuers. The paper documents that issuers with high discretionary accruals have poorer stock performance in the subsequent three years', (p. 1,966). In essence, IPO firms go to the market when their earnings numbers are able to generate a more favourable offer price. This is not too surprising, bearing in mind the attention given to the price/earnings multiple in most IPOs.

Evidence of weak post-listing performance in IPOs not only questions the logic of investing in newly listed stocks but also the extent to which the stocks are initially underpriced. It may also suggest, as argued in Ritter (1991, p.23), that the costs of underpricing for the issuer are lower than is popularly envisioned. Should we, therefore, measure underpricing in relation to a series of prices in a stock's post-listing period?

The important issue is why do such pricing patterns emerge? Ritter (1991) accounts for his US evidence in terms of industry-specific fads.[45] For Hong Kong, rather different explanations can be offered. McGuinness (1993a), based upon empirical and interview-based evidence, accounts for abnormally positive returns in newly listed Hong Kong stocks, in the first few months of listing, followed by a longer-term decline, in three ways. Firstly, there is the possibility that certain parties to an offering may engage in support activities in the initial listing period by holding the stock and encouraging others, through networks and other means, to buy it. Obviously, such support is difficult to sustain over a long period, and it is possible that once an IPO loses its lustre, as media attention wanes following its publicized launch, that such support activities also weaken. All other things being equal, this would precipitate a decline in stock values over the longer term.

The second, and least likely, possibility raised is that a group of de facto market makers might try to manipulate the initial market for IPO stocks by encouraging a speculative rise in stock prices and, upon subsequent profit-taking, liquidate positions. This would also drive prices down in the post-listing period. The third possibility, and perhaps the most compelling, concerns capital commitments made by the pre-listing stockholders in the offerings. It was noted earlier that pre-listing stockholders typically enter agreements to retain their majority interest intact for the first six months of listing. Once these capital commitments elapse, the initial owners in the offerings are then able to liquidate their holdings. McGuinness finds strong positive correlations between the post-listing return performance of Hong Kong IPO stocks and a capital commitment measure (equal to the percentage of equity that the pre-listing stockholders commit to retain for the first six months of listing)[46] for the first six months of listing. A reversal in this correlation is noted thereafter. For the post-listing period between 180 and 250 trading days, these correlations are strongly negative, suggesting that IPO stocks with larger capital commitments fare worse over the longer run.

The interesting question is how have the measures, instituted in the Hong Kong IPO market in recent years, affected both the initial underpricing and longer-term pricing performance of territory-wide IPOs? One can guess that the new measures—including adjustable offer prices, over-allotment options, and book-building— contribute to more realistic offer prices. As a result, initial underpricing levels should be lower than hitherto. The over-allotment option may also be useful in dampening the immediate after-market exuberance evident in many IPOs. As these features are commonly employed in US IPOs, which also exhibit favourable short-term return and unfavourable long-term return patterns, one suspects that the historical pattern could be a recurring one, albeit with some modulation from time to time.

5.8 Concluding Remarks

This chapter has focused on a number of issues pertinent to the pricing and performance of IPOs in Hong Kong and overseas. In understanding these issues, details relating to the mechanics of an issue, the regulatory environment and the rationing procedures for IPO applications were thoroughly examined. The huge subscription rates in recent years, pushed by a flood of mainland investment in the early to mid-1990s, underpinned an unprecedented demand for IPO shares. Through various pressures imposed on the banking system, the authorities were forced to reappraise the way in which IPOs were constructed and applications rationed. Their deliberation on this issue, as we saw, triggered a slew of changes. As such, the Hong Kong IPO market of the mid- to late 1990s is radically different to that prevailing in the 1980s.

Notes

1.   The author would like to acknowledge the comments of two anonymous OUP reviewers for their earlier comments on this chapter.

2.   As set out in Rule 8.08(1), 8-2, 10/95 of the *Listing Rules*. These Rules also state in 8.08(1) that, 'The Exchange will normally accept a prescribed percentage of between 10% and 25% in the case of issuers with an expected market value at the time of listing of over HK$4,000 million because the number of securities concerned will be sufficient to ensure that there is an open market.' (p. 8-3, 9/94).

3.   See *SEHK/SFC Joint Policy Statement on Offering Mechanisms*, 1994.

4.   Barry and Jennings (1993, p.62) for US IPOs indicate that the adjustment essentially occurs at the market open on a stock's first date of listing. This speed of adjustment, at least for the US, points to a very efficient pricing process.

5.   One routinely sees such commitments in prospectus documents. McGuinness (1993a) makes specific reference to this point as follows: 'agreements between pre-listing insiders and the investment bankers to the offerings often exist which restrict the sale of insider holdings in the post-listing period. A typical example of such an agreement, taken from the prospectus of the new issue of Universal Appliances Ltd, is as follows: 'All the existing shareholders of the Company have undertaken to Schroders Asia Limited and to the Company that they will not dispose of any shares within six months from the date of the prospectus save with the prior written consent of Schroders Asia Limited'. (*Source:* The Prospectus Document of Universal Appliances, June 1987, p. 41, Disclosure of Interests, Appendix IV.' (p. 185).)

6.   See *Listing Rules*, Rule 10.07, 10-07, 11/93. Rule 10.07(1)(b) also prohibits controlling shareholders (or the 'registered holder' of such shares), as defined in Rule 10.07, from disposing of stock, between six and 12 months after listing, where such disposals result in the party or parties no longer being controlling shareholders.

7.   Suffice to say that the Exchange provide details on listings via placings in Chapter 7 and Appendix 6 of its *Listing Rules*.

8.   Rule 8.24 of the *Listing Rules* defines what is meant by 'the public'.

9.   See *Listing Rules*, Rule 10.07 pertaining to 'Restrictions on disposal of shares by controlling shareholders following a new listing', pp. 10-07, 10-8, 11/93, 6/98.

10.   Similar kinds of arrangements, albeit with rather different cost structures, are also apparent in the US. Issues of this kind are referred to as firm commitments (see Ritter (1987) for background).

11.   See McGuinness (1993c, pp. 268–269) for a review of the theoretical and empirical evidence in relation to this positive association.

12.   As an indication, the *Fact Book 1996* (pp. 45–46) indicates that only one of the 44 IPOs made to the Hong Kong market in 1996 was constructed on this basis.

13.   See Loughran and Ritter (1993) for account of this, and the reduction of the cost of equity capital, for IPOs pitched during bull markets.

14.   See Ritter's (1984) discussion of initial returns in 'Hot' issue markets in the US.

15.   Listings through IPO, between 1975 and 1979, were made by Far East Hotels and Entertainment Ltd (July 1979) and by Swire Properties (June 1977). Two further listings were made during this period through introductions: Sime Darby Berhad (Dec. 1979) and Mitsui and Co Ltd (Sept. 1976).

16.   See Wong (1991) for background on the rather speculative markets of the 1969–73 period.

17.   As well as Beijing Enterprises, subscription rates of 528 times in GZI Transport Ltd; 892 times in GITIC Enterprises; 523 times in Kin Yat Holdings; 531 times in Sa Sa International Holdings; and 653 times in CATIC Shenzhen Holdings Ltd were observed. Subscription rates were obtained from the *Fact Book 1997.*

18. See Karp (1993) for discussion of these figures.

19. In 1993, in addition to Denway, Tack Hsin Holdings Ltd attracted a subscription rate of 553 times. Subsequently, Arnhold Holdings Ltd achieved a rate of 583 times in 1995 and Guangdong Tannery Ltd a rate of 567 times in 1996. The subscription rates were gleaned from the *Fact Book 1993, 94, 95* and *96*).

20. In an earlier paper, Benveniste and Spindt (1989) also argue that some underpricing is inevitable. They note, *inter alia*, that 'underpricing arises naturally as a cost of compensating investors with positive information about the value of the stock for truthful disclosure of their private information' (p. 358).

21. Twelve global offerings were evident between 1993 and 1994 (see *SEHK/SFC Consultation Paper on Offering Mechanisms* (June 1997, App. 2, p. 1)). All of these were 'H' share issues where some of the shares listed in Hong Kong also dual-listed as depositary receipts in the US (as discussed in Section 7.4).

22. See SEHK/SFC Consultation Paper on Offering Mechanisms (June 1997, Appendix 2, p. 2 for subscription and final offer price details).

23. The level of subscription was just over 100%, 1.03 times (see ibid.).

24. Refer to the *Listing Rules* and Rule 8.08 in particular.

25. See Wardley Cards, Wardley Data Services Ltd (Kerry Properties Ltd, 02, prep: June 8, 1996).

26. See SEHK/SFC (1998).

27. Such a provision was, in fact, evident in the case study example in Exhibit 5.2 (see Kerry Properties Ltd prospectus, p. 24).

28. McGuinness (1993b, p. 382) reports that the correlation between the initial returns and subscription rates on Hong Kong IPOs, for all issues between 1980 and 1990, was +0.644. Initial returns, in this context, measure the difference between the closing price of the stock on the first day of listing and the offer price, all divided by the offer price.

29. See McGuinness (1993b, pp. 382–383) for analysis of this.

30. See Koh and Walter (1987) and Levis (1990) for an account of the rationing schemes in these respective jurisdictions.

31. As disclosed in the *South China Morning Post*, Business Post, April 4, 1997, p. 7. SR was 312.12 times (*Fact Book 1997*, p. 50).

32. This percentage is equal to the number of successful applicants (79) multiplied by the number of shares allocated (216,000), all divided by the 70,000,000 new shares on offer (see ibid.).

33. These findings are made in relation to Rock's (1986) model of underpricing.

34. In particular, the SFC and the SEHK note that, 'The present allocation procedure may encourage certain applicants to apply for large amounts of stock thereby greatly increasing the demand for funds in the banking system upon the close of the offer period, resulting in an increase in short term interest rates. The SFC and the Exchange are concerned about the potential adverse impact on the securities market of Hong Kong. The SFC and the Exchange are conducting a study on the offer mechanism, which, among other things, will consider means to improve the allocation system in IPOs.' (*South China Morning Post*, Business Post, p. 2, May 23, 1997).

35. See Note 18 above. Karp (1993) also provides some interesting statistics about the size of applications funds tied up in the issue. He notes that the issue 'tied up funds equivalent to 40% of the colony's 1991 GDP, about 150% of the Hong Kong dollar M1 money supply and nearly five times the amount of Hong Kong banknotes in circulation.' (Karp, 1993, pp. 62).

36. In excess market return form, the percentage change in the market index between the open and close of trade on the first date of listing can be subtracted from IR. As noted in Beatty and Ritter's (1986) study, this adjustment has minimal effect.

37. Levis (1993) excludes all placings from these initial return figures. Both Aggarwal and Rivoli (1990) and Levis (1993) measure initial returns using the M1 metric described earlier in Table 5.2.

38. Ritter (1984) and Beatty and Ritter (1986) note, for informed investors in Rock's model, the greater the (*ex-ante*) uncertainty of an offering, the greater the underpricing required to compensate the costs of becoming informed.

39. Evidence of a linkage between various proxy measures for *ex-ante* uncertainty and initial IPO returns are well documented (see, for example, Ritter (1984), Beatty and Ritter (1986), and Miller and Reilly,1987).

40. See, for instance, Logue (1973), Neuberger and Hammond (1974), Neuberger and LaChapelle (1983), Tinic (1988), Johnson and Miller (1988), and Carter and Manaster (1990).

41. The quality of reporting acocuntants/auditors to an issue may also have a bearing upon the level of initial returns reported in unseasoned stock issues. The arguments of Titman and Trueman (1986) suggest that higher quality auditors reveal information more accurately than lower quality auditors and, accordingly, receive higher fees. Given this, higher quality auditors should be associated with issues with relatively low *ex-ante* uncertainty levels.

42. See Hensler (1990) for a model of this trade-off. Drake and Vetsuypens (1993) have questioned the significance of the litigation cost-capital raising trade-off. They show empirically that US lawsuits are typically initiated by poor longer term price performance rather than by the level of under- or overpricing.

43. See Goulet (1974) and Welch (1989).

44. Evidence of a strong positive relation between initial returns on local IPO stocks and the incidence of subsequent seasoned equity issues is apparent in McGuinness's (1992) study.

45. In particular, Ritter (1991) notes that his results are 'broadly consistent with the notion that many firms go public near the peak of industry specific fads.' (p. 23).

46. This may not correspond exactly to the percentage of equity retained by pre-listing stockholders.

6. Primary Market Activities II: Seasoned Stock Issues

In contrast to unseasoned offerings of stock such as the initial public offering (IPO) featured in the previous chapter, a seasoned stock issue is an offering of new shares by a corporation that, at the time of issue, has an established listing. Seasoned offerings do not usually involve sale (vendor) shares since existing shares can be sold directly by the vendor through the market where a stock is already listed. All that the vendor need do in such circumstances is submit a sale order through a broker.[1]

The huge amounts of funds raised through Hong Kong's equity markets in recent years reflect the popularity of both the IPO and seasoned stock issue. This second type of primary market activity has received comparatively little attention, however, especially when viewed against the copy and airtime devoted to some of the larger IPO flotations. Despite this, seasoned stock issues feature significantly in the local market and raise more funding, in aggregate terms, than their unseasoned counterpart, as is indicated in Table 6.1. Seasoned issue funds generated around two-thirds of all equity funds raised during the 1995–7 period.

Table 6.1 Seasoned Versus Unseasoned Sources of Equity Funding: 1995–1997

Year	Unseasoned Equity Funds (HK$billions) U^*	Seasoned Equity Funds (HK$billions) S^{**}	Total Equity Funds Raised (HK$billions) T	S/T
1995	8.085	31.091	39.176	0.794
1996	31.216	68.802	100.018	0.68
1997	81.653	165.929	247.583	0.670

Source: Data items Collated from SEHK *Fact Book 1997*, p. 67.

Notes: * Unseasoned equity captures offers for public subscription, sale and by placing.
** Seasoned equity funds refer to categories of 'placing', 'rights issues', open offer', consideration issue', 'warrants exercised', and 'share option scheme' (as defined in the Source, see above).

The unseasoned fund total in Table 6.1 includes capital raised from offers for subscription, sale, and placing. Because of the use of vendor shares in the second of these offer methods, and its possible usage in the third, both primary and secondary offers contribute to the unseasoned dollar figures. In other words, the sums raised flow to both vendor and issuing firm, though one might surmise that the latter is far more important than the former. The seasoned issue totals by comparison, capture funds from new share issues only.

Despite the inclusion of vendor funds in the unseasoned funding totals, seasoned fund-raising activity easily dominates the unseasoned variety. This is not too surprising given the platform for equity funding that a listing offers. For the local market, McGuinness (1992, p. 180) notes that for each of the three years following IPOs in Hong Kong, 20–25% of IPO firms returned to the market to make capital-raising seasoned offerings. For the complete three-year period, nearly half of the firms returned to the market. Studies for other markets, like the United States[2] also highlight the relative frequency with which IPO firms return to the primary market.

As seasoned offerings are much easier to assemble, and are cheaper than the IPO, the fund-raising advantages of subsequent seasoned offerings serve to enhance the value of the initial launch. This also explains why firms are prepared to countenance the heavy direct costs of an IPO.

The material in this chapter is divided into four sections. Non capital-raising seasoned issues, like stock splits and stock dividends, are introduced in Section 6.1. Their capital-raising counterparts then feature in Section 6.2. A case study of the most dramatic of seasoned issues—the rights issue—then follows in Section 6.3. Finally, Section 6.4 presents an overview of corporate funding alternatives.

6.1 Non-Capital Raising Seasoned Issues: Stock Dividends (Bonus/Capitalization Issues) and Stock Splits

Definitions and Distinguishing Characteristics

New share issues by seasoned (i.e., already listed) companies do not necessarily raise funds. There are a number of ways in which new shares can be allocated free of charge to existing stockholders, stock dividends and stock splits being the most obvious methods. Both are frequently used in Hong Kong, although stock dividends are described as bonus or capitalization issues locally. Elsewhere, particularly in the United States, the term stock dividend is preferred. For reasons of consistency, this term is used to connote what local practitioners might understand to be a bonus (or capitalization) issue.

While both stock dividends and stock splits trigger an increase in the number of listed shares of companies engaged in such activities, we are repeatedly told that nothing of value is ever created from such distributions. This is attributed to the fact that such shares are 'given' to existing shareholders (in proportion to existing holdings). Before this assertion is examined and, in this chapter, challenged, the subtle distinction between a stock dividend and split should be appreciated. This distinction can be understood by revisiting Section 4.3. In the example, a company RST had 50 million shares in issue (at par $1.00) prior to the announcement of a one-for-one distribution. For either stock dividend or split, we noted that

50 million new shares would be given to existing shareholders on pro rata terms. Despite differences in accounting treatment, we noted that RST's overall equity value should remain unchanged. As a recap, the accounting arrangements lead to the par halving in the split, and the issued share capital account balance remaining unchanged. In the stock dividend, reserves are capitalized with the par unchanged.

Accounting differences apart, stock dividends and splits are essentially the same. Variants of the stock split can also be arranged to reduce, rather than increase, the number of shares outstanding. These are known as consolidations or reverse splits. A consolidation of two shares into one would halve the number of shares outstanding. To maintain the issued share capital at its original level, the par value would need to double.

The Market Reaction to Stock Dividends and Splits

Based upon comments thus far, it is not obvious why firms might countenance stock dividends or splits. Administrative charges alone would suggest some benefit. Why make the changes if they impose non-trivial costs? There must be a benefit to someone. Empirical studies highlight clear benefits to shareholders. Grinblatt, Masulis, and Titman (1984) note in their study of US stock splits and stock dividends that 'on average, there is a significant increase in a firm's stock price at the announcement and that, in general, this upward revision of the firm's value cannot be attributed to any other contemporaneous announcements', (Grinblatt, Masulis, and Titman,1984, p. 488).

Similar market capitalization gains are also reported in many other studies. Klein's overview of seven US-based studies, including Grinblatt et al.'s (see p. 171), provides a convincing story of a strong and positive announcement effect, apparent in both types of distribution. A similarly strong announcement effect for stock dividends (bonus issues) is also evident in Hong Kong. Guo and Keown (1992), from a sample of cash and stock dividend announcements over the 1984–8 period, detect a pronounced announcement effect for both dividend changes (positive and negative) and stock dividends; however, their findings for the latter are limited by the small number of pure stock dividends available to them. Of the 41 stock dividend announcements scrutinized, only 10 were made without contemporaneous dividend announcements. Despite this, the evidence in Guo and Keown is useful in extending US findings.

To illustrate the positive announcement effect, the earlier one-for-one stock distribution in RST is considered further. With stock value of $10 prior to either a stock dividend or split, and 50 million shares in issue, RST's market capitalization stood at $500 million. Since no new funds are raised in either type of distribution, conventional wisdom suggests no change to RST's market capitalization on the announcement of such a distribution. The evidence clearly contradicts this. What we see in practice is illustrated in Figure 6.1. RST's share price would likely rise on the announcement date (or in the run-up to the announcement, due to information leakage or rumour) but remain relatively stable thereafter, leaving aside the technical ex-date adjustment.

The Importance of the Ex-Date

The ex-date normally occurs a few weeks after the distribution's announcement date.

Stock purchased prior to the ex-date carries an entitlement to the pro-rata distribution; whereas stock purchased after it does not.

In Figure 6.1, the gain in market capitalization on the announcement date should be swift and complete. At least this should be the case if the market is efficient. On the subsequent ex-date, the price of each share should adjust downwards by the appropriate correction factor. In a one-for-one distribution, the post-announcement value of the stock should fall by 50%, ensuring that no change in the market capitalization of the stock occurs around the ex-date. In simple terms, a purchase of one RST share just prior to the ex-date would result in the receipt of two (the purchased share plus one bonus share). As Figure 6.1 shows, the cost of this purchase is $10.10. On the ex-date, or beyond, logic dictates that RST's share price should fall to $5.05 as the accompanying bonus share is no longer on offer. This is all very predictable. The ex-date and distribution terms are known at the announcement date.

But for argument's sake, suppose that events do not unfold as the theory suggests. Suppose instead that RST's price fell to $5.15 on the ex-date. If this had happened, an investor would have profited from buying the stock (plus bonus share) just prior to the ex-date at $10.10 and selling both in the ex-period for $10.30 (= 2@$5.15).[3] Had the ex-price fallen too much, the investor would have profited by doing the opposite. If the price had fallen to $4.95, selling one RST stock (and the accompanying bonus share) prior to the ex-date and buying two RST shares thereafter would have generated a $0.20 profit (ignoring transaction costs). These strategies suggest that, at least on average, the kind of ex- adjustment described in Figure 6.1 should prevail.

Grinblatt et al. (1984, p. 488) note, with reference to US stock dividends and splits, that profitable trading strategies are in fact apparent in the post-announcement period. They point to particular gains around the ex-date. This is clearly a departure from market efficiency.

The Rationale for a Positive Announcement Effect for Stock Dividends and Splits

Liquidity Arguments
The positive announcement effect requires some imaginative reasoning if it is to be explained within the framework of the efficient markets paradigm. Liquidity arguments provide one avenue.[4] Assuming the board-lot size of a stock remains unchanged following a stock dividend or split, overall trading volumes might rise due to increased buying pressure from retail investors able to buy at lower cost. In Hong Kong, the typical board-lot

Figure 6.1 Suggested Share Price Performance of a Stock Subject to Either Stock Dividend or Split

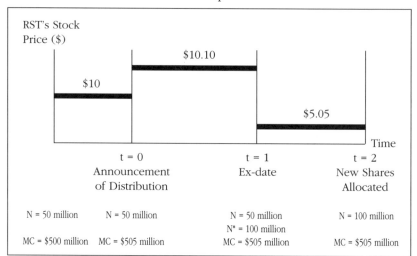

t = 0 – t = 1: Eligible period for Trading with Rights to New Shares (Cum-Distribution Period).
t = 1 – t = 2: Ex-Period.

Notes: Cum-Distribution Period is from the date of distribution announcement (t = 0) to the close of trading on the business day immediately prior to the ex-date. Ex-Period is from the open of trade on the ex-date (t = 1) onwards.

N   The number of shares in issue.
N*   From a pricing perspective, the number of shares in issue is effectively 100 million (despite the fact that the new shares have not yet been distributed).
MC   RST's market capitalization.

size is 1,000 shares. For a share with price $80, this requires, in the absence of more expensive 'odd-lot' trading, an initial investment outlay of at least $80,000. A one-for-one stock dividend or split would approximately halve the share price. If board-lot size remained the same, an increase in demand from small investors would be likely given the reduced cost of one lot of shares (by approximately $40,000). The increased demand could result in the share price rising slightly above the theoretical ex-date value of $40. This would allow an increase in the market capitalization to be explained within the framework of efficient markets.

Evidence for such liquidity increases are elusive, however. Copeland (1972) actually notes a decline in the relative liquidity of US stocks following splits. Murray (1985) provides corroboration of this for US stocks subject to both splits and stock dividends. He also reports a relative decline in liquidity over the longer term (for stocks subject to stock dividends).

There may be a stronger case for liquidity effects in Hong Kong, however. First of all, it is common practice, in all but the largest of distributions, to leave board-lot sizes unchanged. Appendix 6.1 provides anecdotal evidence of this for three splits made in 1996. Only one of these involved a board-lot change. More significant, perhaps, is the relative importance of retail investors to local trading volumes. While markets like the United States are essentially institutionally-based, the SEHK attracts a very significant retail following. This would suggest greater scope for the liquidity effect in stock dividends and splits. Demonstrating this is another matter. Virtually all stock distributions are tied up with cash payments, which mask any mooted price effects in such distributions.

Trading Range and Signalling Arguments

Liquidity arguments have also been used to account for a trading range hypothesis for share prices. Lakonishok and Lev (1987) posit that the preference of small investors for lower prices should be offset against that of the larger investor for higher stock prices. They remark, for stock splits, that 'investors of small means are presumably penalized by high stock prices that deny them the economies of buying stocks in round lots. On the other hand, wealthy investors and institutions will save brokerage costs if securities are priced high because of the fixed per-share transaction cost component'. (Lakonishok and Lev, 1987, pp. 915–16).

The optimal trading range, according to Lakonishok and Lev, results from managers' desire for 'a broad and heterogeneous stockholder base or "wider marketability"' (p. 916). They find, at least for stock splits in the United States, empirical evidence consistent with this. Moreover, the evidence that such distributions are used to rein in share prices suggests, to the casual observer, that high-growth stocks are more likely to be subject to splits. In this sense, stocks splits may act as signals of growth potential.[5]

A signalling theme, where certain kinds of stock distribution convey positive information about future corporate earnings is also evident in Grinblatt et al. (1984). They detect higher post-announcement returns for firms making stock dividends than stock splits. They argue that this finding is consistent with signalling arguments. Specifically, they point to a stock dividend as a costly signal given the capitalization of reserves, which limits 'the firm's ability to pay cash dividends' (p. 464). According to Grinblatt et al., this restriction means that only high quality firms are likely to countenance such costly stock distributions.[6] This point should also be relevant in Common Law jurisdictions, like Hong Kong. Although the legal system in the United States is very different, the issue of defined levels of 'distributable reserves' appears to be a common feature.

Whatever the merits of stock splits and stock dividends, they are overshadowed by fund-raising distributions of stock. Whilst being more expensive to arrange, the latter create an enormous range of corporate investment possibilities for the underlying corporations. Paramount in this, in Hong Kong, is the rights offering.

6.2   Capital-Raising Seasoned Issues: Rights Offerings, Open Offers, Placings, and other Fund-Raising Issues

Rights issues and (private) placings account for around 60% of all seasoned equity funds (see Table 6.2). Particular emphasis is given to the former, which features in larger issues locally.

Table 6.2   Components of Seasoned Equity Funding: 1995–7

Year	Placing (HK$m.)	Rights Issue (HK$m.)	Open Offer (HK$m.)	Consideration Issue (HK$m.)	Warrants Exercised (HK$m.)	Share Option Scheme (HK$m.)
1995	11,510.13	1,289.73	–	9,225.17	8,192.61	873.79
1996	46,111.93	4,653.02	–	10,123.03	5,568.57	2,317.94
1997	78,173.82	16,297.97	213.54	58,859.90	8,327.55	4,056.63
95–7	135,795.88	22,240.72	213.54	78,208.10	22,088.73	7,248.36
Rel.(%)	51.09	8.37	0.08	29.42	8.31	2.73

Source: Data collated from SEHK *Fact Book 1997*, p. 67.

Notes: Unseasoned funds include capital raised under the categories of 'offer for subscription', 'offer for sale' and 'offer for placing'. Seasoned equity funds refer to categories of 'placing', 'rights issues', 'open offer', 'consideration issue', 'warrants exercised', and 'share option scheme'.

Rights Offerings

Rights offerings involve an offer of new shares, at a fixed issue price, to existing stockholders. The number of shares offered to each shareholder is made in proportion to their pre-offer holdings. If an investor holds 20 million shares in a company with 80 million in issue, a one-for-one rights offering would afford he or she the opportunity of acquiring 20 million new shares. If the investor fully exercised the option to buy, he/she could then retain a 25% interest (= 40 million shares/160 million shares) in the company's stock.

Rights issues build upon pre-emptive rights. Essentially, these rights permit stockholders to challenge proposals of stock offerings to third parties.[7] As such, they help to arrest any unwarranted dilution in the percentage holdings of existing shareholders. The terms of such pre-emptive rights normally figure in a company's memorandum and articles of association.

Rights issues are also favoured in the United Kingdom, and other Commonwealth jurisdictions, but are much less popular in the United States. A decline in their use in the United States in recent years now means that such offerings carry considerable novelty value.[8] Where rights still figure, it is of interest to note that both underwritten and non-underwritten forms can be used. In other jurisdictions outside the United States, with Hong Kong being a good example, the non-underwritten rights form is a rarity.[9]

To illustrate the generic features of a rights issue, consider a company with 2,000 million shares in issue. If a one-for-five rights offering has been authorized by the larger body of stockholders, 400 million rights shares will be on offer. This means that every stockholder with five existing shares has an option to buy one new share. The sale proceeds would clearly accrue to the issuing firm. Even if some stockholders choose not to exercise, by either ignoring the invitation to buy or by selling the option(s), all the new shares on offer will be sold at the issue price, given the underwriting commitment. In practice, the burden on the underwriter— who commits to buy unsold shares in the offering at the issue price—is lessened by two factors. Firstly, existing stockholders can apply for excess rights at the time of issue, which allows them to mop up any unexercised rights. Secondly, major stockholders may guarantee the purchase of their pro rata allocation.

Open Offers

Whilst rarely used, the open offer is akin to the rights offering. It differs in one important respect: the options offered to existing shareholders are not transferable. Like the rights offering, though, it involves an offer to existing stockholders to buy new shares. It can also be made on pro rata terms[10]. In an open offer, then, the recipient has only two choices: exercise or ignore the offer to buy. In a rights offering, the recipient can also consider selling the right to a third party. This is normally achieved by way of a sale of the rights (options) through an organized nil-paid rights market. As in a rights offering, existing stockholders can normally apply for excess shares through an open offer.

The greater flexibility attaching to the rights issue probably explains why it enjoys greater popularity. Only two open offers have featured locally in the last five years. This compares with 126 rights offerings over the same period (see Table 6.3).

Placings

In contrast to rights and open offers, placings usually involve the sale of new shares to third parties. Agreements involving existing vendor shares are not unheard of, but are not reflected in the general discussions here or in the data in Tables 6.1–6.3.[11] Suffice it to say, a number of large placings were arranged in 1998 whereby vendors placed (existing) shares with third parties concurrent with an agreement to buy a similar number of new shares in the company. The effect of such arrangements was to maintain the approximate percentage interest of the vendor while allowing an injection of funds into the issuing company. In essence the funds emanate from the placees, the parties receiving the vendor shares. The vendor, as a middleman, uses these funds to finance the new share

Table 6.3   Stock Offerings by Seasoned (already Listed) Companies in
Hong Kong: 1990–1997

| Year | Frequency | | | | Value (HK$million) | | |
| | Rights Issues | Open Offers | Public/ subscription Offers | Total | Funds Raised from Rights | Total Equity Funds Raised | (5)/(6) (%) |
	(1)*	(2)*	(3)*	(4)*	(5)@	(6)@	
1990	13	1	0	14	2,511.12	18,637.92	13.47
1991	12	5	0	17	9,535.43	37,104.12	25.70
1992	23	6	0	29	9,933.13	101,191.61	9.82
1993	23	0	0	23	9,266.07	89,106.80	10.40
1994	19	0	0	19	5,643.12	51,640.16	10.93
1995	9	0	1	10	1,289.73	39,176.30	3.29
1996	22	0	0	22	4,653.02	100,018.25	4.65
1997	48	2	1	51	16,297.97	247,583.03	6.58

Source and notes:
* *Fact Book* ((1990, pp. 76–7); (1991, pp. 80–1); (1992, pp. 81–2); (1993, pp. 81–2); (1994, p. 76); (1995, p. 32); (1996, pp. 51–2); and (1997; pp. 60–1).
@ *Fact Book* (1990, p. 81); (1991, p. 85); (1992, p. 86); and (1997, p. 67).
(6) includes seasoned and unseasoned sums (see Table 6.1, Col. T).
Placings are excluded from the above data.

purchase. In such circumstances, dilution effects are only evident for minority stakeholders (or more precisely parties independent of the vendor). Such arrangements can involve large blocks of stock.

In general terms, placings involve a relatively small number of shares but, unlike the rights offering, occur with considerable frequency.[12] The 222 placings[13] recorded in 1997 bear this out. With over 600 stocks listed at the 1997 year-end, this suggests, even with some companies making more than one placing during the year, that roughly one in three listed companies sought funds through placing.

The size characteristic of the placing is partly a reflection of pre-emptive rights given that, potentially, existing stakeholders are capable of striking out very large placing proposals simply because of unwarranted dilution effects. In general terms, then, the dilution effects engendered by placing may not be that significant on average.[14] Nonetheless, their incidence rate means that huge sums are raised by established companies. Over 51% of all seasoned issue funds, and over 38% of all equity funds raised, over the 1995–7 period (see Tables 6.1 and 6.2) were raised through such means.

The popularity of the placing largely stems from its cost advantage. Despite such issues often being relatively small, and potential economies with regard to fixed costs lost, there are often substantial savings on underwriting costs.[15] In general, underwriting commissions run to around 2% of the gross proceeds raised in rights offerings. Reference to a typical rights offering, like the Styland offering of October 1995, featured in Section 6.3, reveals that expenses absorb around 5.5% of gross funds raised.[16] While such costs are considerably lower than in an IPO, they are noticeably higher than those in a typical placing.

Funding through Warrant and Employee Stock Option Exercise and Consideration Issues

Substantial amounts of seasoned equity funding are also generated from the exercise of equity warrants (over 8%) and from consideration issues (over 29%). Equity warrants, which are discussed in detail in Chapter 10, are similar to traded call options. Both the equity warrant and call option holders have options to buy the underlying stock of the issuer at a fixed exercise price over some defined time interval. The essential difference between the two is that when an exercise notice is served on the issuer, the writer of the equity warrant is forced to issue new shares. Writers of call options, in contrast, sell stock from their existing holdings. The sums in Table 6.2, for equity warrants, reflect the amounts raised from the conversion of equity warrants into underlying shares. Similarly, a separate item for funds raised from new share issues, arising from the conversion of employee stock options into shares, is reflected under the category of 'share option scheme'. Given their exercise characteristics, employee stock *options* are closer to equity warrants than traded call options.[17]

The consideration issue, mentioned above, is defined in the *Rules Governing The Listing of Securities on The Stock Exchange of Hong Kong Ltd*, as follows 'an issue of securities as consideration in a transaction or in connection with a takeover or merger or the division of an issuer' (Rule 7.30, 7-8, 10/95). In this sense, funds may not necessarily emerge from such issues. Instead, assets are likely to be acquired in return for the new shares. The consideration issue is therefore rather different to the fund-raising mechanisms in the foregoing.

In sum, (private) placings are the vehicle through which the bulk of seasoned equity funding is generated. Rights issues lag some way behind but, as noted at the outset, always generate substantial amounts of funding for the companies that use them. They also attract considerable attention given their potential to effect changes in overall market sentiment. This is particularly apparent when larger blue-chip companies launch such issues. For this and other reasons, the rights offering deserves special attention. To shed light on its actual construction, a case study of a typical issue is provided below.

6.3 A Case Study of a Rights Issue[18]

The *Styland Holdings Ltd* rights issue of October 1995 was chosen for the purpose of a case study, although any of several candidates could have been used here. The basic issue details of Styland's one-for-one offering, where one new rights share was offered for every existing stock held, were gleaned from the its Rights Issue Document (27 October 1995), and are summarized below in Exhibit 6.1.

Exhibit 6.1   Key Statistics and Dates in the Styland Hldgs Ltd Oct. 1995 Rights Offering

Issue price	= HK$0.118;	Rights Issue Announcement[19]	26/9/1995
No. of new shares	= 450,857,700;	Ex-rights date	19/10/1995
No. of shares		Record date	27/10/1995
prior to issue	= 450,857,700.	Trading in nil-paid rights	31/10–10/11/1995
		Closing date for acceptance of rights	15/11/1995

Source: Various pages, Styland Holding's Ltd Rights Issue document, 27 October 1995.

Key Dates in a Rights Offering: the Ex-Date, Cum-Rights Period, Ex-Rights Period and the Period for Trading in Nil-Paid Rights

Apart from the announcement date in a rights offering, the most important date to bear in mind is the ex-rights date. This date divides the rights issue into two distinctive periods: the on-rights (or cum-rights) period and the ex-rights period. The on-rights period runs from the rights announcement to the close of trade on the day immediately prior to the ex-rights date. The ex-rights period follows between the ex-date and the closing date in the issue. The ex-date itself indicates the date on which the underlying share sells without entitlement to the rights (options). The record date occurs some days after this ex-date. This is the date from which the company's share registrar commits to establish a record of all those eligible for rights. This also signifies the time from which notices and application forms are likely to be despatched.

In the case of the Styland issue, anyone wanting to participate in the rights issue would have needed to have acquired shares in the company prior to the ex-date, unless attaching rights were acquired separately. Purchasing 1,000 shares in Styland prior to the ex-date of 19 October 1995 would have allowed the buyer the option to buy 1,000 new (rights) shares. This would have to be achieved at the issue price of $0.118 per share and prior to the close in applications.

Anecdotal evidence suggests that the overall period of a rights issue, as measured from rights announcement date to the closing date for acceptances, is around two months in Hong Kong. The Styland case, as indicated in Exhibit 6.1, was characterized by cum-rights and ex-rights periods of approximately four weeks each.

Another key sub-period also exists within the ex-rights period: the period for trading in nil-paid rights. This is an organized market for trading in the options attaching to shares that were acquired prior to the ex-rights date. Basically, it gives investors who want to opt out of the issue, an opportunity to sell their rights. It also enables those without attaching rights an opportunity to acquire them. The workings of this market are taken up in much greater detail later in this section.

Figure 6.2 provides a diagrammatic summary of the various periods and dates that make up a rights issue.

Figure 6.2   Key Dates in the Life of a Rights Offering

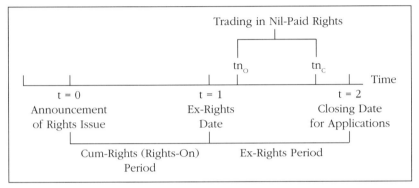

Notes: Cum-Rights period is defined from the announcement date (t = 0) to the close of trade on the business day immediately prior to the ex-date; Ex-Rights period is defined from the open of trade on the ex-rights date (t = 1) to the closing time for submitting applications; tn_O refers to the opening of the organized trading in nil-paid rights market; and tn_C the closing date for trading in nil-paid rights.

The Timing of Rights Share Applications

There is, in fact, little advantage to submitting applications well in advance of the closing date. All applicants, whatever the timing of their submission, receive new shares at the same time. This occurs some days after the closing date.[20] There are also compelling economic reasons for delaying one's submission. The opportunity cost of locking up funds in an application is the most obvious one, given that interest earned on such monies typically accrues to the issuing company (not the investor).[21]

Another reason is the risk of a drop in the value of the underlying below the issue price. To minimize this risk, the more sensible investor will wait until the last feasible date before considering submission. Such an investor would avoid exercise if the stock's price dropped to, for example, HK$0.11 just prior to the closing date. To do otherwise, would mean buying new stock (through the rights) at a premium to secondary market values. Excepting those investors that had expressed an earlier commitment to buy new rights shares, come what may, this course of action would only appeal to the most naive of investors. Where the underlying share's value is appreciably above the issue price, it is safe to assume that most holders of rights will exercise. There is still some risk, though, as the value of the underlying could fall during the ensuing settlement period.

In general terms, then, it is prudent to submit applications for rights shares as close to the expiry date as possible. Nonetheless, major stockholders, particularly those who have undertaken to take up their allowable allocation, may submit applications at the first opportunity. For them, there is less of an advantage in delaying, although interest foregone on monies lodged still makes early submission somewhat irrational. Whatever the timing of the submissions, full subscription is achieved if there are sufficient applications to absorb all shares on offer. Failure to achieve this, leads, as noted earlier, to the underwriter buying all unsold shares at the agreed offer price.

What happened in the Styland case? Reference to closing price data for Styland's stock in Appendix 6.2, for the period encompassing the rights offering, indicates that its price was well above the issue price at the close. Not surprisingly, this led to healthy subscription for the rights shares. Only 5.2 million of around 451 million rights shares on offer were 'left on the table'. Applications for these shares through 'excess rights' easily took care of this residual amount. A massive oversubscription rate of 71.3 times was evident for these shares.[22]

The Relation between Issue Size and the Issuing Discount

As the foregoing indicates, new shares in rights offerings are typically sold at substantial discounts to prevailing market prices. This discount is strongly related to the size of the offering and the level of the issue price itself. To understand this, let us compare actual ex-rights prices to pre-announcement prices in the Styland offering. With a formal announcement date of 26 September 1995, the last available pre-announcement closing price was HK$0.375 (see Appendix 6.2). Let us compare this with the first ex-rights price of HK$0.250.[23] Would investors purchasing stock in the pre-announcement period have lost out by holding their position until the ex-rights date? In a fair market, they should not have. Notice that investors holding stock until the ex-rights period will be entitled to one extra share at an issue price of HK$0.118. This means that they have access to two shares from the ex-rights date. The cost of acquiring the original share in the pre-announcement period (HK$0.375) plus the cost of acquiring the new share (HK$0.118), through the attaching right, was HK$0.493. Given a fair market, this should be approximately equal to the cost of generating the same investment holding at the ex-rights date (= 2@HK$0.250). As the Styland case shows, the ex-rights price adjustment leaves the investor in much the same position, as theory suggests it should.

The Ex-Rights Adjustment

Further exploration of the ex-rights adjustment demonstrates that as shares sell without attaching rights on this date, their value should fall, at the open of trade on the ex-rights date, by the value of the underlying right attaching to each share. In the Styland case, the share value fell by HK$0.14, as it changed from on-rights to ex-rights status (see below).

Last Cum-rights price = HK$0.390; First Ex-rights price = HK$0.250.
Value of rights attaching to one share = HK$0.390 – HK$0.250 = HK$0.14

Based upon this, the value of the option (i.e., right) to buy one rights share, as of the ex-date, was HK$0.14. Fair market pricing in a one-for-one offering would require that the cost of acquiring one share at the last on-rights price, plus the cost of converting the associated right on the share, equal the cost of purchasing two shares at the first ex-rights price. Let R be the last on-rights price and I the issue price. A fair market price for the stock at the ex-rights date (X_F), would then be determined as follows,

$$R + I = 2 \times X_F$$
$$X_F = (R + I)/2 = (0.390 + 0.118)/2 = HK\$0.254$$

As noted, the first ex-rights price, using the opening trade in Styland on the ex-rights date, was HK$0.25. This is very close to the theoretical prediction, based upon the last on-rights price.[24] The stable market conditions in Hong Kong between the close of trading on 18 October and its resumption on the following day, are key in ensuring this (see Appendix 6.2).[25] A large shift in the market overnight would obscure the adjustment. It could still be deciphered, however, after making necessary adjustments for the market change.

The Trading of Nil-Paid Rights

For anyone holding options to buy new shares, three possibilities emerge: convert the options into shares at any time prior to and including the closing date; sell the options prior to the closing date; or simply let them lapse. The second course of action can be pursued through the nil-paid rights market. This, as we saw earlier, opens in the ex-rights period. With most rights issues in Hong Kong, this market lasts for at least one week and opens some days after the record date in an offering. In the case of Styland, it was recognized by the parallel listing on the SEHK of Styland's shares and nil-paid rights. The latter listing, as is always true of nil-paid rights, was somewhat ephemeral. It lasted for only eight trading days, between 31 October and 10 November 1995.

Data for trades in Styland's listed nil-paid rights are shown in Table 6.4. The prices capture the value of an option to buy one new Styland stock where the option is exercisable up to and including 15 November 1995.

To get a closer picture of nil-paid right values, and their relation to underlying stock values, let us consider the closing price for Styland's nil-paid rights of HK$0.106, as of 31 October 1995. Given a corresponding value for the underlying stock of HK$0.239, the intrinsic value of the option appears to be HK$0.121 (= HK$(0.239 – 0.118)). Chapters 10 and 11 will show that the 'golden rule' of option pricing is that an option's

Table 6.4 Data for Styland's Nil-Paid Rights

Date	Closing Price of Nil-Paid Rights	Trading Volume (No. Rights)	Closing Price of Styland Stock	Trading Volume (No. Shares)	Closing HSI
31/10/95	0.106	32,756,000	0.239	1,302,000	9,782.39
02/11/95	0.105	8,450,500	0.235	3,683,000	9,749.36
03/11/95	0.121	8,768,000	0.260	3,184,000	9,855.80
06/11/95	0.110	14,819,000	0.240	9,014,000	9,736.10
07/11/95	0.113	5,726,000	0.242	2,584,000	9,732.41
08/11/95	0.112	3,893,500	0.236	702,500	9,562.45
09/11/95	0.115	4,075,000	0.240	1,236,000	9,497.83
10/11/95	0.142	5,297,500	0.265	8,842,000	9,411.85

Source: Stock Exchange of Hong Kong Daily Quotation Sheets (31/10/95–10/11/95). Extracted from McGuinness (1997b, p. 13).

value (premium) should, at least in the absence of transaction costs, cover its intrinsic value. This intrinsic value reflects the differential between the secondary-market value of the stock and the cost of acquiring the stock through the option (the nil-paid right in this case). The fact that the premium of HK$0.106 lies well below the intrinsic value suggests, at first sight, a violation of basic option pricing principles. If this is so, arbitrage (riskless profit) opportunities should be evident.

Based upon the data, this could be achieved by the following triple-assault: simultaneously short the underlying stock and acquire the nil-paid right. Then exercise the nil-paid right. As there is a notable delay in the settlement of such exercises, borrowing arrangements for the short position would be needed for a period of two to three weeks (i.e., from the date of the trade to about one week after the closing date in the rights issue). Upon receipt of the new rights share, the stock lender could then be repaid, thus extinguishing the short stock position. Ignoring the transaction costs involved, this would suggest a gain of HK$0.015 (per share involved) from the arbitrage strategy. This is around 15% of the premium on the nil-paid right. Even with transaction costs, then, substantial profits are suggested if such an arbitrage trade is possible. There are good reasons to suggest that it is not. Substantial arbitrage profit opportunities would be quickly and gleefully seized if available. This is precisely why such arbitrage profits rarely exist. Pressures exerted, by buying options and selling stock in this case, would easily squeeze any negative differential between option premium and intrinsic value levels.

The arbitrage gain in the example is therefore illusory. Why is this? One reason could be due to the use of closing prices. One cannot trade on closing prices: the market is closed. Put more simply, prices may adjust by the following market open to wipe out potential gains. This is possible. The principal impediment to arbitrage in this case is the restriction on short-sales which applied to the stock in question at the time of the example.[26] This is also the reason why, on other trading days in the nil-paid right in the example (see Table 6.4), similar illusory arbitrage gains appear to obtain. The removal of short-sale restrictions in recent years has probably resulted in the elimination of the kinds of pricing gaps discussed here. It would certainly be difficult to explain their persistence without short-sale restrictions.

All that is offered in this subsection is an insight into the essential pricing of nil-paid rights. Formal valuation models can also be applied.[27] For reasons of brevity they are not considered here.

The Announcement Effect in Rights Issues

Two critical dates are apparent in a rights offering: the announcement date and the ex-date. The latter has been discussed at some length. Assuming efficient market pricing, the pricing adjustment is relatively straightforward. In summarizing the likely pricing effects, the first ex-rights price in an offering will be larger (or smaller) given (i) a higher (or lower) issue price; and (ii) a smaller (or larger) percentage increase in the number of shares outstanding. Because of the apparent predictability of the ex-rights adjustment, greater interest typically centres on the announcement effect of a rights offering, although the assumption of efficient market pricing around the ex-rights date is open to some dispute. Goyal, Hwang, Jayaranan, and Shastri (1994), for rights issues in Japan, cite evidence of positive abnormal returns around such dates. As a backdrop to this, Goyal et al. (p. 278) provide a review of the extant evidence on the issue. This principally revolves around studies in the United States and the United Kingdom. The international evidence they cite suggests either insignificant or negative price effects around ex-dates.

The price reaction of the underlying stock to the announcement of a rights offering is far less obvious. The existence of price-pressure effects, engendered by an anticipated increase in the supply of shares,[28] is viewed as a critical issue. Investors take this supply effect into account at the announcement date, rather than the date when the shares are allotted. This is so because the supply effect can be easily predicted (given the commitment of the underwriter).[29] If price-pressure exists, investors will factor in the shift in the supply curve at the announcement date. Assuming no corresponding shift in demand, a negative price reaction should result. This, of course, is predicated on a downward sloping demand curve for the issuing company's stock.

Major studies by Scholes (1972) and Shleifer (1986) provide conflicting findings on the importance of price-pressure. The earlier of the two studies finds support for a 'substitution' hypothesis, which is consistent with a highly elastic or flat demand schedule. A rightward shift in supply (corresponding to an increase in the number of shares in issue) suggests little or no effect on share price, given such a demand curve. Shleifer's analysis, in contrast, suggests some degree of inelasticity in the demand schedules for corporate stock, and therefore scope for price-pressure.

The issue of a price-pressure effect in a rights offering is further complicated by the possibility of a contemporaneous shift in demand. This is the information effect. As a consequence, both (the anticipated) supply and demand curves for a company's stock may shift at the time of a new issue announcement. Trying to disentangle such price-pressure and information effects is perplexing to say the least. The empirical evidence at least allows some insight into the net effect of rights issue announcements. Unfortunately, the evidence on the price impact of rights issue announcements is not clear-cut, even within particular markets like the United States. Findings seem to vary as much by data period as they do by jurisdiction of trading.

Marsh (1979), on UK rights offerings, for instance, detects some evidence of positive abnormal returns surrounding the actual announcement dates in rights offerings. In contrast, studies like White and Lusztig (1980), on US offerings, suggest significant declines. Whilst a host of other studies can be cited, reference to Tsangarakis's (1996, pp. 21–2) thorough review of rights announcement effects is most expedient. In short, he reports rather 'mixed' findings. Evidence for Hong Kong is rather limited and appears somewhat piecemeal. Lau (1992), for an albeit small sample of 31 randomly selected rights issues, issued between 1980 and 1992, offers some insights. He notes that, in the majority of cases, announcements impact negatively upon stock values.

Most anecdotal accounts for rights offerings in Hong Kong also suggest a negative effect. Media reports habitually refer to the risk of large rights offerings. Teasing out reasons for the dampening effect of such announcements is more difficult. One possibility is a kind of knee-jerk response where stockholders with non-trivial blocks of shares, but with little influence over the issuing company, sell off existing holdings. 'Why should I have to buy new stock simply to maintain my existing percentage holding?' may be the tart reply to the curious onlooker. Rumour of an impending rights issue might also precipitate this effect. This may account for the price declines in some rights issues prior to their formal announcement.

Rights issues may also drain market liquidity by forcing capital to be diverted from investment in the overall market. This has more credence in larger offerings where a tremor-like effect, emanating from the rights issue company, may spread across the whole market. Theoretical models, like Myers and Majluf's (1984), may also be pertinent in explaining a negative announcement effect. They point to an information asymmetry between insider-managers and potential investors that create conditions for issuing firms to overprice stock issues. This could simply be a matter of market-timing with issuers picking peaks in the market to issue. Seasoned issues may also signal cash flow or liquidity weakness in underlying firms.

In contrast to these negative views, positive sentiment could also be generated from a rights issue. This is most likely where investors believe that new investments, derived from the funds raised, will enhance corporate returns. Equally, debt repayment plans may be made possible by rights issues. If the move is seen as a way of staving off a liquidity crisis, this may also impact positively upon sentiment; however, perception is always the key. If investors interpret such a move as a desperation measure, or an indication that the assets of the issuing company are worth less in disposable-value terms than previously thought, they will run for cover.

6.4   Overview of Local Firms Funding Preferences

Considerable attention has been devoted to the structure and dynamics of seasoned issue markets in this chapter. It should be stressed that seasoned issues in Hong Kong, through mechanisms like placings, rights offerings, and consideration issues, account for the lion's share of equity funding in Hong Kong. While pride of place is often given to the IPO, it is worth remembering that for every dollar of funding raised from the unseasoned market, more than $2 are raised in the seasoned issue arena. The activity rates in the seasoned equity arena highlight the reason why so many firms seek listing in the first place: to tap into a liquid pool of potential funding.

Once on the market, though, it is important to ask whether firms prefer the seasoned equity route to other funding routes. A glut of evidence elsewhere suggests that listed corporations have an overwhelming desire for internal funding sources. These sources essentially derive from the working capital of an organization. This can be defined as the balance of current assets over current liabilities. Where a noticeable surfeit exists, corporate managers are likely to draw on these funds before considering any approach to the external debt or equity markets. In many ways this is obvious. The transaction costs involved in issuing new debt or equity are a deterring factor. So are the control issues. Equity issues may result in a dilution of ownership control for major shareholders. In the case of debt, the introduction of a new group of constituents may result in certain constraints.

Is There a 'Pecking Order' of Financing?

The problem for most organizations is that working capital levels are often insufficient to fund substantial real/physical investments. In other words, there comes a point when external funding, either through the capital markets or banks, becomes essential. The evidence in the United States and most other major markets is that debt financing is ferreted out first, before any approach to the equity market is even contemplated. This is, in essence, a pecking order of financing (see Myers, 1984). Firms essentially express a preference for internal financing over debt and for debt over equity. Is this true of the typical corporation in Hong Kong? It may not be. One simple reason is the state of local corporate debt markets which, from our discussions in Section 1.5, may not be that liquid. This clearly limits the scope for primary market activity. Can this be made up by the banks? To some degree it can, although local banks have a reputation for being notoriously selective in channelling funds. This is one of the reasons why they are so healthy. In short, debt financing is not the easiest of options.

A Survey of Chief Executive Officers in local corporations by Kester and Chang (1994) also suggests a preference for seasoned equity over debt financing. In fairness, the sample of opinion surveyed was on the small side, and not that meaningful (statistically). Despite these limitations, the findings are consistent with certain 'facts'. One is that capital structure levels are skewed against debt in local corporations (relative to the levels that might obtain in the typical Western corporation). While now dated, Ip and Hopewell's 1987 analysis of locally-listed firms over the 1970–84 period bears this out. They noted that the mean book-value ratio of long-term liabilities to total assets was only around 8% by the close of their sample period. While this ratio has probably risen somewhat since 1984, it probably still falls some way short of typical levels recorded in the West.[30] Reasons for this are not clear, although the immaturity of local debt markets may be one. Cultural factors may be another. All in all, the picture of financing choices in Hong Kong, and, perhaps, many other parts of Asia, is hardly the mirror image of that in the United States, the United Kingdom and other major Western economies. As a result, equity markets seem to take on a larger role in Asia. This is certainly borne out by the evidence in this chapter and the previous one. The scale of activity in the local equity arena is even more impressive when compared to the size of the market.

Appendix 6.1 Board-Lot Size Adjustments Surrounding Stock Splits: Details for Listed Stocks on the SEHK in 1996

Stock	Board-lot size prior to split	Board-lot size after split
Dah Hwa International Holdings Ltd	2,000	2,000
Distribution details: Split of 1 into 2 (effected on 18/01/96); and interim dividend (ex-date: 29/12/95)		
The Hong Kong Building & Loan Agency Ltd	200	1,000
Distribution details: Split of 1 into 5 and bonus issue of 2 for 1 (effected on 26/06/96); and final dividend (ex-date:13/06/96)		
Triplenic Holdings	2,000	2,000
Distribution details: Split of 1 into 8 (effected on 01/08/96)		

Source: Stocks splitting par values were identified from the SEHK *Fact Book 1996*, p. 49 under the category of 'share subdivisions and share consolidations'. Board-lot sizes were confirmed from various issues of the *Trading Record* of *The Securities Journal* (published by the SEHK). Details of stock and dividend distributions accompanying the stocks splits were drawn from the *January Trading Record 1997* of *The Securities Journal* (March 1997, pp. 28–9; pp. 40–1; and pp. 78–9).

Appendix 6.2 Data for Styland Holdings Ltd's 1995 Rights Issue

Obs	Date	Day	Closing HSI	Closing Price	Trading Volume	Trading in nil-paid Rgts	
01	15//09/95	Fri	9,797.40	0.395	10,380,000	n	
02	18/09/95	Mon	9,770.05	0.405	5,992,000	n	
03	19/09/95	Tue	9,646.14	0.395	8,436,000	n	
04	20/09/95	Wed	9,630.96	0.360	13,262,000	n	
05	21/09/95	Thu	9,536.27	0.375	6,536,000	n	
06	22/09/95	Fri	9,541.87	Tr.s	Tr.s	n	
07	25/09/95	Mon	9,497.88	0.375	18,580,000	n	
08	26/09/95	Tue	9,583.34	Tr.s	Tr.s	n	Announcement
09	27/09/95	Wed	9,650.56	0.270	25,510,000	n	
10	28/09/95	Thu	9,600.56	0.280	9,850,000	n	
11	29/09/95	Fri	9,646.34	0.285	7,113,000	n	
12	2/10/95	Mon	9,724.98	0.295	4,698,000	n	
13	3/10/95	Tue	9,805.46	0.300	2,360,000	n	
14	4/10/95	Wed	9,939.95	0.290	2,198,000	n	
15	5/10/95	Thu	9,888.04	0.295	6,646,000	n	
16	6/10/95	Fri	9,873.90	0.300	3,370,000	n	
17	9/10/95	Mon	9,863.44	0.290	1,719,000	n	
18	10/10/95	Tue	9,730.92	0.280	2,004,000	n	
19	11/10/95	Wed	9,635.06	0.280	13,055,000	n	
20	12/10/95	Thu	9,685.14	0.290	9,016,000	n	
21	13/10/95	Fri	9,883.78	0.300	3,893,500	n	
22	16/10/95	Mon	10,009.28	0.330	2,954,000	n	
23	17/10/95	Tue	10,032.93	0.330	11,608,000	n	
24	18/10/95	Wed	9,973.70	0.390	18,854,000	n	
25	19/10/95	Thu	9,981.61	0.270Xr	20,932,000	n	Ex-Rights
26	20/10/95	Fri	9,895.24	0.265Xr	10,818,000	n	
27	23/10/95	Mon	9,880.53	0.265Xr	16,757,500	n	
28	24/10/95	Tue	9,775.66	0.270Xr	7,906,000	n	
29	25/10/95	Wed	9,841.06	0.260Xr	2,624,000	n	
30	26/10/95	Thu	9,774.48	0.260Xr	1,240,000	n	
31	27/10/95	Fri	9,680.75	0.250Xr	1,423,000	n	
32	30/10/95	Mon	9,672.39	0.255	3,282,000	n	
33	31/10/95	Tue	9,782.39	0.239	1,302,000	t	
34	2/11/95	Thu	9,749.36	0.235	3,683,000	t	
35	3/11/95	Fri	9,855.80	0.260	3,184,000	t	
36	6/11/95	Mon	9,736.10	0.240	9,014,000	t	
37	7/11/95	Tue	9,732.41	0.242	2,584,000	t	
38	8/11/95	Wed	9,562.45	0.236	702,500	t	
39	9/11/95	Thu	9,497.83	0.240	1,236,000	t	
40	10/11/95	Fri	9,411.85	0.265	8,842,000	t	
41	13/11/95	Mon	9,385.22	0.255	2,495,000	n	
41	14/11/95	Tue	9,407.37	0.255	1,506,000	n	
43	15/11/95	Wed	9,431.38	0.255	1,392,000	n	Close
44	16/11/95	Thu	9,367.65	0.250	2,030,000	n	
45	17/11/95	Fri	9,287.90	0.260	780,000	n	

Source: Stock Exchange of Hong Kong Daily Quotation Sheets (15/09/95-17/11/95, inclusive).

Notes: Xa indicates ex adjustment, i.e., when stock goes ex-rights; Tr.s indicates trading suspended in the stock; n indicates no trading in nil-paid rights; and t indicates trading in nil- paid rights. Wednesday 1 Nov 1995 was a holiday on the Exchange.

Notes

1.   Issues of market order would also need to be considered. Selling large blocks of existing stock might destabilize the markets. Sales would also need to meet the requirements of the *Securities (Disclosure of Interests) Ordinance*, Cap. 396.
2.   See, for instance, Goulet (1974) and Welch (1989).
3.   As the bonus share is not distributed immediately, the investor would need to short the bonus stock for a few days (i.e., borrow the stock). This would add some costs to the strategy.
4.   See Copeland (1972, p. 115–16) for a thorough review of the various arguments offered for such a liquidity effect. For reasons of brevity, these are not explored in detail here.
5.   Lakonishok and Lev (1997) allude to this, and note: 'splitting firms exhibited a somewhat higher growth in earnings and especially in dividends than control firms, after the announcement' (page 931).
6.   Moreover, Grinblatt et al. (1984) note: 'firms that expect poor earnings in the future will expect the restrictions to be binding, making it costly to mimic the signals of higher-valued firms.' (p. 464).
7.   Among ordinary resolutions included in the AGMs of Hong Kong listed companies, one often sees a resolution soliciting shareholder support for a general mandate to issue new shares through means other than a rights issue. Typically the mandate allows for an increase in a company's nominal share capital of up to 20% (within a given period—normally around 12 months).
8.   In particular, see Hansen's (1989) account of the 'Demise of the Rights Issue'.
9.   See Rule 7.19(1), 7-3, 10/95 of the *Rules Governing The Listing of Securities On The Stock Exchange of Hong Kong Ltd*, which, inter alia, states: 'In normal circumstances, all rights issues must be fully underwritten.'
10.   For further details of the rights and open offers, see *Fact Book* (1995, p. 21).
11.   The figure of HK$78.173 billion for funds raised via placing in 1997 on the SEHK stems from 222 placings of new shares (see *Fact Book 1997*, pp. 62–6 for a list of such placings).
12.   Readers interested in the guidelines relating to placings in Hong Kong should consult the *Rules Governing The Listing of Securities On The Stock Exchange of Hong Kong Ltd* (especially Rules 7.09-7.12 (7-2 and 7-3, 12/89/10/95) and Appendix 6 of these *Listing Rules*).
13.   Ibid.
14.   Bearing in mind approval of a general mandate to issue new shares of up to 20% of the nominal amount currently outstanding (see Note 7), sizeable dilution of incumbent shareholdings is possible.
15.   One often sees a 'book-building' process in a placing. As we saw in Chapter 5 for IPOs, this tends to lower underwriting risk. As a consequence, underwriting commissions on placings are often markedly lower than on rights issues (see Evans (1999) for discussion of this point in relation to a recent local placing).

16. The Styland Holdings Ltd Rights Issue Prospectus (27 October 1995, p. 34) indicates estimated expenses of HK$2.9 million, relative to gross issue proceeds of approximately HK$53.2 million.

17. Sums raised from the initial sale of equity warrants are not reflected in Table 6.2. Likewise, all other security issues, such as debt and investment fund issues, are excluded from the figures.

18. Much of the discussion in this section of the chapter is built around, and extends, discussions in McGuinness (1997b).

19. See Styland Holdings' Rights issue document (27 October 1995, p. 3) for reference to the directors' announcement of the issue.

20. According to the *Styland Rights Issue Prospectus*, the despatch date for the new scrip was some days after the closing date which would probably have meant a waiting period, from the closing date, of around one week.

21. This is reflected in Styland's issue document where, amongst other things, it states that, 'All cheques will be presented for payment following receipt and all interest earned on such monies will be retained for the benefit of the Company.' (Ibid., p. 9).

22. See the *South China Morning Post, Business Post*, 21 November 1997, p. 2.

23. Details of the opening price, as defined at 10.00am. for the Exchange, were not available. Instead, the price of the first disclosed trade on the ex-rights date of HK$0.25 (see *The Stock Exchange of Hong Kong Daily Quotation Sheets* for 19 October 1995, p. 13) was used.

24. The value of the right attaching to a share can be shown to be equal to $(R - I)/(N + 1)$. For the case under review, the right's value = $(0.390 - 0.118)/2$ = HK$0.136. The actual value, as discussed, was HK$0.14. Theory and practice accord very closely.

25. The Hang Seng Index (HSI) moved by only 23 points (+0.23%) during the intervening overnight period. Opening HSI values were gleaned from real-time, minute-by-minute HSI data for October 1995 provided by Hang Seng Index Services Ltd. The opening value, in this context, reflects the HSI value at 10:01 a.m. (the SEHK's official open is 10:00 a.m.).

26. Enquiries with the SEHK indicate that Styland stock was not eligible for short-selling during 1995.

27. See Bae and Levy (1994), for example.

28. See Scholes (1972) for detailed discussion of this effect.

29. In a strict sense, *force majeure* clauses suggest a small risk of a rights issue being withdrawn.

30. The ratio was, as Ip and Hopewell (1987) point out, already on a rising trend during the data period scrutinized.

7. Dual-Listings, London Trading of Hong Kong Stocks, and American Depositary Receipts (ADRs) in Hong Kong/Mainland PRC Stocks

Some stocks listed on the Stock Exchange of Hong Kong (SEHK) now also trade in other markets.[1] This development is a rather recent one and is in keeping with the globalization and integration of stock trading systems. It also underlines the 'internationalization' of Hong Kong stocks. This process has taken a number of forms: ranging from additional listings of Hong Kong stocks in overseas markets to simple quotations of the stocks on overseas trading systems. The latter development has been particularly important, largely as a result of the interest shown in Hong Kong stocks that trade in London's SEAQ (Stock Exchange Automated Quotation) International system. A recent study commissioned by the Securities and Futures Commission indicates that, in relation to 18 actively traded Hong Kong stocks in London, London volumes have been creeping slowly upwards since the early 1990s. As of the middle of the decade, they were at levels equivalent to over 30% of the stocks' local volumes.[2] The message is clear: London is taking a larger slice of the action than hitherto. The good news for the SEHK, however, as concluded in the same report, is that London's increased volumes have not impacted adversely on absolute volumes in Hong Kong. If anything, the opposite holds. Reference to the spiralling local volumes of the 1990s, reported earlier in Table 1.2, more than supports this.

There is another reason for the SEHK's primacy over Hong Kong stock trading: the local exchange provides both a primary and secondary market for the stocks. In contrast, most stocks traded on SEAQ International do not have recourse to capital-raising facilities in the London market. As most of them are not listed on the official board in London, new equity must be raised in other markets—principally the home market, Hong Kong—where listing exists.

In short, the growing international interest in Hong Kong stock trading does not seem to have undermined the SEHK's hegemony in the trading of Hong Kong stocks. Rather, it reflects positively on investors' appetite for local counters. The China factor has also been important. Stocks with direct links to the Mainland, like the 'H' share and red-chip, or with non-Mainland ownership but clearly defined asset exposure to China, have attracted the gaze of international investors for much of the 1990s. In fairness, this attraction has ebbed and flowed somewhat, the 1998 lull in trading being a retreat from the ebullience of the 1996–7 period. The 1994–5 period also marked a more subdued period of international trading, in the wake of China's Austerity Programme. This followed the booming 1991–4 period when trading in 'B' shares (in Shenzhen and Shanghai) and 'H' shares began. It also marked the rise of the red-chip and the real emergence of London as a trading centre for Hong Kong listed counters.

As well as Hong Kong stock trading, either through overseas listings or quotations on international trading systems, a number of Hong Kong (and Mainland China) stocks can be followed indirectly through the purchase of American Depositary Receipts (ADRs). These, as the names implies, are indigenous to the United States. Depending upon the kind of programme devised for the stocks, ADRs can feature as a listed or unlisted vehicle for gaining exposure to Hong Kong/Mainland China stocks. In the former case, listing may allow capital raising benefits for the company issuing the ADR, as with a listing in the stock proper.

In brief, an ADR is a negotiable receipt issued by a depositary bank in the United States which is backed by a certain number, or fraction, of scrip in the underlying stock. One-for-one (1:1) backing would mean that one ADR covers one underlying share. The ADR is then sold separately in the United States with the underlying scrip retained by a custodian bank in Hong Kong. All features and benefits of the stock should pass to the ADR holder so that investors are accessing the underlying stock without any obvious detriment. As with the London market in Hong Kong stock trading, the ADR market in Hong Kong (and Mainland China) stocks has grown appreciably. This was driven, particularly in the mid 1990s, by investors wishing to open up their portfolios to the burgeoning 'Greater China' market on terms, and in terrain, that were familiar. By allowing United States investors the opportunity to access USD securities with direct exposure to China in their own backyard, ADRs in Mainland China/Hong Kong stocks held considerable appeal for much of the 1990s.

Recent developments in the internationalization of trading in Hong Kong stocks have therefore been considerable and warrant careful attention. Material in this chapter is organized to cover the three essential strands of activity: (i) dual-listings of Hong Kong (and Mainland China) stocks; (ii) the trading of Hong Kong stocks on London's SEAQ International; and (iii) developments in the ADR market for Hong Kong and Mainland China stocks. As a prerequisite to each of these, the motivations behind dual-listings (or dual-quotations) are first considered. The advantages to the constituents involved—issuing companies, investors and exchange forums—are addressed in Section 7.1. The major themes of interest then feature in Sections 7.2 to 7.4. Concluding comments are then drawn in Section 7.5.

7.1 The Motivations and Impact of Overseas Security Listings (or Quotations)

Before listing the various motivations, it is useful to consider how a dual- or multiple-listing is constructed. In theory, a given set of shares—typically being all the shares in issue of a particular class of stock of a company—can be listed on two or more exchanges. A company must first establish a home listing, which would probably be fashioned through an IPO. Once the stock emerges from its initial seasoning period, time may then be ripe for listing overseas. This can often be achieved through an introduction. This allows all existing shares to be listed on an overseas exchange without any recourse to an offer of (existing or new) shares. In theory, then, the same set of shares lists in two places. This gives existing shareholders the opportunity to sell their shares in either of the two markets. Similarly, potential buyers can consider accessing the shares in either jurisdiction. In practice, though, stock is only saleable in the jurisdiction where the seller registers the shares. This complication is returned to later.

Fund-Raising Benefits

With the above as backdrop, overseas listings offer a number of potential benefits to the underlying issuer (company)—capital raising advantages being the most obvious. Once a stock has been opened up to overseas investors, through secondary trading in that market, new stock can be issued in that market. Capital raising benefits could also emerge in another way. Exposure to new investors in an overseas market may fuel demand for new shares offered in the company's home market. To illustrate, consider a company PQR that has 75 million shares in issue. All the shares are dual-listed on exchanges LX (its home market) and SX (its overseas listing). This means that the company has 75 million shares in issue listed in two places (not 150 million shares in issue). Suppose that PQR wishes to enlarge its equity base by issuing 5 million new shares, via placing, and does so wholly through the LX market. The stock's exposure to investors in the SX market may entice them to enter the LX market to buy some of the new shares on offer. Completion of the offer would see the pool of listed stock rise to 80 million shares, with the additional shares listing in both settings. In short, the new shares listed on LX could also potentially enter the share register pertaining to the SX listing.

Company PQR may also be able to alternate between the markets. Raising capital in one setting from new issues and then switching to the other for a subsequent issue may prove optimal. Why would a company like PQR do this? Funds available for new shares, in any given market, are always finite. Once excess demand has been tapped in one market, a subsequent issue may be more favourably pitched overseas. Investors that are continually plugged for funding in one market may become weary, to say the least, of cash calls. Having more than one forum for issuing stock therefore opens up a company to a larger pool of potential buyers. All other things being equal, this should allow a company to sell more new stock on more favourable terms. In essence, the overseas listing may lower a company's cost of equity capital. This is the driving force behind the growth of international or global IPOs.

What about the benefits to the underlying company if instead of listing its stock overseas it simply opens it up for trade on an alternative secondary market? Quotations on SEAQ International fit this description and may serve to raise a stock's profile. In markets like London, where volumes are essentially institutionally driven, buying interest from large institutions and funds may help to boost a stock's kudos in the eyes of international investors. By whetting their appetite for the stock, these same institutional players may be more inclined to enter the stock's primary market on its home exchange.[3]

Liquidity Benefits

Liquidity benefits from dual-listings (and quotations) are also likely. An investor's ability to buy and sell between two or more markets should produce 'feedback' effects. All other things being equal, these effects should raise overall volumes, and suggest some support for prices. This particular benefit should be all the more obvious in cases where time-zone differences exist. A good example is the 'back-to-back' trading in Hong Kong counters made possible by SEAQ International in London (see Figure 7.1), which allows trading in Hong Kong stocks to be extended beyond late afternoon, Hong Kong time, to late evening. With information flows arriving in markets, sometimes rather sporadically and unpredictably, extended trading opportunities have obvious appeal.[4]

Liquidity benefits can also be engineered if a particularly large stock attracts the attention of index funds in an overseas market. If, for instance, the stock were to be included in a major overseas index, once listed there substantial liquidity benefits might result. Funds 'tracking' the index would need to acquire substantial amounts of the stock. This increased buying pressure might spill over into the stock's home market. Again this would help reduce a stock's liquidity premium and, by connection, offer its price greater buoyancy.

Processes of arbitrage might also reinforce liquidity. Arbitrageurs wishing to extract profits from pricing differences would likely zero-in on any dual-listed stock that trades actively in its constituent markets. Where overlapping trading times are apparent, like those for listings between Hong Kong and Singapore and Hong Kong and Tokyo (see Henderson Land for such an example), arbitrage processes should ensure little price deviation.

Increased Business for Brokerage Firms and Exchanges

The net effect of increased trading volumes should be good for all concerned. Underlying corporations gain by being able to market any future stock issue to a larger following of investors; existing investors gain greater liquidity in their stock investments and a boost to the value of their holdings; and the exchanges and brokerage firms involved garner increased commissions and fees.

Benefits to Existing Investors

A number of studies have considered the extent to which existing investors profit from overseas listings. The liquidity benefits, as noted, suggest windfall gains; however, the extant evidence, as appraised in Lau, Diltz, and Apilado (1994, pp. 743–5), appears somewhat mixed. For reasons of brevity, this literature is not reappraised here. Suffice it to say, most studies focus on small numbers of overseas listings in relatively few markets, making it difficult to generalize findings. Lau et al.(1994) take the discussion some way forward, given their use of a large sample (346 US stocks) of dual-listed stocks across a wide range (ten) of foreign markets. They report evidence of a positive 'wealth' effect surrounding the date of acceptance of a foreign listing; however, subsequent returns, determined from a 125-day post-listing period, appear less than impressive.[5]

The positive announcement (or acceptance date) effect of an international listing may also reflect signalling issues. As cogently argued by Alexander, Eun, and Janakiramanan (1988), 'international listing can be interpreted as reflecting management's confidence in its future ability to meet minimum listing requirements of the foreign exchange. It follows that both liquidity and signalling effects, if they exist, may cause a firm's stock price to rise by an abnormal amount around the announcement date of the international listing.' (p. 139).[6]

As for the weak post-listing performance in dual-listed stocks, the interpretation is less clear. However, as with IPOs, the implication is one of markets exaggerating the perceived benefits of listing at listing announcement.

A Modulation of a Stock's Risk Characteristics

The rather lukewarm post-listing performance picture is all the more baffling if a stock's systematic risk level is tempered by overseas listing. If a seasoning process occurs, in a manner akin to that reported in Ibbotson (1975) for US stocks, dual-listings may help stabilize prices and reduce risk levels. Ibbotson's findings suggest a gradual reduction (or seasoning) of stocks' systematic risk levels as they mature on the market. This points to a commensurate rise in a stock's price as its risk premium falls. Does a dual-listing mark a continuation in this seasoning trend? It seems not, in light of studies like Howe and Madura's (1990). The most obvious reason is that an overseas listing of a stock is only likely to occur after a stock has already established itself on its home market. Foreign exchanges are unlikely to welcome overseas stocks unless they can offer substantial investor interest (partly because transaction levies are linked to volumes). Well-established or well-seasoned stocks are more likely to provide this. Issuing corporations, too, are unlikely to countenance initial and annual listing fee payments to an exchange unless they feel some liquidity in the stock is likely on its overseas market. Again, this is more likely to occur in a stock with an established pedigree. Further significant seasoning of a stock's risk, following overseas listing, therefore seems unlikely.

In summarizing the benefits of dual-listings (and alternative stock quotations) to existing stockholders, a windfall gain is apparent around announcement. Longer-term share price performance, if anything, appears slightly negative when assessed relative to an appropriate risk-adjusted benchmark. This, at least, is consistent with stocks experiencing little or no seasoning of their risk characteristics. If the latter did occur, we would be at a loss to explain the extant evidence on post-listing risk-adjusted returns.

7.2 Dual-Listings Involving Hong Kong (and Mainland PRC) Stocks

Excepting ADRs, overseas listings of local stocks (taken here to be SAR and mainland listed stocks), tend to be concentrated in London, Singapore, and Australia. Luxembourg, as noted in earlier chapters, also provides a significant forum for debt issues in locally-listed companies. Debt, investment funds, and ADR listings aside, an indication of overseas equity listings in locally-listed companies is offered in Appendix 7.1. London is one of the major players in this regard with nine local stocks listed. If one were to include companies with a strong local presence, but without local listing, the numbers would be even higher. The Jardine stocks—Dairy Farm International Holdings, Hongkong Land Holdings, Jardine Matheson Holdings, Jardine Strategic Holdings, and Mandarin Oriental—are apt examples.

Secondary and Primary Listings

In a number of countries outside the United States, particularly in former British dependencies, like Hong Kong, or the Commonwealth in general, stocks can often list under either primary or secondary listings. For the SEHK, an overseas issuer—defined as 'an issuer incorporated or otherwise established outside Hong Kong'[7]— is able to list under either category.[8] The various conditions or, more precisely, 'additional requirements, modifications or exceptions' to the general body of rules, pertaining to each type of listed overseas issuer, are set out in Chapter 19 of the *Rules Governing the Listing of Securities on the Stock Exchange of Hong Kong Ltd* (hereafter, the *Listing Rules*).[9]

Issues of Terminology
As a word of warning, the terms primary and secondary listing should not be confused with the terms primary and secondary market. They are very different. The latter, as is evident from Section 1.4, bear upon the actual trading functions of markets. A primary market, for example, is one in which capital is raised for issuers of new securities. In principle, such activity is independent of a security's listed status. An issuer with a secondary stock listing in a chosen jurisdiction can, if required, issue new shares in that

jurisdiction. By the same token, stocks, whether of primary or secondary listed status, invite secondary market activities once the listing is established. Although trading interest is more likely to be concentrated in a stock's primary listed market than its secondary listed market.

The Costs and Obligations for Issuers

In general terms, a secondary listing offers some derogations or exemptions from the listing conditions incumbent upon companies opting for primary listing.[10] Most exchanges that countenance secondary listings also require such a stock to have a primary listing—or some equivalent—on an acceptable overseas market. This essentially means that standards of investor protection and regulatory control, enshrined in the rules governing the market where primary listing exists, meet standards set by the market where secondary listing is sought.[11] Where any conflict in listing rules arises the rules of the stock's principal market typically take precedence.

A secondary listing is also a cheaper way of listing one's stock. For the SEHK, initial and annual listing fees for a stock with secondary listing are approximately 25% of those for a stock with primary listing, although various caveats and qualifications exist. One is that the Exchange may upgrade a stock's secondary listed status, and the fees therein, to the level of a primary listing where it judges the majority of trading to be based on the Exchange.[12] On the downside, the reduced disclosure requirements, for a company holding secondary listed status, typically translate to weaker investor interest and thus reduced liquidity in most markets that entertain such stock listings. Not surprisingly, international investors are more likely to purchase a stock in its home or primary market where, perhaps, greater transparency in that stock is likely. Despite this, arbitrage should ensure that prices in dual-listed stocks, whatever their listed status and locales of trading, only deviate slightly. Certainly, such deviations should lie within levels specified by transaction costs and other market imperfections.

Stocks can also be quoted under a primary listing in two or more markets. Examples of this include HSBC Holdings plc and VTech Holdings Ltd, which have primary listed status in both Hong Kong and London, and CM Telecom International Ltd, which has primary listings in Hong Kong and Singapore.[13] The HSBC Holdings plc case is, perhaps, slightly more complicated than most dual-listings given two tranches of stock: one denominated in Hong Kong dollars (HKD) and the other in British pounds (GB£).[14] While both tranches list locally, virtually all local trading volume, quite naturally, is in the HKD denominated tranche. Changes to the structure of these holdings are on the horizon, however. At the announcement of its 1998 corporate results, HSBC Holdings revealed its intention to consolidate its existing HKD and GB£ stocks and to replace them with new shares, denominated in US dollars. This measure was seen as a prerequisite to a listing in New York, which would broaden its equity trading base from two markets to three.[15] The initial response to the announcement, despite the concurrent announcement of a decline (albeit expected) in its earnings (relative to 1997), was extremely positive.

Some of the advantages noted earlier, pertaining to additional listings, were undoubtedly factored in.

One might hazard that in jurisdictions where primary listings exist, any conflict in a particular area of regulation, is likely to be settled by following the more onerous of the two sets of exchange rules. In this light, the rules of either exchange may predominate. It clearly depends upon the issue and the rules of each exchange. In the secondary/primary dual-listing, we noted that it was generally the rules of the exchange of primary listing that came into force given any obvious conflict. Reference to the specific rules of the exchanges is advised, though, before drawing any conclusions relating to the obligation of issuers under either a primary/primary or secondary/primary dual-listing. The comments made here are only intended to paint the broad picture.

A Special Case of Dual-Listing: Listings of Different Sets of Shares in Different Locales

Stock-issuing companies incorporated in the PRC essentially issue two broad groups of shares: domestic and foreign shares. In contrast to the typical dual-listing—where the *same set* of shares trade on two or more exchanges—markets for 'domestic' and foreign shares in PRC-incorporated companies are necessarily segmented. Aside from the tradeable 'A' share, which sells exclusively between Mainland parties in renminbi, three broad classes of 'domestic' stock are apparent. These all ultimately fall under state-ownership. According to Wu, Xiang, and Zhang (1996) they can be described as' *Guojia Gu* (shares owned by the state), *Faren Gu* (shares owned by other state-owned entities), and *Faqiren Gu* (shares owned by the founding SOEs)' (p. 56, parentheses shown as used). Moreover, all transactions in such 'domestic' shares, including the traded 'A' share, are limited to Mainland parties. The only shares eligible for listing outside the Mainland are those designated as foreign shares.[16]

Accordingly, when PRC-incorporated companies list their foreign stock outside the Mainland, only a fraction of the issuing company's equity will be quoted. This is evident for the SEHK listed 'H' shares (see Section 1.3). In most cases, the number of 'H' shares accounts for between 25% and 30% of the enterprises' outstanding shares. This is quite different to other types of listings in Hong Kong and elsewhere. More often than not, 100% of the shares in issue list, notwithstanding the fact that the actual proportion that can trade at any particular time on an exchange, is contingent upon share registration issues.

Some foreign stocks in PRC-incorporated companies are also subject to restrictions in relation to dual-listings. 'H' shares, for instance, cannot simultaneously trade as 'B' shares in Shanghai or Shenzhen (see Section 1.1). Either the 'B' or 'H' share listing can be used, but not both.[17] Two SEHK listed 'H' shares are, however, listed in London (as so-called 'L' shares).[18] It is also possible for 'H' shares to serve as backing for depositary receipt (DR) programmes, where the receipts are potentially convertible into the underlying 'H' shares. Details of some of these share listings and the mechanisms underpinning the conversion of the DRs to shares are explored in Section 7.4.

One other important issue concerns the relative pricing of foreign and 'domestic' shares in PRC-incorporated entities. Work on this issue by Fang (1997) provides some insight into why the 'A' shares of particular companies on the Shanghai Stock Exchange trade at a premium to corresponding 'B' shares. He notes that: 'Both "A" and "B" shares have the same rights according to their definitions. . . . The domestic investors in China are willing to pay more for the individual "A" shares because of limited number of shares outstanding. The foreign investors, however, are willing to pay less for "B" shares because of the restricted trading conditions and low liquidity' (p. 98).

In other words, foreign investors have greater choice in where they wish to trade foreign shares in PRC-incorporated companies. Even though the same PRC-incorporated stock cannot dual-list as both an 'H' share and 'B' share, foreign investors with a broad interest in exposure to PRC stocks can pick their markets. Domestic investors, in contrast, have much less choice, even if a little permeability in the walls separating domestic and foreign markets exists.

Mok and Hui (1998) also reveal severe underpricing in 'A' share IPOs on the Shanghai Stock Exchange for a sample of offerings, between December 1990 and December 1993. They detect mean underpricing between the offer and first traded prices in the stocks, after adjusting for market movements, of around 289% (p. 464). A comparable mean for the 'B' shares generates a more reasonable level of 26%. Both Fang (1997) and Mok and Hui's (1998) studies point to considerable demand for 'A' shares in both primary and secondary markets. A small number of shares available—with the majority being unlisted, non-negotiable scrip—allied to a tidal wave of investors confronting stock investment for the first time, underpin the results in both studies.[19]

The Importance of Share Registration in the Dual-Trading of Stocks

The convention in most, if not all, exchanges is to report the market capitalization of the stocks they list as being equal to the number of shares outstanding multiplied by the prevailing market price. For stocks in companies such as HSBC Holdings plc, this involves summing the market values of the two tranches in issue: the HKD and GB£ tranches. This practice does not necessarily mean that all stocks reported by an exchange are available for trading on that exchange. As noted earlier, trading also depends upon whether the shares are recorded in a share register recognized by that exchange.

In some cases, the share register may only include a small proportion of the shares in issue. This is often true of stocks in jurisdictions where secondary listing obtains. The majority of stocks, in such cases, appear on a principal register in the stock's home market. This register may, in turn, be the only one that is recognized by the exchange in that home market. Similarly, the exchange, where the secondary listing exists, may also limit trades to shares in the register it recognizes. This would be the stock's branch or overseas register. In the final analysis, decisions relating to the trading eligibility of shares recorded on particular registers rest with the exchanges where the stocks are listed.[20]

The significance of the above is that registration of shares usually requires the owner (or nominee) to have an address in the locale where the register is held. This can mean that most of the shares will be on one register only. Enquiries with share registrars in the SAR indicate that it may be possible for a share owner (or its nominee), with addresses in the locations where registers are held, to register shares on more than one register. Shares can also shift between registers over time. Substantial movement may eventually lead to so few shares on a register that the viability of a listing comes into question.[21] At such a point, a listing may be withdrawn and the branch (overseas) register, to which that listing relates, closed. Remaining owners on the register would then transfer their identities (and shareholdings) to the principal register.

For SEHK listed stocks, 16 share registrars carry out registration activities in the SAR. One of these, HKSCC Registrars Ltd, a wholly-owned subsidiary of the Hong Kong Securities Clearing Co Ltd (see Section 3.3), performs registration activities for all 'H' shares. As of the 1998 year-end, its duties encompassed the registration of the 42 'H' shares then in issue plus four other stocks, one of which was China Telecom (Hong Kong) Ltd.[22]

To summarize, the zeal with which some Asian companies seek stock listings overseas suggests that, at least from the issuing companies' perspective, benefits outweigh costs. This observation may also help to account for the rash of Asian stocks that trade regularly, without listed status, on trading systems in foreign markets. This is particularly true for some of Hong Kong's blue-chip counters which trade with considerable volume in London's SEAQ International trading system. These stocks and the SEAQ International trading forum, which have been touched upon above, are explored in some detail in the following section.

7.3   Trading of Hong Kong Stocks in Markets where Listing is not Required: London's SEAQ International

Characteristics of the SEAQ International Trading Environment

Notwithstanding the London Stock Exchange's (LSE's) cachet as one of the world's major markets, its success in scooping up trades of international stocks owes much to its time-zone advantage. The *Euroclear IFR Handbook of World Stock & Commodity Exchanges 1995* makes this point rather cogently, 'London is situated in a unique time zone which enables its trading hours to cover the whole of the European day plus the afternoon in North America, making London the natural choice for trading in international securities. . . .' (*Euroclear IFR 1995*, p. 610).

This does not explain why London has stolen a march on its European neighbours in the area of international stock trading. Its undoubted reputation, allied to an armoury of financial services surrounding it in the City of London, may be just as compelling a reason for trading stocks in London, as its time-zone advantage.

The structure of trading in overseas stocks on the SEAQ International trading system revolves around market-makers (dealers). For any stock in the Hong Kong sector, a given number of market-makers will be registered to quote two-way prices for the stock during a defined Mandatory Quotation Period (MQP).[23] This period runs from 0930 to 1530 GMT[24] for stocks in the Hong Kong 'country' sector. Converting to Hong Kong time (HKT) means that equities listed on the SEHK can, in principle, trade in Hong Kong between 1000 and 1600 (HKT) and then in London between 1630 and 2230 (HKT), during the summer months. During the winter months, this trading occurs between 1730 and 2330 (HKT).[25] This picture of 'back-to-back' trading in Hong Kong stocks is illustrated in Figure 7.1.

Based upon observations made for extended trading earlier, a number of benefits should emerge from this 'back-to-back' trading, not least of which is the likely gain in volumes arising from trades between the markets. Feedback effects between the markets are also fostered by settlement practices and currency valuations, which typically mirror those in the stock's home market.[26] Minimum order sizes imposed for SEAQ International trades may mean that London's lure is somewhat greater for institutional investors than retail investors.

Differences in institutional participation rates in the trading of Hong Kong stocks on the two markets bear this out. Comparison of average bargain values for Hong Kong stocks traded on the SEHK and SEAQ International in McGuinness (1999a), for the period January 1995 to February 1996, demonstrate levels in London of around ten times those in Hong Kong. Assuming a correlation between average bargain value and investor size, Hong Kong trading in London appears to be very much institutionally-based. The SEHK, on the other hand, has a very significant retail component. As commented upon in Chapter 3, S. 3.1, survey results published in the SEHK *Fact Book 1997* (p. 114) reveal that 53% of the Exchange's total turnover originates from local individuals.

As well as clear differences in institutional participation rates, the structure of the two markets differ considerably. Besides obvious differences in market microstructure—the SEHK is order-driven and SEAQ International quote-driven—SEAQ International only provides a secondary market in many of the stocks it trades. In contrast, stocks quoted on the SEHK have recourse to both primary and market functions, as reported earlier. In some respects, then, SEAQ International is akin to an over-the-counter (OTC) market. The proprietary rights of the LSE mean the trading system is quite unlike most floating OTC forums, however.

Figure 7.1   Time Zones and Trading Periods (HKT) Relevant to the
Trading of Hong Kong Stocks

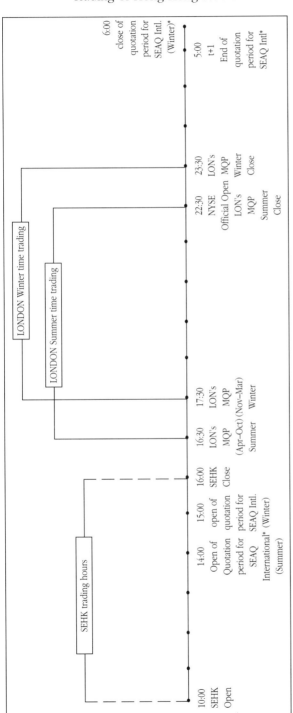

* According to the Euroclear IFR Handbook of World Stock & Commodity Exchanges 1995; 'trading in the International Equity Market can take place 24 hours a day, but quotations may only be input to SEAQ International between 7.00 and 20.00' (page 605).

Notes: • Opening hour and MQP data obtained from IFR Handbook and Guide to the International Equity Market (August 1994), published by the London Stock Exchange. SEHK close changed from 15:45 to 15:55 in September 1995 and 15:55 to 16:00 in February 1998 [see *Fact Books* (1995, p. 6; 1998, p.8)].
        • Adapted from McGuinness (1997a), p. 460.

As SEAQ International only provides a secondary market, unless the stocks are listed in London, a stock's inclusion in the system hinges largely on the whims of market-makers. If a sufficient number of them (normally a minimum of three[27]) agree to offer firm prices in a stock throughout the defined MQP, the stock becomes eligible for trading. While all stocks listed on the SEHK are theoretically eligible, market-making, and hence trading, is generally confined to Hong Kong's blue-chips and some of the larger China plays. This trading preference was reflected by the creation of the Hang Seng London Reference Index (HSLRI) in December 1994.[28] It also testifies to the importance of the London market for Hong Kong stock trades. As the HSLRI dovetails with the Hang Seng Index, it basically gives market participants insights into the market sentiment surrounding Hong Kong stocks from late afternoon to late evening, Hong Kong time.

The Impact of London Trading on the SEHK

Empirical studies on this issue (see Ho et al (1992), Cheung et al (1994) and Cheung and Shum (1995) and McGuinness (1997a, 1999a) for example) suggest, for the most part, that London has had a moderating effect upon local trading behaviour. Cheung et al. (1994) indicate, with reference to HSI data for the SEHK, lower return variances for London quoted Hong Kong stocks (relative to non-London traded stocks) when returns are measured on an open-open and close-close basis. Evidence of a reduction in the systematic risk levels of London quoted Hong Kong stocks trading on the SEHK is also noted in Cheung and Shum (1995) for the period following 4 June 1989.

Interestingly, empirical findings positing some reduction in risk for dual-traded stocks are consistent with theoretical implications offered for dual-listed stocks. Yagil and Forsher (1991) predict risk reduction benefits for dual-listed stocks in markets that are less than perfectly integrated. Leaving aside the difference between dual-traded and dual-listed stocks—which is not a purely semantic distinction—one may be able to generalize these predictions to the dual-trading issue here. Some segmentation occurs because of the time-zone differences.

In terms of trading volume effects, the aggregate benefits of London trading for the SEHK market are not that clear. While London's slice of overall trading in Hong Kong stocks appears to be growing, as indicated in the early part of this chapter, overall volumes on the SEHK have also risen appreciably at the same time. Developments in London, as stated earlier, have not, therefore, been detrimental to the SEHK.

Related evidence in other markets, where listed stocks have been offered for trading on alternative market systems, suggest liquidity benefits (see Khan and Baker (1993)). Khan and Baker consider this situation for stocks listed on the NYSE and AMEX which subsequently obtained trading status, as unlisted stocks, on a US regional exchange. The latter, referred to as an 'unlisted trading privilege (UTP)' in Khan and Baker, appears to improve the stocks' liquidity in their listed environ. They note further that 'results show significantly positive abnormal returns before the SEC's announcement that an exchange has filed an application for UTPs' (pp. 233–5). In this light, extended trading in Hong Kong stocks in London probably has contributed to significant liquidity gains. For those holding the stocks at the time of the dual-trading announcement, a positive windfall may have emerged.

London, due to some overlap in its trading hours with New York (see Figure 7.1), also offers Hong Kong investors an opportunity to trade on US information disclosures in a timely manner. This theme is explored in McGuinness's (1999a) study. The study reports inflated volumes in London trades of Hong Kong stocks on Fridays, which is also reflected in increased volatility in the HSLRI on this day. The increased volumes and volatility levels on Fridays are also noted to coincide with increased macroeconomic disclosure activity in the United States.[29] Interestingly, little correlation between the timing of Hong Kong corporate disclosures and volume and volatility levels is found in McGuinness (1999a).

While the London market provides one opportunity to trade during the US trading day, Hong Kong and Mainland stocks can also be accessed indirectly in the United States. This can be achieved by trading in American Depositary Receipts (ADRs). As argued at the outset, the ADR provides a direct substitute for the underlying stock by capturing all of the underlying benefits and entitlements of the stock. Like the London market, ADR investments in Hong Kong stocks have surged in number in recent years. This market and its development feature in the following section.

7.4 Depositary Receipts (DRs) in Hong Kong and Mainland PRC Stocks

Characteristics of American Depositary Receipts (ADRs)

In the United States, foreign companies can list their shares directly on a US exchange but, more often than not, opt for the ADR route instead. The ADR is a negotiable security that can be traded without delivery of the underlying scrip. Its value is expressed in US dollars. All benefits and claims deriving from the underlying stock are also transferable to the ADR holder in equivalent US dollars.[30] The security comes into being when issued through a depositary bank in the US which, if issued on the behest and instructions of the company responsible for issuing the underlying shares, is deemed a sponsored programme.

In some cases, a distinction is made between depositary shares and depositary receipts to connote, respectively, the sponsored or unsponsored nature of a programme.[31] In most cases, however, the term depositary receipt is used in a generic sense to cover both types of programme. This is the sense in which the term will be used in the ensuing discussions. In any event, anecdotal evidence indicates that most ADR programmes, particularly ones based on Hong Kong and Mainland stocks, are of the sponsored kind.

In virtually all respects, the ADR is equivalent to the underlying share. Why, then, do foreign companies typically choose to list in the United States via the ADR rather than through an official stock listing? Dividends provide one reason. A foreign listed stock would likely pay dividends in the currency denomination of its shares. ADRs, by definition, pay dividends in US dollars, something which is far more palatable to the typical US retail investor. An additional reason is that some institutional investors, like US pension funds, are unable to buy foreign stocks. The ADR, then, provides a legitimate vehicle through which international corporate earning streams can be accessed by such bodies[32].

The Cancellation and Creation of DRs

Once a depositary receipt is in issue, the associated depositary bank takes responsibility for controlling the supply of ADRs in the market and stands ready to cancel and issue new securities when required. At the same time, a custodian bank, in the underlying company's country of origin, holds the underlying scrip and supervizes settlement in the scrip whenever ADRs are created or cancelled.

Given the direct relation between receipt ownership and the underlying share, investors can typically exchange depositary receipts for the underlying shares on demand. Where this occurs, the depositary takes the receipt out of circulation and retrieves the underlying share from the custodian. In this sense, depositary receipts are open-ended investments. Adjustments to their supply stem from both cancellations and, where demand exists, new issues. In the latter, an investor's broker would likely place a requisite amount of scrip with the custodian in the stock's home market. Communication of this by the custodian to the US depositary would then see the requisite number of ADRs issued to the investor. Inspection of prospectuses of companies with outstanding ADR programmes suggests a number of possibilities in relation to the settlement and clearing of local stock, in cases where shares are exchanged for ADRs. The first is the placement of physical scrip, as described in the foregoing, with the custodian (or its nominee). The second is where the arrangement is made through CCASS. This would likely involve a transfer of the underlying shares from an investor's (or his/her broker's) account in the system to the custodian's.

ADRs can also come into circulation through primary market activities, where the underlying stock-issuing company instructs the depositary to issue new receipts. This would require the requisite number of new shares backing the ADRs to be placed with the custodian first. Funds raised from the depositary receipts, less appropriate expenses and fees to be paid to the depositary and custodian, would then accrue to the issuing company.

Arbitrage Between the ADRs and Underlying Stocks

The possibility of ADR creation and cancellation also suggests arbitrage between the depositary receipt and stock markets. A noticeable premium on the stock in its home market, when comparing the USD equivalent price to the ADR price, might prompt such activities. To do this, an investor in the United States could acquire the ADR and convert it, through the depositary bank, into the appropriate number of underlying shares. Subsequent sale of these shares in the home market would then yield a gain. Where the ADR appears at a premium, the same arbitrage logic can be employed but in reverse. An investor could acquire a requisite number of shares in the home market and present them to the depositary for ADRs. These could then be sold at a premium to the purchase price of the stock. As with all pure arbitrage trades, the offsetting transactions must be conducted simultaneously so as to 'lock in' the price-differential. Time delays in conversion might hinder this. In the first arbitrage ploy, for instance, delivery of the shares may take some time. Arbitrageurs wishing to sell stock, at the same time they buy the ADR, may find themselves short of the stock. Borrowing arrangements clearly come at a cost. Other transaction costs, like currency translation, may also erode gains. As always, liquidity problems in either the receipt or underlying is an important issue.

Share Registration Issues
Perusal of prospectus documents suggests that companies with both local stock listings and ADR programmes can resort to a number of models for the registration of their securities. One approach would be to allow all listed shares to enter a principal register in Hong Kong. A register held by the depository in the United States would similarly reflect the beneficial owners of the ADRs, with the underlying shares held with the custodian perhaps appearing on the principal register itself in nominee form (i.e., in the name of the custodian).

Another possibility is the use of two separate registers in Hong Kong: one for the shares directly backing the ADRs (which we can call USD dividend shares) and another, hereafter the principal register, for shares not backing such programmes (HKD dividend shares).[33] The US depositary would also likely hold its own register of ADR holders. While all the shares listed in Hong Kong potentially serve as backing for ADRs, only a proportion of the underlying shares are likely to trade on the local exchange (the HKD dividend shares). The remainder, underlying the ADRs (i.e., USD dividend shares) will be held by the custodian for the beneficial ADR owners.[34]

ADRs in Hong Kong and Mainland PRC Stocks

Large numbers of issues from Mainland China, Hong Kong, and other Asian markets have featured strongly in the surging ADR market. As an indication of this activity, 109 Hong Kong stocks and 29 PRC stocks, as of June 1999, traded under the guise of the ADR in the United States.[35] Summary statistics for these programmes are shown in Table 7.1.

The relative importance of ADR programmes in Pacific-Rim stocks is reflected in Table 7.2, where ADRs are categorized in terms of the country-

Table 7.1   Summary of Trading Features of ADRs on Hong Kong and
Mainland PRC Stocks

	ADRs in Hong Kong stock		ADRs in PRC stocks	
	Number of programmes	Number sponsored	Number of programmes	Number sponsored
ADRs listed on the NSYE	3[a]	3	10[b]	10
ADRs traded on NASDAQ	1	1	–	–
ADRs trading OTC	103	97	10	10
ADRs trading under Rule 144A	2[41]	2	9[42]	9
Total	109	103	29	29

Notes:

a Hong Kong listed ADRs include programmes on HK Telecom, APT Satellite Holdings Ltd
and Asia Satellite Telcom Holdings.

b PRC listed ADRs include programmes on Beijing Yanhua Petrochemical Co Ltd; China
Eastern Airlines Corp Ltd; China Southern Airlines Co Ltd; China Telecom (Hong Kong)
Ltd; Guangshen Railway Co Ltd; Huaneng Power Intl Inc; Jilin Chemical Ind. Co Ltd;
Shandong Huaneng Power Development; Shanghai Petrochemical Co Ltd; and Yanzhou
Coal Mining Company Ltd.

Data Compiled from ADR directory of The Bank of New York Company Inc at http://www.
bankofny.com/adr/aovrview.htm (updated as of 1 June 1999).

affiliation of the underlying stock-issuing companies. In terms of numbers
of companies listed, Australia and Japan are the biggest players in the
region with 320 issues between them. Hong Kong then follows in third
place, and is only 22 issues short of Japan if we combine the mainland
PRC and Hong Kong totals. Corporations from other countries within the
region are noticeably less active. This leaves the 'Big Three'—Australia,
Japan, and the Mainland/SAR—with the lion's share of the issues from the
region. Despite the Asia-Pacific region's prominence, the biggest player,
in terms of number of corporate issues, is the United Kingdom with 236
issues. Other European countries adopt a much lower profile in terms of
number of corporate listings. France had 53 corporate listings, Germany
49, the Netherlands 48, and Italy 40, as of June 1999.

Of the ADR programmes in Mainland stocks, ten traded with listed
status as of June 1999. All of these listed on the New York Stock Exchange
(NYSE). For Hong Kong, listed receipts include programmes in HK
Telecom., APT Satellite Holdings Ltd, and Asia Satellite Telcom. Holdings.
Of the listed PRC ADRs, Shanghai Petrochemical Co Ltd was the first to
list on the NYSE in July 1993.[36] Like the other nine listed depositary receipts
in mainland PRC stocks, it attracts the 'N' share label.

In terms of trading forum, most of the ADRs in Hong Kong and mainland
PRC stocks trade in the over-the-counter (OTC) market. A small number
also trade on NASDAQ. A few depositary receipts are also available through

Table 7.2 Summary of ADRs in Issue According to the Corporate
Identity of the Underlying Stock Issuer

Asia-Pacific Region Country	Number of Issues *	Rest of the World Country	Number of Issues
Australia	160	UK	236
Japan	160	South Africa	96
Hong Kong SAR*	109	India	96
Taiwan	54	Mexico	95
S. Korea	33	Brazil	83
PRC	29	Russia	80
Philippines	22	France	53
Singapore	24	Germany	49
Malaysia	18	Netherlands	48

* Included as a separate entry for comparison purposes.
Source: Data Compiled from ADR directory of The Bank of New York Company Inc. at
http://www.bankofny.com/adr/aovrview.htm (updated as of 1 June 1999).

a so-called Rule 144A mechanism which involves a direct placement of
receipts.[37] Whatever the trading status, listed or otherwise, the various
ADR programmes are generally sponsored. This, as noted, involves the
collaboration of the company responsible for issuing the underlying stock.
Reference to Table 7.1 indicates that all 29 despository receipt programmes
in mainland PRC stocks are of this kind.

Classification of ADR Programmes

The various ADR programmes, other than those driven by Rule 144A, can
be described in terms of Level I, II, and III nomenclature. According to
Anonymous (1993–4), a Level I programme, 'requires only minimal
disclosure to the SEC and trades in the US over-the-counter market on
what are known as "pink sheets". A Level I listed company need not
comply with US Generally Accepted Accounting Principles (GAAP). Issuing
Level I depositary receipts does not allow the company to raise capital or
list on a national exchange' (p. 10).

In contrast, Level II and III programmes involve considerably greater
disclosure requirements but provide for one important advantage: the
possibility of listing the ADRs on the main US exchanges. However, a
Level II programme only accords secondary market status to the depositary
receipts. It does not, as in a Level III programme, provide for fund-raising
possibilities for the underlying corporation. In a Level III programme,
new shares created by the underlying company are first lodged with the
custodian in the home market. The depositary bank is then instructed to
issue a sufficient number of receipts to cover all of these new shares in
the US market. Funds raised from these receipts, less expenses and

commissions, then accrue to the underlying corporation. Of the NYSE and NASDAQ traded ADRs, all, with regard to Hong Kong and Mainland stocks, appear to be in the Level III category.

A Level II programme generally results from a Level I programme being promoted or upgraded to listed status. The genesis of Level I and II programmes is therefore much the same. The general process begins when the organizers of an ADR programme announce that a certain number of ADRs will be traded in an underlying stock on an OTC basis. Brokers nominated by the organizers then buy up stock from interested investors and place the underlying scrip with a custodian. A certain number of depositary receipts, reflecting the number of underlying shares acquired, are then issued by the depositary bank in the United States. These receipts, once sold, then trade on an OTC basis. This provides an opportunity to test the market for the particular ADR. If successful, it may lead to more underlying stock being acquired and further ADRs in the stock being issued. However, secondary market trading in the ADRs may be limited by the unlisted status of the receipts. If a sufficient number of receipts are in issue, therefore, a listing of the instruments, which is tantamount to an elevation of a programme from Level I to Level II status, would seem logical.

The majority of ADR programmes in Hong Kong and Mainland stocks, given their OTC traded status, fall within the Level I category. Why does this route appear to be so popular? Apart from the reduced disclosure requirements, it probably serves as a useful way of raising a company's profile in the world's largest economy.[38] It also serves a useful role, as argued above, in preparing the ADR programme for listed status on one of the major markets.

The Co-Existence of 'H' Shares and DRs
It is possible for PRC-incorporated companies to consider listing their foreign shares as 'H' shares while simultaneously exposing other overseas investors to these shares through depositary receipts. This might suggest the listing of 'H' shares prior to a DR programme, but the reverse is also possible as illustrated by Huaneng Power International Inc's listing on the Exchange in January 1998. This involved 1.25 billion shares, backing American depositary shares (ADSs, hereafter ADRs) listed on the New York Stock Exchange, listing on the local market through an introduction.[39] Normally, the 'H' share listing roughly coincides with the ADR listing, affording holders of both sets of securities the opportunity to make conversions of either the shares into ADRs or the ADRs into shares.

Depositary Receipt (DR) listings outside the United States

Global Depositary Receipts (GDRs) or International Depositary Receipts (IDRs), as they are sometimes referred to, have also taken hold in a number of markets outside the United States. The LSE, in particular, has made significant strides in this area, since its first DR listing in August 1994.[40]

The varying reasons for DR listing, as opined by the LSE, relate to the fact that 'they are often more liquid and easily traded than the underlying shares. DRs can also overcome settlement, foreign exchange and foreign ownership difficulties which may exist in the company's home market.' (*Fact File 1998*, p. 12). The presumption, of course, is that the DR route to listing is less onerous, in many important respects, for the issuing company than a full stock listing. The fact that most of the DR issuers in London hail from 'emerging' markets perhaps bears this out. India (15 issuers) and South Korea (12 issuers) lead the pack. The support offered by the depositary institution may also be a key attraction with international investors in promoting DR programmes.

7.5 Concluding Remarks

Material presented in this chapter highlights the integration of stock market trading, which has led to the dissipation of trades across markets and, at the same time, a surge in overall volumes. For Hong Kong and mainland PRC stocks, widely sought after in numerous jurisdictions, three main developments have been analysed. These relate to (i) the dual-listing of the stocks in other markets, (ii) the trading of Hong Kong stocks on London's SEAQ International, and (iii) the creation of depositary receipt programmes in Hong Kong and mainland PRC stocks. All three developments have occurred at great speed and highlight the 'internationalization' of stocks with linkages to the China markets.

Whilst motives for entering the various markets may differ, companies undoubtedly gain from the increased exposure. For investors in overseas markets, the desire to participate in what many see as 'exotic' markets is the essential driving force. Accessing primary markets overseas, or using the secondary markets in these jurisdictions to promote primary market activities in Hong Kong and the mainland PRC, is clearly the key for Hong Kong and mainland PRC corporations. Selling any product to a particular target also requires sale of that product on terms and conditions with which the buyer is familiar and accustomed. In the case of stocks with underlying interests in 'Greater China', this is more easily achieved in the markets where institutional investors, and capital flows, are most active.

Appendix 7.1 'Local' Stocks Listed in Overseas Markets

LISTINGS ON THE LONDON STOCK EXCHANGE

Stock	Place of Incorporation
Beijing Datang Power Generation[b]	China
Jiangxi Copper Co[b]	China
Zhejiang South East Electric Power	China
CP Pokphand Co	Bermuda
Dailywin Group	Bermuda
Esprit Holdings	Bermuda
VTech Holdings	Bermuda
Wah Kwong Shipping Holdings	Bermuda
HSBC Holdings plc	England[a]

Data was obtained from the London Stock Exchange's record of overseas listings for companies with incorporation in Hong Kong (0), Mainland China (3), Bermuda (21), the Cayman Islands (31), and the Cook Islands (0). Thanks are due to Tim Wood for supplying this information.

Notes:
a Domestic listing; all other stocks were classified as 'overseas listed'.
b Stocks with secondary listing in London (and 'H' share status in Hong Kong). Thanks are due to HKSCC Registrars Ltd for supplying this information.

Notes

1. I would like to acknowledge the comments of an anonymous OUP reviewer for earlier comments on this chapter.

2. In the report's executive summary, the authors state, 'London trading volume for 18 selected sample stocks with active trading in London has been steadily rising, increasing from an average of 13% of Hong Kong volume in 1991 to 35% of Hong Kong volume for the 10-month period ending March 1996. . . .' (See SFC (1997, Chang et al., p. 1)). They also note that a part of 'reported London volume is in fact Hong Kong volume by London transactors, which allows adjustment of the ratio of 35% to 32%' (p. 1).

3. This point is succinctly summarized by Charlton. She remarks:'For a company not considering a London listing, quotation of prices in its securities on SEAQ International is a useful way of obtaining visibility in Europe and other countries, preparing markets for an eventual issue, stimulating interest in the company and in forthcoming new issues or placements, building a secondary market in its securities or a relationship with market intermediaries in the U.K.' (p. 14).

4. Mittoo (1992), for example, based upon questionnaire findings gleaned from Canadian managers reveals general support for this view.

5. Lau et al. (1994) note: 'depending on the listing location, the overall wealth impact of international listing during the post-listing period is either insignificant or negative' (p. 754).

6. These views are prefaced in Alexander *et. al.* (1988) to apply to markets that are at least 'mildly segmented'.

7. See *Rules Governing the Listing of Securities on the Stock Exchange of Hong Kong Ltd*, vol. 1, 1-6, 12/94.

8. Information provided by the SEHK's *Research and Planning Department* indicates that only three secondary listed stocks were on the Exchange as of the 1998 year-end: FAI Insurances Ltd, Guangdong Development Fund Ltd, and The Peninsular & Oriental Steam Navigation Co.

9. This is spelled out in the preliminary section to Chapter 19, which states that, 'The Exchange Listing Rules apply as much to overseas issuers as they do to Hong Kong issuers, subject to the additional requirements, modifications or exceptions set out or referred to in this chapter' (Rule 19.01, 19-1, 5/91).

10. The disclosure benefits of secondary listing are succinctly summarized by Charlton (1995): 'One of the major advantages of a secondary listing is that issuers can frequently obtain certain dispensations from the requirements imposed on those seeking a primary listing. These dispensations generally relate to the application procedures, disclosure requirements to be contained in the listing document and, of particular importance in relation to a listed issuers' continuing obligations. . . .' (Charlton, p. 5, para 4.2).

11. A number of Hong Kong stocks hold secondary listings in overseas markets. It is not always easy to identify stocks with secondary listings, as multiple listings are possible. Dairy Farm International Hlds Ltd, for instance, had, prior to its de-listing from the SEHK in 1994, listings in Hong Kong, Australia, Singapore and London (see Anonymous (March 1992).

12. The reader is recommended to read the various provisions in Appendix 8 of the 'Listing Rules' which broadly cover this issue. Particular attention is drawn to S. 8-9 (A8-9, 1/97).

13. For details, see, respectively, HSBC Holdings Plc Annual Report (1997), Wardley Cards (VTech Holdings Ltd, 01, prep: 23-11-98) and CM Telecom International Ltd's Introduction on The Stock Exchange of Hong Kong Ltd document (1997, p. 112).

14. The tranches listed on the SEHK under stock Codes 5 and 105 (*SEHK Monthly Bulletin* December 1998, p. 48). These listings evolved as follows: In 1991, approximately 1.625 billion shares of HSBC Holdings were issued following a group reorganization whereby HSBC Holdings become the holding company of HongkongBank through a share exchange of four HongkongBank shares for one new HSBC share. The new shares were then listed in Hong Kong and London through introduction (see HSBC Holdings Plc, Introduction to the London Stock Exchange document). The dual-listing arrangement was complicated in July 1992 when HSBC acquired a controlling interest in the Midland Bank by issuing approximately 0.775 billion (GB£) shares to its shareholders. The new GB£ shares were then listed in London and Hong Kong (see Wardley Cards for HSBC Holdings PLC's capital details).

15. See Saunders, Chan, and Kohli (1999). The consolidation was effected in July 1999.

16. Mok and Hui (1998) classify stock ownership of PRC state-enterprises into eight possible categories, 'Non-negotiable stocks: State-Owned Stocks, Founder Stocks (Local), Founder Stocks (Foreign), Legal-Entity Stocks, Employee Stocks. Negotiable stocks: Personal A shares, B shares, and H shares.' (p. 57, note 4).

17. This is borne out by cursory inspection of 'H' and 'B' listings. Thanks are also due to Peter So for his comments on this issue.

18. These are Beijing Datang Power Generation and Jiangxi Copper Co Ltd. In addition, Zhejiang South East Electric Power—which is not currently an 'H' share—is listed as a depositary receipt (see Appendix 7.1 for further details).

19. Mok and Hui (1998, p. 472) allude to this in their conclusions.

20. For SEHK listed stocks, the *Listing Rules*, in relation to overseas stocks (i.e., stocks incorporated outside Hong Kong), for both primary and secondary listed stocks, report that,'Unless the Exchange otherwise agrees only securities registered on the Hong Kong register may be traded on the Exchange' (shown as Rule 19.05(4), 19-2, 5/91, in relation to primary listings, and Rule 19.25(5), 19-11, 11/93, in relation to secondary listings).

21. This broadly captures the reasoning behind United Overseas Bank Ltd's withdrawal of its secondary listing on the Exchange in 1998. For precise details, see 'United Overseas Bank Limited: Withdrawal of Secondary Listing on the Stock Exchange of Hong Kong Limited ("SEHK")'.

22. See SEHK's Monthly Bulletin (Dec., 1998, p. 149) for details of the registrars. Thanks are due to HKSCC Registrars Ltd for supplying information on the companies for which they serve as share registrars.

23. The *Guide to the International Equity Market* (Aug. 1994) states: 'Market-makers are obliged to display continuous two-way prices at which they are prepared to deal in the SEAQ International firm quote securities in which they are registered. This obligation to display exists throughout a prescribed period of the business day called the mandatory quote period (MQP)' (p. 20).

24. Ibid., p. 20.

25. The MQP for Hong Kong Stocks quoted on SEAQ International runs from 09:30—15:30 GMT (see ibid., p. 20).

26. Ibid., p. 51.

27. Ibid., p. 13.

28. The HSLRI is quoted by Hang Seng Index Services Ltd and, like the Hang Seng Index (HSI), is a capital, value-weighted index. As of the 1998 year-end, 29 of the 33 HSI constituents were included in the HSLRI.

29. The concentration of US disclosures on this day is based upon documented findings in Ederington and Lee (1993).

30. See Hui (1993b) for an account of these issues for ADRs on Hong Kong stocks.

31. See Fabozzi, Modigliani, and Ferri (1994, p. 397), for instance, for discussion of this.

32. Thanks are due to Andrew Case for his comments on this issue.

33. This model is evident, for instance, in Huaneng Power International Inc's registration of its 'H' shares (see Huaneng Power International Inc, Listing on the Hong Stock Exchange by way of Introduction, 1998, Appendix IX, IX-1 to IX-2).

34. For the holders of ADRs, the share certificates for the underlying stock may be different to those for the 'HKD dividend shares' that trade locally. As the ADRs are not eligible for local exchange-trading, a conversion of ADRs into 'HKD dividend shares' would necessitate their cancellation and replacement by certificates of the 'HKD dividend share' variety (see ibid. for an application similar to this).

35. As gleaned from a directory of ADR programmes provided by The Bank of New York Company Inc at http://www.bankofny.com/adr/aovrview.htm (updated as of 1 June 1999).

36. See Chao (1995) for further discussion of the trading characteristics of ADRs in PRC stocks.

37. See Chao (1995) for further discussion of this mechanism.

38. Anonymous (Dec 1993/Jan 1994), for a Level I programme, notes: 'One of the most compelling reasons is international exposure for the company name. This is especially true in China, where many companies are depending upon exports for their survival' (p. 10).

39. See Huaneng Power International Inc's Listing on the Hong Kong Stock Exchange by Way of Introduction document.

40. 77 depositary receipts were listed by the close of the 1997 calendar year (see London Stock Exchange Fact File 1998, p. 12).

41. One of the Hong Kong ADRs was shown to have trading status of 'none'.

42. Three of the PRC ADRs were shown to have trading status of 'none' on the Bank of NY homepage. Further enquiries suggest (i) that this indicates incomplete information on the issues and (ii) for these particular issues, a Rule 144A vehicle was used.

8. Share Repurchases, Directors' Dealings, and Corporate Dividend Policies

The materials in Chapters 5 to 7 underline the fact that primary market activities are driven almost as much by market sentiment as by an underlying corporation's need for funding. The contrast between bull and bear market periods—where issues cluster in the former and all but disappear in the latter—is a characteristic of virtually all equity markets.

Market-timing is also critical for corporations repurchasing (or buying-back) stocks already in issue. Such share repurchases are, in fact, the opposite of new issues. While new issues lead to an increase in the number of shares in issue and a siphoning of funds from the market, repurchases do the reverse: cancelling shares in issue and injecting funds into the market for the stock. In this sense, repurchase programmes—which require a mandate from shareholders—add buoyancy to stock values and are more likely than not to be triggered during bear market periods. The surge in local buy-back activity in the last quarter of 1997 in Hong Kong is indicative of this. Not surprisingly, this downturn in market sentiment coincided with a shrinking new issues market.

As the opposite of a new issue, it is logical to consider the share repurchase in relation to the material in Chapters 5 to 7; however, repurchases are not singled out simply because of their antithetical relation to new issues. The scale of local buy-back activity, particularly since the fourth quarter of 1997, means that repurchases constitute a significant type of market activity in Hong Kong. Repurchases are also common in other major markets, like the United Kingdom and the United States. The scale of this activity in the latter is such that a recent article in *Forbes* magazine—in connection with repurchases during 1996 and the early part of 1997—reported that the majority of newly issued shares in the United States were actually offset by repurchases.[1]

For the purposes of this text, repurchases are considered in tandem with two related issues: director share dealings and corporate dividend policy. As share repurchases are typically initiated by a company's directors they appear, on first inspection, to be quite similar to the director share purchase. However, share repurchases—unlike director purchases—are conducted in the name of the underlying corporation and, as such, lead to cancellation of the shares acquired. Director dealings, since they are undertaken specifically in the interests of director(s)—and not the underlying company itself—have no effect on the number of shares in circulation. Regulatory differences are also apparent. For the repurchase, prior approval must be given by a company's shareholders. The same is not true in director dealings, although recent initiatives in the corporate governance area mean that director dealings must be disclosed to the

Exchange in a timely manner, as spelled out in various provisions of the Securities (Disclosure of Interests) Ordinance. Annual corporate reports also contain summary information on such issues for the benefit of the general investment public.

As buy-backs typically have a positive effect on underlying share values, many also see repurchase programmes as an alternative to dividend distributions. The value benefits of repurchase programmes stem from two sources: (i) the inflation of earnings per share figures on the remaining shares, due to the reduction in the number of stocks in issue, and (ii) the support offered to prices by the injection of funds into the market for the stock. In some jurisdictions, where investors face higher marginal income tax rates on income returns than on capital gains, the repurchase may well be preferred to a cash dividend. This is not to say that one precludes the other, as companies engaging in repurchase programmes may well pay sizeable dividends to their shareholders as well. But from an analytical perspective, obvious parallels between dividends and share repurchases can be drawn. In view of this, the dividend policies of locally-listed corporations are also examined and appear as an adjunct to the first two sections of this chapter, which deal, respectively, with local share repurchase activities and director share dealings. An overview of the three areas—repurchases, director share dealings, and corporate dividend policy—is then offered in the final section.

8.1   Share Repurchase Activities[2]

International Comparisons

The United States is without doubt the most active market for share repurchases. In other jurisdictions, like the United Kingdom, Canada, and Australia, buy-backs also occur with some regularity. In a number of countries—particularly within Continental Europe—buy-backs are heavily restrained by regulatory controls and, as a result, occur rather infrequently.[3] Some loosening of these controls is evident in some of these markets, however, with Sweden, for one, proposing amendments to allow buy-back activities.[4] Recent regulatory changes have also made share repurchase activities possible in a number of Pacific-Rim markets. Along with Hong Kong, which has allowed regulated buy-back activities since 1991,[5] New Zealand (since 1993), Japan (since 1994), and Malaysia (since 1997)[6] have instituted regulatory changes allowing such activities in recent years. Such moves were also earmarked in Singapore in 1998, following recommendations by the Review Committee of the Stock Exchange of Singapore.[7]

In most jurisdictions where repurchase activity is admissible—including the Hong Kong SAR, the United Kingdom and other markets with a similar English Common Law inheritance—a buy-back entails the underlying company redeeming shares in circulation for immediate cancellation. In the United States, the practice is slightly different as, instead of share cancellation, the stocks remain in issue—but out of circulation—in the form of corporate treasury stock (CTS). This practice suggests some accounting differences with, instead of a direct debit appearing in the company's issued share capital (ISC) account, as the counterpart to the credit in current assets, a debit is made to a separate CTS account. The dollar book value of shares in circulation is then shown on the balance sheet by offsetting the CTS balance against the ISC balance. The advantage to the US practice is that CTS can be reissued by the corporation if and when required. Apart from this CTS feature, US repurchases are likely to drive market prices in much the same way as they do in Hong Kong. In both markets, a reduction in the number of shares in circulation translates into support for underlying values from such repurchases. Increases in earnings per share, reflecting supply-side changes, and the injection of 'new' funds into the market, on the demand-side, drive this process.[8]

Despite the frequency of buy-backs in Hong Kong, their dollar value is small compared with total equity funds raised in the market. As a guide, the total value of Hong Kong repurchases for 1997 was approximately HK$6.955 billion, in contrast with total equity funds raised over the same period of around HK$247 billion (see Table 8.1).[9] In other words, the value of buy-backs represented approximately 3% of the value of newly issued stock during 1997. Relative to funds raised from IPOs alone—that is, ignoring all seasoned equity issues—a more favourable picture emerges, with share repurchases accounting for approximately 8.5% of unseasoned issue funds.[10] These percentage figures would be much higher if only the last three months of 1997 were considered when repurchase activity peaked and the new issue market—particularly in the months of November and December—almost ground to a halt. Local buy-back activity actually reached its zenith in October 1997, with repurchases in this month alone easily exceeding calendar year levels between 1992 and 1996. Detailed repurchase figures for this month, as well as for the twelve months of 1997, are shown in Appendix 8.1 to further highlight this recent upturn in repurchase activities.

As suggested earlier, the proportion of new stock offset by buy-backs in Hong Kong pales when compared with the United States; although, in the United States, the source of new stock is somewhat different with a large proportion of it stemming from the exercise of employee stock options. These are referred to as Equity Stock Option Plans (ESOPs) in the United States. These call options are typically granted free-of-charge to employees and allow holders the right to buy stock from the underlying issuer on pre-determined terms over some designated future period. The rationale for offering such options is fairly clear: to provide employees with incentives to raise underlying stock values through increased worker productivity and corporate profitability. The benefits of this are captured when the employees purchase new stock from the employer at pre-determined prices, through the exercise of their options, and subsequently

Table 8.1   Buy-Back Activity in Hong Kong: 1992 – March 1998

Month, Year (1)	Value of Buy-Backs (HK$ million) (2)	Range of Closing Hang Sang Index (HSI) Values (3)		Overall Difference in (3) in % Terms[a]
01-12, 1992	699	4297.33 – 6447.11	=	50.03%
01-12, 1993	1,415	5437.80 – 11888.39	=	118.62%
01-12, 1994	2,230	12201.09 – 7707.78	=	-36.83%
01-12, 1995	1,071	6967.93 – 10073.39	=	44.57%
01-12, 1996	1,011	10073.39 – 13530.95	=	34.32%
01, 1997	109	13191.50 – 13868.24	=	5.13%
02, 1997	76	13660.50 – 13102.94	=	-4.08%
03, 1997	301	13507.28 – 12472.33	=	-7.66%
04, 1997	613	12055.17 – 12903.30	=	7.04%
05, 1997	44	13020.78 – 14757.81	=	13.34%
06, 1997	270	13924.34 – 15196.79	=	9.14%
07, 1997	258	14703.73 – 16365.71	=	11.30%
08, 1997	250	16673.27 – 14135.25	=	-15.22%
09, 199	280	13425.65 – 15049.30	=	12.09%
10, 1997	2,720	15128.02 – 9059.89	=	-40.11%
11, 1997	1,202	11255.11 – 9607.91	=	-14.64%
12, 1997	836	11722.94 – 10172.47	=	-13.23%
01-12, 1997	6,960	16673.27 – 9059.89	=	-45.66%
01, 1998	557	10680.57 – 8121.06	=	-23.96%
02, 1998	91	10124.03 – 11480.69	=	13.40%
03, 1998	69	10803.68 – 11810.63	=	9.32%
01-12, 1998	2,950	6660.42 – 11810.63	=	-43.61%

Notes:

a   The values reported for the range for the HSI reflect the chronological ordering of the highs and lows (i.e., if the low occurred prior to the high in the sub-period, the range value is positive).

Monthly and yearly HK$ buy-back totals were provided by R. Halili of Disclosure Inc. in Hong Kong (all were rounded to nearest HK$ million). Closing Hang Seng Index (HSI) values were provided by Hang Seng Index Services Ltd.

sell the stock for profit in the secondary market. The excess return generated, as we saw in relation to the nil-paid right in section 6.3, captures the option's intrinsic value.

As such exercise notices trigger new issues of stock by the underlying company, a dilution of earnings per share, and corresponding fall in share price may follow. Selling pressure in the stock—as the exercising party captures the option's intrinsic value—could also exacerbate the price decline, to the detriment of remaining stockholders. Share repurchase activities may therefore function to counter these effects.

In one sense, the market may be able to anticipate the effects of option exercise from the announcement date of the option issue. This would essentially impound a risk premium into prices. Simply, the risk of dilution would dampen prices, suggesting little or no effect on share prices following option exercise. In practice, this scenario is unlikely. The full effects of option conversion may not be captured, ahead of exercise dates, for two reasons: the timing and number of options exercised cannot be known in advance.[11] Conventional wisdom suggests some negative effects on underlying share prices, especially when large numbers of options are exercised. If this is the case, buy-backs may function as a countermeasure. Directors orchestrating mandated company buy-backs may also see them as a means of ingratiating themselves with option holders. As cogently summarized in recent columns of *Fortune*, this motivation for United States repurchase activities is such that: 'Many of today's buy-backs—most, say some market watchers—are simply a way to pay employees with options without diluting existing shareholders' (Fox, 1997, p. 25).

The fact that a large proportion of employee stock options are granted to senior employees in US institutions—many of whom probably wield significant influence over corporate policy areas, like dividend policy and share repurchase activity—might suggest a conflict of interest where senior management pressure directors to institute buy-back programmes in pursuit of their own self-interest. As this self-interest appears to be to the benefit of the general body of shareholders—a theme which has not gone unnoticed by venerable publications like *The Economist*[12]—shareholders appear to have little to gain by reining in this activity.

As employee stock options are relatively uncommon in Hong Kong—with just over HK$4 million raised in 1997 from share option schemes, accounting for some 1.6% of total equity funds raised[13]—repurchase activities are unlikely to function locally as they do in the United States. Alternative motivations for repurchase activity are more likely to figure, therefore, and are duly considered in later sections.

Methods for Contracting Stock Supply: Comparison of Share Repurchases and Stock Consolidations ('Reverse' Splits)

Like share repurchases, stock consolidations (or reverse splits) serve to reduce the supply of stock in issue, but are quite different to buy-backs in two important respects. Firstly, instead of purchasing existing shares for cancellation—or for conversion into corporate treasury stock, as with US repurchases—consolidations involve an exchange of a smaller number of new shares for all shares previously in issue. Secondly, with respect to the impact upon the par value of the stock, while no specific effect is engendered by a repurchase, the issued share capital account (ISC) balance for the underlying company must remain unchanged in a consolidation—in much the same way as it must with a stock split—which means that the par value of the new shares will increase, relative to the old, in proportion to the exchange factor. To illustrate, suppose 200 million shares are in issue, each with par of $1, and a two into one consolidation is countenanced. If implemented, this would result in 100 million new shares, with par of $2, replacing all pre-existing shares. This would leave the company's ISC account balance unchanged at $200 million: equal to the number of shares in issue multiplied by par. One might also expect the market capitalization of the firm's total equity to be unchanged with the price of each consolidated stock set at approximately twice the old stock's value. The evidence, at least in the United States, is that stockholders generally lose as a result of a reverse split.[14] This being the case, one is left with something of a puzzle: why do stockholders sanction such stock consolidations? One possible answer is offered in Peterson and Peterson (1992, pp. 190–1) where, following US reverse splits, some reduction in trading costs is noted.[15]

Regulations and Mechanics of Share Repurchases in Hong Kong

The general principles, provisions, and regulatory controls relating to local buy-backs are reflected in the local Companies Ordinance (CAP. 32), the Exchange's *Rules Governing the Listing of Securities,* and the Securities and Futures Commission's (SFC's) *Hong Kong Codes on Takeovers and Mergers and Share Repurchases.* From the various provisions therein, three methods for buy-back can be identified: (i) repurchases through 'on-market' transactions; (ii) through 'off-market' transactions; and (iii) through general offers.

Most local repurchase activity is conducted through the 'on-market' method. All of the data shown in Table 8.1 and Appendix 8.1 reflect this method. Once a resolution—requiring shareholder support—is approved, a company can engage in 'on-market' repurchases by buying stock in the open market for cancellation at prevailing market prices. Chapter 10 of the Exchange's Rules Governing the Listing of Securities (herein, the Listing Rules) outlines the various conditions for such a programme. The Listing Rules stipulate that such resolutions should not mandate a purchase of more than 10% of the shares or warrants of the issuer within any financial year (see Rule 10.06(1)(c)) and that a 'cap' be placed on the number of shares or warrants repurchased in a calendar month, equal to 25% of the previous calendar month's trading volume in the securities (see Rule 10.06(2)(a)). Provisions for waivers from the 'cap', and other parts of Rule 10.02, are countenanced, however, in part g of this Rule. The Exchange also recently sought to clarify the conditions for application for such waivers (see SEHK Announcement (1998)), in response to the generally weak volume picture of 1998. In such an economic climate, corporations, with approved repurchase programmes, may feel that the 'cap' effectively undermines any mandate and, as such, acts to the detriment of their wider body of shareholders.

General enquiries suggest that the alternatives to the 'on-market' repurchase—the 'off-market' and general offer methods—rarely figure. While recent cases of the 'off-market' method are not readily apparent, SFC statistics[16] show some activity in the general offer area with three share repurchases made in this way between 1 April 1995 and 31 March

1997. Although general offers are more usually associated with takeover activity in Hong Kong they can be applied in much the same way for repurchases. The third part of the Hong Kong Codes on Takeovers and Mergers and Share Repurchases (here after, the Hong Kong Codes) provide the essential guidelines. To illustrate the workings of such a repurchase, a case study—featuring the Elec & Eltek International Holdings Ltd repurchase of July 1995—is presented below.

Case Study of a Buy-Back through a General Offer

As with all types of general offer, Elec & Eltek International Holdings Ltd's offer was made to all existing stockholders. This entailed an offer by the company to buy up to 30% of the shares in issue—for immediate cancellation—at an offer price of HK$1.08 per share. From *Elec & Eltek International Holdings Ltd's Conditional Cash Offer Prospectus*, this meant that of the 1,004.601 million shares outstanding prior to the offer, a maximum of approximately 301.380 million shares were available for cancellation. As the majority shareholder and 'related parties', holding approximately 489.126 million shares (48.7% of outstanding shares), had made 'irrevocable undertakings'[17] not to include their shares in the repurchase, the remaining shareholders were offered the opportunity to tender additional shares for repurchase in excess of their assured entitlement of 146.738 million shares. These shares were made available to remaining shareholders through excess tenders.[18] It transpired that only 54.818 million shares were accepted for cancellation, raising the majority interest to 51.5%.[19]

The conditional nature of the above offer meant that certain qualifications had to be met before the offer became concrete or unconditional.[20]

Motivations for Share Repurchase Activity

A greater concentration of repurchase activity is always likely in bear market periods. The surge in local buy-back activity in late 1997, as shown in Table 8.1 earlier,[21] aptly reflects this. Knowledge of the general linkage between repurchase activity and market sentiment also means that buy-backs provide signals to investors. As companies have an incentive to buy-back at the end—rather than the beginning—of a bear-run, increased buy-back activity may well alert investors to renewed profit opportunities. The same might also be said about director share purchases. However, the efficient markets paradigm (EMP) would suggest, in relation to the announcement of both, a swift and complete stock price adjustment upon release of this information. In this sense, trading on such information—after the fact—would prove futile. For the 'on-market' buy-back, which is the most widely used repurchase method in Hong Kong, information is also conveyed upon the execution of the buy-back given that the precise dates for consummation are not known in advance. The EMP would suggest the possibility of abnormal returns only by those able to anticipate the timing of such 'on-market' repurchases.

The extent to which the EMP holds with regard to share repurchase and director dealing announcements—and the actual timing of 'on-market' repurchases—is an empirical question and, at least for Hong Kong, awaits further enquiry.

The (Positive) Signalling Arguments

Recent studies in other markets, namely Oyon, Markides, and Ittner's (1994), suggest that buy-backs also signal favourable information about corporate earnings prospects. Since directors with favourable earnings expectations realize that underlying share prices will rise once this information is released, planned repurchases can be carried out at lower cost by scheduling them prior to the relevant disclosures. Recognition of this by investors, means that the repurchase action signals information about the quality of earnings with, other things being equal, a larger repurchase conveying stronger sentiment in relation to future earnings. Survey evidence in the United States highlights the validity of this effect.[22]

A Counter Measure Against the Dilution Effects of Employee Stock Options

The buy-back may be orchestrated, as we saw earlier, with employee stock options in mind. With the exercise of such options forcing underlying companies to issue new stock on agreed terms, a dilution in corporate earnings per share (EPS) may result. In this environment, repurchases could function to mop up a surfeit of new shares—and, by connection—counter a material dilution in EPS. This is somewhat self-serving. In this argument, the buy-back, by offsetting any dilution in EPS, helps preserve the value of remaining unexercised options.

The above motivation for buy-back is likely to be far more important in the United States than markets like Hong Kong where employee stock options still carry some novelty value. The equity warrant is of greater import locally which, much like the employee stock option when exercised, forces issuing companies to sell new shares at an agreed exercise price. In brief, the instrument is akin to a long-term call option and, rather than being distributed free-of-charge to company employees, is sold in the open market. The scale of the dilution effect from such exercise notices however—while potentially greater than those from employee stock options—is still small. To illustrate, the exercise of equity warrants in 1997 raised only HK$8.33 billion on the SEHK: about twice the amount raised from the exercise of employee stock options and equivalent to about 3% of total equity funds raised in the whole market.[23] In this sense, then, both the employee stock option and its more popular cousin, the equity warrant, suggest only limited dilution of EPS numbers in local companies. Unlike the United States then, repurchase programmes are unlikely to be conceived as a counterweight to employee options or warrants.

The Tax Benefits of Repurchase Programmes

The much-touted tax benefit surrounding a repurchase is also less apparent in Hong Kong. In the United States, the so-called double-taxation effect on dividends—where payments are subject to both federal corporate income taxes and personal income taxes—means that buy-backs may feature as a tax-effective substitute to cash dividends.[24] While most investors in Hong Kong would probably agree that buy-backs enhance shareholder value, the capital gains generated are not necessarily preferred to an equivalent cash payment, given the absence of both (financial) income and capital gains taxes. For foreign investors and institutions in the market, the story may be rather different. Their situation clearly depends upon any tax agreement between Hong Kong and their home country, and the extent to which offshore income is taxed in the home jurisdiction. While this is rather difficult to evaluate, the primary role played by local retail and institutional investors in the market suggests a much weaker role for the buy-back as a tax-effective substitute to the cash dividend.

A Response to the Threat of Takeover

Repurchases may also be driven by the threat of takeover. As virtually all corporate buy-backs are conducted 'on-market' and involve the underlying company buying stock from, in the main, parties with relatively small holdings, repurchases tend to raise the percentage stakes of major shareholders. They also swallow up free holdings in the market that can easily fall prey to outside buyers. However, the extent of this—at least in Hong Kong—is limited by the public float requirement for stocks listed on the Exchange.[25]

In short, buy-backs can have a role in helping stave off takeover. Whether this is a good thing or not depends upon the benefits of acquisition activity to the underlying company's shareholders, its consumers, and to the overall economy. The evidence is somewhat mixed on this issue, but one thing is clear: if takeovers are to be avoided, for whatever reason, the corporate buy-back is a relatively cheap and effective means of doing so. This and other defensive measures—like 'golden parachutes'—are examined in the next chapter. Suffice it to say, that most of these defensive strategies are foreign to the local market given the general absence of hostile takeovers.

One interesting irony is that local buy-backs may actually trigger takeovers. Certain provisions in Rule 26.1 of the Hong Kong Codes, for instance, come into play if buy-back activity results in a party with a fractional share interest of less than 35% being forced to cross the 35% majority control threshold. If this were to happen, a general offer would be triggered unless a waiver against this were granted. If a waiver were not granted, the offer would need to be made by the consolidating stockholder (and any related parties) to all other parties holding shares in the company. The Elec & Eltek International Holdings Ltd's share repurchase, through general offer, considered earlier, is a useful reference in this regard. A waiver from the relevant parts of Rule 26.1[26] of the Hong Kong Codes was in fact granted ahead of the repurchase offer in this case. The nature of Rule 26.1 and the general offer mechanism—as it pertains to takeovers—is considered in greater detail in the next chapter.

Consolidation of Share Interest

Aside from takeover concerns, the consolidation of stock ownership brought about by a buy-back may benefit underlying shareholders. By concentrating share ownership, a more direct role in the day-to-day running of the firm may be established resulting in a clearer, and more profitable, strategic plan for the firm.[27]

Adjustments to Working Capital

Less sanguine accounts for repurchase activity can also be made. Some stockholders may believe that a company engaging in buy-back activity is cash-rich and is trying to unload excess working capital. This might not be appreciated for two reasons: (i) shareholders may feel that high yielding investment opportunities are being bypassed; and (ii) that the cancellation of shares and diminution of the company's asset base, brought about by the repurchase, inflates the company's gearing rate and, quite possibly, its credit risk. Both of these points suggest weakness in the corporation's overall strategic plan.

There is also another twist on (i) above. If investors see excessive amounts of working capital being pumped into the market to buy back shares, they may conclude that the company has either a poor strategic plan, or worse, little access to good investment projects. If the share price prior to the buy-backs had impounded an expectation of positive net present value (NPV) projects emerging, news of the repurchase may send stock prices reeling. Not only are excessive amounts of working capital undesirable, but attempts to seemingly fritter the amounts away on nothing better than buy-backs could well raise the ire of shareholders.

On the positive side, the gearing issue raised in (ii) may not be all bad. Buy-backs can lead to a reduction in a company's weighted average cost of capital (WACC). WACC is measured, at least in its simplest form, by weighting the required rates of return on the financing sources of the firm—essentially debt and equity—by the proportion of each in the firm's capital structure. It essentially captures the hurdle or benchmark rate for the evaluation of investment returns within the firm, although the required rates of return on specific investments, due to their risk, may lie above or below the firm's WACC. In simple terms, though, a reduction in the WACC is akin to lowering the height of fences in a steeplechase: it makes it easier for managers to beat their target rate of return.[28] For the managers that might be a good thing when their contracts are up for renewal. To illustrate the use of WACC, suppose that company X has a balance sheet as below and judges the required rates of return (cost of capital) on its debt and (owners') equity to be 7% and 15%, respectively.

$million	B/Sheet of X	$million
Assets 2,000	Owner's Equity: Issued Share Capital & Reserves	1,200
	Debt: Liabilities	800
2,000		2,000

In this case, the simple WACC would be 11.8%.[29] If a large corporate buy-back of, say, $300 million were made, total assets would shrink to $1, 700 million and owner's equity to $900 million.[30] The corporation's WACC would also be lowered to 11.24%.[31]

Only a very large buy-back is likely to materially alter the WACC and, therefore, the firm's hurdle rate. As large buy-outs are probably more typical, again, of the US market, one would not expect local corporate managers to be unduly concerned by the effects of buy-back on either gearing rates or WACC levels. Nonetheless, the effects may explain part of the motivation underpinning buy-backs elsewhere.

Negative Signalling Arguments

We have already seen how this can work when companies weigh into the market with huge amounts of working capital. Buy-backs—and, in particular, their actual timing where mandated 'on-market' directives exist— may also be driven by managers or insiders wishing to conceal a cash-flow problem from its wider body of shareholders and creditors. A stable stock price might allay suspicions or fears on this front. If this can be achieved by the company buying-back its own shares and simultaneously convincing investors that the action is motivated by the shares being cheap, the intervention might help the company stave off cash calls. This would certainly fit in cases where major shareholders pledge their shares as collateral for company or personal loans. A falling share price might cause the creditor to recall the loan and sell the underlying shares (if default occurs). This would not only dilute the ownership interest of the shareholder but could also force him/her, or the underlying company if the debt is a corporate liability, into immediate receivership.

In theory, there are numerous ways in which repurchases could be used to manipulate share prices. Issues of space prevent anything near a comprehensive assessment of these. For interested readers, Dugan and Keef's (1989) lucid account is highly recommended.[32] In practice, one hopes that supervision of markets severely limits the scope of such egregious ploys.

Despite some of the negative views aired, most commentators greet the buy-back as a harbinger of good fortune. This was apparent in the United States during 1997 and most of 1998 when many commentators pointed to soaring levels of buy-back activity as evidence of only one thing: a continuation in the 'bull' run. But much of this activity could have been driven by factors other than the perceived state of the US economy: a reaction to the dilution effects of employee stock options could have been one; the risk of takeover another. The remarkable level of takeover activity in the United States during the 1997–8 period, which also helped to fuel the 'bull' run, strongly points to the latter.

8.2   Director Share Dealings

Unlike the company buy-back, director dealings are undertaken specifically in the interests of the director(s). In this sense, they represent a rather special kind of secondary market activity and, unlike the buy-back, have no effect whatsoever on the number of shares in issue. To many, they provide a more refined insight into the longer-term prospects of the underlying company than the buy-back. A director, purchasing on his/her own account by investing his/her own money—rather than the company's, which would be the case in a buy-back—typically projects a much stronger positive signal to the market. The flip-side of course, is that director sales also project strong signals, but in the opposite direction. It is precisely because directors are informed players that such deals are so closely scrutinized. Directors, as key insiders, are viewed in much the same way as major shareholders by the market-watcher. Even where the directors are not in possession of significant holdings, their insider position would suggest some degree of 'informedness' in their trades.

Table 8.2 provides some insight into both the size and direction of director deals in Hong Kong. The relation between director activity and market sentiment appears somewhat mixed. Unlike the buy-back, where companies seem to weigh heavily into the market during months when the Hang Seng Index (HSI) is falling, director purchases are not uniformly concentrated in declining market periods. Nor, at least at the aggregate level, are director sales necessarily consummated in rising market periods. This may be due to lead times with deals consummated well ahead of anticipated market changes. This is consistent with the stronger signalling role in such deals. The noticeable spikes in net-selling in June and August of 1997, ahead of the precipitous market decline of the last quarter of 1997, provide ammunition for this view. In a similar vein, the spate of net-selling in February and March 1998 was organized ahead of market declines in April, May, and June of that year. In this sense, then, director deals may capture information that is somewhat more prescient than the company-orchestrated buy-back. They may, however, be more concentrated or company-specific than the buy-back, making it harder to see general relationships between aggregate dealing activity and the overall market. In this sense, the avid market-watcher should zero-in on particular directors and companies.

The key provisions relating to the disclosure of director dealings are contained in the Securities (Disclosure of Interests) Ordinance with principal attention drawn to Part III of this ordinance, which deals with 'Disclosure of Interests of Directors, Chief Executives and Their Families'. The principal disclosure requirement for directors and chief executives is that any deal should be communicated to the Exchange in writing within the five day

Table 8.2 Directors' Dealings in Hong Kong: 1995 – June 1998

	Purchases (HK$million) (1)	Sales (HK$million) (2)	Net Total (HK$million) (1) – (2)	Aggregate Total (HK$million) (1) + (2)	Range of Closing HSI Values* (%)
1995	6,425.917	7,388.394	(962.477)	13,814.311	44.57
1996	11,593.686	8,458.621	3,135.065	20,052.307	34.32
Jan 1997	1,624.984	931.615	693.369	2,556.599	5.13
Feb	786.297	231.100	555.197	1,017.397	(4.08)
Mar	1,156.845	509.474	647.371	1,666.319	(7.66)
Apr	2,898.366	398.237	2,500.130	3,296.603	7.04
May	1,374.340	1,062.531	311.809	2,436.871	13.34
Jun	1,285.316	2,187.733	(902.417)	3,473.049	9.14
Jul	1,006.772	595.960	410.812	1,602.732	11.30
Aug	769.991	1,215.045	(445.055)	1,985.036	(15.22)
Sep	1,043.386	685.598	357.788	1,728.984	12.09
Oct	3,282.495	275.836	3,006.659	3,558.331	(40.11)
Nov	780.248	179.005	601.244	959.253	(14.64)
Dec	362.588	264.758	97.829	627.346	(13.23)
Jan–Dec	16,371.628	8,536.892	7,834.736	24,908.520	(45.66)
Jan 1998	1,334.136	856.323	477.813	2,190.459	(23.96)
Feb	287.880	605.950	(318.070)	893.830	13.40
Mar	89.134	446.320	(357.187)	535.454	9.32
Apr	324.919	371.308	(46.389)	696.227	(9.08)
May	495.945	56.025	439.919	551.970	(15.96)
Jun	373.456	32.713	340.743	406.169	(15.38)
Jan–Jun	2,905.474	2,368.639	536.829	5,274.109	(36.82)

* The values reported for the range for the HSI reflect the chronological ordering of the closing daily highs and lows (i.e., if the low occurred prior to the high in the sub-period, the range value is positive and the percentage return is $((HSI_{high} - HSI_{low})/HSI_{low}) \times 100)$.

Monthly and yearly HKD director deals were provided by R. Halili of Disclosure Inc. in Hong Kong. Closing HSI, for computation of *, were provided by Hang Seng Index Services Ltd.

Table Extracted from McGuinness (1998b, p. 45)

period following the execution of the deal. This is in accordance with Section 28(3) of the ordinance. Dealings are also restricted ahead of major, price-sensitive announcements with, amongst other things, directors prohibited from dealing in the stock in their own companies in the month immediately prior to earnings announcements.[33]

While many interpret both director purchases and company buy-backs as bull market signals, some degree of caution should be exercised before leaping into the market on the back of such trades. Leaving aside efficiency arguments—which would suggest that prices react fully and immediately to the news conveyed in such trades and that it is, therefore, too late to benefit after the event—one can conceive of circumstances where buy-backs and director dealings might mislead. The potential for this is, perhaps, greatest with the director trade given the interest such trades command; however, there are limits to such false signalling moves. One would not expect a director to buy heavily into stock that he/she knew to have imminent problems simply because of the personal losses that would result from such interjections. This would be especially true if the director had had only a moderate stake in the company prior to the interjection.

While director deals have the potential to mislead, they can only do so on an occasional basis and, even then, over short-term time horizons. Some degree of market-learning or efficiency must exist such that players with a consistent record of timely purchases are able to convey stronger positive signals when they subsequently re-enter the market.

8.3   Corporate Dividend Policy

As share repurchases, in some respects, serve as a substitute for dividend payments, it is appropriate to compare dividend payment practices in Hong Kong with the buy-back activity already outlined. In any year, the level of dividend paid to shareholders hinges largely upon the level of earnings attributable to stockholders (EAS). If this figure is small or negative, a dividend will probably not be declared. When EAS is at normal levels, a proportion of the amount will be reinvested in the firm (i.e., credited to retained earnings) with the balance being paid out as dividend.

Dividend Payment Practice in Hong Kong

Most dividend payments come in the form of cash. It is also conceivable that payments can come in the following forms: (i) cash payment with scrip option; (ii) cash payment plus stock (i.e., in the form of a bonus issue or a stock split); (iii) a dividend distribution in specie; or (iv) a cash payment with bonus warrants. In method (i), which is commonly employed, shareholders can elect to take a proportion of their dividend in the form of new stock (scrip) or all of their dividend in cash. Method (ii) is slightly different as it entails the underlying company paying an amount of cash and stock as dividend. Similarly, method (iv) entails a given distribution of warrants on the underlying stock, in place of the stock itself, in the distribution. Method (iii) appears the least common, where the shares of a third company, held as a financial asset of the dividend paying company, are distributed in lieu of a cash dividend.

In theory, dividends can also be paid wholly in the form of stock through a bonus issue (stock dividend or capitalization issue) or stock split.[34] In practice, cash is likely to feature as an accompanying payment, with both payments sharing a common ex-date. In terms of the agenda in the Annual General Meeting (AGM), in the case of a final dividend, the cash dividend is likely to feature as the proposed dividend with a separate resolution—also requiring shareholder support—appearing for the stock distribution.

In Hong Kong, the majority of listed companies pay dividends twice yearly: as an interim dividend and a final dividend, which are typically spaced six months apart. This contrasts with markets like the United States where dividends are paid quarterly. Although additional, or special dividends, may be paid to stockholders in Hong Kong listed corporations, these, more than likely, feature as an adjunct to the final dividend payment for the accounting year. To provide an insight into the dividend payment process, details of recent dividends in a representative locally-listed stock— the Hang Seng Bank—are shown in Table 8.3.

As Table 8.3 shows, dividend announcements and payments, for a given company, follow a similar timetable year after year. As well as the observation that interim and final dividends follow a well-defined six-monthly cycle, the lag between financial year-end and dividend announcement is quite predictable. For most listed companies, this is around eight weeks, although annual reports—containing final dividend recommendations from the company's directors—can appear with a lag of up to four or five months (after the accounting year-end).

For most companies in Hong Kong, the accounting year-end is either 31 March or 31 December, with the former clearly chosen to coincide with the fiscal or tax year. Given typical lags between a company's accounting year-end and publication of its annual report, dividend and earnings announcements typically cluster in late February/early March— for companies with a 31 December year-end—and in late May/early June— for companies with a 31 March year-end. A slightly shorter lag is typical between the half-year point and the disclosure date of interim dividends and earnings. Companies with December year-ends typically report their interim figures in early to mid-August and those with March year-ends in early to mid-October. Similar lags can also be envisioned for companies with other accounting year-ends. The popularity of the 31 December and 31 March year-end means that the market is subject to two seasonal reporting periods a year, where trading volumes rise immediately prior to and just after the release of the earnings and dividends figures.

Final dividends, due to their size—which, based upon anecdotal evidence, appear to be about two to three times the size of interim payments—are the key dividend payment. They are also subject to ratification by shareholders, typically at the AGM, held shortly after the company's accounting year-end. In this sense, the final dividend represents a proposed payment, rather than a declaration, by the directors. The interim dividend, in contrast, typically appears as a declared dividend in published mid-year accounts. This difference reflects provisions set out in the Companies Ordinance in Hong Kong.[35] In practical terms, the difference between a proposal and declaration of dividend is largely semantic as

Table 8.3 The Dividend Time-table in a Representative Listed Stock: The Hang Seng Bank (1993–1998)

Announcement Date of Dividend (1)	Type of Dividend, Amount (per Share) (2)	Ex-Date (3)	Payment Date (4)	Accounting Year-End (5)	Profit Attributable to Shareholders (HK$million) (6)	Dividends (HK$million) (7)	Dividend Pay-out Ratio [(7)/(6)]*100 (8)
19 Aug 93	Interim: HK$0.50	09 Sep 93	23 Sep 93	31 Dec 93	2,745.7*	965.8*	35.2*
28 Feb 94	Final: HK$1.15	31 Mar 94	21 Apr 94	31 Dec 93	3,956.5*	2,221.2*	56.1*
					6,702.4	3,187	47.6
15 Aug 94	Interim: HK$0.60	07 Sep 94	19 Sep 94	31 Dec 94	3,107*	1,159*	37.3*
27 Feb 95	Final: HK$2.09	03 Apr 95	19 Apr 95	31 Dec94	4,308*	4,037*	93.7*
					7,415	5,196	70.1
14 Aug 95	Interim: HK$0.60	06 Sep 95	18 Sep 95	31 Dec 95	3,237*	1,159*	35.8*
26 Feb 96	Final: HK$2.30	01 Apr 96	17 Apr 96	31 Dec 95	4,747*	4,443*	93.6*
					7,984	5,602	70.2
05 Aug 96	Interim: 1.26	28 Aug 96	09 Sep 96	31 Dec 96	4,351*	2,434*	55.9*
03 Mar 97	Final: HK$1.82	27 Mar 97	15 Apr 97	31 Dec 96	4,136*	3,515#	85.0*
					8,487	5,949	70.1
04 Aug 97	Interim: HK$1.40	27 Aug 97	08 Sep 97	31 Dec 97	4,982*	2,704*	54.3*
23 Feb 98	Final: HK$2.02	31 Mar 98	16 Apr 98	31 Dec 97	4,381	3,865*	88.2*
					9,363	6,569	70.2
03 Aug 98	Interim: HK$1.40	26 Aug 98	07 Sep 98	31 Dec 98	3,802*	2,678*	70.4*

Source: The Securities Journal, Trading Record (Various Issues) and the SEHK Monthly Bulletin ('dividend announcement', various). Data in Columns (6) - (8) were obtained from Hang Seng Bank Annual Reports and Interim Reports for the period 1993–8.

Notes: * Financial data extracted from Interim Reports for the first six months (1 Jan – 30 June) of each financial year.

     # Financial data for the last six months of each year (1 Jul – 31 December) were also obtained from Hang Seng Bank Interim Reports.

shareholders appear to approve virtually all final dividend proposals when called to do so. This is, perhaps, not too surprising given the dominance of major stockholders—achieved either directly or indirectly, through connected parties—on the boards of typical Hong Kong listed companies. What is more interesting is the scheduling of AGMs which often occur after the final dividend's ex-date. On the one hand, this suggests confidence on the part of the directors that the dividend will be 'declared' by shareholders at the AGM. It also means that shareholders buying the stock ahead of the ex-date, in order to capture the forthcoming dividend, are trading solely on a recommendation. The risk of a change, which can only be a downward revision, according to the Companies Ordinance,[36] is a risk factor, albeit a minor one.

The Ex-Dividend Effect

Whether dealing with interim or final dividends, the ex-date for the dividend generally precedes payment by a period of three to four weeks. This date, as discussed in Section 3.1, signifies the date from which a stock sells without entitlement to a forthcoming dividend. In a stable or flat market, the value of the stock should fall at the opening of trading on the ex-date. In the absence of taxes and transaction costs, this adjustment should be approximately equal to the value of the dividend forgone. Income and capital gains taxes may modify this effect, though.

By considering closing prices for a stock on the day prior to the ex-date (P_{X-1}) and the ex-date itself (P_X), Elton and Gruber (1970) show the difference ($P_{X-1}-P_X$) to be 77.7% of the associated dividend in US stocks. This was determined using 4,000 or more ex-dividend observations. From the 'drop-off' (= ($P_{X-1}-P_X$)/D), they infer a mean *marginal income tax rate* of 36.4%.[37] For Hong Kong, the absence of income and capital gains taxes on local security investments suggests a drop-off much closer to 1. Transaction costs may cause some deviation from this, though the points made in Section 3.1 apply. Any significant departure from a drop-off of 1 suggests potential gains. A drop-off markedly lower than 1 would suggest abnormal returns from buying stock just prior to an ex-date and selling it immediately thereafter. The dividend collected would more than cover the capital loss. Where the reverse occurs, investors should short the stock just prior to the ex-date and close-out the position on the ex-date. The capital gain would exceed the dividend forgone. These kinds of buying and selling pressures should ensure that departures from the drop-off relationship, described in Elton and Gruber (1970, p. 69), are not a recurring feature of markets.

Elton and Gruber also identify investment clienteles. These arise because investors, of a certain tax bracket, gravitate to particular stocks. All other things being equal, high dividend-paying stocks should attract low marginal income tax investors and high-growth (low-dividend paying) stocks should attract higher income tax payers.

The Record Date

Following almost immediately after the ex-date is the record period. During this time the company's share register—which records changes in the ownership of the underlying stock—closes temporarily. Book closure normally commences on the second business day following an ex-date and continues for a period of around five working days. A Thursday ex-date, which is commonly chosen in Hong Kong,[38] therefore suggests book closure between Monday and Friday of the following week. The gap between ex-date and book closure is a reflection of the T+2 settlement system and allows trades just ahead of the ex-date—occurring late Wednesday in the example above—to be settled and recorded in the register prior to book closure. Once the share registrar closes the books, all parties appearing on the register necessarily qualify for dividends.

The Stability of Dividend Payments

As well as the predictability of dividend announcement, payment and ex-dates, many also point to the stability of year-on-year dividend payments. This is particularly true of dividend pay-out ratios—measured by the proportion of dividends paid from profits attributable to shareholders—and is evident in the analysis of the Hang Seng Bank in Table 8.3.

An overwhelming body of evidence indicates that firms are reluctant to change dividend payment levels markedly from one year to the next, and that 'target' dividend levels are typically sought. Ariff and Johnson (1990),[39] in their excellent review of major studies in the area, report a range, for mean target payout ratios in US studies, of between 0.49 and 0.82. These figures are determined from regression analysis. Essentially, a mean target pay-out ratio of 0.5 suggests, other things being equal, that a $1 increase in earnings triggers a $0.50 increase in dividends over the previous period's level. Conducting a similar analysis for Singaporean companies, Ariff and Johnson (1990) find a much lower mean ratio (of about 0.12).[40] Idle speculation would also suggest mean pay-out ratios well below the US range in Hong Kong. Perhaps the lowest mean target pay-out ratios in Asia would be found in Japan. Evidence in Allen's (1992) survey, and from his literature review (p. 55), point to dividends being linked to par values. This also suggests extremely low dividend payments, which is consistent with anecdotal evidence.[41]

The notion of target dividend levels dates back to Lintner's (1956) pioneering field work in the United States and has been uncovered numerous times since across a range of markets and time periods. Kester and Chang's (1994) questionnaire-based survey of chief executive officers of SEHK listed companies unearths this finding in the local context. Considerable empirical evidence also points to share prices being highly sensitive to dividend cuts or omissions (see, for instance, Benesh et al. (1984) for the United States and Guo and Keown (1992) for Hong Kong). The evidence also suggests an asymmetry of market response where increases in dividends, of for example 10%, have only a small positive effect on underlying share prices while cuts of the same magnitude lead to sharp falls.[42]

The adverse reaction to dividend cuts may reflect a view that positive information is released in full to the market whilst negative news is sometimes withheld and, even when released, not revealed in its entirety. Cuts in dividend levels, or worse—their complete omission—may signal to investors an imminent cash-flow problem which may not have been readily apparent from earlier accounting disclosures by the company. Events like the Asian currency crisis spring to mind, where countless companies in the region saw debt assets wither, as the base currencies of debtors tumbled. Unless adequate contingencies for such bad debts are reflected in balance sheets, shareholders are unlikely to know the real value of the company's assets. It is this kind of information gap that helps to explain the significance of dividends in signalling cash-flow strength or weakness.

The asymmetric response to dividend change is argued to be the *raison d'être* for dividend 'smoothing' which reflects, as noted in Lintner's (1956) seminal paper, the wishes of managers and directors to set dividends at long-run target levels and to adjust dividends gradually in accordance with this target level. Raising dividends in one period and then clawing them back in the next would certainly damage shareholder value, if extant evidence means anything. Dividends are only likely to be raised, therefore, if the directors of the underlying corporation are confident that the new dividend level can be sustained.

Cuts in dividends are not easily countenanced. But in some cases a cut might not necessarily signal bad news; although the directors of a company instituting such a change would need to be confident that this view could be relayed to their shareholders. A good example might be where a company has earmarked a new lucrative investment project and, for reasons of project funding, needs to cut dividends. If the project and dividend announcement are made contemporaneously, one might envisage shareholders responding positively to the overall announcement: with the expectation of increased corporate earnings engendered by the new project—and thus the potential for increased future dividends—offsetting the effect of a temporary cut in dividend.

8.4 Concluding Remarks

To some commentators, discussion of dividends amounts to much ado about nothing given the highly speculative nature of the local market, where investors rarely purchase stock in relation to expected dividend streams and move in and out of the market on a whim. Relatively low dividend yields of about 3% would seem to add ammunition to such a view. However, this general sentiment ignores the existence of longer-term players—who are increasingly evident in the field of institutional funds and pension fund management—and a general body of investors who seek out the relatively low-risk, stable income streams emanating from stocks in companies like utilities. Empirical studies also suggest that dividend changes are significant in driving the local market. Dividends therefore matter, even for the most speculative of investors who, even if shunning any interest in such cash distributions, benefits from knowledge that dividend changes have a definite and marked effect on underlying stock prices.

In a similar manner, share repurchases and director dealings have a key role in driving market prices. To non-believers of the EMP, serious study of these events can be used to develop profitable trading rules. To others, who believe in efficient price setting processes, this is anathema. Instead, anticipation of the relevant announcements and execution dates—in respect of the mandated on-market repurchase programme—is the name of the game. Whatever the empirical reality, most would contend that dividends, buy-backs and director dealings have a key role in driving market prices.

Appendix 8.1   Summary Details of Buy-Back Activity in Hong Kong:
1 January – 31 December 1997

Month	Number of Trading Days (1)	Number of Deals		Value (HK$million)	Range of Closing Hang Seng Index Values (5)
		Daily Average (2)	Sum (3)	Sum (4)	
December	21	13.000	273	1,201.69	10,172.47 – 11,722.94(-)
November	20	15.550	311	836.20	9,607.91 – 11,255.11(-)
October	20	18.650	373	2,720.41	9,059.89 – 15,128.02(-)
September	20	3.250	65	280.18	13,425.65 – 15,049.30(+)
August	17	2.706	46	249.59	14,135.25 – 16,673.27(-)
July	20	2.650	53	258.30	14,703.73 – 16,365.71(+)
June	19	4.158	79	270.39	13,924.34 – 15,196.79(+)
May	18	1.889	34	43.93	13,020.78 – 14,757.81(+)
April	22	5.364	118	612.70	12,055.17 – 12,903.30(+)
March	15	2.600	39	301.10	12,472.33 – 13,507.28(-)
February	16	3.250	52	76.40	13,102.94 – 13,660.50(-)
January	22	4.864	107	109.34	13,191.50 – 13,868.24(+)
Calendar Year Totals	230	6.739	1550	6,960.20	9,059.89 – 16,673.27(-)

Notes:
- Signs in parentheses in Column 5 indicate the general trend of the HSI for the calendar months (i.e., a negative (positive) sign indicates that the highest (lowest) closing price for the month occurred prior to the lowest (highest) closing price for the month).
- All computations for buy-backs are based upon daily buy-back data provided by R. Halili of *Disclosure Inc.* in Hong Kong. Computations using the Hang Seng Index (HSI) are based upon data provided by *Hang Seng Index Services Ltd.*

Notes

1. Specifically, *Forbes* Magazine reports: 'almost the entire supply of stock from new stock offerings is being offset by corporate repurchase programmes.' (Hulbert (1997, p. 386)).

2. Much of the material in Section 8.1 represents an extension of an earlier published paper (see McGuinness, 1997c).

3. Leander's (1996) review of European buy-backs suggests that such inactivity reflects tax considerations as well as regulatory constraints.

4. See Fredborg (1997) for details of these proposed changes.

5. The SFC's Hong Kong Code on Share Repurchases marked this event. This Code was later incorporated into the Hong Kong Code on Takeovers and Mergers to form an all-embracing code.

6. For accounts of buy-back activities in Japan and New Zealand, see Shibato (1995) and Bradbury and Westwood (1996), respectively. Thanks are expressed to C.K. Low for information relating to regulatory changes in Malaysia announced in 1997.

7. The *Report of the SES Review Committee*, as Recommendation 46 states that, 'The SERC recommends that the Companies Act be amended to allow companies to buy back stock and keep them as treasury stocks.' (8.1, 29 July 1998).

8. As cogently argued by Hulbert (1997), these favourable supply and demand effects are in stark contrast to those arising from new share issues.

9. Data as supplied by R. Halili of Disclosure Inc. were used to compute this total. HKD sums for total equity funds raised were drawn from the SEHK *Fact Book 1997*, p. 67.

10. These IPO funds were determined from the SEHK *Fact Book 1997*, p. 67 from sub-totals for equity funds raised from an 'offer for subscription'; an 'offer for sale'; and an 'offer for placing'.

11. Thanks are due to Stephen Keef for discussions on this issue.

12. See Anonymous (Apr/May 1998).

13. See SEHK *Fact Book 1997*, p. 67.

14. See Peterson and Peterson (1992, p. 190) for a brief overview of this evidence.

15. As a summary point, Peterson and Peterson (1992) note: 'the reverse split may be used to place the stock price in a more attractive trading range, which, in turn, may be associated with lower transaction costs for shareholders' (page 190).

16. See Securities & Futures Commission, Inserts: *Hong Kong Code on Takeovers and Mergers and Share Repurchases: Statistics of cases during the 12-month periods ended 31 March 1997 and 31 March 1996.*

17. See page 4 of the Prospectus.

18. The possibility that, in addition to all 'assured entitlements' being accepted, sufficient 'excess tenders' were made to reach the ceiling of 301.380 million shares, meant that an increase in the ownership stake of majority parties, from 48.7% to a maximum of 69.6% (= {489.126 million/(1004.601 million − 301.860 million)} × 100), could be countenanced.

19. [= (489.126 million/949.783 million) × 100]. Information on the outcome of this offer was obtained from *Wardley Cards* (Elec & Eltek International Holdings Ltd, W014-W015, published by Wardley Data Services Ltd).

20. According to Elec & Eltek International Holdings Ltd's Conditional Offer Prospectus, the offer would reach unconditional status, 'upon the passing of an ordinary resolution by Independent Shareholders. . . .' (p. 6). The case description indicates that this was achieved.

21. All averages reported are based upon data provided by R. Halili of Disclosure Inc. which is gratefully acknowledged.

22. See Cudd, Duggal, and Sarkar (1996).

23. See SEHK *Fact Book 1997*, p. 67.

24. The punitive effects of taxes on dividends in the US are highlighted in Bagwell and Shoven (1989). They note: 'Even with the new lower marginal tax rates of the 1986 Tax Reform Act, most household shareholders have marginal personal income tax rates of 28 or 33%, meaning that the combined corporate and personal taxes on dividends exceed 50%.' (page 129).

25. Rule 10.06(2), part f, in the Listing Rules makes specific reference to this.

26. See page 5 of the Prospectus for details of the waiver granted.

27. Surveys in other markets typically stress the importance of this factor and the takeover deterrence argument in inspiring repurchasing activity (see, for instance, Cudd and Duggal and Sarkar (1996)).

28. This might be true in the short-term, but with a decrease in the debtholder's cash protection—given the shrinkage in asset levels—a higher cost of debt might be called for.

29. $= \{(0.4 \times 0.07) + (0.6 \times 0.15)\} \times 100$.

30. In the case of the United States, the use of corporate treasury stock as argued earlier, would mean that $900 million would be shown as a net balance on owners' equity.

31. $(= \{(800/1,700) \times 0.07) + ((900/1,700) \times 0.15)\} \times 100)$.

32. See Dugan and Keef, Company Purchase of Own Shares: The Case for New Zealand (pp. 46-49).

33. Similar sentiments also apply to the buy-back, see Rule 10.06(2) part (e) of the Listing Rules (p. 10-5, November 1993). The restrictions, on this issue, in relation to directors, are expressed in Appendix 10 ('Model Code for Securities Transactions by Directors of Listed Companies') of the Listing Rules, Rules A.3 (p. A10-2, November 1993).

34. See Section 6.1 for an account of both.

35. Specifically, Table A of the First Schedule of the *Companies Ordinance* sets out under the heading of Dividends and Reserves, the following: 'The directors may from time to time pay to the members such interim dividends as appear to the directors to be justified by the profits of the company.' (Article 116).

36. Table A, First Schedule of the *Companies Ordinance* states: 'The company in general meetings may declare dividends, but no dividend shall exceed the amount recommended by directors.' (Article 115).

37. Elton and Gruber (p. 69) note that where investors are indifferent with regard to the timing of stock sales, $(P_{X-1} - P_X)/D = (1 - t_i)/(1 - t_c)$, where t_i is the marginal income tax rate and t_c the capital gains tax rate. Given institutional arrangements in the United States, they set t_c equal to $0.5t_i$ (p. 70). Accordingly, a mean 'drop-off' of 0.7767 implies a mean marginal income tax rate of 0.364 (36.4%) in their results.

38. See McGuinness (1997a, p. 462) for evidence supporting this.

39. In Ariff and Johnson, Securities Markets & Stock Pricing, Ch. 27, pp. 303.

40. Ibid.

41. Allen, in an assessment of his questionnaire findings, reports, 'Payments to stockholders are given a relatively low priority in the enumeration of firm objectives. Growth is consistently given the highest priority' (p. 67).

42. Benesh et al (1984) for dividend changes of at least 25% report: 'Market reaction to both dividend omissions and large reductions in dividends is also substantial and significant on days -1 and 0, producing abnormal average returns of -7.7% and -9.6%, respectively. . . . market reaction to large dividend increases is less than conclusive, producing abnormal returns over days -1 and 0 of only 1.4%' (p. 140, day 0 is the announcement date).

9. Acquisitions, Privatizations, and the Corporate Restructuring of Equity Stocks

One of the most dramatic—and most significant—of corporate restructuring exercises is the acquisition. This is common to all markets and, in the Hong Kong SAR, typically operates through a general offer mechanism. This was briefly discussed in the previous chapter in relation to the company-initiated share repurchase. In the case of an acquisition, the offer constitutes a formal invitation to all other holders of outstanding shares to sell to the bidder at a fixed price. The key consideration is the 'trigger' to such an offer, which occurs when a party—or group of 'parties acting in concert', to use the jargon of the Hong Kong Codes on Take-overs and Mergers and Share Repurchases—increases their holding in an underlying stock to a level breaching the 35% control threshold. This trigger point is at the core of most recognized acquisitions in Hong Kong.

The public interest component in listed stocks, normally set at a minimum of 25% of the value of shares outstanding,[1] seemingly underpins this 35% control threshold. As shares in the public domain are often widely held, only a small proportion of them may figure in corporate ballots.[2] If this holds, substantial shareholders with 35% to 40% of outstanding stock could wield control. In other words, such a party (or parties) could guarantee a majority of votes cast. The precise point at which de facto control is realized varies from one company to another. A larger holding of shares in public hands might allow for effective control at a level below 35%, for instance. However, if shareholders in the public domain are more active in corporate affairs than is commonly supposed, a level higher than 35% may be necessary. Some diffusion in holdings, comprising the non-public interest component, might also allow effective control to be exercised at levels well below the 35% threshold. Choosing a threshold to define control is therefore an invidious task. Authorities that design takeover codes with such control thresholds in mind would deliberate on the appropriate level for their market, which explains why such thresholds differ across markets. The United Kingdom, Singapore, and Malaysia have takeover codes akin to Hong Kong's; however, they all judge the control threshold at levels below 35%: Singapore and Malaysia plumping for 25% and 33%, respectively, and the United Kingdom for 30%.[3]

Most quantitative assessments of takeover activity in Hong Kong are based upon the establishment of the Hong Kong Codes' definition of 'control'.[4] But the possibility that effective control may be gained by bidders raising their share interest just shy of the 35% point, means that a wider or more catholic interpretation of the takeover process is required. This is certainly true of back-door listings, which were very common in Hong Kong in the early to mid-1990s. Bidding parties in such listings would typically zero-in on inactively traded stocks and, after establishing a controlling or effective interest, use the listed shell as repository for an assortment of injected assets. The shells chosen were often attractive for two reasons. Firstly, due to the illiquidity of target shares, the target's minority shareholders would often welcome the unsolicited advances of the bidder. And, as the target stock's illiquidity was often a symptom of depressed prices, bids could often be made at basement prices. While considerable attention has been devoted to the regulation of the back-door listing in recent years, the initial use of it may have allowed a number of companies to avoid the rigours and expenses of the conventional IPO route to listing. A large number of red chips can trace their origins to this practice.

Other areas of corporate restructuring, including privatizations, buyouts, and divestitures are also considered in this chapter. Privatizations occur with notable frequency in Hong Kong. This occurs when major stakeholders offer to buy out minority holders in a company. The ultimate goal is to consolidate shareholdings pursuant to a de-listing of the stock. This activity should not be confused with privatizations of state-owned assets. The latter represent sales of government assets. Unlike the privatization to be discussed here, government sales often lead to assets and companies being listed. The privatization featuring here is akin to an acquisition in that major shareholders acquire shares outside their domain. They can also be structured through the general offer mechanism.

Unlike firms that are forced to de-list—for reasons like corporate insolvency—privatizations typically occur in companies that are ongoing concerns but, for various reasons, view listing as being surplus to requirements. This is most likely where secondary market trading in the stock is thin. Not only are minority holders more amenable to offers in such circumstances, but it also means that primary market activities are severely constrained. From the underlying corporation's perspective— and, therefore, that of the majority stakeholders'—this suggests little or no return on listing fees. De-listing might, therefore, be seen as a cost-saving measure. Other companies involved in privatizations might have some liquidity in their underlying stocks but view the disclosure requirements imposed upon them as being rather onerous. Others still may feel that privatization offers some consolidation of control and the potential for increased operating efficiency.

As privatizations often involve general offers, it makes sense to consider them alongside corporate acquisitions. The latter features in Section 9.2 and the former in Section 9.3. These areas are sandwiched between a consideration of the general theory and issues underpinning mergers and acquisitions (Section 9.1) and an analysis of one kind of acquisition, the management buyout (Section 9.4). While generally unheard of locally— excepting, perhaps, the management foray into CITIC Pacific in early 1997—buyouts are routinely observed in markets like the United Kingdom and the United States. Many of them have arisen in financially-stricken firms, where incumbent managers bid to buy out divisions, operations or the whole firm itself. In Asia, the 1997–8 economic climate provided fertile ground for a number of buyout attempts. The mooted reform of mainland state owned enterprises (SOEs) may also offer potential for this kind of activity in China.

Corporate divestitures and a range of other corporate restructuring areas are briefly examined in Sections 9.5 and 9.6. An overview of the Hong Kong SAR's regulatory treatment of corporate restructuring activities is then entertained in the final section. In broad terms, the prevailing ethos encourages self-regulation rather than an intrusive statute-based approach. Competition policy, in particular, has been drawn along such lines. For many commentators, US-style antitrust provisions run counter to Hong Kong's long-established principles of *laissez-faire* economics. As such, a shift to a statute-based approach to mergers and acquisitions looks some way off.

9.1 Mergers and Takeovers

Key Terms and the Distinction between Mergers and Takeovers

The terms takeover, merger, and corporate acquisition are often used interchangeably and cause some confusion to readers. In general business usage, the term acquisition is merely a synonym for takeover. This leaves the key question: what is the difference between an acquisition (or takeover) and a merger?

A merger represents a transaction in which the board of directors of two underlying companies—for example, A and B—reach agreement on terms to combine the assets and share ownership of the two respective companies. A successful outcome, requiring that the directors' proposed terms be approved by both sets of stockholders, leads to the creation of a new or merged entity, C. All shareholders in A and B then become shareholders of C. In contrast, a takeover involves a bidding party offering to buy shares directly from stakeholders in a designated target. A successful conclusion to a takeover would see the target shareholders receiving either securities or cash for their shares. Where a stock payment is involved the target shareholders completely give up all interest in the target but receive an ownership interest in the new parent. Whilst some takeovers are framed in this way, the majority—at least in Hong Kong—involve cash consideration where target shareholders receive no compensating ownership interest in the new parent.

Unlike takeovers, mergers are rarely seen locally. Presumably, the last home-based major merger deal was constructed in 1990 between Asia Insurance Co Ltd and The Commercial Bank of Hong Kong Ltd. Through a Scheme of Arrangement, a new holding company, Asia Financial Holdings Ltd, was set up whereby both sets of stockholders agreed to exchange their original holdings for an agreed number of shares in the new company.[5] Under this scheme both companies became wholly-owned subsidiaries of Asia Financial Holdings Ltd.[6]

The basic framework governing mergers and takeovers in Hong Kong is reflected in the Hong Kong Codes on Takeovers and Mergers and Share Repurchases.[7] These codes, as reported in earlier chapters, are not part of statute but still carry considerable force given their explicit recognition by the SEHK Ltd.[8]

The Motivations Underpinning Mergers and Takeovers

The reasons for a takeover are manifold and are discussed at length in numerous texts in the mergers and acquisitions (M&A) area. For this reason, only a brief account of these motivations is mentioned here.

Popular explanations typically focus on scale economies, where output in a newly consolidated enterprise can be generated at lower unit cost, due to the increase in scale of the operations. This is the cited motivation in most horizontal (or 'same industry') M&As. For the vertical variety, where a producer might consolidate operations with a supplier, certain transfer costs are reduced which may also translate to a reduction in unit costs. Various synergistic gains may also result, not simply in production but across areas like administration, planning, and research and development. Combining teams of managers with expertise in sales and marketing might well impact favourably upon overall turnover, for example. A variety of other motivations also exist ranging from tax advantages, where losses in one firm can be used to offset profits in another, and thus reduce overall tax exposure, to business diversification advantages, reduced financing costs, and market share gains.

M&As as an Instrument of Market Discipline

Those who advocate free and unfettered M&A activity generally view it as an essential disciplining force for the markets. Even if this is true, certain costs may still result. Competition in product and service markets may decline in the face of increased M&A activities. Consumers, faced with higher prices and declining service provision, would be the obvious losers. Undue fear of such detrimental effects—from either merger or takeover—may lead to direct intervention, particularly in markets like the United States where much of the regulation is dealt with under statute. This could result in a merger or takeover being derailed, or the imposition of some form of regulatory control over the new entity's pricing policies. As indicated in the introduction, successive administrations in Hong Kong have eschewed such moves; preferring, instead, an oft-stated policy of positive non-interventionism. This policy has allowed local takeovers to proceed in a generally open and unfettered manner with codes, rather than statutes, dictating the course of events. Of course, the necessary control of 'natural' monopolies in public utility areas, principally in electricity, gas, and water, and in the transportation and telecommunications industries, have required a more 'hands-on' approach from the government. This has taken a number of forms. The imposition of caps on expenditure and income returns, through Schemes of Control,[9] for a number of utility companies, is one example. The creation of certain quasi-government bodies like the Mass Transit Railway Corporation and Airport Authority, and the allocation of government franchises, are others. More recent developments have seen attempts to increase competition in a number of these natural monopolies; the telecommunications industry being an obvious example. These and other areas of 'competition policy' are reviewed in Section 9.7 of this chapter.

Leaving such policy initiatives aside, advocates of M&As generally point to the value of such activities in promoting competition in managerial labour markets. Conventional wisdom suggests that firms that underperform, due to inefficient utilization of existing assets, are more likely to be takenover. Where this happens, the bidder, as the new controlling owner of the company, would likely oust the incumbent management team. In theory, a newly installed management team would then purge existing inefficiencies and raise corporate earnings and—by connection—underlying share prices. This kind of logic suggests that shareholders gain from M&A activity. In some respects they do. Several studies, especially in the United States, highlight positive wealth effects for target firm shareholders just prior to and following the announcement of M&A deals.[10]

Instead of efficient entities absorbing inefficient ones—as received theory suggests—recent evidence points to the exact opposite. Large conglomerates acquiring small, dynamic entities, as a way of jump-starting certain crucial sectors of their own business, underpin this view. The hi-tech industry in the United States is replete with examples of larger outfits preying on smaller ones. The attraction, in most cases, relates to the targets' human resources and entrepreneurial flair.[11] By acquiring such companies, the larger, less dynamic company not only captures an ideas-base but also the property rights and patents that belong to such companies. One without the other is an imperfect prize for the acquirer. If M&A activity is working on such lines—as, increasingly, it seems to be—the Darwinian spirit of the 'survival of the fittest' may well be supplanted by a new creed: 'survival of the biggest'. In this light, M&A activity may have mutated into something that rattles even the stoutest of 'free-marketeers'. If this trend continues, monopoly capitalism may well and truly be foisted on the world. The rise of global alliances and the consolidation of numerous financial services—commercial and investment banking being good examples[12]—may be cues for the future. M&A activity looks to be the key to survival for many entities looking to the twenty-first century and beyond.

The contention, then, that M&A activity instils discipline into managerial labour markets, and enhances shareholder value, is open to dispute. In a more innovative business environment, inefficient companies may languish while more efficient ones are ferreted out by larger versions of the former. Extreme forms of managerial inefficiency should still fall under the hammer of M&As though. Asset-strippers will always pounce when they perceive the disposable value of a company's net assets to be at a substantial premium to market values (market capitalizations).

The Longer-Term Returns from M&A Activities

Motivational issues aside, what is the longer-term prognosis for companies engaged in M&A activity? Studies, like Meeks' (1977) for the United Kingdom, suggest a tale of declining profitability, or 'disappointing marriage'. Gregory's (1997) update on the UK market suggests more of the same. For acquisitions between 1984 and 1992, Gregory finds that acquirers generate relatively poor returns over a 24-month post-acquisition period, He notes: 'the post-take-over performance of UK companies undertaking large domestic acquisitions is unambiguously negative over the longer-term. Under all benchmarks used, this conclusion is unaltered' (pp. 997–8). This finding would seem to be consistent with anecdotal accounts that stress the planning, execution, and rationalization problems inherent in the larger M&As. As such, a conglomerate may be more inclined to court a string of smaller players rather than one big rival. This poses fewer rationalization problems and may come at lower cost.

Loderer and Martin's (1992) update for the United States produces more mixed results, however. Based upon their findings they note:

> on average, acquiring firms do not underperform a control portfolio during the first five years following the acquisition. They simply earn their required rate of return, no more or no less. There is some negative performance for the first three years, especially during the second and third years after the acquisition, but it is most prominent in the 1960s, it diminishes in the 1970s and disappears completely in the 1980s (p. 77).

In short, US acquirers seem to be doing a better job for their stockholders than hitherto.

Defensive Measures Against Takeover

The inflated costs of takeover are driven, in large part, by the resistance of incumbent management, which might involve managers pressuring companies to buy back their own stock. This not only helps in consolidating the percentage control of the major shareholder but also bids-up share prices, making it more costly for the bidder to acquire more shares. These measures, as with a range of others, are aptly described as 'poison pills' or 'shark repellants' by US commentators. Activities like 'greenmail' are synonymous with such labels. 'Greenmail' is really a variant of the buy-back. It entails a company, or its major shareholders, 'buying back' parcels of stock from a bidding party by offering a premium over the bidder's original purchase price. The activity arouses deep-seated concerns, as it should. Much like ransom money, actual payment may be self-defeating. A willingness to offer such premiums may simply encourage others to attack the company ever more vigorously in pursuit of the same. 'Golden parachutes',[13] or compensation packages to managerial teams ousted in takeovers, are another commonly cited defence strategy. Again, these arouse great passion. Like 'greenmail', they are more likely to appear in North American corporations than Asian ones.[14]

Defence Measures in Asia

'Golden parachutes' and other well known 'poison-pill' strategies are quite foreign to Hong Kong, although one or two cases resembling 'greenmail' can be found.[15] In general, deterrence provisions like 'golden parachutes' and 'greenmail' reflect the inherently 'hostile' nature of takeover bids in the United States. 'Cross-holdings' of shares provide a more common form of take-over defence in Asia. They are, perhaps, the most effective means of eliminating takeover. Companies adopting such structures become like citadels, almost impenetrable to outsiders. Japan's *keiretsu* and South Korea's *chaebol* are perhaps the best examples of this arrangement. Both tie together companies within particular industrial groupings. There are some differences though. The *chaebol* is more family-based whilst the *keiretsu* typically extends from a given bank or group of banks. Whatever their specific centre of gravity, both arrangements give rise to interrelated share holding structures.

Restrictions against foreign stock-ownership are also an obvious impediment to takeover. Despite some liberalization in recent years, Indonesia, South Korea, and Taiwan still limit foreign stock-ownership to some degree. Other countries like China, where state-owned enterprises are prevalent, split share capital into 'domestic' and 'foreign' shares (see Section 1.3). By keeping the proportions in favour of the former, the companies are insulated from foreign control.

Structural reasons are only part of the equation. Cultural or unwritten protocols undoubtedly play a role too, which may also explain the 'amicable' nature of Asian acquisitions mentioned earlier. Cross-border deals aside, Hong Kong provides ample evidence of this. As we saw earlier, agreements between the bidding party and major shareholder (in the target) are the usual precursor to takeover. By pushing the bidder's interest across the 35% interest threshold in one fell swoop, such agreements usually trigger general offers. Hostile takeovers are a rarity.

Nonetheless, the perception of takeover, especially in relation to the more virulent cross-border raid, is still likely to be an issue. It may even trigger certain defensive measures. Corporate restructuring activities in Hong Kong, like privatizations, divestments, and group reorganizations, may serve to ward off such threats. Divestments probably offer a cheaper and less stressful way of deterring takeover than privatization. For one, the company does not have to cut itself off from primary market funding. They may also be preferable to group reorganizations which can be inordinately expensive. The evidence also points to 'sell-offs' being very effective in keeping bidders at bay.[16] This may go as far as the target offering the raider a parcel of its prime assets, or a division or subsidiary, to protect its main body of assets.

The cancellation of one or more overseas listings in a stock might also be motivated by such concerns. The Jardine group's decision to de-list five of its companies from the Hong Kong exchange in 1995 ostensibly revolved around such arguments. In a similar vein, some firms may avoid listing, seeing their private status as a more effective means of safeguarding control. Certainly, with the usual 25% 'public interest' requirement for a listed stock on the local exchange, pre-listing parties immediately lose some control when taking their company public. At face value, this might seem unimportant as 75% ownership provides effective control in just the same way as 100% ownership. The risk, of course, is that once the stock has become adequately seasoned, some of the pre-listing parties may be tempted to sell off holdings to third parties. This could arise over something as simple as a family feud. This might induce certain members of the founding family to switch their allegiance to particular minority interest camps.

If, over time, a third party is able to build up a substantial interest, the risk of takeover becomes significant. This might be achieved by breaching the 35% trigger point (see Rule 26 of the Hong Kong Codes). Offers can also be made voluntarily from interest levels well below this threshold. A party with an established interest of 25%, for example, could offer to buy the remaining 75% interest in the target. Success, in this context, would require sufficient acceptances to raise the offeror's interest to at least 50% (see Rule 30 of the *Hong Kong Codes*). Failure to achieve this would see the offer lapse and the offeror's interest remain at 25%.

9.2   Takeovers through the General Offer Mechanism

Voluntary Offers

Voluntary offers occur rather infrequently in Hong Kong, although South China Morning Post Holdings' (SCMP) offer for shares in TVE Ltd in 1996 is one recent example.[17] In this case, the bidder, representing the largest shareholder with an interest just under 35% of the target, voluntarily announced a general offer for the stock. This case was unusual in one other important respect: the original offer generated a counter-offer. This came from Shaw Brothers (Hong Kong) Ltd, which held a stake of just over 30% of the target's shares at the outset of the offer.[18] Again, this constituted a voluntarily offer.

This counter-offer then prompted SCMP to improve its original offer, which was subsequently accepted by the overwhelming majority of the target's stakeholders.[19] The SCMP/TVE case essentially captures a hostile bidding environment. This is the exception to the rule, as pointed out earlier. Major stakeholders in targets are courted, rather than preyed upon, by bidders.

Mandatory Offers: General Offers Triggered by Rule 26 and the 'Creeper' Provision

In general, then, most offers are mandatory. A party (or parties acting in concert) raising its interest from a level below 35% to one above it (i.e., breaching the 35% control threshold) would trigger such an offer. This holds unless the buying parties receive a waiver from the provisions of Rule 26 of the Hong Kong Codes by the Securities and Futures Commission (SFC). A party breaching the creeper provision, as set out in the Hong Kong Codes (see Rule 26.1(c)), would also, in the absence of a granted waiver, trigger a mandatory offer. This occurs when a party (or 'parties acting in concert') increases its ownership interest in a listed stock by more than five percentage points, within any given 12-month period. This increase must originate from an ownership interest of between 35% and 50%.[20]

As the creeper provision relates to situations where control has already been established, general offers triggered by breach of the creeper do not, in a general economic sense, constitute takeover offers. In this sense, only general offers triggered by a party (or parties acting in concert) crossing the 35% threshold are regarded here as formal acquisition offers. This is also the spirit in which takeover activity is generally measured in the SAR. This approach has its limitations though. Effective control can be established at levels below this point. Frenzied buying in stocks by particular investors, which terminates just short of the 35% trigger point, often signifies this type of control.

More than a few listed stocks can lay claim to major stakeholders with ownership interests between 30% and 35%. The attraction of increased holdings for such stakeholders may be limited by the burden and expense surrounding a general offer. The stakeholders may also feel, probably because of a fairly diffuse shareholding structure, that effective control can be established some way short of the 35% threshold. It is this kind of argument that has led to calls for a downward revision of the trigger point. The lower levels cited for countries like Malaysia, Singapore, and the United Kingdom also provide ammunition for such views.

The General Ethos Underpinning General Offers

The Hong Kong Codes set out, with regard to takeovers, mergers, and share repurchases, the following view:

> The Codes seek to achieve fair treatment by requiring equality of treatment of shareholders, mandating disclosure of timely and adequate information to enable shareholders to make an informed decision as to the merits of an offer and ensuring that there is a fair and informed market in the shares of the company affected by take-over and merger transactions and share repurchases. . . .' (Hong Kong Codes, 1.2, page 1.1, March 1992).

In short, the establishment of control places minority shareholders in a rather different position to that prevailing hitherto. While one may quibble about the threshold for the trigger point, the general philosophy would suggest that shareholders should, firstly, be fully informed as to the change in ownership structure of the stock and, secondly, given the opportunity to realize their investment on fair terms if they so desire. It might also be argued that where acquirers cross the 35% threshold without attaining absolute control (i.e., without reaching the 50% ownership point), they should be given the opportunity to do so on terms favourable to all remaining stockholders.

The Determination of the Offer Price

Central to the considerations of 'fairness' and 'equal treatment' is the mechanism by which the offer price is determined. A lower bound for this is stipulated in Rule 26.3(a) of the Hong Kong Codes, which states that: 'Offers made under this Rule must, in respect of each class of equity share capital involved, be in cash or be accompanied by a cash alternative at not less than the highest price paid by the offeror or any person acting in concert with it for voting rights of the offeree within the preceding 6 months. . . .' (See the Hong Kong Codes, Rule 26.3(a), p. 2.79).

Price run-ups in the target's stock, as the bidder increases his/her ownership stake, might suggest a minimum offer price equal to the last traded price prior to offer announcement. This is not necessarily so. The minimum offer price specifically relates to 'the highest price *paid by the offeror . . .*' (italics added). In many takeovers, a substantial holding of stock is agreed between the vendor and bidder at one price. As a consequence, the offer price set, in relation to this one price, could be at a discount to certain traded prices during the preceding six-month period.

Conditional Offers

Once the offer price has been determined it only remains to distinguish between conditional and unconditional offers. The first of these occurs where acquirers increase their interest from below 35% to a level between 35% and 50%. In such circumstances, the offer triggered is contingent upon the acceptance condition, Rule 30.2 of the Hong Kong Codes,[21] which requires that sufficient acceptances be generated from the offer to raise the acquirer's interest to a level of more than 50% of the voting shares. Barring this, the offer fails, with all acceptances from the offer void. The acquirer is therefore left with the same level of holdings obtaining at the outset of the offer. In terms of Exhibit 9.1(a) below, which captures this kind of unsuccessful conditional general offer, the acquirer's interest remains at 37%.

A recent example of a conditional offer failing to reach unconditional status was Hutchison Whampoa's offer for Hong Kong Electric in 1996. This takeover was arranged as part of a general reorganization of the Cheung Kong Group and saw Hutchison trigger Rule 26 of the Hong Kong Codes by raising its interest in Hongkong Electric to 35.01%. As the resulting offer failed to attract sufficient acceptances to raise Hutchison's interest to the 50% threshold, the offer lapsed and was withdrawn. Subsequent reorganization saw Hutchison's post-offer interest in Hongkong Electric of 35.01%, transferred to Cheung Kong Infrastructure.[22]

Clearly, the greater the offeror's desire to reach unconditional status, the greater the chance of a premium on the offer price. Where no such

Exhibit 9.1   Examples of Conditional General Offers

Consider a bidding party BID and a target firm TAR.

Suppose BID's interest in TAR increases, through one transaction, from a stake of 32.2% to one of 37%. This triggers a conditional general offering by BID for all the shares in TAR not currently held by BID. Three possibilities emerge:

(a)   Acceptances of offers raise BID's interest to a level between 37% and 50%.

The offer does not become unconditional (see Rule 30.2 of the Hong Kong Codes) and is withdrawn leaving BID's interest at 37%.

(b)   Acceptances of offers raise BID's interest to a level in excess of 50.0%. The offer is successful (i.e., it becomes unconditional) so all acceptances are paid for by BID at the offer price.

(c)   Acceptances of offers raise BID's interest to a level above 75%. Again, the offer is successful (i.e., it becomes unconditional) so all acceptances are paid for by BID at the offer price, as in (b) above. However, TAR's stock listing cannot normally be maintained unless at least 25% of the stock is in 'public hands'. Subject to the exchange authorities, BID might need to reduce its interest below 75%.

premium arises, one might conclude that the offeror is confident of attaining sufficient acceptances to reach unconditional status. Alternatively, it may signal that the offer price is already a generous one. This would be especially true if bidding pressure forced the minimum possible offer price above what the offeror feels is a fair post-acquisition price. If an offer fails to reach unconditional status, it will either be withdrawn or simply lapse. Furthermore, a revised offer should not be formulated within one year of the original offer, according to the Hong Kong Codes.[23]

When sufficient acceptances are generated from a conditional offer, as described in Exhibit 9.1(b), all acceptances must be honoured. The only complication to this story is if the offer is so warmly received that acceptances raise the acquirer's interest above the 75% mark. Given the public interest requirement for a listed stock—normally prescribed at 25%—the target's listed status may be under threat. Whether this is important or not depends upon the intention of the acquirer to retain listing of the stock. One would expect this to be made known at the outset of the offer. If the intention relayed to target shareholders is that listing should be retained then, following completion of the offer, the acquirer will need to unload some of the newly acquired stock. This, as reflected in Exhibit 9.1(c), occurs shortly after the offer's completion date and typically leads to shares being placed with independent parties. United Power International's offer to the shareholders of Golden Island

(Holdings) Ltd in June 1997 provides a recent example of this.[24] This offer was triggered by the bidding party raising its interest over the 35% threshold to a level just over 49%.

Unconditional Offers

An unconditional offer applies when the acquirer already holds an interest of over 50% of the stock in the target. Accordingly, the acceptance rule (Rule 30.2) does not come into play.[25] This occurs when the acquirer breaches the trigger point, through a given transaction, by raising his/her interest from a level below 35% to one above 50%. The significant issue here is whether the number of acceptances from the offer increase the acquirer's interest to levels above or below the 75% interest threshold. Both of these situations are shown in Exhibit 9.2. Complications arise where this threshold is breached as the listing status of the target may be threatened. As with the overly successful conditional offer in Exhibit 9.1 (c) earlier, excess holdings can be unloaded to restore the 'public interest' level to a level acceptable to the Exchange.

Exhibit 9.2   Examples of Unconditional General Offers

> BID raises interest in TAR, through an agreement, from a level below 35% to a level above 50%. This triggers an unconditional general offer.
> Two possibilities emerge:
> (a) Acceptances raise BID's interest to a level between 50% and 75%. All acceptances are paid for by BID at the offer price.
> (b) Acceptances raise BID's interest in TAR above the 75% threshold. As before, all acceptances are honoured but the stock of TAR will only be eligible for listing if the appropriate exchange authorities deem that a sufficient 'public interest' exists in TAR. To maintain listing BID may need to subsequently place sufficient shares in TAR to restore this 'public interest' to an acceptable level.

A recent case, involving a cash offer by Rapid Growth Ltd for the shares of Chi Cheung Investment Co Ltd in late 1997, was triggered by the acquiring party agreeing to an interest of 50.1% in the shares of the target. The ensuing (unconditional) offer saw Rapid Growth's beneficial interest in the target rise to nearly 87%. Shares were subsequently placed to restore Chi Cheung's 'public interest' component. This resulted in a reduction in Rapid Growth's beneficial interest to a level slightly under 75%.[26]

A final possibility, relevant to both conditional and unconditional offers, is where, following a particularly successful offering, the acquiring party commits itself to buy out all remaining minority interests through a compulsory purchase order. The September 1997 acquisition of Furama Hotel Enterprises Ltd is a good example of this. Lai Sun Development Co Ltd, via its wholly-owned subsidiary Smart Leader Ltd, first triggered a conditional general offer for Furama when it agreed to establish an approximate interest of 45% in the target. The subsequent offer led to a flood of acceptances, raising Smart Leader's interest in Furama to a level bordering 99.5%. While the acquirer declared an initial intention to retain the listed status of the target in its proposed offer document,[27] subsequent events led, instead, to a privatization proposal. The deterioration of the hotel business, and the economy in general, were cited as the key reasons.[28] As a result, a compulsory purchase of all remaining shares was initiated and a subsequent application for privatization filed to the Exchange. The latter was made effective in April 1998.[29]

The Relative Importance of Conditional and Unconditional Offers
To reflect the significance of conditional and unconditional offers, incidence rates in each are summarized in Table 9.1 for the period 1990 to 1997. Only successful bids are recorded, which means that offerings like the ones described in Exhibit 9.1(a) are excluded from the data. Anecdotal evidence suggests that such unsuccessful bids (i.e., conditional offers that remain so) comprise a small proportion of total bids in any year. While precise information was not available on this score, Taylor and Poon's (1991, p. 27) analysis of the 1980–90 Hong Kong takeover market permits some inferences to be drawn. They noted that unsuccessful bids accounted for around 10% of all bids. Assuming this held true during the 1990s, it would partly account for the differential between the number of unconditional and conditional bids in Table 9.1.

Table 9.1   Takeover Activity Rates: 1990–1997

	1990	1991	1992	1993	1994	1995	1996	1997	Total
Conditional Offers	6	9	8	15	7	9	6	7	67
Unconditional Offers	10	6	14	14	8	2	9	21	84
Mergers	2	–	–	–	–	–	–	–	2
Total	18	15	22	29	15	11	15	28	153

Notes: Data recorded for take-overs and mergers in the 1997 SEHK *Fact Book* report offers involved in privatizations (these included three offers through Schemes of Arrangement and one through general offering). These are duly excluded from the figures shown. Enquiries with Research & Planning at the SEHK indicate that only successful bids are reported for 'Take-overs and Mergers' in the various *Fact Books*.
Source: Collated from SEHK *Fact Books* for the years 1990 to 1997.

Comparison with Taylor and Poon's (1991) study also points to an increase in takeover activity rates during the 1990s. For the 1980–90 period, they report 146 successful bids. This compares with 151 over the subsequent eight-year period covered in Table 9.1. Pronounced increases in activity rates are most apparent in 1992, 1993, and 1997. While the figures for 1997 might reflect an increase in business confidence in the run-up to, and establishment of the SAR, the figures for 1992 and 1993 point to a rather different influence: the emergence of 'back-door' listings.

Takeovers Leading to Back-Door Listings

Definition and Characteristics

'Back-door' listings, which became common during the early to mid-1990s, provided the route to listing for many of the stocks now known as red-chips. The process involved an acquirer which, in the case of today's red-chip, emanated from the Mainland, bidding for control of a listed stock. Once acquired, the target stocks were then injected with assets of the acquirer. One of the attractions of this route, particularly during the initial years of activity, was the avoidance of the rigours and expenses of the conventional initial public offering (IPO) route to listing. Poor trading activity and depressed prices in many of the targets often meant that the minority parties in the target were amenable to offers. This picture may not always be accurate but appears to be the one often assumed. In this sense, the back-door listing can be seen as a reactivation of a moribund, or near moribund, shell. A more catholic view of the process would include target companies with ongoing business interests. In this interpretation, all 'shell reactivations' are 'back-door' listings but not all 'back-door' listings are reactivations.

This broader view of the 'back-door' listing is also reflected in pronouncements made by the regulatory authorities in Hong Kong, such as the Stock Exchange of Hong Kong (SEHK)/SFC's joint announcement on 'back-door listings' of May 1993. They also note that a 'back-door' listing can occur in situations where 'the acquirer gains effective management control of the listed issuer without incurring an obligation to make a general offer to shareholders of the listed issuer' (11 May 1993).[30] In other words, the establishment of 'control' is not a prerequisite for recognition of a back-door listing. Effective control may give rise to the same.

'Back-Door' Listings and the Emergence of the Red-Chip

Until the early 1990s, most back-door listings in Hong Kong originated from non-mainland parties and, as reported in Ko (1993), a good number emanated from Australia. Mainland parties have dominated this area since. Of the current flock of red-chips, approximately half owe their origins to the back-door route.[31] Prominent amongst these are names like CNPC (HK), China Aerospace, China Everbright International and Shougang Concord International. Others listing locally through the back-door approach, like CITIC Pacific, China Resources and Guangdong Investment, have graduated to the ranks of the blue-chips by virtue of their size and volume. Their subsequent inclusion in the Hang Seng Index has cemented this. Other current blue-chip constituents, with red-chip origins, like Beijing Enterprises and Shanghai Industrial, listed through the more conventional IPO route.

While 1992 and 1993 saw large-scale activity in back-door listings, relatively little activity has occurred since. To illustrate, as of March 1998, twenty of the thirty-nine red-chips represented in the Hang Seng China-Affiliated Corporations Index came into being through takeover; the remaining nineteen through the IPO. Of the former, only three stocks experienced takeover in the post-1993 period.[32] The slowdown in this area probably stems from two issues: the May 1993 initiative by the SEHK and SFC and the PRC's austerity package of 1994 to 1996. The latter would have caused some contraction in funds for both the financing of acquisitions and subsequent asset injections.

The Relative Costs of Back-Door Listings and Initial Public Offerings
In a truly competitive market, where potential bidders jostle to acquire targets, the effective cost of acquiring a 'shell' should be approximately equal to the costs associated with direct listing. In practice, acquirers would only pursue the back-door approach given an assumed cost discount. Prior to the clampdown on back-door listings in May 1993,[33] many probably saw the process as a convenient way to skip around formal listing requirements. There was also a widely-held view that the indirect approach to listing involved fewer lags and preparatory stages than the direct IPO approach.[34] The initial perceived cost savings may have led to the subsequent inflation of offer premiums. With costs rising, and the convenience savings of the back-door listing threatened by the post-1993 regulatory regime, the flow of 'red-chips' listing via takeover began to ebb. Aside from China's austerity programme, this is as one would expect. All other things being equal, competition should squeeze any cost differential between the IPO and 'back-door' routes to the bare minimum.

The May 1993 SEHK/SFC initiative also increased the direct costs of the 'back-door' approach. More carefully delineated disclosure requirements relating to the acquirer's plans for the acquired company were stipulated. One of the key issues concerned the scrutiny attaching to asset injections and disposals with stipulations that acquisition agreements should contain details of proposed activities in these areas. The 1993 announcement also raised the possibility that, 'If the Exchange forms the view that any injections constitute an attempt to achieve a back-door listing and thereby a circumvention of the Exchange Listing Rules, the Exchange may also decide to treat the issuer as a new applicant for listing.'[35]

9.3 Privatizations

Privatization Methods

The acquisition forms considered thus far, excepting the Furama case, have typically involved retention of the target's listed status. A number of acquisitions, however, are structured each year with the specific purpose of cancelling the underlying target's listed status. These are more commonly known as privatization proposals and can result from acquisitions through general offer or through schemes of arrangement (see S.166 of the Companies Ordinance). Both approaches are examined below.

The regulations and guidelines covering privatization are contained in various parts of the Hong Kong Codes and Companies Ordinance. For privatization through general offer, the Companies Ordinance is germane (see S. 168 and the Ninth Schedule). Part I of the Ninth Schedule sets out provisions for a company, after receiving sufficient acceptances to register a holding of at least 90% of the value of shares in the target, to be able to issue compulsory purchase orders to buyout all remaining interests. The compulsory purchase order of shares in M.C. Packaging (Hong Kong) Ltd in January 1997 is a good example of this route to privatization.[36] This was orchestrated by FTB Packaging Ltd and followed on the heels of their general offer.

Privatizations by Schemes of Arrangement

In recent years, the majority of privatizations have resulted from Schemes of Arrangement. In 1997, three of the four successful privatizations, initiated by major stockholders, were of this type.[37] Such Schemes, which require court sanctioning, are also subject to the provisions of the Hong Kong Codes. Revisions to these Codes, carried out in April 1993, required all Schemes initiated by controlling shareholders to generate overwhelming support from the target's independent shareholders (i.e., those parties independent of the controlling party and parties thereto). The 1993 amendment to the Hong Kong Codes stipulated that:

> In addition to satisfying any voting requirements imposed by law, the scheme of arrangement must be approved by a majority in number representing 90% in value of those shares that are voted either in person or by proxy at a duly convened general meeting by shareholders other than the person seeking to privatise the company and persons acting in concert with him (*Hong Kong Codes*, Rule 2.10(a), page 2.15, April 1993).

The April 1993 amendment led to a number of privatization proposals coming unstuck. Most notable, perhaps, was Peregrine Investment Holdings' attempt to privatize Kwong Sang Hong in early 1997. Following a proposal to acquire the target through a Scheme, Peregrine Investment Holdings garnered support from 87.5% of the value of independent shares mobilized in a public vote. As the vote fell 2.5% short of the required margin, the Scheme was duly dropped, much to the chagrin of the bidder and many of the minority parties. The detailed breakdown of figures in Exhibit 9.3 showed how it worked.

A consultation paper issued by the SFC in February 1998 suggested some unease with the 90% approval rule for privatizations proposed by controlling holders in Schemes.[38] The pendulum had swung a little too far in favour of minority stockholders in some people's eyes.

Following extensive consultations, Rule 2.10 of the Hong Kong Codes was revised, with effect from August 1998 so that, amongst other things: 'In addition to any legal requirements, a scheme can only be blocked by (a) more than 10% in value of the independent shareholders voting in

Exhibit 9.3   Case Study of Peregrine Investment Holdings Ltd's Failed
Attempt to Privatize The Kwong Sang Hong International
Ltd in March 1997

THE KWONG SANG HONG INTERNATIONAL LTD

	No. of Shares (millions)	Interest %
Peregrine Investment Holdings Ltd	322.548[a]	53.09[a]
Independent Shareholders	279.533	46.01
Total	607.496[b]	100.00
Number of Independent Shareholders Voting in Person or by Proxy	≈ 112 million[c]	
Number of Independent Shareholders Blocking Privatization Proposal	≈ 14 million[c]	
Percentage Support (of Voting Independent Shareholders)	≈ 87.5%	

Notes:
a   Figures and percentage obtained from *Wardley Cards* (The Kwong Sang Hong International Ltd, 015, prep: 6/3/97) just prior to the privatization proposal lapsing.
b   Figure determined from The Securities Journal March Trading Record 1997, p. 50 (reconciles with those in note a).
c   For specific details of the vote see Li (1997). She reports that only 40% of the independent shareholders voted (in person or by proxy) and shareholders wielding 14 million of the target's shares declined the offer.
d   Dissenting votes as a proportion of total voting rights ≈ (14 million/607.5 million) × 100 ≈ 2.30%

person or by proxy against the proposal *and* (b) those shareholders holding more than 2.5% of the total voting rights (the 2.5% proposal) . . .' (SFC, Press Release (1998), italics and parentheses reported as shown).

Under the new test, a privatization proposal through a Scheme can meet with success even where support, from the value of independent shareholdings, mobilized in a public vote, falls short of 90%.[39] Had the case in Exhibit 9.3 been subject to the new ruling, the privatization proposal would have seemingly passed, because the 'blocking' vote in Exhibit 9.3 would have fallen below the 2.5% threshold stated in (b) (see note d in Exhibit 9.3). Both conditions (a) and (b) must be satisfied to 'block' a privatization under a Scheme under the new rules.[40]

Mechanisms for De-Listing other than Privatization

Stock Withdrawals

In cases where privatization proposals reach their intended conclusion, the acquirer then applies for a timely withdrawal of the target's listing. Not all de-listings reflect privatizations though. Of the seven withdrawals from the Exchange in 1997, only four were due to privatizations. The remaining three were classified as withdrawals.[41] These are subject, amongst other things, to the passing of a resolution by underlying shareholders, and relate to stocks with primary listings on the SEHK. While the precise conditions for such withdrawals are contingent on the presence or otherwise of alternative market listings,[42] the consequences of de-listing through voluntary withdrawal are much the same as through a privatization: the elimination of listing fees and escape from the regulatory scrutiny of the Exchange and the market. Not that these considerations are, necessarily, the driving force behind decisions to de-list. The motivations may be driven by an assortment of factors.

Poor liquidity in the underlying shares, fear of corporate takeover, and a desire to consolidate ownership and control might figure. For stocks that have experienced subdued trading for some time, balance sheets may be more impressive than market capitalization figures. This would be especially true if the company wanted to showcase its net assets position. Where listing obscures the real value of the company's equity it may even undermine a company's debt financing ambitions.[43] De-listing may be a way around this problem.

Cancellation of Listings

For companies with dual- or multiple-listings, movements of shares between registers can also make overseas listings untenable. Over time, a company's overseas register, for stock trading in that locale, may be seriously depleted. By allowing any remaining members the opportunity to transfer their shares to the principal register, the overseas listing can be scrapped.

Listings can also be cancelled where financial difficulties arise.[44] The spate of corporate liquidations in Asia in 1998 testifies to this. These generally involve the reorganization of corporate groupings with the aim, in the first instance, of paying off creditors. In most liquidations, little or nothing remains for the equity holder after paying-off creditors and liquidation charges. The US approach, which allows companies to reorganize and continue business operations through Chapter Eleven bankruptcy proceedings, may offer greater appeal in such circumstances. Not only does it provide an opportunity for the underlying corporation to payoff the full amount of debt outstanding, through rescheduled future payments, it also offers the possibility of a future residual claim for equity holders.

Listing Suspensions

To round off this section, a few points about 'trading halts' or stock suspensions are helpful. These occur far more often than stock cancellations. A recent paper on the issue by Wu (1998) gives some idea of this for Hong Kong. He notes that they can be driven by the interjection of either the Exchange or SFC or on the behest of the issuer (through voluntary means). He refers to the former as a mandatory suspension. Assessing all suspensions from exchange unification through to December 1993,[45] he notes: 'The mandatory suspensions are all associated with bad news of the company, such as trading fraud, price manipulation and other trading violations. . . . voluntary suspensions are related to the release of the price-sensitive information' (p. 422). The latter made up the bulk of his sample.[46] Wu, in turn, subdivided the latter into events relating to M&As, privatizations, and placements. In terms of valuation effects, his principal finding is that 'there is no evidence that investors are able to make abnormal profits during the post-suspension period' (p. 433), although he does note some positive run-up in prices and volumes of stocks subject to 'voluntary' suspensions in advance of their announcement. This is not unduly surprising in relation to event studies. The post-suspension evidence is good news, though. It indicates some degree of efficiency in the market.

9.4 Buyouts[47]

Buyout History and Characteristics

'Buyouts' represent a further sub-category of acquisition and are a key part of the corporate restructuring landscape in North America and some parts of Europe, such as the United Kingdom. They rarely appear outside of these markets. The closest Hong Kong has come in this regard is, perhaps, the partial management buyout (MBO) of CITIC Pacific in January 1997. This involved the management of CITIC, led by Larry Yung, acquiring almost 15.5% of CITIC's outstanding shares from its parent, China International Trust & Investment Corporation Hong Kong (Holdings) Ltd.[48]

In what way, then, does a buyout differ from other acquisition forms? The key difference is the party orchestrating the raid. In the buyout, one ordinarily assumes that the management of the target company plays a significant role as either the bidding party or the partner to a team of buyout specialists. In the early days of the buyout, during the 1970s and 1980s in the United States and the United Kingdom, managers typically acquired substantial equity interests in such ventures. Banks, for the most part, propped up such deals.

The Increasing Role of Venture Capitalists and Private Equity Financiers
Not surprisingly, the buyout soon came to be known as the leveraged buyout (LBO). Increasingly, though, as reported in accounts like Wright and Robbie's (1996), the buyout has evolved into a creature where venture capitalists or other specialists often capture the lion's share of the available equity. Not surprisingly, Wright and Robbie refer to this type of investment foray as an investor buyout (IBO). As in the United States, where such venture capital has figured more prominently and for a longer period than elsewhere, one commonly assumes some role for the target's management. This may be as the initiator, adviser, or simply the designated management team for the newly acquired entity.[49] The growth of 'hi-tech'

stocks in particular have driven such developments in the United States where existing management in small but dynamic entities seek out financiers, often in the private equity field. Private equity financing affords the financier a direct stake in the operations of the new entity. It also reflects something each partner wants from the other: the private equity financier's desire for ideas and innovative management and the management's for funding.

While private equity financing appears expensive, it is often the only way in which small, innovative, but inherently high-risk operations, can acquire funding. The fact that such financiers take an equity interest is also suggestive of their desire to grab a slice of the potential upside. It also provides a strong signal of the financier's confidence in the venture. Debt-financiers in contrast simply seek repayment of their loan (and the interest thereto) and because of this are more concerned with the downside risk. They can also 'call-back' the loan whenever a default upon interest, or a margin call from the 'marking to market' of collateral, arises.[50]

In sum, then, buyouts, whether of the original LBO kind or the newer investor-led variety, form a particular subset of corporate acquisitions. In other, mainstream acquisitions, like those described in Sections 9.2 and 9.3, bids originate from parties with established share interests in the target. Moreover, these parties are not necessarily in collusion with the target's existing management. More often than not the acquirer seeks the immediate dismissal of incumbents. In contrast, the managers in buyouts are a key driving force behind the deal. Increasingly, they are viewed as an attractive asset to a third party.

The Benefits Arising from Buyout

Much of the buyout activity overseas, particularly in its formative period in the 1970s, arose in response to weakening corporate profits. This was, after all, the *raison d'être* for many buyouts in the early 1980s in the United Kingdom. It was the key reason, but not the only reason. Apart from lagging stock prices, managerial interjections were often motivated by a desire to use specialist positions to effect greater control in the running of the firm's operations. The subsequent earnings performance of many of these allowed a good number to re-enter the market years later through an IPO. In some cases, this process allowed the managerial-entrepreneurs to 'cash-in' by selling off part or all of their equity stakes through the offerings. The Unlisted Securities Market (USM), which was a Second Board to the London Stock Exchange in the 1980s and early 1990s, provided the springboard for much of this.

By realigning ownership and control, the buyout helped eliminate agency costs. These are incurred in ensuring that the agent (managers in this context) act in the best interests of the principal (the equityholders). For companies with diffuse or widely scattered stock holdings, these agency costs may be substantial. They derive not only from monitoring costs but also short-falls in profits brought about by the failure of stakeholders to effectively organize and motivate their managerial teams. Where such diffuse shareholding structures dominate, as they did in the West during the 1970s and early 1980s, no one stakeholder may be able to impose sufficient control over other stakeholders. In such circumstances, attempts to rein in recalcitrant or 'sleeping' managers may well prove futile.

This picture might adequately describe the 'bloated' and inefficient model of Western corporate capitalism of yesteryear. In some corporations, the largest equityholder might well have held a stake of 5% or less. For managers with an agenda geared to self-indulgence, at the expense of the mass of shareholders, the corporate setting of the 1970s would have been Shangri-La. For those with a strategic view for their firms, however, inevitable frustrations would have boiled over. With equityholders unable to offer direction and funding support, growth opportunities were stymied. In these firms, the buyout offered one solution out of the impasse.

The increasing role of institutional investment in the 1980s and 1990s also helped consolidate stockholdings in numerous Western corporations. The second wave of buyout activity helped buttress this. The various alliances between managers and external financiers, like venture capitalists and other private equity firms, have, much like the first wave, been critical in consolidating share ownership. Both the buyout and the increased role of institutional investment have helped in unravelling the 'life-chord' to corporate success: a direct and unfettered link between ownership and control.

The Prospects for the Buyout in the SAR and the Mainland

In the Hong Kong SAR, and its forebear, very little scope has ever existed for the buyout. Earlier chapters provide the clue to this, with most listed companies traditionally able to demonstrate the existence of majority or effective control. This has always meant a clear line of communication between owners and managers. Many listed firms still exhibit a close-knit structure with owners and managers often sharing close family or business ties. Owners and managers may even be one and the same.

Even in the minority of listed companies where shareholdings are more widely dispersed, attempts to wrest control from parties with substantial interests would likely meet with stern resistance. A culture of cordial employee–employer relations, whether driven by Confucianism or some other underlying philosophy, invariably strikes a chord with the casual observer. Economic conditions may also have played a part. An almost continued spurt of economic growth from the mid-1970s to the mid-1990s has certainly inhibited the managerially-inspired buyout.

The recent downturn in Asia in 1997 and 1998 showed that the local market could very well provide fertile ground for such restructuring, although toward the end of the decade, there was only little evidence of activity on this front. This points to the fact that buyouts are not simply a reaction to adversity. The general absence of independent management teams and a lack of local buyout expertise undoubtedly set limits to such activities. A review of sentiment on this issue by McGuinness (1998b), recorded during the middle of 1998, confirmed much of this. Nonetheless, potential developments in the buyout arena are a distinct possibility for some of the smaller Mainland state-owned enterprises.

9.5 Corporate Divestitures

The sale of a subsidiary, division, franchise, or fixed asset would ordinarily characterize a corporate divestment. Numerous studies suggest that units or assets chosen in such 'sell-offs' are likely to be 'failed' initiatives that weaken the overall profitability of the seller's operations. As such, the sales are triggered when the units become a visible drain on resources. Recent research concerning the timing of sales of 'failing' or ill-fitting units, in the area of voluntary divestments, seems to confirm this. Cho and Cohen (1997), for instance, show that firms are more likely to sell less desirable assets when a firm is under-performing. In more ebullient periods, Cho and Cohen suggest a weaker incentive to sell. In such times, the return on failing assets can be masked to some extent by positive company-wide returns, thus concealing managers' earlier failings in acquiring such assets. By connection, one would expect new managers to immediately divest their companies of all ill-fitting units as a means of raising their firm's return on capital employed. This would be particularly advantageous when drawing comparisons with the manager's predecessor.

Divestments can also feature in a more positive light. The sale of value-added assets or activities, as we have already seen, can be very effective in eliminating the threat of takeover. 'Sell-offs' need not be 'voluntary' or subject to the whims of the seller either, as seen in the process of 'asset-stripping', where an aggressive raider ferrets out the value-added parts of businesses.

In many jurisdictions, buyouts have also been largely driven by divestments, particularly in relation to subsidiaries, divisions, and franchises. Thompson and Wright (1991, p. 16), with reference to UK management buyouts, report that the majority of buyouts during the second half of the 1980s were driven through such means. Evidence from the United States, as indicated in the earlier quotation from Weston et al. (1990) (note 49), also points to the existence of involuntary sales made possible by hostile raids.

9.6 'Spin-Offs', Demergers and other Stock Reorganizations

Although some refer to demergers—or 'split-offs'—and 'spin-offs' as part of the divestment process, they really represent a reallocation of existing corporate assets and liabilities from a parent company to a defined subsidiary.

'Spin-Offs'

In the 'spin-off' (SO) the reallocation involves the parent creating a new subsidiary to house a subset of its assets and liabilities. Normally, these relate to a specific area of activity in the parent, as was seen in Cheung Kong's 1996 'spin-off' of its PRC infrastructure assets into Cheung Kong Infrastructure. Unlike the sale of a subsidiary in a 'sell-off', the 'spin-off' results in a shareholder structure mirroring that of the parent. To illustrate, consider the simplified example in Exhibit 9.4 where a parent company PT siphons off $3 billion of a particular class of its assets and $1 billion of liabilities into a new, wholly-owned entity SO. This leads to a $2 billion drawdown in the owners' equity (i.e., issued share capital plus reserves) of the parent.

Exhibit 9.4   Illustration of the Effects of a 'Spin-Off'

B/Sheet of PT Ltd				B/Sheet of SO Ltd			
$ million			*$ million*	*$ million*			*$ million*
Assets	10,000	Issued Share	6,000	Assets 3,000	Issued Share		2,000
	(3,000)	Capital & Reserves	(2,000)		Capital & Reserves		
		Liabilities	4,000		Liabilities		1,000
			(1,000)				
	$10,000		$10,000	$3,000			$3,000
	($3,000)		($3,000)				

In the above, the 'spin-off' company becomes a wholly owned subsidiary of the parent. The consolidated picture would look much as before. The parent's own net asset base would be complemented by a certain number of new SO shares representing its investment interest in its subsidiary. This would be achieved via a new issue of SO shares to PT's stockholders, to replace the existing PT shares in the net asset drawdown.

In some cases, companies are 'spun off' concurrently with a new issue of stock to third parties. This obviously diversifies the stock ownership interest of the 'spun-off' company. This is the manner in which a number of 'spin-offs' have been listed locally. To illustrate, let us amend the example in Exhibit 9.4. In addition to the reallocation of assets and liabilities from PT to SO, consider a 25% increase in the equity base of SO, raising $0.9 billion in proceeds.[51] This would result in SO's assets rising from $3 billion to $3.9 billion and its issued share capital and reserves rising from $2 billion to $2.9 billion. Moreover, PT's stake in SO would be diluted from 100% to 80%.

In the absence of stock or other security offerings, it may be possible, subject to the approval of the exchange where listing is sought, for the new company to gain listing via an introduction. If the 'spun-off' entity inherits the same ownership structure as the parent, and the parent is already listed, one can make the argument that the new entity must satisfy the 'public interest' requirement for stock listing. This is true but trivializes the issue somewhat. Listing eligibility also hinges on other issues. According to the exchange of choice, issues like the stock's prospective market capitalization would figure.[52]

Demergers

Demergers differ from 'spin-offs' in the sense that an existing company, with an already established identity, is broken off from the group and divested to a third party. Other than this, the essential characteristics of the 'spin-off' apply. The demerger of a series of property companies from Winsor Industrial Corporation Ltd (WI) to a wholly owned subsidiary of WI, Winsor Properties Holdings Ltd (WP) in October 1996 serves as a good example of this type of restructuring exercise. In consideration for WP's new ownership of the property companies, WP issued shares to WI shareholders on the basis of one new WP share for every two WI shares held. Upon completion of this, the ownership structure of WP essentially mirrored that of WI, and the 'public interest' component in WI's listing would have figured favourably in any decision to introduce WP onto the local market.[53]

Capital Reconstructions and Group Reorganizations

Capital reconstructions and the creation of new holding companies, for the purpose of relocation of domicile, are also notable activities in the realm of corporate reorganization. The first activity essentially relates to alteration of a company's capital and can take the form of changes to its authorized share capital, issued share capital or both. The second activity, as examined in Section 1.3, occurred with some regularity in the late 1980s/early 1990s and involved the shares of a group's existing holding company being replaced by those of a newly created parent registered in a foreign locale. The reorganization of the HongkongBank Group in 1991, which led to the HongkongBank becoming a fully-owned subsidiary of HSBC Holdings is a good example of this kind of reorganization. As described in Section 7.2, this was organized through a Scheme of Arrangement, which saw approximately 1.625 billion shares of HSBC Holdings issued in exchange for HongkongBank shares in the ratio of one new share for four existing HongkongBank shares. At the same time, the new overseas parent was domiciled in England.[54]

Reorganizations can also involve combinations of mergers, demergers, 'spin-offs', and some of the other acquisition forms considered in this chapter. The somewhat complicated reorganization of the Cheung Kong/Hutchison Whampoa Group in 1996 involved a number of these elements.

9.7 Concluding Remarks

An impressive range of corporate restructuring activities are evident in Hong Kong. Most of the controls on such activities, as we saw, reflect the codes and rules of self-regulatory bodies like the SEHK and those of the market's watchdog, the SFC. In broad terms, successive administrations have eschewed a legislative approach to the control of restructuring activities, like mergers and acquisitions, which seems perfectly congruent with the Hong Kong SAR's commitment to the territory's traditional positive non-interventionist stance. Ignoring the HKMA's foray into the SAR's local stock and futures markets in August 1998, this principle still holds true.

While the Hong Kong SAR government, and its forebear have steered clear of anti-trust provisions and competition laws, attempts to instil greater competition in various product and service markets have been made. The creation of a Competition Policy Advisory Group (described under the sobriquet COMPAG) within the government's Trade and Industry Bureau reflect such moves. A recent Statement on Competition Policy,[55] by the Trade and Industry Bureau, sets out the spirit by which such competition might be fostered and restricted practices constrained. In short, the Statement specifies a number of measures to support its goals, including cooperation with the local Consumer Council to develop codes and practices of behaviour as well as the promotion of administrative and voluntary measures. Legislative intervention is also countenanced but, as emphasized early on in the Statement: 'For Hong Kong, a small and externally-oriented economy which is already highly competitive, the government sees no need to enact an all-embracing competition law' (p. 3).

Regulatory structures to parallel those in the United States, where a panoply of antitrust provisions exist in various states, or in countries like the United Kingdom, and bodies like the European Union, where a whole range of policy initiatives are on the books, seem some way off. The increasing number of 'cross-border' acquisitions suggests that the SAR and the Mainland may face pressures to reassess this situation. The reform of the SOEs in Mainland China will inevitably open more opportunities for 'cross-border' capital flows, and with it the need for clarifications from time to time on the precise measures to be deployed.

Notes

1.   For listed stocks with a market capitalization of HK$4 billion or less (see, in particular, Rule 8.08, 8-2, 10/95 & 8-3, 9/94, The Rules Governing The Listing of Securities on The Stock Exchange of Hong Kong Ltd).

2.   The precise definition of such 'public' holdings was explored in Section 1. 3. For that reason, the exercise is not repeated here.

3.   See Chandrasegar and Baratham (1993) for discussion of these majority control levels.

4.   See Hong Kong Codes, 2.1-2.3, March 1992.

5.   See Recommended Merger Document for Asia Insurance Co Ltd and The Commercial Bank of Hong Kong Ltd, 29 October 1990.

6.   The scheme required the approval of the affected shareholders. In keeping with the Companies Ordinance, shareholder support representing at least 75% of the value of shares (S. 166(2)), in each constituent company, had to be mobilized for approval. This condition, in addition to others, was duly met and the merger consummated.

7.   See amended version of April 1996, published by the SFC.

8.   See Hong Kong Codes, 1.4, page 1.2, March 1992. This point featured in Section 1.3. The panel overseeing the Code can also impose sanctions on those found to be in breach of the Code, with requisite channels also in place for appeal against such measures (see Financial Services Bureau Press Release (1999) for discussion of this process in relation to one such case).

9.   Cheng and Wu (1998, pp. 125–9) offer an excellent guide to the history of Schemes of Control in the territory. They note that public utilities largely fell under such Schemes between 1964 and 1995 and that latter-day arrangements, in a number of sectors, now favour a rather different kind of policy initiative: the opening up of markets to new competition.

10.   For reasons of brevity, a review of these studies is not entertained here. Many reviews can be found elsewhere, such as Krinsky et al.'s (1988, pp. 249–51).

11.   Thanks are due to David Sharam for his input on this issue.

12.   Some limitations on the marriage of investment and commercial banks is apparent in the US due to the Glass-Steagall Act of 1933. Notwithstanding attempts to repeal some of the provisions in this in recent years, the Act provides for some separation between financial services like commercial banking, investment banking, and insurance. The walls separating these have, admittedly, become a little porous in recent years. For an excellent account of these issues, see Anonymous (Mar 1998).

13.   See Krinsky et al. (1988, pp. 253–60) for an excellent review of 'poison pill' strategies.

14.   The 'golden parachute' has come in for particular scrutiny in the US. On the one hand, they discourage managers from wasting corporate resources in fending off takeover bids. They also pose a moral hazard problem as managers may gain at shareholders' expense if managerial under-performance triggers take-over interest. Against this, the sheer size of managerial compensation deals often deters raiders by adding significant costs to the take-over process. This leads to a rather undesirable conclusion: managers with 'parachutes' can under-perform without undue fear of market sanction. This would appear to be detrimental not only to shareholders but also to the general economy. It is this managerial-incentive problem that raises the ire of free-marketeers who see the disciplining role of takeovers as critical to the economy's well-being. They would suggest the elimination of all barriers to takeovers in the name of competition. Paradoxically, as noted earlier, more competition in security markets may mean less elsewhere.

15.   The purchase of a stake by a consortium of investors in Hongkong Land and the subsequent sale of this holding, approximating to 8% of the shares in Hongkong Land, to the counter's major shareholder—Jardine Strategic Holdings— in 1988, while not exactly constituting 'greenmail' in the US sense of the term, was seen by some as a takeover deterrence move by the major shareholder. See Barnes (1988) for a more detailed assessment of the motivations underpinning the agreement.

16.   Loh et al. (1995) provide support for this proposition for 'defensive' divestitures in the United States.

17.   Thanks are due to Larry Chan of the SFC for referring me to this case.

18.   Details gleaned from *Wardley Cards*, TVE (Holdings) Ltd, 011-012, prep: 22 March 1996.

19. Ibid.

20. For purposes of implementation, the lowest percentage ownership level, within the 12-month period, is used as the base point from which to assess the 'creeper'. See Rule 26.1 (c and d), and various notes thereto, in the Hong Kong Codes for specific details of this 'creeper provision.

21. See also Rule 26.2(a) of the Hong Kong Codes and notes thereto. Partial offers (see Rule 28) are exempt from Rule 30.2 (ibid., Rule 30.2). Enquiries with the SFC indicate that partial offers are a rarity. As a consequence, they are ignored here.

22. See *Wardley Cards*, Hong Kong Electric Holdings, 012-013, prepared: 6 March 1997 for further details of the offering and the ensuing reorganization.

23. Rule 31.1(a) sheds some light on this issue, stating: 'Except with the consent of the Executive, where an offer has been announced or posted but has not become unconditional in all respects, and has been withdrawn or has lapsed, neither the offeror nor any person who acted in concert with it in the course of the original offer, nor any person who is subsequently acting in concert with any of them, may within 12 months from the date on which such offer is withdrawn or lapses either: (i) make an offer for the offeree company, or (ii) acquire any voting rights of the offeree company if the offeree or persons acting in concert with it would thereby become obliged under Rule 26 to make an offer.' (See Hong Kong Codes, Rule 31.1(a), p. 2.98)

24. For specific details on this offering, see *Wardley Cards* for Golden Island (Holdings) Ltd, 010-012, 10 Nov 1997.

25. See Note 1 to Rule 26.2 for further elaboration.

26. Details of the offer and Rapid Growth's subsequent placing of shares in Chi Cheung were gleaned from *Wardley Cards*, Chi Cheung Investment Co Ltd, 016, 1 April 1998.

27. See Lai Sun Development Co Ltd Discloseable Transaction document, 23 July 1997, p. 7.

28. The decline was such that Lai Sun Development felt it 'inappropriate to implement any steps to maintain a public float of shares of the Company as any sale or new issue of shares of the Company could likely only be effected at a material discount to the price per share under the cash offer' (*Wardley Cards*, Furama Hotel Enterprises Ltd, 010, prepared 23 March, 1998).

29. See Wardley Cards (010-011; prep: 23 March & 30 March, 1998) for a detailed description of the chain of events leading up to Furama's de-listing.

30. The opening statement in this joint announcement allows a clearer insight into the formal definition of 'back-door listing' used by the SEHK and SFC. It states: 'Recently a number of concerns have been raised by participants in relation to the increase in the number of proposed acquisitions of controlling interests, or major listed stakes in issuers whereby the acquirer gains effective management control of the listed issuer without incurring an obligation to make a general offer to shareholders of the listed issuer. There has been widespread speculation that such acquisitions are being used as a means to circumvent the requirements for new applicants as set out in the Exchange Listing Rules. A "back-door listing" can occur when purchaser acquires control of, or a major stake in a listed issuer as described above, and then simultaneously or shortly thereafter injects assets into the listed vehicle' (parentheses shown as used, Joint Announcement: "Back-door Listings", SEHK/SFC, 11 May 1993).

31. See De Trenck's 'partial list of red-chips' as of 1 May 1997 for a more precise assessment (De Trenck et al. (1993, pp. 79-80)).

32. Thanks are due to HSI Services Ltd for providing details on both the IPO listing dates and acquisition dates relevant to each constituent.

33. The joint announcement was entitled 'back-door listings' and was issued by the SEHK and SFC on 11 May 1993 (See *South China Morning Post*, 11 May 1993, p. 2, Business Post).

34. See Ko (1993) for discussions on this theme.

35. This declaration formed a part of the following passage: 'Upon any announcement relating to an intended acquisition of a controlling or major stake in a listed issuer . . . , the Exchange will also remind prospective purchasers, in writing, that: (a) where injections and/or disposals are proposed as part of the acquisition the Exchange, pursuant to its powers under the Exchange Listing Rules, may treat the issuer as a new applicant for listing. If the Exchange forms the view that any injections constitute an attempt to achieve a back-door listing and thereby a circumvention of the Exchange Listing Rules, the Exchange may also decide to treat the issuer as a new applicant for listing. Alternatively, such injections or disposals may result in a review of the issuer's listed status; . . .' (Joint Announcement: "Back-door Listings", (Joint Announcement: "Back-door Listings", SEHK/SFC, 11 May 1993).

36. A number of qualifications are pertinent. One is that notification of purchase orders must be given to minority parties within four months of an offer. Minority parties may also seek recourse through the courts against such orders if claims are made within two months of the the purchase order being served (see Companies Ordinance, Ninth Schedule, Part I, 4, p. 480).

37. The three targets in the Schemes were Consolidated Electric Power Asia Ltd (document dated: 1 November 1996), The East Asiatic Company Ltd (document dated: 5 May 1997) and CDW International Ltd (document dated: 19 March 1997). The remaining privatisation, involving M.C. Packaging (Hong Kong) Ltd (document dated: 9 January 1997) stemmed from a general offer. The companies involved were identified from the *Fact Book 1997*, p. 53.

38. See SFC (February 1998).

39. The SFC's Press Release (1998) also reminds us that, by virtue of the local Companies Ordinance, this support level must exceed 75% for Hong Kong incorporated companies.

40. As a further illustration, suppose the controlling shareholder of a company C with 1,000 million shares in issue wished to privatize C through a Scheme. If he/ she held 60% of the outstanding stock and half of the independent shareholders mobilized their stock for voting purposes, the privatization proposal would succeed if at least 175 million shares were used in support. If 176 million shares were used in such a way, 88% support would be garnered from the voting independent shareholders. But, as the dissenting parties' position—represented by a block of 24 million shares—fails to exceed 2.5% of the total value of voting rights in C (= 25 million shares), the proposal would succeed. Under the old provisions in Rule 2.10 it would not.

41. See *Fact Book 1997*, p. 53.

42. See *Fact Book 1997*, p. 49 for an overview of the Exchange's conditions for voluntary withdrawals of listing.

43. Thanks are due to David Sharam for raising this issue.

44. A range of reasons for cancellation (as summarized in the *Fact Book 1997*, p. 48, under Suspension and Cancellation of Listing') are evident. One is where 'There are insufficient securities of the issuer in the hands of the public' (p. 48).

45. Wu (1998, pp. 421–2) adopted a parsimonious approach by including only 'news-related suspensions'. By also excluding suspensions in the same company within the space of 30 days, he was able to classify 522 suspensions.

46. 31 were classified as 'mandatory' and 491 'voluntary' (see ibid. (p. 422)).

47. Much of the discussion in the following area is an extension of McGuinness (1998b).

48. See *Wardley Cards* for CITIC Pacific Ltd 017 (prep: 4 August 1997) for further details of this acquisition agreement. Other notable MBOs in Asia include the 1994 buyout of London Sumatra in Indonesia by the Napan Group (see Yu (Dec 1994/Jan 1995) for details).

49. This is captured by Weston et al.'s definition of the LBO in the US. They note: 'an LBO is defined as the acquisition, financed largely by borrowing, of all the stock, or assets, of a hitherto public company by a small group of specialist investors. This buying group may be sponsored by buyout specialists . . . or investment bankers that arrange such deals and usually includes representation by incumbent management, although hostile LBOs are not unknown' (p. 393).

50. See Section 3.1 in relation to collateralized (stock) borrowing arrangements. The same principles apply to the situation described here.

51. Remember that this is not 25% of $2 billion. The amount raised depends upon the sale price of the stock. If the par value for SO's issued share capital was $1 per share, 0.5 billion shares would be sold at $1.80 per share.

52. Practice Note 15, issued by the SEHK, deals with the listing requirements relating to 'spin-offs'. (See The Stock Exchange of Hong Kong Ltd, Practice, Note 15.).

53. See Introduction Document for Winsor Properties Holdings Ltd listing on the SEHK, 14 October 1996 and *Fact Book 1996*, p. 47 for details of the demerger. This demerger is also explored in McGuinness (1998b).

54. See Scheme of Arrangement Document, The HSBC, February 01, 1991.

55. See Statement on Competition Policy (1998).

10. Equity Derivatives I: Options

The global proliferation of derivative securities now means that exposure to positions in equity stocks can be achieved without physically holding stock. Derivatives with features allowing conversion into underlying stock in the SAR are now numerous and include options, warrants, futures, convertibles, and swaps. Options and warrants are considered first—given their obvious similarities—in this and the following chapter. Coverage of futures and other equity derivatives follows in Chapter 12.

As the option is the building block for many other derivatives, it makes sense to examine this security in some detail first. In broad terms, an option is an entitlement to either buy or sell a share, or any other security, currency or commodity, at some future date at some predetermined exercise (or 'striking') price. This description, in regard to an option to buy, would also characterize the warrant, which is keenly followed locally. Understanding of the subtle difference between the two products requires, however, a clear appreciation of options and options theory.

While warrants have been in evidence for quite some time in Hong Kong—with initial issues going back as far the 1970s—traded options only arrived quite recently. Notwithstanding this, progress and interest has been swift with an array of equity options on the Stock Exchange of Hong Kong (SEHK) and various index options on the Hong Kong Futures Exchange (HKFE) attracting considerable volume. With various positions in over-the-counter (OTC) markets complementing these traded options products, Hong Kong can now boast one of the largest and most active options markets in the Pacific Rim. This is all the more remarkable given that options, as little as five years ago, were viewed by many in the territory as an arcane and unknown quantity. The rising sophistication of trading and the growing role of risk-management—of which the option is central, given its hedging role—represent key developments. Hedging apart, where derivatives are used to protect underlying cash positions, speculators and arbitrageurs in derivatives can easily effect changes in cash prices.

Analyses that suppress the burgeoning role of derivatives are, therefore, much like a vignette—a snapshot with background deliberately obscured. To some, this metaphor is very telling as derivatives are seemingly hidden but always 'lurking' in the background. The calamitous events surrounding Barings and Orange County easily arouse this view. However, the consensus position is rather different. Most now appreciate that inadequate risk-management policies were responsible for these and other debacles—not the derivative itself. Where adequate internal and external regulation of positions prevail, derivatives appear to offer a stabilizing influence. A number of researchers note that derivatives typically lessen overall cash-market volatility. This is not too surprising, as options, and many other derivatives, enhance risk-management through their hedging role. They have also been lauded for their role in the price-discovery process. This suggests, in contrast to popular mythology, that derivatives contribute to more robust and transparent markets.

Formulation of regulatory policy in the derivatives arena necessitates an erudite appreciation of the properties of such instruments. Without this, arguments for or against intervention carry little weight, although concerns of this nature may not always figure in the minds of the prime-movers of policy: the politicians. The aim of this chapter, and Chapters 11 and 12, is to strip away some of the mystery surrounding options and other derivatives

The basic characteristics of options are first explored in this chapter. The key features of call options are then introduced in Section 10.2, along with essential terms such as time value, intrinsic value, gearing, and delta. Similar material for the call's partner—the put option—follows in Section 10.3. Stoll's (1969) put–call parity relation and the pivotal Black and Scholes (1973) valuation model are then outlined in Sections 10.4 and 10.5. Discussion of popular investment strategies in locally-traded options then follow in Section 10.6 with concluding remarks drawn in Section 10.7.

10.1   The Characteristics of Options and Their Markets

OTC Versus Exchange-Traded Derivative Products

Derivatives, like many other securities, trade either through organized exchanges or privately on OTC type markets. Trading in the latter probably accounts for around 50% of all outstanding positions and, in some derivative products—like swaps and forwards—all positions are confined to OTC trades.[1]

Significantly, credit risk, or counterparty risk, is reduced for exchange-traded derivatives. For futures and options contracts, for instance, the presence of a clearing house serves to reduce, if not eliminate, counterparty risk. In terms of technical jargon, the clearing house provides novation by agreeing to interpose itself between counterparties where default arises. The clearing house backs this up with guarantee funds to ensure that it can intervene when and if required. Investors in OTC derivatives, in comparison, do not have recourse to such protection and depend critically upon the creditworthiness of the counterparty. For this reason and others, most investors probably prefer the more regulated exchange-traded product. Others, who might wish to shy away from the prying eyes of exchange officials and market regulators, might feel more comfortable in the freer and more mobile OTC arena. While others still may see the OTC market as a more convenient outlet for trading on customized terms. This largely explains why swaps, which are essentially tailor-made by specific counterparties, fit so well into the OTC market. For those looking for standardized terms, exchange-traded products would clearly be preferable.

The general illiquidity of OTC products also means that most parties to OTC derivatives have to take their positions all the way through to settlement or expiry. An interesting irony is that exchange-traded options offer one route to hedge a variety of illiquid OTC positions.

In terms of exchange-traded options, the largest trading centre is the Chicago Board Options Exchange which, when it opened for trading in 1973, became the first significant market for organized options.[2] The second largest international centre is the London International Financial Futures Exchange (LIFFE). The origins of organized trading in equity options in London go back to 1978 when options emerged on the London Traded Options Market. These were subsequently absorbed by LIFFE following a merger between the two entities in 1992. Equity options are also apparent in a number of Asian markets with the SEHK being one of the leading lights, with listings dating back to September 1995.

Options Defined: Calls, Puts, and Exercise Terms

To introduce the various features of options, it is useful to categorize the instrument in terms of its option form and exercise style. The most basic distinction is between the call and put.

> Calls are options to *buy* underlying securities at a specified strike price at some future date. Puts are options to *sell* underlying securities at a specified price at some future date.

Options, whether of the call or put variety, can also be categorized by American or European exercise style. The labels have little to do with geography or the location of trading. In simple terms, the American call (or put) confers the right to buy (or sell) the underlying at any date up to and including the option's expiration date. The European option in contrast only allows for exercise at expiration. As options can broadly be described in terms of their call/put form and exercise style, an option can be placed into one of four broad categories: American call; American put; European call; or European put. This is a little simplistic though, as options can also be distinguished by the delivery conditions pertaining to the underlying.

Traditionally, most options have involved physical delivery. A call option with such terms—when exercised—involves the option holder buying a physical asset from the option writer at the agreed strike price. More and more options now involve cash payment features (in lieu of physical delivery). When exercising a call with such a feature, the investor submits a notice to buy the asset as before. Rather than delivering an asset, the writer transmits a cash payment to the investor. This cash payment is based upon the difference between some settlement price in the underlying, at the time of exercise, and the predetermined strike price. In short, the settlement price should reflect the market price of the underlying at the time of exercise. To illustrate, suppose an investor has a call option with strike $10 on stock X. Where physical delivery obtains, the investor receives the stock from the writer after paying $10. This will occur only if X's cash market price is higher than $10. By selling X in the market for $15, for example, the investor would generate a gain of $5. This is referred to as the option's intrinsic value. What would happen in the absence of physical settlement? Obviously, a cash payment of the same could be made from the writer to the investor. The settlement price would, of course, be the prevailing market price for X: $15, in the example.

For cash-settled options, there is a further complication. This comes in the form of the Asian option where settlement prices are determined by averaging prices on the underlying over some specified period. This period can range from just a few hours to a few weeks but always covers the period in the immediate run-up to option expiry. As a result, the Asian option is incompatible with American exercise style (and, therefore, applies to European options only). In a strict sense, locally traded Hang Seng Index (HSI) options—available on the HKFE—are European options with Asian settlement features. The average of quotations on the HSI, recorded at five-minute intervals during the final trading day of such contracts, determines the final settlement price. This is then compared to the strike price in the option to determine the cash payment, if any, to the investor. Numerous index options embody this kind of Asian or average rate settlement feature.[3] By deriving an average price for settlement, attempts to manipulate the underlying cash market, so as to generate profits on an option position, are made that much harder.

Where physical delivery of the underlying is mandated, Asian settlement features are clearly impracticable. The physical delivery requirements of traded equity options on the SEHK, therefore, preclude such Asian settlement features. In the light of the foregoing comments, six broad categories of option emerge. Leaving aside the distinction between cash and physical settlement, a call or a put can have one of two European exercise styles (with Asian or non-Asian settlement features where cash-settlement conditions apply) or an American exercise style, as illustrated in Exhibit 10.1.

Exhibit 10.1 Categorization of Option Types

	EXERCISE FORM		
Option Form	*EUROPEAN(1)*	*EUROPEAN(2)*	*American*
CALL	A[b].	B[a].	C[b].
PUT	D[b].	E[a].	F[b].

Notes: European (1) offers exercise against a given (probably closing) settlement price. European (2) offers a settlement pay-out by comparing the exercise price to some average (or weighting of prices) over a prescribed period. Referred to as a European option with Asian exercise terms.
a   Cash-settlement only.
b   Physical or Cash-Settlement Permissible.

HSI options fall into categories B and E in the illustration. The SEHK's equity options, which are American in exercise style, fall into categories C and F. The same would apply to exchange-traded equity options in all of the major trading centres—Chicago, London and Amsterdam. For those with a liking for European terms, privately-arranged equity options can always be arranged through the OTC markets.

Most attention in the following will be directed to American options given the dominance of this exercise form, particularly in the realm of exchange-traded equity options.

Long and Short Positions and the Concept of Open Interest

Analyses of options typically focus more attention on investors than issuers. In terms of accepted terminology, the investor is in a long position and the writer (or issuer) in a short position. The writers of call options, when served with an exercise notice from the buyer, commit to sell the underlying to the option investor at the agreed strike price.

It goes without saying that for every long position, a short position is evident somewhere. This is equivalent to the trite expression that 'for every buyer, there must also be a seller'. It does not mean, however, that every seller of an option is a writer. A seller may, for instance, be closing-out a long position (i.e., selling an option acquired earlier).

The concept of open interest is a useful one in appreciating the interplay of buying and selling in options markets. For any investor, this describes the number of 'open' positions in a particular class of derivative. If, for instance, an investor A originally wrote three call options on a specific asset X with given terms and then subsequently acquired two of these options in the secondary market, A would have open interest of one position—or net interest of one short position. Likewise, a player that bought three call options in X and subsequently sold the same has open interest of zero.

As an example of the computation of open interest, consider a market in a call option on an underlying stock PQR with given strike and expiry terms. Consider five possible players in this market (A, B, C, D, and E) across four days of trading (t = 1 to t = 4). Suppose at t = 1, A buys five options from D. As shown in Exhibit 10.2, A is therefore long in five contracts and B short in five. This also records their open interest, which for the overall market is the sum of net short or net long positions. At t = 2, one contract is traded. The trade between A and D on this day is an offsetting one for both parties: A sells one contract from his holdings and D buys one contract to offset one of his/her short positions, which results in open interest for the market of four contracts. For D, the offset does not lead to the cancellation of the short position, but logically implies exposure to only four of his/her five short contracts outstanding. Similar principles are applied in Exhibit 10.2 for representative trades between parties A, B, C, D, and E for days t = 3 and t = 4.

Exhibit 10.2 The Computation of Open Interest

Investor	Day:	t = 1	OI	t = 2	OI	t = 3	OI	t = 4	OI
A		5l	5l	1s	4l	–	4l	2s	2l
B		–	0	–	0	7l	7l	–	7l
C		–	0	–	0	1l	1l	1s	0
D		5s	5s	1l	4s	–	4s	1l	3s
E		–	0	–	0	8s	8s	2l	6s
Volume (no. of contracts)		5		1		8		3	
Open Interest			5		4		12		9

Both retail and institutional players are able to write and invest in options—a key feature of the option that helps to distinguish it from the equity warrant, which is always written by the issuer of the underlying asset. An equity warrant on Swire Pacific 'A' stock, for instance, would be written by Swire Pacific. A call or put option on the same could, in contrast, be issued by a range of third parties. Equity warrants are also typically issued in one batch, while equity options can be written at any time between their introduction and expiry. The calculation of open interest in Exhibit 10.2 aptly demonstrates this situation.

10.2   The Characteristic Features of Call Options

To illustrate the essential features of call options, consider a fictitious American option on stock RST. Suppose that the call has expiry of 31 March 200x and can be written at any time between 1 January 200x and the day prior to expiry. Suppose that on a specific date during the life of the option, let's say 21 January 200x, the underlying stock's value (V_{RST}) is $11.20. Given a strike price (X) on the option of $10 and a conversion ratio of one—which allows one option to be converted into one underlying RST share—a market price for the option of $3 emerges. This market price is known as the premium.[4] Exhibit 10.3 summarizes the key features of this option.

Premium, Intrinsic Value and Time Value

The premium depends, principally, on two things: (i) the differential between the value of the underlying and the strike price (V_{RST} – X); and (ii) the time remaining to expiry.

In the example, purchase of the option for $3 would allow the holder to buy one stock from the option writer for $10 which could then be sold in the cash market for $11.20. This $1.20 gain, referred to as intrinsic value, would not, of course, cover the premium paid. The option investor pays a premium greater than $1.20 not for the privilege of immediate option conversion but for the opportunity to buy RST at a pre-determined

Exhibit 10.3 Summary of the Characteristics of an *American 3-Month Call* Option on Stock RST

Conversion ratio	= 1
Strike price (X)	= $10
Premium (P)	= $3
Value of underlying stock (V_{RST})	= $11.20
Gearing = V_{RST}/P	= 3.73
Intrinsic value	= $1.20
Time value	= $1.80
Intrinsic value	= Max. ($V_{RST} - X$, 0)
Premium	= Intrinsic Value + Time Value

Option is priced 'into-the-money' when $V_{RST} - X > 0$; 'at-the-money' when $V_{RST} - X = 0$; and 'out-of-the-money' when $V_{RST} - X < 0$.

price over some defined future period. A speculative investor purchasing at the market-determined premium of $3, would surely hope (and expect) that the value of RST would rise sufficiently by the expiry date to garner at least $3 of intrinsic value. If at expiry, V_{RST} rises to $13.05, the investor would be able to realize intrinsic value of $3.05 and generate an overall net profit (ignoring transaction costs) of $0.05.

Investors can of course sell options prior to expiry. At any time prior to expiry, an option always carries some time value. This is the key to option pricing and reflects the market's evaluation of the upside potential in the underlying in the period prior to option expiry. Essentially, longer time to expiry and greater volatility in the underlying translate to increased time value.

As the premium is always equal to intrinsic value plus time value, time value represents the residual component of value. The time value component of the option featured in Exhibit 10.3 is $1.80 (= $3 – $1.20). At option expiry, time value is always zero so that option value is wholly intrinsic value. In contrast, intrinsic value can be zero at any time prior to expiry. This occurs where $V_{RST} - X <,= 0$. In such cases, it is irrational to exercise as one can buy on terms at least as favourable through the cash market. This logic explains why intrinsic value cannot be negative. Where intrinsic value is positive, the call option is said to be 'in-the-money'. Call options are 'at-the-money' when the value of the underlying equals the strike and 'out-of-the-money' when this value falls below the strike.

The foregoing also suggests that investors are better off selling existing holdings of options than exercising them. Option exercise is equivalent to realizing intrinsic value and giving up time value. For any significant time to expiry, some time value is likely and, assuming liquidity in the options market, it makes more sense to sell the option.[5] In this respect, there is no obvious advantage to an American call option over a European call. This is true in the absence of dividends on the underlying. There may be an advantage to an American option when dividends feature, though. In cases where relatively large dividends are paid on the underlying, it may be optimal to exercise just prior to the ex-dividend date.[6]

The Concept of Leverage (Gearing)

One of the key reasons investors buy options is the leverage (gearing) such instruments offer. This means that investors wishing to gain exposure to the underlying stock can do so through the option at a fraction of the cost of the underlying. In Exhibit 10.3, the gearing rate of 3.73 times indicates that the cost of buying one option—which allows access to one underlying share—is 26.79% of the cost of RST stock. However, as we shall see later this gearing advantage, like any other kind of margin arrangement, is a double-edged sword. While it reduces the cost of entry, it also levers up the volatility of percentage returns. As a result, options are likely to shed a much greater proportion of their value than the underlying in a bear market. The good news for the investor is that the maximum loss on an option—the premium—is always a fraction of the cost of the underlying stock.

To understand gearing, suppose that one day after purchasing the RST option, V_{RST} rises by $0.10. This represents an increase in the value of the underlying of 0.9%. Given an immaterial change (of only one day) in the time remaining to maturity, the call premium should rise by approximately $0.10 to $3.10 (intrinsic value = $1.30; time value = $1.80).[7] Exposure to the upside in RST, through the option, allows a percentage return of over three times that on RST. Equally, a $0.10 decline in RST, over the same one-day period, would have generated a 3.33% loss on the option, compared with a 0.9% loss on the stock.

The Writer's Position

Thus far, little has been said about the writer of a call option. In particular, what are the obligations facing such a party? These depend upon whether the writer's position is 'naked' or 'covered'. For the writer of a 'naked' call option, underlying stock is not held in treasury. In the event of an exercise notice being served by the investor, the writer goes to the cash market to acquire the underlying and then sells it—as required through the option—at the agreed exercise price.

In contrast, the writer of a 'covered' call option buys (or holds) the underlying stock at the time the option is written. Consequently, the writer is able to deliver any stock to an investor exercising the call by selling from treasury. In effect the 'covered' call writer's position represents two positions: a long position in the underlying and a short position in the call. Not surprisingly, therefore, the writer's profit profiles for 'naked' and 'covered' positions are quite different.

For the option featured in Exhibit 10.3, profit profiles, using possible values for stock RST at the option expiry date, are shown in Table 10.1 and Figure 10.1. These relate to both 'naked' and 'covered' written positions and cover expiry values on RST of $4, $8, $12 and $16. With respect to the 'covered' written position, it is assumed that the writer acquired the underlying sometime earlier for $9.

The profit profile for the writer of the 'naked' position is straightforward. It is the exact opposite of that of an investor purchasing the call for $3 and holding it until expiry. In other words, there is a zero-sum game between the investor and 'naked' option writer. Gains for the latter translate to losses for the former, and vice versa. From Table 10.1 and Figure 10.1, it is also apparent that the investor has 'capped' downside and 'uncapped' upside. Naturally, the reverse applies to the writer of the 'naked' position given the foregoing.

The situation for the 'covered' option writer is very different and requires some careful analysis. Given a value for RST of $4 at expiry, the option would expire worthless. An exercise notice would not, therefore, be submitted from the writer's counterparty (the investor); however, this is not the end of the story. The writer loses on his/her stock covering given a decline in its value of $5 ($9 – $4). This is not realized, but it is still a loss nonetheless. As this loss is partly offset by the premium collected from

Table 10.1 Comparisons of the Profit Profiles for 'Naked' and 'Covered' Call Option Writers

(i)   'Naked' Writer's Position

Value of RST at Expiry	Premium Collected	Intrinsic Value Paid	Profit/Loss
$4	$3	$0	$3
$8	$3	$0	$3
$12	$3	($2)	$1
$16	$3	($6)	($3)

(ii) 'Covered' Writer's Position (RST Stock Purchased for $9.00 some time Prior to Sale of Option)

Value of RST at Expiry	Premium Collected	Capital Gain/Loss	Profit/ Loss
$4	$3	($5)*	($2)
$8	$3	($1)*	$2
$12	$3	$1	$4
$16	$3	$1	$4

Figures in parentheses represent losses.
* Indicates unrealized capital gains/losses.

Figure 10.1 Comparison of 'Naked' and 'Covered' Call Writer's Profit
Profiles at Expiry

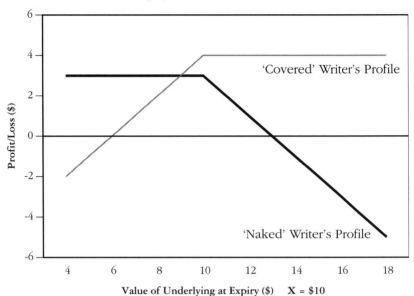

Based upon a call sold on 21 January, 200X on the following terms: premium = $3; Strike =
$10; conversion ratio = 1; value of the underlying at the time of option issue = $11.20; and
option maturity of 31 March 200X [see Exhibit 10.3].

the earlier sale of the option, of $3, the writer's overall loss is $2. Had RST
risen, instead, to $16 at expiry the picture would have been very different:
the writer would have received an exercise notice to sell stock for $10
and, having purchased it earlier for $9, would have realized a $1 capital
gain. Adding this to the premium, leads to a gross profit of $4.

The situation described for the 'covered' call writer is akin to that of
the 'naked' writer in the sense that the upside gain is limited and the
downside loss unlimited (insofar as the value of the underlying is positive);
however, the favoured direction of market change is opposite. The key
issue in the 'covered' writer's strategy is income enhancement. This can
only be achieved where the writer purchases the underlying at a discount
to the option's strike price. Anecdotal evidence suggests that this is quite
feasible as writers often buy heavily into the underlying prior to a call
option issue. Such buying pressure may well contribute to an increase in
the value of the stock and thus generate a more favourable premium for
the option sale. A less cynical view would suggest the writer's foresight in
two areas: (i) buying the underlying prior to a rise in stock values; and (ii)
selling options at a subsequent market peak.

As a final point, option exercise has no effect on the number of shares
in issue in the underlying company, irrespective of the nature of the
writer's position. Chapter 11 shows that for equity warrants the situation

is completely different: the writer, as issuer of the underlying, issues new stock upon receipt of an exercise notice, which suggests an opportunity for the issuer to raise capital twice—once when the warrant is issued and again upon exercise. The exercise effect also triggers a dilution in the earnings per share of the underlying company. These effects are clearly not evident in traded call options, although they are found in another kind of option: the employee stock option (ESOP), covered in Section 8.1.

The Valuation of Call Options and the Behaviour of Time Value

It is one thing to understand the profit profiles to the writer and investor, it is another to understand how the premium of the option behaves. Fairly complex models exist for this purpose. Their complexity arises from an appreciation of time value. This is not only a function of time to maturity, but also of intrinsic value and the volatility of the underlying.

The 'Golden Rule' of Option Pricing

Before getting into the knotty issue of time value, it is important to be aware of the 'golden rule' of option pricing: premium must always be at least equal to intrinsic value. This applies to both calls and puts.

To see this, reconsider the example in Exhibit 10.3. Had the premium on the RST option been less than the intrinsic value of $1.20, arbitrageurs would have extracted riskless profit by simultaneously buying options and shorting a corresponding number of the underlying. Settlement of the short stock position would have been achieved through option exercise. Suppose that the premium had been $0.80 (rather than $3). An arbitrage gain, ignoring transaction costs, of $0.40 ($11.20 − $10 − $0.80) would have emerged for every option purchased and stock shorted.

Arbitrageurs seizing on such opportunities induce a self-correcting mechanism in to the markets: option premiums rise due to increased buying pressure and stock values fall due to the opposite. This narrows the gap between premium and intrinsic value. Assuming costless arbitrage, and liquidity in both the option and underlying, arbitrage should continue until the premium at least covers intrinsic value. In theory, transaction costs would allow an option premium to dip slightly below the option's intrinsic value.

The Importance of Time Value

As noted, the behaviour of this component is at the heart of all option pricing models. Time value represents a payment over and above the intrinsic value for the possibility that the value of the underlying will rise between purchase and expiry dates. All things being equal, the greater the time remaining to expiry and the greater the volatility of the underlying, the greater time value.

Time value, at any given point, is also a function of intrinsic value, which adds a further complication to the modelling process. Theory states that, at any given time to expiry, time value is at a maximum when an option is priced 'at-the-money'. The logic for this claim is as follows. As an option moves further and further 'out-of-the-money', for a given time to expiry, investors see less potential for positive intrinsic value at option expiry and, accordingly, premium shrinks. Equally, time value will shrink as an option moves deeper and deeper 'into-the-money', for a given time to expiry. In such cases, large sums of intrinsic value can be wiped out by adverse movements in the value of underlying. In contrast, no intrinsic value is at stake when an option is priced 'at-the-money'. This means that a fall in the value of the underlying is less damaging to the option. It also means that any increase in the value of the underlying immediately translates to an intrinsic value gain.

Figure 10.2 broadly captures the behaviour of the time value component (as shown by the difference between the premium and intrinsic value lines) for a given time to expiry. Line #2, which records higher time value for all values of the underlying, reflects a longer time to expiry than Line #1.

The Option Delta (δ) and its Link with Time Value

Delta (δ) captures the curvature of the premium function (as shown in Figure 10.2). It measures the ratio of a dollar change in premium to a corresponding dollar change in the underlying. The δ moves between a range of zero and one as a call option moves from being deeply priced

Figure 10.2 Typical Option Valuation Profiles for Calls with a Given Time to Expiry

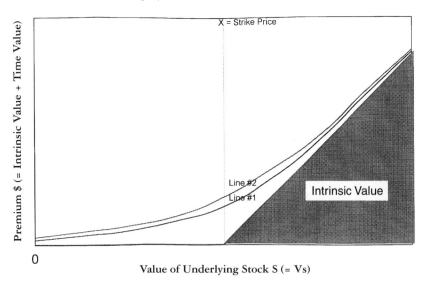

Line #1: Option premium with 1 month to expiry
Line #2: Option premium with 2 months to expiry
Time Value = Premium − Intrinsic Value

'out-of-the-money' to being deeply priced 'into-the-money'. By intuition, δ approximates to 0.5 at the 'at-the-money' point.

The behaviour of time value is best illustrated using real examples. SEHK traded call options on the Hongkong and Shanghai Banking Corporation (HSBC) stock (see Table 10.2, A) highlight how time value varies both with respect to time to expiry (for a given strike price) and intrinsic value (for a given time to expiry). Consistent with theory, time value is higher on the more distant month (January) options, for all strikes. Time value also peaks for options priced closer to the 'at-the-money' point, whatever the expiry date. For December call options, for example, the time value associated with the $180 strike call exceeds that for the $190 call: the former being $3.50 away from the 'at-the-money' point and the latter $6.50. Other comparisons also yield the same insight with time value dissipating as one moves further away from the 'at-the-money' point (for a given expiry date).

The above observations are also corroborated in Table 10.2, B for call options on the *London* International Financial Futures Exchange (LIFFE). In short, one would expect the two behavioural traits for time value—one cross-sectionally based and the other time based—to be evident in all efficiently priced options markets.

The Relationship between Gearing and Delta

While gearing tells us that option premiums are attractively priced relative to the underlying, we know from earlier discussions that the variance of rates of return on options are magnified by gearing. The extent of this depends upon the option's δ.

To illustrate, return to the example in Exhibit 10.3. Consider an increase in the value of RST of $0.10 (as before) and a δ on the option of 0.90. The latter, which is consistent with the option being deeply priced 'into-the-money', suggests an increase in the premium of $0.09, for a $0.10 gain in the underlying. This increase translates to gains of 0.89% and 3%, respectively, in the stock and option. In other words, for a small increase in the value of the underlying, the rate of return on the option is approximately 3.37 times that on the stock. Equally, a small decline in the value of the underlying would have meant that returns on the option would have been negative but 3.37 times higher in absolute terms. The difference in these returns reflects both the gearing and delta of the option. As the δ increases, the differential in returns is magnified. Had the δ been 1.00, the ratio of rates of returns (on the option to the stock) would have been 3.73 times. This corresponds to the option's gearing (see Exhibit 10.3).

The issue above is complicated when large changes in the value of the underlying are considered. There are two reasons for this: an option's δ and time value both change when such large shifts in the value of the underlying occur. This has important implications, especially when δ is used for hedging. We will see this later when the topic of delta-hedging is introduced.

Table 10.2   Decomposition of Call Option Premiums into Intrinsic and Time Value Components

Panel A: HSBC Options Traded on the SEHK
HSBC Stock = HK$183.50

Strike:		$170	$175	$180	$185	$190	$195	$200	$210
December Call Options	Intrinsic Value	13.50	8.50	3.50	0.00	0.00	0.00	0.00	0.00
	Time Value	1.10	1.98	3.73	4.51	2.82	1.46	0.61	0.10
	Premium	14.60	10.48	7.23	4.51	2.82	1.46	0.61	0.10
January Call Options	Intrinsic Value	13.50	8.50	3.50	0.00	0.00	0.00	0.00	0.00
	Time Value	5.69	7.50	9.51	10.00	7.80	6.57	5.08	2.91
	Premium	19.19	16.00	13.01	10.00	7.80	6.57	5.08	2.91

Intrinsic values are based on a closing value for HSBC stock of 22 Dec 1997 of HK$183.50. Market price data for the options was obtained from *South China Morning Post*, Business Post, p. 8, Tuesday, 23 December 1997. Strikes of $165, $220 and $230 in December calls and $220 in January calls were also available.

Panel B: Marks & Spencer Call Options Traded on the London International Financial Futures Exchange (LIFFE)
M&S Stock = 581.5p (£5.815)

Strike:		550p	600p
July Call Options	Intrinsic Value	31.50	0.00
	Time Value	7.00	14.50
	Premium	38.50	14.50
October Call Options	Intrinsic Value	31.50	0.00
	Time Value	28.00	36.50
	Premium	59.50	36.50
January Call Options	Intrinsic Value	31.50	0.00
	Time Value	40.50	47.00
	Premium	72.00	47.00

Premiums and option terms determined from *Financial Times (WEEKEND)*, 23/24 May 1998, p. 17.
Two observations are apparent in Panels A and B: (i) for a given time to expiry, the closer the option to the 'at-the-money' position, the greater the time value; and (ii) for a given strike price, the longer the time to expiry, the greater the time value.

10.3 The Characteristics of Put Options

Much of what has been said about call options applies to put options. The major difference, of course, is that the put is an option to sell rather than buy. By virtue of this, intrinsic value is generated when buying the underlying stock in the cash market and selling it, at a higher strike price, through the option. Where the strike is less than or equal to the value of the underlying, the put's intrinsic value is zero. In sum, standard theory tells us that the intrinsic value for a put on stock S is:

$$\text{Max } (X - V_S, 0).$$

From the perspective of the put option writer, there are two possible positions: a 'naked' written position and a 'covered' written position. The former is straightforward and simply means that the writer commits to buy underlying stock—without any position in the stock itself—whenever the put option investor serves an exercise notice. The 'covered' written position is a little more complicated. It entails the writer being short in the put and short in the underlying. Upon receipt of an exercise notice, therefore, the writer buys stock from the option investor and simultaneously uses this newly acquired stock to 'close-out' his/her short stock position.

To appreciate the profit profile of the put option writer at expiry, both positions are considered through numerical example (see Table 10.3 and Figure 10.3). In this example, a stock S with current value of $69 is considered. A put option is then written on S for a premium of $4 with expiry date in three months' time and a strike of $65. The projected profit profile at expiry, for both 'naked' and 'covered' written positions, is then reflected for expiry date values in S of $50, $60, $70, and $80.

The profit profile to the 'naked' put option writer is straightforward. It represents the mirror image of the profile of a put option investor acquiring the option at $4 and holding it all the way through to expiry. As with the 'naked' call option writer and investor, profits across both parties sum to zero. The same cannot, of course, be said when the put writer's position is 'covered'.

The 'covered' writer actually gains when the underlying falls in value. For an expiry value in the underlying of $60, the writer reaps a profit of $8 (see Table 10.3). As an exercise notice will be served at expiry—given intrinsic value of $5 on the option—the writer is forced to buy stock at the strike of $65. This stock once acquired is then used to 'close-out' the short stock position—opened earlier at $69—for a $4 profit. With the premium collected of $4, this translates to an overall gain of $8, ignoring all transaction costs. At the other end of the spectrum, an expiry value of $80 in the underlying suggests a loss to the writer. Moreover, the loss exposure is unlimited, which is also true of the 'naked' writer's position, but the direction of exposure is markedly different as shown in Figure 10.3. As with the 'covered' call writer's position, the 'covered' put provides a strategy for income enhancement. This is evident from the comparison of the upside

Table 10.3   Comparisons of the Profit Profiles for 'Naked' and 'Covered' Put Option Writers

(i)   'Naked' Writer's Position

Value of S at Expiry	Premium Collected	Intrinsic Value Paid	Profit/Loss
$50	$4	($15)	($11)
$60	$4	($5)	($1)
$70	$4	$0	$4
$80	$4	$0	$4

(ii)   'Covered' Writer's Position (RST Stock shorted for $69.00 at time Option is Sold)

Value of S at Expiry	Premium Collected	Capital Gain/Loss	Profit/ Loss
$50	$4	$4**	$8
$60	$4	$4**	$8
$70	$4	($1)*	$3
$80	$4	($11)*	($7)

Figures in parentheses represent losses.
*   Indicates unrealized capital gains/losses.
**   Transaction costs associated with short position in stock are ignored.

Figure 10.3   Comparison of 'Naked' and 'Covered' Put Writer's Profit Profiles at Expiry

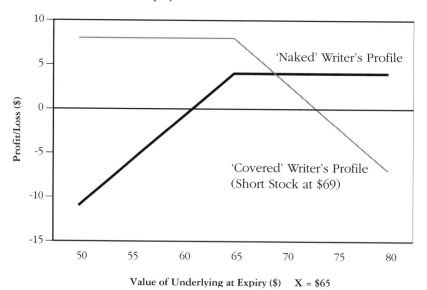

Figures depict example in Table 10.3 where the put is written three months prior to its maturity. It is sold with a conversion ratio of 1; premium of $4 and strike of $65.

gain on the 'covered' and 'naked' positions in Table 10.3, where a differential of $4 is apparent: equal to the short sale price of $69 less the put option strike of $65.

The Time Value Component of the Put Option Premium

Time value behaves in much the same way for puts as for calls. For one, it is highest for a put of a given strike series, the longer the time remaining to expiry. It also increases on puts of a given expiry date, as the value of the underlying moves closer to the 'at-the-money' point. These observations are confirmed by considering, as before, real data for SEHK traded and LIFFE equity options. This data is shown in Table 10.4.

The relation between the put option premium and the value of the underlying is shown in Figure 10.4. The key difference between this and Figure 10.2—for the call option—is that the δ of the put is negative. It varies from levels approximating zero, for puts deeply 'priced-out-of-the-money', to minus one, for positions deeply priced 'into-the-money'.

One other key difference between puts and calls is the fact that, in the absence of dividends, exercise style matters. This is due to the fact that the intrinsic value of a put always has an upper 'cap' equal to the difference between the strike price and the lowest valuable obtainable on the underlying. In theory, the latter is $0. In reality, security values normally have a minimum floor approximating to $0; such as $0.01. This being so, a put option on a stock S, with strike $10, could not possibly record a

Figure 10.4 Typical Option Valuation Profiles for Puts with a Given
Time to Expiry

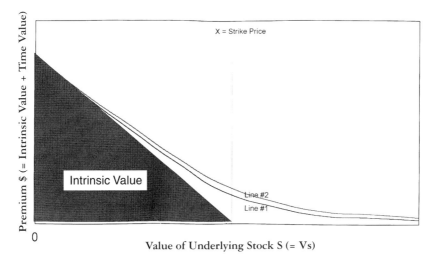

Line #1: Option premium with 1 month to expiry
Line #2: Option premium with 2 months to expiry
Time Value = Premium − Intrinsic Value

Table 10.4   Decomposition of Put Option Premiums into Intrinsic and Time Value Components

Panel A: HSBC Options Traded on the SEHK
HSBC Stock = HK$183.50

	Strike:	$170	$175	$180	$185	$190	$195	$200	$210
December Put Options	Intrinsic Value	0.00	0.00	0.00	1.50	6.50	11.50	16.50	26.50
	Time Value	0.98	1.86	3.72	4.45	2.65	1.41	0.58	0.02
	Premium	0.98	1.86	3.72	5.95	9.15	12.91	17.08	26.52
January Put Options	Intrinsic Value	0.00	0.00	0.00	1.50	6.50	11.50	16.50	26.50
	Time Value	4.87	6.74	8.80	9.85	7.66	5.87	4.33	2.13
	Premium	4.87	6.74	8.80	11.35	14.16	17.37	20.83	28.63

Intrinsic values are based on a closing value for HSBC stock of 22 Dec 1997 of HK$183.50.
Market price data for the options was obtained from *South China Morning Post*, Business Post, p. 8, Tuesday, 23 December 1997.
Strikes of $165, $220, and $230 in December puts and $220 in January puts were also available.

Panel B: Marks & Spencer Put Options Traded on the London International Financial Futures Exchange (LIFFE)
M&S Stock = 581.5p (£5.815)

	Strike:	550p	600p
July Put Options	Intrinsic Value	0.00	18.50
	Time Value	14.00	20.00
	Premium	14.00	38.50
October Put Options	Intrinsic Value	0.00	18.50
	Time Value	26.50	29.00
	Premium	26.50	47.50
January Put Options	Intrinsic Value	0.00	18.50
	Time Value	29.50	35.50
	Premium	29.50	54.00

Premiums and option terms determined from *Financial Times (WEEKEND)*, 23/24 May 1998, p. 17.
Two observations are apparent in Panels A and B: (i) for a given time to expiry, the closer the option to the 'at-the-money' position, the greater the time value; and (ii) for a given strike price, the longer the time to expiry, the greater the time value.

value exceeding its maximum intrinsic value of $9.99. Whenever put premiums gravitate to this theoretical level, investors are likely to exercise them early. In such circumstances, the benefits of time are overwhelmingly negative as additional time offers little or no potential for upside benefit but huge potential for downside loss.[8]

10.4 Put–Call Parity

Knowledge of the characteristics of puts and calls leads usefully to an equilibrium pricing theorem that incorporates both: Stoll's (1969) *Put–Call Parity Theorem*. This holds for European style options and tells us that for a put and a call, with the same terms on the same underlying stock S, the following holds:[9]

$$V_S + P_S - C_S = X / (1 + r)^t$$

where V_S is stock value; P_S the premium for a put on S; C_S the premium for a call on S; X the strike in the call and put; t the time to option expiry; and r the riskless rate of interest.

To illustrate, consider European put and call options written on stock S with the same terms of issue: same strike, expiry dates, and conversion ratios (equal to one). Based upon this, an investment strategy involving the purchase of one share in S, the purchase of one S put option, and the sale (shorting) of one S call option yields a guaranteed pay-off at the expiry dates in the options equal to the strike X. Consider expiry values of S of $10, $20, and $30 to illustrate. With a strike on the put and call of $20, the values of the put–call parity portfolio, at expiry, is $20. This is so, whatever the value of S at expiry, as is shown in Exhibit 10.4.

Exhibit 10.4 An Illustration of Stoll's Theorem of Put–Call Parity Theorem

	Portfolio	*Share price of S at option expiry dates*		
		$10	$20	$30
Values	Long in one S share	10	20	30
at	Long in one S put	(20 – 10)	0	0
Expiry	Short in one S call	0	0	– (30 – 20)
	Sum of values at expiry	20	20	20

Investments in the underlying share and put option, and a short position in a corresponding call, therefore guarantee an expiry pay-off equal to the strike price in the options. In a fair market, the cost of assembling the three-legged portfolio would equate to the present value of the portfolio's expiry pay-off. As this pay-off occurs with certainty, the appropriate discount rate is clearly the riskless rate. In the case of continuous compounding, we typically see the put–call parity result expressed as,

$$V_S + P_S - C_S = X.e^{-(r \times t)}$$

It should be recognized, however, that this relation does not hold for American options. As noted earlier, whilst European and American calls on the same underlying with the same terms have the same value, an American put is always more valuable than a European put.[10] Dividends add a further complication, even when the options considered are European. While ex-dividend effects have, at least in theory, countervailing effects on the call and put premiums—enhancing the latter and damaging the former—they result in a diminution of the underlying share's value. This suggests a re-interpretation of the European put–call parity theorem as follows,[11]

$$P_S - C_S = X.e^{-(r \times t)} - (V_S - D)$$

where all terms are as before, and D is the present value of the dividend (measured by discounting the known or estimated dividend from its ex-date back to present).

The Arbitrage-Free Properties of Put–Call Parity
For European style options, uncontaminated by ex-dividend dates, marked departures from put–call parity often signal arbitrage opportunities. Such opportunities depend, crucially, upon liquidity in the options and underlying as well as transaction costs being less than the perceived gross profit from the strategy. An example of such an arbitrage opportunity is constructed in Appendix 10.1. The first opportunity captioned relates to the situation where the cost of assembling the put–call parity portfolio (i.e., the left-hand side (LHS) of the theorem) is markedly higher than the present value of the guaranteed pay-off (i.e., the right-hand side (RHS) of the theorem). Arbitrageurs seizing on this would short the put and stock and buy the call, and invest the proceeds at the riskless rate until the options' expiry date. These proceeds would more than cover the payment of the strike price obligation, resulting from the creation of the diametric opposite of the put–call parity portfolio. This would leave an excess constituting arbitrage profit. Arbitrage strategies are also evident where the LHS value of the put–call parity theorem is markedly lower than the RHS, and are illustrated in the second caption of Appendix 10.1.

While call and put options with the same terms are routinely available in most markets, clear insights into put–call parity are hindered by the predominance of American exercise styles. Despite this, a litany of studies have sought to test put–call parity using such options. In general, these reveal only moderate departures from Stoll's original relation. More refined insights are offered in studies like Kamara and Miller's (1995) which focus on European options. They note, after adjusting for dividends and transaction costs, for options on Standard & Poor's 500 US stock indices, that departures from put–call parity 'are less frequent and smaller than those found in earlier PCP studies using American options' (PCP = put–call parity, p. 538). They also suggest that even where *ex-ante* profit opportunities exist, liquidity risk often frustrates the realization of such gains.

To illustrate the principle of put–call parity for locally-based options, two examples are considered in Table 10.5. One for American equity options traded on the SEHK and the other for European HSI options traded on the HKFE. In the first case, the illustration chosen shows a departure from put–call parity of less than 1%. This could, in all likelihood be explained away by transaction costs, or the fact that the early exercise advantage of American puts causes a natural deviation from Stoll's European put–call parity result. The larger LHS value in the illustration is, in fact, consistent with this.

For the European HSI index options, contract value is measured by a multiplier of HK$50 per index point. In virtually all respects, the index option can be treated just like any other option. Despite its European form, however, sizeable departures from put–call parity result. In the illustration these are around 1.5%. The significant transaction costs involved in constructing the underlying index probably account for this. Variable costs, like brokerage commissions, are not the problem as these are paid at a flat rate. Fixed costs, though, mount up when 33 constituents have to be assembled. To effectively arbitrage, either the underlying index has to be purchased or sold short; both of which entail some effort and inconvenience. Attempts to mirror the cash index by holding or shorting the index's principal stocks is an alternative—though a somewhat imperfect one. More realistically, HSI futures would likely feature as the substitute in any arbitrage strategy. But this entails something called *basis risk*. This is an issue that is taken up in Chapter 12. Consideration of arbitrage strategies between cash, futures, and options is also considered.[12]

Dividend effects should also be considered in illustration B in Table 10.5 as the HSI's constituents are not adjusted for ex-dividends effects. In any event, the short time remaining to option expiry, and the fact that any dividend effects are diffused across the whole index, would suggest that dividends have minimal effect on the results in Table 10.5. Over a year, the story would be rather different. Dividend yields on the HSI, of around 3% to 4%, would impound much more strongly on the premiums of longer-term options.

In sum, the general evidence suggests that put–call parity holds, at least in approximate terms. The importance of this result, is that an approximate value for a put naturally follows from the premium on a call on the same underlying with the same terms. As the demand for call options is typically greater than for puts, most option valuation models deal exclusively with calls. Put–call parity is then invoked to compute an approximate value for an equivalent put. The most well-known of the call valuation models, the Black and Scholes (B&S) model, is briefly surveyed in the following.

Table 10.5   Illustrations of Put–Call Parity for Locally-Traded Options

SEHK TRADED EQUITY OPTIONS

Exercise style: American

Consider HSBC January $185 strike put and call options*.
V_{HSBC} = $183.50; P_{HSBC} = $11.35; C_{HSBC} = $10.00;
r = 0.06 (an approximation of bank deposit rate); and t = 40/365.

$$P_{HSBC} - C_{HSBC} + V_{HSBC} = 11.35 - 10 + 183.50 = \$184.85$$
$$X/e^{r \times t} = 185e^{-(0.06 \times 0.1096)} = \$183.79$$

% departure from P–C Parity = {(184.85 − 183.79)/183.79} × 100
= 0.58%

Data obtained for closing option and stock values for HSBC as of 22 December 1997
from *South China Morning Post*, Business Post, p. 8, Tuesday, 23 December 1997.

* Dividends are not a complicating factor due to the absence of ex-dividend dates in
HSBC stock between 22 December 1997 and the expiry date in the options.

HKFE TRADED HSI OPTIONS

Exercise style: European (one index point = $50)

Consider HSI December 10,400 Call and Put options.
HSI = 10,172.47 points; P_{HSI} = 498 points; C_{HSI} = 133 points;
r = 0.06; and t =9/365.

$$P_{HSI} - C_{HSI} + V_{HSI} = 10,172.47 - 133 + 498 = 10,537.47 \text{ points}$$
$$= 10,537.47 \times \$50 = \$526,873.50$$

$$X/e^{rt} = 10,400^{-(0.06 \times 0.0247)} = 10,384.63 \text{ points}$$
$$= 10,384.63 \times \$50 = \$519,231.50$$

% departure from P–C Parity = {(10,537.47 − 10,384.63)/10,384.63} × 100
= 1.47%

Data obtained for closing option and HSI values for HSI options as of 22 December
1997 from *South China Morning Post*, Business Post, p. 8, Tuesday, 23 December
1997.

10.5 Option Valuation Models: Black and Scholes (1973)

Black and Scholes' (B&S) pathbreaking contribution to security pricing, through the publication of their 1973 paper on European call-option valuation, really marks the genesis of organized options trading. While options were evident in disparate locations and forms prior to 1973, the B&S option-valuation model gave impetus to option trading by allowing dealers, investors, and writers access to a model form to validate 'fair' premium levels. It is more than coincidence, then, that the first major market for organized options trading—The Chicago Board Options Exchange—came into being in 1973. The very same year that B&S's seminal paper came into print.

The Model was proposed for options on non-dividend paying securities in real (continuous) time in markets unfettered by transaction costs and taxes. Rates of return on the underlying security are also assumed to follow a random walk with the variance on such returns assumed to be constant over time. The final Model form is shown in Exhibit 10.5.

Exhibit 10.5 The Form of the Black and Scholes (1973, p. 644) Model

$$V_O = V_S \cdot N(d_1) - E \cdot e^{-(r \cdot t)} \cdot N(d_2)$$

where V_O = call premium; V_S = value of underlying; N ($\cdot$) is a standard normal cumulative density function;

$$d_1 = [\ln(V_S/E) + (r + 0.5\sigma^2) \cdot t]/(\sigma \cdot \sqrt{t});$$

E = Exercise price; r = risk-free rate; t = time to expiration; σ^2 is the variance of the underlying security's annualized rate of return; and

$$d_2 = [\ln(V_S/E) + (r - 0.5\sigma^2) \cdot t]/(\sigma \cdot \sqrt{t})$$

(note that different notation is given for the above in Black and Scholes).

By noting that d_2 is equivalent to $(d_1 - \sigma \cdot \sqrt{t})$, the B&S Model is also reported, in a rather more user-friendly manner, as follows,

$$V_O = V_S \cdot N(d_1) - E \cdot e^{-(r \cdot t)} \cdot N(d_1 - \sigma \cdot \sqrt{t})$$

$$d_1 = [\ln(V_S/E) + (r + 0.5^2) \cdot t]/(\sigma \cdot \sqrt{t})$$

The only major pitfall when applying the B&S Model manually is to ensure the correct interpretation of the N($\bullet$) operator to d_1 and $(d_1 - \sigma \cdot \sqrt{t})$. Reference must be made to standard normal tables with N($\cdot$) capturing the area under this distribution to the immediate left of the actual d_1 or $(d_1 - \sigma \cdot \sqrt{t})$ values. To illustrate, suppose, in a certain example, d_1 equals 0.51. From standard normal tables, the area to the right of this point is 0.305 (i.e., 30.5% of the area under a standard normal curve). N(0.51) therefore equates to 0.695. If d_1 had been -0.51, N(-0.51) would instead have been 0.305, due to the symmetrical nature of the standard normal distribution around its mean of zero. While these subtleties are often lost on the typical trader or dealer, students of finance should beware, given that manual computations are routinely requested in many examinations.

The significance of $N(d_1)$ should also be emphasized. This captures the call option delta = (dollar change in premium/dollar change in the value of the underlying). Inspection of V_O indicates quite clearly that the rate of change of premium with respect to the value of the underlying (= $\delta V_O/ \delta V_S$) equates to $N(d_1)$.

A simplified case study is shown in Appendix 10.2 to illustrate application of the B&S model. The first example, in caption A, is faithful to the original outline of the model as it relates to a European call on a non-dividend paying stock. Inevitable biases result, though, when the model is applied, without adjustment, to European or American call options on dividend paying stocks. Black's (1975) commentary—'fact and fantasy in the use of options'—offers suggested adjustments in this context. Caption B reflects this suggested adjustment for European call options on dividend-paying stocks by modifying the example of Appendix 10.2, A.

The adjustment is straightforward and, following the instructions of Black, simply requires that an adjusted stock price (V_S') is used instead of V_S in the Model. This adjustment is achieved by 'subtracting the present value of dividends likely to be paid before maturity from the stock price' (p. 41). This requires that both the ex-dividend date and dividend to be paid are known in advance. The predictability of dividend payments schedules and the stability of dividends makes this problem less onerous than it might seem.

For American call options on dividend paying stocks, the situation is a little more complicated. The Model has to be calculated twice: firstly, where the option remains unexercised, so that V_S' substitutes for V_S in the formula and secondly, where the option is exercised just prior to the ex-dividend date—in which case V_S replaces V_S' and t, the time to expiry, is replaced by t', the time to the ex-date. These calculations are reflected in caption C of Appendix 10.2. The largest of the two B&S option values is then chosen as the premium.[13] The two-step procedure again requires that dividends are known in advance. As acknowledged in Black (1975), the procedure serves only as an approximation. Many subsequent papers have gone to great lengths to delineate more precise valuation adjustments.[14]

The critical question is, after adjusting for dividends and exercise style, does the B&S Model provide accurate call option valuations? Answers to this question typically allude to the model's widespread usage as proof of its intrinsic worth and, therefore, reliability. By the same token, its almost universal deployment, albeit in a number of forms, might suggest something of a self-fulfilling prophecy. If trading is commonly dictated with reference to the model's predictions of 'fair' value, then, not surprisingly, gaps between actual and model prices are likely to narrow. Its longevity, in the face of competing models, and the proliferation of options globally, lends greater support to the first of the two arguments.

The literature does, however, point to certain biases when comparing B&S Model predictions with actual prices. Black (1975) points to actual prices deviating from Model prices in a number of 'systematic' ways. Relative to the Model, he notes: 'Options that are way out of the money tend to be overpriced, and options that are way into the money tend to be underpriced. Options with less than three months to maturity tend to be overpriced' (page 64).

Subsequent empirical analyses, namely MacBeth and Merville's (1979), confirm biases with the Model in relation to near-expiry options and options priced far from the 'at-the-money' point. However, for the latter, evidence diametrically opposite to Black's is offered. Deep 'in-the-money' options appear overpriced relative to the Model, with deep 'out-of-the-money' options showing the opposite. In a sense, the contradictory evidence is comforting to advocates of the B&S Model as it calls into question the original biases suggested in Black (1975). Moreover, MacBeth and Merville (1979) suggest that the divergence from Black's findings, 'may, at least in part, be the result of a non-stationary variance rate in the stochastic process generating stock prices' (p. 1186). Simply put, σ^2, the variance of the underlying security's annualized rate of return, assumed constant in the B&S Model, changes over time.

Certainly, most would contend that σ varies through time, although the process governing this is seemingly a mystery to all but a few rocket-scientists. This does not seem to have stymied the Model's popularity. Nor does evidence of the superior accuracy of other models.[15] The greatest accolade offered to the Model's founders is, perhaps, the way it commonly features in the calculation of implied volatilities. Assuming equality between actual and Model prices, and given one equation with known values for t, E, V_s and r, direct inferences to σ can easily be made. This implied volatility can then be used within the same trading day to gauge deviations between actual and Model prices.[16]

The above discussion offers only a partial sketch of the various tests of the B&S Model and other competing models.[17] Notwithstanding this, the almost universal deployment of the B&S Model probably reflects not only its overall reliability but also the convenience and ease with which it can be applied.

10.6 Features of Locally-Traded Options

SEHK Traded Stock (Equity) Options

Trading in stock options began in earnest in September 1995 with the introduction of puts and calls, with various strikes and expiry months, on

286 A GUIDE TO THE EQUITY MARKETS OF HONG KONG

HSBC. As confidence and liquidity in the market has grown, a number of other stocks have been added to the list of eligible underlying securities. The speed of this development has been such that, as of mid-1998, 17 stocks were eligible for options trading on the local exchange. Details of these—including their launch date and option lot size—are shown in Appendix 10.3. These options, as noted earlier, offer American exercise and require physical delivery of the underlying upon exercise.[18]

The options market operates separately from the Exchange's trading system for its other listed securities, with all trades in options made from members' office terminals. Its trading independence is also buttressed by the presence of a designated clearing house—referred to by the acronym SEOCH—which promises to novate SEOCH members' positions in the market (Note 18, p. 10). Trading itself takes place through an electronic matching system, known as TOPs.[19] The trading process is also complemented by market-makers who stand ready to quote bid/asking prices for any orders that fail to attract matches within TOPs. In this sense, order-driven and quoted-driven trading features are intermeshed.

All of the stock options are available in put and call form with a variety of prescribed strike prices. The intervals between the strikes depend upon the value of the underlying. Strike price intervals for stock prices between HK$50 and HK$200 and HK$200 and HK$300 are HK$5 and HK$10, respectively.[20] The HSBC options considered in Tables 10.2 and 10.4 earlier provide apt illustration.

The number of strikes on a call or put, for a given underlying and contract month, largely reflect movements in the value of the underlying. The requirement that at least two 'in-the-money' and two 'out-of-the-money' contracts be available at all times, means that large price movements in the underlying may result in the introduction of new strikes in options of a given type (put or call) and given expiry. In terms of expiry, five contract months exist for any given strike series: 'the nearest three months as well as the following two quarterly expiry months.'[21] As of June 1998, for instance, calls or puts on given stocks had strike series for the expiry months of June, July, August, September, and December. The last permitted day of trading in all cases occurs on the 'Business day immediately preceding the last business day of the contract month'.[22]

Equity call options—as elsewhere—appear more popular than puts. Approximately 59% of stock options traded during 1997 were of the call variety.[23] Offsetting positions, rather than leaving positions 'open' for possible exercise, also seems to be the preferred route for the overwhelming majority of option investors. Using 1997 figures, only 13% of total stock option volume was met by subsequent exercise.[24]

A Sample of Popularly Employed Options Trading Strategies

Straddles and Strangles
To illustrate the workings of stock options, a simple example of a popular option-based strategy, known as a straddle, is constructed using recent

options data on Cheung Kong (CK). Table 10.6 provides an illustration of the pay-offs at expiry for both the buyer and seller (writer) of such a straddle. A long (short) straddle consists of the purchase (sale) of an equal number of put and calls on a given underlying with the same terms (i.e., same strike price and expiry). As shown in Figure 10.5, a purchaser of a straddle gains when either the value of the underlying moves sharply downward or upward. The writer gains when the converse holds. In general terms, an investor would be motivated to purchase a straddle if he/she believes an increase in the volatility of the underlying is likely. Sellers of straddles would clearly be motivated by expectations counter to that of the buyer's. In a fair market, though, one would expect premiums to reflect the overall market's perception of the underlying's volatility. If this market perception accurately captures this volatility during the term of the options, both investor and writer should just break even.

A variant of the straddle is the strangle. A long position in such a construction involves the purchase of the same number of puts and calls on the same underlying with the same expiry. Unlike the straddle, though, the strike prices in the calls and puts are different.

As with the long straddle, the long strangle is appropriate for those betting on an increase in volatility. If it can be constructed at a lower premium than a straddle, it may well be preferred. For the writer, betting on a fall in market volatility, the strangle will be preferred to a straddle if it extracts a higher premium.

Combining Long and Short Positions in Calls and Puts: Synthetic Positions
Using the puts and calls featured in Figure 10.5, other popular strategies can also be assessed. The combination of a long position in a call and a short position in a put generates a profit profile mirroring a long position in the underlying. This construction is known as a synthetic long position. As an illustration, consider, as before, ten contracts in both CK January $48 calls and CK January $48 puts. The profit profile at expiry for a long position in the former and a short in the latter is shown in Table 10.7 and Figure 10.6.

The diametric opposite of the synthetic long is the synthetic short. This is constructed by buying puts and shorting calls. For the CK options above, the profit profile obtained at expiry can be ascertained by multiplying the profit flows in the synthetic long by -1. For comparison, the expiry date profit profile of the synthetic short position is also shown in Figure 10.6.

The beauty of a synthetic position, is the low cost involved. To create a profit profile akin to the long synthetic in Table 10.7, an investment outlay of HK$48,000 (= 10,000 shares * HK$48) in CK would be required. This compares with a net premium payment of only HK$2,300 in the synthetic. Of course, the synthetic long is only a short-term position and evaporates at option expiry. Transaction cost differences between the cash and option market positions are likely to figure as well, although one would expect such costs to comprise a small fraction of the pay-offs in both cases.

Table 10.6   Long Straddle: Buy 10 Contracts in CK January $48 Calls and 10 Contracts in CK January $48 Puts

Call premium = $3.00; put premium = $2.77; CK cash = $48.

Stock Value at Expiry ($)	Intrinsic Value of Call at Expiry per option ($)	Intrinsic Value of Put at Expiry per option ($)	Gross Profit at Expiry* ($)
40	0	8	1000 × 10 × (8 – 5.77) = 22.3k
42	0	6	1000 × 10 × (6 – 5.77) = 2.3k
44	0	4	1000 × 10 × (4 – 5.77) = -17.7k
46	0	2	1000 × 10 × (2 – 5.77) = -37.7k
48	0	0	1000 × 10 × (0 – 5.77) = -57.7k
50	2	0	1000 × 10 × (2 – 5.77) = -37.7k
52	4	0	1000 × 10 × (4 – 5.77) = -17.7k
54	6	0	1000 × 10 × (6 – 5.77) = 2.3k
56	8	0	1000 × 10 × (8 – 5.77) = 22.3k

At expiry, the investor purchasing the straddle breaks-even if the settlement level of Cheung Kong is either $53.77 or $42.23.

* The board lot size for CK options is 1,000 options (see Appendix 10.3).

Data obtained for closing option and stock values for Cheung Kong as of 22 December 1997 from *South China Morning Post*, Business Post, p. 8, Tues., 23 December 1997.

Figure 10.5   Comparison of Profit Profiles at Expiry for Long and Short Straddles in CK Stock Options

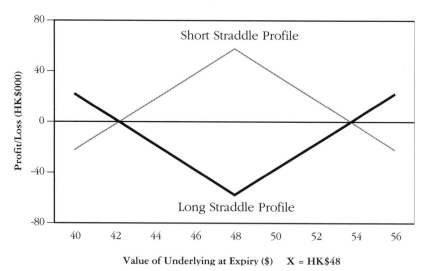

Value of Underlying at Expiry ($)   X = HK$48

Based upon the example in Table 10.6 for 10 call and puts in January (1998) CK Options [see Table 10.6 for further details]. Transaction/margin costs ignored.

Table 10.7   Synthetic Long Position: Buy 10 contracts in CK January
$48 calls and short 10 contracts in CK January $48 puts

Net premium paid = 1000 × 10 × ($3.00 − $2.77) = $2.3k

Stock Value at Expiry ($)	Intrinsic Value of Call at Expiry per option ($)	Intrinsic Value Payment on Put at Expiry per option ($)	Gross Profit at Expiry* ($)
40	0	(8)	1000 × 10 × (-8 − 0.23)= -82.3k
42	0	(6)	1000 × 10 × (-6 − 0.23)= -62.3k
44	0	(4)	1000 × 10 × (-4 − 0.23)= -42.3k
46	0	(2)	1000 × 10 × (-2 − 0.23 = -22.3k
48	0	0	1000 × 10 × (0 − 0.23) = -2.3k
50	2	0	1000 × 10 × (2 − 0.23) = 17.7k
52	4	0	1000 × 10 × (4 − 0.23) = 37.7k
54	6	0	1000 × 10 × (6 − 0.23) = 57.7k
56	8	0	1000 × 10 × (8 − 0.23) = 77.7k

*   The board lot size for CK options is 1,000 options (see Appendix 10.3).

Data obtained for closing option and stock values for Cheung Kong as of 22 December 1997
from *South China Morning Post*, Business Post, p. 8, Tues., 23 December 1997.

Figure 10.6 Comparison of Profit Profiles at Expiry for Synthetic Long
and Synthetic Short Positions in CK Stock Options

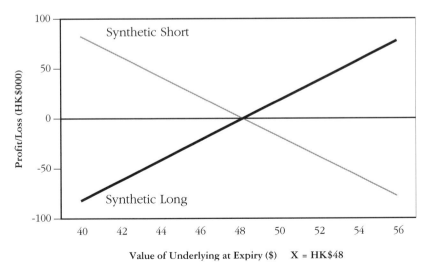

Value of Underlying at Expiry ($)   X = HK$48

Based upon 10 Calls and Puts in CK January (1998) Options [see Table 10.7 for further
details of profiles]. Transaction costs and margin ignored.

The Issue of Margin

Short option positions do, however, attract an additional cost: the establishment of margin, which must be 'marked-to-market' at regular intervals. Initial margins on such positions depend, amongst other things, on the life of the option and its level of intrinsic value. Figures provided by the Exchange for the 'typical minimum margin required' suggest initial levels of up to 22%.[25] The higher initial margin payments apply to 'in-the-money' options where the risk of option exercise at expiry is clearly greater. Such margin payments essentially serve as a deposit to cover the writer's intrinsic payment liability at expiry. Where no such exercise notice is received, or where the writer 'closes-out' his/her position prior to expiry, the margin deposit can be returned in full. As long as the short position remains open, though, margin adjustments may be required. Additional sums would need to be added whenever movements in the underlying raise the option's intrinsic value.

In essence, a short position in an option is risky because the downside is unlimited, which provides a similar risk exposure to a futures contract. Margin provisions do not apply to fully covered written positions though. Investors in stock options are also exempt from such requirements due to their downside risk being limited to the cash premium paid.[26]

As options are a generic product, option strategies and principles easily carry over from one market to another. With this in mind, additional investment strategies in the options field are analysed in the following in relation to index options traded on the HKFE. This provides an opportunity for us to look at other key exchange-traded options products available in the Hong Kong SAR.

HKFE Traded Stock Index Options

Various options contracts are available on stock indices on the HKFE. The May 1998 introduction of contracts on the Taiwan Weighted Index invites exposure to three market indices via options. The other two being the local HSI and red-chip index. The most long standing of these is the HSI options contract which was introduced in March 1993. Its contract (settlement) months follow those of futures contracts on the index. This is done to allow trading between the HSI options and HSI futures. This interaction, which is examined further in Chapter 12, is key to effective hedging and arbitrage between the markets.

HSI options are European in exercise style with automatic cash settlement arising at expiry, where any intrinsic value obtains. This automatic exercise feature is achieved via the HKFE's Clearing House. The cash difference—if intrinsic value exists at expiry—is determined by comparing the average of the HSI, taken at five minute intervals on the expiry date, with the option's strike and multiplying this difference by HK$50. The expiry date in this context is taken to be the penultimate business day of the contract month with actual settlement of any intrinsic value following one day later.[27]

As an example, consider HSI 10,000 January call options, quoted at the close of trading on 22 December 1997. This option had a premium at the time of quotation of 722 points.[28] If one purchased the option, it would have provided an option to 'buy' the index for a strike of 10,000 points at the penultimate business day of the contract month (26 January 1998 was the expiry date). The premium indicates that one contract had a value of HK\$36,100 (= 722 × HK\$50).

If at expiry, the settlement price had been 11,000 points, 1,000 points of intrinsic value would have been payable to the investor, yielding a gross profit of HK\$13,900 (= (1,000 − 722) × HK\$50). As the investor promises to 'buy' the index for 10,000 points, a cash settlement of 1,000 points multiplied by HK\$50 would be made to the investor by the clearing house. Similarly, the assigned counterparty to the investor would be obliged to make the same cash payment to the clearing house. As with all options markets, the clearing house acts as the interface between the brokers of counterparties (i.e, it provides novation). To protect against possible default and, therefore, clearing house intervention, margin, as in other options products and markets, is required on short positions.

To illustrate the workings of HSI options, certain spread trading strategies are introduced. These involve positions in two or more options of the same type and are attractive to the more conservative investor. Notable constructions like bull and bear spreads allow 'caps' to be placed on gains and losses. For calls, two types of construction spring to mind: the bull call-spread and the bear call-spread. The former involves a long and short position in a call with higher strike on the short. The latter similarly entails both a long and short position in the same call, but a higher strike on the long call. An example of a bull call-spread in HSI options is shown in Table 10.8 (and illustrated in Figure 10.7). The counterparty's profit profile at expiry can also be obtained by multiplying the bull call-spread investor's profit profile by -1. This is, in fact, the profit profile of the bear call-spread investor.

A notable characteristic of both bear and bull call-spreads is the reduction of premium, achieved by netting short and long positions. This comes at a cost, though, in the form of a 'cap' on the investors' maximum returns.

Similar profit profiles can also be generated for put spreads. The profit profile for a bull put-spread, which involves shorting a higher strike put, is shown in Table 10.9 for HSI January 9,800 puts and HSI January 10,000 puts. Again, the counterparty's profit profile, which characterizes that of the bear put-spread investor, is obtained by multiplying the profits in Table 10.9 by -1. As with bull and bear call-spreads, the put-spread strategies allow for reduced loss on the downside in exchange for a 'cap' on the upside return (see Figure 10.8). Other spreads, like calendar spreads, where opposite positions are taken in options of the same type with different expiry months, also perform a similar function. Spreads are therefore an effective means of capturing some upside potential, from a particular directional play, for relatively low premium.

Table 10.8   Bull Call-Spread: one long contract on HSI January 10,000 calls (premium = 722 points) and one short contract on HSI January 10,200 calls (premium = 615 points)

Net cost = (722 − 615) points = 107 points*

Index at expiry	Premium collected or (paid) in index points	IV on 10,000 call (pts)	IV on 10,200 call (pts)	Overall Profit (pts)
9,500	(107)	0	0	(107)
9,700	(107)	0	0	(107)
9,900	(107)	0	0	(107)
10,100	(107)	100	0	(7)
10,300	(107)	300	(100)	93
10,500	(107)	500	(300)	93
10,700	(107)	700	(500)	93

* See Note 28 for source of premiums.

Figure 10.7   Comparison of Profit Profiles at Expiry for Bull and Bear Call-Spreads in HSI Options

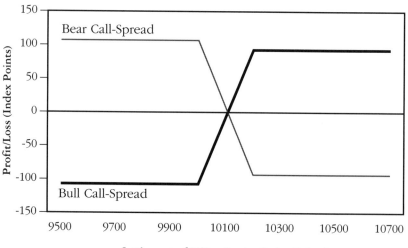

Settlement of HSI at Expiry (Index Points)

Bull Call-Spread is depicted in Table 10.8 for HSI Options. A corresponding Bear Call-Spread is given by the profit profile of a direct counter-party to the Bull Call-Spread trader (i.e., multiply the profit index profile of the Bull Call-Spread trader by -1). See Table 10.8 for data details. All transaction and margin costs are ignored.

Table 10.9 Bull Put-Spread: one long contract on HSI January 9,800 puts (premium = 563 points) and one short contract on HSI January 10,000 puts (premium = 637 points)

Net Premium Collected = (637 − 563) points = 74 points*

Index at expiry	Premium collected or (paid) in index points	IV on 9.800 put (pts)	IV on 10,000 put (pts)	Overall Profit (pts)
9,300	74	500	(700)	(126)
9,500	74	300	(500)	(126)
9,700	74	100	(300)	(126)
9,900	74	0	(100)	(26)
10,100	74	0	0	74
10,300	74	0	0	74
10,500	74	0	0	74

* See Note 28 for source of premiums.

Figure 10.8 Comparison of Profit Profiles at Expiry for Bull and Bear Put-Spreads in HSI Options

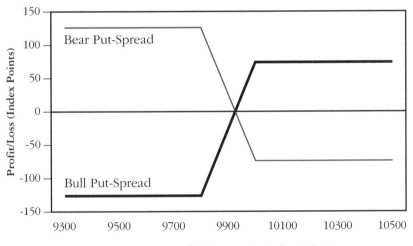

Bull Put-Spread is depicted in Table 10.9 for HSI Options. A corresponding Bear Put-Spread is given by the profit profile of a direct counter-party to the Bull Put-Spread trader (i.e., multiply the profit index profile of the Bull Put-Spread trader by -1). See Table 10.9 for data details. All transaction and margin costs are ignored.

The Hedging Benefits of Options

The range of possible option constructions is in fact huge and the examples in the foregoing, for stock and index options, are intended to give only a flavour of the possibilities. For many, however, options and other derivatives are simply a means of hedging an underlying position. The hedging example constructed below in Exhibit 10.6A provides an illustration of this key role.

Exhibit 10.6A   A Case Study for the Use of Options as Hedge Instruments

Suppose as of March 01, 200x you commit to buy a portfolio $PORT_s$ at May 30, 200x. The current value of $PORT_s$ is $2 million. The risk is that its value will rise in the interim. Call option contracts on index IDX for May 30, 200x expiry currently have a premium of $0.0125 million. Assume that this consists of $0.01 million intrinsic value and $0.0025 million of time value (where IDX = 10,000 points, X = 9,800 points and the contract multiplier is $50).

Also assume that relative to IDX, $PORT_s$ has β of 1.25.

A 1% rise (fall) in IDX should therefore translate into a 1.25% increase (decrease) in $PORT_s$'s value.[29]

To hedge the cash market commitment, how many IDX call options should be acquired? Alternatively, how many IDX options would be needed to offset the loss associated with a rise in the value of $PORT_s$ of, say, 25%? This eventuality would be consistent with a 20% appreciation of IDX (given the assumed β of 1 for IDX and of 1.25 for $PORT_s$). We should also remember that time value in the options will be zero at expiry.

To offset the 25% increase in $PORT_s$, a $500,000 gain on the option portfolio at expiry would be required. The number of options that would need to be acquired (= n) at 1 March, 200x, to generate this is as follows,

$$+\$500,000 = \{[(1.20 \times 10,000) - 9,800] \times \$50\} \times n - (\$12,500 \times n)$$
$$n = 5.128 \text{ contracts}$$

As only discrete numbers of contracts can be traded, the suggested hedge is five long contracts in May Call IDX Options. If at expiry a 20% rise in $PORT_s$ does occur, the actual gain on the hedge would be $487,500. This, then, would be quite effective in hedging the risk on the cash position.

But what about the downside? When netting the overall position, the greatest exposure to loss would be if $PORT_s$ was $1.95 million or higher at expiry. Given corresponding IDX levels at expiry, this would suggest an overall loss (from the hedge) of $12,500. At lower levels of IDX, the hedger actually gains overall given the modest loss of premium on the five options compared to the reduced cost of acquiring PORT$_s$. Exhibit 10.6B shows the profits (losses) on the hedge and cash market position at the expiry date, for various values of PORT$_s$.

Exhibit 10.6B   Profits on the Overall Hedge and Cash Market Position at Option Expiry (Based upon a Long Hedge of 5 IDX Options as Described in Exhibit 10.6A)

IDX at Expiry	PORT$_s$ at Expiry Position ($ millions)	Profit (loss) on Cash Position ($ millions)	Profit (loss) on Options ($ millions)	Overall gain (loss) ($ million)
12,000	$2.500	($0.50)	$0.4875	($0.0125)
11,000	$2.250	($0.25)	$0.2375	($0.0125)
10,000	$2.000	$0	($0.0125)	**($0.0125)**
9,900	$1.975	$0.025	($0.0375)	($0.0125)
9,800	$1.950	$0.050	($0.0625)	($0.0125)
9,000	$1.750	$0.250	($0.0625)	$0.1875
8,000	$1.500	$0.500	($0.0625)	$0.4375

The hedging example above demonstrates the strength of options in hedging: they are effective in removing much or all of the downside risk but leave open a large proportion of cash market gains if the market moves favourably. This reflects the relatively low premium when using options as a long hedge. Not all hedging instruments are like this. In fact, many are designed to remove exposure completely so that the returns on the hedge and cash market offset each other whichever way the market moves. Arranging to buy the portfolio forward would effectively do this.

The long hedge described for call options is also appropriate where an investor has a short cash position, given the requirement to purchase stock at some future date. The hedging function described could also have been mirrored by shorting put options.

For a long cash market position, the risk is a fall in the cash value of the underlying. Similar hedging principles apply with, this time, a suitable number of long put or short call positions on the underlying fulfilling the hedging role.

For market-makers (dealers) who hold option inventory, or are exposed to short positions, hedging instruments can be devised to shield against small adverse movements in the underlying. This works in relation to the δ of the option and is designed to guard against losses over short periods. This issue is examined in detail in Chapter 11.

10.7 Concluding Remarks

The basic principles underpinning the mechanics and pricing of options have been set out in detail in this chapter. Options are truly powerful instruments in controlling risk and creating a variety of possible profit profiles, as the various investment and hedging strategies demonstrate. Warrants also offer such benefits. Nonetheless, there are a number of distinct differences between warrants and options. These range from issues of market microstructure, where exchange-traded options and warrants are considered, to specific differences in the issue and exercise process. The material presented in the foregoing provides the essential background to assess these differences.

Appendix 10.1 Arbitrage Opportunities Stemming from Mispricing in Call and Put Options

Consider European call and puts on the same underlying S.*

X	= \$8.50;
Time to expiry	= 3 months;
V_s	= \$9.52;
Premium of put	= \$0.08;
Premium of call	= \$1.07; and
Riskless interest rate	= 4% per annum.

LHS of the P–C theorem: \$9.52 – \$1.07 + \$0.08 = \$8.530;
RHS of the P–C theorem: $(8.50) \times e^{-(0.04 \times 0.25)}$ = \$8.415.

Where LHS value > RHS value,
short put, buy call & short stock, raising proceeds of \$8.530
(= \$0.08 – \$1.07 + \$9.52).
Invest \$8.530 for 3 months at riskless rate of 4%.
Future proceeds = $8.53 \times e^{(0.04 \times 0.25)}$ = \$8.616.
Obligation from shorting put, shorting stock and buying call, 3 months
later is X = \$8.50

Arbitrage profit in 3 months' time = \$8.616 – \$8.50 = \$0.116.
Present value of profit = $0.116 \times e^{-(0.04 \times 0.25)}$ = \$0.115.

Assume data as above, except put premium = \$0.05 and call premium
= \$1.25.

LHS of the P–C theorem: \$9.52 – \$1.25 + \$0.05 = \$8.320;
RHS of the P–C theorem: $(8.50) \times e^{-(0.04 \times 0.25)}$ = \$8.415.

Where LHS value < RHS value,
buy put, short call & buy stock, giving outlay of \$8.32
(= \$0.05 – \$1.25 + \$9.52).
Borrow \$8.32 to cover outlay.* Repayment at option expiry =
$8.32 \times e^{(0.04 \times 0.25)}$ = \$8.404.
Return from P–C parity portfolio at expiry = \$8.50.

Arbitrage profit in 3 months time = \$8.500 – \$8.404 = \$0.096.
Present value of profit = $0.096 \times e^{-(0.04 \times 0.25)}$ = \$0.095.

* No dividends are paid on the underlying stock.
\# Borrowing and lending rates are assumed equal.

All transaction costs (excluding borrowing costs) are ignored. In reality, the costs of shorting or buying stock, taxes, commissions, and bid-asking spreads (which are assumed to be zero in the above) would need to be considered. These might eat up most or all of the profit thus making arbitrage untenable. Issues of illiquidity might also lead to this result.

Appendix 10.2   Example of the Application of the Black and Scholes (1973) Model

A: European Call Options on Non-Dividend Paying Stocks

Example: suppose the price of stock S is $4.30. Three-month call options written on S have a strike price of $4.10 and a maturity date in 73 days' time. The annual risk-free rate is 7% (continuously compounded), the annualized standard deviation on share price returns is 30% and the conversion ratio of the call option is one.

V_s = $4.30; E = $4.10; r = 0.07; t = 73/365 = 0.20; σ^2 = 0.30.

d_1 = 0.53	$d_1 - \sigma\sqrt{t}$ = 0.39
$N(d_1)$ = 0.70	$N(d_1 - \sigma\sqrt{t})$ = 0.65
V_o = $0.38	

Implied Statistics from the B & S Valuation
Intrinsic Value = $0.20; Time Value = $0.18; Gearing = $4.30/($0.38/1.00) = 11.32 times; and Delta (= $N(d_1)$) = 0.70.

B: European Call Options on Dividend Paying Stocks

Consider the Example in A above, but suppose that an ex-dividend date on S occurs in 48 days' time where the dividend to be paid per share, payable in 75 days' time, is known to be $0.10.

Recalculate Black and Scholes (1973) with all terms as before, except replace V_s by

V_s' (= $4.30 - 0.10 \times e^{-(r-t')}$) = 4.20   (t' = 48/365)

d_1 = 0.35	$d_1 - \sigma\sqrt{t}$ = 0.22
$N(d_1)$ = 0.64	$N(d_1 - \sigma\sqrt{t})$ = 0.59
V_o = $0.31	

C: American Call Options on Dividend Paying Stocks

Consider the example in A and, in addition to the inclusion of the dividend described in B above, assume American exercise style.

Step 1: Recalculate Black and Scholes (1973) with t = 0.20 and all other terms as before, except replace V_s by V_s' (= $4.30 - 0.10.e^{-(r \times t')}$) where t' = 48/365).

V_o = $0.31 (as in B above)

Step 2: Recalculate with all terms as in A but using t' (= 48/365) instead of t.

d_1 = 0.58	$d_1 - \sigma\sqrt{t}$ = 0.47
$N(d_1)$ = 0.72	$N(d_1 - \sigma\sqrt{t})$ = 0.68
V_o = $0.325	

The highest of the two valuations is then used as the 'fair' option premium.

Appendix 10.3   Details of Stock Options Available for Trading on the
                    SEHK

Stock	Launch Date	Lot Size Option	Stock
Cheung Kong Holdings	25/09/95	1,000	1,000
China Resources	14/07/97	2,000	2,000
China Telecom*	15/05/98	2,000	2,000
CITIC Pacific	23/10/95	1,000	1,000
CLP Holdings	18/12/95	500	500
Hang Seng Bank	09/12/96	100	100
Henderson Land Devel.	18/12/95	1,000	1,000
Hongkong Electric Hold.	16/02/98	500	500
Hong Kong Telecom	23/10/95	400	400
Hopewell Holdings	26/02/96	1,000	1,000
HSBC Holdings	08/09/95	400	400
Hutchison Whampoa	18/12/95	1,000	1,000
New World Develop.	05/08/96	1,000	1,000
Shanghai Ind. Hold.	14/07/97	1,000	1,000
Sun Hung Kai Prop.	18/12/95	1,000	1,000
Swire Pacific 'A'	09/10/95	500	500
Wharf Holdings	05/08/96	1,000	1,000

Source: Underlying stock list (except China Telecom.), launch date, and options lot size obtained from: SEHK homepage (at http://www.SEHK.COM/english/Markets/options/options. htm (for 28/08/97); * data for China Telecom obtained from: http://www.SEHK.COM/english/ Markets/options/What_New.htm; and data for stock lot sizes obtained from the *SEHK Monthly Bulletin*, May 1998.

Notes

1.   See Anonymous (March 1995, p. 22).

2.   Options in equity stocks are also traded on the following US exchanges: The American Stock Exchange; The Philadelphia Stock Exchange; The Pacific Stock Exchange; and The New York Stock Exchange.

3.   One possible pricing model for average rate options is offered in Levy (1992). Newer forms of Asian options also allow for an averaging of the strike price over some defined period (see Bouaziz, Briys, and Crouhy (1994) for the valuation of such options).

4.   In practice, there will be a difference in the buy and sell price, with dealers making markets to buy options at the bid premium and sell them at the asking premium. For convenience, this is ignored.

5.   However, option sale may be frustrated in the immediate run-up to expiry, leaving little manoeuvre for anything other than exercise.

6.   It is virtually impossible to sell call options just prior to an ex-date as everyone in the market anticipates an imminent fall in the option's intrinsic value on the underlying's ex-date. If option holders believe that the ex-adjustment will be such that the option premium on the ex-date will be less than the option's intrinsic value prior to this date, they should exercise (see Alexander, Sharpe and Bailey (1993, pp. 730–1) for further discussion of the possibility of early exercise for American options on dividend paying stocks).

7. We assume that the option's time value remains unchanged, which is reasonable given the minuscule time change and small increase in the underlying (as we will appreciate in later discussions).

8. See Hull (1989, pp. 112–15) for an excellent account of the valuation difference between American and European puts.

9. Stoll (1969) considers a situation where 'options are held to maturity'. This essentially captures the situation for European options.

10. Reference to Hull (1989, pp. 115–16) is recommended for a discussion of the precise modifications to put–call parity for American exercise style.

11. The form shown is equivalent to that used elsewhere (see, for example, Zivney (1991, p. 132)). See also Klemkosky and Resnick (1979) for detailed discussion of the dividend adjustment formulation in the put–call parity result.

12. The recent empirical results of Fung, Cheng, and Chan (1997) for arbitrage on the HSI are pertinent.

13. As recommended in Black (1975, pp. 41–2).

14. These include contributions from Geske (1979), Geske and Roll (1984), and Whaley (1981).

15. MacBeth and Merville (1980) show empirically, for instance, that an alternative model, 'the Cox call option valuation model for constant elasticity of variance diffusion processes', exhibits superior performance.

16. Although as MacBeth and Merville (1979) and others have noted, options with different terms on the same underlying often exhibit rather different implied volatility levels. Such differences, as noted in MacBeth and Merville's (1979) empirical analysis, 'systematically related to the difference between the stock price, the exercise price, and the time to expiration' (p. 1174, as shown, excepting notation symbols).

17. For more exhaustive discussions of developments in this literature, particularly in relation to the refinement of tests of the Black and Scholes model through the 1980s and 1990s, see, amongst others, Choi and Wohar (1994).

18. For the precise provisions relating to both of these terms, see *Understanding Stock Options (And Their Risks)*, p. 12.

19. This is described by the Exchange as, 'an electronic, screen-based auto-matching system (Traded Option System—TOPs). It is based on an existing system which is used by Deutsche Terminborse, DTB, the German Futures and Option Exchange from whom the Exchange purchased a licence to use the software.' (http://www.SEHK.COM/english/Markets/options/options.htm (page 1)).

20. See *Fact Book 1997*, 'Contract Specifications for Stock Options', p. 108.

21. Ibid.

22. Ibid.

23. As indicated in the *SEHK Monthly Bulletin* (January 1988, p. 159). 1,648,748 stock option contracts were traded during 1997, of which 976,107 were calls.

24. 217,111 contracts were exercised in 1997 (See *SEHK Monthly Bulletin* (January, 1988, p. 159).

25. See SEHK homepage (at http://www.SEHK.COM/english/Markets/options/options.htm (28 Aug 1997) for precise details.

26. Ibid.

27. See HKFE homepage (at http://www.hkfe.com/products/spec/options/html for further details).

28. See *South China Morning Post*, Business Post, p. 8, Tuesday, 23 December 1997. The foregoing illustrations (Figures 10.5–10.8) simplify the real situation; closing (rather than real-time prices) are used; and all transaction costs (including bid-ask spreads) and margin issues are ignored.

29. This assumes the validity of the Market Model (as in Sharpe 1963).

11. Equity Derivatives II: Warrants, Convertibles, and Swaps

As warrants are so closely related to call options, many of the terms introduced in Chapter 10 apply wholly, or with slight qualification, to the material in this chapter. To avoid unnecessary repetition, readers are advised to familiarize themselves with the content of Chapter 10 before bravely jumping into warrant territory.

In very simple terms, a warrant usually involves an entitlement to buy some underlying asset at a predetermined price over some future period. Recent innovations like the put warrant, which confers an option to sell rather then buy, mean that the presumed call feature may not always apply. Not withstanding this, the call type of warrant is still, by far, the dominant form of locally-listed warrant. Accordingly, the call feature is implied whenever the term 'warrant' is used in the following. The put prefix (i.e., put warrant) figures whenever this feature is absent.

What is the difference between a warrant and a traded call option? The answer to this question depends upon the type of warrant we consider. For SEHK-traded warrants, there appear to be two broad categories: the equity warrant and the derivative warrant. The equity warrant can only be written by the company responsible for issuing the underlying security. In contrast, a traded call option can, in theory, be written by anyone. This also means that upon exercise of the equity warrant, new shares are issued by the writer. In the case of the traded call option, a transfer of ownership in the underlying security occurs.[1,2] This is true whether the writer has a 'naked' or 'covered' position. In essence, then, an equity warrant raises new funds for the underlying issuer. A call option exercise, in contrast, triggers a secondary market transaction. This offers a fairly clear and precise distinction. The same cannot be said, however, when comparing the derivative warrant to the call option.

The derivative warrant is really a hybrid of the call option and equity warrant. In other words, it falls somewhere between the two. The derivative warrant is, in fact, a warrant issued by a third party, not by the company responsible for issuing the underlying security, as is the case in an equity warrant. By connection, the exercise effect of the derivative warrant is equivalent to that in a call option: securities already in issue are transferred from writer to investor. The derivative warrant therefore looks, feels, and smells just like a call option. In what way is it different? Principally, in terms of its life expectancy and the way in which it is traded. Warrants, whether of the equity or derivative type, are generally issued with a longer time to expiry than a call option. They are also, at least in Hong Kong, traded much like a stock. Options, in contrast, trade through a separate system (TOPs, as we saw in Section 10.6 for the SEHK's equity options) and also clear through a different entity.

With regard to the life expectancy issue, the derivative warrant, according to the SEHK's Rules Governing the Listing of Securities (hereafter, the 'Listing Rules') 'must normally expire not less than six months and not more than two years from the date of listing.' (Rule 15A.37, 15A-11, 6/98). For equity warrants, an even longer term can be countenanced. The Listing Rules require that such a security must have a minimum term of one year and a maximum of five years.[3] In contrast, traded options are normally written for periods from one month up to twelve months. For SEHK-traded equity options, as we saw in Section 10.6, various maturities up to a maximum of nine months are possible.[4]

There are also other subtle differences between the (derivative and equity) warrant and the call option. The nature of the underlying asset can be quite different as comparisons between equity options and listed warrants on the SEHK reveal. For the former, the underlying assets typically experience active trading and report market capitalization levels at the higher end of the spectrum. The Exchange's warrants, in contrast, cover an array of individual stocks, stock baskets, and indices. Traded options are also standardized in terms of their strike, maturity, and exercise features. This standardization means that there will always be a given number of calls and puts on eligible underlying stocks at any time. This is not the case for warrants.

Equity and derivative warrants are also typically issued in a single batch and by a single issuer.[5] The discussion in Chapter 10 reminds us that exchange-traded options can be written by a wide range of players with new positions created at any time, by various parties, during the trading life of the option.

In sum, then, warrants and traded call options have many similarities. They can still be distinguished along a number of lines, however. Aside from the exercise effects of derivative warrants and call options, a number of key differences exist between call options and warrants (of both the equity and derivative variety). The nature of the underlying, the time to expiry, the standardization of terms, the trading and clearing systems used, and the issue mechanisms employed all help to distinguish the warrant from the traded option.

Differences aside, the material in this chapter will show that options and warrants perform very similar roles for investors. Other option-based instruments, like the convertible and exchangeable bond are also considered. Both are debt-based and, at the discretion of the holder, can be converted into shares. For convertibles, the shares acquired are those of the underlying issuing company. In the exchangeable bond, conversion results in shares of a third party being acquired. For pedagogical reasons, both instruments are assessed alongside the debt–equity swap which, like the convertible and exchangeable bond, allows the holder to convert corporate debtholdings into underlying equity. Aside from this common feature, the arrangement of the debt–equity swap is very different to an option-based security.

As the warrant holds such a special fascination with local investors, most of the material in this chapter is devoted to this topic. In this regard, Sections 11.1 to 11.3 outline the key terminology, characteristics and international standing of locally-based warrants. The hedging role of warrants and various product innovations in the warrant field are then assessed in Sections 11.4 and 11.5. Convertibles, exchangeable bonds and equity swaps then feature in Section 11.6. Finally, Section 11.7 offers an overview of the various option-based securities surveyed.

11.1 Warrant Terminology

The term premium is common to both traded options and warrants. Some caution is recommended, though, as it carries a very different meaning when applied to warrants. Convention has it that, in relation to warrants, the premium refers to time value. For traded options, the premium is the market price of the option (time value plus intrinsic value). This is quite different.

Another area of confusion concerns the use of the term 'covered warrant', which is commonly used with reference to the locally-based 'derivative warrant'. This is misleading. The standardized terminology in the Listing Rules informs us that the 'covered' warrant is one kind of derivative warrant. Derivative warrants are formally recognized as being either collateralized derivative warrants (CDWs) or non-collateralized derivative warrants (NCDWs).[6] The collateralized derivative warrant captures what many regard to be a 'covered' warrant.

The Listing Rules require that the issuer of a CDW holds sufficient of the underlying to ensure that all potential exercise notices are 'covered'. This 100% coverage requirement means that the construction of the CDW may be somewhat more onerous than the NCDW.[7] Nonetheless, the issuer of an NCDW must conform to the various standards set out in the Listing Rules. Amongst other things, the Exchange makes provision for a guarantee to operate in lieu of some of these.[8] Cursory inspection of issue documents for derivative warrants indicates that the NCDW form has, at least in recent years, been the preferred vehicle for derivative warrants. Enquiries with the Exchange, as of late 1998, indicated that all listed derivative warrants were of the NCDW variety.

To reiterate, the term 'warrant' is used in the following in relation to both equity and derivative warrants. American exercise style will also be assumed throughout, although recent innovations in warrants mean that a handful of warrants have been made on European terms.

11.2 Background Statistics on the Hong Kong Warrant Market

In terms of standard criteria like numbers of listings, trading turnover, and market value, the derivative warrant overshadows the equity warrant in Hong Kong (see Tables 11.1 and 11.2). As of October 1997, 400 of the 585 warrants listed on the Exchange were of the derivative variety, comprising 59% of total warrant value. Likewise, the lion's share of warrant volume occurs in the derivative warrant.

The ascent of the derivative warrant has been swift. Until the early 1990s, the equity warrant was easily the most popular of the two warrant types. A sea-change occurred between 1992 and 1996, when numerous derivative warrant issues arrived on the market. While, in absolute terms, the number of equity warrant listings is broadly comparable with the situation in the early 1990s, the rash of derivative warrant issues in recent years has reduced the relative standing of the equity warrant somewhat; so much so that by late 1997 it accounted for only 35% of all warrant listings (compared to 95% in 1990).

Within the derivative warrant sector, all of the current issuers are major investment banks. This reflects changes to the Listing Rules in recent years which prohibit majority stakeholders in the underlying acting as 'third party' issuers.[9, 10] In the early years of Hong Kong's derivative warrant market, several issues were made by parties with controlling interests in the underlying. In response to fears that issuers might be able to manipulate warrant prices through control of the underlying, the authorities quickly cut off this route to listing. As shown in Table 11.1, B, as of late 1997, the dominant issuers, in terms of number of listings, were Merrill Lynch (58 issues), Credit Lyonnais (44 issues), Deutsche Bank (33 issues), and the Union Bank of Switzerland (31 issues).

Relative to stocks, HKD turnover in warrants appears rather small and, in aggregate terms, approximated to 7.3% of locally-listed stock volumes at the end of 1997. Warrants are considerably more active in 'turning over' their value than stocks, however. The velocity (or speed of circulation) of trading, measured by the ratio of market turnover to market value, captures this. For warrants, this ratio, using 1996 year-end figures, was around 2.58 times as compared with 0.41 times for stocks (see Table 11.2). From this viewpoint, the local warrant market is extremely active.

In terms of the warrant market's overall value, combined warrant values have ranged in recent years from somewhere between 0.5% and 2% of ordinary stock values. Like the HKD turnover figures, the figures require some careful interpretation. At a superficial level, the figures suggest a relatively unimportant market. This belies the reality, though, as warrants, due to their inherent gearing (leverage), are inevitably priced at a large discount to the value of the underlying. This means that market capitalization comparisons between stocks and warrants offer a less than perfect insight into their relative importance. This, of course, is true of

Table 11.1 Characteristics of Hong Kong's Listed Warrant Market

PANEL A: NUMBER OF EQUITY AND DERIVATIVE WARRANT LISTINGS

Year[a]	Equity Warrants	Derivative Warrants	Total Number of Warrants Listed
1986	25	0	25
1987	77	0	77
1988	114	2	116
1989	115	2	117
1990	134	7	141
1991	153	21	174
1992	211	59	270
1993	228	69	297
1994	212	74	286
1995	161	83	244
1996	156	219	375
Oct 1997	185	400	585
1997	187	346	533

a Year-end figures, excepting figure for October 1997.

Source: Figures for 1992 were extracted from the *Fact Book 1996*, p. 69; figures for 1993–7 from the *Fact Book 1997*, p. 96. Figures for 1986-91 were supplied by the SEHK's Research & Planning Department.

PANEL B: DERIVATIVE WARRANT ISSUERS

	Issuer	No. of Issues		Issuer	No. of Issues
1	ABN AMRO Bank NV	12	13	Macquarie Bank Ltd	4
2	Bankers Trust Intl plc	19	14	Merrill Lynch Intl & Co CV	58
3	Bear Steams Co Inc	12	15	Morgan Stanley (Jersey) Ltd	20
4	BZW Warrants Ltd	21	16	NatWest Financial Products plc	13
5	Canadian Imperial Bank	15	17	Nomura Intl (HK) Ltd	4
6	Citibank NA	12	18	Paribas Capital Markets Group Ltd	5
7	Credit Lyonnais F P (G) Ltd	44	19	Peregrine Derivatives Ltd	26
8	Credit Suisse F B (HK) Ltd	4	20	Robert Fleming & Co Ltd	12
9	Deutsche Bank AG	33	21	Salomon Inc	3
10	Goldman Sachs Intl	4	22	SGA Societe Generale Acceptance NV	13
11	Indosuez W-1. Carr (D) Ltd	24	23	Swiss Bank Corp, HK	2
12	ING Baring Financial Products	8	24	Union Bank of Switzerland	31

Total No. of Derivative Warrant Issues   399

Data was compiled from the 399 derivative warrant listings recorded on the Exchange's Web-site: (http://www.sehk.com.hk/english/Markets/cash/Stock/stkList/Warrants.htm) as of 24 November 1997.

Table 11.2 Warrant Value and Trading Turnover Levels

PANEL A: MARKET CAPITALIZATION COMPARISONS

Year	Market Capitalization Levels (HK$ billion)				Ratio of Warrant
	Equity Warrants (1)	Derivative Warrants (2)	All Warrants (3)	Ordinary Shares (4)	Value to Ordinary Share Value (%) (3)/(4)
1992	15.014	10.268	25.282	1330.64	1.90
1996	15.334	33.154	48.489	3475.89	1.40
1997	7.263	9.129	16.392	3202.63	0.51

Year	Trading Turnover Levels (HK$ billion)				Ratio of Warrant
	Equity Warrants (1)	Derivative Warrants (2)	All Warrants (3)	Ordinary Shares (4)	Turnover to Ordinary Share Turnover (%) (3)/(4)
1992	29.768	61.913	91.681	700.58	13.09
1996	35.031	80.825	124.856	1412.24	8.84
1997	60.243	215.666	275.908	3788.96	7.28

Source: Figures for stock and warrant trading turnover and warrant market capitalization for 1992 and 1996 were extracted from the *Fact Book 1996*, p. 26 & 69; the same figures for 1997 were extracted from the *Fact Book 1997*, p. 96.

Stock market capitalization levels were drawn from *The Trading Record* (TR) of *The Securities Journal* (December 1992 TR, p. 10; and December 1997 TR, p. 9). Ordinary share market capitalization and turnover figures were extracted from *Fact Book 1997*, p. 4.

any comparison between a derivative and its underlying. A 'notional' value offers an alternative to this. This captures the value of all the underlying securities a derivative is exposed to (or can, potentially, be converted into). It is far more helpful than the absolute value of the derivative, when making comparison with 'cash market' valuations.

Finally, in relation to capitalization levels, individual derivative warrants must normally satisfy a minimum valuation of HK$50 million for listing purposes.[11] Minimum valuation levels are also stipulated in relation to the value of the underlying shares in derivative warrants. For derivative warrants written on an individual share, for instance, a 'public float capitalization' of at least HK$4 billion in the underlying is required.[12] Additional requirements, for basket warrants, where warrants are written on two or more underlying shares are also specified. These are discussed in greater detail in Section 11.5.

Hong Kong's Warrant Market: An International Overview

Warrants have had a strong presence in Europe for some years, with the United Kingdom, Germany, and Luxembourg, in particular, boasting sizeable markets. Based upon figures collected from BZW Securities Ltd for 1995, McHattie (1996) reports that 'Germany is easily the largest of the European warrant markets, with around US$5 billion of major warrant issues' (p. 207). This still lags some way behind Hong Kong, though, given a comparable figure, for exchange-traded products at the 1996 year-end, of around US$6.2 billion (see Table 11.2 earlier for HKD figures, converted at HK$7.8/US$1). Comparisons using more recent data would provide a less flattering picture, given the 1997–8 'meltdown' in warrant values. In view of this, comparison with other Asian warrant markets may be more meaningful. All, or most, of these buckled under the strain of the Asian financial malaise, particularly during the final quarter of 1997.

Other than Hong Kong, Japan and Singapore have carved out notable warrant markets in the region. Comparisons with Singapore are routinely made when assessing Hong Kong's development in any area of the securities industry, due to similarities in the economies' size, structure and business cultures. According to the Stock Exchange of Singapore (SES) *Fact Book 1997* (p. 66), Singapore had, as of the close of 1996, listed warrants on 98 companies which generated a combined market value of SGP$2.439 billion. Using an exchange-rate of SGP$1.3/US$1, this approximates to US$1.9 billion, a figure which languishes some way behind the US$6.2 billion valuation for Hong Kong listed warrants.

Hong Kong's warrant market, when compared to Japan's, looks less impressive, however. Anecdotal evidence suggests that warrants on Japanese stocks are more readily traded than the warrants of any other countries' stocks.[13] Despite this, their affiliation to their home-base is quite remote in many cases. McHattie (1986) reports, in this vein, that, 'Japanese warrants are generally denominated in US dollars, issued in the Euromarkets, and traded primarily in London' (p. 204). In comparison, warrants on Hong Kong stocks primarily trade in the SAR. The figures quoted thus far for Hong Kong relate solely to local listings which are denominated, for the most part, in Hong Kong dollars and written almost exclusively on locally-listed stocks. Comparisons with Japan are also problematic due to the exclusion of over-the-counter (OTC) based warrants from the Hong Kong figures. If these were factored in, the margin of Japan's assumed dominance would inevitably narrow.

Lastly, warrants in North America appear to be diffusely traded given an array of trading locations and the seeming dominance of the OTC market. Reliable comparison with Hong Kong, and other major warrant centres are therefore rather difficult to gauge.[14]

11.3 Characteristics of Warrants

To highlight the principal features of a warrant, a working example of a derivative warrant is constructed in Exhibit 11.1A below.

Exhibit 11.1A   The PTY–PQR 200x Warrant

> Consider a party, PTY, which is in the process of issuing 100 million warrants on a listed stock PQR, with the following terms: conversion ratio = 0.1; exercise price = $15; time to expiry 9 months; and issue price $0.50. Also assume that, at the time of issue, the value of PQR's stock was $18.00.

As is the convention with derivative warrants, the issuing party's name, PTY, appears first in the warrant description followed by the underlying security's name. The final detail in the warrant description is the year of expiry which, for reasons of generality, is referred to as 200x. An equity warrant on PQR with expiry of 200x would appear as a PQR 200x warrant and would be clearly distinguishable from the derivative variety.

The details in Exhibit 11.1A reveal that PTY will raise $50 million before costs. In most markets, a placing would be used to raise such funds. Subscription risk in such cases is reduced given an agreement to sell the warrants directly to a particular party or parties at the issue price. Once in issue, the conversion terms of the warrant allow for 100 million warrants to be converted into 10 million PQR shares.

For the potential investor, various issue details can be gleaned from Exhibit 11.1A. Four of these, the intrinsic value and time value components of the warrant price and the gearing (leverage) and premium (%) of the warrant are summarized in Exhibit 11.1B.

Exhibit 11.1B   Key Statistics for the PTY–PQR 200x Warrant

Gearing (leverage)	= $18/($0.50/0.10)	= 3.6 times
Intrinsic Value*	= $18 - $15	= $3
Time Value*	= $5 - $3	= $2
Premium (%)	= {[((0.50/0.10) + 15)/18] – 1}	= 11.1%

* Intrinsic and time values are calculated for a holding of 10 warrants.

Gearing

Gearing for warrants, as with options, is central to their marketability. The gearing rate of 3.6 times for the warrant in Exhibit 11.1A/B indicates that the cost of buying ten warrants—allowing access to one underlying stock— is 27.8% (= (1/3.6) × 100) of PQR's value. For retail investors especially, warrants offer an attractively priced alternative to direct stock ownership. As we saw for options, this comes at a cost in the form of increased return volatility. Figures 11.1 and 11.2 highlight this for the turbulent 1997 trading year.

During bull markets, warrants typically go into overdrive. The appreciation in Robert Fleming's Hong Kong Covered Warrants Index of 114% between 2 January and 7 August 1997, eclipsing a 26% rise in the

Figure 11.1 Cumulative Returns of the Fleming Hong Kong Covered
Warrant Index (FWI) Versus the Hang Seng Index (HSI):
January – December 1997

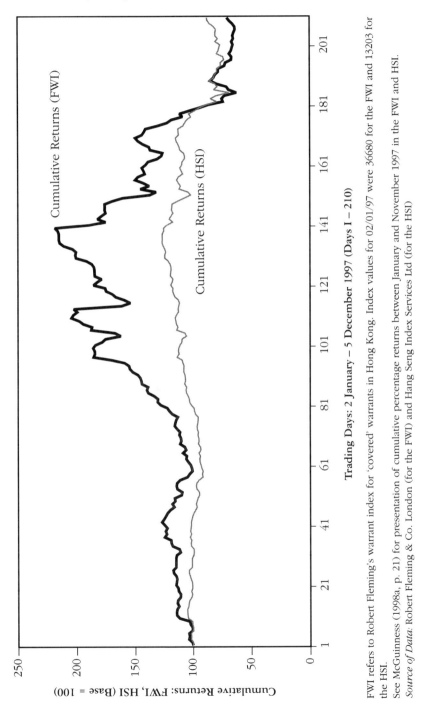

FWI refers to Robert Fleming's warrant index for 'covered' warrants in Hong Kong. Index values for 02/01/97 were 36680 for the FWI and 13203 for the HSI.

See McGuinness (1998a, p. 21) for presentation of cumulative percentage returns between January and November 1997 in the FWI and HSI.

Source of Data: Robert Fleming & Co. London (for the FWI) and Hang Seng Index Services Ltd (for the HSI)

Figure 11.2   Cumulative Returns of the Fleming Hong Kong Covered
Warrant Index (FWI) Versus the Hang Seng Index (HSI):
July 1994 – December 1997 (Base Date, 1/7/94 = 100)

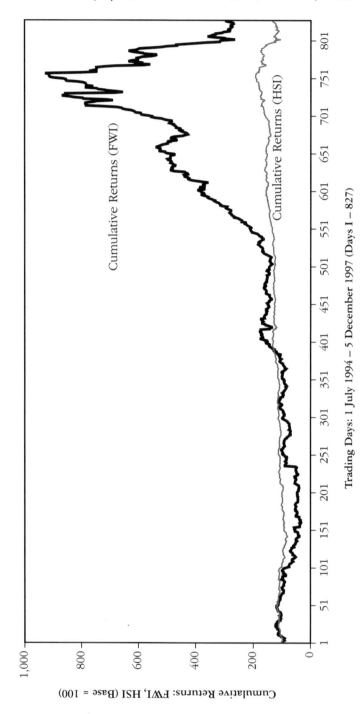

FWI refers to Robert Fleming's warrant index for 'covered' warrants in Hong Kong. Index values supplied for FWI began from 1/7/94 when the FWI was recorded with value 8634 (the value of the HSI on 1/7/94).

Source of Data: Robert Fleming & Co. London (for the FWI) and Hang Seng Index Services Ltd (for the HSI)

Hang Seng Index (HSI) over the same period, is an apt demonstration of this (see Figure 11.2).[15] During bear markets, warrants wreak chaos on investors' balance sheets. The period from 7 August to 30 November 1997 is a potent reminder of this. This saw a decline in local derivative warrants, as measured by Robert Fleming's Hong Kong Covered Warrants Index, of around 70%.[16] The corresponding decline in the HSI was 37%. In sum, warrants, like options and any other leveraged instrument, exhibit much greater return volatility than do their underlying assets. The greater the leverage, of course, the greater the volatility.

Time Value and Intrinsic Value

The principles relating to intrinsic value and time value (or premium, in the case of warrants) apply in much the same way for warrants as for options. In this regard, much of what was said in Section 10.2 applies here as well.

Realization of intrinsic value is rather different for investors of warrants though. Unlike some options which enjoy automatic exercise features, the warrant holder must vigilantly watch the market in the run-up to expiry. Failure to serve an exercise notice on the issuer, where intrinsic value in the warrant is evident at expiry, would prove to be very costly. Provisions in the Listing Rules, which require issuers to publicize imminent expiry dates, serve as timely reminders for the more dilatory.[17]

The general observations surrounding time value for options also hold for warrants. Essentially, time value increases:

(i)   the greater the time to expiry (for a given strike price) and (ii) the closer the instrument is priced to the 'at-the-money' point (for a given time to expiry).

Finding data to demonstrate these behavioural traits for warrants is not always easy. For equity warrants, it is somewhat unusual for a company to issue more than one warrant category with the same expiry date. For derivative warrants, the task is a little easier. The three derivative warrants on Hong Kong Telecom (Hong Kong Tel.) in Table 11.3, extracted from a total of 18 listed issues on Hong Kong Telecom at the time, provide apt demonstration of this. All three of the derivative warrants selected share an expiry date within one day of each other. With different strikes on the three derivative warrants we are able to demonstrate the time value-intrinsic value relation we observed earlier for options. That is, for a given time to expiry, time value increases as the difference between the value of the underlying and strike narrows (see (ii) above).

Unfortunately, insights into the time value property captioned in (i) are not so easy to demonstrate. One would need to find derivative warrants on the same underlying with the same strikes, but differing times to expiry to do this, which is a practical impossibility.

Table 11.3   Decomposition of Warrant Prices into Intrinsic Value and
Time Value

DERIVATIVE WARRANTS TRADED ON THE SEHK

	Warrant Price	*Ordinary Share Price*	*Exercise Price*	*Share/ Warrant*	*Expiration Date*
ABN-HKTel 98	0.130	14.75	16.61	0.100	Jun 12
ML-HKTel 98	0.118	14.75	18.00	0.100	Jun 11
UBS-HK Tel 98	0.250	14.75	15.03	0.100	Jun 11

Source: South China Morning Post, Business Post, p. 7, 23 December 1997. Conversion
ratios of 0.100 are not stated but implied from the data.

	'In-the-Money'(+) or *'Out-of-the-Money'(–)($)*	*Intrinsic* Value ($)*	*Time* Value ($)*
ABN-HKTel 98	-1.86	0.00	1.30
ML-HKTel 98	-3.25	0.00	1.18
UBS-HK Tel 98	-0.28	0.00	2.50

* All calculations based upon values for 10 warrants given a conversion ratio of 0.1.

The Premium (%)

This statistic is widely and routinely calculated by warrant traders and
issuers and is defined below.

$$\text{Premium (\%)} = \{[(W_p/CR) + X]/ Vs - 1\} \times 100$$

where W_p refers to the market price of a warrant; CR the conversion ratio; X
the strike price; and Vs the value of the underlying.

For further illustration, the premium (%) figures for the AN-HK Tel. 98,
ML-HK Tel. 98 and UBS-HK Tel. 98 warrants featured in Table 11.3 are
21.4%, 30.0%, and 18.8%, respectively.

It is often suggested that a warrant with a negative premium (%), or
discount (%), is undervalued. In the absence of transaction costs and any
liquidity problems in the warrant or underlying, the premium (%) for a
warrant should be at least zero. Where a sizeable discount (%) is evident,
an arbitrage opportunity probably exists. In such cases it becomes optimal
to buy the warrant and simultaneously sell the underlying stock. The
settlement of the stock sale can then be arranged by exercising the warrant.
In this particular context, the pay-off, ignoring transaction costs, is positive
and equal to $V_s - W_p - X$ (where V_s is the value of the underlying, W_p is
the warrant price, X the exercise price and CR is 1).

Transaction costs and/or illiquidity in the warrant or underlying stock
may impede or limit any potential arbitrage returns. In this sense, it is
possible for a small discount (%) to persist in the market. In most cases,
however, discount (%) figures are quickly seized upon by arbitrageurs.

As a consequence, arbitrage opportunities suggested by a discount (%) figure at the close of trading may be illusory. As trades cannot be conducted on the closing prices, the arbitrage opportunity may well disappear by the following day's open.

The premium (%) should also be adjusted in the event of a stock split, stock dividend, or other capitalization change in the underlying. Adjustments to either the conversion ratio or exercise price of the warrant typically result in such cases. The precise form of this adjustment should be spelled out in the warrant issue document. A one-for-one (1:1) stock split would approximately halve the market value of a stock and, to protect an investor holding a warrant on the underlying, either the conversion ratio would double or the exercise price halve. Either would leave the premium (%) unchanged. Failure to recognize the adjustment in the calculation of the premium (%) would lead to spurious conclusions being drawn.

The Interaction of Delta and Premium (%)

The delta (δ) was introduced in Chapter 10, S. 10.2 for call options. It carries much the same meaning for warrants. Most market-watchers will be aware that, like a call option, a warrant's δ increases from 0.5 to 1 as it moves deeper and deeper 'into-the-money'. The more astute will also recognize that, as this happens, the warrant's premium (%) shrinks. In fact, a discount (%) is likely when the warrant δ approaches 1. The reasons for the inverse relation between δ and premium (%) are explored in the following.

If one takes the definition for the premium (%) given earlier and, for simplicity, consider a warrant with a conversion ratio of one, the premium (%) becomes,

$$[(Wp + X - V_s)/V_s] \times 100 = \{[Wp - (V_s - X)]/V_s\} \times 100$$

Delta/Premium(%) Relation where the Warrant has Positive Intrinsic Value
If the warrant has positive intrinsic value (i.e., $V_s - X > 0$), the premium (%) simply represents time value/V_s. Given this, as time value shrinks as the warrant advances further and further 'into-the-money', the premium (%) will clearly fall. Discussions in Chapter 10 illustrated that the δ on a call instrument increases with the value of the underlying.

Delta/Premium(%) Relation where the Warrant has Zero Intrinsic Value
When a warrant is priced 'at-the-money' ($V_s = X$) or 'out-of-the-money' ($V_s - X < 0$), intrinsic value is obviously zero. No one, in other words, would exercise the warrant under such circumstances. Unlike intrinsic value, though, $V_s - X$ in the premium (%) formula is not constrained to be zero. As the warrant moves deeper and deeper 'out-of-the-money', the premium (%) gets larger and larger. In the limit, imagine that V_s falls to zero. The

premium (%) would equal positive infinity (= (Wp + X)/0). As the warrant moves deeper and deeper 'out-of-the-money', there is also a commensurate decline in δ. As a consequence, the premium (%) and δ move in opposite directions for both 'in-the-money' and 'out-of-the-money' warrants.

11.4   The Role of Delta in the Hedging Strategies of the Warrant Investor and Issuer

Options serve a central hedging role. The same is also true of warrants. As illustrated in Section 10.6, option-based hedges are relatively straight-forward to construct; although, where the hedge is constructed for a short time period, careful attention must be paid to the δ in the option or warrant.

To illustrate the fundamentals of the delta hedging approach, suppose the δ of a call option or warrant is 0.50. If one wishes to hedge a short position in the underlying, this suggests a delta hedge of two long positions in the option or warrant (= 1/δ). If the underlying share then rises by $0.10, the value of the options or warrants will rise by the same (2 × $0.50). Equally, a long position in the underlying stock could be hedged by writing call (options) or warrants. This might occur, for instance, where a fund manager runs a designated fund in a particular group of stocks and, within his/her year of evaluation, has already achieved the benchmark return. As the fund manager must retain the portfolio structure, he/she is likely to protect the position—and the end-of-year bonuses that go with it—by hedging. Shorting (writing) call options or warrants is one possibility. Another is to purchase a certain number of put options or put warrants on the underlying.

The delta can also be used to help writers of short positions (in options or warrants) determine a hedge in the underlying. A writer of an option or warrant with δ of 0.5, could hedge his/her short position by taking two long positions in the underlying, for instance. This particular aspect of hedging is examined in detail here for derivative warrants. Specific attention is given to the writer of NCDWs, rather than of the alternative type of derivative warrant—the CDW. In the CDW, the writer is required to hold sufficient of the underlying to cover all possible exercise notices, anyway. As the long position of the CDW writer cannot be easily adjusted, it is somewhat different to a hedge portfolio. In any event, it is constructed with a different purpose in mind: to enhance the issuer's income return under bull market conditions. Section 10. 2/Figure 10.1 illustrated how this worked for 'covered' call option writer.

An Illustration of the Hedge Approach

If a δ hedging approach is adopted by the writer of a NCDW, a long position in the underlying will be held and adjusted with changes in the value of the underlying. To shed light on this, an example, as discussed in McGuinness (1998a), is set out in Exhibit 11.2.

Exhibit 11.2   Example of the Construction of the Issuer's δ Hedge
Portfolio

Suppose an issuer writes 10 million derivative warrants, each with the
following terms: conversion ratio 1; exercise price $10; and time to expiry
of nine months. The value for the underlying stock (V_s) is $15 and the
warrant price $8 which leads to gross funds raised of $80 million.

If the δ of the above warrant were 0.75, the writer would need 7.5 million
underlying stocks to completely hedge his/her position. This complete
hedge might be constructed if the writer, shortly after issuing the warrant,
senses a change in market sentiment. Normally, we assume that writers of
call options and warrants pitch their issues at market peaks, hoping to
collect funds without the need for subsequent payments of intrinsic value to
the investor. If the writer gets it wrong, and more ebullient market
conditions emerge, the writer might wish to assemble a long cash position,
simply to hedge against the risk of future payments of intrinsic value.

To illustrate, suppose a hedge portfolio is constructed shortly after the
warrant issue in Exhibit 11.2. What happens if V_s subsequently rises by
$0.10? Given a warrant δ of 0.75, each warrant would also rise in value by
$0.075. In this setting, the value of the hedge portfolio, and the writer's
short warrant position, would be equally affected. The shareholdings and
warrants would each rise in aggregate by $0.5625 million with the increased
exposure on the latter cancelled out by the gain on the former. If the
opposite occurs, the writer may well rue his bad luck in hedging. But this
misses the point. Hedging is designed to minimize exposure. If a loss on
a hedge is offset by a gain on the derivative, this objective is satisfied. We
can see this in the example, as the short warrant position can be offset
(repurchased) by the writer at lower cost which, in turn, offsets the loss
on the hedge.

The Risks Implicit in δ Hedging

One complication in the δ hedging approach, is that δ changes with the
value of the underlying. As a consequence, adjustments to the underlying
hedge portfolio must be made to maintain the effectiveness of the hedge.
A falling stock price and δ would require a proportionate reduction in the
hedge portfolio for instance.[18] While this becomes less onerous as more
and more warrants are 'closed-out', the transaction costs of these hedging
adjustments are likely to be substantial. More importantly, actual
adjustments may be hindered by liquidity. As explored in McGuinness
(1998a), the illiquidity of δ hedges during the October 1997 'meltdown' in
the markets meant that a number of warrant issuers were unable to sell
from their hedge portfolios in a timely fashion. This illiquidity triggered
substantial losses for some issuers.[19] The massive decline in warrant values
meant that deltas on warrants were squeezed, in many cases, from levels
well above 0.5 to levels nearer zero. For those hedging short warrant

positions, this signalled substantial cuts to long hedge positions. Unfortunately, delta hedging requires that the adjustments are made in small increments as prices fall. With few buyers and a glut of sell orders, adjustments were virtually impossible to make. For many hedgers of warrant issues, substantial price adjustments probably occurred before they could unwind their hedge positions. By this time, huge losses on their hedge positions would have been racked up.[20]

The transaction costs associated with fine-tuning hedge positions, as well as the risks of being overexposed during volatile periods, mean that complete hedging is unlikely. Hedging techniques for the warrant writer are not confined to positions in the underlying given an array of derivative products that can serve the same function. In an index call, for instance, it would be rather expensive to assemble a physically-based hedge and, in all likelihood, an index derivative would be preferred.

Instead of the long position being a hedge, the short position could be the hedge. A short warrant position can often function as a hedge against an illiquid or committed long position in the underlying. One should also note, as mentioned earlier, that a long cash position for a 'covered' call or warrant writer does not constitute a hedge (see Figure 10.1).

A hedge-like portfolio can also be convenient cover for market manipulation. Sales of large blocks of stock, disguised as part of a hedge, could drive underlying stock and warrant values down. If this is done to allow the writer of a call or warrant to buy back his/her warrants at basement prices, it is clearly outright manipulation of the market. If the writer then reacquires the stock, with fundamentals subsequently restored, he/she may not lose anything on the stock foray, although all his/her exposure to the warrant would have been eliminated. This kind of strategy is one that market regulators would clearly monitor. It should also be limited to small, developing markets.

11.5   Innovations in Hong Kong Listed Warrants

Put Warrants

As the put embodies an option to sell the underlying, intrinsic value exists when the value of the underlying is less than the warrant's exercise price. The investor, in such circumstances, can buy the underlying in the cash market and then sell it through the put warrant at a higher strike. In practice, most put warrants in most markets appear to be cash-settled with the writer making a cash payment at expiry equivalent to the warrant's intrinsic value. This procedure is all the more convenient if the put warrants are traded on stock indices or baskets. In previous years, put (as well as call) warrants—with cash-settlement features—have also been issued on gold and foreign exchange.

Until recently, the put warrant was something of a novelty with only a smattering of issues evident locally. The onset of the Asian currency crisis in late 1997 changed all that, triggering a flurry of such instruments in the first two quarters of 1998. As we saw in Section 10.3/Figure 10.3, put investors are not the only parties that gain from such instruments in a market downturn. Issuers do too—in terms of income enhancement—if short positions in the underlying are established prior to the put issue. The timing of put warrant issues in 1998 is clearly consistent with this.

A number of puts have also featured recently on the SEHK for non-Hong Kong market indices: stock codes 2189 and 1909, for put warrants on the US Standard & Poor's index, issued by Morgan Stanley and Peregrine Derivatives, respectively, are good examples. Warrants on indices closer to home, like those issued by Peregrine Derivatives and UBS on the Taiwan Stock Exchange Weighted Index are also worthy of comment in this regard, although these, which were listed on 23 April 1997, embody call features.[21]

Call-Spread Warrants

It has been assumed throughout that warrants embody American exercise features. This, like the assumed call feature, is no longer necessarily true either. The listing of call-spread warrants, which embody European exercise style, are proof of this. Various call-spreads have been available on the SEHK since June 1994.[22] In addition to their unusual exercise style, these also feature an upper 'cap' on the amount of intrinsic value payable at expiry. This produces a discount on the market price of such call-spreads. As a result, call-spreads offer much higher levels of gearing relative to 'uncapped' warrants (with comparable terms).

In an ebullient market, the 'cap' feature of the call-spread might deter investors. Under stable market conditions, however, the call-spread is likely to generate more interest. Its gearing advantage, allied to the fact that gains from 'modest' appreciation in the underlying, are unlikely to be impeded by the 'cap' are the selling features.[23]

Call-spreads replicate a bull call-spread strategy in equivalent equity options on the underlying. As we saw in Chapter 10, Section 10.6/Figure 10.7, this translates to one long and one short position in call options on the same underlying where both calls have the same expiry, but the short position has the higher strike. The bull *call-spread warrant* is demonstrated in Exhibit 11.3 below.

The call-spread in Exhibit 11.3A is equivalent to a long call option on LMN with strike $80 and a short call option on LMN with strike $110. Assuming market prices, at the issue date, for the $80 and $110 strike call options, of $17 and $2, respectively, the net premium paid is $15 (= $2 – $17). The returns at expiry for this option strategy are shown, for a range of possible values on LMN, in Exhibit 11.3B. In brief, the maximum return at expiry is $15. This is equivalent to the 'cap' on the PTY— LMN 200x CS warrant's intrinsic value of $30 less the $15 cost of acquiring it. A 'cap' also occurs on the downside, which is equivalent to the PTY—LMN 200x CS warrant being priced 'out-of-the-money' at expiry. In this case, the initial purchase cost of the warrant of $15 represents the loss.

Exhibit 11.3A   Example of a Call-Spread Warrant, the PTY—LMN 200x
CS Warrant

Suppose a call-spread is currently being issued by third party PTY on a
stock LMN with the following terms: expiry in 9 months' time; conversion
ratio of 1.00; and exercise price of $80.00. Furthermore, assume that an
'upper cap' of $110 is placed on the value of LMN's stock for the purpose of
capping intrinsic value at expiry to a maximum of $30. In addition, the
value of LMN stock at the issue date is $88.00 and the initial market price
for the call-spread is $15.

For the PTY—LMN 200x CS warrant,

Gearing	= [$88.00/(15/1.00)]	= 5.87 times
premium (%)	= {[(15/1.00) + 80.00)/88.00] - 1} × 100	= 8%
Intrinsic value	= $8.00; Time Value	= $7.00
Maximum rate of return (if the warrant is purchased at its issue price)		= 100%

Exhibit 11.3B   Possible Cash-Flow Returns to the Bull Call-Spread
Strategy in Options at Expiry

Stock Value ($) at Expiry	Net Premium paid ($) (i)	Intrinsic value ($) received on long position(at expiry) (ii)	Intrinsic value ($) paid on short position(at expiry) (iii)	Total net Cash-flow Return($) (iv)
60	(15)	0	0	(15)
80	(15)	0	0	(15)
100	(15)	20	0	5
120	(15)	40	(10)	15
140	(15)	60	(30)	15

Other Developments: Basket and Regional Warrants

Summary description of all local warrant listings on the SEHK can be
gauged from the Exchange's web-site.[24] Of the 578 listings recorded as of
24 November 1997, 179 were reported as equity warrants. The remaining
399 listings were, naturally, derivative warrants. Of the latter, the majority
(281 listings) were simply labelled as call warrants. Three put warrants
aside, the rest of the derivative warrants were either basket warrants (100),
regional call warrants (14), or exotic warrants (1).

Basket warrants, which are written on two or more stocks, have proved
immensely popular since around the mid-1990s. Many of the underlying
baskets relate to theme groups of counters like blue and red chips and
stocks in certain sectors. Property, hotel, conglomerate, banking, and
petrochemical stocks being notable in this regard. The regional call warrant
complements the basket warrant. These emerge where one or more of

the underlying securities have listed status in an overseas market.[25] A number of these relate to conglomerate stocks, or are written on particular stock sectors, like properties. As such, they can be regarded as regional basket call warrants.[26] Nine of the fourteen regional warrants identified as of 24 November 1997 fitted this description. Of the remaining five, four were written on Hongkong Land and one on Jardine Matheson Holdings. Both stocks clearly have a strong presence and historical association with Hong Kong. Neither was listed in Hong Kong when the warrants on these underlying counters were issued. Hence, the prefix regional in the description of the warrants.

The emerging basket warrant market has prompted regulators to assess various features of the basket product. Pronouncements relating to (i) the minimum weightings given to the underlying constituents, (ii) the capitalization of the 'public flotation' in each of the constituents and (iii) the bases offered for any cash-based settlement have figured in recent years.[27] The third issue has, perhaps, aroused the most interest.

The 'Issuer Settlement Option'

Until very recently, a number of issuers of derivative warrants were able to exercise an option in relation to the terms of settlement of the warrant. In other words, they were given a choice at the time of notification of exercise as to the precise form of intrinsic value payment to the investor. This created some uncertainty for the investor. Would they get shares or cash? Changes to the Listing Rules in June 1998 effectively curtailed this issuer-option. The requirement now is that issuers disclose the precise form of any intrinsic value payment to the investor at the time of issue.[28]

One justification for the old 'issuer settlement option' was the flexibility it afforded the issuer for hedging. Physical hedges, as we have seen, may be very illiquid, particularly during a market free-fall. The option to be able to hedge using other more liquid, cash-based securities, when physical stock holdings become illiquid, would have been an attractive one for the issuer. For the investor, uncertainty typically translates to increased risk. Consider the following: an investor hedges a short stock position with a derivative warrant where the expiry date on the warrant coincides with his/her intended repayment date on the short position. The investor, in this case, needs the stock to close-out his/her short position. The risk of a cash payment—made possible under the old issuer settlement option— would have penalized the investor by forcing him/her to incur additional transaction costs in acquiring the underlying stock. Liquidity risks would also have had to have been factored in. For some investors, the uncertainty engendered by the old 'issuer settlement option' would have undermined the attractiveness of warrants embodying such features. It would certainly have damaged their price, to some degree. Like all trade-offs in finance, the loss of flexibility for the issuer, under the new system, should generate a compensating pay-off. All other things being equal, this should come in the form of increased issue prices. Testing this is far from easy, though.

All other things are not equal. The primary market for warrants in the second half of 1998—as in the first half—all but disappeared in the face of poor investor sentiment.

Callable and Exotic Warrants

In other markets, developments like callable warrants are noteworthy. These have featured in the United States since the early 1980s (see Schultz (1993)). They give issuers the opportunity to redeem warrants within a defined expiry period. In this regard, the warrant embodies a call provision similar to that found on some corporate bonds and, in some jurisdictions, government bonds. In Hong Kong, repurchase mandates for equity warrants, which allow up to 10% of warrants outstanding to be repurchased, offer something close to this. Once the mandate is approved, the issuer has some discretion in timing the conferred 'option' to buy back the warrants. These, like share buy-backs, have been quite popular in recent years.

A very recent innovation in Hong Kong is the exotic warrant. An example is the Morgan Stanley exotic call (issuer's cash option) on New World Development with expiry date of June 1998 (identified as stock code 1994 by the exchange). This embodied a reset feature which allowed the issuer to reset the exercise price within a limited period of the warrant's launch.[29]

11.6   Convertibles, Exchangeable Bonds, Debt–Equity Swaps and Other Equity Swaps

Convertible Debt Securities

Warrants can also be written on debt securities, although they do not seem to figure significantly in the Hong Kong SAR. Option-based instruments, with a direct linkage to debt, like convertibles, appear more popular. These are quite different to debt warrants which trade separately from the underlying debt. Convertibles really consist of an option and bond rolled into one. Conversion of the option leads to a certain amount of the principal (face value) of the debt being exchanged for a certain number of shares of the issuing company. In this sense, the convertible is a hybrid—or half-way house—between a debt security and an equity security.

The terms of conversion depend upon the actual 'strike' price of the option. Once the option is exercised debt is sacrificed for underlying stock, in relation to this 'strike' price. In general terms, convertibles carry American exercise terms allowing the exchange to be achieved at any time between purchase and bond redemption. In a debt warrant, no such exchange takes place. Instead, the warrant provides terms on which debt can be purchased at some future date. No interest, or access to capital appreciation on the underlying debt, is therefore offered unless the warrant is exercised. Convertibles in contrast provide direct access to interest income—in the form of a fixed coupon—and capital gains on the debt for as long as they remain unexercised.

Investors, in a sense, get the best of both worlds with a convertible: access to a fixed-income debt security with potential to access the upside of equity market returns. This should enable the issuer to sell the security at a premium to a comparable non-convertible bond (with the same credit risk, maturity, and coupon rate). Equally, the issuer could sell the convertible bond for a similar price to such a comparable bond, but offer a lower coupon. This is the way it normally works. The convertible therefore plays a significant role in reducing the issuer's cost of funding.

The example in Exhibit 11.4 illustrates the essential features of a convertible.

Exhibit 11.4 A 1.5% 200x convertible bond on stock PQR

Suppose a company PQR issues US$80 million of face value debt at a coupon interest rate of 1.5% per annum with maturity, in exactly two years' time. At an exchange-rate of HK$7.8/US$1, the principal value of this debt issue is HK$624 million. Suppose that the debt trades in US$1,000 board lots, and that investors have an option to convert the debt into the shares of the underlying company at a conversion price of US$10.00. If the value of the underlying stock is US$11.00, the following key statistics emerge:

Conversion ratio	=	US$1,000/US$10	=	100 shares
Conversion price	=	US$1,000/100	=	US$10
Conversion value	=	100 × US$11	=	US$1,100

The example shows that an investor acquiring the convertible has an option to surrender US$1,000 face value of PQR debt for 100 shares in the underlying issuer. This is the conversion ratio. Two related statistics, the conversion price and conversion value, are inferred from this ratio: the former obtained by dividing the principal (US$1,000 in this case) by the conversion ratio and the latter by taking the product of the conversion ratio and the stock's underlying value.

Lower Bounds for Convertible Bond Valuations

Many studies tell us that, due to arbitrage, the *conversion value* provides a theoretical minimum for convertible bond value. To illustrate, if the PQR convertible was priced at US$1,080 (per US$1,000 of face value debt), an arbitrage gain could be generated. This would be achieved by *simultaneously* buying one lot of the convertible and shorting 100 PQR stocks, with the short position subsequently closed-out through bond conversion. Ignoring transaction costs, this strategy would yield US$20 (=-$1,080+$1,100) profit. With the incentive to buy the convertible and sell the underlying in large numbers of lots, market pressures would ensure suitable price adjustments. These adjustments should be sufficient to push the convertible bond's value to a level at least equal its conversion value. In practice, a convertible might trade slightly below this level due to transaction costs and/or illiquidity in the underlying or convertible bond.

It also stands to reason that an equivalent bond, with the same credit rating, maturity, and coupon rate as a convertible bond—but without an option to convert—should sell for a lower price than the convertible. As the convertible bond represents such an equivalent bond plus an option, all bundled into one security, this is hardly surprising. In short, the option to convert must be worth something.

One of the problems of applying the above theory—at least as far as convertibles in the Hong Kong SAR is concerned—is the absence of deep and liquid corporate debt markets. So, even where convertibles exist, equivalent bonds may not. While the local Exchange lists a wide array of debt securities—numbering 265 at the close of April 1998—volume levels appear very low.[30] This might also mean that even where equivalents exist, pricing comparisons with convertibles might not be that meaningful. Most acknowledge that exchange-traded debt constitutes only a small proportion of market-based debt though, with many issues trading OTC.

Euroconvertible Bonds

Convertibles have proved extremely popular with local corporations over the last five years or more, although the events of late 1997 and early 1998 have weakened demand for the product somewhat. Most of the major convertible issues in local companies have, hitherto, been issued in euroconvertible form. Traditionally, the 'euro' prefix has been taken to connote a security denominated in a currency different to that of its chosen locale of trading. This definition is no longer sufficient as most bonds and notes traded on the SEHK, despite being listed in US dollars, are not commonly regarded as Euro securities. This also seems to be true of bonds listed throughout Asia, which principally trade in US dollars. The proliferation of listings in securities with currencies foreign to their area of trading now means that the euro prefix carries a geographical interpretation as well; with the bulk of trading in eurobond securities, naturally, in Europe.

Euroconvertibles, as with bonds in general, are placed through 'book-runners' who take on the role of placing the bonds with investors.[31] This often results in placements to institutional players from the three major trading continents: Europe, North America, and Asia. The success of many local issues has been such that a number of book-runners have also been able to exercise over-allotment options, resulting in increases in the size of many issues by as much as 15%.

A number of euroconvertibles have listings in European markets, with Luxembourg seemingly preferred by the majority of local issuers of euroconvertibles. Despite this, the majority of trading often occurs outside recognized exchanges, on parallel, dealer-based markets.[32] These are often more liquid than the exchange-based markets. They also have tie-ups with international clearing systems like CEDEL and Euroclear. All of this begs an obvious question: Why do companies list their debt on major exchanges if a substantial part of the secondary market lies outside such exchange perimeters? The major reason is that many institutions are only allowed to invest in listed securities. Because of the greater disclosure requirements, and ongoing obligations, that exchange-listing entails, investor protection should be enhanced by exchange-listing. In other words, issuers of corporate debt often pay listing fees because it opens up the market for their debt. All other things being equal issuers should be able to generate more favourable prices. The same line of reasoning also helps explain why 'open-ended' investment funds sometimes list. They really have no reason to, from a secondary market perspective. Remember, the bid price of such units is simply the fund's net asset value per share.

The Exchangeable Bond

Exercise of a convertible requires the issuing company to issue an appropriate number of new shares, which results in some dilution of the underlying company's earnings per share figures. One security that is often compared to the convertible, but does not produce such dilution effects, is the exchangeable bond. This can be structured in much the same way as a convertible, but provides a subtle nuance not evident in the convertible: upon conversion, the issuer exchanges existing shares in issue for the outstanding debt.

In theory, there are three ways in which such an exchange can take place. Firstly, in markets where corporate treasury stock (CTS) is allowed, companies can use existing CTS balances to 'cover' conversion notices. A notice from an investor requesting debt conversion can then be settled by releasing the requisite number of shares from CTS to cancel the debt. As CTS is not available to local corporates, this mechanism currently lies off-limits. Whether this remains to be so is a good question, given moves afoot to assess the efficacy of CTS. Amongst other things, the creation of CTS would provide more ideal conditions for the issue of exchangeable bonds.[33]

A more likely construction for the exchangeable bond is where the stocks in issue relate to an investment in a third party. One recent local example of this is Lai Sun Development Co Ltd's exchangeable guaranteed bond issue of 1997. With maturity designated for 2004, the key feature of this bond is the option granted to holders to exchange the debt for the shares of a third company—Asia Television Ltd—albeit on the proviso that Asia Television Ltd attains listing in its shares prior to 1 June 2001.[34]

The third form for an exchangeable is where the issuer offers stocks in a subsidiary as 'cover' for the written option. A recent example of this form is Shanghai Industrial Investment Treasury Co Ltd's Guaranteed Exchangeable Bond, which is convertible into the shares of Shanghai Industrial Holdings Ltd.[35]

Recent press commentaries also suggest that the exchangeable bond form is being studied by the Exchange Fund Investment Ltd. as a means for disposing of some of the government's local stock holdings, acquired in its foray into the markets in August 1998. The mechanism would also fit in very nicely with one of the government's much vaunted policy objectives: to develop debt markets for high quality paper. Chapter 14 returns to this theme, and to the role of the Exchange Fund Investment Ltd.

As a final point, new products and new twists on existing products are constantly emerging. The recent sale of a convertible bond on Teco Electric & Machinery, a Taiwanese concern, with an option allowing conversion of the bond into either the underlying stock of the issuer or the stock of other companies in the Teco group, is a clear reminder of this. This bond, which might be described as a convertible/exchangeable bond, was singled out for the award of 'most innovative deal' by *Finance Asia* magazine in its 1998 Deal Awards for Asian banks.[36] It is cited as the first bond of its kind by the publication.

Other Options Embedded in Convertibles or Exchangeable Bonds

The option in a convertible or exchangeable bond can also be coupled with one granted to the issuer in the form of a call provision. This allows the issuer to retire the bond early within a specified period immediately prior to the bond's maturity date. Investors can, of course, avoid such provisions by exercising just ahead of any call provision period. The imposition of such a provision normally reduces (increases) the market price (yield) of a bond. Complications also arise in terms of the strategies for conversion, and the actual valuation of the convertible, when such provisions exist.[37]

A number of local companies issuing convertible bonds have also sought to make the issues more attractive to investors by attaching a put option to the convertible instrument, allowing investors the option to sell the bond to the issuer on prescribed terms.

Debt–Equity Swaps and Other Equity Swaps

Debt–equity swaps typically surface during times of economic duress and largely feature when debtor organizations are unable to meet coupon or principal payments in a timely manner. Where attempts to restructure the payments flounder, the creditor might view a swap of the debt holding into the underlying equity of the issuer as the only real chance of extracting some pay-back from the debtor. This is only likely to appeal, however, where positive net asset value in the debtor company exists: holding shares in a company with liabilities in excess of the dollar disposable value of assets means the equityholder receives nothing if liquidation subsequently results.

Where the debt–equity swap materializes, the creditor simply forgoes his/her debt holding for an equity stake in the company. This is akin, in some respects, to a buy-out, as discussed in Section 9.3. If a substantial new equity stake results, a complete managerial overhaul of the debtor company is likely with the erstwhile creditors acting to install new directors through their newly acquired voting rights. Many other corporate changes would also surely follow.

Equity swaps are quite different to the swap arrangement featured above. They are structured between two parties, for example investor I and counterparty C, where I agrees to swap the returns on a given index (or stock basket) with C for an alternative income stream. A good example of this is where, for a given stock index, I can arrange to swap the gain on the index (capital plus dividend) with C in return for a floating-rate return— connected to some market rate.[38] Such swap arrangements may confer certain cost-saving benefits.[39] For I's counterparty C, in the above, one imagines that the equity-linked returns can be generated at a substantial cost discount to either constructing the index or buying it through the market (particularly given the 'front-end' charges some fund managers are prone to levy, even on passive index funds). For I, there is a presumption that he/she wishes to switch from direct equity investment to floating rate investment (on debt-based instruments). This being so, the swap avoids the inconvenience and costs of I having to sell the index and buy the equivalent debt instrument (associated with the floating-rate return). The swap arrangement may also allow I the opportunity to generate returns well above those on a commercial 'floating-rate' deposit (of the same notional amount).

The above account represents a rather simplified view of an equity swap and one must be cognizant of the credit-risks facing each of the counterparties. The income returns agreed can fail to materialize if either party acts egregiously or simply goes bankrupt. Careful credit analysis is always critical. This is particularly important in relation to OTC products like swaps where contract novation is not possible. Chapter 13 revisits this subject, examining risk-management issues surrounding equity derivatives.

11.7 Concluding Remarks

In Hong Kong, warrants are widely regarded as a cheap alternative to holding stock and, given the liquidity and sophistication of the market, offer a series of views and opportunities on an array of securities and indices. While retail investors might see the warrant as a speculative play, it also offers hedging and capital raising functions to other users. For corporations with future commitments to repurchase securities, the (call) warrant offers an attractive insurance policy. Similarly, fund managers with a committed long position in stock, might see a (put) warrant as a means of locking in returns on their portfolios and their associated end-of-year bonuses.

For many issuers, the warrant is a useful capital-raising device. Both equity and derivative warrants raise substantial sums in the primary market. The equity warrant, of course, offers a second stage of funding, if and when an exercise in the underlying is made. For other warrant issuers, the hedging properties of short positions are attractive, especially when used against a long cash-market position.

While the various benefits of warrants have been outlined in some detail in this chapter, it is also clear that warrants move in and out of favour with investors as market conditions change. These changes in investor sentiment appear far more marked than is the case with many of the underlying cash market products which are often purchased for their long-term benefits. The shorter term of the warrant, allied to its geared nature, means that the adverse effects of a general market downturn are far more acute. The effects may also be irreversible during the term of a given warrant. The October 1997 cataclysm in Hong Kong's warrant market saw many warrant values tumble almost overnight. By the end of this crisis many of the instruments were so deeply 'priced-out-of-the-money' that their values were firmly glued to a minimum of HK$0.01 per security. With the chances of recovery slim—given the short term of such securities— some investors would have sought alternative domestic uses for the scrip.

The bear market of late 1997 and 1998 has, at least in the minds of many retail investors, tarnished the image of the warrant. For those that lost most of their investment in such products, a return to the market may well be some way off. This reticence may well remain until the stellar returns, associated with warrants of yesteryear, reappear in the next major bull market. Warrants may then become popular once again.

Notes

1. As a reminder, employee stock options (ESOPs), as introduced in Section 8.1, are very much like equity warrants. They enjoy the same kind of exercise feature. The reader should appreciate that the traded call option is very different from the ESOP.

2. Apart from the time interval from issue date to expiry, the equity warrant has similarities with the nil-paid right discussed in Section 6.3. As the nil-paid right is listed for only a few days, it represents a short-term version of an equity warrant. For both the nil-paid right and the longer-term equity warrant, the effect of exercise is the same: an issue of new shares by the underlying company with a corresponding dilution in corporate earnings.

3. See Rule 15.02, 15-1, 5/91, Listing Rules. The Listing Rules distinguish between warrants and derivative warrants. The former is referred to as an equity warrant in this chapter for reasons of clarity.

4. See Understanding Stock Options (And Their Risks), p. 28.

5. Apart from bonus issues, increases in the number of 'open' positions, following the original issue date, are uncommon in warrants.

6. See Listing Rules, Chapter 15A, 'Derivative Warrants' (and Rule 15A.06, 15A-2, 6/98 in particular).

7. According to Rule 15A.07 of the Listing Rules, '"collateralized warrants" are derivative warrants where the issuer owns all of the underlying securities or other assets to which the collateralized warrant relates and grants a charge over such securities or assets in favour of an independent trustee which acts for the benefit of the warrantholders.' (15A-02, 6/98, quotes as shown).

8. See Rule 15A.15, 15A-3 of the Listing Rules which makes reference to the possible use of a guarantee in lieu of provisions set out in Rules 15A.13 and 15A. 14 for NCDW issuers (see 15A-3, 6/98).

9. See Exchange Announcements, New Derivative Warrant Regulations, Dec. 1993. *Inter alia*, this states that, 'Warrants issued by controlling shareholders or by persons with effective management control are no longer considered suitable for listing.'

10. Specific prohibitions relating to a third party issuer are set out in Rule 15A. 26, 15A-7, 6/98 of the Listing Rules.

11. See Rule 15A.38, 15A-11, 6/98 of the Listing Rules.

12. See *Listing Rules*, Rule 15A.28, 15A-7/8, 6/98. Part (2) of this ruling deals with the specific conditions relating to the underlying's listing on a recognized overseas exchange.

13. McHattie (1996) notes that, 'The Japanese warrants market is the most famous, infamous, and easily the largest warrants market in the world' (p. 203).

14. See ibid. (pp. 191–201) for an overview of the US warrant market.

15. R.Fleming, London are gratefully acknowledged for provision of this data.

16. See McGuinness (1998a) for a detailed account of this market decline.

17. For derivative warrants, Rule 15A.84, 15A-22/23 of the Listing Rules is pertinent.

18. Writers might also act in ways that are contrary to the hedging strategies suggested through δ. As the δ increases as a warrant moves deeper and deeper 'into-the-money', for example, the writer may, instead of buying underlying stock to increase his/her proportionate hedge, short stock. This might occur if the change in δ is such that a negative premium (%) emerges and the writer, for reasons of arbitrage, simultaneously buys warrants in issue and sells from the hedge portfolio. After the discount (%) has been eliminated, the writer might then consider rebuilding the hedge cover. Thanks are due to Eric Wong of the Exchange's Listing Department for comments on such hedging practices.

19. See Pritchard (1997) and Horsewood (1997a) for details of some of the losses incurred by issuers during this period.

20. Tuesday 28 October 1997 provides apt demonstration of how quickly, and how far, prices can fall. The HSI plummeted from its previous day's close of 10,498.2 to 9,295.2 points, all within the first two minutes of trading on the 28th. Closing and intra-day HSI values were supplied by HSI Services Ltd.

21. See New Listings (July 1997, p. 26). Also see Horsewood (1997) for discussion of these issues and of plans for the listing of other warrants on regional stock indices in Hong Kong.

22. The first three of these were the Peregrine–Swire Pacific 'A' CS '95 warrant, the UBS–Hong Kong Telecom CS '96 warrant and the UBS–Hang Seng Bank CS '96 warrant (see Bennett, Chen and McGuinness (1995) for more details).

23. See ibid. for details.

24. SEHK homepage (at http://www.sehk.com.hk/english/Markets/cash/Stock/ stkList/Warrants.htm).

25. Specifically, the Exchange reports that, '"R" stands for regional derivative warrants with one or more underlying shares not listed on the Exchange but listed on the other stock exchanges recognized by the Exchange' (Exchange Announcement: New Category of derivative warrants, 17 June 1997).

26. Thanks are due to the Listing Division for their help with enquiries concerning this data.

27. For (i) and (iii), see exchange Announcement: New Measures Relating to the Listing of Derivative Warrants (5 Sept 1997). For (ii), see Exchange Announcement: Public Float Capitalization and Market Capitalization for Derivative Warrant Issues: Introduction of Qualifying Period (May 1997).

28. See Rule 15A.43, 15A-11, 6/98 of the Listing Rules.

29. See issue document (p. 8) for reset conditions. This, and other forms of exotic option, are detailed in a recent Exchange announcement (see Exchange Announcement: New Category of derivative warrants, 17 June 1997).

30. Turnover was reported to be less than HK$1 billion for debt trades in April, compared with a level of over HK$111 billion for 672 listed ordinary shares (See *SEHK Monthly Bulletin* (May 1998, p. 9)).

31. For a ranking of major 'book-runners' involved in the placement of Asian Euroconvertibles, see Gailey (Dec. 1996/Jan. 1997, p. 53) for issues during the first 10 months of 1996.

32. Fabozzi notes in this regard, that, 'Although Eurobonds are typically registered on a national stock exchange, the most common being the Luxembourg, London or Zurich exchanges, the bulk of all trading is in the over-the-counter market. Listing is purely to circumvent restrictions imposed on some institutional investors who are prohibited from purchasing securities that are not listed on an exchange' (page 166).

33. See Report of Financial Market Review (1998, S.4.42 & 4.43) for mooted CTS consultations.

34. See Wardley Cards, Lai Sun Development Co Ltd, 020 (prep: March 12, 1997).

35. The guarantee in this case was provided by Shanghai Industrial Investment (Holdings) Co Ltd which held the requisite number of shares in Shanghai Industrial Holdings Ltd relating to the exchange arrangements. See Extel News for details.

36. See Deal Awards (December 1998/January 1999, pp. 50–1).

37. Brennan and Schwartz (1977) provide important contributions in both areas.

38. See Ghassemieh, Shaw, and Wilson (1997, p. 87) for a detailed example of this particular application.

39. For some specific details, See ibid. (p. 86).

12. Equity Derivatives III: Futures

For those attuned to local market conditions, Hang Seng Index (HSI) futures numbers are just as important as underlying cash numbers.[1] This reflects the prescient quality of HSI futures. A strong premium over the cash index typically arouses bullish market sentiment. Much like the shepherd who welcomes a red sky at night, a strong premium on closing HSI futures bodes well for subsequent movement in the cash-based HSI. Certainly, buying activity in the Hong Kong sector of London's SEAQ International—which opens shortly after the Hong Kong close—is likely to be spurred by such a premium. In a similar fashion, a closing discount on the futures might trigger selling.

Aside from the timely insights futures offer—essentially, in aiding predictions of subsequent price movements in the underlying—they have several other uses. First and foremost, they provide a low-cost vehicle for hedging cash-market exposure. The significant gearing rates on futures, which can be as much as 20 times, also make them a favourite of the speculator.[2] Other players, like the arbitrageur, are also attracted to the product. Arbitrageurs ensure that pricing gaps between futures and the underlying cash (or spot product) conform to acceptable levels. If, for instance, futures appear too expensive relative to the underlying cash instrument, arbitrageurs sell the futures and buy the cash market, thus setting in motion pressures that squeeze the price differential. Arbitrageurs therefore contribute to fairer pricing in the cash market. In short, they enhance the price discovery process. As we shall learn in the following, futures trading involves the interplay of hedgers, speculators, and arbitrageurs.

How does a futures contract differ from the option-based products examined in Chapters 10 and 11? In simple terms, a futures obligation is a promise to perform. Defining a futures contract as a promise to either buy or sell some underlying asset at a given price at a designated future date, highlights the essential difference. Investors in options, and related products like warrants, enjoy an entitlement or 'right' to do something—not an obligation. It should be said, though, that the writers of options commit to buy or sell (or execute cash settlement) where an option investor serves an exercise notice on them. Even so, the commitment in futures works on both sides of the contract: the buy and sell side. As we shall see later, the buyer commits to buy (or take delivery of) the underlying asset. The seller, as the buyer's counterparty, ensures this can be achieved by agreeing to sell the asset on the predetermined terms at the designated future date.

To fully appreciate futures, description of the essential mechanism and obligations enshrined in such contracts is first set out. Section 12.1 makes an inroad by sketching out their defining characteristics. Futures and forward contracts are compared, and the role of the clearing house, on a futures exchange, is also assessed given its role in ensuring counterparty compliance with the terms of their agreement. As forward contracts trade outside organized exchanges, counterparties are not afforded the protection of an exchange-based clearing house. Despite the fact that forward contracts look much like futures, this feature drives a clear demarcation line between the two. Settlement and liquidation of futures positions, and the behaviour of the basis in a futures contract—defined as the price differential between futures and underlying cash values—then figure in Sections 12.2 and 12.3. The principal local futures products are then introduced in Section 12.4 and, via worked examples, analysis of their risk-return characteristics and margin features made. Major trading strategies are then described in Sections 12.5 to 12.7.

Lastly, developments in the local futures industry, relating to products and trading and risk-management systems, are examined in Section 12.8. As we saw in Section 1.7 and Section 2.1, the events of October 1987 were a turning point, ushering in a radical programme of reform. The Hong Kong Futures Exchange's (HKFE's) status, as one of the world's premier derivatives markets, owes much to these changes. Its success in index futures also offers a blueprint for other exchanges.

12.1   Salient Characteristics of Futures

Key Terms: Settlement Price, Settlement Date, and Long and Short Positions

The two key terms in a futures contract are the futures (or settlement) price and the settlement date. The latter is the date at which the commitment must be carried out or 'settled' and the former the agreed price of settlement. Every contract clearly has a buyer and a seller. The buyer is said to be in a long position and the seller a short position. The positions, though briefly introduced earlier, are summarized as follows: when buying a futures contract, one is said to be in a long position. This entails a commitment to buy (or take delivery of) the underlying asset at the agreed settlement price on a designated futures date. The opposite applies to the seller who, deemed to be in a short position, commits to sell (or deliver) the underlying at the agreed terms.

The very essence of a futures agreement means that positions are set up without an initial transfer of funds between buyer and seller. Instead, the agreed price—the settlement/futures price—is paid at the expiry or settlement date in the contract. The initial cost of constructing a position, for either buyer or seller, therefore appears negligible, with the bulk of these costs likely to be made up of brokerage commission. A fractional amount of the settlement/futures price, known as margin, has to be placed on deposit, however, when opening a futures position. While satisfactory completion of the terms of the futures agreement leads to return of this deposit, interest on the deposit may not be forthcoming. The significance of margin is returned to in later discussions. Suffice it to say, that margin deposits, which may be somewhere between 5% and 20% of a contract's value, allow for considerable leverage.

Membership Firms and Client Accounts

As futures are always exchange-traded, all transactions must be struck through members of the appropriate exchange. Members as licensees of an exchange trade as a principal (for themselves) or as an agent for a client. The latter is probably more typical. Members offering this brokerage function vouch for the creditworthiness of their trading clients. They also take responsibility for their financial integrity (as does the client with the member). This, as the market crisis of October 1987 reminds us, can result in losses for member firms. As these losses represent the profits of other counterparties (or member firms), trading privileges may be suspended until such losses are made good.

Profits and Losses on Futures Positions

Futures provide what the economists would know as a zero-sum game. The profit to one party is the loss to the counterparty, as the example presented below in Exhibit 12.1 aptly illustrates. It also shows the essential mechanism of a futures contract.

Exhibit 12.1   Case Study of the Profits and Losses to Counterparties in a Futures Contracts

> Suppose a futures contract is written on asset ABC where the settlement (futures) price is $10 and delivery is in one month's time (Party B buys this contract, party S sells it).
>
> Suppose, in one month's time the price of ABC is $15. B therefore purchases asset ABC from S for $10 and realizes a profit of $5 if he/she immediately sells ABC in the cash market (an unrealized profit of $5 is apparent otherwise). In contrast, S buys asset ABC in the cash market (assuming a 'naked' position) for $15 and sells it to B through the futures contract for $10, thus incurring a loss of $5.

As transaction costs in futures trades are normally a trivial proportion of contract value, they are ignored in Exhibit 12.1. The example demonstrates that the buyer of the futures contract gains when the cash value of the underlying rises above the agreed settlement (or futures) price. The seller loses under such circumstances.

The zero-sum outcome is contingent on one issue: both parties keeping their side of the bargain. What would happen if S failed to deliver asset ABC to B? To begin with, B would not be able to realize the paper profit on the position of $5 and S, the delinquent party, would seemingly have escaped his/her obligation (and loss). In the first instance, the member firm of the defaulting client would be called upon to make immediate payment to cover the loss. Failure to comply could result in the clearing house of the appropriate exchange suspending the trading privileges of S's member firm and, if the debt remains outstanding, taking over its whole trading position. This would entail payment of B's profit in the form of cash, or the delivery of asset ABC at the agreed settlement price to B's member firm. This captures novation: the clearing house's commitment to guarantee profits on (members') positions. Subsequent recompense would then be sought by the clearing house against the defaulting member firm. Where the member of the defaulting client wishes to avoid such sanctions, as is likely, payment of the loss will be made and legal recompense against the defaulting client subsequently sought.

There is one complication to the example in Exhibit 12.1. Clearing houses of futures exchanges typically promise to novate the net position of their members (and not the individual positions of members' clients). As long as B's member firm is in profit on its net client position, a clearing house's guarantee holds. If B, however, were a client in a member firm showing a loss on its net client position, B might fall outside such guarantee provisions,[3] in which case B would need to deal directly with his/her own member firm. This issue is examined in much greater detail in Section 12.8 with specific reference to the October 1987 episode. Client defaults on long HSI futures positions at this time forced approximately one-third of the HKFE's membership to be suspended.[4]

The Principles of Margin

Thus far, the margin deposit placed by parties to a futures contract has been ignored. Its purpose, as the following will show, is to protect member firms and, in turn, the clearing house against client defaults. If a margin of 20% were required to open the futures position on ABC in Exhibit 12.1, B and S would have placed $2 with their brokers at the commencement of their futures position. The respective member firms would then ensure that this payment is made available to the appropriate exchange's clearing house. This means that the net amount of margin collected on all client accounts should be sufficient to cover monies despatched into a clearing house account for that member.

A subsequent default by S would, as suggested above, result in S's initial margin being used to reduce the arrears. Where physical delivery is mandated, the default might entail the clearing house buying asset ABC through the cash market for $15 and selling it to B for $10, to ensure contract fulfilment. Events, as noted earlier, would then lead to the $5 loss incurred by the clearing house being reimbursed by S's member firm. This would occur as a payment from the member firm's margin balance at the clearing house, leaving the member firm with arrears of $3.

Additional margin payments are also required by clients where unrealized paper losses accumulate, offering additional protection to members. In general, members are responsible for the maintenance of margin on all positions undertaken by their clients. Unlike margin placed for stock trading, margin payments placed for futures can be returned to the client if the client realizes a profit on his/her position. In the case of stock trading, the margin is paid off once an investor's position is liquidated. The process of 'marking-to-market' is much the same for both stock and futures however (but may vary from exchange to exchange).

As always, the beauty of margin is the leverage it offers. The downside is that losses on futures can accumulate well in excess of the initial margin placed, which can be appreciated by examining the return profiles of short and long positions in futures. These are shown in Figure 12.1, using the futures/settlement price of $10 for commodity ABC, featured in Exhibit 12.1. The profiles highlight the inherent risk of futures trading, with returns unlimited both on the upside and downside.[5] Comparison with earlier profiles for options and warrants reveals that while writers of 'naked' options and derivative warrants suffer unlimited downside risk, the loss to the investor is always 'capped'. Futures positions, like uncovered short positions in options and warrants, are not, therefore, for the faint-hearted. Where futures are used to hedge an underlying cash position, the issue is rather different, as seen in Section 12.5.

Commodity Futures vs. Financial Futures

Thus far, we have assumed physical delivery of the underlying at the settlement point in a futures contract. This is the essential characteristic of

Figure 12.1   Comparison of Profit Profiles for Long and Short Positions in Futures

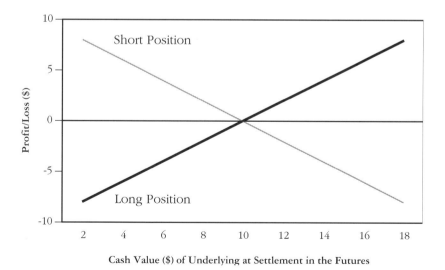

Long & Short Futures/Settlement Price = $10 (profiles constructed using futures on asset ABC, as featured in Exhibit 12.1)

commodity futures which, until the early 1970s, were the principal futures trading vehicle. These basically relate to contracts on metals, petroleum, and agricultural produce. The development of financial futures in the last twenty years or so has meant that vast numbers of contracts exist without physical delivery of the underlying. Stock index futures, interest rate futures, Treasury Bond futures, and currency futures are good examples. The cash settlement terms used on such contracts, relating to the payment or receipt of the gross profit on each position, are a necessity in futures on stock indices. The cost and effort required in assembling the underlying would clearly make physical delivery untenable. Imagine having to construct the S&P 500 contract.

Basically, most of what has been said so far applies without qualification to cash-settled, financial futures contracts. To see this, let us modify Exhibit 12.1 by changing the underlying commodity ABC to a financial asset. The cash-based settlement feature of financial futures would mean that B's profit of $5 would require a cash payment of the same from S. As no physical delivery is required, the settlement process is, in theory, much simpler. In a commodity futures contract, the buyer and seller face some liquidity risk: the selling party has to buy the asset in order to deliver it to the buying party and the buyer, in turn, has to sell the asset in the cash market to realize a profit. Other than this, all of the features described in the foregoing, like the principles of novation, margin, and the zero-sum nature of futures trading, apply with little qualification.

Futures and Forward contracts

To the casual observer, forwards and futures appear indistinguishable. Both, for instance, have the same essential features: fixed settlement prices and dates. The mechanisms for realizing profit also appear to be much the same; however, as we have seen in earlier chapters, forwards are not exchange-traded. At one level, this allows investors to trade in forwards on their own account, instead of through the registered member firms of an exchange. At another level, the novation feature apparent in futures does not apply.

A final characteristic of the forward is that, unlike a futures contract, its terms are rarely standardized. In particular the quality and composition of the underlying asset, settlement dates, and settlement prices are subject to private negotiation between buyer and seller. As a rule, the standardized features of futures makes them considerably more liquid than similar forward contracts. Consequently, commitments in futures can be unwound by taking offsetting positions in the same contract. This often happens if a trader sees a paper profit on a position or wishes to 'cap' a paper loss. The principles relating to such offsetting trades are set out in Section 12.2. These principles are critical to an appreciation of futures as many traders, particularly in financial futures like HSI futures, engage in 'day-trading' where positions are routinely offset. This may occur within minutes of a position being opened.

12.2 The Liquidation of Futures Contracts

To illustrate how an investor might offset or liquidate outstanding futures positions, the example in Exhibit 12.2 is considered.

Exhibit 12.2

Suppose that December 200x futures contracts on a Troy Ounce of Gold first became available, on a recognized exchange, on 1 September 200x with a settlement date prescribed as the penultimate business day—30 December 200x—of the settlement month. Suppose that the following settlement/futures prices obtain on the contract between 20 September and 23 September 200x.

	Closing settlement/futures prices (US$)
20 Sept 200x	301
21 Sept 200x	297
22 Sept 200x	299
23 Sept 200x	292

Suppose further that the initial margin requirement on the futures contract is 10% of its contract value and that transaction costs are negligible.

Consider an investor selling one contract on 20 September and subsequently offsetting this position by buying one contract on 23 September. Margin of $30.10 (i.e., 10% of $301) would have initially been placed (and returned after the offsetting trade on 23 September).

What is the investor's exposure in the above offsetting trade? Two positions, with two offsetting promises or commitments, are held. These guarantee a profit of $9 at the settlement date of 30 December 200x. How do we know this? Suppose that the cash price of gold on 30 December turns out to be $320. This would result in a loss on the short position of $19, given a commitment to sell gold for $301, and a profit on the long position of $28, given a commitment to buy gold at settlement at $292. Overall this translates to a net gain of $9. Assuming physical delivery, this would mean buying one Troy ounce of gold at $292 and selling the same for $301. Whatever cash price is evident at the settlement date, the net profit is always the same: $9. This process does not negate the promissory nature of futures. The offsetting nature of the promises simply extinguishes all market exposure.

When will the investor, in the example described in Exhibit 12.2, realize the $9 profit? This depends upon the settlement terms. If, as with most commodity futures, physical settlement is required, the $9 profit would only be realized at settlement. This would involve buying a troy ounce of gold, through the long position, for $292 and simultaneously selling the same for $301, through the short positions. Cash settlement makes things considerably easier as it allows member firms to credit the guaranteed profit, associated with the offset, to client accounts shortly after the actual offset has occurred. In time-value-of-money terms, there is an obvious advantage to cash settlement.

To illustrate the liquidation or offsetting principle further, let us consider a further example. Using the data in Exhibit 12.2 as before, suppose one long position is opened on 21 September 200x for a settlement price of $297. By the close of the following day, the investor might be tempted to offset this position given an increase in the contract's futures price. By shorting the contract at the new futures price of $299 he/she could lock in a gain of $2. Again, whatever the cash value for the underlying at settlement, the return is always the same. For physical settlement, this translates to a commitment to simultaneously buy gold for $297 and sell it for $299 at the settlement date of 30 December 200x.

Contract Liquidation and Open Interest

The level of open interest in a futures contract has much the same meaning as described for options in Chapter 10, Exhibit 10.2. It captures the number of unliquidated (or 'live') long or short positions outstanding. To illustrate, consider trades executed through three member firms—A, B, and C— across three days of trading: $t = 1$, $t = 2$, and $t = 3$. Suppose that on $t = 1$, A buys three contracts from B; on $t = 2$, C buys three contracts from A; and on $t = 3$, A buys three contracts from B. The volume on each day is clearly three contracts. The open interest levels are 3, 3, and 6 on each respective day, as shown in Exhibit 12.3.

Exhibit 12.3 An Illustration of the Concept of Open Interest When Applied to Futures

Investor	Day:	$t = 1$	OI	$t = 2$	OI	$t = 3$	OI
A		3l	3l	3s	0	3l	3l
B		3s	3s	–	3s	3s	6s
C		–	0	3l	3l	–	3l
Volume (no. of contracts)		3		3		3	
Open Interest (no. of contracts)			3		3		6

As Exhibit 12.3 shows, the liquidation of A's long client position on t=2 removes open interest on this member account to zero. As B still has three outstanding short positions and C now has three long positions, open interest remains at three positions for t=2. Its level rises to six contracts on t=3, despite the liquidation of A's client position, due to three outstanding long positions for C and three new long ones for A.

In general, a build-up of 'live' positions is likely in the initial phase of a contract's life followed by a series of offsetting transactions as settlement nears, the net effect being an inverted U-shape in the number of outstanding positions. This is captured in Figure 12.2 for the HKFE's June 1998 HSI futures contract for trades between 2 March and 29 June 1998.

Figure 12.2   The Behaviour of Open Interest in Financial Futures: June
1998 HSI Futures

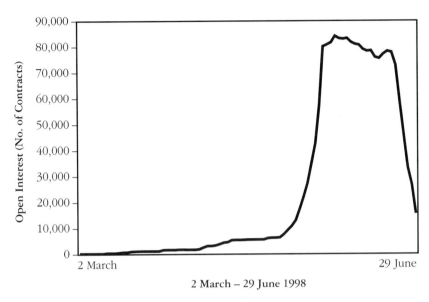

2 March – 29 June 1998

Closing Open Interest Levels, 2 March – 29 June 1998
Source of Data: HKFE

The tail-off in open interest, as expiry nears, may not be as dramatic as
portrayed in Figure 12.2 for commodity futures. Many farmers take positions
in commodity futures simply to guarantee the sales price of their produce.
A farmer selling coffee in South America, with an anticipated harvest date
in January, might want to lock in the sales price of his produce by selling
a certain number of January coffee futures. As long as the produce is
available at the settlement date in the futures, all price risk would be
eliminated. The important point, in relation to open interest, is that the
position remains open all the way to settlement.

It is conceivable that farmers, facing uncertainty over the precise harvest
date in their crop, might elect to short futures with more distant settlement
dates. This situation is considered in Section 12.5. We will see that where
the crop becomes available prior to the settlement date, the farmer is able
to hedge his/her cash position by offsetting the short position. Where this
occurs, the farmer's open interest is extinguished prior to settlement.

12.3 The Basis in a Futures Contract

The futures/settlement price is likely to differ from the cash price of the
underlying at any time prior to the settlement date. In general terms, the
longer the time remaining until settlement, the greater the possible disparity

between futures and cash prices. This difference is known as the basis. It is typically reported as futures price less cash price. All other things being equal, it should converge to zero as settlement nears.

The 'Cost-of-Carry' Relationship

The basis for a financial futures contract behaves in a slightly different manner to that on a commodity futures contracts. As virtually all local contracts are of the former type, the basis relation in financial futures is considered first. Finance academics and practitioners depict this relation using the following 'cost-of-carry' model,

$$F_t = C_t \times (1 + r - d)^T \tag{1}$$

where F_t is the price of a futures contract at time t; C_t is the cash market value of the underlying ; r is the annualized cost of borrowing; d is the annualized dividend yield on the underlying; and T is the time remaining to settlement in the futures contract.

In continuously compounded form, the above is often written as,

$$F_t = C_t \times e^{(r - d) \times T}$$

where e is the exponential function, and dividends and interest are paid on a continual basis throughout the year (see Cornell and French (1983b, p. 4), for instance, for presentation of the above form[6]).

The theoretical futures price determined in (1) is deemed to be an equilibrium or arbitrage-free price. It holds in conditions where transaction costs and all frictions, like restrictions on short-selling, are absent. Other assumptions, like dividends on the underlying being known (and therefore riskless), lending and borrowing rates being equal and short stock positions being attainable at zero cost, are also reflected in (1). This all means that (1) is an approximation to reality; although the same could be said of virtually any model in finance. The result in (1) is illustrated in Exhibit 12.4.

The arbitrage strategy in (b) is self-financing because the the stock purchased through the the futures contract is used to repay the stock borrower.

Only where the futures price approximates to $101 in Exhibit 12.4, do such arbitrage opportunities disappear.[8] As both of the above strategies yield riskless profits, departures from F's $101 value represent disequilibrium. However, as arbitrage opportunities are always limited by transaction costs, some deviation from (1) is inevitable.[9] Short-sellers of stock, for instance, face borrowing costs. In (b) of Exhibit 12.4 these are not taken into account (as one would expect given the perfect markets assumption underpinning the 'Cost-of-Carry' Model). While the stock lender is in fact compensated for dividends foregone, no interest charge is apparent

Exhibit 12.4 An Illustration of The 'Cost-of-Carry' Model

An asset ABC has a current cash price (C) of $100 and pays dividends of $5 per year, payable in two equal instalments, the first of which is in six months' time. Assume that the riskless cost of borrowing (r) is 7% per annum. Based upon (1), the futures price F on a contract with six months to settlement (i.e., T = 0.5) should be $100.995.[7]

To demonstrate the arbitrage nature of (1), let us assume that the futures market for asset ABC is in a disequilibrium state.

(a) Suppose F = $103. This being so, the following strategy becomes optimal: sell futures for F = $103; purchase ABC for $100 by borrowing for 6 months at the riskless rate of interest. This strategy is not only self-financing but also yields a riskless cash profit of $2 in 6 months' time, as shown below.

	Cash flows ($)	
	t = 0	t = 0.5
Borrowing	100	(100)
Purchase of ABC	(100)	–
Interest	–	(3.50)
Dividends on ABC	–	2.50
Futures Receipts	–	103
Net Balance	$0	$2

(b) Suppose instead F = $99. The following strategy would have been optimal: buy futures for F = $99; short ABC for $100 and invest proceeds for six months. Again, this strategy is self-financing and returns an arbitrage cash profit in six months' time [see notes 10, 11].

	Cash flows ($)	
	t = 0	t = 0.5
Stock Sale Receipts	100	–
Interest	–	3.50
Dividends on ABC	–	(2.50)
Futures Payments	–	(99)
Net Balance	$100	(98)

on the stock lending arrangement. In reality, collateral, representing the value of the borrowed stock (105% of the value, in the case of Hong Kong), will be placed with the lender's broker. As such, either the returns on the collateral will be retained by the stock lender, or a separate interest charge levied. Whichever obtains, the arbitrage gain in (b) will be adversely affected.[10, 11]

Empirical Evidence in Relation to the 'Cost-of-Carry' Model

For Hong Kong, a study by Yau, Schneeweis, and Yung (1990) indicates that, after accounting for transaction costs, the disparity between actual and theoretical HSI futures prices is minimal. They reach this conclusion using daily data between May 1986 and December 1988, and assessing theoretical futures prices in terms of the continuously compounded form of (1). They also note fewer instances of mispricing after the 1987 crash with less than 5% of their data points exhibiting mispricing levels in excess of transaction costs.

Fung and Fung (1997) also offer some evidence of mispricing when using intra-day data between April 1993 and May 1995. Their study is a little different to Yau et al.'s (1990) though, as they test arbitrage between HSI options and HSI futures. This was clearly not possible in Yau et al.'s study as HSI options were still on the drawing board at the time of their study. As such, the arbitrage form tested in Fung and Fung (1997, p. 39) is a variant of the 'Cost-of-Carry' Model (1) referred to in most other studies of the arbitrage process. For reasons of brevity this is not introduced here. Nonetheless, they note that, 'Eliminating or accounting for most factors that affect the traditional efficiency of derivative markets (tracking error, uncertain dividend payout, the tax timing option, transaction costs, differential rates of borrowing and lending), we can still find some mispricing, although it is not economically significant' (p. 44, parentheses shown as used).

Anecdotal evidence indicates that the basis in many financial futures is quite variable, even over short time periods. Dividend yields in Hong Kong in recent years, of around 3% to 4%, and relatively high interest rates, suggest conditions under which locally-based financial futures would have traded at premiums to cash-market prices. Accepting deposit rates as the interest rate (r) in the 'Cost-of-Carry' Model, suggests a substantial positive (r − d) carry of around 200 basis points for much of the 90s (see Section 12.8). Cursory inspection of recent HSI futures prices in Hong Kong, as shown in Figure 12.3, suggests otherwise. Both the direction and absolute size of the basis are clearly subject to considerable variation. While most of this would probably occur within bounds set by transaction costs, transaction costs alone allow for considerable movement in the basis. Notwithstanding this, the basis behaves in accordance with theory in one important respect: it typically converges to zero as settlement approaches. As shown in Figure 12.3 this translates to a reduction in the size and volatility of basis movements as settlement nears.

A small amount of basis may still be evident at settlement, however, as shown in Figure 12.3. This reflects the practice of using some average of cash prices to determine the final settlement price. In the case of HSI futures, quotations from the HSI cash market (i.e. the SEHK) are taken at five-minute intervals during SEHK trading hours on the penultimate business day (last trading day) of the contract month.[12] These are then averaged to determine the final settlement price in the contract. This accounts for the slight deviation between the closing cash price (i.e., the HSI at the close of 29 June 1998) and the final settlement price in Figure 12.3. Were the final settlement price to be determined solely on a closing price, as is done in some financial futures, the basis would be zero.[13]

Figure 12.3   The Behaviour of the Basis in Financial Futures

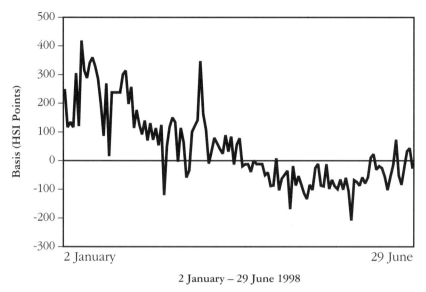

JUNE 1998 HSI FUTURES: FUTURES PRICES—CASH HSI PRICES

2 January – 29 June 1998

Source of Data: Closing Daily HSI ('Cash' Market) Values were provided by HSI Services Ltd and Closing Daily Futures/Settlement Prices for June 1998 HSI Futures by the HKFE

The Basis in Commodity Futures

For commodity futures, which involve physical delivery of the underlying, one typically observes a positive basis at any time prior to settlement. Most commentators note that this premium results from storage, insurance, and other inconvenience costs associated with holding a cash position in the underlying. To illustrate, suppose that we have a commitment to sell a commodity C in exactly one month's time. One way of guaranteeing the sales price on C is to short a futures contract on C with the appropriate settlement date. Given various holding costs, one would expect the cash value of C to be at a discount to the futures/settlement price. Basically, investors will only suffer the inconvenience and holding costs associated with C if its cash price provides due compensation for this. Ideally, this discount should at least cover the 'out-of-pocket' holding and inconvenience costs of the commodity. For futures on such commodities, the relation in (2) is commonly cited.

$$F_t = C_t \times (1 + (r + s) - d)^T \qquad (2)$$

where all terms are as in (1) and S represents the annual cost of carry of the underlying as a percentage of C_t.

Intuitively, this is a straightforward modification of (1) where holding costs are simply added to interest rate costs. The arbitrage principles for financial futures would also apply as in earlier examples, albeit with r + s replacing r. As many commodities fail to generate income, d is often treated as zero in the above.[14]

The combined effect of interest and carrying costs therefore explains why most commodity futures, with some time to settlement, trade with a positive basis. Although, as with financial futures, this basis should converge to zero as settlement nears.

The Terms Backwardation, Contango and 'Normal Backwardation' and their Relation to the Basis

As far back as Keynes (1930, pp. 142–4), the term backwardation was used to describe negative basis on a forward or futures contract. The opposite, a premium of futures (or forward) prices over cash, was known as a contango. Contemporary usage of the terms has altered somewhat with many now using backwardation (contango) to describe a negative (positive) carry relation when rolling over futures positions. Such roll-overs are examined in greater detail in Section 12.8. In brief, a negative carry or backwardation, in the contemporary sense of the term, captures a situation where futures prices on near-term contracts are at a premium to distant month prices.[15] This benefits investors long in the spot or near-month contract since such an investor is able to re-establish his/her long position at a discount to the sale (liquidation) of his/her spot position.

Where roll-overs are executed close to spot-month expiry, the original and latter-day meanings of backwardation are equivalent as spot-month futures prices should approximate to underlying cash values. A lower futures price on a more distant contract therefore suggests negative basis on that contract. Where roll-overs are consummated well ahead of the spot's expiry, the situation may be rather different: more distant-month prices could be lower but both spot and distant-month prices could still be at a premium to the cash market.

What about normal backwardation? This term still retains the meaning given to it in the seminal works of Keynes (1930, pp. 144) and, later, Hicks (1946). It exists if (i) futures prices offer a downwardly biased expectation of the cash price; and (ii) the bias widens with time to futures expiry. In this sense then, normal backwardation, captures something more than a negative basis in futures prices. The bias in the story of normal backwardation, as conceived in Keynes, stems from the differing risk attitudes of speculators and hedgers. According to Keynes, speculators gravitate toward long futures positions; hedgers do the opposite. In his story, hedgers have greater need to enter the market. In Keynes's day, most of the hedgers would have been farmers wanting to lock in the sales price of their anticipated harvest. Speculators, with less need to enter the market, know that without their participation, the hedger cannot trade futures. They are also assumed to be risk averse in Keynes's story. For hedgers to entice speculators to trade, then, some premium must be offered. In this account, this amounts to a reduction in the futures price below its 'fair' or expected value. Hedgers therefore have to short contracts at a lower price than they would ordinarily prefer. Speculators have the comfort of being able to buy the underlying at some future date on terms that offer an expected discount to the price at settlement. Why do the hedgers trade on such terms? Without the cooperation of the speculator they would clearly be in a worse position. In this story, then, normal backwardation not only presupposes something about the directional trades of speculators and hedgers, it also tells us that speculators call the tune.

Backwardation and contango, whether in original or contemporary guises, are relatively straightforward to assess empirically. Testing normal backwardation is much less so. Despite this, various attempts have been made to assess its validity. The evidence to date appears very mixed. The testing procedure is complicated by the fact that the assumed 'risk premium' for speculators must be just that and not a reflection of any superior information. As eloquently argued in Chang's (1986) detailed examination of normal backwardation for a variety of agricultural commodity futures: 'A test of the theory of normal backwardation is not based on whether the market ever provided speculators with profits in any periods; instead it is based on whether or not a risk premium is systematically (in the statistical sense) rewarded to naive speculators . . .' (p. 195–6, parentheses as shown).

Chang (1986) also notes that the assumptions implicit in normal backwardation necessitate 'a rise, on the average, of futures prices during the life of each contract' (p. 194). As strong evidence of this was provided, Chang concluded in favour of normal backwardation for the futures scrutinized in his study.[16] Subsequent studies, like Kolb's (1992) of 29 commodity futures markets, suggest widespread departures from normal backwardation and that normal backwardation may be both time- and product-specific. In summarizing his findings, he notes that: 'In general, the results . . . show that normal backwardation is not normal—only a few commodities show prices that rise over the life of the futures contract. However, some commodities exhibit normal backwardation very strongly' (Kolb, 1992, p. 76).

12.4 The use of Margin in Futures Contracts

As we noted earlier, whenever investors open a position in a futures contract, they are required to place initial margin (= fixed % of contract value) with their member (brokerage) firm. Payments made to the client's brokerage account can then be made available to the clearing house to cover possible arrears on positions.

Once a position has been opened, maintenance margin requirements also apply. As the maintenance margin levels may differ from initial margin levels, variation margin adjustments are likely as futures prices change. To help illustrate this, an example using the most actively traded futures contract in Hong Kong, the HSI futures contract, is constructed, and shown in Exhibit 12.5. Before appreciating the effects of margin though, some consideration of the features of the HSI contract are required.

'Marking-to-Market' of Positions: The Case of the HKFE's HSI Futures Contract

Running on the heels of stock index futures developments in the United States, the HKFE introduced its own index futures—the HSI futures contract—in May 1986. The underlying, as we know from earlier discussions, is a value-weighted index based on 33 of the local market's most actively traded stocks.

Four contract months are always available with settlement always on cash terms. Settlement occurs on the last business day of the contract month with trading possible right up to the penultimate business day. As the HKFE requires that contracts be available for the current (spot) month, next calendar month, and subsequent two quarter months[17], HSI futures for the months of January, February, March, and June would be available during January of any year. By February, the February contract would take on the mantle of spot month contract. In addition to the existing March and June contracts, a September contract would be added to replace the lapsed January contract. By March, contracts for March, June, and September would remain with an April contract introduced to replace February. Similar logic would apply to subsequent months to ensure the defined sequence of spot, next month, and subsequent two calendar month contracts is maintained.

Whatever the contract month, HSI futures have a contract value equal to their quoted settlement/futures price multiplied by HK$50. To illustrate the operation of HSI futures and the margin, spot-month futures contracts for March 1995 are considered in Exhibit 12.5.

For both the short (S) and long (L) investor the same initial margin must be placed to record one 'open' position. If three contracts were either shorted or purchased, HK$135,000 would therefore need to be placed by each investor (see note 18). Comparisons with contract value— equal to HK$432,450 when the contracts were opened as of 20 March 1995—suggest leverage of nearly ten times.

After establishing initial margin, subsequent debit and credit entries are made to the accounts to record the investor's accumulated profit or loss on his/her position. We assume, for means of the illustration in Exhibit 12.5, that this was done shortly after the close of trading on each day. This reflects inter-day 'marking-to-market'. Increasingly, more and more exchanges are demanding that their members 'mark-to-market' client accounts on an intra-day basis. This might involve debits and credits being recorded at the end of morning and afternoon sessions.

The 'marking-to-market' illustrated in Exhibit 12.5 is of the inter-day variety. As of the close of 21 March, it is apparent that investor S has accumulated a paper gain to the detriment of the counterparty, L. The

Exhibit 12.5 An Illustration of Margin for HSI Futures Contracts

Consider a long and short position held between 20 March, 1995 (close) and liquidated (offset) at the close of trading on 24 March 1995 in March HSI Futures. Suppose the initial margin per HSI futures 'open' position was HK$45,000 and the maintenance margin HK$36,000.[18] Based upon this, the margin accounts for the long and short investor would face the following credit (positive) and debit (negative) entries at the end of each trading day.

	Settlement Price	Long (L) Investor's Margin	Short (S) Investor's Margin
Mon., 20 Mar 1995	8,649	45,000	45,000
Tues., 21 Mar 1995	8,610	(1,950)	1,950
Wed., 22 Mar 1995	8,515	(4,750)	4,750
Thu., 23 Mar 1995	8,502	(650)	650
Frid., 24 Mar 1995	8,515	650	(650)

See Hang Seng Index Futures: market Review for March 1995 for closing prices. This is a simplified illustration only.

gain (loss) to S (L) is 39 points. At HK$50 per point per contract, this leads to S's account being credited with HK$1,950 and L's debited with the same. The 95-point change in the futures price of the contract between the close of the 21 and 22 March again leads to paper gains for S and losses to L. This entails a credit of HK$4,750 to S's account and a debit of the same to L's. As long as the positions remain 'open', this daily adjustment to the margin account will continue. The sum of these adjustments reflects each investor's accumulated profit or loss and allows the investor and member firm to be aware of possible profits or losses in the event of liquidation. As illustrated earlier, where a client defaults on a loss in excess of his/her outstanding margin balance, the risk is borne by the client's member firm.

Suppose that the positions were offset just prior to the close of trading on 24 March. This would involve L selling one February HSI futures contract and S buying one contract. The balance of debit and credit adjustments to each investor's margin account would then indicate the gross profit or loss realized on each position. Investor S would obviously be the winner, realising a gain of HK$6,700 (= (8,649 − 8,515) × HK$50). As reflected in Exhibit 12.5, this is the balance of the margin adjustments (= HK$(1,950 + 4,750 + 650 − 650)). The same, of course, is true for L where a gross loss of HK$6,700 is evident. The profit for S would meet with a cash payment from the HKFE's clearing house with L's loss, in turn, being paid from his/her margin balance to the clearing house. In this sense, S receives the cash profit plus the return of all the initial margin if he/she so requires. For L, only HK$38,300 of the initial margin can be returned. This is not the whole story, however, as both parties would have incurred some transaction costs in opening and liquidating their positions. While detailed account of these is not made here, anecdotal evidence suggests that inclusion of these would lead to a marginal reduction in S's overall profit (and a marginal increase in L's loss).

Interestingly, with maintenance margin levels at HK$36,000 per contract, at the time of the example, neither L nor S would have suffered losses sufficient to mandate margin calls. Had the futures price fallen to 8,468 points, instead of 8,515 points, on 22 March though, a margin call would have been triggered on L's account. The accumulated paper loss at this point would have been HK$9,050 (= 181 points @ HK$50 per point) for L. An additional payment of HK$50 would have been required, had L not taken steps to extinguish his/her open position (see note 18).

It is also possible for investors to remove sums in excess of the maintenance margin level, though in practice a sufficient buffer of funds might be left to avoid the risk and inconvenience of subsequent margin calls. Margin calls, when they occur, normally require immediate electronic payment. In a number of markets, failure to meet such calls would lead to immediate liquidation of accounts by the client's brokerage firm. These and other provisions would be spelled out in margin account agreements between member firm and client.

12.5 Hedging with Futures

The illustrations thus far primarily concern ways in which futures can be used to derive speculative profit. Long positions are constructed where an investor is bullish about the underlying and short positions where the opposite applies. This being so, a futures trade between speculators can only occur where the two traders have diametrically opposite views about the value of the underlying. Not all trades are speculative though, as many investors buy and sell for hedging purposes. It is this hedging function that accounts for the volumes in many futures contracts, as Keynes (1930) appreciated in his account of 'normal' backwardation.

For instance, where market sentiment for the underlying is generally bullish, very few investors are likely to want to short futures for speculative reasons (unless their expectations or beliefs are radically different to the majority). Hedgers, as recognized earlier, might be willing counterparties if they have a commitment to sell the underlying at some future date or a desire to lock in returns on a long cash position. In either case, futures would feature as a short hedge. Hedgers therefore add a very important component to liquidity. One can see this when comparing volumes in cash and futures markets. When cash markets are subject to strong negative sentiment, volumes often dry up with very few buyers evident in the market. In contrast, futures on the underlying might still trade actively. This reflects hedgers wishing to buy to hedge short cash positions (or established future commitments to buy the underlying) and speculators wishing to short futures. The marriage of such long hedge positions with speculators desire to sell keeps volumes flowing.

Concrete examples of both types of hedge are highlighted in Exhibit 12.6 and 12.7 in the following.

The Long Hedge

As noted above, investors with short cash positions or established future commitments to buy an underlying asset face the risk of an increase in the value of the underlying. To hedge this risk, an appropriate number of futures on the underlying can be acquired. Exhibit 12.6 provides an illustration in relation to an established commitment to buy stock at a designated future date.

Exhibit 12.6 A Case Study of a Long Hedge

Suppose that you are required to buy a portfolio of stock ($PORT_S$) at the upcoming December year-end, which is three months from now. The portfolio is currently worth $10m and has an overall β of 1.25. Assume that IDX futures serve as the hedging tool and that the futures price on the December contract is currently 8,000 points ($25 per point) and is equal to the cash value of the IDX (i.e., the basis of the contract is currently zero).

In relation to $PORT_S$, the IDX has β of 1. Therefore, a 1% rise (fall) in the IDX should translate into a 1.25% increase (decrease) in the value of $PORT_S$.[19]

The number of IDX futures contracts required to hedge the proposed purchase of $PORT_S$ = 1.25 × $10 million/$0.2 million ($0.2 million is the contract value of IDX futures (= 8,000 × $25)) = 62.50 contracts (The investor should therefore long 62 IDX futures contracts.)

(a) Suppose that at settlement on 30 December 200x, the IDX is at 7,500 points:
Profit on the hedge = 62 × (7,500 − 8,000)*$25 = −$0.775 million

The profit on the cash market position (where a 6.25% change in the IDX, suggests a 7.8125% decrease in $PORT_S$) = $(10 million − 9.21875 million) = +$0.78125 million
Overall Gain = +$0.00625 million

(b) Suppose that at settlement on 30 December 200x, the IDX is at 8,500 points:
Profit (loss) on the hedge = 62 × (8,500 − 8,000)*$25 = +$0.775 million

The profit on the long cash market position (where a 6.25% change in the IDX, suggests a 7.8125% increase in $PORT_S$) = $(10 million − 10.78125 million) = -$0.78125 million
Overall Gain = -$0.00625 million

If scenario (a) were to emerge, we might rue our bad luck in deciding to hedge. Sometimes it may be better not to hedge. Various examples illustrate this situation. One of the most well known being the case of Kashima Oil, a Japanese importer of oil, which, during the 1980s, bought US dollars forward to lock in the rate of exchange for USD oil imports.[20] The significant appreciation in the yen during the 1980s and 1990s meant that Kashima were eventually forced to use more yen than would otherwise have been the case. To say that this is bad luck misses the point though. The whole point of hedging, as we argued earlier with warrants (see Section 11.4), is to lock in returns to a narrow range of definable outcomes. One cost of doing this, is that upside gains on the underlying are necessarily sacrificed. The object is to eliminate downside risk. The case in Exhibit 12.6 demonstrates how this can be achieved.

Why are we unable to generate a perfect hedge in the example in Exhibit 12.6? The principal reason is that the number of contracts for a perfect hedge is 62.50 and only discrete numbers of contracts can be traded. The hedge is also evaluated assuming the β on the underlying portfolio is stable at 1.25. If this changes, the hedging strategy may not be quite as effective as suggested. In reality, a perfect hedge is something that can only be aspired to. The construction of an effective hedge, which 'lock in' returns to a narrow band of values, is the goal.

The Short Hedge

Hedging a long cash market position with futures requires construction of a short hedge. This helps safeguard against a fall in the future price of the underlying asset. To illustrate, suppose a fund manager holds an HSI fund and is evaluated on his/her performance over a calendar year. Suppose the fund manager's annual target is 20% and, as of early October, this goal has been met. If the manager feels that the HSI may fall in value between October and December, either liquidation of the portfolio or a hedging strategy would be recommended. Normally, the former is preferred. It is cheaper to arrange. However, the fund manager runs a designated portfolio. He is therefore obligated to hold the portfolio and should hedge his/her exposure. Exhibit 12.7 illustrates how this might work.

Short hedges are also commonly used by farmers, as noted earlier. The perennial problem for any farmer is to try to estimate the likely market price of his/her produce at harvest. This price hinges upon the global supply of the product at the time of the harvest. If climatic conditions are good and supply is high (low), produce prices will be low (high). To insure against a lower than expected price, the farmer could short futures contracts on the underlying. To add definition to this point, a numerical example is shown in Exhibit 12.8.

As noted earlier, it may be difficult to match futures settlement with the intended selling date in the underlying cash position. In such cases, a longer-dated futures contract should be shorted and offset by a long

Exhibit 12.7 A Case Study of a Short Hedge

Suppose the value of the HSI portfolio is HK$4 million and the December HSI futures contract has a futures price of 12,500 points (contract value = 12,500 × HK$50 = HK$625,000). Assume that the basis on this contract is zero as of early October. To hedge his/her portfolio, the fund manager should sell 6.4 contracts (= HK$4 million/HK$0.625 million). As only discrete numbers of contracts can be sold, 6 should be shorted.

(a) Suppose at the end of December, the HSI falls to 11,000 points
Gain on cash position
= ((12,500 − 11,000)/12,500) × HK$4 million =   −HK$0.480 million
Gain on futures position
= 6 × (12,500 − 11,000) × HK$50 =   +HK$0.450 million

    −HK$0.030 million

(b) Suppose at the end of December, the HSI rises to 14,000 points
Gain on cash position
= ((14,000 − 12,500)/12,500) × HK$4 million =   +HK$0.480 million
Gain on futures position
= 6 × (14,000 - 12,500) × HK$50 =   −HK$0.450 million

    +HK$0.030 million

Exhibit 12.8

Suppose on 20 April, 200x, the spot price of a bushel of wheat is $3. A farmer expects to reap his crop in August and anticipates a harvest of 10 million bushels. To ensure revenues of at least $3 per bushel in August, the farmer should sell 1,000 August Wheat futures contracts (assuming one futures contract is for 10,000 bushels of wheat). As of 20 April, 200x, the futures/settlement price on this contract was $3.20 (cash price = $3.00).

Price of a bushel of wheat in August	Sales revenue per bushel in the Futures contract	Gain or loss per bushel from Futures contract
$2.50	$3.20	$0.70
$3.00	$3.20	$0.20
$3.50	$3.20	-$0.30

The farmer 'locks in' revenue of $3.20 per bushel (wheat is delivered at $3.20 per bushel).

position in the same futures contract when required. To illustrate, suppose that rather than an August futures contract, a September contract was used in the example in Exhibit 12.8. Suppose that as of 20 April 200x, the futures/settlement price of the September contract was $3.23. If the cash market price of wheat, in August, had been $2.91, and the September contract was offset at $2.93 as of this date, the following would result:

Gain from the futures contract = $(3.23 – 2.93) = $0.30 per bushel
sale price of wheat   = $2.91
Overall revenue   = $3.21 per bushel

The above reflects a basis level, at the time of offset in the September contract, of $0.02. Had the basis been narrower still, even greater revenue would have accrued to the farmer. To reflect this, suppose that the September futures price instead of being $2.93—at the time of offset— was $2.92. This suggests a basis of only $0.01 and implies:

Gain from Futures contract   = $(3.23 – 2.92) = $0.31 per bushel
sales price of wheat   = $2.91
Overall revenue   = $3.22 per bushel

Hedging Risks for both Short and Long Hedges

Basis Risk
Basis risk always limits the effectiveness of futures-based hedging strategies. Where the settlement date and underlying cash position have the same settlement date, as in the examples in Exhibit 12.6 and 12.7, this problem disappears. This is because a basis of zero (or a level approximating to zero, in the case of an Asian type settlement price) can be predicted at settlement. This allows the precise change in basis, and its effect on the hedge, to be gauged.

Quantity Risk
For the farmer or any other producer of a commodity, there is a further risk element: quantity risk. While price risk can easily be hedged through futures or forwards, the farmer (or any other producer) can never be certain that he has shorted exactly the right number of contracts. Too many, and he/she will be forced to buy extra produce through the cash market to meet the delivery requirement imposed by the surfeit of contracts. Too few, and the farmer faces price risk on the excess produce uncovered by the futures. The farmer also has to be concerned about the quality of his produce.

Futures as a Proxy for Portfolio Realignments

Futures can also be used to fine-tune the risk level or volatility of a portfolio. This is a well-known application. A fund or institution wishing to reduce its weighting to the Hong Kong market might see the sale of HSI futures as being preferable to the sale of some of its stock holdings, for instance. The principal advantage would be the transaction cost savings from such a move. Retaining portfolio weightings may also serve to build trust with the local retail market. This might be an important consideration for institutions wishing to tap Hong Kong's considerable retail market.

In addition to hedging and outright speculation, futures are commonly used for two other purposes: spread-trading and arbitrage. Both are examined below.

12.6 Spread-Trading Strategies in Futures

This approach captures the trading approach of the 'conservative speculator'. This sounds like a contradiction in terms, but is appropriate for investors with a particular view on the direction of the market but with some desire to reduce their exposure to potential loss. The spread occurs when a trader takes concurrent long and short positions in a futures contract on the same underlying. The spread derives from the fact that settlement dates on the contracts differ. Examples of spread-trades, using July and August futures contracts on an asset RST, are shown in Exhibit 12.9.

Exhibit 12.9 Illustrations of Spread-Trading Strategies in Futures

Consider July and August futures contracts on an asset RST.

	July futures price (1)	August futures price (2)	Spread (2) – (1)	Cash price of RST
14-07-97	$20.00	$21.10	$1.10	$19.80
15-07-97	$20.80	$21.50	$0.70	$20.30

The following strategy would have been beneficial: on 14-07-97, long July futures and short August futures; offset two positions on 15-07-97 (short July futures and buy August futures). Overall gain (ignoring transaction costs) = $(20.80 − 20.00) + $(21.10 − 21.50) = $0.40. Consider further data for July and August futures contracts on asset RST.

	July futures price (1)	August futures price (2)	Spread (2) – (1)	Cash price of RST
21-07-97	$20.10	$20.80	$0.70	$19.70
22-07-97	$20.40	$21.80	$1.40	$20.20

The following strategy would have been beneficial: on 21-07-97, short July futures and long August futures; offset two positions on 22-07-97 (long July futures and short August futures). Overall Gain (ignoring transaction costs) = $(20.10 − 20.40) + $(21.80 − 20.80) = $0.70.

In the first strategy in Exhibit 12.9, where the investor is long in the near-month and short in the distant-month contract, the spread narrows from $1.10 on the 15 July to $0.70 on the 16th. It is this reduction in spread that accounts for the $0.40 gross profit. Had the opposite occurred, a loss would have arisen. In the second spread strategy, the investor is short in the near-month and long in the distant-month contract. This yields a profit when the spread widens. To profit from either of the scenarios considered, a crucial condition must be satisfied: liquidity must be evident in both the spot and distant-month contracts. As distant-month contracts are notoriously illiquid, the spread-trading strategy may not work as theory suggests. This liquidity problem is an issue even in products which have highly liquid spot contracts. HSI futures would probably fit this description. Although liquidity in spot and next-month contracts would allow for the strategy, especially when spot expiry looms.

Liquidity issues aside, the transaction costs for spread trades are often lower than those pertaining to outright long or short positions. Most exchanges are also likely to offer some dispensation on the margin requirements. Clearly, the exposure of members, and their clearing houses, is significantly reduced by the offsetting nature of the positions.

12.7 Arbitrage

This normally takes one of two forms: (i) taking opposite positions in a futures contract and the underlying cash position; or (ii) taking opposite positions in futures contracts on the same underlying that are traded in two different places. The Nikkei 225 futures contract provides for the second of these, given its trading on SIMEX in Singapore and Osaka in Japan. As we saw in Chapter 7, examples of this kind of arbitrage also apply to dual-listed stocks, especially those listed in similar time zones.

As the first type of futures-based arbitrage activity was featured in Section 12.3, it is only considered briefly here. We saw that arbitrage-based models provide users with formulae for determining the fair spread between futures and cash prices. Any movements outside of these spreads are then evaluated in terms of transaction costs and liquidity risk. If the departures are sufficient to cover both of these, arbitrage trades are likely to be initiated. As the seasoned arbitrageur is only likely to trade in the most liquid of cash and future products, the transaction cost issue is the overriding concern.

Arbitrageurs typically trade on small margins (i.e., small pricing discrepancies net of transaction costs). Much like a wholesaler, they buy and sell heavily on low mark-ups. The volumes traded also serve to reduce transaction costs well below those of any competing individual investor. This reflects the economies involved and the bargaining power the arbitrageur has in negotiating commission rates. This is another compelling reason for having deregulated brokerage commissions (see Section 3.1). As arbitrageurs—at least in theory—promote 'price-discovery', some would argue that fixed brokerage impedes arbitrage and, by connection, competitive pricing processes.

What does the empirical evidence tell us? In certain areas, like stock index arbitrage, there is ample evidence of mispricing.[21] In the spirit of Grossman and Stiglitz's (1980) impossibility theorem for efficient markets, complete arbitrage is a fallacy. If prices were completely arbitraged, the potential gains for arbitrageurs would disappear. So would the arbitrageur. And if this happened, prices could not, logically, be arbitrage-free. It is this circularity of reasoning which suggests some scope for arbitrage activity.

Some commentators also apply the arbitrage label erroneously. Much of the so-called 'arbitrage' we see is, in fact, risky. This may be because the 'arbitrageur' operates between cash and futures markets with slight delay. One reason is that a large trade in one market can move the corresponding cash or futures market favourably. A good example is where a hedger with long cash and short futures positions decides to unwind his cash position ahead of the corresponding hedge. Even with a slight delay, the selling pressures imposed in the cash market might work favourably in the hedger's favour. Without appreciating the original hedge position, and the delay in the liquidation of the two positions, the casual observer might mistakenly view the whole exercise as index arbitrage.

Stock Index Arbitrage and Cash-Market Volatility

The advent of financial futures, and stock index futures in particular, have led some to argue that large trades in futures induce increased volatility in underlying cash markets. Index 'arbitrageurs' are seen as the main culprits. While commonly supported by large sections of the press, such views hold little water when subjected to closer scrutiny. Edwards (1988), based upon an empirical study of US stock index and interest rate futures between 1973 and 1987, reaches a very clear conclusion on the issue: 'Volatility has not increased because of futures trading' (p. 437). Studies of the local market also yield similar conclusions (see Freris, 1990).[22]

Many other studies have looked at the transmission issue using causality tests. Findings from such studies are contentious, at best. As eloquently argued by Edwards: 'Even if futures price volatility "leads" cash price volatility, it may simply be because futures markets process more quickly the same information available to cash markets' (p. 434, quotation marks used as shown). Evidence that volatility in futures prices exceeds that in cash prices is not, therefore, a cause for great concern.[23]

12.8 Developments in Futures Trading in Hong Kong

Historical developments in futures trading, at least prior to the creation of the HKFE in 1984, were spelled out in Section 2.1. In view of this, they are not reappraised here. The cataclysmic events of the October 1987 market crash are worth examining in greater detail, though. The direct effects of the Crash on the futures industry at the time and its effect in reforming the industry are evaluated.

The Restructuring of Futures Trading: The Post-Crash Period

The Events of October 1987

The period prior to the Crash was one of unbridled growth for the HKFE. Its newly launched HSI futures contract had proven to be an overwhelming success, amassing huge volumes, in the month preceding the Crash, of around 600 million contracts (see Chapter 2, Figure 1.2). This 'honeymoon' was brought to an abrupt end on Tuesday, 20 October 1987. Due to an unprecedented sell-off in New York, on the evening (HKT) of Monday 19 October, the authorities decided to close both the SEHK and HKFE.[24] Extraordinary measures, perhaps, for extraordinary times.

The complete removal of liquidity from the markets meant that losses on outstanding long futures positions could not be accurately gauged. The true severity of the losses only came to light on Monday, 26 October, when the markets reopened. Despite this, it became clear fairly early on in the crisis that a number of trading members would not be able to meet margin calls on their net client positions. In fact, several members argued vehemently that the market closure had exacerbated the problem, by denying their clients the opportunity to square outstanding long positions.[25] It may also have sparked a larger correction than might otherwise have been the case. Comparisons with other markets, like the United States (see Figure 12.4), lend more than a modicum of support to this view. In short, the closure did little to buttress Hong Kong's reputation as a financial centre, especially with all other major centres remaining open, during the melee.

Upon opening, on Monday, 26 October 1987, over one-third of the SEHK's value was wiped off its board. The effects on positions in HSI futures were duly magnified given the generous leverage offered on such products. So much so, that some brokers, with clients unable to meet margin calls on existing positions or losses on liquidated long positions, were pushed into bankruptcy. The effects, though perhaps not their true ferocity, had been widely anticipated days earlier. This had allowing a rescue package to be mounted to support the market. This involved an initial injection of HK$2 billion into the Hong Kong Futures Guarantee Corporation to ensure that the HKFE was able to guarantee all profits for members holding net short positions. In the event, the scale of defaults was larger than anticipated. Losses of HK$1.8 billion were racked up in the first week of trading alone.[26] This precipitated a further injection of HK$2 billion to the 'lifeboat'. All in all, the Hong Kong government provided around HK$2 billion of support with the rest coming from an assortment of banks and healthy member firms.

Member firms responsible for the HK$1.8 billion default, after being suspended from futures trading, were made liable for full repayment of losses. Losses were 'capped' by the Guarantee Corporation taking over and liquidating the positions of each defaulting member.[27] With the 'life boat' supporting this action, writs were duly issued to each defaulting member requesting payment of losses. Anticipated delays, and failures, in

Figure 12.4 Movement of HSI Cash and Futures Relative to the United States Market During the October 1987 Crash

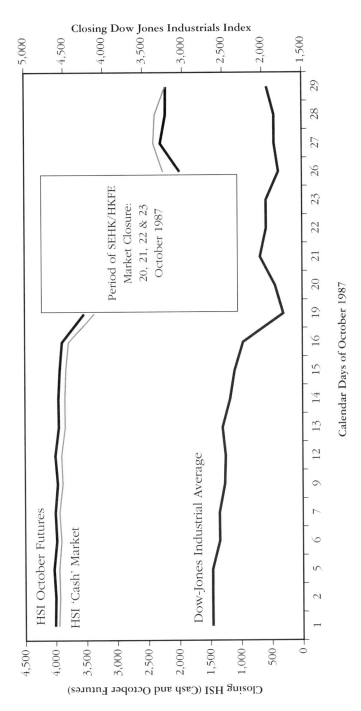

Source of Data: Datastream for Closing Dow-Jones Values; the HKFE for Closing HSI October 1987 Futures; and HSI Services Ltd for Closing HSI ('Cash' Market) Values

the payment of such sums necessitated additional steps. One included the imposition of a special 'lifeboat' levy on all stock and futures transactions. This remained in force until the mid-1990s.

The whole débâcle raised a number of questions, not least of which was the very feasibility of futures trading in Hong Kong.[28] To most, it seemed incredible that the entity charged with supporting the clearing of trades on the HKFE, the Guarantee Corporation, could be so poorly funded. It was reputed to have held only HK$22.5 million in capital prior to the Crash.[29] The total absence of risk-management systems necessitated a complete overhaul of the Exchange. In the first instance, changes in the management and supervision of the clearing and guarantee bodies were initiated. Changes to the capitalization requirements and trading status of members followed. A rash of other changes, on the heels of the government commissioned *Report of the Securities Review Committee* (hereafter the *Report*), published in May 1988, were also set in train. Paramount amongst these was the reorganization of the HKFE's clearing and guarantee functions. This was brought about by the creation of the HKFE Clearing Corporation in 1989. As a wholly-owned body of the HKFE this replaced the old contractual basis relating to guarantee and clearing activities. Previously, the HKFE had contracted out clearing duties to the International Commodities Clearing House (Hong Kong), a body wholly-owned by the International Commodities Clearing House (London) (ICCHL), and its guarantee operations to the Hong Kong Futures Guarantee Corporation.[30] Amongst other things, the new 'in-house' guarantee and clearing arrangement served to combat deficiencies, identified in the Report. Not least of which was the segmentation of risk management operations between the erstwhile clearing and guarantee parties.

The October 1987 Crash, though painful, forced changes that, in more clement times, would never have been countenanced. In this sense, the experience was a salutary one. The radical changes instituted in the years following the Crash have, without doubt, paved the way to a more robust futures market.

Product and Microstructure Developments

Despite a plethora of new products in recent years, the HSI futures contract is still the HKFE's *pièce de résistance*. As the HKFE generates revenues from the turnover of its products, primarily through the interest earned on margin deposits placed by members and through the various transaction, clearing, and member fees it collects, the profitability of the Exchange has moved almost in tandem with the volumes recorded on its premier product. The HKFE has also made extensive changes to its product list. The products available, as of mid-1998, are summarized in Table 12.1.

New products, like HSI options, have reduced the percentage contribution of HSI futures to overall HKFE volumes. Nonetheless, HSI futures still account for around 80% of annual volumes (measured by number of contracts traded in 1997).[31] HSI options come in next with

Table 12.1   Exchange-Traded Futures Products in Hong Kong

Product	*Date Introduced*
Gold	August 1980
HSI Futures	May 1986
HSI Options	March 1993*
Stock Futures	March 1995^
Rolling Forex	
(DM and Yen)	November 1995
(GBP)	September 1996
3-Month HIBOR Futures#	September 1997
Hang Seng China-Affiliated Corporations Index Futures	September 1997
Hang Seng China-Affiliated Corporations Index Options	September 1997
HKFE Taiwan Index Futures	May 1998
HKFE Taiwan Index Options	May 1998

Notes:
* These relate to 'short-dated' options. 'Long-dated' options were subsequently launched in July 1996.
^ Contracts are now available on 17 stocks. Originally, contracts were introduced on two stocks—HSBC Holdings Ltd and Hong Kong Telecom Ltd—in March 1995.
\# HIBOR futures were relaunched on this date, having previously been traded on the HKFE.
All dates and contract details were obtained from the Hong Kong Futures Exchange.

around 14% of total volumes (accounting for approximately 1.147 billion contracts traded during 1997). The remaining volumes are due to trades, in order of importance, in rolling forex contracts, red-chip futures, three-month HIBOR futures, stock futures, and red-chip options.[32] Despite the falling percentage contribution of HSI futures, its volumes have grown consistently in absolute terms (see Figure 2.2, Chapter 2). So much so that record monthly volumes, of over 800,000 contracts, were realized in October 1997.[33]

Developments in market microstructure have also been significant. The shift to an electronic, screen-based system, known as the Automated Trading System (ATS), has been the central development in this area. This operates through a market-making system and has displaced the old 'open outcry' system of trading for all products, other than the HSI futures and HSI options contracts. The latter are scheduled to pass into the ATS fold in the second-half of 1999.

The conventional 'open outcry' system, which involves the matching and execution of buy and sell orders on an open 'trading-pit', still has its supporters, given the immediacy it offers. However, most would contend that electronic systems are more efficient. It is against this background that an international trend towards electronic futures trading has gathered momentum. A number of the larger exchanges, like the Deutsche Terminborse and the French futures exchange Matif have already shifted to electronic trading mode. The new Eurex market embodies this approach.

This came into being following an alliance between Deutsche Terminborse and the Switzerland Options and Financial Futures Exchange which was announced in 1997 and consummated in 1998.[34] This involves, amongst other things, a tie-up in the partner exchanges' trading and clearing systems. Matif entered the fray, as Eurex's third exchange partner, shortly after the announcement of the link between the two founding partners.[35] The new electronic trading environment has upped the ante for other major exchanges, like the London International Financial Futures Exchange (LIFFE). An electronic trading system for futures trading on LIFFE is, in fact, in the pipeline.[36]

Electronic trading is therefore part of a new package of exchange consolidation. The other is the coalescence and harmonization of clearing systems. This issue, which is also affecting non-derivative exchanges, is taken up further in Section 14.3. Other major developments in futures markets include the use of electronic systems for 'after-hours' or extended trading in products that trade under conventional 'open outcry' system during regular trading hours.[37] A number of exchanges have already embraced this approach.

The SAR government as a Futures Player: The Market Intervention of August 1998

August 1998 also marked a watershed in local futures trading given the SAR government's direct intervention in the futures markets. Estimates at the time suggest that the government, through the Hong Kong Monetary Authority (HKMA), injected around 15% of the value of the Exchange Fund into both stock and futures markets.[38] The intervention involved heavy buying in the cash and spot HSI futures markets for a two-week period running from 14 August through to the last trading day of the August (spot) futures month, 28 August. The final day of this intervention alone, saw a new daily trading turnover record of HK$79 billion on the SEHK.

The HKMA's actions were specifically aimed at hedge funds that were allegedly short in large numbers of spot (August) HSI futures contracts. The hedge funds were argued to be extracting large profits from the markets by virtue of a double play. This entailed borrowing large amounts of Hong Kong dollars, to finance short positions in the local currency, and simultaneously selling HSI futures.[39] This was viewed by the government as outright manipulation, designed, as a result of pressure imposed on interest rates from currency borrowings, to weaken stock prices and generate large paper gains on short futures positions. These profits were argued to be well in excess of the costs of the currency positions taken.

The HKMA's Counter against HSI Futures 'Roll-Overs'
One of the key features of the government's strategy was to ensure that speculators wishing to retain short positions in HSI futures paid for the

privilege. The central pillar in this was the HKMA's intervention in the HSI futures market, designed to raise the cost of 'rolling over' short positions. Realizing that currency speculators would have to buy spot HSI futures, to liquidate outstanding short positions, and sell next-month contracts, the HKMA sought to inflict costs on both sides of the 'roll-over'. This was achieved by the HKMA buying heavily into August (spot) futures and selling September (next-month) futures. This culminated in a premium on August futures prices (over September futures) of over 600 points on the last trading day of the spot-month (see Figure 12.5). The effectiveness of this initiative is difficult to gauge. Currency speculators sensing the growing intensity of the spread-trading intervention may well have re-established their short positions on acceptable terms ahead of the intervention, This could have been done in the penultimate week of August, or early part of the spot's final trading week (see Figure 12.5).

McGuinness's (1999b) analysis of HSI futures 'roll-overs' offers some insight into this issue. The analysis shows that, based upon historical evidence, 'roll-overs' from spot to next-month contracts typically yield positive returns for investors in short positions.[40] This applies to all days in the final week of trading apart from the last trading day. This 'positive carry' is noted to be a reflection of the typical differential between interest rates and HSI dividend yields. Using bank deposit rates, McGuinness (1999b) shows that the average differential was around +200 basis points between September 1993 and August 1998. Interestingly, as the time to spot expiry increases, mean 'roll-over' returns also increase slightly. This is also accompanied by reduced variance around such means, suggesting more favourable 'roll-over' returns, for short-sided players, on days well ahead of spot expiry. If speculative currency players, involved in the recent foray into the markets, had acted in accordance with this, some may well have 'rolled-over' positions prior to the HKMA's intervention. Relatively low volumes in the next-month contract, right up to the end of the spot's penultimate week of trading, might well have frustrated this, however.[41] It is also likely that the 'roll over' return pattern, of reduced mean (and higher variance) as spot expiry nears, is a reflection of trading effects. As argued in McGuinness (1999b): 'If hedgers have a greater propensity to 'roll-over' positions than other parties and, as is so often assumed, inhabit the short side of the market, ROLL values may well narrow as spot expiry nears simply because of increased buying pressure in the spot- and selling in the next-month contract.' (the variable ROLL equates to the 'roll-over' measure described in Note 40).

So, even if liquidity allows—which it may not—increased 'roll-over' activity is likely to squeeze potential gains. In this sense, then, it is questionable whether sizeable 'roll-overs' can be achieved more favourably well in advance of spot expiry. The HKMA's action, at least in respect of its ploy to force a futures discount on the next- (September) month contract, would seem well-motivated in this light. The spread-trading strategy of buying August and selling September contracts also served another important purpose: it helped hedge the government's accumulated cash

Figure 12.5   The Behaviour of Settlement Price and Open Interest for August and September 1998 HSI Futures: 3–28 August, 1998

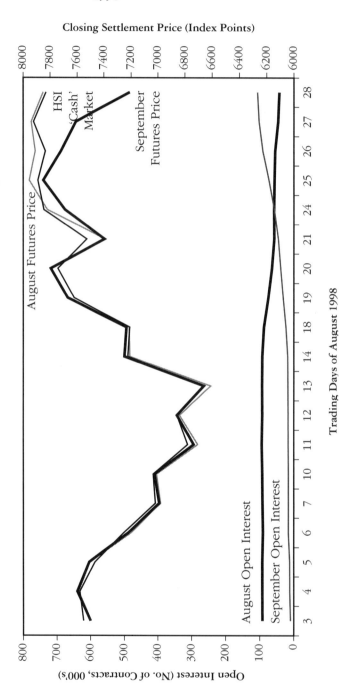

Last Trading Day in August HSI Futures: 28 August 1998 (17 August was a holiday).
Source of Data: The HKFE for all closing daily HSI futures prices and open interest figures; HSI Services Ltd for closing HSI 'cash' levels.

market position into September 1998. In relation to the merits of the SAR government's stock and futures intervention, opinion seems well and truly divided. Whether there will ever be a consensus remains to be seen.[42]

12.9 Concluding Remarks

In concluding the material on equity derivative products, this chapter has sought to highlight the crucial role played by hedgers, speculators, and arbitrageurs in the local futures market. The sheer size of this market and its burgeoning growth, particularly in its talisman, the HSI futures product, have given the HKFE a handsome lead over most other Asian derivatives exchanges. This is all the more impressive bearing in mind the trials and tribulations of 1987 when the local futures market came within a whisker of collapse. The resuscitation of futures owed much to the restructuring of the HKFE and the creation of new clearing and guarantee systems. These changes, along with a list of new, successful products and trading links with other major exchanges, have made Hong Kong a veritable tour de force in the trading of derivatives. Other than Japan, the HKFE would seem to have a lead on its rivals in Asia.

New challenges are always on the horizon. SIMEX's relaunch of a Hong Kong-based index futures contract in late 1998 is one such example. This kind of development is not unusual. Many of the major exchanges around the world trade contracts on overseas products; the HKFE being one (namely, HKFE Taiwan Index Futures and Options, Table 12.1). The pre-eminence of the HSI futures contract and the immediacy of information on the constituents in the SAR inevitably give local traders and the HKFE a distinct advantage. Despite some concerns on the issue, SIMEX's venture may lead to greater interest in HSI futures. Processes of arbitrage, for one, would suggest some benefits as Singaporean investors and institutions trading in SIMEX compare prices with Hong Kong. Admittedly, 'tracking' error limits the extent of this arbitrage as the two indices are different. Nonetheless, the correlation of return movement between the two is extremely high.

Competition in other areas, as with the trading of Hong Kong stocks in London, has, if anything, boosted local volumes over the years. The same will likely hold in the case of futures and other derivatives. Even where competition seems more threatening, it may still offer benefits. If exchanges are forced to look for efficiency gains—as with the development of cross-margining arrangements and links with other clearing houses—the community at large gains.

Notes

1.   As a reminder, the 'cash' HSI is computed using prices of the constituents determined on the SEHK.

2.   Gearing rates were introduced in Section 11.2 for warrants. They carry much the same meaning for futures. A gearing rate of 20 captures the ratio of contract value/margin. The margin represents the initial deposit required to open a position.

3.   This consideration was, in fact, raised during the October 1987 crisis for clients holding profitable short positions in HSI futures in member firms with net losses on overall client positions (see To (1987) for further discussion). Broad principles are difficult to outline as the conditions underpinning such eventualities may vary from exchange to exchange and over time. Additional layers of protection, including compensation funds, are conceivable, depending upon the exchange in question.

4.   At the peak of the crisis, the HKFE suspended 43 of its members (see Anonymous (Oct 1987)). Some members were able to subsequently pull funds together to cover losses on their net trading positions and were therefore able to seek reinstatement.

5.   As the value of ABC cannot fall below zero, the downside of the long position investor (L), and the upside of the short position investor (S), have theoretical limits. However, a cash value of $0 for ABC at the settlement date would render a loss (profit) of $10 for L (S). In terms of the initial margin, this suggests rates of return of 400% and -400% for L and S, respectively. In reality, then, returns are effectively unlimited in both directions for L and S.

6.   This is based upon their derivation of a form which serves as an approximation to this. This is shown as,

$$F_t = C_t \times [e^{r \times T} (1 - d/r) + d/r] \text{ (See Cornell and French (1983a, p. 678))}.$$

7.   The annual dividend yield (d) used is 5% [= ($5/$100) × 100]. This is an approximation as the true compound yield should be 5.0625% [= $(1+0.025)^2 - 1$]. Use of the continuously compounded form of (1)—as outlined—would suggest a slight departure from the $100.995 value presented (although it would still be approximately equal to $101).

8.   To illustrate, buying futures at $101, shorting asset ABC for $100 and investing $100 for six months yields a cash return in six months' time = $(100 + 3.50 – 101 – 2.50) = $0. If selling futures at $101 and purchasing ABC for $100 through borrowings for six months, the cash return in six months' time = $(101 + 2.50 – 100 – 3.50) = $0.

9.   For a discussion of arbitrage activities in the pricing of HSI futures contracts in Hong Kong see Terpstra and Mumford, pp. 129–32.

10.   See Cornell and French (1983a, pp. 692–3) for discussion of how constraints on the use of a short-seller's proceeds in the US affect arbitrage in determining the 'cost-of-carry' result.

11.   The cash flows shown in (b) of Exhibit 12.4 are a more accurate description of an investor selling from existing treasury, with the futures subsequently used to restore the stock position. This is, in fact, described under the guise of a 'stock replacement strategy' in Stoll and Whaley (1987, p. 17). The negative cash amount relating to dividends would then reflect dividends lost by the stock seller (instead of compensation to the stock lender).

12.   See *HKFE HSI Contract Specifications* for further details.

13.   This assumes that the futures and cash markets close at the same time. For HSI futures and the HSI this has not always been the case. As of June 1998, though, both markets closed daily at 4.00 pm.

14.   Reference to Hull's (1989, pp. 47–50) excellent account of the relation between cash and futures prices, using continuously compounded forms for a range of commodity types, is strongly recommended for an in-depth analysis of commodity futures pricing.

15.   See Hecht (1997) and Edwards and Cantor (1995) for examples of this usage.

16. Chang (1986, p. 207) also noted some evidence of increased returns for larger speculators in one of the three futures markets surveyed, suggesting some forecasting ability for such players in this market.

17. See *HKFE HSI Contract Specifications*.

18. Thanks are due to the HKFE for supplying information on 'Client Margin Rates' in HSI Futures. These rates came into effect on 28 February 1995 and represent the 'minimum' margin that members have to draw from clients. The margin figures refer to 'full rates' (not 'spread rates' which relate to spread spreads— to be discussed later) applicable per lot. The discussion in this area (pp. 344–6) is a simplified account of the margin process and is not intended to capture the actual process which will be client/member specific. The 'minimum' rates in the example apply to clients (not members) and, subject to the HKFE, are revised over time.

19. Assuming the validity of the Market Model (as in Sharpe (1963)).

20. See Anonymous (Apr 1994).

21. Yadav and Pope (1990) reach this conclusion in their assessment of US studies of arbitrage using stock index futures.

22. Freris, in his analysis of the daily behaviour of the HSI between January 1984 and September 1987, contends that, 'The introduction of stock futures trading in Hong Kong had no measurable effect on the stock price volatility' (Freris (1990, p. 414)).

23. Tang's (1996) comparison of volatility levels in the HSI and HSI futures, for the period from March 1993 to January 1995, provides local confirmation of this. Greater inter-day (or 'close-to-close') volatility was apparent in the futures. With the exception of the lunch-break period, Tang also noted greater intra-day volatility levels for the futures.

24. See Fell (1992, pp. 195–6) for an account of the personnel and bodies involved in this decision.

25. During the week of 26 October 1987, a group of defaulting members lobbied the Hong Kong government on the grounds that client losses, which they were liable to pay to the clearing house, should be subject to some ceiling set by the HKFE, given the unwarranted closure of the Exchange (see To and Sendzul (1987)).

26. One member firm alone defaulted to the tune of HK$645 million. For a detailed description of the defaulting parties and their losses, see To, Ko, and Chan (1987).

27. This involved the sale of 25,000 long positions in October and November contracts in the trading days between 27 October and 1 November 1987 (See Sendzul (1987) for details).

28. The authors of the Hay-Davidson Report, commissioned shortly after the local market crash, saw fit to raise this very question as part of their preliminary investigations (see *Report of the Securities Review Committee*, (1988, p 141)).

29. See Sendzul and Glain (1987) for details.

30. This, like its clearing partner, included the ICCHL as an equity player (see *Report of the Securities Review Committee* (pp. 175–7)) for details of the ownership basis of the Guarantee Corporation as well as the precise form of the contractual terms between the guarantee and clearing bodies and the HKFE). The Guarantee Corporation enjoyed a 20% ICCHL equity stake and holdings from an assortment of major banks.

31. See yearly volume figures reported on the HKFE homepage (at http://www.hkfe.com/dataset/stat/s6.html).

32. Rankings based upon source as in Note 31. The basic principles of the futures mechanism are much the same for all the products shown. Rolling forex contracts, introduced in 1995, are a little different in one important respect: they do not have a given settlement date. As a consequence, open positions automatically 'roll-over' until an offsetting position is established.

33. The earlier monthly record of 601,005 contracts, realized in October 1987, was, in fact, breached three times during 1997.

34. See Kharouf (1998) for detailed discussion of the alliance.

35. See ibid. and Sales (1998) for details of the technological implications of the partnership.

36. See Maguire (1998) for details of these plans.

37. See Caveletti (1998) for an excellent summary of some of these developments.

38. See Lloyd-Smith (1998).

39. As we saw in Section 2.2, much of the currency speculation was probably arranged via forwards. As such, little or no up-front capital was required.

40. 'Roll-over' returns were measured by the differential between next- and spot-month closing futures prices all divided by spot futures price.

41. Press reports at the time (notably Van Der Kamp (1998)) suggest little evidence, based upon volumes and open interest, of substantial 'rolling-over' activities prior to the final few days of the August 1998 spot contract.

42. Some commentators suggested that the government might use provisions in the Securities Ordinance, relating to the creation of 'false and disorderly markets' (S. 135), to punish unnamed hedge funds allegedly manipulating the markets. This course of action, for whatever reason—perhaps due to time considerations—was not pursued. In any event, the government's decision to intervene suggested little possibility of sanction through such means. One market-watcher even noted that, 'If the government does not regard its actions as market manipulation, then it surely cannot accuse hedge funds of creating a false market by acting in the opposite direction' (Webb (1998a)).

13. The Control and Management of Risk for Derivatives[1]

Derivatives, as reflected by the space given to them in this text, are central to all deliberations about equity markets and, much like incendiary devices, can have an explosive effect on corporations and markets if mishandled. Despite this, the majority of players use derivatives for rather benign purposes. Hedgers and arbitrageurs would seem to fit this description. The hedger, for instance, uses the derivative as a mechanism for reducing risk exposure. Arbitrageurs take offsetting positions in cash and derivatives markets and, at least in theory, extract profits with relatively little risk. They also aid the price discovery process by bolstering efficiency in the cash market. Despite the sober ploys of these players, it is the third major user of derivatives—the speculator—who grabs the headlines. Huge financial losses on speculative derivative plays in Orange County and Barings still remain in the public consciousness. These and some of the other major cases, as summarized in Table 13.1, remind us that investors and market regulators need to be cognizant of the risks involved in 'open' (speculative) derivative plays. Moreover, all kinds of derivatives, not just ones of the equity variety, have the potential to wreak havoc on financial markets.

In the face of some of the spectacular derivative loss cases, a number of pronouncements and interventions, from august bodies like the Basle Committee for Banking Supervision, the Bank of England, and the Group of Thirty, have emerged in recent years. These have been significant in establishing codes and rules for the risk-management of derivatives.[2] Much of this emphasis has been driven by politicians fearful of a market 'meltdown' caused by one or more errant users of derivatives. The paramount issue in all of this has been quantitative risk-assessment, operationalized through concepts like value-at-risk (VAR). Increased

Table 13.1 Summary of Publicized Derivatives-Based Losses

Procter & Gamble	$157 million loss on swaps[a]
Metallgesellschaft	$1,000 million loss on futures and swap hedges[b]
Codelco	$210 million loss from copper futures[c]
Wisconsin Investment Board	$95 million loss on swaps[d]
Salomon Brothers	$175 million loss adjustment for swaps[e]
Kashima Oil	$1,500 million unrealized loss in FX forwards[f]
Showa Shell Sekiyu	$1,100 million loss on FX futures[g].
Bank of Tokyo-Mitsubishi	$50 million loss on swaps[h]
Industrial Bank of Japan	$85 million loss on swaps[h]

[a] See Loomis (1995); [b] Edwards and Canter (1995); [c] Anonymous (March 1994); [d] Barr (1995); [e] Shirreff (1995); [f] Anonymous (April 1994); [g] Clifford (1993); and [h] Reuters (1997).

surveillance and governance of privately-negotiated over-the-counter (OTC) trades is also seen as a way of reining in over-exposure. The various strands of thought on these issues, as well as their state of development locally, are assessed in this chapter. This also helps to provide a topical overview of the materials in Chapters 10–12.

Before appraising the finer points of risk-management control and evaluation for derivatives, some familiarity with the various risk dimensions, implicit in derivative use, is essential. The materials in Chapters 10–12 offer some insight into this by broadly alluding to two key dimensions. The first is price risk, engendered by leverage in 'naked' or speculative plays. The second is the risk of counterparty default, apparent for both speculators and hedgers in OTC trades. These two risk areas are the most commonly referred to and are reassessed in Section 13.1. Other dimensions of risk, like operations and supervisory-based risk, then feature in Section 13.2. Despite these components being interrelated with price and counterparty (credit) risk, demarcation lines can still be drawn. Approaches to the risk-management of OTC derivatives then feature in Section 13.3 with an analysis of the VAR concept, and its role in identifying exposure, carried out in Section 13.4. An overview of the current state of play in the risk-management of derivatives is then offered in Section 3.5.

13.1   The Principal Dimensions of Risk: Market and Counterparty (Credit) Risk

Various accounts in the field of risk-management refer to as many as six risk factors. As a guide, the International Organization of Securities Commissions (IOSCO) delineate risk as such.[3] The six areas pertain to credit risk, market risk, liquidity risk, settlement risk, operations risk, and legal risk. Discussion of the first two of these is entertained below. For reasons of convenience and logic, liquidity risk is subsumed under the heading of market risk and legal and settlement risks under the rubric of counterparty risk.

Market Risk

As mentioned, market risk really has two facets: price risk and liquidity risk. Liquidity risk is most apparent in OTC markets where the absence of secondary markets often requires traders to take positions all the way through to settlement or expiry. It can also be a problem in some exchange-trades; spread-trades in futures being an obvious example. In essence, liquidity risk results in both trading delay and, by connection, price risk.

For price risk, the issue is one of adverse market movement rather than the ease with which positions can be offset. Large numbers of speculative proprietary trades in futures, options or swaps ultimately result in significant price risk. The more than 20,000 contracts held by Barings in Nikkei 225 Futures on SIMEX and in Osaka in early 1995 highlight this issue.[4] The impact of adverse market movements when holding such speculative positions can be and, in the Barings's case was, devastating. This has been appreciated for some time and the burning question is how such large speculative positions develop in the first place. The existence of effective internal monitoring systems should operate to prevent such exposure. One can only conjecture that such systems were absent in many of the publicized derivative loss cases, including Barings. This issue is examined in Section 13.2.

The recent financial troubles of a number of hedge funds further highlight the market risk of derivatives.[5] Many of these funds, though not all, take directional views on particular assets and markets through highly-leveraged derivative plays. As noted in Section 3.5, such funds can inflict huge losses on their proprietary investors when the strategies go awry. Not all hedge funds easily fit into this speculative mould, though, with some steering clear of derivatives completely or even limiting exposure through the use of derivatives for more benign purposes, like arbitrage (of the riskless rather than the risky variety).

Large speculative positions may also have damaging effects upon the markets housing such trades. Again, the Barings incident is pertinent given the effect of the losses on SIMEX and the Nikkei 225 contract itself. Large speculative positions may also endanger the very existence of derivatives markets. In extreme cases, like the 327 treasury futures fiasco in Shanghai, where position limits on futures contracts were blatantly violated, organized exchanges may be forced to suspend trading temporarily thus extinguishing liquidity in listed products.[6]

Risks Implicit in Hedging
While speculative trading in derivatives is fraught with danger, hedging and arbitrage activity in such products are thought to carry relatively few risks. In such cases, a position in the underlying asset is held and operates as an offset to the derivatives position taken. Losses experienced by Metallgesellschaft (MG), where derivatives were used for the explicit purpose of hedging, have led to some revision in this view, however. A substantial part of the loss in the MG hedging operation arose from the 'rolling over' of futures contracts.[7] As eloquently argued in Cantor and Edwards' (1995) account of the MG collapse, MG's 'roll-over' of long positions was undertaken in anticipation of a continuation of a 'negative carry' relation in energy futures prices.[8] Had this continued, MG would have been able to re-establish long positions in more distant-month contracts at a discount to liquidated near-month values (see the discussion of 'roll-overs' in Section 12.8). The reversal to a 'positive carry' relation in 1993 proved disastrous forcing MG to buy new contracts at a premium to the old ones.

Losses in cases like Showa Shell Sekiyu, where counterparties were allowed to continually 'roll over' loss-making forward positions, highlight the weakness of automatic 'roll-over' mechanisms.[9] Aside from unpredictable changes in the near-to-distant month differential in futures prices, hedging can also come unstuck due to a lack of liquidity in the hedge or an unpredictable change in its basis (where forward or futures instruments are used).

Counterparty Risk

Credit or counterparty risk is a perennial problem in OTC-based contracts. As such positions now account for a larger proportion of the global value of outstanding derivative positions than exchange-traded positions, this issue cannot be easily dismissed. Moreover, some derivatives, like swaps, are particular to OTC markets.[10] The catchphrase 'know your 'counterparty' clearly has profound meaning. It is also wise to know the legal standing of your counterparty. There may be several reasons why a contract may be void or unenforceable which vary according to jurisdiction and the nature of the counterparty. The case of the London Borough of Hammersmith and Fulham,[11] where the user of the derivatives, after succumbing to large losses, argued that derivatives were outside its legal remit, is case in point. This issue of *ultra vires*, or unlawful use of the product, is a clear reminder to all counterparties to check on the legitimacy of their trades. Attempts have also been made to enforce *ultra vires* elsewhere.

Other significant legal disputes, like the case between Gibson Greetings and Bankers Trust, highlight other possible issues of dispute between counterparties.[12] Disputes over documentation and terms may also arise. Some legal complexities can be reduced, however, through the use of standardized documents. International Swaps and Derivatives Association (ISDA) Master Agreements are helpful in this regard.[13] In sum, any kind of legal risk should be incorporated into the category of counterparty risk since a counterparty should establish its legal rights and obligations, as well as those of its opposite number, before committing to any derivatives position.

To some extent, credit risk can be reduced through cash management procedures like netting where mutual obligations between parties are offset (see Hendricks (1994)). Derivatives can also be found to protect against counterparty risk, as the rise of the credit derivative shows.[14] There is still no substitute for a thorough credit evaluation of one's counterparty, though. This can be achieved using quantitative models of credit risk.[15] In addition, models like J.P.Morgan's CreditMetrics™, can be applied to portfolios to enable VAR numbers to be calculated in response to a counterparty default or credit-rating change.

As noted in Chapters 10 to 12, exchange-traded products carry minimal credit risk by virtue of the novation promised in such trades. This may be reason enough to attract some players to the exchange-traded arena; however, we know from earlier discussions that the novation guarantee, on many exchanges, only extends to members. Individual investors, with paper profits on positions, may not therefore be protected if their positions are established through loss-making or defaulting members. Inadequate risk-management controls on an exchange, as was evident for the HKFE in October 1987, might also threaten the novation promise. Clearly, credit risk is a non-trivial issue, even on organized exchanges.

13.2 Other Risk Factors: Operations and Supervisory-Based Risks

Media commentaries have focused on the risk of misguided managers, or errant employees, wreaking devastation on their own firms through proprietary derivative trades. This raises the spectre of surveillance risk. Until recent years, it had been assumed that most corporates and investment banks were principally involved in derivatives for hedging or arbitrage purposes and, as such, were not unduly exposed to the market. This assumption may no longer be entirely true. Many of the major derivative losses in the 1990–5 period were significant because they related to the proprietary trades of investment banks. The movement from essentially client-based investment to a mix of client- and proprietary-based investment, has inevitably led to much greater exposure for banks.[16]

Most accounts of publicized losses in derivatives cite poor or ineffective supervision of positions as the key issue. The suggestion of unauthorized trading, in a number of notable derivative loss cases (Codelco and Barings, for example), is an extreme and obvious example. Losses in Daiwa Bank between 1984 and 1995—of $1.1 billion—and by Sumitomo Corporation—of $1.8 billion between 1987 and 1996—also highlight the significance of surveillance risk for debt and commodity trades as well.[17]

Operational risks are also apparent. Within this category, several risk factors can be identified. Hoffman and Johnson (1996, p. 61), with regard to the business operational risks of Bankers Trust, identify five broad risk areas pertaining to people, technology, relationships, physical assets, and external/regulatory issues. Many of these risks, like computer glitches, are well understood given their potential to severely dent operating profits. This is well known, especially in the light of cases, such as that of Kidder Peabody, where computer program errors were cited as a possible explanation for a $350 million overvaluation of bond holdings.[18]

The loss of a key trader is also a major risk for any derivatives trading house given the potential damage this can cause to the entity's competitive advantage. Informational asymmetries between management and the trading desk itself, also raise the possibility of unexplained trades. As with supervisory-based risks, the consensus seems to be that more frequent and rigorous audits of traders' positions are warranted in order to validate the actions of both the traders and the systems they use.

The 'off-balance-sheet' accounting treatment of derivatives may also mean that shareholders are unable to judge the real risks associated with their investments. A number of accounting changes have arisen of late with the specific intention of remedying this. The US-based Financial Accounting Standards Board (FASB), through FASB 119 ('Disclosure about

Derivative Financial Instruments and Fair Value of Financial Instruments') is one example.[19] This seeks, amongst other things, to increase the transparency of derivative positions. The regular disclosure of VAR figures also has potential in reminding investors of the true risk exposure of their investments. As revealed in Jorion (1996, p. 47), VAR figures, which we shall review in Section 13.4, are increasingly available to the investment community. He reports that some banks in the United States even give details of VAR figures in annual reports. Others may not be as adventurous, but still provide details of their off-balance-sheet commitments in note form in their annual reports.

As well as reporting information to external parties, internal accounting procedures are likely to be helpful. The significance of this is revealed by recent losses reported by the Industrial Bank of Japan of around US$85 million, which were revealed after the Bank had switched to a new 'mark-to-market accounting method'.[20] The obvious advantage of having rigorous internal control systems in place is that adverse changes in operational profits can be quickly spotted and remedial action sanctioned.

13.3   Risk-Management Approaches to OTC Derivatives

Much of the regulation in the derivatives area in recent years has been spawned by losses in OTC products. Barings and Metalgessellschaft aside, which both involved trades in futures, most of the major losses appear to have been concentrated in privately-negotiated derivative trades. This is not unduly surprising given the comments in the foregoing. Issues of liquidity and counterparty default in many OTC positions burn brightly. This seems to be widely appreciated. IOSCO, in respect of its own delineation of risk factors for derivatives, notes on this matter that such risks 'are not unique to OTC derivative transactions, but are of special concern due to the volume, scope, and variety of OTC transactions, the degree of interrelatedness of participants, the "opaqueness" and uncertain liquidity of OTC "markets", and the complexity of and potential leverage in such instruments.' (Technical Committee of IOSCO (1994, p. 1), quotations used as shown).

The special risk-management issues associated with OTC derivatives have also been given explicit recognition locally by the Securities and Futures Commission (SFC). In a document issued in March 1995, the SFC, in relation to Parts I and II of ISOCO's July 1994 report on the 'Operational and Financial Risk Management Control Mechanisms for Over-the-Counter Derivatives Activities of Regulated Securities Firms',[21] embraced the various provisions therein as 'a statement of minimum best practice for registered persons in respect of their management control systems and procedures for OTC derivatives activities' (page i).[22] The 'registered persons' in this regard, refer to those registered (and licensed) with respect to three major local ordinances: the Securities Ordinance, the Commodities Trading Ordinance and the Leveraged Foreign Exchange Trading Ordinance[23].

Subsequent surveys by the SFC have also shed some light on the practices of locally 'registered persons' in the OTC derivative arena.[24] The first of two surveys, based upon 645 'registered person' responses, suggested a relatively limited role for OTC derivative activities given that 'outside banks and unregulated issuers, only 33 registered firms engage in any form of OTC derivatives activity in Hong Kong' (SFC, 1997, p. 1). Of these, however, the SFC noted that the majority set limits on credit risk and market exposure, conducted marking-to-market of positions at least on a daily basis and prepared 'regular reports on derivative activities'.[25] Evidence of counterparties with generally sound credit ratings was also apparent. All in all, the general findings indicated that local OTC derivative players embraced sound and clear financial risk-management policies. Surveys often tell you this, however, as the more egregious often steer clear of invitations to volunteer information.

A second SFC survey of 48 registered firms revealed something about the nature of OTC derivative positions taken. Of the 24 firms in the sample 'indicating some involvement in OTC derivative activities', the majority engaged in foreign exchange business (in terms of numbers of positions) and were not, in general, in the business of holding proprietary positions. More than 50% of the respondents reporting OTC involvement were noted to be managing OTC positions 'booked' under the name of one or more of their affiliates in jurisdictions outside of Hong Kong. The SFC (April 1997) noted on this issue that: 'For many large international investment houses, this type of activity constitutes the only part of their OTC derivatives activities in Hong Kong' (p. 4). In sum, then, the second survey suggested a rather limited role for direct, proprietorial OTC derivative activities in the local market.

13.4　The Value-at-Risk (VAR) Concept and its Contribution to Risk-Management

One of the key issues to emerge from the SFC surveys of local OTC derivative activities was the attention given to the management of market-risk. Most organizations in Hong Kong and overseas typically allude to measures like the 'marking-to-market' of positions, the setting of position limits and the use of stress testing, as being instrumental in the control of market exposure levels. More and more organizations around the globe also seem to be embracing the value-at-risk (VAR) concept, which offers a quantitative evaluation of an entity's day-to-day exposure to loss. Its arrival has been marked by a proliferation of software pioneered, amongst others, by J.P. Morgan, Chase Manhattan, CS First Boston, Bankers Trust, and Deutsche Bank.[26]

VAR's origins can be traced to J.P. Morgan and the Group of Thirty (G30).[27] Subsequent developments, like the 1996 Basle Capital Accord, have led to the VAR concept taking on a central role in the risk-management policies of international banks.[28] The Accord specifically allows for a choice between 'standardized' and 'internal' approaches to the measurement of market risk, with the latter opening the door to VAR numbers in establishing an entity's capital at risk (in relation to both derivative and non-derivative positions).

The Basle Capital Accord, in relation to the use of internal models (see Part B of the Accord), stipulates, amongst other things, that VAR be calculated on a daily basis to characterize an upper bound for the dollar value of potential losses at a confidence level of 99%. The upper bound for potential losses is, in turn 'an instantaneous price shock equivalent to a 10-day movement in prices' (p. 44). In theory then, the probability of losses exceeding one's VAR estimate, computed over a subsequent 10-day holding period, should be 1% or less.[29]

The critical issue, perhaps, is the capital requirement or charge emanating from a bank's VAR computations. The Accord makes it clear that: 'Each bank must meet, on a daily basis, a *capital requirement* expressed as the higher of (i) its previous day's value-at-risk number measured according to the parameters specified . . . and (ii) an average of the daily value-at-risk measures on each of the preceding sixty business days, multiplied by a multiplication factor' (p. 45, italics as used).

The Accord stipulates further that the multiplication factor in the above meet a level of at least three. These stipulations on internal models also come with an array of additional requirements including the use of stress testing and scenario analysis. VAR is therefore one part, albeit a key part, of a risk-management approach for those adopting the procedures set out in Part B of the Accord (rather than the standardized approach in Part A).

The composition of the Basle Committee, which include the governors of central banks housed within the Group of Ten (G10), means that the Accord carries force directly within the G10 arena subject, where appropriate, to the assent of the requisite national authorities. Its provisions have also been embraced further afield, where supervisory authorities have taken steps to accept some, or all, of its provisions. The SAR is one such example, given steps taken by the Hong Kong Monetary Authority (HKMA) to revise the capital adequacy regime, relating to banks under its purview, in late 1997. This involved two initiatives: an amendment to the Seventh Schedule of the local Banking Ordinance and *A Guideline Issued by the Monetary Authority under Section 16.10* of the Banking Ordinance (hereafter the *Guideline*). These changes essentially paved the way for the broad acceptance of the Basle Accord, within certain parameters set by local conditions. Amongst other things, the HKMA made provision for certain banks to obtain a 'de minimus exemption' from the provisions of the new market risk regime, where a bank's exposure to market risk was deemed minimal.[30] They also made provision for the internal models approach, enshrined in Part B of the Basle Capital Accord, to figure as one of three possible methods for market-risk measurement for banks without such de minimus exemptions.[31] Banks adopting the new market-risk measures would, in effect, report two capital adequacy ratio figures to the HKMA: one to reflect the banking standards already in force and the other, the new adjusted ratio, to reflect market-risk.[32] Recent annual reports for some local banks also contain information on the two types of capital adequacy ratio.[33]

As the VAR technology has been widely accepted by a host of securities firms, which ostensibly lie outside the direct remit of the Basle Capital Accord guidelines, the VAR concept has extended across the whole of the financial services industry. In all cases, firms benefit from knowing the amount of capital that can be freed up for productive investment. In the absence of quantitative standards, large amounts of funds may be tied up unnecessarily leading to opportunity costs for individual firms and the economy in general. The irony to some, is that the multiplication factor of three, adopted in the Basle Capital Accord, promotes this in some senses and may encourage banks to plump for the 'standardized' approach.[34]

VAR also offers advantages beyond the issues of firm-wide capital adequacy. One is that it can be decomposed, in so-called incremental form, across products and traders. Ho, Chen, and Eng's (1996) decomposition of VAR into VAR betas or 'blocks' aptly demonstrates the former. The decomposition of VAR across trading positions is equally meritorious. By being able to examine a trader's contribution to a bank or corporation's VAR, insights into the risk–reward pay-off of the trader's portfolio easily emerge. One imagines that the errant trader would be more easily identified through this approach. This is all the more significant given the rather myopic preoccupation of securities firms in rewarding traders solely on the basis of revenues generated. Barings and others would undoubtedly have benefited from knowing something about the risk–return performance of their traders.[35]

Approaches to the Calculation of VAR

VAR itself is a generic approach to risk and, as indicated, can be applied across products to provide a dollar value of company-wide risk exposure. In this sense, it is considerably more powerful than particular sensitivity measures applied to individual products (like duration for the price sensitivity of bonds to interest rates). In pursuit of a company-wide VAR measure, three general approaches are apparent: historical correlation-covariance analysis, historical simulation, and stochastic (Monte Carlo) simulation. The simulation approaches are considerably more complex than the first approach to VAR.[36]

In the first approach to VAR, historical correlations are computed for various products across risk factors and then information is aggregated to form a company-wide VAR measure. This correlation-covariance approach is easier to apply than either the historical or stochastic simulation approaches. However, it relies upon a number of questionable assumptions. In particular, Reid (1996) opines that the correlation method 'assumes the returns on risk factors are normally distributed, the correlations between risk factors are constant and the delta (or price sensitivity to changes in a risk factor) of each portfolio constituent is constant' (p. 3).

Evidence of 'fat-tails' in the distribution of returns would seem to undermine the assumption of normality.[37] The upshot of such tails, as cogently argued by Paul-Choudhury (1996), is that 'Outlying events (a technical euphemism for crashes) are more common in the real world than the normal distribution would suggest' (p. 23, brackets as shown). Options, as suggested, also pose a significant problem in the correlation approach given the non-linear relationship, as captured through delta, between option premium and underlying share value. In such cases, simulation approaches seem to be preferred, despite the increased complexity of such approaches.[38]

The possibility of conditional (i.e., time-dependent) volatilities is also a worry for users of the correlation-based VAR approach. This is, perhaps, one of the reasons why bodies like the Basle Committe for Banking Supervision require capital levels to be at set at levels that are at least three times average daily VAR figures (computed over a preceding 60-day period).[39]

The essential differences between the various approaches to VAR raise an obvious question: does VAR vary significantly across the three approaches for any given firm or portfolio? Hendricks' (1996) application of VAR models to foreign exchange portfolio data, over the 1983–95 period for 1,000 randomly chosen portfolios, addresses this issue. Twelve categories of model are selected from three basic types of approach to VAR in this analysis.[40] In his conclusion, he notes that 'historical examination of twelve approaches to value-at-risk modelling shows that in almost all cases the approaches cover the risk that they are intended to cover' (p. 55).

While Hendricks' paper provides some comfort for VAR users, Beder's (1995) investigation raises some questions. Three hypothetical portfolios are examined by Beder by using a variety of historical and Monte Carlo simulations (see Table 1 in Beder (1995, p. 13)). The hypothetical portfolios were chosen to differ in terms of asset composition and so-called optionality. While only three portfolios were featured in this study, against 1,000 in Hendricks', the essential differences in asset composition of the portfolios provide a new angle on the stability of VAR. Beder notes considerable variation in VAR results[41] across the portfolios and concludes that 'the 99% VAR changes significantly based on the time horizon, data base, correlation assumptions, mathematical models, and quantitative techniques that are used' (p. 23).

VAR results may well exhibit some stability when used for a particular type of asset or portfolio, as in Hendricks' analysis of foreign exchange portfolios. Further standardization of model assumptions might also be helpful in the pursuit of meaningful VAR numbers. The potential variance in VAR numbers, across models and portfolios, does not undermine the present need for quantitative evaluations of a bank's capital at risk, however. Rather, it indicates that bank should consider VAR in relation to the precise portfolios they hold and, perhaps, err on the side of caution by accepting VAR numbers at the higher end of the spectrum.

Overview of the VAR Approach

While the various VAR models appear to be helpful, they are not, nor are they intended to be, a panacea for the ills associated with market risk. However, they do offer a warning device against overexposure arising from the use of both derivative and non-derivative based products. It should be stressed that they are not a safeguard against fraudulent or unauthorized trading activities prevalent in many of the publicized derivative loss cases. If fraudulent trading activity is present and trades are either disguised or hidden, VAR will not lead to the identification of such trades. Effective supervisory controls should be in place to ensure that the VAR numbers produced are meaningful. Internal controls for the auditing and surveillance of positions are clearly vital precursors to the application of VAR.

VAR, for all its merits, cannot be used on its own. It is probably a futile exercise to quantitatively assess market risk up to the 99th percentile (for a one-day holding period) if the risks pertaining to the counterparty, legality of contracts, or supervisory controls are not measured. As cogently summarized by Beder, quantitative evaluations only tell part of the story:

> Many risk variables such as political risk, liquidity risk, personnel risk, regulatory risk, phantom liquidity risk, and others cannot be captured through quantitative techniques. Yet, as demonstrated by recent, well-publicized losses, such variables can cause significant risk. For this reason, VAR must be supplemented not only with stress testing but also with prudent checks and balances, procedures, policies, controls, limits, random audits, and appropriate reserves' (Beder (1995), p. 23).

The principal advantage of VAR is that it provides an indication of the necessary capital protection for trading positions and means that capital in excess of this can be freed up for more productive uses. In addition, VAR should be seen as a tool to complement existing systems for risk management, particularly those which focus on the supervisory and operations-based risks of the organization.

13.5 Concluding Remarks

Attention in this chapter has focused on the common risk factors associated with derivatives. While most of the discussion has dealt squarely with issues of market and credit-based risk, other risk areas, relating to supervisory and operational-based risks, are also critical. Invoking VAR numbers, in an attempt to capture an entity's market exposure, without taking adequate steps to supervize trading documentation and systems would probably offer very little benefit in risk-management terms. At worst, quantitative assessments might mislead, especially where only a portion of trades are reflected in the figures. As realtors are apt to say, there are only three things that matter: location, location, and location. For an entity trading derivatives, the repetitious bullets might well apply to supervisory controls.

A clear demarcation was also made in the foregoing between exchange-traded and OTC-traded derivatives. With the various risks in the latter generally at levels well in excess of those for exchange-traded products, arguments for further regulation in the burgeoning OTC-derivatives area have been well heeded. Others also argue that guidelines offered in recent years by bodies like IOSCO, in particular countries, are sufficient and that further regulation might prove counter-productive by forcing OTC business offshore. Critics always aver, however, that this old chestnut is used to justify inaction. This may be a little disingenuous, as regulatory controls might well be very effective if mandated with a global remit. The difficulties in organizing this and making it effective surely weigh heavily on the minds of regulators around the world.

Convergence of regulatory standards can also be achieved by authorities, in the more heavily regulated jurisdictions, liberalizing their own standards. Again, this may be driven by a desire to keep derivatives on shore rather than off. SEC approval in late 1998 of new rules, which allow for a new kind of registration mode for US OTC derivatives dealers, appears to be of this ilk. For those broker-dealers embracing the new trading status, the new rules afford certain risk-management and margin benefits.[42] All in all, these benefits would seem to provide greater incentive for US OTC derivatives dealers to book their business onshore, than might have been the case hitherto.

Notes

1.   Much of the following is based upon a paper entitled 'The Control and Management of Risk for Derivatives: A Survey' by Paul B. McGuinness. This paper was, in turn, an extension of a consultancy report written by the author whilst employed as a consultant for the National Bank of New Zealand. Comments made by Martin Lally and Leslie Young on earlier drafts of the survey paper are also gratefully acknowledged.
2.   As an indication, see Bank of England (1995) and Basle Committee on Banking Supervision (1996).
3.   See Technical Committee of IOSCO (1994, p. 1).
4.   See Lim, Yu, Sargent, and Shimomura (1995) for an in-depth analysis of the trading strategies employed in the Barings case.
5.   See Anonymous (October 1998a) for an excellent review of some of these cases.
6.   See Davies and Yu (1995) for further details.
7.   A US subsidiary of MG was held culpable (see Edwards and Cantor's (1995) overview).
8.   See Edwards and Cantor (1995, pp. 218–24) for detailed discussion of the historical 'backwardation' of oil energy futures prior to 1993.
9.   See Anonymous (February 1993).

10. For guidelines on the control of OTC derivatives, see the Technical Committee of the International Organisation of Securities Commissions (IOSCO), July 1994. In addition, the Basle Committee on Banking Supervision 1994 have also published guidelines focusing on operational and risk-management issues for OTC derivatives. For specific guidelines on the market and credit risks associated with OTC derivatives, useful reference can also be made to the findings of the US based Derivatives Policy Group (see Compton's (1995–6) overview of OTC derivatives regulation) and to Kambhu, Keane, and Benadon's (1996) assessment of a global survey carried out in 1995 by The Bank for International Settlements.

11. For background discussion of this ruling, which was made in the House of Lords in January 1991, see Anonymous (May 1991). The issue has also been raised regarding derivative losses in other markets (see Bancroft (1995)) and suggests that before any consideration can be given to credit or market risk, the legal footing of the contract and the counterparty should be well-established.

12. After incurring large losses on derivatives positions, Gibson Greetings argued that Bankers Trust had sold them securities that were inappropriate for their business (see Holland (1994) for further details).

13. See Levine and Sotunde (1996) for discussion of the features and application of the ISDA Master Agreement to its intended domain: OTC market transactions.

14. See Neal (1996, p. 19-24) for an overview of three of these kinds of instruments described under the rubric of credit swaps, credit options, and credit-linked notes.

15. As indicated in Davidson (1996), the technology and expertise for credit assessments is widely available.

16. See Van Duyne (1995) for discussion of this trend.

17. See Walker (1995) for discussion of the losses in Daiwa and Anonymous (June 1996) for those in Sumitomo.

18. See Mayer (1995).

19. See Woodward, Siegel, and Qureshi (1996) for detailed discussion of FASB 119.

20. See Reuters (1997).

21. See Technical Committe of IOSCO (1994).

22. See SFC (1995).

23. Thanks are due to the SFC for its clarification of this issue.

24. See SFC (April 1997).

25. See SFC (April 1997, p. 2) for details of these findings and others.

26. See Heron and Irving (1996, p. 16) for an overview of the suppliers of VAR software.

27. For background on its origins, see Cooper (1996) and Reed (1996, p. 2).

28. One of the most significant developments in the regulatory control of derivatives and the measurement of derivative risk is the promulgation of the recent Basle Capital Accord, published through the Basle Committee on Banking Supervision (1996). This report specifies capital requirements for certain international banks that operate in countries comprising the Group of Ten (see Elderfield (1996) for a brief summary of the implications of the Accord) and builds upon earlier initiatives like the Group of Thirty's.

29. Another way of interpreting the confidence level is as in Reed (1996). He notes that 'the BIS rules, known as the Basle Capital Accord, specify a 99% confidence interval (i.e., actual losses on the portfolio should exceed the VAR estimate not more than once in every 100 days)' (Reed (1996, p. 3)).

30. See, in particular, S. 14 of the *Guideline.*

31. The other approaches entertained were the 'standardized' method, as set out in Part A of the Basle Capital Accord, and the CAD or Capital Adequacy Directive, as set out by the European Union for market risk (see, in particular, S. 17 of the *Guideline*).

32. Specifically, see S. 8 of the *Guideline.*

33. See the Hang Seng Bank's Annual Report for 1997 (p. 133) for instance.

34. Elderfield (1996, p. 10), in the immediate aftermath of the Accord's publication, offers a notable account of such opinion.

35. Van Duyne (1995) offers a lucid account of VAR as a vehicle for rewarding traders in this trade-off.

36. For details of the characteristics of the three methods, Leong (1996) and Stambaugh (1996) offer useful accounts.

37. For a brief review of this finding, see Hendricks (1996, p. 41).

38. See, for instance, Leong (1996, p. 11).

39. Hopper (1996), with regard to the issue of conditional volatility, outlines a number of methodologies for obtaining meaningful VAR measures when volatilities are time-dependent. One of the methodologies reviewed in Hopper, which involves a Bollerslev style GARCH approximation for conditional volatility, is offered through J.P. Morgan's RiskMetrics™ service.

40. Equally weighted and exponentially weighted moving-average approaches and historical simulation approaches.

41. Beder (1995) notes with regard to the VAR approaches surveyed, that 'the magnitude of the discrepancy among these methods is shocking, with VAR results varying by more than 14 times for the same portfolio' (page 12).

42. See Jacklin and Woo (1998) for a description of this new trading category and detailed enumeration of the key benefits to OTC derivative dealers registering under the new category.

14. An Overview of Market Trends and Recent Developments

As an overview, key developments and likely trends in the markets are explored in this final chapter. Much of the analysis in this area revolves around the Asian financial malaise of 1997 and 1998, and the lessons learnt from this rather painful experience. The retreat of overseas banks and institutions, in particular, and the ensuing 'liquidity crunch' highlighted a major deficiency in virtually all Asian markets: the absence of deep and liquid markets for corporate debt securities. With overseas lenders, and Japanese banks in particular, effectively issuing a moratorium on new lending, the East Asian financial crisis exposed a gaping hole in corporate funding. To many, this gap could have been plugged had debt markets played a substantive supporting role. The experience in Western markets, particularly in the United States and the United Kingdom, shows that debt financing is evenly shared amongst banks and markets. This not only takes pressure off the banks, but also generates certain spin-off benefits for equities. By drawing in new institutional investors, such markets enhance liquidity and lower funding costs. Improvements in corporate credit ratings, and an easing of pressure on inter-bank rates, would also be healthy by-products of this. Both would contribute to a reduction in the risk premium of local stocks. It is small wonder then that local politicians and regulators see debt market development as a key strategic goal for the SAR.

Proposals for a Second Board on the SEHK, like the debt market initiative, are also intended to widen funding choices. Essentially targetted at small to medium sized firms, its undoubted aim is to entice scores of Mainland companies to 'tap' the market for new funds. This would not only offer investors greater scope in their investment selections, but also galvanize the investment picture in the real economy. A Second Board would also place Hong Kong on a par with other major markets that serve small to medium sized companies: London's Alternative Investment Market (AIM), Tokyo's Second Section, and Singapore's SESDAQ market being good examples. In various ways, then, both the mooted debt and Second Board developments are instrumental in strengthening the SAR's role as a capital-raising centre. These developments are mentioned in Section 14.1.

The creation of the Exchange Fund Investment Ltd is then examined in Section 14.2. This body is charged with managing the Exchange Fund's local equity portfolio, amassed during the HKMA's intervention in the local markets in August 1998. While the *modus operandi* of the intervention was broadly spelled out in Chapter 12, little was said about the intervention in terms of its impact upon market supervision or the possible conflict of interest stemming from the HKMA's supervisory role, as an adjunct to the office of the Financial Secretary. Other effects, like the impact on market liquidity are also assessed given that, in a number of stocks, the effective 'free-float' was reduced below levels previously obtaining. In short, the intervention was unparalleled and the issues that relate to it, like the management of the Exchange Fund Investment Ltd and its precise role, deserve some attention.

The advent of electronic or Internet trading is also another major development. This is a truly global phenomenon and is assessed in Section 14.3. It offers enormous potential in generating new, competing trading systems and exchanges. Thus far, Internet trading has not had this effect in Hong Kong, acting instead on the periphery of existing systems. Only a handful of members of the SEHK currently offer access to their brokerage services through the Internet, with all orders routed through to the SEHK. In this sense, Internet trading serves as a complement to more traditional order-routing techniques which involve telephone communication between investor and broker. Regulations governing electronic trading are still at a formative stage and an overview of how these might evolve is critical to an appreciation of trading systems in the twenty-first century.

More traditional exchange forums are also responding to the Internet threat and will need to evolve to meet this challenge. The trend towards 'de-mutualization', introduced in Section 2.1, is one example of this. So is the move towards exchange cooperation and merger. Recent merger activity amongst US exchanges, as well as the London/Frankfurt joint venture to dual-list 300 of their leading stocks, points to engagement, rather than outright competition, as the new strategy for exchange survival. Consolidation of derivatives trading, especially in Continental Europe (see Section 12.8), and moves towards common clearing and settlement systems are also part of this trend. Issues relating to the various consolidations, mergers, and exchange 'de-mutualization' form the content of Section 14.4.

As a conclusion to the whole text, the reasons behind the Asian financial crisis of 1997 and 1998 are briefly explored in Section 14.5. The whole experience proves that even well-managed economies with sound governments, strong banks, and healthy risk management systems—as befits a description of Hong Kong—sometimes fall prey to the profligate policies of neighbouring countries. The crisis, which largely emanated from Thailand and Indonesia and spread like wildfire to The Philippines, Malaysia, South Korea and (later on) Japan, highlighted one important thing: the resilience of the regional hubs, Hong Kong and Singapore. It also offered one or two other instructive insights. Apart from the potential benefits offered by liquid debt markets, it highlighted the need for cooperation between the region's trading partners. Issues of transparency also came to the fore. Deficiencies in relation to corporate disclosure and governance were clearly signalled. Stories of numerous banks and corporations overladen with debts, in several South-East Asian Countries, stirred debate on this issue.

The debt situation would not have been so bad had they been denominated in local currencies. With a good many in US dollars, and with little or no attempt to hedge the implicit currency risks, the currency devaluations, when they came, hit with tremendous ferocity. The question on everyone's lips, admittedly with the benefit of hindsight, is why were such risks not adequately measured and managed? From a measurement perspective we come back to that catch-all, transparency. Without this, there is little prospect of any meaningful stab at risk management.

14.1   The Restructuring of Debt Markets and its Potential Impact upon the Local Equity Market

A number of eminent speakers in Hong Kong have pointed to the immaturity of regional debt markets as a key factor behind the recent financial crisis. Withdrawals of HKD deposits, spurred by currency devaluation fears in late 1997 and much of 1998, led to pressure on the funding base of many banks. Attempts to shore up liquidity deficiencies through inter-bank transactions more often than not provided the solution. The net result, though, was unwelcome pressure on HIBOR. An active debt market, by freeing corporations from the constraints of bank financing, would ultimately release some pressure from the inter-bank market when it most needed it. It would also help to address the widely perceived assets–liabilities mismatch of many local banks where funding is predominantly short term (via deposits) and lending long term (often in mortgaged asset form). It is on these grounds that the Financial Secretary, Donald Tsang, and other luminaries, have argued so vehemently for a wider set of funding choices.

The debt market initiative also reflects a desire on the part of local regulators and market-players to provide a greater mix of securities for international investment funds. The Mandatory Provident Fund (MPF) scheme will undoubtedly attract renewed institutional interest and it is hoped that funds generated from local savings find their way back into local markets. While the SAR's equity markets appear well placed to absorb a good portion of these funds, it is unclear how the debt markets will fare. Despite an increase in the number of official debt listings and OTC-based fund-raising activities in the debt area, liquidity is a perennial problem.

While the MPF might be seen as one vehicle for reviving interest in this arena, changes to the structure of the debt market are essential. Issues of debt quality and type are also critical. The SAR government appears to recognize this given various pronouncements calling for an increase in the supply of high quality, fixed-interest paper.

A substantial portion of locally-issued corporate debt is floating-rate debt and may not satisfy the needs of institutional investors who are likely to be key players in the formation of MPF programmes. To encourage greater interest in this area, initiatives like the Hong Kong Mortgage Corporation (HKMC), created by the Hong Kong government in 1997, are key. Amongst other things, the HKMC has a mandate to purchase mortgage assets from local banks and other deposit-taking companies (DTCs). Using the cash-flow returns on these assets as backing, it can then issue fixed-interest bearing securities to the investment populace. This process of *securitization* is critical to the development of Hong Kong's debt markets. The combined role of the MPF, in searching out new, fixed-interest quality paper, and the HKMC, in supplying it, are fundamental strands of the government's debt-development policies. Spillover effects, as argued at the outset, should also add buoyancy to local equity markets.

The Nature of Asset-Backed (Collateralized) Securities

The origins of asset-backed securities can be found in the United States, where securitization of both corporate and government bonds has been big business for many years. The forebear of the STRIP, or 'separate trading of registered interest and principal of securities', provides an example of securitization in the area of US Treasuries.[1] The STRIP acronym is also an apt description of its construction, where a bond's constituent interest (coupons) and face value (principal) payments are 'stripped out' and sold separately as zero-coupon securities. To illustrate, consider a collection of 7% US Treasury bonds with exactly two years to maturity. These could be unbundled, given coupons payable in two equal instalments per year, into four constituent securities: one for each of the coupons of $3.50 (per $100 of face value) receivable in six, 12, and 18 months' time, and one for the final payment of coupon plus face value of $103.50 in 24 months' time. STRIPS these days are created by the US Treasury (see note 1). Prior to the origination of this market, a similar process of 'stripping' was carried out by intermediaries acquiring Treasuries and unpackaging constituent period cash flows. This resembled what we now know as securitization. In simple terms, new securities were issued backed by underlying collateral. The collateral, in the case of the antecedents of the current-day STRIP, being underlying Treasuries.

Securitization is most commonly associated with the pooling of mortgage loans. The work of the *Federal National Mortgage Association* (or Fannie Mae, to use the accepted sobriquet) in the United States is a good example. This body accepts a specific role in supporting the US mortgage market and like its relative, the *Federal Home Loan Mortgage Corporation* (or so-called Freddie Mac), actively buys and pools mortgages in issue. Using the pooled mortgages as backing (or collateral), new debt-based securities are then issued. This is described as a 'pass through' arrangement since all receivables on the mortgages 'pass through' to the new security holders.[2] The receivables are the interest and repayment of principal on the loans which, instead of being paid to the originating bank, 'pass through' to the new security holders via the mortgage association or corporation. As owners of the underlying mortgage assets, the mortgage corporations' new securities are fully-backed or collateralized. This is the spirit in which the work of the HKMC is expected to progress.

The Role of the Hong Kong Mortgage Corporation (HKMC)

Like its US counterpart, the HKMC fulfils a critical supporting role by offering a secondary mortgage market. In the first instance, this will help banks rearrange balance sheets by allowing them to unload excess mortgage assets. Until recently, excess holdings for local, authorized banks were deemed to be mortgage holdings over and above a 40% 'ceiling' on the proportion of outstanding loans in property mortgage form, as stipulated by the HKMA.[3] The removal of the 'ceiling' in 1998, driven by weakening property values, was made possible, in large part, by the very existence of the HKMC. As this body now provides a mechanism for banks to unload excess mortgage holdings, the old 'ceiling' may be viewed as less valuable than hitherto. Previously the 'ceiling' was designed to limit banks' exposure to the vacillations of local property values. Critics aver, however, that the 'ceiling's' removal has strengthened the hand of banks in its dealings with the HKMC.

Whatever the possible misgivings of the 'ceiling's' removal, most agree that the new secondary mortgage market, made possible by the HKMC's arrival, provides a welcome boost to the primary mortgage market. The very fact that banks can pass mortgage holdings on should give them greater confidence in issuing new loans. The fact that the HKMC will also make its own credit assessments before purchasing loan assets, means that banks also need to ensure that new loans are of a sufficiently high quality. This is also a healthy by-product of the HKMC. As in virtually all securitization programmes, some level of credit enhancement is likely.

The HKMC therefore offers a route to a substantial increase in the size of the primary mortgage market without endangering quality ratings. This would have undoubtedly weighed heavily in its favour when the HKMC was first mooted. HKMA forecasts at that time suggested that by the year 2005, residential mortgage loans would account for around 50% of GDP, having already risen from 8.3% to 31.3% between 1980 and 1995.[4] In the absence of new mortgage providers, fears of a decline in mortgage loan quality, as existing banks stretched to meet increasing demand for new loans, seemed quite legitimate.

The HKMC, as a body owned by the Exchange Fund, has received some 'seed' money from its parent. It has also raised funding from a number of recent debt issues. These have helped finance some of its mortgage purchase commitments. The Corporation has also set out to promote fixed-interest rate mortgages by entering into a 'fixed-rate mortgage pilot scheme'.[5] In this scheme, the HKMC has arranged to buy fixed-interest rate mortgages as they originate from two banks: Dao Heng and Chase Manhattan. Amongst other things, the fixed-rate mortgage market should help to stabilize the property and equity markets against unwarranted interest rate movements. Donald Tsang, the Financial Secretary and Chairman of the HKMC, has also consistently pointed to the asset-liability mismatch problem in local banks. This, as noted earlier, describes a situation where lending is predominantly long-term and funding (deposits) short-term. This explains why virtually all mortgages in Hong Kong have, hitherto, been arranged on floating rate terms.[6] The HKMC's venture into fixed-interest rate mortgage products is therefore a timely one.

Lastly, in connection with the principal issue of interest here, the HKMC has made some headway in its programme of debt market development. This has largely been achieved through the issue of fixed-interest (unsecured) notes. As we saw earlier in this text, trading in these notes, as in Exchange Fund bills and notes and Hong Kong Airport Authority and Mass Transit Railway Corporation notes, is made via registered dealers with clearing and settlement achieved through the HKMA's Central Moneymarkets Unit (CMU).

In the longer-term, the HKMC is likely to issue collateralized (mortgage-backed) securities. In short, debt secured on recently acquired mortgage assets. This initiative, as described in its 1997 annual report, represents the second phase of its programme. With regard to debt market development this is, without doubt, the most promising area. To reiterate, most expect the supply of quality, fixed-interest paper from this initiative, and the demand from investors wishing to park funds through the MPF scheme, to be the driving force behind local debt market developments.

More recent pronouncements, like the proposals to list Exchange Fund notes on the SEHK, should complement the government's HKMC and MPF initiatives by raising the profile of marketable debt.[7]

The Development of a Second Board for the SEHK

Talk of the need for a Second Board on the SEHK has been rife for some time. Interest in the issue resurfaced with the publication of an exchange consultation paper on the matter in 1998 (see SEHK (1998, May)). Responses from the exercise were sufficiently encouraging for the exchange to issue a subsequent news release (see SEHK (1998, October)) confirming its intention to develop the new board through a specially constructed Second Market Working Group. As a forum for funding 'low-cap' local and Mainland stocks the market has huge potential. The history of markets catering for small to medium firm stocks, in other jurisdictions, has been a rather chequered one, however. The meteoric rise of London's Unlisted Securities Market (USM) in the 1980s, and its subsequent decline is a potent reminder of this. The Alternative Investment Market (AIM) now stands as the successor to London's original second market, the USM.

Small to medium firm stocks are, by their very nature, risky investment propositions. This raises very natural concerns about their liquidity. Without the prospect of active secondary markets, the very purpose of a second board—as a primary market forum—may be compromised. Grappling with this issue of liquidity is therefore key and requires controls over the quality of stocks listed and clear rules on their accounting disclosures and continuing obligations. Obvious derogations from rules applying to stocks listed on main boards clearly apply. Finding the balance between the magic words of 'transparency' and 'accountability' and allowing a free-flow of small to medium sized corporations access to the markets, requires some skill. Nonetheless, the track record of the SEHK in running its 'main' board augers well for its new, and timely, 'second' board venture.

14.2 The Market Intervention Policy of August 1998 and its Longer-Term Effect on Market Stability and Developments

The gravity of the SAR government's decision to intervene in its own stock and futures markets in August 1998 can hardly be understated. While the background to this intervention was largely spelled out in Section 12.8, its effects continue to unravel. By a number of yardsticks, though, the intervention was an outstanding success: the restoration of some semblance of interest rate stability and reduced volatility in the HSI, in the months following the intervention, being the best measure of this. The government can also claim that its intervention was a timely one given the large windfall return on its investment portfolio in the immediate aftermath of the intervention. Some commentators like *The Economist*, however, are less inclined to offer such plaudits. They suggest the timing was rather fortuitous, occurring just prior to the Russian debt crisis, which triggered a 'flight to quality' and losses for hedge funds (holding short positions in 'risky' debt), and prior to a series of interest cuts by the US Federal Reserve.[8] The latter was, perhaps, the more important of the two events, allowing some weakening of the local currency against other regional currencies, like the yen. This is only part of the story, though. The measures instituted by the HKMA, in the aftermath of August 1998, to inject more liquidity into the inter-bank markets (see Section 2.2), are also compelling reasons behind the hedge fund retreat. Whatever the reasons for the SAR government's success, the move represented a bold and calculated gamble. It was also unprecedented in both its scale and intensity.

Government Ownership of Securities

The HKMA's intervention is not the first time governments, or agencies thereof, have intervened in markets. Many governments around the world routinely invest in overseas treasury bill and bond markets. Government rescues of ailing banks and other major financial institutions, whether listed or unlisted, also mark another obvious form of direct intervention. The US government's rearguard action in salvaging Long Term Capital Management in 1998 being a recent case. Government intervention therefore takes many forms and is typically justified in terms of 'public interest' issues.

Certain governments also hold large equity stakes in listed corporations. Government ownership of stock in public listed companies is not, in itself, unusual. In most cases, though, this is a residual holding following the sale of a company, as a hitherto fully-fledged state asset, to the public. These state privatizations have been common throughout much of the 1980s and 1990s in countries as diverse as the UK, Australia, New Zealand, the PRC, and Poland (as well as several other Eastern European countries). Telecommunications stocks around the world typify such ownership structures where as much as 30% to 40% of the listed stock can be beneficially owned by the state. 'H' shares, as we saw in earlier chapters, are a good example of 'partial privatizations' locally, although these are slightly different. The PRC government or a municipal body wields majority control by holding the non-'H' share component of the company's issued share capital which is not allowed to trade outside the Mainland.

There is also a history of government stock ownership in Hong Kong, as was revealed from questions levelled at the Secretary for Financial Services, Raphael Hui, in the chambers of the Legislative Council in November 1998. One of these questions sought clarification on the government's record of stockholdings in locally-listed companies. Amongst other things, the reply indicated that the Exchange Fund had had a role in local equity investment since 1981 and had held substantial interests (10% or more) in one or two listed stocks, such as the Cross Harbour Tunnel Co, between the early 1980s and early 1990s. Once again, it comes as no surprise to learn of a government's investment interest, albeit in limited form, in listed stocks. The same cannot be said of futures, though, given an assertion that the Exchange Fund had not, prior to its intervention in August 1998, purchased futures on the local market.[9]

The Arguments for and against the HKMA's 1998 Stock and Futures Intervention

Despite a history of governments around the world participating in markets, the sheer scale of the SAR government's 1998 intervention was simply staggering. Views on its merits, quite naturally, were wide-ranging. To some, holding steadfastly to 'free-market' principles, the intervention was ill-advised and served to undermine the SAR's reputation as a free and unfettered port of call for securities trading. This view was, and still is, widespread but can be challenged on a number of fronts. Firstly, for some, albeit a vocal minority, of those venting their concerns, the rhetoric may have had more to do with the size of their balance sheets than economic ideology. To be fair, the self-interest argument can also be used in reverse: many retail investors, seeking an opportunity to sell in an otherwise illiquid market, rejoiced in the HKMA's intervention simply because it offered a way out of the market. Refuting the position of the 'anti-interventionists', simply on grounds of self-interest, clearly invites a similar riposte.

More substantive criticism of the 'anti-interventionist' position can be made by questioning whether the 'free-market' environment such commentators wished to preserve actually existed. Can markets be 'free' when a small number of players, as media reports at the time suggested, act to manipulates prices? Yes, Hong Kong's markets were, and still are, 'open'. But general opinion would suggest that they were far from 'free' in the run-up to the August 1998 intervention. Arguments lambasting the HKMA's intervention on the grounds of undermining 'free-market' principles often fail to acknowledge this point. As the government would no doubt argue, extraordinary events sometimes require extraordinary measures.

Others have argued that the alleged manipulation should have been dealt with by invoking existing regulations or developing new ones. The difficulties and time involved in pursuing such a course of action are self-evident. Should one defend oneself against attack when bullets are flying or seek redress after the battle has been lost? The carnage resulting from delay could have been devastating. Most, quite rightly, offered an Armageddon-type scenario for Hong Kong, in the event of a decoupling of the exchange-rate, with sharp falls in the currency accompanied by a massive capital outflow. In the event, most expected the link to withstand the battering, but accepted that failure to attack the speculative 'double-play' strategy[10] would simply invite speculators to move in and out of the markets, generating considerable interest rate volatility in the process.

Additional measures to add transparency to the markets have, in any event, followed on the heels of the intervention. An issue that has also received attention is the legitimacy (or legality) of the government's intervention. Section 135 of the Securities Ordinance, which refers to the creation of 'false and disorderly markets',[11] would seem to apply to the actions of the alleged and unnamed manipulators. A burning question for some, however, is whether the government's subsequent intervention contravened provisions in this statute, or any other related statute. The answer, given exemptions provided to the state through provisions in the Interpretation and General Clauses Ordinance,[12] seems to be no.

One issue of greater substance, perhaps, is that of a possible conflict of interest arising from the government's holdings. As a legislator and supervisory body, clear guidelines are obviously necessary to assuage any doubts on this matter. The *Exchange Fund Investment Ltd* (EFIL) which was set up in October 1998, was devised, amongst other things, to do precisely this by giving clear definition to the government's obligations in relation to its investment holdings. This body and its remit is examined below.

The Role of the Exchange Fund Investment Ltd (EFIL)

To appreciate the duties of this body, which broadly entail the management of the SAR government's portfolio of local stock holdings, acquired through the auspices of the HKMA and its Exchange Fund, a breakdown of its investment holdings is necessary. Based upon a press release made by the body on 26 October 1998, the portfolio of Hang Seng Index (HSI) constituents was created for a cost slightly in excess of HK$118 billion.[13]

Over 34% of this amount was used in the purchase of one stock: HSBC Holdings. Precise figures on shares held were also revealed with interest in three stocks—New World Development, Cheung Kong Holdings, and Swire Pacific 'A'—at levels in excess of 10% of all shares outstanding. Amongst other things, the Board of the EFIL gave assurances that any changes to the holdings of these stocks, of 1% or more, would comply with the reporting requirements enshrined in the Securities (Disclosure of Interests) Ordinance.[14]

The figures reported also allowed for a more refined assessment of the size of the 'free-float' in the constituent stocks. This essentially refers to the proportion of stock held in small investor hands and normally is the component of stockholdings that drives liquidity. Ordinarily we often assume a 'free-float' of around 25% of a stock's shares given the 25% 'public' interest requirement 'normally' prescribed by the Exchange. Although, as we noted in Section 1.3, stocks with market capitalizations of HK$4 billion or more may be allowed to have a 'public' interest percentage lower than 25%.[15]

While the government's intervention may not have directly affected the definition of the 'public interest' component, the effective 'free-float' would have been materially reduced. In fact, analyst estimates reported in the press, suggest that the government's intervention precipitated a fall in the 'free-float' of some companies of over 20%.[16] To some, the fall in the available supply of shares may well have contributed to the rise in share prices in the months following the intervention, though, in defence of the HKMA and the government, the intervention built in a risk premium into the market with many fearing that subsequent sale of the stock would drive down the market. Issues of when and how such sales are made dictate the size of this risk premium. Nonetheless a risk premium, or dampening effect on stock prices, exists. In the event, the EFIL has made it clear on several occasions that any disposals would be carefully managed with a view to minimizing any deleterious effects on the markets. Recent pronouncements on the issue point to the possible use of various vehicles, including share repurchases and the construction of exchangeable bonds to off load up to HK$100 billion of the portfolio.[17]

14.3 Electronic Trading and the Rise of Internet Trading

The Emergence of the Internet

The potential of the Internet in shaping financial market systems is so immense that by the first decade of the new millennium, virtually all trade could be routed through this medium. Already a number of major exchanges have reacted to this prospect by allowing their members, as both principals and agents, a role in electronic trading. The SEHK, as noted in the introduction, has, quite naturally, embraced this approach.

The Internet as an Order-Routing Facility

The proviso, of course, is that all trades find their way into established exchange-based trading systems. This requires formal registration of the Internet-service providers by the regulatory authorities in the jurisdictions chosen for trading. In general terms, two forms of order-routing are apparent: one where orders are transmitted directly to an associated brokerage arm of the supplier and another where the supplier transmits orders to one of an array of nominated member (broker) firms. The latter aptly describes the order-routing service provided by Asia's pioneer in Internet order-routing, Boom Securities,[18] which provides trading access to the SEHK via selected member firms of the Exchange.

If order-routing is the way forward for electronic trading, the Internet will essentially provide another forum through which recognized broker members receive client orders, the only difference being that once a client is registered with a broker member, the Internet rather than the telephone serves as the instrument of instruction. This has obvious appeal, especially during heavy trading periods, when telephone contact with a broker representative may be far from easy. It also holds greater appeal when routing orders from overseas, given the cost of telephone communication.

The convenience of being able to route orders directly through the new medium should be all the more obvious once volume levels return to Asian markets. Despite this, many still see a role for the more conventional approach. For one, the traditional method of directing orders is not only more human but can also be more valuable. This is especially so if one's account representative is able to avail him/herself of timely information. The Internet can do much the same, but it often requires the user to skilfully scroll through masses of information. While this detailed information is often of value to the more erudite, it may be viewed as a distraction by others. Despite this reservation, the Internet's speed and convenience will probably result in more conventional order-routing techniques being marginalized.

The 'big bangs' of the last decade or so, which paved the way for the elimination of fixed/minimum brokerage commissions on stock trades, in markets like the United States (in 1975) and the United Kingdom (in 1986), have provided fertile territory for Internet development. Nonetheless, as noted in Section 3.1, minimum brokerage commissions in Hong Kong limit the extent to which Internet suppliers are able to compete in cost terms. As with some discount brokers overseas, Internet brokers have been particularly adept at cutting costs where competition allows. The prime difference, though, is that this is often achieved by providing 'value-added' services, like data links and up-to-the-minute information flows. For the time being at least, Internet stock broking services will probably have to focus more on the latter in marketing their wares in Asia. Inevitably, though, fixed brokerage commissions will succumb to international pressures. The proposed 'de-mutualization' and merger of the SEHK and HKFE will probably hasten this change.

The Internet as a Fully-Fledged Digital Market

The challenge for existing exchanges, many of whom enjoy monopoly status through statute, is to ensure that the Internet augments rather than weakens their central role. This challenge throws up a host of regulatory problems; the most obvious being the 'floating' nature of the medium which seemingly defies current jurisdictionally-based standards. Regulation on a global, rather than local, level is therefore inevitable. The advent of 'super-regulators'—as we saw in Chapter 2—and their likely cooperation in developing common regulatory structures in the major markets is a likely first step. How this pans out over the longer term is anyone's guess.

The sight of alternative cybersystems relegating some existing exchanges to a rather peripheral role is one very real possibility. Unless existing changes can 'add value' there is a real prospect of many of them disappearing. This probably underpins the various moves by exchanges around the globe to 'de-mutualize'—as the Australian Stock Exchange (ASX) has done—or consolidate via joint venture or merger. This restructuring theme is analysed below.

14.4   Equity Trading Systems and Exchanges in the Next Millennium: A Story of Mergers, Joint Ventures and Ownership Reform

The Trend Towards De-Mutualization

The issue of ownership reform was fleetingly discussed in Section 2.1 in relation to the de-mutualization of the Australian Stock Exchange (ASX) and the mooted SEHK/HKFE reorganization. The ASX's move was overwhelmingly approved by its members in late 1996. This was not the first exchange to shed its sedentary form for a more incisive, corporate structure. The Stockholm Stock Exchange (SSE) presaged ASX's move in 1992 when its members agreed to it becoming a subsidiary of the Stockholms Fondboers AB—a stock-issuing company. This was achieved through a subsequent stock issue by the parent with new shares allocated on a 50:50 basis between existing SSE members and listed issuers.[19] Another European exchange, the Amsterdam Stock Exchange, joined the fray in 1996 when its members decided to endorse a similar move. Through the creation of a parent company, the Amsterdamse Beursholding, new shares were subsequently issued to three constituents—existing members, issuers, and institutions—in the ratio 50: 25: 25.[20]

While the new structures generally lend themselves to more innovative and proactive ownership and management structures, members still act as the medium through which trades are routed. As we argued in Section 2.1, this facilitates a separation of ownership and trading rights. This is the central principle behind the proposed 'de-mutualization' of the SEHK and HKFE.

Whether the transformation of hitherto membership-based entities, as in the ASX, SSE, and Amsterdam Stock Exchange, into public limited companies is a model for others to follow, is too early to tell. In Australia's case, its hand was forced largely, according to *The Economist*, by resurgent Asian markets and the growing migration of Australian stock trades.[21] Like most membership-based structures, ownership change can be a rather slow and drawn out affair with, often, only a small number of exchange 'seats' changing hands each year. Membership, then, lends itself to the continuity and preservation of the established order. This is all well and good when exchanges are doing well, but proves to be somewhat unwieldy in less clement times. *The Economist*, commenting prior to the ASX's vote on de-mutualization, captured this exquisitely:

> Mutuality, say its critics, is a recipe for inertia. . . . each of the 527 individual and 99 corporate members has the same voting power—putting the smallest semi-retired individual stockbroker on the same footing as SBC Warburg Australia, the country's biggest stockbroker. The small provincial brokers, who prefer a quiet life, can block reforms such as extended trading hours or faster settlement times.' (Oct 1996, p. 93).

The spiralling growth in the value of 'seats', converted into tradeable shares, following the corporatization and listing of the ASX on its own bourse in 1998, has allowed many erstwhile members to cash in their holdings for handsome profit. This, amongst other things, has contributed to a more institutionally-based shareholding structure.

The Process of De-Mutualization in Asia

Will other Asian exchanges follow the lead of the ASX? The Singapore International Monetary Exchange (SIMEX) and the Stock Exchange of Singapore (SES) have announced that they will. Under the reorganization, both will become wholly-owned subsidiaries of a new exchange body.[22] Indications are that the new Singaporean body will come on line towards the end of 1999, with a listing penned for some time later.[23] As we know, the SEHK and HKFE propose to do much the same.

New ownership structures may invite certain unpalatable consequences for brokers: the removal of fixed brokerage commissions being one. As we noted earlier in this chapter, Asian brokers have been particularly resistant to change, despite moves in most Western markets in the last two decades to deregulate. New ownership structures, involving new constituents and a possible consolidation of shareholdings, would likely weaken the position of smaller brokers who, by and large, place greater store by fixed commissions. With exchange competition accelerating, fixed commission structures appear to be way past their 'sell-by' date.

Nonetheless, not everyone is rushing to embrace the new approach. A number of major exchanges still cling to the traditional model where 'seats' (or unquoted shares) change hands privately. Demutualized exchange structures, despite the success of the ASX, since its 'de-mutualization' and listing in late 1998, are still in their infancy. Only time will tell whether such models achieve what they are intended to. As we will learn in later discussions, the success of 'de-mutualized' forms hinges very heavily on the regulatory structures imposed on the new breed of entity. Where exchange owners are able to influence their share values, as they are at least in theory able to do, in the new model, an inherent conflict of interest exists. For reasons of transparency and accountability, then, de-mutualization requires careful redefinition of market regulation. Initiatives to reinforce and, perhaps, redefine the powers of a nominated independent regulator are central to this.

The Proposed SEHK/HKFE Reforms

The slate of reforms proposed for Hong Kong's securities markets, announced in March 1999,[24] invite three stages of restructuring. If the proposals are approved by the membership of the two exchanges, the Stock Exchange and the Futures Exchange will be de-mutualized and consolidated, along with their clearing houses, into one new entity.[25] In the final stage, the new entity will list on the market. What are the implications of these reforms for existing exchange members? First, member seats (shares) will be converted into tradeable shares in the entity, this preserving their ownership stake.[26] Changes in ownership structure are likely, however, once the tradeable shares attain listed status. Some erstwhile members may seek to 'cash in', or even add to their new shareholdings. These buying and selling pressures suggests a gradual change in the ownership configuration of the new body as it becomes 'seasoned' on the market. Radical changes to the structure are unlikely to be countenanced, though. Restrictions on share ownership levels will certainly figure. Fear of a concentration of shareholdings amongst a few players or, even worse, a takeover by competing concerns, underpin this.[27]

Motivations Behind the Reforms

In brief, a perceived conflict between members as *owners* and *users* of the existing exchange bodies drives the reform. As suggested for the ASX in its previous incarnation, attempts to shift membership-based exchanges in new strategic directions are often stymied by the entrenched interests of members. To some, the traditional model operates first for its members and second for the wider community of investors and issuers. Smaller brokers in particular have more to lose from competition and are often quite adept at mobilizing their 'seats' and those of similar parties to frustrate change. Reference to the attempted reform of the Exchange in 1991, discussed in Section 2.1, and attempts to remove fixed brokerage commissions provide ammunition for such accounts.[28] The changes to ownership envisioned under the new 'de-mutualized' structure, may serve to break up, if not weaken, the various cabals that resist change. Consolidation of holdings amongst the larger brokers is a distinct possibility.

Smaller brokers, given their resource limitations, may well feel the desire to 'cash in' once their shares become marketable. This would not, in theory, affect their trading rights and, more importantly, many large brokers would probably be willing parties for their trades.[29] Some larger brokers may even see this as a means of eliminating recalcitrant shareowners.

More significantly, all stakeholders in the new body benefit as its earnings streams improve. As noted in Section 2.1, the current ownership model prevents this by prohibiting dividend distributions to members. Under the new, proposed regime, they become eligible for such payments as long as they hang on to their traded shares.[30] Obviously, the earnings potential of the new entity also bears upon the valuation of their shares. In essence, then, the new model radically alters the incentives of the exchanges' stakeholders. All will have a vested interest to see more incisive policies at work. By introducing competition in the markets, the commission income of brokers may initially fall, but increased volumes over the longer-term should more than make up for this. This should, in turn, impact favourably on the value of the tradeable shares and also enhance income returns. All in all, the new model points to a more robust, business-like structure.

One of the weaknesses of the new model, however —and it is a major weakness—is that a profit-oriented body sits rather uneasily with a prescribed slate of public duties. How can we be sure that it will not maximize profit to the detriment of the public? Unless regulations dictate otherwise, it will be the instrument of its new masters: its shareholders. Their interest in seeing underlying share valuations appreciate may mean that short-term considerations are placed before the longer-term good of the market. A 'get-rich-quick' mentality of creating conditions for shares to rise, and then dumping them to reap gains, may enhance the welfare of some shareholders, but would do nothing for the market's credibility. Suppose new shareholders attempt to dilute internal controls in order to generate more new listings (and, therefore, listing fees). Such a myopic policy would destabilize the markets over the longer term. The huge expansion in listings between 1969 and 1973 in Hong Kong, when three new exchanges opened, proves how vulnerable a market can be when the worm turns. Strict regulatory controls over Hong Kong's new exchange entity will need to be in place, before the new shareholdings list. This is clearly envisaged and planned for.

The present system, while having its failings, actually militates against the 'get-rich-quick' philosophy. Even if some members embrace this philosophy, the absence of dividends and freely-tradeable ownership rights, severely weakens their incentive to pursue rash and, essentially, speculative strategies. On the other side of the coin, the existing model, as we have argued, encourages inertia and the continuation of uncompetitive trading practices that benefit the greater body of members (but not the wider public).

To harness the advantages of a 'de-mutualized' exchange, then, very careful consideration has to be given to the regulation of such structures. The creation and enforcement of the requisite regulatory framework lies at the very heart of local exchange reform (assuming the reforms come into effect).[31]

In sum, the proposals meted out for Hong Kong, having just surfaced at the time of writing, are set to radically alter the financial market place. In many ways, we can only speculate on the changes ahead. But one thing is clear. Even if the reforms fail to satisfy the exchange members, other radical reforms will inevitably be pushed through, possibly through statute, to deliver the competition the government sees as vital to the long-term success of financial services.

Consolidation of Exchange Structures and Trading

It is quite possible for an exchange to merge with another without dispensing with the membership model. All members of the separately-constructed exchanges could become members of a newly consolidated exchange. Mergers and consolidations have occurred with considerable frequency in recent years along these lines. Many more are likely to follow. The marriage of the National Association of Securities Dealers, Inc (NASD) and the American Stock Exchange, Inc (AMEX) in 1998 is, perhaps, the most notable of the recent pairings.

Technology drives many of the link-ups, with many smaller exchanges drawn to larger ones simply because of their comparative trading/risk-management know-how. The costs and difficulties in upgrading trading technology are prohibitive, especially for smaller exchanges, where the investment may only be a means of preserving market share rather than increasing it. For the larger exchanges, smaller exchanges provide, amongst other things, a means for widening exposure to new investors, issuers and intermediaries.

Consolidation is also apparent between derivative and cash markets. The 1998 merger between Sweden's derivatives exchange (the OM Group) and the Stockholm Stock Exchange being a recent example.[32] Consolidation across countries, particularly in the derivatives arena, is also likely. The creation of Eurex provides ample evidence of moves in this direction already. Scores of futures exchanges in the PRC have also been closed down or merged with larger provincial ones in the last ten years or so.

There are also obvious regulatory advantages to consolidation. Ensuring compliance with standards is certainly cheaper and more efficient when applied through only one (or a few) exchange bodies. The consolidation of regulatory agencies, in particular countries and trading blocs, like the EU, also complements this process. For many, greater transparency, engendered by greater and more efficient regulatory control, could have saved Asia from the cataclysmic events of 1997 and 1998. Had certain banks and institutions, in a number of Asian countries, been more closely regulated throughout the 1990s, the Asian currency crisis could well have been avoided. This message is heard time and time again. Hindsight is a glorious thing. Nonetheless, should lightning strike again, the lessons of 1997 and 1998 will prove salutary.

14.4   Lessons Learned from the Asian Financial Crisis of 1997 and 1998

The 1997–8 malaise was different to earlier crises, such as the October 1987 crash, in one very important respect: local markets functioned without any real hiccoughs. Risk management and clearing systems were tested to the full and proved, beyond doubt, their resilience. This was an achievement, bearing in mind the near collapse of the futures exchange, and the closure of the two exchange bodies, only ten years earlier when a similar tempest hit Hong Kong's shores.

What, then, were the reasons behind the Asian financial crisis? Was it the result of profligate financing and investment policies, the 'crimes' of the financial system's great usurper, the hedge fund, or some other reason? As argued in several leading publications at the time, speculators only speculate when the fundamentals are in their favour. This now appears to have been the case, with huge debt burdens, compounded by enormous currency exposure, the norm in many affected countries. In essence, then, the hedge funds lit the fuse, but someone else provided the dry tinder for the financial conflagration. The fundamental problems seem to relate to lax lending policies, poor regulation of the markets and, what some might call, 'crony capitalism', in one or two of the worst affected countries. As argued at the outset, Hong Kong and Singapore, in particular, were buffeted by the storm but weathered it largely because of their demonstrable strength in the key areas alluded to: banking, market regulation, and the rule of law. Despite disingenuous suggestions to the contrary, this owes much to the city-states' British antecedents.

The Extent of the Currency Turmoil

To appreciate the severity of the crisis, and its domino effect on economies in the region, it is worth revisiting the currency turmoil of 1997. As shown in Table 14.1, massive devaluations were witnessed in the Indonesian

Table 14.1   Summary of Currency Devaluations of the Won, NT$, Rupiah, Baht, Ringgit, Peso, Singaporean $ and Yen against the US$

Exchange-rates (US$ per X)								
Date	X: Won	NT$	Rupiah	Baht	Ringgit	Peso	Sing$	Yen
30 June 1997	0.0011260	0.03596	0.000411	0.04049	0.3961	0.03791	0.6993	0.008722
31 Jan. 1998	0.0006555	0.0294290	0.0000947	0.01892	0.2386	0.02335	0.5834	0.007877
% Gain by US$ against Currency X	41.79%	18.16%	76.96%	53.27%	39.76%	38.41%	16.57%	9.69%

Note: All exchange-rates obtained from Datastream

rupiah (77%), Thai baht (53%), South Korean won (42%), Malaysian ringgit (40%) and Philippine peso (40%) between mid-1997 and early 1998.

As Figures 14.1 to 14.3 show, much of the decline can be linked to attempts, by the countries affected, to peg their currencies as closely as possible to the US dollar. While only Hong Kong adopted an official linked-rate policy, countries such as Thailand and Malaysia 'shadowed' the 'greenback' fairly closely during the early to mid-1990s. This was largely achieved through central bank intervention. Other currencies, like the Philippine peso, New Taiwanese dollar, South Korean won and Indonesian rupiah also 'tracked' the US dollar to some degree, although the latter two experienced a gradual decline against the US dollar throughout the early to mid-1990s. While the co-movement of many of Asia's currencies with the US dollar may have won the hearts of many of Asia's debtors, whose liabilities were often denominated in US dollars, exporters would have been less enamoured with the actions of their central banks. With the US dollar appreciating strongly during the period from July 1995 to July 1997, as we can see from the USD/DEM and USD/JPY rates in Figure 14.1, the exchange-rate policies were making South-East Asian exports considerably more expensive, especially for European and Japanese buyers.[33]

Nominal exchange-rates are one thing. What about real exchange-rates? In countries like Thailand, which effectively pegged its currency to the US dollar prior to the baht's forced devaluation, product and service prices were rising at a faster pace than corresponding prices in the United States and other benchmark countries. Both the rising US dollar and excessive local inflation, brought about by large infrastructure and development programmes, were in fact combining to weaken the country's competitiveness.[34] To highlight this, consumer-price-index figures taken for Thailand between 15 July 1995 and 15 July 1997 indicate an annualized compound inflation rate of 4.79%, nearly twice that of the United States for the same period.[35]

A significant current-account deficit was also building at the same time in Thailand. Speculators normally smell blood in such circumstances. A widening deficit typically signals currency weakness. In fairness, though, the current account, being only one side of a country's balance of payments (BP), provides only part of the story. The way in which the deficit is financed also matters. This is picked up through the capital account which indicates the extent to which a country's (private and public-sector) capital liabilities are rising or its overseas assets falling. While detailed discussion of the BP is somewhat removed from this text's remit, a current-account deficit, which is tantamount to a diminution in a country's assets, can cause alarm if it is funded by short-term inflows of capital. As argued in *The Economist*:

> When their exchange-rate crisis struck, both Mexico and Thailand had current
> account deficits of 7–8% of GDP. . . . By itself a large current-account deficit
> does not foreshadow a currency crisis. But look where the money comes

Figure 14.1 Performance of USD Spot Exchange Rates Against the Deutschmark and Yen: 1990–1998

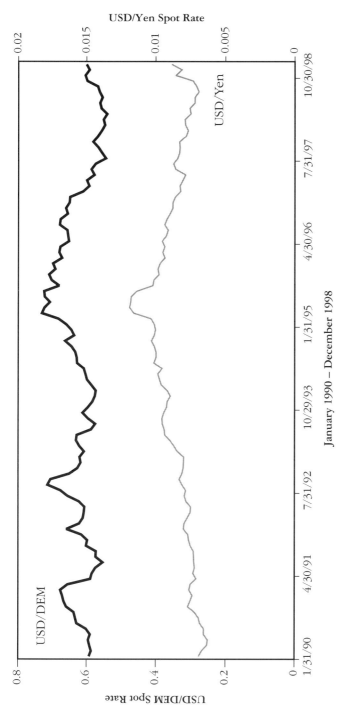

Source of Data: Datastream

Figure 14.2   Performance of USD Spot Exchange Rates Against the
Korean Won and Indonesian Rupiah: 1990–1998

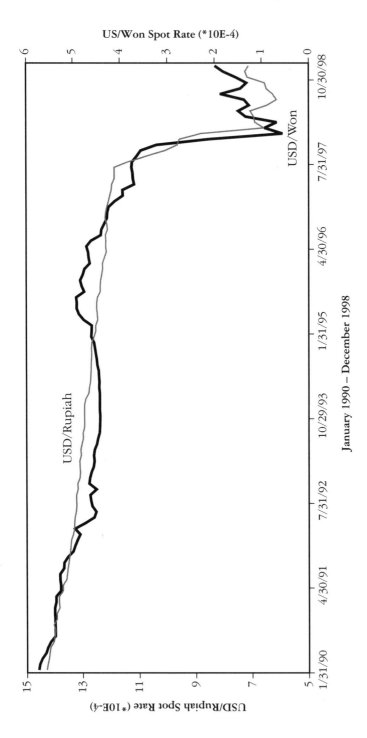

Figure 14.3   Performance of USD Spot Exchange Rates Against the
New Taiwan Dollar, Thai Baht, Malaysian Ringgit, Filipino
Peso, and Singapore Dollar: 1990–1998

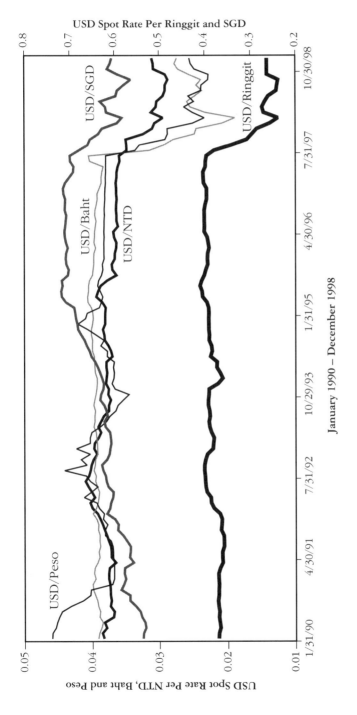

Source of Data: Datastream

from. If its current-account deficit is financed by flighty short-term capital rather than long-term foreign direct investment, a country is vulnerable to sudden capital outflows.' (Anonymous (Oct 1997, p. 89)).

A current-account deficit therefore raises certain flags. Despite this, most commentators, including this author, blithely went about their business untroubled by the potential problems mounting in Thailand. Some others have immodestly claimed credit in predicting Thailand's downfall but discreetly sweep other predictions, like a collapse in Europe and North America, under the proverbial carpet. Selectivity seems to be a trait of many a financial 'expert' where hubris is never in short supply.

The Ensuing Contagion

Explaining what happened in Thailand is one thing, but why did the malady spread so virulently across South-East Asia? Confidence, or the lack of it, played a huge part in the ensuing chaos. With Thailand, and then Indonesia, succumbing to 'Asian flu', creditors, quite naturally, went on the defensive. Loans were called and existing credit lines cancelled. Many international banks reacted like this across Asia, viewing Thailand as an indicator of generally weak Asian credit risk. This reinforced selling pressure on a number of currencies, precipitating declines across the board. Only Hong Kong, where an implacable Currency Board held (see Section 2.2), and the Mainland, where convertibility was limited to current-account transactions, stood firm. The loss of that precious commodity, confidence, does not mean that most of the economies affected were, in a rational sense, fundamentally strong. Many, as suggested at the outset, were blighted by a variety of woes. As argued in accounts like Chris Patten's *East and West*, the correction and the loss of confidence seems a little overdone.[36]

Where were the hedge funds in all this? Probably in the midst of the chaos. With arsenals of funds under their control, they, undoubtedly, reinforced the sentiment of the day. But for every Asian currency contract they shorted in the spot and forward markets, someone else somewhere was buying. Markets do not, despite the pronouncements of financial journalists, function in one direction only. Nonetheless, the pressure of selling orders set the tone. Position limits could have helped by restricting the number of positions certain players can take in certain products. This works very effectively on organized exchanges to prevent individual players from 'cornering' the market. Unfortunately, imposing such a regime in the opaque, floating OTC arena, where most currency trading is conducted, is next to hopeless. For it to have any effect, increased disclosure in all OTC transactions would have to come first. Nonetheless, Asian regulators and politicians clamour for greater control and governance of international capital flows. Their exhortations, by implication, call for change in the OTC arena. Attempts to regulate OTC market activities should not be confused with capital or exchange controls, however. Increased disclosure surrounding capital flows and the enforcement of position limits (if feasible) do not impede capital movement as such. They serve as protective devices against those with a less than altruistic view of economies and societies. What is the prognosis for the future? Most of the countries afflicted by the 'Asian flu' will hopefully institute reforms to foster the over-used, but vitally important concepts, of transparency and accountability. Just as Hong Kong prospered in the aftermath of the 1987 crash, Asia is likely to do so in the first decade of the new millennium, as long as real attempts are made to the close the 'fault-lines' in the banking and market sectors. This can only be achieved through increased disclosure and competition in all areas of the banking and securities markets.

Notes

1. See Fabozzi et al. (1994, pp. 330–2) for an account of the origins of STRIPS.
2. In addition, a Ginnie Mae (Government National Mortgage Association) operates as a guarantor of mortgage 'pass-throughs' arranged by external parties. The Ginnie Mae and Freddie Macs are, in fact, outgrowths of the more established Fannie Mae. For a precise description of their evolution and their specific roles in the US secondary mortgage market, see Fabbozi et al. (1994, pp. 481–2).
3. The 40% rule was promulgated as a *guideline* [see HKMA (1998, July)]; hence the use of the term 'ceiling' in the foregoing.
4. See Lee (1996b, p. 6) for details of this forecast and a review of the changes in this proportion.
5. See HKMA Press Release (1998, March).
6. See Tsang (1998), for example.
7. See SEHK Consultation Paper (1999).
8. See Anonymous (1998c, Oct).
9. See Financial Services Bureau Press Release (1998).
10. Involving hedge funds shorting both the currency and HSI futures contract, as described in Section 12.8.
11. As referred to earlier in Section 12.8 (see note 42).
12. See Webb (1998b), in particular, for discussion of such provisions.
13. See Exchange Fund Investment Ltd (1998) Press Release.
14. See ibid.
15. See Rule 8.08 of The Rules Governing the Listing of Securities on the Stock Exchange of Hong Kong Ltd.
16. See Oldfield (1998).
17. See Yiu and Ibison (1999) for discussion of this.
18. See BOOM homepage, http:/www.boom.com for details of its service.
19. See Anonymous (1992).
20. See Chernoff (1996) for more details.
21. See Anonymous (Oct 1996a).
22. See Speech, Deputy Prime-Minister of Singapore, Lee Hsien Loong (Lee 1998, para. 23). Lee reports that 'The Committee on Governance of Exchanges has proposed, and the government has agreed, that SES and SIMEX should be de-mutualized, as well as merged into a **single integrated privately-held stock company**. A new holding company will be formed, which will wholly own SES and SIMEX as subsidiaries.' (Lee 1998, para. 23, 4 Nov 1998, boldface as published).
23. See ibid (1998, Para. 46 & 48).
24. See *A Policy Paper on Securities and Futures Market Reform*, 1999.

25. Notwithstanding the point made in Chapter 2 (see Note 2) that the authorities are seemingly prepared to forge ahead with the esssential reforms even if members' approval is not forthcoming. Affirmation of this, in the runup to the votes, has also been apparent (see Yiu, 1999).

26. See A Policy Paper on Securities and Futures Market Reform (1999, Para. 8.4).

27. See ibid [Para. 8.14(a)].

28. The then Chairman of the SEHK, Mr Edgar W.K. Cheng, made specific reference to the latter in the SEHK Annual Report, 1997, (pp. 12–13) in relation to a proposal to introduce some degree of negotiability into commissions. This was rejected by the majority of brokers.

29. Reference to the separation of ownership and trading rights in the new entity is made liberally throughout the policy paper (see A Policy Paper on Securities and Futures Market Reform (1999., Para. 7, 'Executive Summary, for example).

30. Ibid (Para. 8.8).

31. See ibid (Para. 8.15-8.19) which details the 'strengthened regulatory function' implicit in the reform.

32. For more details of its organizational structure, see Stockholm Stock Exchange *Fact Book 1998*, p. 1.

33. Comparing USD/DEM and USD/JPY rates between 31 July 1995 and 31 July 1997, the USD appreciated by 24.83% against the DEM (changing from US$0.72427 to US$0.544425/DEM) and 25.63% against the yen (changing from US$0.011358 to US$0.008446/yen). All exchange-rates were obtained from Datastream.

34. *The Economist* provides compelling evidence of this, given a reported 25% increase in the real baht/yen exchange-rate between 1993 and 1996 (see Anonymous (Oct 1997, p. 90)).

35. From CPI indices supplied by Datastream, Thailand's index rose from 106 to 116.4 points and the US's from 152.5 to 160.5 points.

36. See Patten (1998).

References

A Draft for a Composite Securities and Futures Bill, 1996, The Securities and Futures Commission, Hong Kong, April.

A Guideline issued by the Monetary Authority under Section 16(10), 1997, Banking Ordinance: Maintenance of Adequate Capital Against Market Risks, Hong Kong Monetary Authority, November.

A Policy Paper on Securities and Futures Market Reform, 1999, Government of the Hong Kong Special Administrative Region, March.

Aggarwal, R. and Rivoli, P., 1990, 'Fads in the Initial Public Offering Market?', *Financial Management*, 19, Winter, 45–57.

———, Leal, R. and Hernandez, L., 1993, 'The Aftermarket Performance of Initial Public Offerings in Latin America', *Financial Management*, 22(1), pp. 42–53.

Agrawal, A. and Tandon, K., 1994, 'Anomalies or Illusions? Evidence from Stock Markets in Eighteen Countries', *Journal of International Money and Finance*, 13, pp. 83–106.

Alexander, G.J., Eun, C.S. and Janakiramanan, S., 1988, 'International Listings and Stock Returns: Some Empirical Evidence', *Journal of Financial and Quantitative Analysis*, 23(2), pp. 135–51.

———, Sharpe, W.F. and Bailey, J.V., 1993, *Fundamentals of Investments*, 2nd Ed., Prentice- Hall.

Allen, D. E., 1992, 'Some Features of Dividend Policy in Japan', *Managerial Finance*, 18(1), pp. 49–69.

Allen, F. and Faulhaber, G.R., 1989, 'Signalling by Underpricing in the IPO Market', *Journal of Financial Economics*, 23, pp. 303–23.

Anonymous, 1975, 'How to be Smart without Really Trying', *Business Week*, 17 March, p. 68.

Anonymous, 1987, '43 Barred from Futures Market', *South China Morning Post*, pp. 1, 28 October.

Anonymous, 1991, 'British Local Authority Swaps: We're a Special Case, Old Chap', *The Economist*, 11 May, p. 74.

Anonymous, 1992, 'The Trading of Hong Kong Stocks in Foreign Markets', *The Securities Journal*, March, pp. 22–4 & 26–7.

Anonymous, 1992, 'International Stockholm Stock Exchange', *The Wall Street Journal*, 27 June, p. A6.

Anonymous, 1993, 'Shell Game: Shell's Foreign Exchange Disaster', *The Economist*, 27 February, p. 80.

Anonymous, 1993a, 'Switzerland', *Euromoney*, World Equity Markets Supplement, May, pp. 47–52.

Anonymous, 1993b, 'Transferring Hong Kong Corporate Domicile', *International Corporate Law*, 25, May, pp. 27–8.

Anonymous 1993/94, 'Depositary Receipts: New Money Drives DR Market', *Asiamoney*, December/January, pp. 10–12.

Anonymous, 1994, 'Investigation Probes Codelco's London Connections', *Platt's Metals Week*, 65(12), March 21, p. 8.

Anonymous, 1994, 'Determined Loser', *The Economist*, 16 April, p. 82.

Anonymous, 1994, 'Plunging into Foreign Markets', *The Economist,* 17 September, pp. 86 & 89.

Anonymous, 1995, 'The Collapse of Barings: A Fallen Star', *The Economist*, 4–10 March, pp. 19–22.

Anonymous, 1996, 'Sumitomo Loses $1.8 Billion', *Japan Times* Weekly International Edition, 36(25), 24–30 June, pp. 1 & 6.

Anonymous, 1996, 'Settled, At Last', *The Economist*, 13 July, p. 78.

Anonymous, 1997, 'Finance and Economics: The Wild West of the East', *The Economist*, 12 July, pp. 67–8.

Anonymous, 1996a, 'Bonzer Bonanza', *The Economist*, 12 October, pp. 80–1.

Anonymous, 1996b, 'A Japanese Cross-Holding Puzzle', *The Economist*, 5 October, p. 71.

Anonymous, 1997, 'Something Horrible Out There', 18 October, pp. 89–90.

Anonymous, 1998, 'Finance and Economics: The Great Escape', *The Economist*, 14 March, p. 86.

Anonymous, 1998, Share Buybacks: A Popular Option', *The Economist*, 25 April – 1 May, p.84.

Anonymous, 1998, 'A Hitchhiker's Guide to Hedge Funds', *The Economist*, 13 June, p. 76.

Anonymous, 1998a, 'Hedge Funds: A Guide', *The Economist*, 3 October, p. 92.

Anonymous, 1998b, 'Windfall for Brokers as Exchange Goes Public', HK Standard, Business Section, 15 October, B06.

Anonymous, 1998c, 'Fair Shares', *The Economist*, 31 October, p. 79.

Anonymous, Review & Outlook, 1998, 'Long-Term Backlash', *The Asian Wall Street Journal*, 13 October, p. 12.

Ariel, R.A., 1990, 'High Stock Returns Before Holidays: Existence and Evidence of Possible Causes', *The Journal of Finance*, 45(5), pp. 1611–26.

Ariff, M. and Johnson, L. W., 1990, *Securities Markets & Stock Pricing*, Singapore: Longman Publishing.

Bae, S.C. and Levy, H., 1994, 'The Valuation of Stock Purchase Rights as Call Options', *The Financial Review*, 29(3), August, pp. 419–40.

Bagwell, L.S. and Shoven, J.B., 1989, 'Cash Distributions to Shareholders', *Journal of Economic Perspectives*, 3(3), Summer, pp. 129–40.

Bancroft, M. A., 1995, 'Orange County's Ultra Vires Defence Raises Questions of Over Protection', *Financial Regulation Report*, February, pp. 6–7.

Bank of England Supervision and Surveillance: Implementation in the United Kingdom of the Capital Adequacy Directive (1995), No. S&S/1995/2, April.

Banking Ordinance (Amendment of Seventh Schedule) Notice 1997, August, Hong Kong.

Banz, R.W., 1981, 'The Relationship Between Returns and Market Value of Common Stocks', *Journal of Financial Economics*, 9, pp. 3–18.

Barclay, M.J., Holderness, C.G. and Pontiff, J., 1993, 'Private Benefits from Block Ownership and Discounts on Closed-End Funds', *Journal of Financial Economics*, 33(3), pp. 263–91.

Barnes, W., 1988, 'Puzzle over Land Retreat', *South China Morning Post*, Sunday Money, 8 May, p. 1.

Barr, P. G., 1995, 'Poor Oversight Cited in Wisconsin Swaps Loss', *Pensions and Investments*, 3 Apri, p. 35.

Barry, C.B. and Jennings, R.H., 1993, 'The Opening Price Performance of Initial Public Offerings of Common Stock', *Financial Management*, 22(1), pp. 54–63.

Basle Committee on Banking Supervision, 1996, Amendment to the Capital Accord to Incorporate Market Risks, January.

Beatty, R.P., and Ritter, J.R., 1986, 'Investment Banking, Reputation and the Underpricing of Initial Public Offerings', *Journal of Financial Economics*, 15, 213–32.

Beder, T. S., 1995, 'VAR: Seductive but Dangerous', *Financial Analysts Journal*, September/October, pp. 12–24.

Beecham, B. J., 1996, *Monetary and Financial System of Hong Kong*, Hong Kong: Hong Kong Institute of Bankers.

Benesh, G., Keown, A. J. and Pinkerton, J. M., 1984, 'An Examination of Market Reaction to Substantial Shifts in Dividend Policy', *Journal of Financial Research*, 7(2), pp. 131–42.

Bennett, J. A., Chen, A. H and McGuinness, P.B., 1995, 'Innovations in Derivative Products: The Call-Spread Warrant', *The Securities Journal*, January, pp. 22–5.

Benett, J.A., Chen A.H. and McGuiness, P.B., 1996, 'An Analysis of Capital Guaranteed Funds', *Internàtional Review of Economics and Finance*, 5(3), 1996, pp. 259–68.

Benveniste, L.M and Spindt, P.A., 1989, 'How Investment Bankers Determien the Offer Price and Allocation of New Issues', *Journal of Financial Economics*, 24, pp. 343–61.

———— and Busaba, W.Y., 1997, 'Bookbuilding Vs. Fixed Price: An Analysis of Competing Strategies for Marketing IPOs', *Journal of Financial and Quantitative Analysis*, 32(4), December, pp. 383–403.

Bessembinder, H. and Chan, K., 1995, 'The Profitability of Trading Rules in the Asian Stock Markets', *Pacific-Basin Finance Journal*, 3, pp. 257–84.

Black, F. and Scholes, M., 1973, 'The Pricing of Corporate Liabilities', *Journal of Political Economy*, May–June, pp. 637–59.

————, 1975, 'Fact and Fantasy in the Use of Options', *Financial Analysts Journal*, July– August, pp. 36–41 & 61–72.

BOOM homepage (http:/www.boom.com).

Bouaziz, L., Briys, E. and Crouhy, M., 1994, 'The Pricing of Forward Starting Asian Options', *Journal of Banking and Finance*, 18(5), pp. 823–39.

Bradbury, M. and Westwood, M., 1996, 'Accounting for Share Repurchases', *Chartered Accountants Journal of New Zealand*, 75(3), April, pp. 28–31.

Brennan, M. and Schwartz, E.S., 1977, 'Convertible Bonds: Valuation and Optimal Strategies for Call and Conversion', *The Journal of Finance*, 32(5), December, pp. 1699–1715.

Brock, W., Lakonishok, J. and LeBaron, B., 1992,' Simple Technical Trading Rules and the Stochastic Properties of Stock Returns', *The Journal of Finance*, 47, pp. 1731–64.

Carter, R. and Manaster, S., 1990, 'Initial Public Offerings and Underwriter Reputation', *Journal of Finance*, 45, 4, 1045–67.

Cavaletti, C., 1998, 'After-Hours Systems See Sunlight', *Futures*, June, pp. 70–5.

Chan, M.W.L., Khanthavit, A. and Thomas, H., 1996, 'Seasonality and Cultural Influences on Four Asian Stock Markets', *Asia Pacific Journal of Management*, 13(2), pp. 1–24.

Chan, P. and Ku, G., 1997, 'Banks Question HKMA Decision to Restrict Access to Emergency Funds', *South China Morning Post*, Business Post, 30 October, p. 2.

Chandrasegar, C. and Baratham, S., 1993, 'Takeovers and Mergers in Singapore, Malaysia and Hong Kong', *Asia Business Law Review*, 1, January, pp. 3–8.

Chang, E. C., 1986, 'Returns to Speculators and the Theory of Normal Backwardation', *The Journal of Finance*, 40(1), March, pp. 193–208.

Chao, V.T., 1995, 'Accessing China Through Depositary Receipts', in *Investing in Chinese Securities*, pp. 183–192, Hong Kong: Asia Law and Practice.

Charlton, J., 1995, 'Secondary Listing: The Issues', *THC Conference: The Complete Guide to Listing*, 16–17 October, Hong Kong.

Chen, D.F., 1989, 'The Month-of-the-Year Effect as a Profitable Trading Rule in the Hong Kong Common Stock Market', *Hong Kong Journal of Business Management*, 7, pp. 19–33.

Chen, N.-F., 1997, 'Defending the Dollar in a Crisis', *South China Morning Post*, Saturday Focus, 22 November, p. 18.

Cheng, A., Copeland, L. and O'Hanlon, J., 1994, 'Investment Trust Discounts and Abnormal Returns: UK Evidence', *Journal of Business Finance and Accounting*, 21(6), pp. 813–31.

Cheng, L.K. and Wu, C., 1998, *The Hong Kong Economic Policy Study Series: Competition Policy and the Regulation of Business*, City University of Hong Kong Press.

Chernoff, J., 1996, 'Dutch Bourse to Become Publicly Traded Company', *Pensions & Investments*, 13 May, p. 18.

Cheung, Y-L and Lui, Y-H, 1992, 'A Note on the Information Content of Relocating Corporate Domicile: A Trading Volume Approach', Accounting and Business Research, 22(88), pp. 377–80.

————, Ho, Y.K. and Wong, K.F., 1994, 'Return and Risk Premium Seasonalities in Three Emerging Asian Markets: Hong Kong, Taiwan and Korea', *Journal of International Financial Management and Accounting*, 5(3), pp. 223–41.

————, Ho, Y-K., Pope, P. and Draper, P., 1994, 'intraday Stock Return Volatility: The HK Evidence', *Pacific Basin Finance Journal*, 2, pp. 261–76.

————, 1995, 'A Small Cap: A Big Return', *The Securities Journal*, January, pp. 14–16.

———— and Shum, C-K., 1995, 'International Stock Exchange Listing and the Reduction of Political Risk', *Managerial & Decision Economics*, 16, pp. 537–46.

Cho, M.H. and Cohen, M.A., 1997, 'The Economic Causes and Consequences of Corporate Divestiture', *Managerial and Decision Economics*, 18(5), August, pp. 367–74.

Choi, S. and Wohar, M.E., 1994, 'S&P 500 Index Options Prices and the Black-Scholes Option Pricing Model', *Applied Financial Economics*, 2(6), pp. 249–263.

Chowdhry, B. and Sherman, A., 1996, 'The Winner's Curse and the International Methods of Allocating Initial Public Offerings', *Pacific-Basin Finance Journal*, 4, pp. 15–30.

Clifford, M., 1993, 'Shroff: Shell-shocked in Japan', *Far Eastern Economic Review*, March 04, p. 58.

CM Telecom International Ltd.: Introduction on The Stock Exchange of Hong Kong Ltd. document, 25 September, 1997.

Code on Unit Trusts and Mutual Funds, 1995, Securities & Futures Commission, 2nd. Ed., February, Hong Kong.

Companies Ordinance, Cap. 32, published by the HK Government.

Commodities Trading Ordinance, Cap 250, Published by the Government Printer, HKSAR.

Compton, P., 1995/96, 'OTC Derivatives Regulation' an 'Voluntary Oversight of OTC Derivatives', *London Business School's Institute of Finance and Accounting Newsletter*, 8, Winter, pp. 1–4.

Condoyanni, L., O'Hanlon, J. and Ward, C. W. R., 1987, 'Day of the Week Effects on Stock Returns: International Evidence', *Journal of Business Finance and Accounting*, 14(2), pp. 159–74.

Connolly, R. A, 1989, 'An Examination of the Robustness of the Weekend Effect', *Journal of Financial and Quantitative Analysis*, 24(2), pp. 133–70.

Cooper, G., 1996, 'Comment: The Value of VAR', *Risk* (Value-at-Risk Supplement), June, p. 1.

Copeland, T.E., 1972, 'Liquidity Changes Following Stock Splits', *The Journal of Finance*, 34(1), March, pp. 115–41.

———— and Weston, J.F., 1983, *Financial Theory and Corporate Policy*, Addison-Wesley Publishing Co., 2nd Ed.

Cornell, B. and French, K. R., 1983a, 'Taxes and the Pricing of Stock Index Futures', *The Journal of Finance*, 38(3), June, pp. 675–94.

————, 1983b, 'The Pricing of Stock Index Futures', The Journal of Futures Markets, 3(1), pp. 1–14.

Cross, K., 1973, 'The Behaviour of Stock Prices on Fridays and Mondays', *Financial Analysts Journal*, November–December, pp. 67–9.

Cosandier, P. A. and Lang, B. R., 1981, 'Interest Rate Parity Tests: Switzerland and Some Major Western Countries', *Journal of Banking and Finance*, 5(2), pp. 188–200.

Crowder, W.J. and Hoffman, D.L., 1996, 'The Long-Run Relationship Between Nominal Interest Rates and Inflation: The Fisher Equation Revisited', *Journal of Money, Credit and Banking*, 28(1), pp. 102–18.

Cudd, M., Duggal, R. and Sarkar, S., 1996, 'Share Repurchase Motives and Stock Market Reaction', *Quarterly Journal of Business and Economics*, 35(2), pp. 66–76.

Davidson, C., 1996, 'Risk Where Credit's Due', *Risk* Technology Supplement, June, pp. 54–5 & 57.

Davies, B. and Yu, D., 1995, 'Shanghai Shanghaied', *Asiamoney*, October, pp. 15–20.

Dawson, S.M., 1982, 'Is the Hong Kong Market Efficient?', *The Journal of Portfolio Management*, Spring, pp. 17–20.

———, 1984, 'Underpricing New Share Issues: Is Singapore an Immature Market?', *Singapore Management Review*, 1–10.

——— and Hiraki, T., 1985, 'Selling Unseasoned New Shares in Hong Kong and Japan: A test of Primary Market Efficiency and Underpricing', *Hong Kong Journal of Business Management*, 3, pp. 125–34.

———, 1987, 'Secondary Stock Market Performance of Initial Public Offers, Hong Kong, Singapore and Malaysia: 1978–84', *Journal of Business Finance and Accounting*, 14(1), Spring, pp. 65–76.

Deal Awards 1998, *Finance Asia*, Dec. 1998/Jan. 1999, 3(3), pp. 48–56.

DeBondt, W.F.M and Thaler, R.H., 1987, 'Further Evidence on Investor Overreaction and Stock Market Seasonality', *The Journal of Finance*, 42, pp. 557–81.

——— and Thaler, R.H., 1985, 'Does the Stock Market overreact', *The Journal of Finance*, 40, pp. 793–805.

De Long, B. and Shleifer, A., 1992, 'Closed-End Fund Discounts', *Journal of Portfolio Management*, Winter, pp. 46–53.

De Trenck, C., Cartledge, S., Daswani, A., Katz, C.A. and Sakmar, D., 1998, *Red Chips and the Globalisation of China's Enterprises*, Hong Kong: Asia 2000 Ltd.

Drake, P. D. and Vetsuypens, M. R., 1993, 'IPO Underpricing and Insurance Against Legal Liability', *Financial Management*, 22(1), pp. 64–73.

Dugan, R. and Keef, S., 1989, *Company Purchase of Own Shares: The Case for New Zealand*, New Zealand: Victoria University Press for the Institute of Policy Studies.

Dyl, E., 1977, 'Capital Gains Taxation and Year-End Stock Market Behavior', *The Journal of Finance*, 32(1), pp. 165–75.

Ederington, L. H. and Lee, J. H., 1993, 'How Markets Process Information: News Releases and Volatility', *The Journal of Finance*, 69(4), pp. 1161–91.

Edwards, F. R., 1988, 'Futures Trading and Cash Market Volatility: Stock Index and Interest Rate Futures', *The Journal of Futures Markets*, 8(4), pp. 421–39.

——— and Cantor, M.S., 1995, 'The Collapse of Metallgesellschaft: Unhedgeable Risks, Poor Hedging Strategy, Or Just Bad Luck?', *The Journal of Futures Markets*, 15(3), pp. 211–64.

El-Baroudi, G., 1992, Investing without Frills', *Canadian Banker*, July/August, pp. 52–5.

Elderfield, M., 1996, 'Basle Accord: Final Market Risk Capital Standards Published', *Financial Regulation Report*, January/February, pp. 7–10.

Elec & Eltek International Holdings Ltd. Conditional Cash Offer Prospectus, August 7, 1997.

Elton, E. J. and Gruber, M. J., 1970, 'Marginal Stockholder Tax Rates and the Clientele Effect', *Review of Economics and Statistics*, 52(1), pp. 68–74.

Euroclear IFR Handbook of World Stock & Commodity Exchanges 1995.

Evans, D., 1999, 'HSBC Stands by its Placement Decision', *South China Morning Post*, Business Post, 26 May, p.2.

Exchange Fund Ordinance, Cap. 66, Published by the Government Printer, HKSAR.

Exchange Announcement, 1993, 'New Derivative Warrant Regulations' (The Stock Exchange of Hong Kong Ltd.), *The Securities Journal*, December p. 42.

Exchange Announcement, 1997, 'Public Float Capitalisation and Market Capitalisation for Derivative Warrant Issues: Introduction of Qualifying Period' (The Stock Exchange of Hong Kong Ltd.), May.

Exchange Announcement, 1997, 'New Category of Derivative Warrants', (The Stock Exchange of Hong Kong Ltd.), 17 June.

Exchange Announcement, 1997, 'New Category of Derivative Warrants' (The Stock Exchange of Hong Kong Ltd.), *The Securities Journal*, September, p. 32.

Exchange Announcement, 1997, 'New Measures Relating to the Listing of Derivative Warrants' (The Stock Exchange of Hong Kong Ltd.), 5 September.

Exchange Fund Investment Ltd., 1998, 'Statement by Mr. T. L. Yang, Chairman of the Exchange Fund Ltd.', Press Release, 26 October.

Eye on Securities, 1996, 'Knowing the Exchange Rules (Part Seven)', 19, Issued as a *Supplement to the Securities Journal*, September,.

Fabozzi, F. J., Modigliani, F. and Ferri, M.G., 1994, *Foundations of Financial Markets and Institutions*, Prentice-Hall International Editions.

Fact Book (issues 1986–97, inclusive), published by The Stock Exchange of Hong Kong Ltd.

Fact file 1998, 1999, London Stock Exchange.

Fama, E. F., 1965, 'The Behaviour of Stock Market Prices', *The Journal of Business*, 38, pp. 34–105.

———, 1970, Efficient Capital Markets: A Review of Theory and Empirical Work', *Journal of Finance*, 25, May, pp. 383–417.

———, 1991, 'Efficient Capital Markets II', The Journal of Finance, 46(5), pp. 1575–1617.

——— and French, K R, 1992, 'The Cross-Section of Expected Returns', *The Journal of Finance*, 47(2), pp. 427–65.

Fang, Z., 1997, 'No Gains from Dual Listing in the Shanghai Stock Exchange', *Advances in Pacific-Basin Financial Markets*, 3, pp. 91–100.

Fell, R., 1992, *Crisis and Change: The Maturing of Hong Kong's Financial Markets*, Hong Kong: Longman.

Ferguson, R. and Hitzig, N. B., 1993, 'How to Get Rich Quick Using GAAP', *Financial Analysts Journal*, May/June, 49(3), pp. 30–4.

Filsner, G., 1997, 'How to Assess the Impact of Charges on a Fund's Return', *South China Morning Post*, Sunday Morning Post, 9 March, p. 10.

Financial Services Bureau Press Release, 1998, 'LCQ8: Involvement of Exchange Fund in Markets', 4 November.

Financial Services Bureau Press Release, 1999, 'LCQ5: Takeovers and Mergers Code', 26 May.

Finn, F.J. and Higham, R., 1988, 'The Performance of Unseasoned New Equity Issues-Cum-Stock Exchange Listings in Australia', *Journal of Banking and Finance*, 12, 333–51.

Fisher, I., 1930, *The Theory of Interest: As Determined by Impatience to Spend Income and Oppoortunity to Invest It*, New York: The MacMillan Co. (Reprinted by Augustus M. Kelley Publishers, 1986).

Fox, J., 1997, 'The Hidden Meanings of Stock Buybacks', *Fortune*, 136(5), 8 September, pp. 24–5.

Fredborg, L., 1997, 'International Briefing: Sweden', *International Financial Law Review*, 16(4), April, p. 56.

French, K. R., 1980, 'Stock Returns and the Weekend Effect', *Journal of Financial Economics*, 8, pp. 55–69.

French, S., 1997a, 'Index-Tracking Fund Takes Off', *South China Morning Post*, Sunday Morning Post, 6 April, p. 12.

———, 1997b, 'Top Funds Tracker Targets Hong Kong', *South China Morning Post*, Sunday Morning Post, 1 June, p. 10.

Freris, A. F., 1990, 'The Effects of the Introduction of Stock Index Futures on Stock Prices: The Experience of Hong Kong 1984–1987', in Rhee, S. G. and Chang, R. P. (Ed.), *Pacific Basin Capital Markets Research*, Vol. 1, North-Holland: Elsevier Science Publishers B.V. , pp. 409–16.

———, 1991, *The Financial Markets of Hong Kong*, Routledge.

FSB homepage (at http:/www.info.gov.hk/fsb), Financial Services Bureau.

Fuller, R.J. and Farrell, J.L. jr., 1987, *Modern Investment and Security Analysis*, McGraw-Hill International Ed.

Fung, J. K-W., Cheng, L. T-W. and Chan, K-C., 1997, 'The Intraday Pricing Efficiency of Hong Kong Hang Seng Index Options and Futures Markets', *The Journal of Futures Markets*, 17(7), pp. 797–815.

——— and Fung, A. K-W., 1997, 'Mispricing of Index Futures Contracts: A Study of Index Futures Versus Index Options', *The Journal of Derivatives*, Winter, pp. 37–45.

Gailey, C., 1996/1997, 'Convertibles Appeal to Fixed-Income Investors', *AsiaMoney*, December/January, pp. 49 & 52–3.

Gerson, M. and Lehrman, T., 1998, 'Most Hedge Funds Play it Safe', *The Asian Wall Street Journal*, 21 October, p. 12.

Geske, R., 1979, 'A Note on An Analytical Formula for Unprotected American Call Options on Stocks with Known Dividends', *Journal of Financial Economics*, December, pp. 375–80.

——— and Roll, R., 1984, 'On Valuing American Call Options with the European formula', *Journal of Finance*, 39, pp. 443–55.

Ghassemieh, R., Shaw, W. and Wilson, R., 1997, 'Equity Index-Linked Derivatives', in *Asian Equity Derivatives Handbook*, Hong Kong: Asia Law and Practice, pp. 71–88.

Glosten, L. and Milgrom, P., 1985, 'Bid, Ask and Transaction Prices in a Specialist Market with Heterogeneously Informed Traders', *Journal of Financial Economics*, 14, pp. 71–100.

Goettzmann, W. and Ibbotson, R.G., 1994, 'Do Winners Repeat?', *Journal of Portfolio Management*, 20(2), pp. 9–16.

Goodstadt, L., 1981, 'The Chinese Puzzle of 1997', *Euromoney*, August, pp. 109–20.

Goulet, W.M., 1974, 'Price Changes, Managerial Actions and Insider Trading at the Time of Listing, *Financial Management*, 3, pp. 30–6.

Goyal, V., Hwang, C-Y., Jayaraman, N. and Shastri, K., 1994, 'The Ex-Date Impact of Rights Offerings: The Evidence from Firms Listed on the Tokyo Stock Exchange', *Pacific-Basin Finance Journal*, 2, pp. 277–91.

Gregory, A., 1997, 'An Examination of the Long Run Performance of UK Acquiring Firms', *Journal of Business Finance & Accounting*, 24(7), & (8), pp. 971–1002.

Grinblatt, M.S., Masulis, R.W. and Titman, S., 1984, 'The Valuation Effects of Stock Splits and Stock Dividends', *Journal of Financial Economics*, 13, December, pp. 461–90.

——— and Hwang, C.Y., 1989, 'signalling and the Pricing of New Issues', *Journal of Finance*, June, pp. 393–420.

——— and Titman, S., 1992, 'The Persistence of Mutual Fund Performance', *Journal of Finance*, 47(5), pp. 1977–84.

Grossman, S.J. and Stiglitz, J.E., 1980, 'On the Impossibility of Informationally Efficient Markets, *The American Economic Review*, 70(3), June, pp. 393–408.

Gruber, M., 1996, 'Another Puzzle: The Growth in Actively Managed Funds', *The Journal of Finance*, 51(3), pp. 783–810.

Guide to the International Equity Market, 1994, London Stock Exchange, August.

Gultekin, M.N. and Gultekin, N.B., 1983, 'Stock Market Seasonality: International Evidence', *Journal of Financial Economics*, 12, pp. 469–81.

Guo, E.Y. and Keown, A.J., 1992, 'The Impact of Dividend and Bonus Issue Announcements on the Hong Kong Exchange: An Empirical Investigation', in Rhee, S.G. and Chang, R.P. (Ed.), *Pacific-Basin Capital Markets Research*, Vol III, North Holland: Elsevier Science Publishers B.V.

Hang Seng Bank Annual Report, 1997.

Hang Seng China Enterprises Index, brochure, HSI Services Ltd.

Hang Seng China-Affiliated Corporations Index, brochure, HSI Services Ltd.

Hang Seng Index Futures: Market Review for March, 1995, *The Securities Journal*, May, p. 42.

Hansch, O., Naik, N. and Viswanathan, S., 1996, 'Do Inventories Matter in Dealership Markets? Evidence from the London Stock Exchange', *London Business School Working Paper*, IFA 225.

Hansen, R.S., 1989, 'The Demise of the Rights Issue', Review of Financial Studies, 1(3), 289–309.

Harris, L., 1986, 'A Transaction Data Study of Weekly and Intradaily Patterns in Stock Returns', *Journal of Financial Economics*, 16, pp. 99–117.

Harrison, M., 1997, *Asia-Pacific Securities Markets*, 3rd. Ed., Hong Kong: Financial Times Financial Publishing Asia Pacific.

Hecht, A., 1997, 'Cantango's Curse: And the Beauty of Backwardation', *Barron's*, 6 October, mw12.

Hendricks, D., 1994, 'Netting Agreements and the Credit Exposure of OTC Derivatives Portfolios, *Federal Reserve Bank of New York Quarterly Review*, Spring, pp. 7–18.

————, 1996, 'Evaluation of Value-at-Risk Models Using Historical Data', *Federal Reserve Bank of New York Policy Review*, April, pp. 39–69.

Hensler, D A, 1990, 'Underpricing of Initial Public Offerings: A Litigation Costs Explanation', *University of Portland Working Paper*.

Heron, D. and Irving, R., 1996, 'Models: Banks Grasp VAR Nettle', *Risk* (Value-at-Risk Supplement), June, pp. 16–18 & 21.

Hicks, J. R., 1946, *Value and Capital*, Oxford University Press, 2nd Ed.

HKFE HSI Contract Specifications, Hong Kong Futures Exchange Ltd.

HKFE Annual Report 1997, Hong Kong Futures Exchange Ltd.

HKFE homepage (at http://www.hkfe.com), Hong Kong Futures Exchange Ltd.

HKFE Clearing Corporation Ltd.: Rules and Procedures, 1998.

HKMA, Annual Report, 1997.

HKMA, 1997a, 'Management of Interbank Liquidity', Monetary Management Department, The Hong Kong Monetary Authority, in Lui, Y.-H. (Ed., Moderated by Jao Y. C), *Hong Kong Financial System in Motion*, Hong Kong: Hong Kong Institute of Bankers, pp. 21–31.

HKMA, 1997b, 'The Interest Rate Structure in Hong Kong', External Department, The Hong Kong Monetary Authority, Lui, Y.-H. (Ed., Moderated by Jao Y. C.), *Hong Kong Financial System in Motion*, Hong Kong: Hong Kong Institute of Bankers, pp. 32–40.

HKMA, 1998, 'Monetary Survey of Hong Kong 1993–1997', Quarterly Bulletin, Hong Kong Monetary Authority, February, pp. 15–21.

HKMA Press Release, 1998, March, 'Signing Ceremony of the Fixed Rate Mortgage Pilot Scheme', the Hong Kong Monetary Authority, 18 March.

HKMA Press Release, 1998, July, 'Withdrawal of the HKMA's 40% Guideline, the Hong Kong Monetary Authority, 28 July.

HKMA Press Release, 1998, September, 'Strengthening of Currency Board Arrangements in Hong Kong', Hong Kong Monetary Authority, 5 September.

HKMA Press Release, 1999, 'Backing Arrangements for Coins in Circulation and Interest Payments on Exchange Fund Bills and Notes', Hong Kong Monetary Authority, 1 February.

Ho, T. S.-Y., Chen M. Z.-H. and Eng, F. H.-T., 1996, 'VAR Analytics: Portfolio Structure, Key Rate Convexities, and VAR Betas', *The Journal of Portfolio Management*, Fall, pp. 89–98.

Ho, Y-K., 1990, 'Stock Return Seasonalities in Asia Pacific Markets', *Journal of International Financial Management and Accounting*, 2(1), pp. 47–77.

———, Cheung, Y-L., Draper, P. and Pope, P., 1992, 'Return Volatilities and Trading Activities on an Emerging Asian Market', *Economic Letters*, 39, pp. 91–94.

——— and Cheung, Y-L., 1994, 'Seasonal Pattern in Volatility in Asian Stock Markets', *Applied Financial Economics*, 4, pp. 61–7.

Hoffman, D. and Johnson, M., 1996, 'Operating Procedures', *Risk*, 9(10), October, pp. 60–3.

Holland, K., 1994, 'A Lingering Black Eye at Bankers Trust', *Business Week*, 14 November, p. 42.

Hong Kong Codes on Takeovers and Mergers and Share Repurchases, Securities & Futures Commission, Hong Kong, April 1996.

Hong Kong Futures Exchange Ltd.: Rules, Regulations and Procedures, 1998.

Hong Kong Investment Funds Yearbook 1997, 10th. Ed., The Hong Kong Investment Funds Association.

Hong Kong Securities Clearing Co. Ltd., Annual Report 1997/98.

Hong Kong Securities Clearing Co. Ltd. Home page (at http://www.hkclearing.com.hk/p4/htm).

Hong Kong Monetary Authority, 1997, A Guideline Issued by the Monetary Authority under Section 16.10 (Banking Ordinance), 'Maintenance of Adequate Capital Against Market Risks', November.

Hopper, G., 1996, 'Value at Risk: A New Methodology for Measuring Portfolio Risk', *Federal Reserve Bank of Philadelphia Business Review*, July/August, pp. 19–31.

Horsewood, R., 1997a, 'Hong Kong Turmoil Hits Warrant Dealers', *Risk*, 10(11), Nov., p. 6.

———, 1997b, 'Flavour of the Month', *Asia Risk* (supplement to *Risk*), June, pp. 17–20.

Howe, J.S. and Madura, J., 1990, 'The Impact of International Listings on Risk: Implications for Capital Market Integration', *Journal of Banking & Finance*, 14(6), pp. 1133–42.

How, J.C.Y. and Low, J.G., 1993, 'Fractional Ownership and Underpricing: Signals of IPO Firm Value', *Pacific Basin Finance Journal*, 1(1), March, 47–65.

HSBC Holdings PLC, Introduction to the London Stock Exchange document, 25 March, 1991.

Huaneng Power International, Inc., 1998, Listing on the Hong Kong Stock Exchange by Way of Introduction document, 19 January.

Hudson, R., Dempsey, M. and Keasey, K., 1996, 'A Note on the Weak Form Efficiency of Capital Markets: The Application of Simple Technical Trading Rules to UK Stock Prices'—1935 to 1994', *Journal of Banking & Finance*, 20, pp. 1121–32.

Hui, K., 1993a, 'Going Global, But How Far?', *The Securities Journal*, September, pp. 4–6.

———, 1993b, 'US Equity Strategy 101', *The Securities Journal*, September, pp. 12–13.

Hulbert, M., 1997, 'Putting Their Money Where There Mouths Are', *Forbes*, 159(8), 21 April, p. 386.

Hull, J., 1989, *Options, Futures, and Other Derivative Securities*, Prentice-Hall International Eds.

Humphreys, G., 1990, 'Rethinking the Revolution', *Euromoney*, May, pp. 107–13.

Hung, M., 1993, 'Have Stock, Will Travel: The Exploration of Foreign Markets Continues', *The Securities Journal*, September, pp. 8–9.

Ibbotson, R.G., 1975, 'Price Performance of Common Stock New Issues', *Journal of Financial Economics*, 3, pp. 235–72.

——— and Sinquefield, R.A., 1979, 'Stocks, Bonds, Bills and Inflation: Uodates', *Financial Analysts Journal*, July–August, pp. 40–4.

Introduction Document for Winsor Properties Holdings Ltd. listing on the SEHK, 14 October, 1996.

Ip, Y.-K. and Hopewell, M., 1987, 'Corporate Financial Structure in Hong Kong', *Hong Kong Journal of Business Management*, V, pp. 21–31.

Jacklin, N. and Woo, T., 1998, 'SEC Approves "Broker-Deal Lite" Rules for OTC Derivative Dealers', *Financial Regulation Report*, November, pp. 18–19.

Jaffe, J. and Westerfield, R., 1985, 'The Week-End Effect in Common Stock Returns: The International Evidence', *Journal of Finance*, 40 (2), June, pp. 433–54.

Jain, B. A. and Kini, O., 1994, 'The Post-Issue IPO Operating Performance of IPO Firms', *Journal of Finance*, December, 5, pp. 1699–1726.

Jao, Y.C., 1998, 'The Working of the Currency Board: The Experience of Hong Kong 1935–1997', *Pacific Economic Review*, 3(3), pp. 219–41.

Jensen, M.C. and Meckling, W.H., 1976, 'Theory of the Firm: Managerial Behavior, Agency Costs and Ownership Structure', *Journal of Financial Economics*, 3, pp. 305–60.

Johnson, J.M. and Miller, R.E., (1988), 'Investment Banking Prestige and the Underpricing of Initial Public Offerings', *Financial Management*, 17, pp. 19–29.

Joint Declaration of the Government of the United Kingdom of Great Britain and Northern Ireland and the Government of the People's Republic of China on the Question of Hong Kong, 1984 (Joint Publishing (H.K.) Co. Ltd., 1996).

Jorion, P., 1996, 'Risk²: Measuring the Risk in Value at Risk', *Financial Analysts Journal*, November/December, pp. 47–56.

Kamara, A. and Miller, T. W. Jr., 1995, 'Daily and Intradaily Tests of European Put-Call Parity', *Journal of Financial and Quantitative Analysis*, 30(4), December, pp. 519–39.

Kambhu, J., Keane, F. and Benadon, C., 1996, 'Price Risk Intermediation in the Over-the-Counter Derivatives Markets: Interpretation of a Global Survey', *Federal Reserve Bank of New York Economic Policy Review*, April, pp. 1–15.

Karp, J., 1993, 'Shroff: Singapore on the Line (Part 2)', *Far Eastern Economic Review*, 156(8), 25 February, p. 62.

Keasey, K. and McGuinness, P.B., (1995), 'Underpricing in New Equity Listings: A Conceptual Re- Appraisal', *Small Business Economics*, 7, pp. 41–54.

Keim, D.B., 1983, 'Size-related Anomalies and Stock Return Seasonality: Further Empirical Evidence', Journal of Financial Economics, 12, pp. 13-32.

Kerry Propeerties Ltd. Prospectus (for Placing and Public Offer), 23 July, 1996, Hong Kong.

Kester, G.W. and Chang, R.P., 1994, 'Executive Views on Corporate Financial Policy in Hong Kong: Dividends and Capital Structure', *Research in International Business and Finance*, 11B, pp. 20–22.

Keynes, J.M., 1929 (1st Ed., 1923), *A Tract on Monetary Reform*, MacMillan and Co. Ltd.

Keynes, J.M., 1930, *A Treatise on Money*, Vol 2. ('The Applied Theory of Money'), MacMillan & Co. Ltd.

Khan, W.A. and Baker, H.K., 1993, 'Unlisted Trading Privileges, Liquidity, and Stock Returns', *The Journal of Financial Research*, 16(3), pp. 221–36.

Kharouf, J., 1998, 'German Engineering Goes a Long Way', *Futures Cedar Falls*, 27 (1), pp. 78–81.

Kim, S.-W., 1993, 'Capitalizing on the Weekend Effect', Journal of Portfolio Management, 19(2), 93–99.

King, S.R. and Remolona, E.M., 1987, 'The Pricing and Hedging of Market Index Deposits', *Federal Reserve Bank of New York Quarterly Review*, 12, pp. 9–20.

Klein, L.S., ' 1989, 'Stock Distributions: A Review and Synthesis of the Literature', *Journal of Accounting Literature*, 8, pp. 165–80.

Klemkosky, R. and Resnick, B., 1979, 'Put-call Parity and Market Efficiency', *The Journal of Finance*, 34, pp. 1141–55.

Knight, F., 1921, *Risk, Uncertainty and Profit*, Boston: Houghton Mifflin Co.

Ko, E., 1993, 'Clampdown on Backdoor Listings', *The Securities Journal*, June, pp. 14–15.

Koh, F. and Walter, T., 1989, 'A Direct Test of Rock's Model of the Pricing of Unseasoned Issues', *Journal of Financial Economics*, 23, pp. 251–72.

———, Lim, J. and Chin, N., 1992, 'The Signalling Process in Initial Public Offerings', *Asia Pacific Journal of Management*, 9(2), pp. 151–65.

Kolb, R. W., 1992, 'Is Normal Backwardation Normal?', *The Journal of Futures Markets*, 12(1), pp. 75–91.

Koseki, M., 1997, "Big Bang' Foundations Set in Place', *Japan Times Weekly International Edition*, 23–29 June, pp. 1 & 6.

Krinsky, I., Rotenberg, W.D., and Thornton, D.B., 1988, 'Takeovers: A Synthesis', *Journal of Accounting Literature*, 7, pp. 243–79.

Lakonishok, J. and Lev, B., 1987, 'Stock Splits and Stock Dividends: Why, Who, and When?', *The Journal of Finance*, 42(4), September, pp. 913–32.

Larson, J. C. and Morse, J. N., 1987, 'Intervalling Effects in Hong Kong Stocks', *Journal of Financial Research*, 4, Winter, pp. 353–62.

Lau, S-T., Diltz, D. and Apilado, V.P., 1994, 'Valuation Effects of International Stock Exchange Listings', *Journal of Banking and Finance*, 18, pp. 743–55.

Lau, Y.F. Lawrence, 1992, 'Rights Issues and Investor Returns in Hong Kong', MBA Project Report, The Chinese University of Hong Kong.

Leander, E., 1996, 'Nigel Taylor Orchestrates a Rare European Buyback', *Global Finance*, 10(8), August, p. 24.

Lease, R.C., McConnell, J.J. and Mikkelson, W., 1983, 'The Market Value of Control in Publicly Traded Corporations', *Journal of Financial Economics*, 11, pp. 439–71.

Lee, Hsien Loong, 1998, Speech given at The SES 25th Anniversary Celebration Dinner, 4 November (@ http://www.mas.gov.sg/).

Lee, I., Pettit, R.R. and Swankoski, M.V., 1990, 'Daily Return Relationships Among Asian Stock Markets', *Journal of Business Finance and Accounting*, 17(2), pp. 265–84.

Lee, P., 1996a, 'The AMS Second Terminal System: The Future of Securities Trading', *The Securities Journal*, March, pp. 18–19.

———, 1996b, 'A Hong Kong Fannie Mae: The Benefits', *The Securities Journal*, May, pp. 6 & 8–9.

Leger, J. M., 1994, 'Hong Kong: Fun with Funds', *Far Eastern Economic Review*, 21 April, 157(16), p. 86.

Leland, H. and Pyle, D., 1977, 'Information Asymmetries, Financial Structure and Financial Intermediation', *Journal of Finance*, 32, pp. 371–87.

Leong, K., 1996, 'Techniques: The Right Approach', *Risk* (Value-at-Risk Supplement), June, pp. 9–11 & 13–14.

Levine, I. and Sotunde, M.-T., 1996, 'Does the Master Pass Muster?', *Risk*, 9(10), October, pp. 36–7 & 39–40.

Levinson, H., 1992, 'Keiretsu Relations Changing', *Japan Times Weekly International Edition*, 10–16 August, p. 18.

Levis, M., 1990, 'The Winner's Curse Problem, Interest Costs and the Underpricing of Initial Public Offerings', *The Economic Journal*, 100, March, pp. 76–89.

———, 1993, 'The Long-Run Performance of Initial Public Offerings: The UK Experience 1980– 1988', *Financial Management*, 22(1), Spring, pp. 28–41.

Levy, E., 1992, 'Pricing European Average Rate Currency Options', *Journal of International Money and Finance*, 11, pp. 474–91.

Li, S., 1997, 'PIH to Seek Privatisation Review', South China Morning Post, Business Post, 6 March, p. 1.

Lintner, J., 1956, 'Distribution of Incomes of Corporations among Dividends, Retained Earnings and taxes', *American Economic Review*, 46, May, pp. 97–113.

————, 1965, 'The Valuation of Risk Assets and the Selection of Risky Investments in Stock Portfolios and Capital Budgets', *Review of Economics and Statistics*, 47(1), pp. 13–37.

Lim, S-H, Yu, D., Sargent, S. and Shimomura, K., 1995, 'The Nine Days that Sank Barings', *Asiamoney*, April, 6(3), pp. 15–22.

Lloyd-Smith, J., 1998, '$70b Market Showdown', *South China Morning Post*, 29 August, p. 1.

Lo, C., Besjak, J.R. and Toms, H., 'Voluntary Corporate Divestitures as Antitakeover Mechanisms', *The Financial Review*, 30(1), February, pp. 41–60.

Loderer, C. and Martin, K., 1992, 'Postacquisition Performance of Acquiring Firms', *Financial Management*, Autumn, pp. 69–79.

Logue, D.E., 1973, 'On the Pricing of Unseasoned Equity Issues: 1965–1969', *Journal of Financial and Quantitative Analysis*, 8, 91–103.

London Stock Exchange home pages, press releases at http://www.stockex.co.uk/n_info].

Loomis, C. J., 1995, 'Untangling the Derivatives Mess', *Fortune*, 20 March, pp. 32–42.

Loughran, T. and Ritter, J.R., 1993, 'The Timing and Subsequent Performance of New Issues: Implications for the Cost of Equity Capital', Unpublished Manuscript, July, University of Illinois at Urbana-Champaign.

Low, C. K., 1998, 'Securities Regulation', in Kan, F. (Ed.), *The Business Guide to Hong Kong*, Reed Academic Publishing Asia, pp. 125–44.

Lui, Y. H., 1991, 'The Foreign Exchange Market', Ho, Y.-K., Scott, R. H. and Wong, K. A. (Ed.), *The Hong Kong Financial System*, Hong Kong: Oxford University Press, pp. 187–214.

MacBeth, J.D. and Merville, L.J., 1979, 'An Empirical Examination of the Black-Scholes Call Option Pricing Model', *The Journal of Finance*, 34(5), December, pp. 1173–86.

———— and Merville, L.J., 1980, 'Tests of the Black-Scholes and Cox Call Option Valuation Models', *The Journal of Finance*, 35(2), May, pp. 285–301.

Machina, M.J. and Rothschild, M., 1990, 'Risk', in Eatwell, J., Milgate, M. and Newman, P., (Ed.), *The New Palgrave: Utility and Probability*, London: MacMillan Reference Books, pp. 227–239.

Madhavan, A., 1992, 'Trading Mechanisms in Securities Markets', *The Journal of Finance*, 47(2), June, pp. 607–41.

Maguire, F., 1998, 'Liffe Accelerates Screen Launch', *Futures Cedar Falls*, 27(7), pp. 18.

Malkiel, B.G., 1977, 'The Valuation of Closed-End Investment Company Shares', *The Journal of Finance*, 32(3), June, pp. 847–59.

Markowitz, H.M., 1952, 'Portfolio Selection', *The Journal of Finance*, 7, pp. 77–91.

Marsh, P., 1979, 'Equity Rights Issues and the Efficiency of the U.K. Stock Market', *Journal of Finance*, 34, September, 839–62.

Marston, R.C., 1976, 'Interest Arbitrage in the Euro-Currency Markets', *European Economic Review*, 7, pp. 1–13.

Mayer, M., 1995, 'Joe Jett: Did the Computer Make Him Do It', *Institutional Investor*, March, pp. 7–12.

McDonald, J., 1989, 'The Mochiai Effect: Japanese Corporate Cross-Holdings', *Journal of Portfolio Management*, 16(1), pp. 90–4.

McHattie, A., 1996, The Investor's Guide to Warrants, Second Ed., Financial Times Pitman publishing.

McGuinness, P.B., 1992, 'An Examination of the Underpricing of Initial Public Offerings in Hong Kong: 1980–90', *Journal of Business Finance & Accounting*, 19(2), January, pp. 165–86.

————, 1993a, 'The Post-Listing Return Performance of Unseasoned Issues of Common Stock in Hong Kong', *Journal of Business Finance and Accounting*, 20(2), pp. 167–94.

————, 1993b, 'Investor- and Issuer-Related Perspectives of IPO Underpricing', *OMEGA International Journal of Management Science*, 21(3), pp.377–92.

————, 1993c, 'The Market Valuation of Initial Public Offerings in Hong Kong', *Applied Financial Economics*, 3, pp. 267–81.

————, 1997a, 'Inter-Day Return Behaviour for Stocks Quoted 'Back-to-Back' in Hong Kong and London', *Applied Economics Letters*, 4, pp. 459–64.

————, 1997b, 'Hong Kong's Market for Rights Offerings: Characteristics and Trends', *The Securities Journal*, November, pp. 10–14.

————, 1997c, 'Share Repurchase Activities in the Local Market', *The Securities Journal*, December, pp. 24 & 26–30.

————, 1998a, 'Turbulence in the Hong Kong Warrant Market: A Recap of the Events of October 1997', *The Securities Journal*, January, pp. 20–4.

————, 1998b, 'Buy-Outs, Divestments & Director Share Dealings', *Capital*, August, 129, pp. 40 & 42–6.

————, 1999a, 'Volume Effects in Dual Traded Stocks: Hong Kong & London Evidence, forthcoming in *Applied Financial Economics*.

————, 1999b, 'Timing Derivative Roll-overs: The Case of HSI Futures'.

Meeks, G., 1977, *Disappointing Marriage: A Study of the Gains from Merger*, University of Cambridge Department of Applied Economics Occasional Paper 51, Cambridge University Press.

Miller, M. H., 1995, 'Do We Really Need More Regulation of Derivatives', *Pacific-Basin Finance Journal*, 3, pp. 147–58.

Miller, R.E. and Reilly, F.K., 1987, "An Examination of Mispricing, Returns, Uncertainty for Initial Public Offerings, *Financial Management*, 16, pp. 33–8.

Minto, R., 1997, 'The Big Fizzle?', *Euromoney*, September, p. 14.

Mittoo, U.R., 1992, 'Managerial Perceptions of the Net Benefits of Foreign Listing: Canadian Evidence', *Journal of International Financial Management and Accounting*, 4(1), pp. 40–62.

Mok, M. K., 1988, 'Interdaily Return Efficiency in HK's Stock Market in Recent Years', *HK Journal of Business Management*, VI, pp. 91–111.

————, 1990, 'The Lunar and Western New Year Effects and Influence from Major Markets: A Cross-Country Comparison', *Proceedings of the Third Symposium on Cross-Cultural Consumer & Business Studies*, Hawaii, USA, December, pp. 80–91.

————, Lam, K. and Cheung, I., 1992, 'Family Control and Return Covariation in Hong Kong's Common Stocks', *Journal of Business Finance & Accounting*, 19(2), January, pp. 277–93.

———— and Hui, Y.V., 1998, 'Underpricing and Aftermarket Performance of IPOs in Shanghai, China', *Pacific-Basin Finance Journal*, 6, pp. 453–74.

Monthly Market Statistics, published by The Stock Exchange of Hong Kong Ltd., September 1995.

Mossin, J., 1966, 'Equilibrium in a Capital Asset Market', *Econometrica*, 34(4), pp. 768–83.

Murray, D., 1985, 'Further Evidence on the Liquidity Effects of Stock Splits and Stock Dividends', *The Journal of Financial Research*, 8(1), Spring, pp. 59–67.

Myers, S.C., 1984, 'The Capital Structure Puzzle', *Journal of Finance*, 39, July, pp. 575–92.

———— and Majluf, N.C., 1984, 'Corporate Financing and Investment Decisions when Firms have Information that Investors do not have', *Journal of Financial Economics*, 13, pp. 187–221.

Naik, N., Neuberger, A. and Viswanathan, S., 1994, 'Disclosure Regulation in Competitive Dealership Markets: An Analysis of the London Stock Exchange', London Business School Working Paper, IFA193.

Neal, R. S., 1996, 'Credit Derivatives: New Financial Instruments for Controlling Credit Risk', *Economic Review (Federal Reserve Bank of Kansas City)*, 81(2), pp. 15–27.

Neuberger, B.M. and Hammond, C.T., 1974, 'A Study of Underwriters' Experience with Unseasoned New Issues', *Journal of Financial and Quantitative Analysis*, pp. 165–77.

—————— and LaChapelle, C.A., 1983, 'Unseasoned New Issue Price Performance on Three Tiers: 1975–80', *Financial Management*, 12, pp. 23–8.

New Listings, 1997, *The Securities Journal*, July.

News Release, 1998, 'Tick Rule Reinstated', The Stock Exchange of Hong Kong Ltd., September 4.

Oldfield, S., 1998, 'Intervention Squeezes Liquidity 14pc', *South China Morning Post*, Business Post, 28 October, p. 1.

Oyon, D., Markides, C.C. and Ittner, C.D., 1994, 'The Information Content of Common Stock Repurchases: An Empirical Study', British Journal of Management, 5, Special Issue, June, pp. 65–75.

Paisley, E., 1991, 'Blinkered Brokers: Hong Kong Exchange Members Rebuff Reform', *Far Eastern Economic Review*, 29 August, p. 49.

Pang, K.-L., 1988, 'An Analysis of Hong Kong Stock Return Seasonality and Firm Size Anomalies for the Period 1977 to 1986', *Hong Kong Journal of Business Management*, 6, pp. 69–90.

Patten, C., 1998, *East and West*, MacMillan Publishers Ltd.

Paul-Choudhury, S., 1996, 'Frontiers: Optional Extras', *Risk* (Value-at-Risk Supplement), June, pp. 23 & 25.

Pierog, K., Stewart, J., Schoenfeld, S. and Alpe, R., 1987, 'International Trading Scene Booming', *Futures: The Magazine of Commodities and Options*, 16(9), pp. 56–9 & 88.

Peterson, D.R. and Peterson, P.P., 1992, 'A Further Understanding of Stock Distributions: The Case of Reverse Stock Splits', *The Journal of Financial Research*, 15(3), Fall, pp. 189–205.

Poterba, J.M. and Summers, L.H., 1986, 'The Persistence of Volatility and Stock Market Fluctuations', The American Economic Review, December, 76(5), pp. 1142–51.

Pritchard, E., 1997, 'Warrants Burn Issuers as well as Investors', *South China Morning Post*, Markets Post: Monitor, 28 October, p. 12.

Recommended Merger Document for Asia Insurance Co. Ltd. and The Commercial Bank of Hong Kong Ltd., 29 October 1990.

Reed, N., 1996, 'Variations on a Theme', *Risk* (Value At Risk Supplement, June, pp. 2–4.

Report of the Securities Review Committee, 1988, 'The Operation and Regulation of the Hong Kong Securities Industry', May, Hong Kong.

Report on Financial Market Review, 1998, Financial Services Bureau, Government of the HKSAR, April.

Report of The SES Review Committee, 1998, Singapore, 29 July.

Reuters, 1997, 'Change in Accounting Uncovers a $670m Loss', reported in *South China Morning Post*, Business Post, 23 May, p. 16.

——————, 1997, *The South China Morning Post*, Markets Post, 19 September, p. 1.

Review Editorial, 1998, 'Liberte, Egalite, Equity': Look Out Crony Capitalism', *Far Eastern Economic Review*, 16 April, p. 70.

Reynolds, N., 1997, *South China Morning Post*, Sunday Morning Post Money, 2 November, pp. 1 & 3.

Ritter, J.R., 1984, 'The 'Hot Issue' Market of 1980', *Journal of Business*, 57, pp. 215–40.

——————, 1987, 'The Costs of Going Public', Journal of Financial Economics, 19, pp. 269–81.

———, 1991, 'The Long-Run Performance of Initial Public Offerings', *Journal of Finance*, March 1991, pp. 3–27.

Rock. K., 1986, 'Why New Issues are Underpriced', *Journal of Financial Economics*, 15, pp. 1051–69.

Rogalski, R. J., 1984, 'New Findings Regarding the Day-of-the-Week Returns over Trading and Non- Trading Periods: A Note', *The Journal of Finance*, 39(5), pp. 1603–14.

Roll, R., 1983, 'Vas Ist Das?' The Turn-of-the-Year Effect and the Return Premia of Small Firms', *Journal of Portfolio Management*, Winter, pp. 18–28.

Ross, S, 1976, 'The Arbitrage Theory of Capital Asset Pricing', *Journal of Economic Theory*, December, pp. 343–62.

Rozeff, M. S. and Kinney, W. R. Jr, 1976, 'Capital Market Seasonality: The Case of Stock Returns', *Journal of Financial Economics*, 3, pp. 379–402.

Rules Governing the Listing of Securities on The Stock Exchange of Hong Kong Ltd., 1989, 3rd.Ed., Updated to 6/96.

Rules of the Exchange, The Stock Exchange of Hong Kong Ltd., Reprinted March 1997.

Sales, R., 1998, 'Alliance Threatens Liffe's Open Outcry', *Wall Street and Technology*, 16(5), pp. 32–6.

Saunders, A. and Lim, J., 1990, 'Underpricing and the New Issue Process in Singapore', *Journal of Banking and Finance*, 14, pp. 291–309.

Saunders, D., Chan, P. and Kohli, S., 1999, 'HSBC to List on Wall Street', *South China Morning Post*, Business Post, 23 February, pp. 1 & 3.

Scheme of Arrangement Document, The HongKong and Shanghai Banking Corporation, 1 February, 1991.

Schoenfeld, S. A., 1987, 'Can it Rise from the Ashes', *InterMarket*, February, 6(2), pp. 24–9.

Scholes, M., 1972, 'The Market for Securities: Substitution Versus Price Pressure and the Effect of Information on Share Price', *Journal of Business*, 45, pp. 179–211.

Schultz, P., 1993, 'Call of Warrants: Timing and Market Reaction', *The Journal of Finance*, 68(2), June, pp. 681–96.

Securities (Disclosure of Interests) Ordinance, Cap. 396, Hong Kong Government, 1991.

Securities Ordinance of HK (Chapter 333), published by the Hong Kong Government Printer.

Securities & Futures Commission, 1997, (pp. 1–12), Insert 2 (of 9): Hong Kong Code on Takeovers and Mergers and Share Repurchases: Statistics of cases during the 12-month periods ended 31 March 1997 and 31 March 1996.

Securities & Futures Commission, 1997, (pp. 1–12), Insert 4 (of 9): Authorised Mutual Funds and Unit Trusts, 31 March.

Securities and Futures Commission Ordinance, Cap. 24, Published by the Government Printer, HKSAR.

Securities and Futures Commission Annual Report 1997/98 ('Meeting the Challenges of Change').

SEHK Annual Report 1997, 1998.

SEHK Consultation Paper 1999, 'Consultation Paper on The Proposed Market Infrastructure for Trading Exchange Fund Notes', January, The Stock Exchange of Hong Kong Ltd.

SEHK homepage (at http://www.sehk.com).

SEHK, 1998, May 'Consultation Paper on a Proposed New Market for Emerging Companies', The Stock Exchange of Hong Kong Ltd.

SEHK, 1998, October, 'News Release', The Stock Exchange of Hong Kong Ltd., 7 October.

SEHK, 1998, 'Announcement: Share Repurchase Programme', 5 November.

SEHK Monthly Bulletin, various issues, The Stock Exchange of Hong Kong Ltd.

SEHK/SFC, 1993, Joint Announcement: 'Backdoor Listings', May.

SEHK/SFC Joint Policy Statement on Offering Mechanisms, 1994, published by The Stock Exchange of Hong Kong Ltd. and the Securities & Futures Commission, 4 November.

SEHK/SFC Consultation Paper on Offering Mechanisms, 1997, published by The Stock Exchange of Hong Kong Ltd. and the Securities & Futures Commission, June.

SEHK/SFC, 1998, Joint Policy Statement: Offer Mechanisms, Hong Kong, 24 February.

Sendzul, A., 1987, 'Futures Loss Pegged at $1.8 Billion', *South China Morning Post*, Business Post, 4 November, p. 1.

Sendzul, A. and Glain, S., 1987, 'Urgent Talks on Rescue of Futures', *South China Morning Post*, Business Post, 24 October, pp. 1 & 3.

SES Fact Book 1997, Stock Exchange of Singapore.

SES Press Release, 1999, 'Revision of Brokerage Rates', (from http://www.ses.com.sg/).

Seyhun, H.N., 1986, 'Insiders' Profits, Costs of Trading and Market Efficiency', *Journal of Financial Economics*, 16, pp. 189–212.

SFC, 1995, 'Core Operational and Financial Risk Management Controls for Over-the-Counter Derivatives Activities of Registered Persons', Hong Kong, March (* also re-printed therein).

SFC, 1997, 'Report of the Surveys on the Over-The-Counter Derivatives Activities of Registered Firms', Hong Kong, April.

SFC, 1997, 'Offshore Trading of Hong Kong Stocks: Migration of Trading or a Growing Pie?', report prepared for the SFC by The Sandra Ann Morsilli Pacific-Basin Capital Markets Research Center, Securities & Futures Commission, Hong Kong, May (co-authored by Chang, R., Oppenheimer, R.H. and Rhee, S.G.).

SFC Annual Report, 1998–99.

SFC, 1998, 'A Consultation Paper on a Review of the Hong Kong Code on Takeovers and Mergers', The Securities & Futures Commission, Hong Kong, February.

SFC, Press Release, 1998, 'Revised Hong Kong Code on Takeovers and Mergers to Become Effective on 1 August 1998', 24 July.

SFC Press Release, 1998, 'Illegal Short Selling', September.

SFC Press Release, 1999, 'Regulation of Share Margin Financing', January 7.

Sharpe, W. F., 1963, 'A Simplified Model for Portfolio Analysis', *Management Science*, 9(2), pp. 277–93.

————, 1964, 'Capital Asset Prices: A theory of Market Equilibrium under Conditions of Risk', *The Journal of Finance*, 19(3), September, pp. 425–42.

————, 1982, 'Factors in New York Stock Exchange Security Returns, 1931–1979', *The Journal of Portfolio Management*, Summer, pp. 5–19.

Shibata, Y., 1995, 'Buyback', *Global Finance*, 9(10), October, p. 22.

Shirreff, D., 'Danger—Kids at Play', *Euromoney*, March 1995, p. 43–6.

Shleifer, A., 1986, 'Do Demand Curves for Stocks Slope Down?', *The Journal of Finance*, 41(3), July, pp. 579–90.

Smiles, V., 1984, 'Deregulation: The Shakeout Begins', *Asian Business*, April, p. 32.

Smirlock, M. and Starks, L., 1986, 'Day-of-the-Week and Intraday Effects in Stock Returns', *Journal of Financial Economics*, 17, pp. 197–210.

Stambaugh, F., 1996, 'Risk and Value at Risk', *European Management Journal*, 14(6), pp. 612–21.

Statement on Competition Policy, 1998, Trade and Industry Bureau, Government of the Hong Kong Special Administrative Region, May.

Stoll, H. R., 1969, 'The Relationship Between Put and Call Option Prices', *The Journal of Finance*, 24(5), pp. 801–24.

———— and Whaley, R. E., 1987, 'Program Trading and Expiration-Day Effects', *Financial Analysts Journal*, March–April, pp. 16–28.

Stock Exchange of Hong Kong Ltd. News Release, 1998, 'The Stock Exchange Agrees to Become a Public Body', 1 December.

Stock Exchange Unification Ordinance, CAP. 361, Published by the Government Printer, HKSAR.

Stockholm Stock Exchange Fact Book 1998.

Styland Holdings Limited Rights Issue Prospectus, 27 October, 1995.

Tang, G. Y-N., 1996, 'Return Volatilities of Stock Index Futures in Hong Kong: Trading Versus Non-Trading Periods', *The Journal of Derivatives*, Fall, pp. 55–62.

Taylor, D. and Poon, M., 'Charting Hong Kong's Takeover Game', *The Securities Journal*, August 1991, pp. 26–8 & p. 30.

Technical Committee of the International Organisation of Securities Commissions (IOSCO)*, 1994, 'Operational and Financial Risk Management Control Mechanisms for Over-The-Counter Derivatives Activities of Regulated Securities Firms', July.

Teoh, S.H., Welch, I. and Wong, T.J., 1998, 'Earnings Management and the Long-Run Market Performance of Initial Public Offerings', *The Journal of Finance*, 53(6), December, pp. 1935–74.

Terpstra, R. H. and Mumford, V., 1994, 'Derivative Instruments: Index Linked Options & Futures', in Terpstra, R. H., (Ed.), *Manual of the Securities Industry*, 2nd Ed., Hong Kong: The Stock Exchange of Hong Kong Ltd. and the Asia-Pacific Institute of Business of The Chinese University of Hong Kong, pp. 121–54.

The Bank of New York Co. Inc. home pages (at http://www.bankofny.com/adr/aovrview.htm, updated as of 1 June 1, 1999).

The Basic Law of the Hong Kong Special Administrative Region of The People's Republic of China, 1990 (Joint Publishing (H.K.) Co. Ltd., 1996).

The Hong Kong Mortgage Corporation, Annual Report 1997 (year end: 31st December).

The Stock Exchange of Hong Kong Ltd. Practice Note 15, 1997, 'Practice with Regard to Proposals Submitted by Issuers to Effect the Separate Listing on the Exchange or Elsewhere of Assets or Businesses Wholly or Partly within their Existing Groups', May.

Thompson, R.S. and Wright, M., 1991, 'UK Management Buy-outs: Debt, Equity and Agency Cost Implications', *Managerial and Decision Economics*, 12, pp. 15–26.

Thornton, D. L., 1989, 'Tests of Covered Interest Rate Parity', *Federal Reserve Bank of St. Louis Review*, 71(4), pp. 55–66.

Tinic, S.M., 1988, 'Anatomy of Initial Public Offerings of Common Stock', *Journal of Finance*, 43, pp. 789–822.

Titman, S. and Trueman, B., 1986, 'Information Quality and the Valuation of New Issues', *Journal of Accounting and Economics*, June, pp. 159–72.

To, E., 1987, 'Tighter Rein May be Kept on Brokers', *South China Morning Post*, Business Post, 31, 1 October, p. 1.

———— and Sendzul, A., 1987, 'Brokers Lobby for Easy Terms', *South China Morning Post*, Business Post, 30 October, p. 1.

————, E., Ko, M. and Chan, C-K., 1987, 'Guarantors Sue Brokers for $1.8 billions', *South China Morning Post*, 29 October, p. 1.

Tricom Holdings Ltd. Prospectus (for New Issue and Offer for Sale), 30 September, 1994, Hong Kong.

Tsang, D., 1998, Speech given during the Signing Ceremony of the Fixed Rate Mortgage Pilot Scheme, 18 March.

Tsang, F., 1996, 'The Lunar New Year Effect', The Securities Journal, March, pp. 20–1.

Tsangarakis, N.V., 1996, 'Shareholder Wealth Effects of Equity Issues in Emerging Markets: Evidence from Rights Offerings in Greece', *Financial Management*, 25(3), Autumn, pp. 21–32.

Understanding Stock Options (And Their Risks), The Stock Exchange of Hong Kong, Traded Options Division, January 1998.

Uhlir, H., (1989), 'Going Public in the F.R.G.', in Rui. Guimaraes, B. Kingsman and S. Taylor (eds.), *A Reappraisal of the Efficiency of Financial Markets*, New York: Springer-Verlag.

United Overseas Bank Limited: 'Withdrawal of Secondary Listing on the Stock Exchange of Hong Kong Limited ("SEHK")' notice, 1998, *South China Morning Post*, Business Post, 19 May, p. 2.

Van der Kamp, J., 1998, 'Signs of Pain Emerge as Screw Starts to Turn', *South China Morning Post*, Markets Post, 27 August, p. 14.

Van Duyne, A., 1995, 'Whose Risk? Whose Reward?', *Euromoney*, May, pp. 60–2.

Walker, J. L., 1995, 'Daiwa's Losses Spell a Scandal Too Far', *International Financial Law Review*, 14(12), December, pp. 12–14.

Wardley Cards (Various issues), Wardley Data Services, Hong Kong.

Webb, D., 1998a, 'Letters to the Editor: HKMA Brings Return to '87', *South China Morning Post*, Business Post, 20 August, p. 2.

———, 1998b, 'Secrecy is the Enemy of Free-Market Philosophy', *South China Morning Post*, Business Post, 4 September, p. 2.

Webb, S.E., Officer, D.T. and Boyd, B.E., 1993, 'An Examination of International Equity Markets Using American Depository Receipts (ADRs)', *Journal of Business Finance and Accounting*, 22(3), April, pp. 415–30.

Welch, I., 1989, 'Seasoned Offerings, Imitation Costs and the Underpricing of Initial Public Offerings', *Journal of Finance*, June, pp. 421–49.

Weston, J. F., Chung, K. W. S. and Hoag, S. E., 1990, *Mergers, Restructuring and Corporate Control*, Prentice-Hall.

Whaley, R. E., 1981, 'On the Valuation of American Call Options with Known Dividend', *Journal of Financial Economics*, June, pp. 207–11.

White, R.W. and Lusztig, P.A., 1980, 'The Price Effects of Rights Offerings', *Journal of Financial and Quantitative Analysis*, 15(1), March, pp. 25–40.

Wong, A.W.F., 1976, 'The Implementation of the Resettlement Program', in Iglesias, G.U. (Ed.), *Implementation: The Problem of Achieving Results, A Casebook on Asian Experiences*, The Philippines: Eropa, pp. 268–308.

Wong, L. and Chan, P., 1997, 'Red-Chip Application Deluge Draws $200b', *South China Morning Post*, Business Post, 24 May, p. 1.

Wong, K.A. and Chiang, H.L., 1986, 'Pricing of New Equity Issues in Singapore', *Asia Pacific Journal of Management*, 4(1), pp. 1–10.

———, 1991, 'The Hong Kong Stock Market', in Ho, Y. K., Scott, R. H. and Wong, K. A. (Eds.), *The Hong Kong Financial System*, Hong Kong: Oxford University Press, pp. 215–34.

———, Hui, T. K. and Chan, C. Y., 1992, 'Day-of-the-Week Effects: Evidence from Developing Stock Markets', *Applied Financial Economics*, 2, pp. 49–56.

Wong, M.C.S., 1997, 'Fund Management Performance, Trend-Chasing Technical Analysis and Investment Horizons: A Case Study', *Omega, International Journal of Management Science*, 25(1), pp. 57–63.

Woodward, S., Siegel, J. G. and Qureshi, A. A., 1996, 'FASB 119 & Derivative Financial Instruments: Disclosure and Fair Value', *National Public Accountant*, 41(1), January, pp. 18–21 & 44.

Wright, M. and Robbie, K., 'The Investor-led Buy-out: A New Strategic Option', *Long Range Planning*, 29(5), pp. 691–702.

Wu, L., 1998, 'Market Reactions to the Hong Kong Trading Suspensions: Mandatory Versus Voluntary' *Journal of Business Finance & Accounting*, 25(3)&(4), pp. 419–37.

Wu, Y.W., Xiang, B. and Zhang, G., 1996, 'Ownership Structure Reform and Corporate Performance: An Empirical Evaluation of Chinese Shareholding Companies', *Hong Kong Journal of Business Management*, 14, pp. 53–66.

Yadav, P. K. and Pope, P. F., 1990, 'Stock Index Futures Arbitrage: International Evidence', *The Journal of Futures Markets*, 10(6), pp. 573–603.

Yagil, J. and Forshner, Z., 1991, 'Gains from International Dual Listings', *Management Science*, 37(1), January, pp. 114–20.

Yam, J., 1998a, 'The Hong Kong Dollar Link', *Hong Kong Monetary Authority Quarterly Bulletin*, May, pp. 45–59.

Yam, J., 1998b, 'A Modern Day Currency Board System', Hong Kong Monetary Authority (@www.info.gov.hk/hkma/pub/public/mdcbs/content/htm).

Yau, J., Schneeweis, T. and Yung, K., 1990, 'The Behaviour of Stock Index Futures Prices in Hong Kong Before and After the Crash', in Rhee, S. G. and Chang, R. (Eds.), *Pacific-Basin Capital Markets Research*, North-Holland, pp. 357–78.

Yiu, E., 1998, 'Yam Unveils 7-Point Plan', *South China Morning Post*, Sunday Money, 6 September, p. 1.

—— and Ibison, D., 1999, 'EFI to Unload about $100 b of portfolio', *South China Morning Post*, Business Post, 17 March, p. 1.

——, 1999, 'Government Conceals Cudgel in Stock-Market Reforms Push', *South China Morning Post*, Business Post, 9 June, p. 1.

Yu, D., 1994/1995, 'Repackaged LBOs Sprout New Roots', *AsiaMoney*, December/January, pp. 12–13 & 15.

Zivney, T. L., 1991, 'The Value of Early Exercise in Option Prices: An Empirical Investigation', *Journal of Financial and Quantitative Analysis*, 26(1), March, pp. 129–38.

Zuckerman, D., 1998, 'Bond Market Still Punishes Hedge Fund', *The Asian Wall Street Journal*, 5 October, p. 20. 'Repackag

Index

Index compiled by Françoise Parkin